MW00674014

When should I travel to get the best airfare?
Where do I go for answers to my travel questions?
What's the best and easiest way to plan and book my trip?

frommers.travelocity.com

Frommer's, the travel guide leader, has teamed up with **Travelocity.com**, the leader in online travel, to bring you an in-depth, easy-to-use resource designed to help you plan and book your trip online.

At **frommers.travelocity.com**, you'll find free online updates about your destination from the experts at Frommer's plus the outstanding travel planning and purchasing features of Travelocity.com. Travelocity.com provides reservations capabilities for 95 percent of all airline seats sold, more than 47,000 hotels, and over 50 car rental companies. In addition, Travelocity.com offers more than 2,000 exciting vacation and cruise packages. Travelocity.com puts you in complete control of your travel planning with these and other great features:

> **Expert travel guidance from Frommer's** - over 150 writers reporting from around the world!
>
> **Best Fare Finder** - an interactive calendar tells you when to travel to get the best airfare
>
> **Fare Watcher** - we'll track airfare changes to your favorite destinations
>
> **Dream Maps** - a mapping feature that suggests travel opportunities based on your budget
>
> **Shop Safe Guarantee** - 24 hours a day / 7 days a week live customer service, and more!

Whether traveling on a tight budget, looking for a quick weekend getaway, or planning the trip of a lifetime, Frommer's guides and Travelocity.com will make your travel dreams a reality. You've bought the book, now book the trip!

Also available from IDG Books Worldwide:

U^{the}nofficial Guide® to Cruises
2001

Kay Showker

with

Bob Sehlinger

Every effort has been made to ensure the accuracy of information throughout this book. Bear in mind, however, that prices, schedules, etc., are constantly changing. Readers should always verify information before making final plans.

IDG Books Worldwide
An International Data Group Company
909 Third Avenue
New York, New York 10022

Produced by Menasha Ridge Press

UNOFFICIAL GUIDE is a registered trademark of
IDG Books Worldwide, Inc.

ISBN 0-02-863792-5
ISSN 1083-1460

Manufactured in the United States of America

10 9 8 7 6 5 4 3 2 1

2001 edition

Contents

List of Illustrations

Laurels for the Laborers

It goes almost without saying that a book of this scope—covering more than 100 cruise lines with upward of 300 ships sailing to destinations from the North Pole to the South Pole and around the world—is the work of many people. It required extensive research, interviews with passengers, seemingly endless discussions with specialized travel agents and other people knowledgeable about cruises, not to mention the incredible amount of follow-up due to the constantly changing nature of the industry.

So many people were tireless in their effort to help that it would take another book to name them all, but we would be remiss not to mention some. Michael Brown, editor of *Cruise and Vacation Views,* helped every step of the way. Steve Gordan, publisher and managing editor of Star Service, which issues reports and evaluations on hotels and cruise ships worldwide for its travel agency subscribers, generously allowed us access and use of the publication's material.

Lloyd Cole of Valerie Wilson Travel, NY; Dr. Bradley Feuer, Pace Travel, Lake Worth, FL; and Lisa Haber, Cruise Professionals, Baltimore, gave us plentiful insights and never seemed to tire of our endless questions.

We are grateful to all our public relations friends at the cruise lines who helped us check the nitty-gritty details that can drive you crazy and who have been our hosts over the years without any obligation whatsoever. Rich Steck, formerly of Royal Caribbean Cruise Lines, and Julie Benson, Princess Cruise Lines, went above and beyond the call of duty and have our everlasting gratitude.

TEXT CONTRIBUTIONS

Time constraints in writing a book such as this make it impossible for two people to visit and revisit every ship prior to our deadlines, as we would want to do. We called on colleagues for help, particularly on writers who specialize in cruising and are as qualified as we to write this book.

Some folks contributed material written specifically for the book, others shared their knowledge from recent cruises or allowed us to use material from recent research published elsewhere, while still others reviewed or helped with the updating of information we had written.

Specifically for Part Two, sections were written by Ann Kalosh (Abercrombie & Kent International); Matt Hannafin (Alaska's Glacier Bay Cruises and Tours/Commodore Cruise Line); Dave Houser (Cruise West); Betsy McNeil (Commodore Cruise Line); and Ted Scull (P&O Cruises) and for Part Three, Ted Scull (Norwegian Coastal Cruises and European Cruise Ferries) and Dave Houser (Freighter Cruises), who not only wrote parts of this book but also generously contributed their insights and information to many of the cruise lines and ships profiled in Part Two; and Susan Milne, who prepared the itineraries. Continuous input also came from Georgina Cruz, Marcia Levin, and Molly Staub.

Many other writing colleagues shared their firsthand experience with us, too. We particularly want to thank Arlene and Sam Blecker, Ernest Blum, Deborah Boyd, Anne Campbell, Michael Brown, Jerry Brown, Lisa Chickering, Jeannie Porterfield, George Devol, Michael Driscoll, Marilyn Green, Mary Ann Hemphill, Francis Kay Harris, Elizabeth Harryman, Paul Lasley, Henry Magenheim, and Joan Scobey.

Many, many friends, friends of friends, travel agents, and cruise passengers along the way willingly gave us their time for interviews, helped with ship ratings, phoned and sent us letters about their latest cruise, and to them we express our heartfelt thanks.

Last but not least, we thank the staff of Menasha Ridge Press, who worked tirelessly on the manuscript, researching, and checking facts.

Kay Showker
Bob Sehlinger

Introduction

About This Guide

How Come "Unofficial"?

The material in this guide has not been edited or in any way reviewed by the cruise lines profiled. In this "unofficial" guide we represent and serve you, the consumer. If a ship serves mediocre food, has cramped cabins, or offers poor shore excursions, we will say so. Through our independence, we hope we can make selecting a cruise efficient and economical and your cruise experience on target and fun.

Making It Easy

In the nearly two years it took to write this book, Kay had pinned on a wall in front of her a note that read: "This book has one purpose: To help readers select the right cruise—i.e., the cruise that's right for them." She kept it there to make sure we never lost sight of that goal.

Most guides to cruising approach their subject on a ship-by-ship basis, giving only the briefest attention to the cruise line and emphasizing ships— the hardware. But people don't buy ships, they buy cruises, and those cruises—the software—have been designed according to cruise lines' business plans, which define the types of cruises they offer. The cruise lines are challenged daily by their competitors and all the other leisure products vying for your attention—from the latest car and computer to a Disney vacation—to make their cruises irresistible. Yet, they freely admit that although there's a cruise for everyone, not every cruise is for everyone. What it boils down to is that you can listen to Beethoven's Ninth Symphony played by an amateur band, or you can hear it played by the New York Philharmonic. It's the same music, but it's going to come out differently.

This book is designed to help you recognize the differences. By understanding the cruise lines and the experiences they offer, you will be able to recognize the different types of cruises available and identify the ones likely to appeal to you. Each line offers cruises with features that distinguish them from the others. It is these features, or "style" as we call it, that are the essence of the cruise experience.

A Carnival cruise is a Carnival cruise, for example. Each Carnival ship offers a "Fun Ship" vacation, and, except for the cruise's length and destinations, the experience varies little among Carnival ships. Carnival has designed it that way.

The same is true of Royal Caribbean Cruise Line, Holland America, Seabourn, and every other line that has built ships of a class or style from the same mold. On the other hand, a Carnival cruise is as different from a Princess, Holland America, Crystal, or Seabourn cruise as night is from day.

As cruise lines continue to standardize their operations to keep costs down and distinguish themselves from their competition, it becomes more important for you (or your travel agent), as you select a cruise, to understand the line and the type of cruises it offers. With that goal in mind, this guidebook is organized in three parts:

"Part One: Planning Your Cruise Vacation" covers basic information on what cruises contain, tips on finding the best values, and preparing for your cruise.

"Part Two: Cruise Lines and Their Ships" profiles all major, "mainstream" cruise lines that sell primarily to U.S. and Canadian travelers. At the end of Part Two are ships also in the mainstream, but not necessarily on this side of the Atlantic. Most are based in Europe, cruise less-traveled routes, and cater mainly to Europeans.

"Part Three: Cruising Alternatives" describes other options, such as river, adventure, and expedition cruises, plus freighters, coastal ships, cruise ferries, and sailing ships.

LETTERS, COMMENTS, AND QUESTIONS FROM READERS

Many who use the *Unofficial Guides* write to us with questions, comments, or their own strategies for planning and enjoying travel. We appreciate all such input, both positive and critical. Readers' comments are frequently incorporated into revised editions of the *Unofficial Guides* and have contributed immeasurably to their improvement. Please write to:

Kay and Bob
The Unofficial Guide to Cruises
P.O. Box 43673
Birmingham, AL 35243

Please put your return address on both your letter and envelope; the two sometimes become separated. Also, include your phone number if you are available for a possible interview. And remember, our work often requires that we be out of the office for long periods, so forgive us if our response is slow.

A Reader Survey is included at the end of the book. We urge you to copy or clip it out, add your impressions, and send it in.

Cruising: A Look Back, a Look Ahead

Modern cruising in 2001 marks its thirty-fifth anniversary. December 19, 1966, is recognized as a landmark because on that date a series of cruises was launched that, for the first time, was created and packaged as a mass-market product and sold on a year-round basis. The ship, the *Sunward* of the Norwegian Caribbean Line (later to be named the Norwegian Cruise Line), sailed from Miami to Nassau with 540 passengers on the first 3- and 4-day cruises to be offered year-round between Miami and the Bahamas. No one, including the creators, imagined where that small step would lead. Indeed, many in the steamship business dismissed the idea as crazy, declaring there was not enough of a market to support such cruises.

Cruising, of course, did not actually start in 1966; it evolved over a time span of 150 years. But it's true that until the 1960s the closest most people got to a big ship was on the big screen, either in movies about glamorous people living romantic lives, or in newsreels of the duke and duchess of Windsor arriving on the Queen Mary, or F. Scott and Zelda, the Astors, the Vanderbilts, and other celebrities sailing stylishly to Europe aboard an elegant oceanliner.

From the start of the first regular transatlantic steamship service by Samuel Cunard in 1840, a voyage on a great liner became the ultimate dream shared by people worldwide. In the early days, a sea voyage was more of an expedition, requiring passengers to endure hardships with few amenities on board ship or at ports. Passenger comfort, even in first class, was not a priority, but as competition developed and steamship travel gained popularity, each generation of ships brought enhanced comfort.

Then, too, throughout the late nineteenth century and up to World War I, ships carrying passengers had other purposes. Among them was transporting thousands of immigrants to the New World and a new life. To meet the demand—and reap large profits—many steamship companies were born and ships built, and, except for the war years when the vessels transported troops, oceanliners paraded across the Atlantic and Pacific in an endless stream, with the world's elite in their top decks and the huddled masses below.

Then in 1921, passage of the Immigration Act, intended to slow the torrent of new arrivals, forced steamship companies to change course. To make up for lost revenue from steerage, companies created cabin, or tourist, class in the several decks below first class and unwittingly took the next step toward modern cruising. Although a voyage remained a means of getting from one continent to another, it was no longer a pastime only for the privileged. Cabin class did not have the elegance and panache of first class, but it wasn't bad. It found a ready market in the GIs who had fought in Europe and wanted to return with their families, immigrants who had made good and wanted to visit relatives in their homelands, and America's growing middle class, who wanted to emulate the celebrities and aristocrats in first class.

THE GOLDEN AGE

The Roaring Twenties was a golden age for steamship travel. It was a time of new prosperity, blithe spirits—and Prohibition in America. With alcoholic beverages legal at sea, ship companies offered a new type of short cruise—the party, or booze, cruise—that made getting there half the fun.

Meanwhile, passenger comfort was enhanced. The first-class main lounge sought to make aristocratic passengers feel at home by echoing the elegance of a chateau, with wood, marble, and an open fireplace. The space was used for many activities—as a smoker by day and for entertainment, such as bingo, films, or dancing, in the evening. At dance time, furniture was cleared away. Reflecting the era's social code—as they always have—ships until the 1920s maintained separate smokers for men and lounges for ladies.

In the dining room, passengers sat at long tables on chairs bolted to the floor (ships did not have stabilizers). In 1910, Ritz restaurants, replicating the setting of their shore-side operations, introduced round tables and carpeted floors in first class on ships of Hapag-Lloyd of Germany. The style soon became the standard for other ships. Private bathrooms were available in first class on the grandest liners, but in cabin class, passengers shared bath facilities until the 1950s. Air-conditioning was introduced by P&O Lines in the 1930s, but did not become common until the 1950s.

The first indoor swimming pool appeared in 1910 on the *Olympic* of White Star Line. (It was the first of the line's three superliners; the others were the *Titanic* and the *Gigantic,* later renamed *Britannic.*) Known as a plunge bath, it had a balcony where others could watch the bathers. The first permanent outdoor pool was introduced in 1926 on the *Roma* of Italian Lines. Until the late 1950s, the top deck was fitted with machinery and off-limits to passengers. Today, it's usually a sports deck.

A NEW ERA

After weathering the Great Depression and another war, oceanliners resumed their traditional role, and by the 1950s were conveying hordes of students to Europe and masses of refugees to U.S. shores. The glamour returned with the comings and goings of a young Liz Taylor and the sailing of Grace Kelly to her fairyland prince. After World War II, the addition of radar and improved navigational equipment made passenger ships safer and more accurate regarding arrival times, enabling operators to plan reliable itineraries. By the mid-1950s, most oceanliners had stabilizers. Radios were added in staterooms. The tradition to separate first class and tourist class on transatlantic service continued, but in 1958, Holland America launched the *Rotterdam,* which could be converted to one class. Meanwhile, dark clouds gathered over oceanliners' futures. By decade's end, most elite passengers had taken flight—literally.

The final blow came in 1958, when the first commercial jets streaked across the Atlantic, cutting travel time from five days to just over five hours. Instead of dying out, however, the ships changed course and became part of the revolution that took place on the sea as well as in the sky.

THE CRUISE REVOLUTION

The turnaround of the 1960s brought radical changes. New cruise lines, untethered to the past, exchanged formality for fun and brought a new atmosphere to shipboard life. The barriers of separate classes were removed, and the space was used for sports, recreation, and entertainment, turning the ships into floating resorts. Getting there was no longer half the fun. It was the fun. Passengers no longer bundled under blankets in deck chairs. Instead, they bounced in aerobics classes, swung at golf and tennis balls, plunged into the sea with masks and fins, soaked in hot tubs, and luxuriated in shipboard spas. Bingo survived, but it now competed with jazzy casinos, Broadway shows and discos, wine and piano bars, comics and cabarets. New and younger passengers were attracted by the activity and informality. Families with children, too, were finding cruises to be an ideal vacation.

But change came wrapped in skepticism. For example, the hot news in 1968 was the new, mod look of the *S.S. Independence.* With a red, orange, and yellow sunburst splashed across the length of its sides and a riot of interior color, it was quickly dubbed the psychedelic ship. A trade magazine's story on the shakedown cruise called it a "floating water pad for the turned on generation" and suggested that "dancing until the wee hours . . . , the informal atmosphere of the one-class ship, and ever-changing program of top-talent entertainment may prove a real drawing card."

The 1970s began with Royal Caribbean Cruise Lines making its debut with a fleet of ships built specifically for Caribbean cruising. It was followed two years later by Carnival Cruise Lines, which developed the "Fun Ship" concept to scuttle the elitist traditions of oceanliners and appeal to a mass market of younger, first-time passengers from all walks of life.

As the revolution's final irony, the spectacular growth in cruise vacations really took off in the 1970s, when cruise lines joined forces with airlines, which had almost put the steamship companies out of business. The union created air/sea programs that combined air transportation and ground transfers with a cruise in one package at one price. The programs enhanced the value of cruise vacations, simplified their purchase, and eliminated hassles for travelers. With the packages, cruise lines virtually brought their ships to people's doorsteps, regardless of where they lived. The marriage enabled cruise lines to base their ships in warm-weather ports from where they could cruise year-round and to fly passengers from faraway places to begin their cruises. A relaxed, informal holiday in the sun, available year-round, became the essence of modern cruising. Flying passengers to their ships saved time and enabled lines to offer shorter, less expensive cruises that fit into the national trend toward shorter vacations. It also allowed cruise lines to open new parts of the world to cruising; itineraries multiplied. No matter how many cruises a person took, new ones remained. Or so it seemed, until the oil crisis of the early 1970s, when dark clouds again threatened the future of vacations at sea.

Then, in 1978, despite skyrocketing fuel prices and predictions that cruising was doomed, Carnival Cruise Lines ordered a large, technologically advanced passenger ship. It became the forerunner of the 1980s superliners. Two years later, Norwegian Cruise Line shocked the cruise world by buying the fabulous *France* and transforming her into the *Norway*. The floating resort set cruise trends for the decade, introducing innovations including a variety of entertainment lounges, a theater for Broadway-scale productions, a shopping plaza, and a "sidewalk" cafe. Holland America followed with *Nieuw Amsterdam* and *Noordam,* twin ships with square sterns that allowed over 20 percent more deck space for recreation, including 2 swimming pools. The ships also introduced computer keys to open cabin doors and other innovations.

Princess Cruises' stylish *Royal Princess,* which debuted in 1984, set new standards of comfort with all outside cabins fitted with minibars, television, and baths with tubs in every category. About the same time, the *QE2* introduced the first Golden Door spa at sea, first computer learning center, and first satellite-delivered newspaper.

Among the most interesting entries was the *Windstar* in 1986, a cruise ship with computerized sails. *Windstar* married the romance of sailing under canvas with the comforts of a cruise ship and the electronic age. At the same time, Carnival's superliners, *Holiday, Jubilee,* and *Celebration,* were introduced. Their madcap design totally changed the look of ship interiors and the use of public space.

Yet nothing since the *Norway* caused as much excitement as the 1988 debut of Royal Caribbean Cruise Line's *Sovereign of the Seas.* The world's largest cruise ship at the time, she became the pacesetter for the 1990s. Among her features was the first shipboard atrium, rising through five decks and creating a new environment. The ship offered such numerous and varied entertainment and recreation options that passengers needed several cruises to experience them all. As the decade closed, some old lines disappeared in mergers, and new lines popped up. Health and fitness facilities were integrated into cruising. Healthful foods were readily available. Well-equipped gyms, elaborate spas, VCRs, cable television, and world-wide direct-dial telephones were rapidly becoming standard amenities. Small boutique ships, including those of the Seabourn and Silversea lines, brought new levels of luxury to cruising. Special-interest lines were finding their niche. Increased interest in adventure and nature cruises caused some traditional cruise lines to add them. Environmental concerns had a major impact on cruise ship technology. The late 1960s and early 1970s saw the conversion of oceanliners to cruise ships and the first ships built specifically for cruising, but the 1980s became the decade of innovation, particularly aboard ships designed to sail in warm climates. People who might never have considered taking a cruise booked them.

IN THE NEW MILLENNIUM

The 30-year cruise boom shows no signs of letting up. In that time, the number of passengers has swollen from under 500,000 annually to over 5.5 million. Eleven of the 22 members of the Cruise Lines International Association, the major cruise trade association, did not exist 15 years ago.

The 1990s were a blockbuster decade, with more than three dozen new ships costing an estimated $12 billion in the water and another $12 billion committed for four dozen more ships by 2003. Most of the ships are bigger, with more dazzle, and travel specialists are asking, "Where's the sky?"

The ships over 75,000 tons—and particularly those over 100,000 tons—represent a new generation of megaliners. Most have new design features and facilities—such as the highly publicized 18-hole miniature golf course on the *Legend of the Seas,* the virtual-reality theater on Princess

Cruises' *Grand Princess,* and the interactive computers on Celebrity's *Century* and *Galaxy.* But the capper may be the *Voyager of the Seas,* the first of the three 142,000-ton ships being built by Royal Caribbean, which debuted in November 1999 with cruising's first rock-climbing wall and ice rink.

Along with innovations, cruise lines are enhancing the cruise experience. Passengers will find larger standard cabins on most new ships and more verandas in the mid–price range. They will also find that more dining options are fast becoming standard on new ships, as are more entertainment choices, more sports opportunities, and larger, more elaborate spas.

Lines faced with intense competition (particularly in the Caribbean) are branching out and offering itineraries worldwide. The immediate impact of so many new ships will be to keep prices down. It also will accelerate the need for lines to define their style and differentiate themselves from the competition. That should help distill the options for you. But you still need to make the right choice, and helping you do that is what this book is designed to do.

We Want to Hear from You

At the end of this book, you will find an
Unofficial Guide Reader Survey. We invite you to use it.
Tell us about your cruise and how we can
make this a better book.

Part One

Planning Your Cruise Vacation

Understanding Cruises

THE CRUISE PACKAGE

Although it's possible (and sometimes desirable) to buy the components of a cruise vacation à la carte, most cruises are sold as complete packages. The basic package includes:

1. Shipboard accommodations.

2. Three full-service dining room meals daily (breakfast, lunch, and dinner), plus alternative breakfast, lunch, and late-night buffets. On most ships, room service meals do not cost extra. Many ships also offer options, such as early-bird breakfast, morning bouillon, and afternoon events, including tea, pizza snacks, ice cream parties, wine and cheese tastings, and poolside cookouts.

3. All shipboard entertainment, including music, dancing and shows in the lounges, discos, live bands, Las Vegas–style productions, nightclubs, karaoke, and movies.

4. All shipboard sports and recreational facilities, including swimming pools, health club or exercise room, promenade or jogging track, Jacuzzi, sauna, library, game room, and child-care facilities. (Spa and beauty treatments and some specialized sports equipment often cost extra.)

5. All shipboard activities, including the casino, on-board games and contests, lectures, demonstrations, and children's program (where applicable, babysitting services are extra).

6. Stops at ports of call on the itinerary.

7. Round-trip airfare* to and from the port city.

8. Transfers* (ground transportation) from the airport to the ship and from the ship to the airport.

* See the section "What Happened to 'Free' Air?"

Port charges (about $120 per person on a seven-day Caribbean cruise) may not be included in the advertised cruise price. If not, the line's brochures will show the cost for each cruise.

Taxes, optional shore excursions, alcoholic beverages and soft drinks, casino play, on-board shopping, and tips are not included in most cases. On a few very upscale lines, tipping and wine and alcoholic beverages are included in the cruise price. On some, tips are pooled (you are asked to contribute a suggested amount per day to be divided among all staff except officers and senior staff). We include a section on tipping in Part Two.

CRUISING'S UNFORTUNATE STEREOTYPES

You have probably heard that "cruising is not for everyone." But that's like saying travel is not for everyone. If you like to travel, you will almost certainly enjoy cruising. It's that simple. Cruising, however, has accumulated unfortunate stereotypes, which continue to recycle.

Myth No. 1: I'll Be Bored   Many people, particularly men and younger, active folks believe cruising is dull and sedentary. They picture bulk loaders crowding buffets while active folks sit bored and unstimulated. Sorry, not so.

Today, most cruises offer around-the-clock activities. Ships have exercise rooms with quality equipment, jogging tracks, pools, and daily exercise classes. Some larger ships have volleyball and basketball courts. At ports of call, a variety of sports—from golf to cycling, snorkeling to kayaking—are offered. There are far more opportunities for sports and athletics than most of us have at home. If you go on a cruise and sit on your butt, that's your decision.

For the active but less athletic, most ships offer swimming, shuffleboard, table tennis, walking areas, and spa amenities, including hot tubs and saunas. Many ships offer yoga or stretching classes. At night, for the energetic, there's dancing in many forms, from ballroom to reggae to line dancing to salsa.

A range of organized activities targets gregarious and fun-loving people. Versions of television game shows are popular, as are more traditional events like bridge tournaments, arts and crafts classes, and dancing lessons. Most cruise ships have casinos, and almost all have bingo.

If learning is your goal, dozens of cruises specialize in providing educational experiences and exploration of a region accompanied by experts. Like floating graduate schools, these cruises may focus on political and natural history or offer lectures on topics unrelated to the ship's destinations.

Finally, there is no place better than a cruise ship to relax. The favorite cruise activity for many people is curling up in a comfortable deck chaise with a good book. Even a big ship with constant activity offers quiet spots for meditation, reading, or just enjoying the beauty of the sea.

Myth No. 2: Cruising Is for Rich People; I Can't Afford a Cruise   If you take a vacation of three or more days during which you stay in hotels and eat in restaurants, you can afford a cruise.

Let's compare cruising to a modest vacation: Vic and Edna's one-week trip to Gatlinburg, Tennessee, and the Smoky Mountains. Driving from their home near Cleveland, Ohio, Vic and Edna spent about $200 on gas for the Chevy. They averaged $65 a night plus tax for motels, or $498 for the week. For breakfast and lunch, it was Shoney's- or Denny's-type restaurants. They'd go more upscale for dinner, and they liked beer or wine with their meal. Total for seven days' food: $388. In the mountains they mostly hiked and drove around. One day, however, they played golf; on another they visited a museum and a theme park. On the Friday before heading home, they rented horses for half a day. Golf, admissions, and horses came to approximately $190. Recapping:

Vic and Edna's Splendid Vacation

Lodging	$ 498
Gas	$ 200
Meals	$ 388
Admissions	$ 190
TOTAL	$ 1,276

During the same period, Royal Caribbean, a good middle-of-the-market line (not super-budget or super-luxury), offered a seven-night southern Caribbean cruise on *Monarch of the Seas* for $699 per person, including round-trip airfare from Cleveland to the home port. The cruise visited San Juan, St. Thomas, Martinique, Barbados, Antigua, and St. Maarten. Commodore, a small line with an old but commodious ship, offered seven nights in the Caribbean for a remarkable $499 per person! Even better values can be had with Celebrity and Holland America's promotional fares, which can go as low as $599 for nicer cabins on even newer ships.

These were promotional rates, not the "rack" rates listed in the brochures. The point is: On the seven-night cruise, Vic and Edna could have enjoyed the amenities of a full resort, dined in grand style, danced to live music, visited six beautiful tropical islands, and soaked in a whirlpool under the Caribbean moon for about the same amount they spent on their road trip. We are not suggesting Vic and Edna should swap the Smokies for the Caribbean, only that they could afford to do so if they are inclined.

Myth No. 3: Cruises Are Stuffy, Elitist, and Formal   Most cruises are none of the above, though the description might fit some passengers. A few cruises resemble floating debutante balls, but these are easily avoided. Cruises cover a broad range of dress and social protocols. You can choose a cruise at whatever level of formality or casualness feels right for you. Overall, cruises have become very casual and informal. Even on "formal" nights— such as the captain's welcome-aboard party and/or farewell party—half of the men wear business suits, and women don cocktail or party dresses. On the most informal ships, like Carnival, where you can wear anything short of a burlap bag, people dress to the nines—and it's often the men more so than the women. And they love it.

Myth No. 4: Cruises Are Too Regimented for Me   Granted, it takes organization to get everyone on board a cruise ship. It takes similar regimentation to get everyone off at the end of the cruise. In between, meals are often served at specific times at assigned tables, but many ships assign dinner only. At ports, you need only get back on board before the ship sails.

Some folks lump cruises into the same category as whirlwind bus tours— eight countries in five days and that sort of thing. A cruise might visit eight countries in five days, but you will have to check in and unpack only once. That's the beauty of cruising—you can hang out on the ship and just enjoy the ride, or you can get off at each port and pursue your own agenda.

Myth No. 5: I'm Afraid I'll Get Seasick   Well, you might, but the vast majority of people don't, particularly on a Caribbean cruise, where the ocean is usually as smooth as bathwater. Even those who get queasy in a car can usually handle a cruise. Over-the-counter antinausea medications like Bonine (doesn't make you drowsy) or Dramamine get most folks over the acclimatization period of the first few hours at sea. Bring some; you may never need it, but having it is comforting. Usually, Dramamine or Bonine is available from the purser's desk or your cabin steward.

If you are really worried, buy Sea Bands—a pair of elasticized wristbands (similar to a tennis band), each with a small plastic disk that applies pressure to the inside wrist, according to acupuncture principles. They are particularly useful for people who have difficulty taking medication. Sea Bands are sold in drug, toiletry, and health-care stores and can be ordered from Travel Accessories, P.O. Box 391162, Solon, OH 44139; phone

(440) 248-8432. If you take precautions and become seasick anyway, the ship's doctor can administer more powerful medication.

In regard to seasickness, remember: Don't dwell on your fear, and if you become queasy, take medicine immediately. When you deal with symptoms quickly, relief is fast.

Minimize the probability of getting seasick by choosing an itinerary in calmer waters: Alaska's Inside Passage, the Caribbean, the Mediterranean, and the Gulf of Mexico. Less smooth are voyages on the Atlantic, Pacific, or Indian Oceans or the South China Sea.

Myth No. 6: I'm Apprehensive about Walking on a Moving Ship   If you are not agile or fit on land, you might envision tortuous trips down narrow gangways or climbing ladders through tiny hatches while the ship rolls and pitches. But generally, if you can handle a hotel, you can handle a cruise ship. Large vessels have wide, carpeted halls and slip-resistant outside decks. Elevators serve all passenger decks, so using the stairs may not even be necessary. Passengers use no tricky ladders or tiny hatches.

Modern cruise ships have stabilizers, and even in bad weather and heavy seas they are amazingly stable. Small ships, depending on their draft and build, may be more subject to the motion of the ocean and are a little more challenging to get around. Being smaller, however, there's less territory to cover. Most ships launched in the last ten years were built with consideration for healthy passengers as well as those with ambulatory disabilities. Many modern ships offer wheelchair-accessible cabins and ramps.

A TYPICAL DAY ON A CRUISE

Let's say we're cruising the Caribbean. You can start your morning with an early-bird breakfast or a walk or jog around deck, or you can have breakfast from the menu in the dining room. Late sleepers can order breakfast from room service or catch the breakfast buffet, which stays open later than the dining room. It usually is served on the "lido" deck—a casual indoor/outdoor dining facility on the same deck as the swimming pool or sports facilities. The lido buffet has longer and more flexible hours, enabling you to come and go at will.

Days at sea are the most relaxing of the cruise itinerary. The casino, shopping arcade, spa, exercise room, and shore excursion desk are open. Programs and activities are virtually nonstop on large ships; most folks, however, hang out by the pool or on deck to enjoy the beauty of the sea and the relaxing movement of being under way. The captain may update passengers over the public address system on the ship's progress toward the next port. The captain or cruise director may also point out interesting sights.

Lunch works much like breakfast: you can eat in the dining room and order from the menu, or you can stay in your swimsuit and eat burgers or pizza by the pool, where there is likely to be a music combo playing upbeat rhythms. You can join the pool games—a good way to meet people—or just watch or ignore them. You then might work out, read, nap, play bridge, learn the latest dance steps, or attend orientation lectures about the next port. Recently released movies are shown in the ship's movie theater or on cabin television in the afternoon. On some ships, afternoon tea is a big deal—white gloves and all. At cocktail hour, there is usually live music by the pool, often with special drinks or appetizers, or happy hour in one of the bars.

As dinner approaches, it's time to dress for the evening. The dress code generally is specified on the daily agenda slipped under your door every evening. It is also spelled out in the cruise line's brochure, so you can pack accordingly. (More information on dress codes is available in this section under "Preparing for Your Cruise.")

Some passengers stroll the deck before dinner, particularly at sunset, a beautiful time at sea. Others have a drink in one of the lounges. Dinner in the dining room is a social culmination of the day's activity. Spirits are always high.

After lingering over several well-prepared courses, it's off to the show-room, where live entertainment, ranging from Las Vegas–style variety shows to Broadway musicals, is offered nightly. After the show, early risers and those who had a long day of touring retire to their cabins. The more nocturnal or party-minded guests head for the casino, disco, or a lounge with entertainment. By now, it's time for the midnight buffet, on many ships the chefs' most creative venue. Each night may have a theme—pasta, salads, desserts, barbecue, and so on. But, at least one night will be the Grand Buffet. Bring your camera; every platter is a work of art. Before turning in, stretch out in a chaise longue on deck with a glass of wine. Breathe in the balmy salt-sea air and be caressed by the warm breeze. Lose yourself among the million stars of the Caribbean night.

Usually, cruise ships sail through the night and arrive at the next port early in the morning. If you have been smart and risen in time to enjoy the early morning—the most beautiful time at sea—you can watch your ship dock. It's interesting and fun. After breakfast, the captain announces that the ship has been cleared by local officials and that passengers may disembark. Those signed up for shore excursions are given last-minute instructions about when and where to meet and are normally first to go ashore.

Although port calls range from three hours to two days (with an overnight at dock), most are five to ten hours—hardly enough time to sample an island or city. As you disembark, crew members remind you of the sailing time and make sure you are carrying your cruise identification, which you must present to reboard. Once ashore, some people explore on foot, taking walking tours, shopping, and perhaps trying a shoreside restaurant. Others hire a cab for a driving tour, whereas still others are on shore excursions purchased aboard ship.

Shore excursions take many forms. Some are passive (bus tour), but others are active (snorkeling, sailing, hiking, biking, or fishing). Surprisingly, many folks, particularly experienced cruisers, stay aboard ship. It's quiet—almost empty of passengers—but it's in full operation except for casinos and shops. Lunch is served on schedule in the dining room.

At least 30 minutes before sailing, you reboard the ship. Just before castoff, go topside to watch the crew prepare for departure. Leaving port is always interesting, and a ship's higher decks offer a great viewing platform. Once at sea, the ship settles into its normal nighttime routine, and you join it.

So Many Cruises to Choose From

To the first-time cruiser and many veterans, the number of cruise lines, ships, and itineraries is staggering. Travel agencies that sell only cruises ease their customers into the array of choices by comparing cruise lines with well-known hotel chains, and such a comparison is useful. They might see Commodore Cruise Line, for example, as offering Budget or Quality Inn cruises. Carnival is the Holiday Inn of cruises. Holland America and Celebrity Cruise Line are up a notch, perhaps at the Hyatt level.

Ritz-Carlton cruises might appeal to the most discriminating cruisers and are at the upper end of price, service, and amenities. Ships in this class include Crystal Cruises' *Crystal Harmony* and Cunard's *Seabourn Sun*. Boutique cruises overlap the deluxe category and include the smaller, all-suite ships of Radisson Seven Seas, Silversea, Seabourn, and Sea Goddess, and the cruise/sail ships of Windstar.

Be aware that none of the hotel chains mentioned (except Radisson and Hyatt) have anything to do with cruising, and these are only a handful of the lines available. Though the foregoing may help you see where you fit into the general scheme, you must dig much deeper to find your perfect cruise.

Getting Your Act Together

Cruises vary widely. To pinpoint your requirements and preferences in a cruise, you need to ask yourself dozens of questions. Once you settle on what you want, it's easier to match your demands and budget with the appropriate line and ship.

What Is My Vacation Budget?

Unless price is no object, start your planning with your budget. How much can you afford, and what are you willing to spend for your cruise? Consider what you must or may add to the cruise price: port charges and taxes, shore excursions, shopping, drinks and dinner wine (on most ships), gambling in the casino, spa services, laundry, and tips for crew members. Once you figure your uppermost limit for all costs, you can begin to explore what kind of cruise you can buy.

Although we will revisit this issue in the section "How to Get the Best Deal on a Cruise," let's say three-day cruises start at about $280 a person, assuming two to a cabin. Seven-day cruises begin at about $550, and ten-day cruises are about $800 and up. These prices are deeply discounted and represent the least you would expect to pay, usually for a cabin without windows.

How Many Days Do I Want to Cruise?

Your available vacation time and budget are factors in your answer. Generally, the larger your budget, the more cruise days you can buy. That is, the longer the cruise, the more it will cost. If your budget isn't up to the number of days you have your heart set on, you still have options. First, trade luxury for cruise days; consider a cruise on a less luxurious ship. The fee for a week on an upscale ship will easily buy two weeks on a midrange vessel. However, don't veer too far from your lifestyle or expectations, or you will be disappointed with your cruise. Second, cruise during the off-season, when prices are lowest. Third, settle for the least expensive cabin. Once aboard, all passengers have the same privileges, eat the same meals, and enjoy the same entertainment. Unless you plan to spend an extraordinary amount of time in your cabin, you probably can tolerate less expensive accommodations. We're not talking about special suites, just the difference between the highest deck outside cabin (with a window) and the lowest deck inside cabin (no window). For example, on a seven-day Celebrity Cruise Line itinerary to Bermuda, the upper deck outside cabin costs more than twice as much as the lower deck inside cabin.

In the Caribbean and Mexico, a seven-day cruise is about right for your first trip, but if you can't afford the time or money, a three- or four-night cruise will give you a good enough overview of ship life that you can determine whether cruising is something you'll enjoy again in the future.

Where Do I Want to Go?

You can cruise just about anywhere there is enough water to float a ship. This includes all of the world's oceans and seas and many rivers. Where

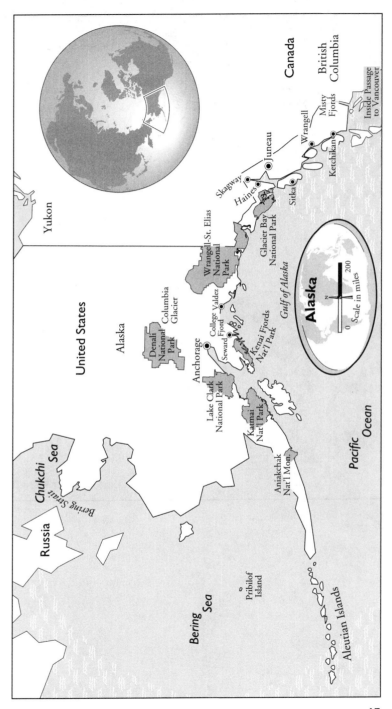

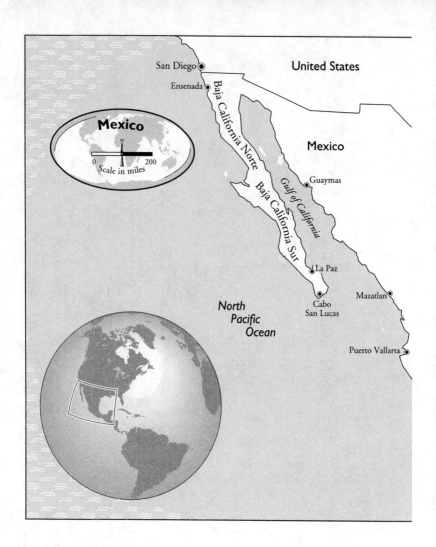

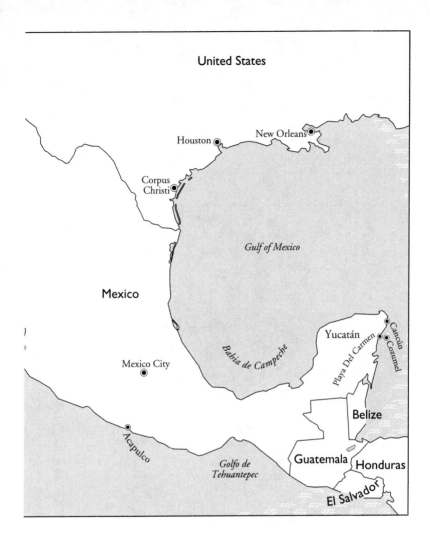

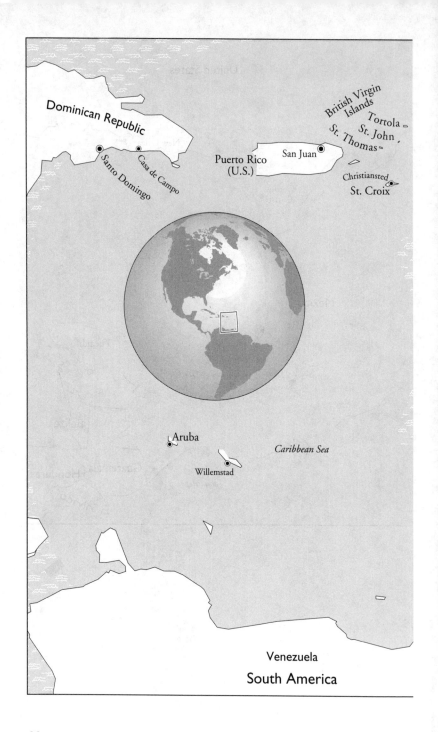

Dominican Republic

Santo Domingo

Casa de Campo

Puerto Rico
(U.S.)

San Juan

British Virgin
Islands

Tortola

St. John

St. Thomas

Christiansted

St. Croix

Aruba

Caribbean Sea

Willemstad

Venezuela

South America

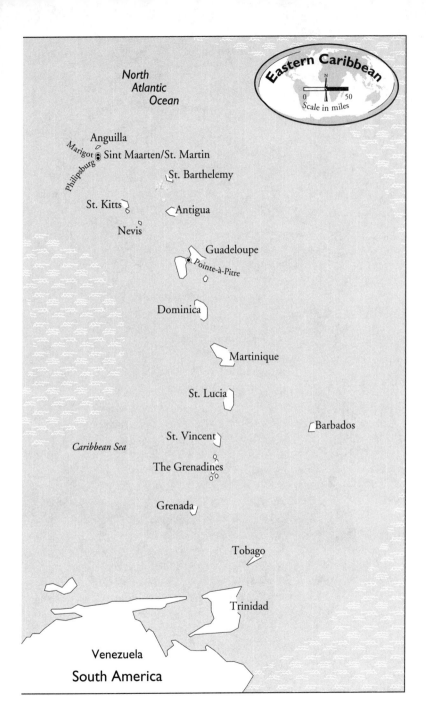

North
Atlantic
Ocean

Eastern Caribbean

N

0   50
Scale in miles

Anguilla
Marigot
Sint Maarten/St. Martin
Philipsburg
St. Barthelemy

St. Kitts
Antigua
Nevis

Guadeloupe
Pointe-à-Pitre

Dominica

Martinique

St. Lucia

Barbados

Caribbean Sea
St. Vincent

The Grenadines

Grenada

Tobago

Trinidad

Venezuela
South America

21

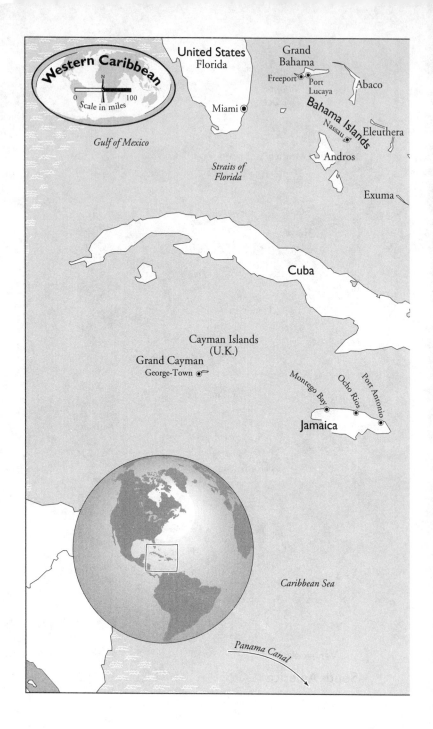

Western Caribbean

N

0   Scale in miles   100

United States
Florida

Gulf of Mexico

Miami

Straits of
Florida

Grand
Bahama

Freeport Port
Lucaya

Abaco

Bahama Islands

Nassau   Eleuthera

Andros

Exuma

Cuba

Cayman Islands
(U.K.)

Grand Cayman
George-Town

Montego Bay   Ocho Rios   Port Antonio

Jamaica

Caribbean Sea

Panama Canal

22

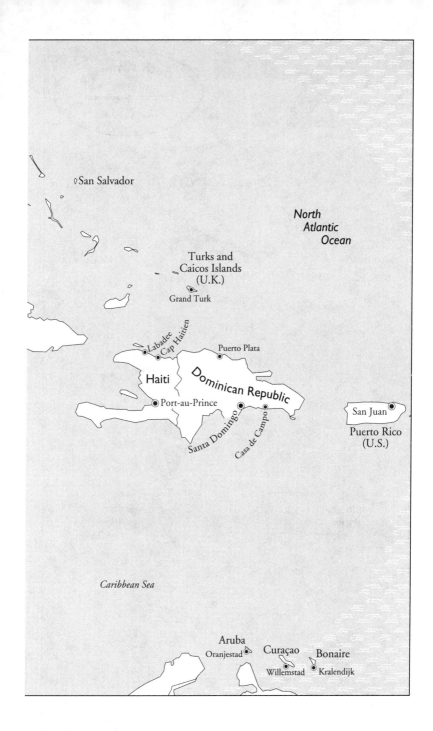

24

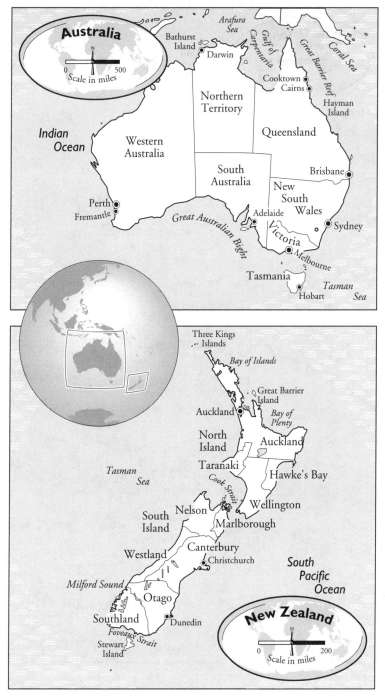

Australia

N

0   500
Scale in miles

Arafura Sea

Gulf of Carpentaria

Great Barrier Reef

Coral Sea

Bathurst Island

Darwin

Cooktown
Cairns

Hayman Island

Northern Territory

Queensland

Indian Ocean

Western Australia

South Australia

Brisbane

New South Wales

Perth
Fremantle

Adelaide

Sydney

Great Australian Bight

Victoria

Melbourne

Tasmania

Tasman Sea

Hobart

Three Kings Islands

Bay of Islands

Great Barrier Island

Auckland

Bay of Plenty

North Island

Auckland

Taranaki

Hawke's Bay

Tasman Sea

Cook Strait

Wellington

Nelson

South Island

Marlborough

Westland

Canterbury

Christchurch

South Pacific Ocean

Milford Sound

Otago

Southland

Dunedin

Foveaux Strait

Stewart Island

New Zealand

N

0   200
Scale in miles

25

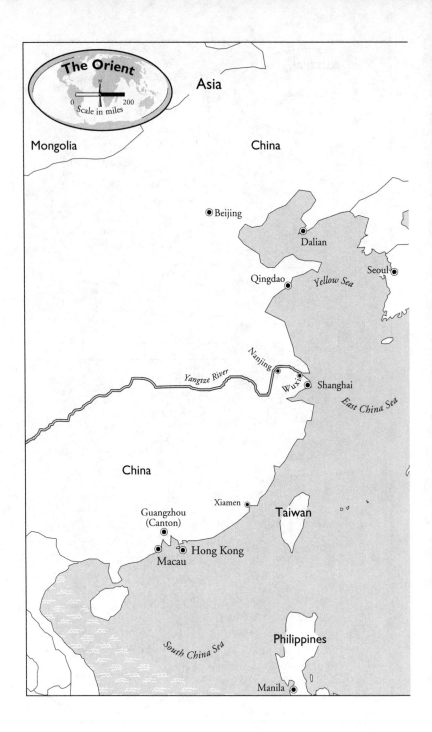

The Orient

Asia

Mongolia

China

Beijing

Dalian

Seoul

Qingdao

Yellow Sea

Nanjing

Yangtze River

Wuxi

Shanghai

East China Sea

China

Xiamen

Taiwan

Guangzhou
(Canton)

Hong Kong

Macau

South China Sea

Philippines

Manila

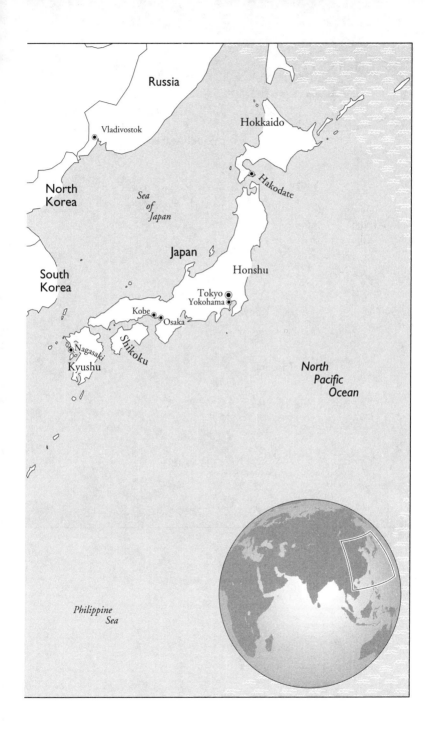

Russia

Vladivostok

Hokkaido

North
Korea

*Sea
of
Japan*

Hakodate

Japan

South
Korea

Honshu

Tokyo
Yokohama

Kobe
Osaka

Nagasaki
Kyushu

Shikoku

*North
Pacific
Ocean*

*Philippine
Sea*

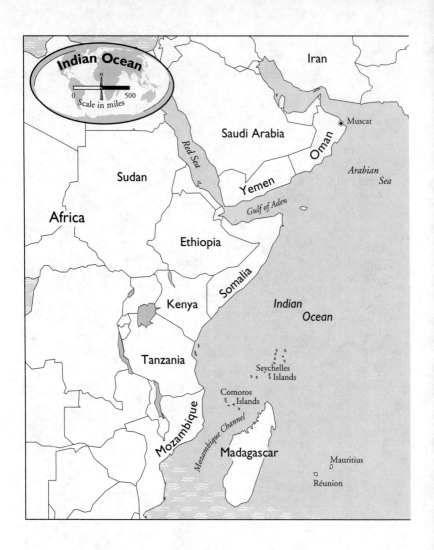

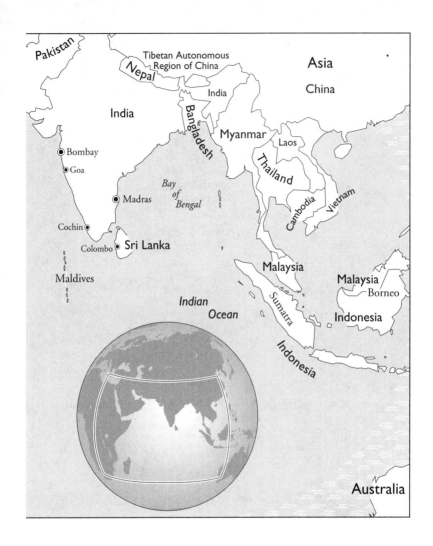

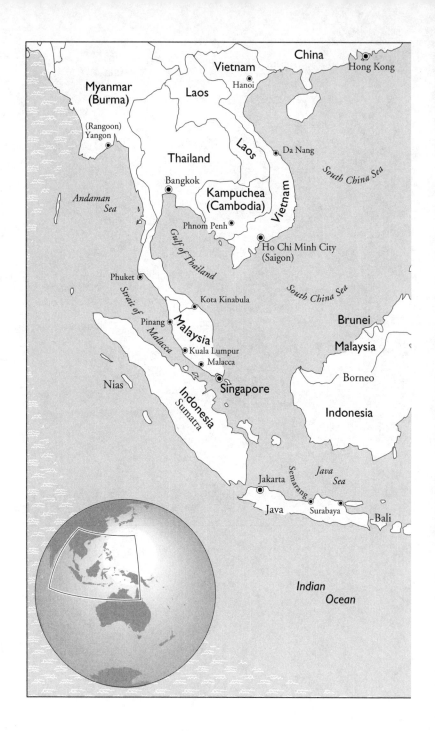

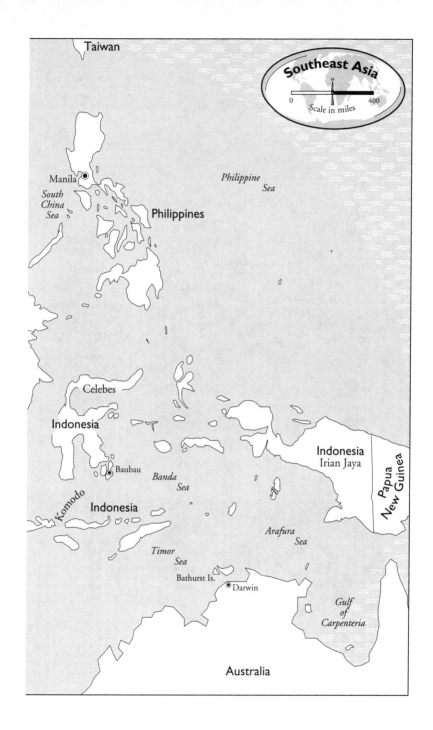

Taiwan

Southeast Asia

0   400
Scale in miles

Manila

Philippine
Sea

South
China
Sea

Philippines

Celebes

Indonesia

Indonesia
Irian Jaya

Papua
New Guinea

Baubau

Banda
Sea

Komodo

Indonesia

Arafura
Sea

Timor
Sea

Bathurst Is.

Darwin

Gulf
of
Carpenteria

Australia

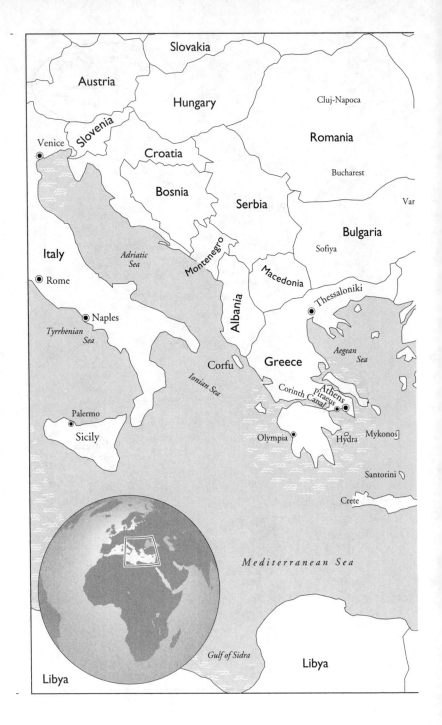

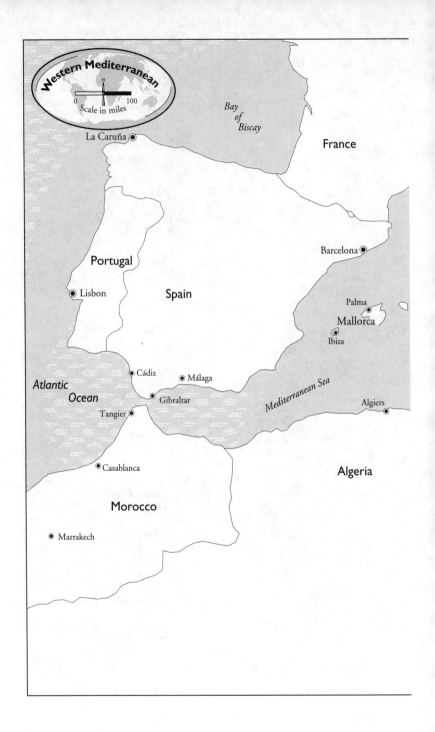

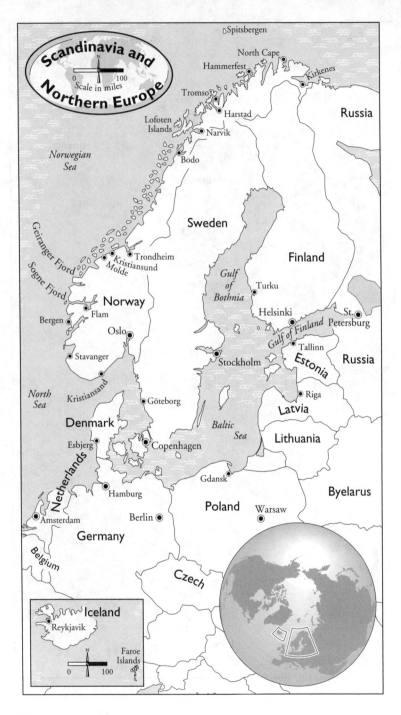

Scandinavia and
Northern Europe

0   100
Scale in miles

Spitsbergen

North Cape
Hammerfest
Kirkenes
Tromso
Harstad
Lofoten
Islands
Narvik
Bodo

Norwegian
Sea

Russia

Sweden

Finland

Geiranger Fjord

Trondheim
Kristiansund
Molde

Sogne Fjord

Norway

Flam
Bergen
Oslo

Stavanger

Gulf
of
Bothnia

Turku

Helsinki

St.
Petersburg

Gulf of Finland

Tallinn

Estonia

Russia

Stockholm

North
Sea

Kristiansand

Göteborg

Riga

Latvia

Denmark

Baltic
Sea

Lithuania

Esbjerg

Copenhagen

Gdansk

Byelarus

Netherlands

Hamburg

Poland

Warsaw

Amsterdam

Berlin

Germany

Belgium

Czech

Iceland

Reykjavik

Faroe
Islands

0   100

36

you want to cruise depends primarily on your own "wild goose." It also hinges on your preferred style of cruising and whether you enjoy the destinations or the ship more.

Some destinations, including Alaska and Europe, are seasonal. Others, including the Caribbean and Mexico, are year-round. Almost all cruises worldwide are tailored to the market and the weather. Many to the Caribbean and Mexico, for example, are festive and high-spirited, emphasizing activity and fun. Mild temperatures allow time outdoors, and passengers tend to be younger. By contrast, Alaskan, Canadian, North Atlantic, Scandinavian, and Baltic Sea cruises are more passive, focusing on the beauty of the forests, islands, fjords, and glaciers. For these northerly venues, longer cruises and colder temperatures contribute to a more sedate experience and attract families or older passengers. Mediterranean itineraries generally revolve around antiquities and port cities of southern Europe, north Africa, and the Middle East. Most ships visit a port each day, and sight-seeing is the backbone of the vacation. On ships where English is spoken and the majority aboard are Americans, the clientele is age 50 and older and affluent. On cruise ships where Europeans predominate, passengers are younger, and sun and fun are emphasized, like in the Caribbean.

Hawaiian cruises occupy the middle, emphasizing both festivity and scenery, though passengers are older on average than those in the Caribbean. For other North Pacific, South Pacific, Indian Ocean, and South China Sea settings, the distance of the cruise areas and home ports from the United States ensures an older, wealthier market. Like Mediterranean cruises, sight-seeing and cultural attractions are the focus.

Though a great way to see exotic places without shuffling among hotels, cruises allow only a cursory glimpse of the countries visited. Ten hours in Venice on a cruise is no substitute for visiting Italy. Even in the Caribbean, short stopovers on small islands leave much undiscovered.

Some travelers use cruising to sample cities and countries to determine whether they might want to return later for a more prolonged visit. If you are interested in further exploring a destination, consider the add-ons most lines offer at the beginning and end of cruises. Two- or three-night packages include a hotel and some sight-seeing. They are usually well priced and can be booked at the time you buy your cruise.

Defining the Caribbean   On a map with the arm of the compass pointing north, the islands closest to the United States are the Greater Antilles; they include Cuba, the Caymans, Jamaica, Haiti, the Dominican Republic, and Puerto Rico. All but Cuba are visited by ships from U.S. ports and have daily, direct air service from major U.S. cities.

The Bahamas and the British colony of the Turks and Caicos lie north of the Greater Antilles and southeast of Florida. They are entirely in the Atlantic Ocean, but because their tropical environment is similar to that of the Caribbean, they are viewed as part of the region. The Bahamas, not the Turks and Caicos, are cruise stops; both have air service from the United States.

In the eastern Caribbean are the Lesser Antilles, starting with the Virgin Islands in the north and curving south to Grenada. The northern of these many small islands are called the Leewards and comprise the U.S. and British Virgin Islands, Anguilla, St. Maarten, St. Barts, Saba, St. Eustatius, St. Kitts, Nevis, Antigua, Barbuda, Montserrat, and Guadeloupe. The south islands, called the Windwards, include Dominica, Martinique, St. Lucia, Barbados, St. Vincent and the Grenadines, and Grenada.

The Virgin Islands, St. Maarten, Antigua, Guadeloupe, Martinique, St. Lucia, Barbados, and Grenada are frequent cruise stops and have direct air service from the United States. The others are reached through local airlines, and most are stops for small ships, particularly during winter cruise season. In the south are Aruba, Bonaire, Curaçao, and Trinidad and Tobago, which lie off Venezuela. In the western Caribbean off the Yucatán Peninsula are the Mexican islands of Cancún and Cozumel.

Along the 2,000-mile Caribbean chain, nature has been extravagant with its color, variety, and beauty. Verdant mountains rise from sun-bleached shores. Between towering peaks and the sea, rivers and streams cascade over rocks and hillsides and disappear into mangrove swamps and deserts. Fields of flowers, trees with brilliant blossoms, and a multitude of birds and butterflies fill the landscape. The air, refreshed by tropical showers, is scented with spices and fruit.

Yet, what makes the Caribbean islands unique is their combination of exotic scenery and the kaleidoscope of diverse cultures. The people and their cultures have evolved from traditions, music, dance, art, architecture, and religions from around the world.

When Do I Want to Go?

Cruises follow the sun, visiting destinations during their best weather. Hence, for some exotic destinations and such seasonal cruise areas as Alaska, the British Isles, Canada, and Antarctica, you have only a two- to five-month window of opportunity. For the Caribbean, Mexico, Hawaii, and the Orient, among others, cruises are available all year.

Following is a sampling of popular destinations and cruising seasons.

Africa	Year-round, but mostly May–October for north Africa; November–April for eastern and southern Africa

Alaska	May–September
Asia and the Orient	Mainly October–March
Baltic	May–October
Bermuda	May–October
Black Sea	April–October
Canada	May–October
Caribbean	Year-round
Hawaii	Year-round
India and Southeast Asia	Year-round; mostly November–April
Mediterranean	March–November
Mexico	Year-round
New England	May–October
Panama Canal	September–May
South America	North coast, year-round; other areas, September–April
South Pacific	Year-round; mainly November–April

For every area, periods of peak demand are called high season; moderate demand, shoulder season; and low demand, low season or value season. Usually high season occurs when good weather in the cruise area coincides with times when people want to take vacations. In the Caribbean, that's between Christmas and the middle of April and from June 15 to August 15. Yet within high season are often valleys when prices are likely to be their lowest for the year, offering you an opportunity to save a bundle. In the Caribbean, for example, immediately after the Christmas–New Year holiday demand drops, the first two weeks in January offer value season rates. If you can be flexible, shifting cruise dates a week or two may offer big savings. Always check the period immediately before or after your selected dates to find out your options.

The January–April market targets seniors and Northerners seeking a respite from the winter. Although weather in summer is not as good as between January and April, families create high demand during midsummer when school is out. When demand tapers off, shoulder season follows, giving way to low season as cruise demand continues to decline.

During high season, ships generally are full (more crowded), and cruises are more expensive (because demand is high). If your plans are flexible, it is usually possible to identify several times in the year when your destination's weather is predictably good but cruise demand is moderate or low. Cruising during these periods provides lower prices, less crowded ships, and good weather. Caribbean cruises in November and early December before Christmas are good examples. Hurricane season is over, prices are low, and ships are significantly less crowded. Early May for Alaska is another excellent time.

If your travel schedule is not flexible, shoulder seasons (early June or late August) may be your best bet.

What Sort of Lifestyle or Activity Level Am I Seeking?

As Baby Boomers enter middle age and relative affluence, and as younger couples and families discover the economy of cruise vacations, cruising's demographics are changing. On most midmarket cruises of two weeks or less, passengers are amazingly diverse. Responding to a widening range of energy and interests among these passengers, lines have developed activities that offer something for almost everyone.

Even so, lines continue to fine-tune their product for their primary markets. Thus, although Celebrity Cruise Lines might develop programs and activities for younger clients, these cruisers continue to be a secondary market. The line's real focus is the 45–65 age group. That means a younger person will have a good time on Celebrity, but an over-40 will probably have a better time because the cruise is built around the latter's preferences.

How cruise lines serve their primary, secondary, and even tertiary markets makes relevant the question, "What sort of lifestyle or activity level am I seeking?"

In each of our cruise line and ship profiles, we pinpoint the style, tenor, and activity level of the cruises offered. Look for an activity and social mix that seems right for you, but don't get bogged down in demographics. Many older people are active, athletic, and like to party, while many young people appreciate a sedate cruise and may spend their days doing nothing more than reading in a lounge chair.

The choice to participate in activities or party all night is entirely yours. Do, however, pay attention to the ship's size. A small ship carrying 250 or fewer passengers may have only one or two lounges and limited deck space. If you don't care for a full day or evening of shipboard activity, you'll enjoy its low-key ambience. Large ships have the resources to offer considerable variety. Carnival Cruise Line, for example, pretty much wrote the book on party cruising, but even on a Carnival ship it is possible to relax. Ships carrying 1,000 or more passengers have plenty of places to escape the festivities.

Most ships offer a variety of dance music. Many even have separate nightclubs offering different types of music, dancing, and entertainment.

Cruise lines design their promotional brochures to appeal to their target markets. If you identify with the people and activities depicted in the brochure, you probably will feel at home on one of that line's ships. Lines that do not cater to families, for instance, do not feature them in their literature. Study the brochures from your travel agent. Are the passengers pictured your age or of varied ages? Is the emphasis on shipboard activities or ports and scenery? Does shipboard life look like a 24-hour party, or do photos show a more laid-back experience? On-board facilities need no interpretation. They're spelled out.

What Level of Formality Do I Prefer?

Most cruises give passengers an opportunity to play dress-up. On certain evenings in the main dining room, men wear jackets, tuxedos, or dark suits, and women wear cocktail dresses or gowns. Most ships have a dress protocol that passengers are expected to observe. (See Dress Codes in the section "Preparing for Your Cruise.")

Formality (or lack thereof) is a way cruise lines set themselves apart. A luxury line targeting highly affluent passengers almost always will be more formal than a midmarket line. Family and budget lines are less formal, and adventure cruises are usually the most informal.

The bottom line is how much formality you want. The great majority of cruises vary attire from night to night and won't punish someone who breaks the dress code. If, for example, a man wears a dark suit instead of a tuxedo for the captain's party, no one will turn him away. On the other hand, even an informal ship might ask passengers not to wear shorts and tank tops in the dining room and be strict about it. Most passengers don't spend a lot of time worrying about formality, but if it's important to you, check the ship's dress code before you book.

What Standards Do I Require for Dining and Food Quality?

Food—its quality and the overall dining experience—is cited by most passengers as a critical element of their cruise. The fare on cruise ships is generally very good—impressive considering that shipboard meals represent the ultimate extension of catered banquet dining.

Feeding 300 to 1,400 persons at a sitting is challenging under any circumstances. Doing it at sea with attention to detail, quality ingredients and preparation, and beautiful presentation is one of cruising's miracles. Ships have made an art of serving palatable food to crowds of diners. Hotel food and beverage managers could learn a lot from cruise ship chefs.

However, you can't expect the same excellence from a galley serving hundreds of dinners as you can from an upscale restaurant cooking to order for a small number of guests. A few small ships rival better restaurants, but they are the exception.

The quality of meals and sophistication of the dining experience vary considerably among ships. Although luxury ships serving fewer passengers in single seatings have the greatest potential for serving memorable meals, midmarket lines like Celebrity have shown they can approach similar standards of excellence serving larger numbers.

If you have a refined palate and eat exclusively in the finest restaurants, you may meet your dining requirements only in the high-end group of cruise ships. If, however, you dine regularly in restaurants of varying quality, are acquainted with the world's major cuisines, and understand the limitations of cruise food service, you will find numerous ships capable of meeting or exceeding your expectations.

For those not hung up on gourmet food, suitable cruises are many and, even better, among the most affordable. You can use your cruise dining experience to broaden your culinary horizons, or you can save bucks aboard a ship specializing in good, but less expensive, American fare.

Many people pay for food much fancier than their taste requires. Meat-and-potatoes people get a better deal putting their dollars into a cabin upgrade on a midmarket line rather than paying for fancy food on a luxury line.

Cruise lines have tended to offer good dining room meals or good buffets, but seldom both. Holland America and Celebrity are notable exceptions. Almost all lines have cut back on the midnight buffet, except for one extravaganza when chefs go all out to show off their culinary skills.

Weather and lifestyle have clearly affected cruise dining. Because most ships spend all or part of the year in the Caribbean and Mexico, where passengers remain in their bathing suits most of the day, the lines found that it makes sense and saves money to expand the lido breakfast and lunch. Lido dining also gives passengers relief from the regimentation of dining room hours.

How Gregarious Am I (Are We)?

Generally, it's easier to meet folks on a small ship. There are fewer passengers, and you see the same people more often. Conversely, on a large ship, the only folks you see regularly are your dinner table companions (hope you like them!). On larger ships, if you meet somebody you would like to see again, get their name and cabin number. We once met a nice woman checking in on the 2,300-passenger *Monarch of the Seas*. In a week aboard, we never again saw her.

Large ships offer many social settings. It's possible to meet people in bars, lounges, and nightclubs; on shore excursions; in the health club; around the pool; and in the casino. But the easiest time to meet them is at planned activities. Whether it's aerobics and line dancing or bridge and wine tasting, such activities help people with similar interests come together.

The style of a cruise is important. If you are gregarious, you might prefer a ship that promotes a party atmosphere. If you are more solitary or are taking a romantic cruise with your significant other, you may prefer a less frantic social agenda.

Most cruisers solve the problem of companionship by taking lovers, friends, relatives, or all of the above with them. As on Noah's ark, the majority of passengers arrive already paired up. This is attributable in part to the double-occupancy norm for cabins. Solo passengers pay a hefty "singles supplement" for the privilege of having a cabin to themselves. Ships schedule gatherings where singles can meet, and some try to seat singles at the same dining tables, but singles generally have to scout around to find other people who are flying solo.

The Other Passengers: What Kind of People Am I Most Comfortable With?

The less expensive the cruise, the more varied the passengers. Aboard a recent, affordable four-day Premier (Big Red Boat) cruise were retired seniors, middle-aged professionals, 20-something newlyweds, a bowling team from Pennsylvania, families with young children, a group of pipe fitters, and college students on spring break.

On upscale cruises of two weeks or longer, the cost ensures that passengers are somewhat more affluent and perhaps less diverse. On a seven-day Caribbean or Mexico cruise with midmarket lines, such as Royal Caribbean, Princess, Celebrity, and Holland America, you will find more seniors, more professionals, fewer tradespeople, fewer families with children (except during summer), and fewer people younger than age 25. Passengers are even less varied on the same lines' seven-day or longer cruises to the more expensive destinations of Alaska and the Mediterranean.

On the most upscale lines, including Seabourn, Radisson Seven Seas, and Silversea, the average passenger is older than age 55 and affluent. Passengers younger than age 20 are likely traveling with parents or grandparents. Some lines don't take children or discourage their presence because they do not have the facilities or atmosphere for them. Couples account for 80% of those on board. Singles are likely to be widows, widowers, or mature singles able to afford the lifestyle.

For our profiles of cruise lines and ships, we carefully scrutinized their passengers so you'll know what to expect. We believe the inclusion of this information is one element that makes this book different from other guidebooks on cruises. If you have strong feelings about who your fellow passengers will be, pay close attention to these descriptions.

What Kind of Itinerary Do I Prefer?

Among itineraries, there's a world to choose from. You can have mostly days at sea, mostly days in port, or a balance of the two. Your cruise can be educational or just fun. There are theme cruises where entertainment or education is the focus, such as a jazz festival, and cruises where specific activities are emphasized, such as scuba diving, sailing, or viewing wildlife.

Start by deciding how much time at sea versus time in port you prefer. If you are more interested in visiting ports, seek an itinerary with many of them. (Be aware that when a ship visits more than five ports on a seven-day cruise, some stops will be half-day.) Port-intensive itineraries are most plentiful on Mediterranean and eastern Caribbean cruises. Compare itineraries for different lines listing the same ports. When figuring your time in each port, remember that your ship must clear customs on arrival before passengers are allowed to disembark. A ship making port at 8 a.m. may not put passengers ashore before 9 or 9:30 a.m. Most ships require passengers to be aboard 30 minutes or more before leaving port. Thus, your time in port could be trimmed by an hour or more coming and going.

Another important consideration, if you want to maximize your time in port, is whether your ship ties up at the dock or anchors offshore. Having to use a tender (a small commuting boat) to reach shore can take a big bite out of your port time. The larger the ship, the more likely the need to use a tender. The published itinerary or your travel agent will provide information on tendering.

Many passengers—usually experienced cruisers—relish the serenity of being at sea. In recent years, they have been very vocal in opposing cruise lines' cramming ports into their itineraries to attract first-time cruisers who commonly perceive value in the number of ports visited. It's more difficult to find itineraries featuring days spent at sea than to uncover itineraries with daily port calls. Most three-, four-, and seven-day cruises spend more daylight hours in port than at sea. Longer cruises typically feature more time at sea. Itineraries list days spent under way as "cruising" or "at sea."

A map highlighting ports of call in the world's cruise areas shows the hundreds of ports ships can add to their itineraries. With the possible exception of the Atlantic coast of Africa, most ports are close enough to one another to allow a port visit every day. Fortunately, most itineraries of seven or more days strike a balance. A typical seven-day itinerary includes two days at sea. Three or four days of cruising is typical of 10-day itineraries; 4 to 5 days on 12- to 14-day itineraries.

Repositioning cruises are the best buys for those who crave more days at sea. They are also the best bargains. They occur at the end of the season in a cruise area when lines reposition their ship(s) by dispatching them to other areas where new seasons are beginning. Thus, Princess repositions some of its Caribbean fleet in April (the end of Caribbean high season) to the Pacific Northwest for summer cruises to Alaska. Royal Caribbean at the same time might dispatch ships from the Caribbean to Europe or the Mediterranean. Repositioning cruises stop at some ports, but there usually is a high ratio of sea days to days in port. Because such voyages occur only twice a year, they are difficult for lines to promote, and passage usually is discounted significantly.

Specialized Itineraries and Specialized Ships
Passengers aboard most large ships determine for themselves how they will use their time. Specialty cruises, by contrast, focus on a specific activity or pursuit. Some may specialize in whale-watching, others in exploring ancient ruins. Sometimes the vessel sets the focus. Smaller, 80- to 150-passenger ships can dock in small ports and anchor in secluded coves. This facilitates fishing, swimming, snorkeling, scuba diving, and water skiing (participants carry their own sports equipment) and makes a difference in the way passengers use their time.

Traditional ships sometimes offer theme cruises. For example, professional football players may be aboard and reruns of famous games are shown. Passengers should inquire about themes and book the cruise only if they're interested. A cruise ship can be the medium for countless activities and themes. For additional information on specialty cruises, see "Part Three: Cruising Alternatives."

Big Ships vs. Small Ships
Hardly a week passes that some cruise line doesn't announce plans for another ship—bigger and, of course, better than the last. But bigger isn't necessarily better for a cruise.

New words have crept into the cruise lexicon. Not everyone agrees on their definitions, but these are the currently accepted parameters:

Megaliner: a cruise ship with a basic capacity (i.e., two people per cabin) of 2,000 or more passengers.

Superliner: a cruise ship with a basic capacity of about 1,000 to 2,000.

Midsize: a cruise ship with a basic capacity of 400 to 900.

Small ship: a cruise ship with a basic capacity of under 400.

Boutique ship: a luxury cruise or expedition ship with a basic capacity of under 300.

Oceanliner: generally, any oceangoing passenger vessel, but tends to be used for former steamships that provided transatlantic and worldwide service and have since been converted into a cruise ship.

Until you sail on small ships, you may not realize their special pleasures. Small ships are fewer, but more diverse in style than larger ones. They range from traditional sailing ships, such as Star Clipper's tall ships, to computer-driven ones like Windstar Cruises', and in the degree of comfort and service from the modest vessels of American Canadian Caribbean Lines to Cunard's ultraluxurious *Sea Goddess* twins. Prices likewise vary from the moderate Windjammer Barefoot Cruises to très cher Seabourn Cruises.

It's difficult to generalize, but all small ships are cozy, imparting warmth never felt on a superliner. The smallest ones, such as American Safari's 12- and 21-passenger ships, are like private yachts—yet are often surprisingly affordable.

Small ships are people-sized. It's easy to learn the layout on the first day. Life aboard is casual, even on the most luxurious ships. Informality and friendliness go hand in hand. Passengers are fewer, and making friends is easy—an advantage for singles. The congenial atmosphere also enhances interaction between passengers and crew, who are likely to call you by name from the first day.

Small ships with their shallow drafts, turn-on-a-dime maneuverability, and fewer passengers can gain access and acceptability in places where large ships simply cannot go. Their size makes them welcome at private islands and exclusive resorts and allows them to nudge into shallow bays and hidden coves. Their ports tend to be offbeat and uncommercialized.

Some small cruisers have bow ramps, enabling them to disembark passengers directly onto beaches or into remote villages. Others carry Zodiacs and/or sea kayaks to transport passengers into wilderness. Some have retractable marinas, enabling passengers to water-ski from the ship.

A small ship offers exclusivity, even if unintended. Seating is unassigned at single seatings for meals. On deluxe ships, dining is even at the time of your choosing. There are no crowds, no long lines, almost no regimentation. Best of all, on shore, you don't feel like part of a herd.

Today's superliners and megaliners are self-contained floating resorts with facilities that operate almost around the clock. The bigger the vessel, the more the ship becomes the focus and ports matter less.

For small ships, destinations are key, and sight-seeing is the main activity. They offer more varied and unusual itineraries than larger ships can and often carry experts to discuss destinations and accompany passengers on shore excursions.

Small ships draw experienced, discriminating, and independent travelers who enjoy low-key ambience and appreciate what is not available as much as what is. They neither want nor need nonstop activities. A few small vessels have tiny casinos and small-scale entertainment, but most substitute conversation and companionship for chorus lines and cabarets.

The smaller size attracts all age groups. Sailing ships, particularly wind-jammers, draw the young and adventuresome, attracted by the lower price and the opportunity to work alongside the crew. Deluxe ships and those with longer itineraries attract older travelers, many of whom are young in spirit and intellectually curious. They appreciate an island's culture and are eager to interact with the locals.

Sound appealing? Then consider one of the three basic types of mini-ships: Ultraluxurious liners offer privacy and pampering, exclusivity and elegance, tastefully opulent suites, gourmet dining, and often formal evenings. In sharp contrast are adventure-oriented ships, whose destinations are chosen for their natural beauty, wildlife, or cultural interest. Activities include hiking and birding. Cabins usually are modest, service minimal, and cooking down-home, with limited choices. They appeal to people who spurn luxury but are keenly interested in participatory travel. A third type strikes a middle ground, offering comfortable but not lavish accommodations, good food, and attentive service. There is some adventure, some history and wildlife, and some time for sports. Evening entertainment includes games, movies, local talent, and guest speakers.

Even with these choices, small-ship cruising is not for everyone. Some would find it boring or confining. But if you abhor lines or regimentation, operate on your own juices, yearn for a more intimate environment, or want to try trimming the sails or floating in luxury, small ships might be right for you.

Old Ships vs. New Ships

Poets praise the beauty of sailing ships. But observers of classic cruise ships like the *QE2* have been equally captivated by noble grace that is both massive and subtle. Examine the *Norway* closely and discover there is scarcely a straight line in her. Alas, such ships will never be built again.

Are old or new vessels better? The debate rages. Classic ships still in service, as opposed to those merely old, offer ambience that no newer ship can duplicate. But the newest cruise vessels have advantages only dreamed of in 1960. Because there are well-maintained and up-to-date older ships in service, you have a choice between the old and the new afloat. Find your preference by surveying what each type of ship has to offer.

Notice first the appearance of any vessel, old or new. The newest ships are designed from the inside out to provide more and better public rooms and the most amount usable deck space. These vessels spend most of their days in calm seas. None will cut through the North Atlantic at full speed to maintain a schedule, so the fine lines and razor-sharp bow of the *QE2* aren't needed. Instead, new ships have squared sterns and chunky super-structures that provide many benefits internally but none externally.

As with some prima donnas, most new ships have one or two good angles. Publicity materials show profile shots and aerials of raked stems and funnels and broad decks for recreation. But approach the ship in person, and you see what she really looks like: a full-figured lady from bow to stern.

Once inside your cabin, however, you may forget your ship's outward appearance. The space available to modern designers has generally made possible standard, usually larger, cabins for everyone. Some older ships like Commodore's *Enchanted Isle* and American Hawaii's *Independence* offer comfortable space in every cabin, but they can't match the improved bath-rooms and lighting of newer ships.

Luxury vs. Midprice and Economy Cruises

Spending more on a cruise does not necessarily get you more or better facilities. Some of the most extraordinary spas, gyms, pools, lounges, and showrooms are found on the megaships of affordable midmarket lines Car-nival and Royal Caribbean Cruise Lines. Dropping big bucks likewise will not ensure that your ship is newer, nicer, or more competently and cour-teously staffed. (Check the ratio of passengers to crew. The lower the ratio, the more service you should get.)

Booking a luxury cruise may get you a larger cabin (suites aboard Seabourn Cruise Line) and almost certainly buys a roomier bath with tub and shower.

Regarding food, luxury lines have the edge. Usually they feed fewer pas-sengers at a single seating spanning a couple of hours. Passengers arrive at the dining room a few at a time, like at a restaurant ashore. The staggered arrivals allow the galley the flexibility to provide more choice and cook dishes to order. Most midmarket and economy cruises have two seatings for each meal. When their seating is called, passengers blow into the din-ing room like marines hitting the beach. Surprisingly, however, the quality of meals on some luxury ships is only marginally better than that of better midmarket lines. Midmarket Celebrity Cruises makes dining a top prior-ity and serves meals comparable to those on cruises costing much more. Generally, the extra dollars for a luxury cruise buy exclusivity. For those who can afford it, that's saying a lot.

SPECIAL PEOPLE WITH SPECIAL NEEDS

Some passengers require special services or accommodations. If you are a honeymooner, single, disabled, require a special diet, or plan to travel with young children or teens, read on.

Singles

Safety and security, comfort, convenience, companionship, fun, and freedom—all are reasons that cruises are among the fastest-growing options available to travelers who want to go it alone.

A cruise ship is about the safest, most secure environment you can find. A woman might hesitate to talk with someone in a hotel bar, dine alone in a fancy restaurant, or walk alone into a nightclub, but such barriers don't exist on a ship.

Furthermore, the fun is at your fingertips. The nightclub, disco, casino, and theater are walking distance from your cabin. Relieved of the need for an escort and with ready-made companions for dinner or activities, single people—men and women—vacation on their own terms.

Cruise prices are based on two people sharing a cabin. For one person to occupy a cabin alone, cruise lines impose an extra charge over the per-person double-occupancy rate. This "single supplement" varies from 10 to 100 percent (expressed as 110–200 percent), depending on the line, ship, itinerary, season, and cabin category. The most frequent charge is 150 percent for all except suites, which usually go for 200 percent. Brochures always publish the rate. Your choices are to pay it, bring a friend, or take one of these options:

Guaranteed Single Rate   You pay a set price published in the brochure, which is comparable to the low end of a per-person double-occupancy rate. The line assigns your cabin at embarkation. You don't have a choice, but you do have a guarantee of price and privacy.

You are likely to be assigned an inside cabin. If you select low season (October in the Caribbean), the start of a new season (May in Alaska), or a repositioning cruise when the ship is unlikely to be full, you might get a nice outside cabin. Royal Caribbean Cruise Line and Norwegian Cruise Lines offer a guaranteed single fare, which includes air transportation. Some lines do not show a guaranteed single rate in their brochure, but will accept a reservation when bookings are light. Be sure to ask.

Low Single Supplement   Some lines have single supplements of 15 percent or less. Seabourn offers 110 percent on some cruises; Silversea has a few at 125 percent, though most are at 150 percent. In all cases, you pay slightly more than the per-person double rate, but you get privacy, and in the case of Seabourn and Silversea, all accommodations are deluxe suites.

Flat Rate Clipper Cruises, Star Clipper, and some other lines charge a flat rate for single occupancy. You pay more, but are ensured privacy and choice.

Guaranteed Share   The line plays travel matchmaker. You pay the perperson double-occupancy price, and the line matches you with a cabin mate (same sex and smoking preference). If the line does not find a suitable

Cruising for Singles

S = Single cabins available
GSP = Guaranteed share program available
Single Supplement = Percentage of fare based on per-person double
    occupancy rate

Cruise Line	S	GSP	Single Supplement
Abercrombie and Kent	No	No	150–200
Alaska's Glacier Bay	No	No	175
American Canadian	Yes	Yes	175–200
American Hawaii Cruises	Yes	No	100–160
Carnival Cruise Lines	Yes	Yes	150–200
Celebrity Cruises	Yes	No	200
Clipper Cruise Line	Yes	Yes	150
Club Med	Yes	No	125–150
Commodore Cruise Line	Yes	No	200
Costa Cruise Lines	Yes	No	150–200
Cruise West	Yes	No	175
Crystal Cruises	No	No	125–200
Cunard Line	Yes	No	140–200
Delta Queen Steamboat	Yes	Yes	150–200
Disney Cruise Line	No	No	175–200
Holland America Line	Yes	Yes	150–200
Norwegian Cruise Line	Yes	No	175
Orient Lines	No	No	125–200
P&O Cruises	Yes	No	160–200
Premier Cruise Lines	Yes	No	125
Princess Cruises	No	No	150–200
Radisson Seven Seas	No	No	Varies by cruise
Royal Caribbean	Yes	No	200
Royal Olympic Cruises	No	Yes	Varies by cruise
Seabourn Cruise Line	No	No	Varies by cruise
Silversea Cruises	No	No	Varies by cruise
Star Clippers	No	Yes	150–200
Windstar Cruises	No	No	175–200
World Explorer Cruises	No	No	150–200

mate, you get the cabin to yourself at no extra charge. The savings—and
drawbacks—are obvious. It's a bit of Russian roulette. You stand a better

chance of having a cabin to yourself during low season or on a repositioning cruise. Some lines don't publicize a guaranteed share program, but accept a reservation. Be sure to ask.

Single Cabin   Some older ships have single cabins. The price is set but not necessarily comparable to a per-person double rate. More likely, a surcharge has been built into the price.

Find single cabins on American Hawaii: *Independence* (24); Premier: *Big Red Boat II* (14); Cunard: *QE2* (145), *Caronia* (36); and P&O: *Victoria* (22).

Also, some lines charge singles minimal or no surcharge for less desirable cabins, such as inside rooms with upper/lower berths.

Helpful Hands

Golden Age Travellers (Pier 27, The Embarcadero, San Francisco, CA 94111; (415) 296-0151), offers about 300 cruises a year and provides a cabin-mate matching service and lower supplements based on bargaining clout. Limited to those age 50 and up. Annual fee is $10 per person; $15 per couple.

Travel Companion Exchange (P.O. Box 833, Amityville, NY 11701; (800) 392-1256; (631) 454-0880), offers membership, a matching service, and bimonthly issues of a 20-page newsletter for $99 (first-time enrollment rate; regular annual rate is $298).

Finally, watch for specials and find a knowledgeable travel agent to help you. A smart, experienced agent knows which, when, and how cruise lines make special deals for singles, and they can often unearth ways that advance purchase and special promotional fares, even though based on double occupancy, can be applied to single travelers.

Other Tips for Sailing Solo   The cruise industry has a long way to go in handling the singles market. The probability of finding love at sea varies according to age group. Twenty-somethings should look to the Caribbean on cruise lines that target a younger market, though the average passenger age remains above age 35.

Singles wanting to meet people should participate in activities, shore excursions, and sports. Small ships generally are preferable to large ones because it is easier to mix and the staff works harder to involve you in the ship's social life.

Among small ships, adventure and educational cruises are singles' best choices; camaraderie quickly develops among passengers. Also, the number of unattached men is likely to be higher than on traditional cruises.

If you're 40-something or an older single woman who loves to dance, book a ship with gentlemen hosts—single males, age 50 or older, who dine and dance with all unattached women—no favoritism or hanky-panky allowed. Crystal, Cunard, Delta Queen, Holland America, and Royal Olympic Cruises have them.

On singles cruises offered four times annually, Windjammer Barefoot Cruises all but guarantees a 50–50 ratio of males and females. Ages vary widely. You get no break on price—the single supplement is 150 percent—unless you are willing to share.

A common complaint we hear from singles concerns table assignment for dining. Some singles are discontented because they're seated with married folks. Others are annoyed because they're seated with other singles and resent the cruise line playing matchmaker. Response varies, but your best bet is to submit a written request in advance outlining your preference in dining companionship. Aboard, if you are disenchanted with your table mates, ask the maître d'hôtel to move you.

Honeymooners

If there is a better honeymoon option than a cruise, we can't think of it. There is nothing more romantic than balmy nights and sunny days under a Caribbean or Mediterranean sky. Your cabin is your honeymoon suite; room service usually is complimentary, so you never have to leave unless you want to. Forget the car, unpack only once, and still visit exotic places. Many lines (with advance notice) will provide a cozy table for two in the dining room. Regardless, tell the cruise line you are newlyweds. You will probably get preferential treatment, a bottle of champagne, flowers in the room, a souvenir photo, or even a cabin upgrade.

If you are contemplating a cruise honeymoon, consider: If you marry on Saturday, Sunday or Monday departures are most convenient. Check on the availability of bathtubs versus showers if that is important to you. Ask whether room service is available at all three meals and whether you can choose from the regular menu (room service menus are often limited).

Nonambulatory Disabled Passengers

Many people who use a wheelchair or other mobility aids have discovered the pleasures of cruising firsthand. However, you need to be very direct and specific when exploring your options. Dining rooms, showrooms, or public rest rooms are not wheelchair-accessible on many ships. A few small ships have no elevators; on others, particularly older ships, elevators do not serve every deck. Most ships require that you bring your own wheelchair, often one that is collapsible or narrow-gauge. Do not count on a lot of wheelchair-accessible facilities or cabins. On the most wheelchair-accessible ships, no more than two dozen cabins will have wheelchair-accessible bathrooms, and there usually is no way to get a wheelchair into a regular cabin's bathroom. If you need an accessible cabin, book well in advance. We list the number of wheelchair-accessible cabins available under each line's Standard Features and ship's Cabin Specifications. Look for a ship with a lot of elevators relative to its complement of passengers. Divide the number of passengers by the number of elevators. Generally, the lower the calculated number, the less time you will spend waiting for elevators.

It is important that you book your cruise through an agency specializing or experienced in travel for the handicapped.

If you power your own wheelchair, unaided by a companion, bring something to extend your reach. A rubber-tipped teacher's pointer is good, a collapsible one is ideal. You need the pointer to reach elevator buttons, some light switches, and the closet rod and higher storage space in your cabin, even in some wheelchair-accessible rooms.

Make sure that dining rooms, rest rooms, showrooms, lounges, promenade decks, and the pool areas are wheelchair accessible. Determine whether gangways are accessible at ports. If tenders are used, will you be able to board in a wheelchair? In the dining room, will your table accommodate your wheelchair, or must you shift to a regular chair? If you cannot shift yourself, will you need a companion to help or are crew members allowed to assist? Can crew members help in your cabin and elsewhere aboard ship? Must you sign a medical waiver or produce documentation from your physician to obtain a wheelchair-accessible cabin? No matter how dependable your travel agent is, call the cruise line and double-check all important arrangements yourself.

Partially Ambulatory Disabled

If you use a wheelchair sometimes but can walk a little way, you will do fine on most ships large enough to have elevators. You will be able to get around your cabin and into the bathroom on foot. A collapsible wheelchair will enable you to cover longer distances. Crutches are iffy on ships, walkers better, but the safest way for the partially ambulatory to get around is in a wheelchair.

Larger ships have wide passageways, spacious public areas, and, most likely, an adequate number of elevators. Smaller ships often have tight passageways, steep stairs, and no elevators. Older vessels may have bulkhead doors with raised thresholds, blocked passageways with steps to the next level, and no elevator access to some decks.

Choose a cabin near the elevators. Book one with a shower (with metal chair or stool); many ships' bathtubs are higher and/or deeper than yours at home. Ask whether the cabin's bath has sturdy hand grips.

Consider booking an itinerary on calmer water, like Alaska's Inside Passage or the Mississippi River. If you cruise on the open sea, choose a cabin on a lower deck in the vessel's center; this area is least susceptible to motion.

Passengers with Sight and/or Hearing Impairments

Most people with sight or hearing impairments travel with a nondisabled companion. Regardless, inform your cabin steward of your disability. In the event of an emergency, he should know to check your cabin immediately to make sure your companion is with you and to assist you if the aide isn't. If you are hearing-impaired, your steward should be given permission to enter your cabin in an emergency if there is no response to a knock.

Passengers with Diet Restrictions

Diet restrictions usually pose no problem on cruise ships. The galley will prepare meals to your specification and serve them at regular seatings in the dining room. Orthodox religious practitioners who must verify that a meal is prepared in a certain way should ask whether such verification will be possible. All lines request advance notice—two to three week—for specific needs. We provide this information under cruise lines' Standard Features. Also, cruise line brochures detail procedures for diet requests.

Families with Younger Children

Although some lines are equipped to handle younger children, we do not recommend cruising for kids younger than age five. Lines that really want family business advertise that fact. If you have young children and want them to enjoy the cruise, but do not necessarily want to tend them 24 hours a day yourself, book with a line specializing in family cruises. Its ships will have play areas and supervised activities and sometimes a separate swimming pool for children. Best, the chaperoned children's program provides a respite from constant parenting. If, however, your rich Aunt Hattie wants to treat you and your little nippers to a luxury cruise, don't decline because the ship's brochure doesn't picture kids. Little ones on essentially adult cruises fare reasonably well. Although planned activities may be few or none for them, your children will revel in the adventure of being at sea.

Usually, the children's center will be a sort of seagoing day care or in-cabin babysitting. If both in-cabin babysitting and all-meal room service are available, you've got it made. Sign up for second seating in the dining room, or go late if there is only one. Let the kids enjoy room service in the cabin, or take them to the buffet or informal dining area. Then turn the fed-and-scrubbed munchkins over to the sitter and head for the dining room. Of course, you can take your children to the dining room, but if they are age six or younger, once may be enough.

If your ship has a children's program, your kids will be on the go all the time. However, we've seen children who scarcely countenance their parents at home refuse to leave them and go to the children's center aboard ship.

Cruising for Children

This chart includes only those cruise lines with facilities for children; for details, see the line's profile in Part Two. Many lines not included on this chart accept children and offer cruises appropriate for them, but have no special facilities for children. Also, note that age limits vary from "no age restriction" to "no children younger than age 18 permitted." Always check with the cruise line before making plans.

(A) Varies by destination
(R) Reduced third or fourth berth rate, regardless of age
(S) Seasonally
* Varies with ship, consult cruise line
** Under age 10 not permitted

Cruise Line	Age Limit for Child Discount	Air/Sea Rate**	Baby-Sitting Avail.	Special Shore Excursions	Teen Center/ Disco	Playroom/ Youth Center	Youth Counselors
Abercrombie & Kent	(R)	Yes	Some	Yes	No	No	Some
American Canadian Caribbean Line	No	Yes	No	Some	No	No	Some
American Hawaii	18	Yes	Yes	No	Yes	Yes	Yes
Carnival	(R)	Yes	Yes	Some	Some	Yes	Yes
Celebrity	12	Yes	Yes	Yes	Some	Yes	Yes
Commodore	(R)	Yes	Yes	Some	Yes	Some	Some
Costa	*	Yes	Yes	Some	Yes	Some	Yes
Crystal	12	Yes	Yes	No	Yes	Yes	Yes
Cunard	*	Some	Yes	(S)	Some	Some	Some
Delta Queen	16	Yes	No	No	No	No	No
Disney	Yes	Yes	Yes	Yes	Yes	Yes	Yes
Holland America	12	Some	Yes	Some	No	Some	Yes
Norwegian	(R)	Yes	Yes	Some	Yes	Yes	Yes
Premier Cruise Lines	(R)	Yes	Yes	No	Yes	Yes	Yes
Princess	(R)	No	Yes	Some	Some	Some	Yes
P&O Lines	NA	NA	Yes	NA	Some	Yes	Yes
Royal Caribbean	(R)	Yes	Yes	(S)	Most	Most	Yes
Royal Olympic	12	Yes	Yes	No	(S)	(S)	(S)

To avert this issue, before you leave home explain how things work and negotiate what time you will spend together and apart. If your children are too young to negotiate such deals, save the family cruise for another year or put the kids into the children's center and deal with any fallout.

Consider accommodations: Cabins are much more confining than children's homes or bedrooms. Your kids will size up your cabin in about ten seconds and figure there is not much to do there. From that point, they will be obsessed with running loose around the ship. Anticipate this response. Set limits in advance about bedtime, naps, meals, and parental private time, and plan for each day. Television, when available, is usually limited to a news channel, movies, and information about the ship and shore excursions. Therefore, bring games, books, and toys to keep the children reasonably content in the cabin.

If you can afford it, putting the children in an adjoining cabin is best. If you buy kids their own cabin, the cruise line will usually include airfare. If you bunk the young ones in your cabin, you have to buy their airfare as an "add-on." A few cruise lines offer a discount on a connecting cabin, where available, especially during low seasons.

Families with Teens

Teens do pretty well on cruises. They are old enough not to need constant supervision, will definitely eat their money's worth of food, and collect new experiences they can talk about back home. Teens are allowed to enjoy everything aboard except the casino and some lounges. On some ships, teens accompanied by parents are allowed in the disco and other adult areas. Family and midmarket ships often have clubs where teens can dance and arcades with Ping-Pong, pool, or electronic games.

A cruise is a totally new environment for children—some embrace it with gusto, eager to learn, to find every nook and cranny, but others are intimidated and need help. For the right kids, it's a fabulous, fun, learning experience. With teens, as with younger kids, negotiate and set your limits before you leave home. Because teens can be messy and monopolize the bathroom, we double our recommendation that you get them an adjoining cabin. Finally, though we believe teens on their own are safe aboard ship, we suggest you keep them under tight rein ashore. If this is your first cruise and you have qualms about taking children, go without them and size up the situation. All of you might enjoy it more if you know the territory.

Additional Information

In both the Cruise Line Standard Features and the cruise ship profiles, we include a section on children's facilities. These references are a start. Also consult *Family Travel Times* (40 Fifth Avenue, New York, NY 10011; (888) 822-4FTT, www.familytraveltimes.com), an online publication of TWYCH (Travel With Your Children) that frequently reports on family cruises, down to the last playpen and high chair. Annual subscriptions are $39, which buys you access to six online issues.

A Word of Warning

One person's darling can be another person's pain in the neck. We have received a surprising number of complaints from readers about children on their cruises. However, most referred to cruises during holidays, spring break, and summer, when there can be 300 or more children aboard a ship. In such cases, even people who adore children might find their patience wearing thin if the children are rowdy and ill-behaved or if the cruise lines fail to supervise them adequately. As cruise popularity and family travel increase, the two converge with greater frequency. The simple fact is that cruising is a wonderful family vacation.

If you do not want to cruise with children, avoid holiday periods, particularly on mass market lines that promote family travel and cruise to the most popular Caribbean, Mexican, and Alaskan destinations. If, however, these are the only times you can travel (if you are a teacher, for example), search for ships that sail off the beaten track or focus on enrichment rather than entertainment. Finally, an experienced travel agent should be able to help you find the right ship—or the ones to avoid.

Shopping for and Booking Your Cruise

GATHERING INFORMATION

Now that you have outlined your requirements and preferences, compare them against the profiles of the cruise lines and ships described in this book. After you identify several lines that seem to meet your needs, obtain their promotional brochures through a travel agent or by contacting the lines directly using phone numbers and addresses in the profiles.

A travel agent specializing in cruises or selling them routinely can be a good source of information. Many agents can provide firsthand information about ships and lines. Also, many will put you in touch with clients willing to share thoughts and opinions. However, always understand from a self-interest perspective that cruise lines pay the agent a commission on every cruise the agent sells.

In addition to obtaining promotional materials, buy several Sunday newspapers: (1) one in a primary geographic market for the cruise industry, including New York, Chicago, Dallas, or Los Angeles; (2) your local paper; and (3) the paper of the largest city within 200 miles of your home. The travel sections in these papers indicate where the deals are. If you live in a medium-sized city like Charlotte, North Carolina, you may uncover cruise deals in the Atlanta paper that beat anything in your local paper.

Finally, here are some helpful magazines, periodicals, and Internet sites: Cruise Critic on America Online (access with Keyword: Cruise Critic); www.cruisemates.com, written and hosted by Anne Campbell, former author of *Fielding's Guide to Worldwide Cruises* and a veteran cruise writer; and www.cruise411.com. Their candid ship reviews are based on firsthand experience. They also have cruise line information, news updates, information on promotions, and best deals. AOL's Cruise Critic also has a "Caribbean Ports of Call" feature by this book's author, Kay Showker.

Cruise Week, a two-page weekly industry newsletter available by fax or e-mail, is produced by an editor who has reported on the industry for many years. It's directed to the travel industry, but consumers interested in tracking news about cruising will find it a timely resource. Annual subscription: $125. Write to Lehman Publishing Co., 910 Deer Spring Lane, Wilmington, NC 28409, or call (800) 593-8252; fax: (910) 790-3976; e-mail: cruzweek@aol.com; web: www.cruise-week.com.

Cruise Reports offers evaluations and firsthand comments by travel agents. Annual subscription: 12 issues, $70 for printed version, $50 for e-mail version; the e-mail version includes photos not featured in the printed issues. Write to 25 Washington Street, Morristown, NJ 07960, or call (973) 605-2442; e-mail: cruises@gti.net; web: www.cruise-report.com.

Cruise Travel magazine is unabashedly rah-rah cruising and contains no critical content, but it's a good source of information. Its six issues a year contain ads from dozens of cruise discounters, consolidators, and cruise specialty travel agents. Subscriptions run about $12 a year in the United States, $32 in Canada. Write to P.O. Box 342, Mt. Morris, IL 61054, or call (800) 877-5893.

Ocean & Cruise News reports on the industry and reviews a different ship in each issue. A much-publicized annual evaluation of lines and ships in the February issue is based on subscribers' votes, which tend to reflect seasoned cruisers' preferences for established lines. Subscriptions are $30 annually for 12 issues. Write to P.O. Box 92, Stamford, CT 06904, or call (203) 329-2787; web: www.oceancruises.com.

Porthole is by far the most attractive and lively magazine on cruises. It offers a range of interesting articles by knowledgeable writers. Annual subscription: $19.95. Write to P.O. Box 469066, Escondido, CA 92046, or call (800) 776-PORT; fax (760) 738-4805.

HOW TO READ A CRUISE LINE BROCHURE

Cruise brochures are very elaborate. Because they contain so much information, we offer a systematic approach to evaluating and understanding their contents.

Look at the Pictures

All photos in the brochures have been carefully chosen to excite the people for whom the cruise line tailors its product. If you identify with the activities depicted, this may be a good cruise line for you. Pay attention to ages of the people shown.

Sizing up the Ships

Look at the ships. Are they too big, too small, about right, or you don't care as long as they float? Most brochures also contain a deck-by-deck schematic of the ship. Concentrate first on the ship's layout, looking for features important to you. If you work out, look at the relative size of the exercise room and try to find a photo of it so you can check the equipment. If you have mobility problems, look for elevators. Because upper decks offer the best views at sea, note inside and outdoor public areas, particularly on the top two and promenade decks.

Itineraries

Read the itineraries, making preliminary selections on where and how long you want to cruise. On what days and at what times does the cruise begin and end? Do these work for you? Focus on a couple of cruises. Read the itineraries, observing how much time the ship spends at sea and in port, how much cruising is during waking hours, and whether the number of ports and the time allowed to see them suits you.

For practice, let's look at a ten-day itinerary from Copenhagen to London/Tilbury.

Day	Date	Port	Arrive	Depart
Sunday	June 4	Copenhagen		6 p.m.
Monday	June 5	Baltic Sea	Cruising	
Tuesday	June 6	Helsinki	8 a.m.	6 p.m.
Wednesday	June 7	St. Petersburg	8 a.m.	
Thursday	June 8	St. Petersburg		6 p.m.
Friday	June 9	Stockholm	4 p.m.	
Saturday	June 10	Stockholm		3 p.m.
Sunday	June 11	Cruising		
Monday	June 12	Oslo	8 a.m.	5 p.m.
Tuesday	June 13	Cruising		
Wednesday	June 14	London/Tilbury	7 a.m.	

The cruise sails at 6 p.m. Sunday, allowing several options. Because most flights from the United States to Europe depart in the late afternoon and evening, a person living in the eastern United States could work most or all of Friday and catch an evening flight to Copenhagen, arriving Saturday morning. They would have until about 3:30 p.m. Sunday to rest and see Copenhagen. Alternately, they could fly out Saturday evening and arrive in Copenhagen on Sunday morning with four or five hours at their disposal before boarding. A third possibility, of course, would be to arrive before Saturday and enjoy a leisurely weekend. The first day at sea is a wonderful start, providing a chance to catch up on jet lag and become familiar with the ship.

This cruise calls on four ports, not counting ports of origination and termination. This is fewer than average for a ten-day cruise, but all are major cities. The itinerary gives lots of time in each port. In St. Petersburg and Stockholm, the ship anchors overnight. If you're interested in St. Petersburg and Stockholm, this works well. If not, it's a long time in port. Full days (8 a.m. to 5 or 6 p.m.) are planned in Helsinki and Oslo. In total, the cruise is 229 hours, of which 153 hours (67 percent) are at sea and 76 hours (33 percent) are in port. However, only 71 hours of the 153 hours at sea are during waking hours (7 a.m. to 10 p.m.).

Rates

Flip to the rate charts to determine whether the cruises you like fall roughly within your budget. We do mean roughly: Almost nobody pays the brochure rates. Brochure rates are helpful only in providing a base for calculating discounts. You should anticipate paying 25 to 50 percent less depending on the line, ship, itinerary, season, and market condition. In "How to Get the Best Deal on a Cruise," we describe available discounts.

Most lines present their fares in a chart like the one below for Royal Caribbean International Cruise Line's *Rhapsody of the Seas'* seven-night Alaska itinerary.

The fares are per-person, based on two persons sharing a cabin (double occupancy). If the per-person fare for a cabin on Main Deck, Category F, in spring/summer is $1,499, you and your spouse or companion would pay $2,998 ($1,499 x 2) for the cabin.

For singles supplement, see "Singles" in this chapter for a rate explanation.

As many as five persons may share a cabin, depending on its configuration. Rates for the third, fourth, and fifth persons are deeply discounted, sometimes as much as 66 percent off the double-occupancy fare. Let's say Tom, Ed, John, and Earl are willing to share a "B" Deck, Category I cabin that goes for $1,249 per person double occupancy. The line will charge the double-occupancy price ($1,249) for two of the four men, and the third/fourth person rate of $649 for the remaining two. Thus, the tab for all four would be:

Rhapsody of the Seas Rate Chart

Holiday cruises—add $250 to special holiday cruises. Single Guarantee Program guests add $500.

Cat.	Deck	Description	Base	Season
R	Bridge	Royal Suite, King/Queen	$7,679	$8,449
A	Bridge	Owner's Suite, 2 Queens	5,979	6,579
AA	Bridge	Royal Family Suite, Accommodates 8 people	5,979	6,579
B	Bridge	Grand Ocean View Suite, 2 Twins	5,079	5,589
C	Bridge	Superior Ocean View Suite, 2 Twins	4,229	4,659
D	Commodore	Superior Ocean View Stateroom, 2 Twins	3,429	3,779
E	Main, A, and B	Family Stateroom, Accommodates 6 people/Ocean View	3,179	3,499
F	Main	Larger Stateroom, Ocean View/2 Twins	2,879	3,169
H	A	Larger Stateroom, Ocean View/2 Twins	2,679	3,079
I	B	Larger Stateroom, Ocean View/2 Twins	2,579	2,979
J	Bridge	Superior Stateroom, Inside	2,449	2,849
K	Bridge, Commodore, Main	Larger Stateroom, Inside	2,349	2,749
L	A, B	Larger Stateroom, Inside	2,299	2,699
M	Bridge, Commodore, Main	Stateroom, Inside	2,249	2,649
N	A, B	Stateroom, Inside	2,199	2,599
O	A	Stateroom, Inside	2,099	2,499
P	A	Stateroom, Inside	1,999	2,399
Q	B	Stateroom, Inside	1,949	2,349
S		Single Guarantee Program (provides single occupancy of staterooms—assigned at Royal Caribbean's discretion*)	1,999	2,049
SH		Special Share Program (pairs you with a person of same sex and smoking preference)	1,499	1,599
Third & Fourth Person			999	999

Accommodations in categories R–D have a private bathroom, vanity area, closed-circuit TV, radio, and phone.

Accommodations in categories E–Q have two twin beds that convert to a queen size, private bathroom, vanity area, closed-circuit TV, radio, and phone.

Rates include port charges. Air transportation and certain taxes and fees ($6.50–12.50 per person per cruise) are additional.

All rates quoted in U.S. dollars, per person, double occupancy.

Royal Caribbean International
RHAPSODY OF THE SEAS℠

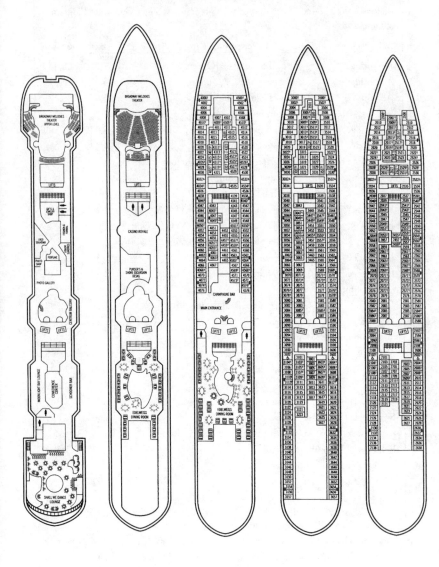

| Mariner Deck | Promenade Deck | Main Deck | "A" Deck | "B" Deck |

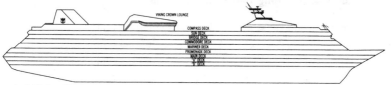

Length: 915'• Beam: 105.6'• Draft: 25'• Gross tonnage: 75,000 tons • Passenger capacity: 2,000 double occupancy • Total staff: 765 • Cruising speed: 22 knots

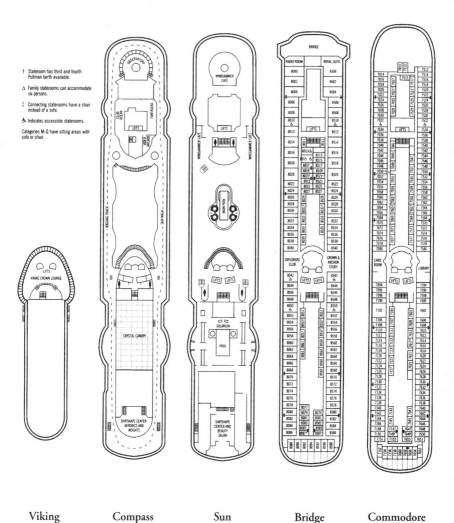

† Stateroom has third and fourth Pullman berth available.

△ Family staterooms can accommodate six persons.

: Connecting staterooms have a chair instead of a sofa.

& Indicates accessible staterooms.

Categories M-Q have sitting areas with sofa or chair.

Viking
Crown Deck

Compass
Deck

Sun
Deck

Bridge
Deck

Commodore
Deck

63

Person 1	$1,249	Cruise Only
Person 2	$1,249	Cruise Only
Person 3	$649	Cruise Only
Person 4	$649	Cruise Only
TOTAL	$3,796	

Usually, for cruise lines that bundle airfare to the port into the total price of the cruise, the airfare is normally included only for the two persons paying the double occupany rate. The cruise line will arrange airfare, often at a discounted rate, for the third and fourth persons.

If Tom, Ed, John, and Earl want to split the cost of their Royal Caribbean cruise equally, here's the way the finances average out:

Cruise Fare for All Four Guys	$3,796
Final Cost Per Person	$949

Because most cabins are small with tiny bathrooms and little storage, we do not recommend cruising with more than two persons in a cabin unless your budget dictates it. If you do elect to cruise with extra people in your cabin, select your roommates with care. Make sure everyone is compatible regarding smoking, snoring, and sleeping hours. Most of all, be tolerant and bring your sense of humor. Start with a cruise in a warm clime; when you can spend more time on deck than in your cabin. One reason a cabin on a Caribbean or Mexico cruise is much less significant than one on a chillier itinerary relates to the amount of time you are likely to spend in your cabin. In the Caribbean, you do little more than sleep and change clothes there. Finally, pack light.

Sailing Dates

Check the sailing dates of cruises that interest you, looking for those compatible with your schedule. Check dates around these to see if a slight shift puts you into a lower-priced season.

Cabin Category and Ship Deck Plans

Now look at the types of cabins available. Many brochures include floor plans for several types of cabins showing their size, configuration, and placement of furniture and fixtures. Some brochures include color photographs of cabins.

Although some upscale lines offer only suites, most ships provide a choice of cabins. The top of the line—usually on the top decks—are the palatial owner's suite or royal suite, comparable to the presidential suite in a good hotel. Next are a small number of one- or two-bedroom suites, followed by a larger number of mini- or demisuites. Suites, particularly on newer ships, often have verandas. After these deluxe accommodations come standard cabins, which account for about 85 percent of accommodations on most ships. And now, on more and more of the new, large ships, even some standard cabins have verandas. Outside standard cabins with a window are generally preferred to inside standard cabins without windows but are more expensive. Usually, the higher the deck, the higher the cabin's price.

Standard cabins on ships built since 1988 generally are the same throughout the ship. Windows may decrease in size as you descend from deck to deck. Although the Royal Caribbean International chart does not specify whether the window view is obstructed, this information is provided on most rate charts.

Cabins toward the middle of the ship are considered more desirable than cabins on either end, because center cabins are closer to stairs and elevators and are less affected by the ship's back-and-forward motion (pitching). The side-to-side motion (rolling) is more pronounced the higher you go and is felt least on lower decks. The most stable cabins are at the water line near the center of the lower passenger decks—the best cabins for travelers prone to motion sickness. But the fact is, on large cruise ships, you will feel very little motion of the sea, except perhaps on the highest decks.

Before selecting a cabin category, study the ship's deck plan. Normally, the schematic is near scale and is color-coded for cabin category. Checking the Royal Caribbean rate chart with the ship schematic for *Rhapsody of the Seas,* you see the most expensive accommodations are on the Bridge Deck, the fourth-highest of ten decks. They are centrally located mini-suites with verandas, and the Bridge Deck is removed from noise of the galley, engines, lounges, pool area, and showroom.

Check the drawing for decks where passengers walk or jog. Avoid cabins beneath jogging tracks or promenades. Similarly, avoid cabins where the window overlooks a track or walkway. Pinpoint lounges, showrooms, the casino, discos, and other potentially noisy, late-night areas. Avoid cabins directly above or below them. Engine noise may be audible in lower-deck cabins toward the stern. Even veteran cruisers have difficulty gleaning this information from a deck plan, but a knowledgeable travel agent knows how to check out these details when you ask. Analyze what you get for a few dollars more or less. In the chart above, for example, an outside cabin on "B" Deck is only $50 more than an inside cabin on the higher Bridge Deck.

A PRELIMINARY LOOK AT DISCOUNTS AND INCENTIVES

You should now know whether you are interested in a cruise offered in the brochure you are reading. If you are, the next step is to check the line's price incentives and discounts.

MINI-SUITE WITH
PRIVATE BALCONY

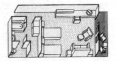

(Category A)

Large bedroom with twin beds, which make up into a comfortable queen-size bed. Sitting room area and private balcony for entertaining. TV. Spacious closets. Refrigerator. Bath with tub and shower.

OUTSIDE DOUBLE WITH
PRIVATE BALCONY

(Category BA, BB, and BD)

Two lower beds, which make up into a comfortable queen-size bed. TV. Spacious closet. Refrigerator.

OUTSIDE OR
INSIDE DOUBLE

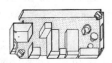

(Category CC, C, D, EE, E, FF, F,
GG, G, H, I, J, K, L, and M)

Outside staterooms have a picture window. Two lower beds, which make up into a comfortable queen-size bed. Many staterooms with two upper berths. TV. Spacious closet. Refrigerator. GG has a queen-size bed. G has one lower bed and one upper berth, and portholes.

Although the cruise market continues to grow, supply (the number of ships and cabins) has historically run several years ahead of demand, with more cabins to fill than people to fill them. With more than 40 new ships coming on line in the next several years, competition will put pressure on cruise lines to cut deals to keep their ships filled, and a buyer's market will prevail.

Incentives and discounts offered in the lines' brochures are varied. First, the line prices according to times of greatest demand. High season is most expensive, followed by shoulder season, then low season. Savings may not be spectacular, judging from the brochure prices.

Remember: Fares in the brochure are base prices to which discounts are applied. Also, ships are less crowded and cabin upgrades more readily available during low and shoulder seasons.

After studying seasonal discounts, check early-booking discounts. Lines offer fairly substantial discounts to travelers who are willing to book six months to a year ahead. The line has use of your money in advance and gets critical information on whether a particular cruise is filling. Early-booking discounts commonly are 15–45 percent off the seasonal rate or a two-for-one deal. Either way, early-booking incentives are generally the largest discounts given directly by the lines. You get other benefits, too: your choice of cabin, the most direct air routing, and your dining-room seating preference (if the line bases seating on first-come, first-served). That's the kind of information available in fine print or from an experienced travel agent.

Cruise lines also may offer cabin upgrades, credit for shipboard purchases, receptions with the captain, or a couple of nights at a hotel at the originating or terminating port. In addition to early-booking discount, almost all lines offer other discounts (often up to 50 percent) to repeat passengers. Many discounts from cruise lines, travel agents, wholesalers, and consolidators never appear in the cruise lines' basic brochures. For help in finding them, read the section "How to Get the Best Deal on a Cruise."

ROUND-TRIP AIRFARE

Unless you live within driving distance of your cruise's originating port, you will require transportation to it. Until recently, most lines included air transportation in the cruise cost and promoted it as "free air." But times are changing.

What Happened to "Free" Air?

First, check the cruise brochure to determine whether prices include air transportation. When lines include air transportation in their packages, they agree to fly you round-trip from specific "gateway" cities. These gateway cities vary among cruise lines but usually include all major U.S. and

Canadian cities and many smaller cities. If air transportation is part of the cruise package but your gateway city is especially far from the port, an air supplement—extra charge—may be levied.

Until recently, air/sea packages were touted as all-inclusive, with "free" airfare. Nothing, of course, was ever free. Cruise lines built air transportation into the cruise cost and called it "free." By buying in advance and in large volume, lines could negotiate big discounts on airfares. These discounts enabled the cruise lines to offer complete vacation packages—the cruise with airfare—for a good price. Since 1997, however, cruise lines have increasingly published their rates as "cruise-only" fares and sell the air transportation as an "add-on." The reason for the change is that demand for air travel has increased and airlines have radically reduced the availability and size of discounts for cruise lines. Simply put, airlines can fill their planes without offering reduced fares. Today, cruise lines can obtain the discounts required for a good air/sea package only by buying airlines' least desirable flights, including late-night flights, circuitous routes, and multiple stops. Luxury cruise lines are the exceptions, as they continue to offer air-inclusive packages to ensure that their customers get the most direct and convenient flights.

At the same time, passengers often are discovering they can get better airfares and routing on their own. Plus, they receive their tickets well in advance. Often with air/sea packages, airlines issue tickets only at the last minute (in order to distribute passengers equally among available flights). The practice panics cruise passengers near departure who wonder where their tickets are. Passengers also are irritated because flights arranged by the cruise lines are often not eligible for frequent-flier mileage, and when they are, passengers or their travel agents must call the airline and provide frequent-flier numbers after the tickets have been issued.

Much as they may be reluctant to surrender their most successful marketing vehicle—one-price-buys-all—many lines have concluded there's greater benefit in "unbundling" the package.

In the "unbundled" cruise package, the air "add-on" is calculated from the passenger's gateway city and is printed in the cruise brochure. When you buy the line's air add-on, transfers are included. When you purchase your air transportation independently or use frequent-flier awards, you can usually buy airport transfers from the cruise lines. Carnival, for example, offers one-way and round-trip transfers, which must be booked 14 days in advance; price varies with location. Without such an arrangement, you must set up your own transfers. This seems complicated, but a travel agent can handle such details for you—and we advise you to let them, so that you still pay one inclusive price for a "seamless" package. Despite these new realities, lines' add-on fares usually are lower than you can get on your own. Nevertheless, shop before you buy; ask your travel agent to help.

When air transportation is included, the cruise line and airline determine your flight time and routing. You can request a change or particular routing through your travel agent. Many cruise lines maintain "Air Deviation" desks to handle requests from passengers who want to change their assigned routing. Changes can cost $75 (as if you changed a ticket directly with an airline), and an additional air supplement may be charged if no seats are available in your designated airfare category.

If you arrange (and pay for) your own air transportation, the cruise fare will be decreased because you are not using the air allowance. The amount is shown at the bottom of the rate sheet as "Cruise Only Travel Allowance." The allowance, for example, is about $250 on one-week Caribbean cruises.

Price, however, isn't the only consideration in buying an "air add-on" deal. When a line arranges your air transportation, it also arranges for your luggage to go directly to the ship. Once you check your luggage at your home airport, you won't see it again until it's delivered to your cabin. Also, the cruise line will meet your plane and transport you from the airport to the ship. At cruise's end, some lines provide this luggage and transportation service for both cruise-only and air-inclusive passengers.

During busier times, cruise lines may fly you to the port city a day in advance and provide hotel accommodations. If you live in the western United States and are sailing from an eastern port, the cruise line may fly you to the port city on a late-night flight with arrival between midnight and 9 a.m. More considerate lines arrange hotel day rooms where you can rest before boarding your ship later in the day. Similar arrangements are sometimes made for Eastern passengers embarking on the West Coast and passengers on European or Asian cruises.

The line, when it puts you in a hotel, assumes responsibility for transporting you to the pier. If you are to be accommodated in a hotel before embarkation, pack an overnight bag; you may not have access to your luggage until you're aboard ship.

Most air transportation is coach class. Your travel agent can arrange seat assignments, boarding passes, and upgrades (when available).

If you are cruising during autumn (excluding holiday periods) or when airfares are discounted in your city, or if you can reach the port on a discount airline (like Southwest), you may want to book your own air travel to save money. If you can book your flights at or near the cruise line's air allowance, you will be able to choose your airline, assure a good flight itinerary, accrue frequent-flier miles, and receive your tickets well before your departure date.

If you choose the air-inclusive package or buy air transportation as an add-on, take these precautions:

1. Call early to reserve. Passengers are assigned on a first-come, first-
   served basis to the seats allocated in the cruise line's bulk-purchase

agreements with airlines. Cruise lines contract for a specific number of seats for every cruise—when they're filled, the line has to scramble for additional ones. That's when you're likely to get a circuitous routing.

But, to put this in perspective: The airline crunch comes at holiday times—Labor Day, Thanksgiving, Christmas—and can be exacerbated by bad weather. So, if you plan a cruise during a holiday period, arrange it early, buy your airfare from the cruise line, and save yourself a pile of headaches. As a veteran travel agent advised, "Passengers should seriously consider taking the air/sea package from the cruise line during the winter months, especially if they are flying from a cold-weather gateway. If there are weather- or equipment-related delays, the cruise line will help air/sea passengers get to the ship. If passengers have booked their own air, they are on their own if they miss the ship. Passengers who do their own air would be well advised to purchase third-party travel insurance that covers trip interruption, delay, or cancellation due to weather- or equipment-related problems."

2. Ask your travel agent when you can expect your tickets. Most cruise brochures tell this in the fine print. If not, your travel agent will know from experience or can ask the cruise line. Normally, they arrive two to three weeks before departure. Smaller cruise lines generally deliver earlier than the big guys do.

3. If you have a specific route you want to fly to your departure port, tell your travel agent when you book or as soon as possible so that your plane tickets can be issued properly. If you receive tickets requiring layovers and a change of planes, have your agent contact the cruise line's Air Deviation desk.

How to Get the Best Deal on a Cruise

To get a good deal on a cruise, know the players and how the game is played. In the case of cruising, game rules pivot on the unalterable reality that a cruise is a time-sensitive product. If a cabin is not sold by sailing time, it loses all of its value. This makes selling cruises like playing "Beat the Clock." From the time a cruise is announced, the line is on a countdown to sell all the cabins. The immense expense of operating a cruise ship makes the selling a high-pressure, big-stakes endeavor.

For consumers, the time sensitivity is a major plus. Any time a dealer must make a sale or write off the inventory (empty cabins, in this case), wheeling and dealing are likely, and it almost always benefits the buyer.

However, we emphasize there's more to buying a cruise than its price. If you allow yourself to be influenced only by "getting the best deal," you are likely to end up on the wrong cruise.

The Players: Cruise Lines

Lines have sales offices and can sell cruises directly to consumers. But as many as 95 percent of all cruises are sold through travel agents or other players, and you usually get a better price buying from them. To their credit, cruise lines are loyal to the agents who sell their product and won't undercut the prices available to them. Practically, the lines don't want the bother, plus it wouldn't be cost-effective. It costs cruise lines far more to maintain sales offices to serve the general public than it does to maintain a sales network through travel agencies. The only time it might be a better to deal directly with the cruise line is when you're pier hopping—showing up at the pier, bags packed, and negotiating with the ship's boarding officer for a walk-on rate for any available accommodation. Few people have time to do this. We should also note that some cruise lines are now selling directly to consumers on the Internet, although not necessarily at discounted prices. Such sales are in their infancy, and it's too early to know their impact on prices.

The Players: Wholesalers and Consolidators

Wal-Mart founder Sam Walton taught Americans that the more of something you buy, the lower the price should be. Businesspeople call it buying in quantity, or volume discounting. In cruising, travel wholesalers and consolidators are volume buyers. Booking well in advance, they buy large numbers of cabins on specific cruises with the intention of reselling the cabins at a profit. Advance purchasing and volume discounts, coupled with the fact that the cruise lines do not have to pay commissions, allows wholesalers and consolidators to buy at prices substantially below what an individual could obtain. Some cabins that go unsold can be returned to the cruise company by a certain date; others are bought on a nonreturnable basis. In the latter case, the wholesaler or consolidator absorbs the costs of any cabins he doesn't sell. The biggest cruise discounts available to any player go to wholesalers and consolidators who buy cabins in bulk on a nonreturnable basis. Wholesalers and consolidators sell to travel agents and, often, directly to consumers. If the wholesaler sells a cruise through a travel agency, the wholesaler pays the agent a commission.

Some cruise lines refuse to sell their inventories to these middlemen. Note that wholesalers and consolidators generally deal with lines having large ships, or they offer the best deals on a limited number of ships and lines. If they spread themselves too thinly over the spectrum of cruises, they diminish their clout with specific lines. Remember: It's in the wholesaler's or consolidator's interest to steer you to ships where they get the best deal. That may not be in your best interest.

The Players: Travel Agents

Travel agents act as sales representatives of the cruise lines. Unlike wholesalers and consolidators, they don't buy cabins. Instead, they sell from the line's inventory on commission. Like cruise lines and wholesalers, however, agents earn the most when they sell in volume.

Some full-service travel agencies specialize in cruises, whereas others are cruise-only agencies, selling nothing but cruises and cruise-related travel. The latter sell so many cabins for certain lines that they earn "override commissions"—a commission on a commission. There is usually a volume threshold where the override kicks in. General travel agencies and independent agencies cash in on override commissions by joining a consortium, a group of agencies that pool their sales to receive the overrides.

To make the most in commissions and overrides, agents push selected cruise lines, known in the industry as preferred suppliers. If the line that interests you is among your agent's preferred vendors, great. If not, your agent will probably try to interest you in a line with which the agency has such an arrangement. Be sure to ask for the one you want.

Because most cruises are sold by travel agents, it is critically important for cruise lines to develop extensive systems of loyal travel agents. Competition among cruise lines to influence agents is so heated that consumers sometimes become pawns in a marketing chess game. Recently, for example, Holland America awards its agencies bonus points redeemable for chocolate, picnic lunches, or dinners in local restaurants. Such incentives may influence agents' recommendations and narrow consumers' choices. These are all reputable cruise lines, but they are not necessarily a good fit for all of an agent's customers. Good agents place their client's needs and preferences first, but some agents go for the largest commissions and the most goodies.

Some agents sacrifice part of their commission or override to make a cruise more affordable to a good customer. Some agencies selling cruises in volume take lower commissions to underprice other agencies. In many locations, competition among agencies for cruise business is as keen as it is among cruise lines, particularly with the proliferation of cruise-only agencies. And now with airlines' decreasing agents' commissions, the competition for cruise business has grown hotter.

In the final analysis, buyer beware. Protect yourself best by developing a long-term relationship with a knowledgeable travel agent who works to put you on the cruise right for you.

Helping Your Travel Agent Help You   When you call a travel agent, ask whether he or she has cruised. Firsthand experience is invaluable. If the answer is no, find another agent or be prepared to give your agent copious direction. Ask who your agent's preferred vendors are. Just asking that question will tell the agent you are a savvy buyer. Compare the agent's recommendations with information in this guide. Request permission to contact other clients who have been on the cruise line recommended, and ask your friends. Someone you know may have sailed on the line.

To help your travel agent obtain the best possible deal, do the following things:

1. Determine from brochures, friends' recommendations, and this book where and when you want to cruise, which lines offer the kind of cruise that most appeals to you, and how much you can spend.

2. Check cruise ads in the Sunday travel section of your local newspaper and compare them to ads in the newspapers of a key cruising market (New York, Philadelphia, Los Angeles, Phoenix, Dallas, Chicago, Boston, Washington, or Atlanta) near you. Look for deals that fit your plans and that include a line you like. Also, read ads in specialty magazines, such as *Cruise Travel.*

3. Call consolidators or retailers whose ads you have collected. Ask about their offers, but do not book your trip with them directly.

4. Tell your agent about cruises you find, and ask if he or she can match or beat the price. The newspapers' deals will probably be a good benchmark against which to compare alternatives proposed by your agent. Be aware that promotional ads are often bait to get your attention. The "lead" price probably applies to a limited number of cabins on a specific sailing. This element is probably the trickiest part of obtaining the best deal. Every ship has 6–20 categories of cabins. Often, unless you can pinpoint the date, itinerary, and cabin category being advertised, it may be hard to know whether you are getting a good deal. Nobody said this was easy.

5. Choose among options uncovered by you and your travel agent. Whatever option you elect, have your agent book it. It may be commissionable (at no additional cost to you) and will provide the agent some return on the time invested on your behalf. Also, your agent should be able to help you verify the quality and integrity of the deal.

How the Game Is Played: The Sales Countdown

Cruise lines work well in advance to schedule cruises and develop promotional brochures. It is essential to roll out marketing campaigns quickly to avoid panic sales as sailing dates near.

Most itineraries and dates are announced 10–14 months in advance. Particularly attractive dates on popular ships and itineraries sell out quickly. Likewise, cruises to seasonal destinations like Alaska fill fast. The highest- and lowest-priced cabins sell out first. Usually the last cruises to fill are low- and shoulder-season cruises to year-round areas. Many consumers used to wait for last-minute discounts available when cruise lines hit the panic button. The lines finally wised up, reasoning that early-booking discounts could generate cash flow and indicate sales prospects for each cruise. Although some distress selling continues, cruise lines are learning to control the inventory more efficiently. Now, natural disasters, political crises, and other sudden events beyond the cruise lines' control are likely to cause fire sales.

Escalating Base Rate Model

To see how this works, let's examine a pricing model adopted by several prominent cruise lines. When the cruise is announced, the line advertises a base fare, discounted from the brochure figure by, say, 40 percent. The line warrants that the discounted base fare may increase as the countdown progresses, but will never be lower. Therefore, a consumer who books a November cruise in the preceding April would pay less than a passenger who books in June. That passenger, in turn, would pay less than someone booking in August, and so on.

This strategy allows the line and the travel agent to tell the customer that "this cruise will never be cheaper than today." The customer knows that the rate may rise, but will never be lower. The line can maintain the discounted rate if the ship is filling slowly, or raise it incrementally as the cruise approaches being sold out. We call this the escalating base rate model.

Identifying the pricing model is useful because it's then easier to understand what the cruise line does to nudge the ship to capacity. Pay attention: What the cruise line tells the customer is that the base rate will never be cheaper than today. That's very different from telling the customer the base rate is the deepest discount available.

In practice, cruise lines operate two pricing systems. Primary is the escalating base rate system. If the cruise sells to near capacity, only that system will be employed. If sales lag behind expectations, however, the line goes to its separate and collateral model: the special situations system.

Special Situations System

Special situations initiatives—usually time-limited and tightly targeted efforts for boosting sales—run concurrently with and independently of the escalating base rate system. Examples of such initiatives include a deeply discounted senior citizen's rate, a direct mailing to previous customers offering a big discount, a regional campaign, or a heavily discounted group sales overture to a large company for their executives or employees.

Each special situation initiative targets a carefully selected market segment. Initiatives may run sequentially or concurrently but usually are short-lived and end when the cruise sells out. What is really important about special situation initiatives is that the discount offered might be much greater than the base rate discount. If you can locate such an initiative, you may have found the lowest possible fare. If the special is advertised in Atlanta and you live in Buffalo, the package's air component will be useless to you. However, if you can buy the cruise-only part of the special and arrange affordable airfare from Atlanta, you've got a deal.

A common special situations approach is for the cruise line to join forces with specific travel agents. Like travel agents who have preferred suppliers, cruise lines have preferred retailers. When a cruise is not selling to expectations, the line will enlist its favorite big-volume agencies to help move the remaining cabins. Because the line is anxious to sell the cabins, it develops promotions with these agents featuring extra-deep discounts and special incentives, such as cabin upgrades or discounted air add-ons. Many preferred agencies sell cruises only and field hundreds of toll-free calls daily. If they have an especially juicy deal to offer, they can sell lots of cabins fast. Big-volume, cruise-only agencies advertise in magazines, including *Cruise Travel, Travel & Leisure,* and *Condé Nast,* and in large-market newspapers.

The Dump Zone

In the cruise marketplace, anything can happen. Some lines are either unequipped to nudge effectively or aren't very good at it. Sometimes, lines expert in special situations campaigns don't fill their cruises. The upshot is that a goodly number of empty cabins may be sold at distress prices during the final eight weeks before sailing, especially in the off-season.

When time is short, agents and cruise lines know it is much easier and less complicated to sell a cruise to someone who doesn't require air transportation to the port. Florida is a huge market for late-breaking deals because of its large population of retirees and its proximity to ports. Major ports on the Pacific Coast and northeast likewise enjoy distress sales. If you live within easy driving distance of a major cruise ship port, you live in a dump zone.

You are well situated to benefit from last-minute discounts, but you probably will have no choice in cabin selection or dining room seatings.

Discount Alphabet Soup

Before you shop for discounts, pick the cruise type that appeals to you. Once you start looking, don't get sidetracked by price. Instead, stay doggedly on the trail of the cruise that meets your needs. Never equate cheapest with best, but don't equate it with worst, either.

More than a dozen types of cruise discounts are commonly offered, other than seasonal discounts. As you encounter them, be aware that catchy marketing come-ons, like "Two-for-One" or "Sail Three Days Free," aren't always what they seem. For example, a promotion advertising 50 percent off on the second person in the cabin (a frequent gimmick) is nothing more than 25 percent off for both (you probably could have done better with an early-booking discount). The best method for comparing rates, with or without discounts, is to calculate the per diem (per day) cost of your cruise vacation. Add the cruise cost and the airfare cost if it isn't included, plus taxes, port charges, and other applicable fees (transfers, etc.). Divide the total by the number of nights you will stay on the ship or in hotels included in the package.

Work Sheet
Cruise Cost _____
Airfare (if not included) _____
Transfers (if not included) _____
Other _____
TOTAL _____
Total divided by number of nights = _____ per day

Always compare apples to apples. Some cruising areas are more expensive. For example, Caribbean cruises should be compared to Caribbean cruises, not to Alaskan or Mediterranean cruises. Remember also that cruise lines are not created equal. Comparing a seven-day Commodore (Quality Inn) cruise with a seven-day Silversea (Ritz-Carlton) cruise is meaningless. The cruise line profiles in Part Two will describe the differences.

Early-Booking Discounts

The more common of two kinds of early-booking discounts, the escalating base rate model, was described earlier. Each line has a different name for it. Royal Caribbean International, which pioneered the strategy, calls its program Breakthrough Rates. Escalating base rates are capacity-controlled and can be withdrawn or escalated without notice. Most of the major lines employ capacity-control pricing. The second type of early-booking discount is the flat cut-off date. If you book before the specified date, you get the discount. This, too, is common practice on selected itineraries. Passengers who pay in full by a specified date (as much as six to nine months before the cruise) receive a 10 to 20 percent discount. This discount is popular with Crystal, Silversea, and others in the luxury market.

Free Days

Passengers are offered 7 days' cruising for the price of 6, or 12 for the price of 10. Variations include complimentary days (with hotel) in the port city before and/or after the cruise, or "book a seven-day cruise and receive a free two- or three-day land package." Divide the double-occupancy price by the number of days in the package to get a per diem cost for comparative purposes.

Two-for-One and Second Passenger Cruises Free

The deal is that two passengers cruise for the price of one, but some tricky math is involved. Pick your cruise and cabin category and find the double-occupancy price per person, air included, on the brochure's rate chart. The two-for-one price is this rate less the cruise line's air cost for one person from your gateway city.

Let's say the brochure's air-inclusive double-occupancy rate is $2,000. Have your travel agent call the cruise line to learn the round-trip airfare cost from your gateway city. This amount is subtracted from $2,000, and the remainder is your cruise-only cost for two persons. You must then make your own air arrangements or buy airfare from the cruise line as an add-on. Celebrity, Princess, Costa, and Holland America frequently offer two-for-one promotional fares. They work well if you can travel to and from the port on frequent-flier miles or by car. If you have to pay for air, however, comparative math might demonstrate that a discounted air/sea package is a better deal.

Two-for-one offers come and go with supply and demand. It's difficult to keep up with them. Normally, two-for-one fares are offered far in advance with a cut-off date to secure early bookings. They also might pop up on short notice. Such fire-sale fares aim to boost short-term sales and can be withdrawn at any time.

Flat Rates

This is an early-booking program in which every cabin in the ship, except probably the luxury accommodations, is sold for the same flat rates (one for inside cabins and one for outside cabins) on a first-come, first-served basis. The earlier you book, the nicer your cabin. Flat rates are usually cruise only, but airfare may be purchased as an add-on. Flat rates are frequently offered by Princess, Crystal, and Norwegian Cruise Lines.

X Percent Off Second Passenger in a Cabin

In this very common discount offered by many cruise lines, the first passenger pays the double occupancy brochure rate and the second passenger gets 40 to 70 percent off. Some simple averaging demonstrates that this works out to a discount of 20 to 35 percent per passenger.

Reduced Rate Air Add-Ons

If you purchase airfare from the cruise line separately (as opposed to included in the cruise price), that is an air add-on. Sometimes cruise lines will couple a discounted cruise-only rate (no airfare) with a very attractive air add-on. This usually occurs when the cruise line is able to negotiate an exceptionally good bulk airfare purchase with an airline from a specific gateway city. In essence, the cruise line is passing some of their savings along to the consumer. Typically, this kind of deal applies only to specific cities and is offered only for a short time. It often results from an airline's slow sales and its need to stimulate air travel from a particular area, as opposed to being a cruise line initiative.

Senior Citizen Discounts

Because seniors have traditionally been the backbone of the cruise market, they are one of the first groups targeted for a discount program if a line is having difficulty filling a cruise. Usually the discount requires that one person sharing the cabin must be at least 55 years old. The size of discount varies, as does the inclusion of airfare.

Kids or Third/Fourth Passengers Go Free or at Reduced Rate

This discount is a fairly common for lines like Carnival, Celebrity, and Premier that target families and younger cruisers. Third and fourth persons or children sharing a cabin cruise free or at a substantial discount. Airfare for the third/fourth person or children is usually not included. Third/fourth person rates are generally part of a cruise line's basic rate structure (rather than promotional fares). They normally appear in the cruise line's brochure and are applicable year-round. Their promotional use might come into play seasonally by being reduced or waived altogether, perhaps in summer to stimulate family travel or in the shoulder season to stimulate first-timers to buy a cruise when three or four friends can share the cost.

Back-to-Back or Contiguous Segments Discounts

The seven-day cruise is the most popular product offered by any cruise line, as it suits the vast majority of people in terms of time and cost. However, there are people who have both the time and means for longer cruises. To satisfy both groups, the cruise lines have several choices. They may break longer cruises into seven-day segments, enabling a passenger to board in one port and depart from another. Or, they may offer two 7-day segments with different itineraries as one 14-day cruise, offering the second week at a greatly reduced price. For example, a ship departing from Miami that sails one week to the eastern Caribbean and the next week to the western Caribbean. In combining the two, the only port repeated in 14 days is Miami, the departure port. Throughout our cruise line profiles we highlight ships whose itineraries lend themselves to this sort of coupling and who offer attractive discounts for the second segment.

Repositioning Cruises

When a cruise line moves a ship from one cruise area to another, this is called a repositioning cruise—and it represents one of the year's biggest bargains. Rather than dispatch a ship empty, lines sell their repositioning cruises, and to attract as many passengers as possible, they offer them at very attractive prices. The majority of repositioning cruises are in spring and fall when the great "migration" of ships occurs—mostly when ships that have spent the winter on Caribbean, Panama Canal, and Mexico cruises are dispatched to Alaska or to New England/Canada and/or Europe for the summer; and again in autumn, when these ships return.

Repositioning cruises with interesting and unusual itineraries, such as from the Caribbean to New England via the Eastern Seaboard, are unlikely to have as much of a discount as those with few ports of call, such as transatlantic crossings. Those with more days at sea, however, appeal to folks who really love to cruise and cherish having uninterrupted days or weeks at sea.

Group Discounts

Persons traveling together can almost always negotiate a group rate. The larger the group, the better the rate. For a big group, at least one free berth or cabin is customarily provided for the organizer. What constitutes a group varies among cruise lines, but eight or more persons traveling together and occupying at least four cabins generally can obtain a discount, extra amenities, or a cabin upgrade.

Standby Rates

Lines may offer deeply discounted standby rates for specific itineraries and sailing dates. Normally, you rank your ship, departure, and cabin preferences and submit them to the line with a deposit. If your preferred date is available, the line notifies your travel agent at least 30 days in advance. If you are offered your first choice, the deposit is nonrefundable. Airfare is additional.

Cabin Upgrades

Four basic ways to get a cabin upgrade are:

1. *Advertised or Unadvertised Specials*   Usually publicized only to travel agents, upgrade programs give them a powerful selling tool. Upgrades apply to specific sailings and can be guaranteed by the agent and line at time of booking. Such specials allow consumers to buy the cheapest fare and be upgraded from one to five cabin levels.

2. *Soft Sailing Upgrades*   A soft sailing refers to a cruise that is likely to depart at substantially less than full capacity. Booking the least expensive cabin category on a low- or shoulder-season cruise offers the best opportunity for receiving an upgrade. Early booking an inside cabin on a ship with few inside cabins (study the ship's deck plans) might result in upgrading to an outside cabin.

3. *Guarantees*   If a cruise is sold out of the cabin category you request when booking, the line will offer a guarantee, promising a cabin in your preferred category or better. You pay the same rate as for the cabin you requested, including early-booking or other applicable discounts. Because guarantees are offered only when a cruise is sold out or oversold in a requested category, chances of getting the upgrade are good. The downside is that you cannot specify your preferred cabin location.

4. *Paid Upgrades*   A number of lines, particularly on soft sailings, sell upgrades. Sometimes the upgrades are as little as $15 per person per cabin category.

Confusion among passengers regarding cabin-upgrade availability often leads to frustration and disappointment. A travel agent wrote us:

> *PLEASE, PLEASE tell your readers that cabin upgrades are a privilege and not a right. . . . With most ships sailing at [near] 100 percent capacity, most people have a slim-to-none chance of getting upgraded—and almost certainly not from an inside cabin to an outside cabin. Many cabin upgrades are given at the time of booking, but "guaranteed cabin categories" do not mean guaranteed upgrades—these are based solely on availability. The only thing that is guaranteed is that they will get a cabin in at least the category they are booked in! Former passengers and people who book the earliest are the most likely to get upgrades, if they become*

available. If a certain cabin category is that important to someone, they should book it and pay for it, and not hope to be upgraded to it. . . . Plus, any travel agent that tells [clients] to take a "guaranteed" or "run of ship" rate to increase their chances of being upgraded, is setting up their clients for disaster. The agent may say one thing, but the client hears the word "upgrade" and thinks this is a given. Then when it doesn't happen, the client gets angry with the travel agent and the cruise line.

Free Stuff

Cruise lines might offer cameras, binoculars, and other goods as booking incentives. Or, freebies may be tied to a theme cruise; for example, a photography cruise sponsored by a camera manufacturer.

Organizational Discounts

Cruise lines commonly develop relationships with organizations like the American Automobile Association or AARP. Check for discounts available through organizations to which you belong.

Credit Card Programs

Some cruise lines have credit card programs. Whenever you use the credit card, you accrue points or "cruise dollars." These can be applied toward a cruise or taken as a credit to spend aboard. Cardholders receive mailings promoting discounts, and charging a cruise on the card may result in cabin upgrades. Similarly, miles accrued on the American Express program offering one mile for every dollar charged are redeemable for cruises.

Travel Agents' Discounts

We have found that agents selling the same discount program for a cruise often quote different prices. Usually the difference is small, 2 to 5 percent. What's going on is that some retailers are sacrificing part of their override commissions to lowball the competition. Big-volume, cruise-only agencies routinely do this, but local agents frequently will knock a few dollars off their commission to retain a good customer. Ads that claim "We will beat or match your best offer" usually mean an agent is rebating some commission to his or her clients. But beware of this practice. Commissions represent an agent's costs and profit. As any businessperson knows, if you give away your profit, you will end up with red ink.

Cruise Loan Programs

Pioneered by Princess, cruise loan programs are seen by the lines and travel agents as "a tool for taking away one of the clients' biggest stumbling blocks: paying in full for a cruise before sailing." Loans may also help sellers trade the customer up. Basically, you borrow your cruise's cost on a revolving line of credit (like most credit cards) and pay off the loan in 24, 36, or 48 installments, like a mortgage or car loan. The main difference between a mortgage or car loan and a cruise loan is that the former are secured by pledging your home or car as collateral. Because there is nothing to pledge as collateral on a cruise loan, interest rates are much higher. In 2000, the lowest annual percentage rate for a cruise loan was 13.29 percent; the highest, 28 percent. Loans are administered by participating banks that are unaffiliated with the cruise lines. If you obtain the lowest interest rate on a 36-installment loan, the monthly payment for a seven-day cruise costing $4,252 per couple is $144 per month. Multiply the $144 by 36 months to see you'll actually be paying $5,184 for your cruise. Most people would do better taking out a loan on their own.

Lost in the Information Haze

Deals come and go so rapidly that a travel agency has to be knowledgeable, well staffed, and computerized to keep on top of the action. Though big cruise-only agencies are the best equipped to handle the information flood, even they occasionally lag.

The National Association of Cruise Only Agencies can provide a list of member agencies in your area. Discount agencies usually advertise widely. Always check the reliability of any agency with whom you do business.

CRUISING THE INTERNET FOR CRUISES

Cruise information on the Internet has increased 1,000 percent in the last two years. There are thousands of Web sites to investigate. Even if you're a wiz at searches, you'll still need a great deal of time and infinite patience to find the facts you need. Cyberspace is chaotic. We can't organize it for you, but here are facts that can help you navigate the ocean of information.

Essentially, cruise-related information on the Internet is precisely that—information. You can ask questions and order brochures, but only a few cruise lines have taken the next step enabling you to buy a cruise directly from them on the Internet. (Online customers pay by credit card.)

Renaissance Cruises launched the first online direct-booking service in 1997, followed by Windjammer Barefoot Cruises. By 1999, Carnival Cruises and Royal Caribbean had moved to online selling; Holland America Line (a Carnival sister company) plans to take the concept further by offering consumers a "virtual tour" of its ships and cruises. Other lines have been watching these developments and are beginning to follow suit. The best way to find out if a particular cruise line is selling online is to check out its Web site. The Web addresses for all major cruise lines and many small, specialized ones are included in this book.

Information is also available from these sources:

- Cruise associations: Trade organizations, including Cruise Lines International Association, which have their own Web sites (www.cruising.org).

- Travel agencies: Hundreds of agencies have Web pages, and others participate through their trade organizations. Most take bookings online or via e-mail.

- Travel publications: Major travel magazines, such as *Travel & Leisure* and *Travel Weekly*, and book publishers, including IDG (which publishes this book), have Web sites.

- Individuals: Recognized travel experts and some people who consider themselves cruise experts or are interested in cruises have created their own sites.

- Subscriber services, such as AOL, have programs on cruises.

The typical cruise line Web site offers about the same information available in a cruise brochure. However, fares are likely to be sample prices only. Cabin sizes or configurations aren't specific. You usually can request a brochure by e-mail (you may be required to give a phone number or e-mail address), but such sites are most useful when you know where and when you plan to cruise. Information, of course, covers the host cruise line only.

Some sites are well done, fun, clever, and even amusing, and they are getting better. Others are basic and slow to upload—you would learn more by reading the line's brochure. The best sites have special features, such as itineraries with links to maps and port information or the facility to search by ZIP code for travel agencies near you. Often, the site is linked to other cruise-related information. For example, American Hawaii Cruises' site is linked to "Whales of the Wild," which lists whale-watching cruises.

The range of information is as broad as it is voluminous—Princess Cruises' site runs 1,000 pages! There is no uniformity in presentation, style, or amount of detail. On Windstar Cruises' site, you can go through a typical day on board, see a sample dinner menu, review itineraries with sailing dates, and read about special fares and onboard credits for Internet users. Holland America's site offers a cruise match program. Click on your preferences in destinations, ships, ports of embarkation and cruise duration, and appropriate Holland America cruises with fare ranges will be recommended. Carnival Cruises, with one of the most extensive sites, offers pictures and descriptions of each cabin category, including drawings of cabin layouts—a rare feature. These three sister lines are linked to each other.

For news, guidance, and evaluations, America Online's "Cruise Critic" is maintained by a team of cruise specialists and knowledgeable persons.

Included are candid, continuously updated ship reviews and evaluations on more than 100 ships, with descriptions on facilities, activities, amenities, itineraries, and fellow passengers; news on industry developments; and features ranging from seasickness to bargains. The Cruise Critic library contains AOL members' trip reports and travel tips.

Similar information is available from www.cruisemates.com, a new site by veteran cruise writer Anne Campbell and a group of established writers who specialize in cruises. When Campbell cruises, she offers daily reports with video. In addition to constantly updated information on special deals, Cruisemates promotes several specially priced cruises throughout the year. Campbell and others host message boards where people can ask questions or post their opinions on cruises, ports, and related matters.

The first all-travel audio Web site was created by knowledgeable radio talk show and television personalities Elizabeth Harryman and Paul Lasley. "On Travel" is essentially radio on the Internet (you must have audio capability). It offers timely coverage on cruises, often on location, and includes conversations with cruise executives and shipboard personnel.

Cruise Opinion (www.cruiseopinion.com) claims to have the largest database of cruise ship reviews on the Web. All are recently written and based on personal experiences. Each reviewer evaluates the ship in 40 categories using a rating of 0 to 100 and describes the cruise experience. Most reviews were provided within the last year. A recent check showed nearly 2,000 reviews on file, with more added daily.

CruiseReviews (www.cruisereviews.com) is more limited but more current. The site lists about 20 major cruise lines and all their ships. About a third had been reviewed recently. Those we checked were short, but pointed.

Online Auctions

The latest twist in discounting is auctioning cruises online at such sites as www.onsale.com and www.allcruiseauction.com. If ever there were a need for "buyer beware," it is here. We know that some people have scored true bargains, but we also hear of people bidding more for a cruise than they would have paid through their travel agent.

The bottom line is: If you want information, cruising the Internet can be useful and fun. It can also be frustrating and time-consuming. You will learn quickly which sites are worthwhile. Be cautious about comments on message boards, forums, and chat rooms from unidentified sources whose reliability you can't check.

We believe that this book—we say in all modesty—together with cruise lines' compendiums and a knowledgeable travel agent (particularly for first-timers), remains the most efficient and effective way to help you select the right cruise—that is, the cruise right for you.

PULLING IT ALL TOGETHER

You know the players and how the game is played. Now it's time to put your knowledge into action.

Step 1. To Agent or Not to Agent

Your first big decision is whether to use a travel agent. This guide, cruise lines' brochures, Sunday newspaper travel sections, and cruise specialty magazines will enable you to narrow your choices. Even so, a reliable travel agent can contribute immeasurably in offering advice and facilitating the process. If you have a travel agent who has served you well, particularly if you're a volume customer, you should use him or her. If you don't have a regular agent, ask your friends for recommendations. Try to select a travel agent near your age or one who shares your interests and lifestyle. Make sure the agency has a good reputation and that the agent with whom you are dealing is experienced in selling cruises. Using a travel agent will not cost you more; the cruise line pays any commissions.

Step 2. Narrow Down

Using this book and the other material, make a priority list of four lines, ships, and cruises. Be flexible. Also be alert to the possibility of travel agents pushing their preferred suppliers, which may not be on your list.

Step 3. Scout the Discounts

Using information collected from newspaper travel sections and other sources, ask your agent if he or she can meet or top any special deals you have found. Call a few high-volume cruise-only agencies on your own. Ask about cruises on your priority list, then ask what's the best deal the agency is selling. Always ask for the bottom-line cost in dollars rather than the per-centage discount. Repeat the quote to the agent and verify what is included (airfare, accommodations, transfers, and so on). Take notes.

Never fall into the trap of buying a cruise simply because it sounds like a great deal—especially if you are buying your first cruise. Your top prior-ity is to determine which cruise is right for you. Only then is it time to scout deals. The best way to ruin your cruise vacation is to book the wrong ship in an effort to save a few dollars.

Step 4. Buy Early or Buy Late

As we said, the biggest discounts are usually given for buying early (four to six months before sailing) or late (during the last month). First-time cruis-ers have greater choice and peace of mind taking the early-bird route. Experienced cruisers are in a better position to play the best deal game. But any time you hold out for a deal, you decrease your options on getting the cabin, dining room seating and airline routing you prefer. In the long run, these factors are much more important to the quality of your cruise than saving $50 or $100.

Step 5. Give the Seller a Price to Beat

When you've narrowed the field to one or two cruises and you're ready to buy, call the four or so retailers who quoted the best prices in your first round of inquiries. Say, "I've been quoted a price of $X for this particular cruise, can you beat it?" Give your travel agent a chance to match it. If he can't, he may be able to verify the deal's integrity or uncover hidden problems. If the deal is commissionable, have your agent book it, or if the agent has invested a lot of time on your behalf, offer a $50 or $100 consultation fee. You will probably find the agent more receptive to working with you in the future.

Step 6. Check It Out

If you decide to buy from an agency outside your city or state, try to determine whether it's bonded and a member of its local Better Business Bureau and/or Chamber of Commerce. Also check whether it's a member of the American Society of Travel Agents (ASTA), the National Association of Cruise Only Agencies (NACOA), or Cruise Line International Association (CLIA). Membership isn't a guarantee of ethical business practices, but the organizations have a vested interest in maintaining the good reputation of cruising and try to attract only upstanding members.

> *American Society of Travel Agents*   (703) 739-2782
> *Cruise Line International Association*   (212) 921-0066
> *National Association of Cruise Only Agencies*   (305) 663-5626

To find out how consolidators and wholesalers respond to questions about their affiliations and accreditations, we called all of the cruise discounters advertising in *Cruise Travel* and *Condé Nast* magazines. Some agencies were gracious and seemed to understand that customers have a right to check their credentials. An amazing number, however, were surly and uninformative. "Who are you?" and "What do you need to know that for?" were typical responses. Representatives from four agencies said they didn't know the answers to our questions but would call us back. Of course, we never heard from them. When you call to check an agency, accept nothing less than complete courtesy, openness, and cooperation. Life's too short, and your cruise is too important to deal with rude salespeople. Remember to show the same respect. Good travel agents will work hard for you, but they can spot someone on a fishing expedition.

Step 7. Protect Yourself

When you pay for your cruise, use a credit card and insist that the charge be run through the cruise line's account, not the agency's account. This precaution is important. Financially shaky agencies sometimes use customers' payments to settle agency debts instead of securing the customer's booking. When these agencies fold, the customer is often left with no cruise and no refund. Paying with a credit card allows you to cancel payment if the cruise is not provided as promised.

Protect your cruise investment with travel insurance. Most comes with lots of bells and whistles, but three things should concern you: (1) loss of your paid fare if you must cancel or if your cruise is interrupted, (2) the potentially huge costs of emergency medical evacuation, and (3) major medical expenses while traveling that your primary health insurance doesn't cover.

Though overpriced at about $5–8 per every $100 of coverage, travel insurance nevertheless is a prudent expenditure. You never know when you might become ill, have a death in the family, or miss your sailing because of a flight cancellation or delay.

Although travel insurance coverages can be purchased separately, they are usually "bundled." We recommend you purchase good coverage for trip cancellation/interruption and emergency medical evacuation. Trip cancellation/interruption insurance covers the insured traveler and traveling companion(s) against losses caused by illness, injury, or death. Most policies cover losses resulting from the interruption of your trip by the death, serious injury, or serious illness of a close family member back home. American Express and Travelers offer coverage for the illness, injury, or death of a business partner.

If you cancel your cruise before departure, your cancellation/interruption insurance will reimburse you for the cruise's full cost less any refund you receive from the cruise line. Though cancellation and refund policies vary, most lines provide a full refund if you cancel 61 or more days before your departure date. Remember that these policies cover only the extent of your investment. If you are buying a $1,500 cruise, you don't need $10,000 in insurance.

Ideally, insurance will allow you to cancel your trip for any reason. Most policies, however, stipulate situations that qualify for coverage. At a minimum, insist on being covered for death, injury, illness, jury duty, court appearances, accidents en route to the airport or pier, and disasters at home, including fire or flood. The same coverage applies to your traveling companion(s). If you buy a cruise at the double-occupancy rate and your companion must cancel, your policy should cover the single supplement if you want to continue alone.

Policies usually cover airline or shipworker strikes, but not hurricanes, earthquakes, or other disasters at scheduled ports of call. Cruise lines reserve the right to alter the itinerary once under way to avoid bad weather or other problems.

The fine print in many policies can be tricky, and seemingly innocuous loopholes limit the carrier's obligation. One essential question regarding cancellation/interruption insurance is whether it covers preexisting conditions: any for which you were treated by a physician in the 60 days (90 days in Maryland) before the policy was purchased. In better policies, if the preexisting condition is controlled by medication, it is covered. In insurance company language, however, "controlled" is very different from "treated." If you have high blood pressure and medication maintains it at normal, safe levels, your condition is controlled. If you have a tumor and are receiving radiation, carriers would say you are being treated, but that your condition is not controlled. If your tumor caused you to cancel your cruise, the policy would not reimburse you. We recommend that you question the insurance carrier directly about any health problem, obtaining written confirmation if necessary.

Pregnancy is covered by most policies if you cruise during your first two trimesters. If a complication arises, the policy will pay. Amazingly, if you deliver your baby normally while on a cruise, you are not covered. Many cruise lines won't accept a pregnant passenger in her third trimester.

Another potential land mine in cancellation/interruption insurance is operator failure. What if your travel agent, airline, or cruise line goes belly up? Although brochures and most policies say they will pay in the event of operator failure or default, fine print sometimes defines failure and default as bankruptcy. Because many businesses fail without declaring bankruptcy, this is an important distinction. Note that most policies exclude the failure of the company that sold the cruise (usually a travel agent) or the company that sold the insurance. If you buy insurance from a travel agency, you're covered if the cruise line or airline fails, but not if the agency fails. This is yet another reason you should pay for your cruise with a credit card and insist that the charge be run through the cruise line's account, not the travel agent's.

Trip interruption coverage, sold with trip cancellation policies, supplements what you recover from the cruise line if something goes wrong during your trip. If a family member dies, for example, and you must fly home from a port mid-cruise, the interruption coverage will pay for your plane ticket home, plus reimburse you for the unused portion of your cruise (less any refund you receive from the cruise line). The policy also would pay the single supplement of your cabin companion if he or she remains on the cruise.

Bundled with trip cancellation/interruption is emergency medical evacuation insurance. This pays to transport you to a place where you can obtain quality medical care. In the Caribbean and more remote cruise areas, you might prefer not to entrust your care to local doctors. The insurer in conjunction with a qualified physician usually must verify your condition and authorize the evacuation. Once authorized, the insurer usually selects the means of transportation.

As a rule, evacuation insurance does not cover hospital stays, doctors, diagnostic procedures, treatments, or medications, though medical coverage sometimes is bundled with a comprehensive trip cancellation/interruption policy. Ask your primary health insurance, Medicare, or HMO whether you are covered for medical attention required when traveling abroad. If you are not covered, buy supplemental insurance.

If you book an upscale cruise and pack Rolex watches, gems, and other valuables, check your homeowners policy to determine what's covered when you travel. If you aren't covered, take out a rider. When you travel, carry your valuables on your person, not in checked luggage. Even better, leave them at home.

Travel insurance is sold by travel agents and cruise lines, but is generally underwritten by insurance companies. The broadest is the Travel Guard Gold Comprehensive policy, which may be more than cruisers need. Travel Guard also markets a less expensive Travel Guard Cruise and Tour package. Here are several major insurers and their policy names and phone numbers:

> *Access America Service Corporation Access America Cruise Policy*
>   *(800) 284-8300*
> *CSA Travel Protection   (800) 234-0375*
> *Mutual of Omaha Cruise and Tour   (800) 228-9792*

When shopping for travel insurance, remember that language in the brochure is marketing language. The language in the policy legally defines the carrier's obligations.

If your cruise line offers its own policy, compare it with one or more of the policies listed above or one offered by your travel agency. If the cruise policy is comparable, buy it. The line has a greater interest in your satisfaction than does an insurance company and may be more helpful in a crisis.

When you buy cruise insurance, know when it takes effect. Some policies start from the time of deposit; others take effect when the trip begins: at the airport, at the port, or when you board the ship.

Every cruise brochure has fine print regarding payment/cancellation/ insurance coverage. Read it. They also have—usually in large type to get your attention—information on the line's insurance package. Review it carefully.

WHAT'S THE REAL COST OF A CRUISE?

Some readers report being surprised by all the extras that are not covered by their cruise fare: items like port charges, beverages on board, spa services, photos taken by the ship's photographer, shore excursions, wine tastings, and even designer ice cream treats. Although all these things add up to a hefty sum, we don't consider them to be "hidden" charges. Except for port charges, such purchases are optional. Any travel provider will try to sell you stuff; it's like the popcorn or beer vendors at the ballpark: You know they'll be there and that they will be expensive. Buy or not as you see fit, but don't be surprised by their presence. The cruise lines find these services to be very lucrative profit centers, which help them keep basic cruise prices down. Because most folks don't like to scrimp on their vacation, however, it's wise to anticipate these expenditures. Even the little stuff like beverages and photos can tack on $200–400 to a week-long cruise. So be forewarned.

Concerning port charges, after some lawsuits in Florida seeking to redress the less than forthright ways that certain cruise lines represented port charges, almost all cruises from Florida to the Caribbean now include port charges in the cost of the cruise rather than tack them on as a separate charge. Nonetheless, take a close look at port charges, particularly for Europe and Asia.

Preparing for Your Cruise

A cruise may be about the easiest vacation you can take when it comes to making preparations because so much is done for you, particularly when you buy an air/sea package. During the cruise, entry formalities are handled by the ship for its passengers in most cases, sparing them the need to fill out immigration forms or clear customs in each port of call.

In most ports you can simply walk off your ship after it has been cleared by local authorities, spend the day sight-seeing, shopping, enjoying a sport or other pleasant pursuits, and return to your ship without having to do anything more than pass through metal detectors for security reasons and show your boarding pass. It's remarkable, if you stop to think about it or compare it to a trip by air visiting similar locations.

The destination of your cruise will make some difference—the more exotic the location, the more you may have need for planning ahead, perhaps for inoculations, visas, and the like. And of course, the weather during your cruise will determine the wardrobe you select.

Such advice may seem obvious to those who have traveled, and if it does, let this information serve simply as a reminder or checklist. Even the most seasoned travelers have been known to pack their cruise tickets in their checked luggage or leave their traveler's cheques at home.

CRUISE LINE BROCHURES

The easiest place to start your preparation is by reading the large compendium of the cruise line from which you selected your cruise. It has a wealth of useful information. To be sure, much of it is glossy pictures and promotional puff to entice you to take a cruise, but almost all contain several pages, usually toward the rear, aimed at answering the questions people ask most often.

They are the specifics about dining hours, smoking/nonsmoking provisions, paying for incidentals on board ships, embarkation and sailing times, and similar tips. In this book, too, each of the major cruise line profiles in Part Two includes a chart entitled Standard Features, which will answer similar questions pertaining to a specific cruise line and its ships.

CRUISE LINE VIDEOS

Most cruise lines have videocassettes of the cruise you are taking that they would be happy to send you—for a fee. Most cost about $15. Essentially, it is a promotional video, but it will give you an idea of what to expect, particularly if your cruise is to an area of the world in which you have not traveled previously. You will probably receive a flyer from the cruise lines to order the tape directly from a distributor. Vacations on Video (phone (602) 483-1551; fax (602) 482-0785) is a major distributor of cruise videos.

TRAVEL DOCUMENTS

You do not need a passport or visa for cruises in the Caribbean, Alaska, Mexico, Panama Canal, New England, Canada, Bermuda, or Hawaii—that's about 90 percent of the cruises sold in the United States. However, it's a good idea to carry your passport or some documentation that bears your photo because airlines—and many cruise lines—require a photo identification. What's more, it's always smart to have a passport for travel outside the United States—as much for your returning to the United States as for any reason. If you do not have a passport, you will need to have proof of citizenship, such as a certified copy of your birth certificate. Personally, we would never leave U.S. shores without our passports. It facilitates your travel wherever you are, and it's the best identification you can carry. Never pack your passport in your suitcase; carry it with you at all times.

Aliens residing in the United States need to have valid alien registration cards and passports. All non-U.S. citizens must have valid passports and necessary visas when boarding any cruise ship departing from and returning to U.S. ports.

Passengers on most other cruises—in Europe, former Soviet bloc countries, Asia, Africa, South America—are required to have a valid passport and in some cases may need visas. A valid passport usually means one that will not expire for at least six months.

Often, on cruises in these destinations, ship authorities will ask you to surrender your passport when you check in and will keep it until the end of your cruise. This enables them to clear the ship more quickly in foreign ports. In such cases, you do not need to worry about giving over your passport to the ship. The passports are locked away securely and are taken out only if local authorities ask to see them.

TRAVEL REQUIREMENTS

Specific requirements for visas and vaccinations depend on the ports of call on your cruise. Normally, this information will be provided by your cruise line or travel agent. However, obtaining the necessary visas and any other documentation required for embarkation, debarkation, and reentry into the United States is your responsibility; if you do not have the proper documents, you will be denied boarding.

U.S. passengers under 18 years of age are usually not allowed to board a cruise ship at initial embarkation without proper proof of identification. No refund of the cruise fare will be given to passengers failing to have such identification. Documents that will be accepted as proof of identification vary with each cruise line. You will need to inquire in advance if the information is not provided in the cruise line's brochure, which it usually is—in the fine print.

Children traveling with anyone other than their parents or legal guardian must have permission in writing for the child to travel. Failure to comply with this requirement can also result in denial of boarding.

DRESS CODES AND PACKING

What to pack will be determined by your ship, its destinations, and, to some extent, the itinerary. An adventure cruise might be three weeks long, but not a single night will be formal or even very dressy. The dress code is usually explained in the cruise line's brochure. Also, we note it in the Standard Features in each cruise line's profile in Part Two.

There are no limits on the amount of luggage you can bring on board, but most cabins do not have much closet and storage space. More important, because you are likely to be flying to your departure port, you need to be guided by airline regulations regarding excess baggage.

Despite the image you may have about fancy parties and clothes, the reality is that shipboard life is very casual. You will spend your days in slacks, shorts, T-shirts, and bathing suits. Lightweight mix-and-match ensembles with skirts, shirts, blouses or T-shirts, shorts, and slacks are practical. Colorful scarves are another way to change the look of an outfit. For women, cocktail dresses are appropriate for evening wear.

Men usually are asked to wear a jacket at dinner in the dining room. If you do not have a tuxedo, bring a dark suit and white shirt. Add a selection of slacks and sport shirts, and one or two sports jackets. If you are heading for a warm weather cruise—Caribbean, Mexico, Hawaii, Tahiti—pack as you would for any resort destination. Lightweight, loose-fitting clothing is ideal, and cotton or cotton blends are more comfortable than synthetic fabrics for the tropics. Include two bathing suits if you are likely to be spending much time in the sun and at the beach. And don't forget a cover-up for the short jaunt between your cabin and the pool or other outside decks, since cruise ships ask passengers not to wear bathing suits in the public rooms.

Take along cosmetics and suntan lotion, but don't worry if you forget something. It will most likely be available in shipboard or portside duty-free shops. Sunglasses and a hat or sun visor for protection against the sun are essential. A tote bag comes in handy for carrying odds and ends, and plastic bags for wet towels and bathing suits on returning from a visit to an island beach. You might also want to keep camera equipment in plastic bags as protection against the salt air, water, and sand.

The first and last nights of your cruise are casual, and the nights your ship is in port almost always call for informal dress. At least one night will be the captain's gala party, where tuxedos for men and long dresses for women are requested, but not mandatory.

Bring your most comfortable walking shoes for shore excursions. Tennis, deck, or other low-heeled rubber or nonskid shoes are recommended for walking about the ship, up and down gangways, getting in and out of the ship's tenders, and for sight-seeing. And you will need a sweater for breezy nights at sea or for the air-conditioning in the dining room or shore excursion bus. A small flashlight, a fold-up umbrella, and a light jacket are often handy.

Pack lightly. For a one-week or shorter cruise, you should be able to fit everything you need into one suitcase. But most of all, be comfortable. You do not need to rush out and buy an expensive wardrobe. Obviously, if your cruise is in a cool or cold climate, you will need to plan accordingly. A Baltic or Scandinavian cruise in summer is likely to encounter colder temperatures than you might think—similar to a New England fall—but then can quickly turn to a hot summer day. Plan for layers when the weather is uncertain.

As we mention elsewhere, it's a sound practice to have a small carry-on bag for your medications and cosmetics and to include a change of clothing for your first afternoon aboard your ship, in the event there is a delay in the delivery of your luggage. Also, bring a foldaway bag to carry all those souvenirs, gifts, and duty-free bargains that probably won't fit in your suitcase.

Every evening, an agenda for the following day is delivered to your room; it states the dress code for the following evening. It may be:

Casual	Comfortable daywear, such as slacks, shorts, jeans, but some cruise lines will state specifically that T-shirts, tank tops, or shorts are not allowed in the dining room for dinner.
Informal	Dresses and pantsuits are suggested for the ladies; jackets for the men, but ties are optional.
Formal	Cocktail dresses or gowns for the ladies, and tuxedo, dinner jacket, or dark business suit for men; jacket and tie are required.

As a general rule, the lineup will be like this:
3–4 nights: one formal, one informal, and one or two casual.
7–8 nights: two formal, two informal, two or three casual.
10–14 nights: three or four formal; four or six informal; four or five casual.

You are asked to comply with the ship's stated dress code, if for no other reason than out of respect for your fellow passengers. Generally, the suggested attire is respected throughout the evening or at least until after the shows in the main showroom and the late-night buffet when it is a gala event. Often, those who want to stay up late for the disco or casino change to more comfortable dress, if they prefer.

COSTUMES

Some ships still have one night as a masquerade party, and others have theme nights for which some people bring an outfit—for '50s and '60s night or country and western night, a musical instrument or props for the passenger talent show, or a costume for the masquerade parade. It's entirely up to you whether or not to participate. The cruise line's brochure usually tells you about theme night, or you can ask your travel agent for theme nights featured on your cruise, if you want to join in. If you don't have space for a costume, the cruise staff can help you make one.

SPORTS EQUIPMENT

If you plan to play golf or tennis frequently, you might want to bring your own equipment, and of course, you'll need the appropriate clothes and shoes. Ships that have golf practice facilities sometimes supply the equipment for a nominal fee. Inquire.

Fins and a snorkeling mask, particularly if you have one fitted with your eyeglass prescription, are bulky, but might save you a $10–20 fee each time you go snorkeling on your own. If you buy the ship's shore excursions, the equipment is included. Scuba gear is usually included in dive packages, too, and, except for your regulator, is impractical to bring on a cruise.

Hiking boots, jogging shoes, riding attire, and other sporting gear will depend entirely on you and the nature of your cruise. For adventure or expedition cruises, such as to Antarctica, your cruise line will give you ample information about dress and the equipment you need.

MONEY MATTERS

Dollars are readily accepted throughout the Caribbean and indeed throughout most of the world, as are traveler's cheques and major credit cards. In Europe or Asia, the ship's purser or front office usually offers foreign currency exchange facilities, or the ship brings someone aboard to provide the facility in each port of call.

If you do exchange money (it's a great opportunity to teach kids about other currencies—French francs in Martinique, Dutch guilders in Curaçao, pesos in Mexico), exchange only small amounts for your immediate use. Seldom will you have time to exchange the money back before returning to your ship, and you lose money every time you make the exchange.

Even with U.S. dollars, always carry small denominations—ones, fives, tens. Chances are, if you are owed change, it will be returned in the local currency. Incidentally, U.S. coins are seldom accepted in foreign countries and are impossible to exchange except in quantity at foreign exchange banks. Likewise with foreign coins when you want to exchange them back into U.S. currency. Most become souvenirs.

Major credit cards have become the currency of travelers worldwide. On a cruise, you will often find them the most convenient method of payment for settling your account aboard ship, for shopping at duty-free shops, and for payment of local restaurant or hotel bills. However, do not expect to use them in off-the-beaten-track locations. The Cuna Indians of the San Blas Islands—an exotic stop on Panama Canal cruises—want your greenbacks.

PRESCRIPTION MEDICINE AND OTHER MEDICAL REQUIREMENTS

As with any trip, whether on land or sea, you should have all your required medicine with you and carry it in your hand luggage, not packed in your suitcase. As a further precaution, bring copies of your prescriptions—and for your eyeglasses, too.

If you have dietary requirements, you or your travel agent should communicate them to your cruise line at the time you book your cruise. Most ships can accommodate normal requirements of low salt and low fat, but more complex ones that require special stores be carried aboard require planning. Do not take anything for granted. Inquire. For example, many ships do not normally stock skim milk. In each of the cruise line profiles in Part Two under Standard Features, the amount of advance notice a cruise line requires to handle special diets is indicated.

Cruise ships that travel beyond coastal waters are required to have a doctor on board, and most large ships have nurses and adequate medical facilities for normal circumstances. The doctor and nursing staff have daily office hours, which are always printed in the ship's daily agenda, and they are always on call for emergencies. There are charges, generally reasonable, for most medical services.

SUNBURNS

You will need to take precautions against the sun when you are on a Caribbean, Mexican, or Antarctic cruise. The sun in these regions is much, much stronger than the sun to which most people are accustomed. Always use a sunscreen with an SPF of 15 or higher, and do not stay in the direct sun for long stretches at a time. Nothing can spoil a vacation faster than a sunburn.

LEARNING THE LINGO

Cruise ships have a language all their own. Though it is not necessary to enroll in a Berlitz course to learn it, becoming familiar with a few terms will be worthwhile so you won't feel lost at sea, if you will forgive the pun.

Passengers don't reserve rooms on a ship, they book cabins, which cruise lines sometimes call by a fancier name, staterooms. The price level of a cabin

Who's Who on the Cruise Ship

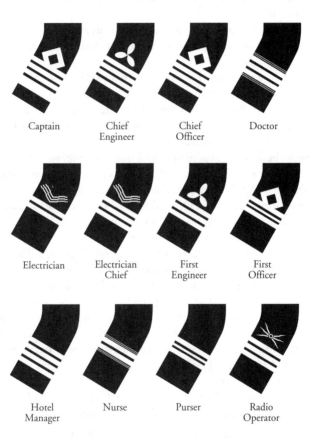

| Captain | Chief Engineer | Chief Officer | Doctor |

| Electrician | Electrician Chief | First Engineer | First Officer |

| Hotel Manager | Nurse | Purser | Radio Operator |

Second Engineer

Second Officer

Uniform designations of Seabourn Cruise Line; other cruise lines may vary.
Courtesy of Seabourn Cruise Line.

is known as its category. A cabin rate per person in a double occupancy cabin is called basis two.

When you reach your ship, you will board or embark; when it's time to leave the ship, passengers disembark. If the ship arrives at a port where it cannot pull into the dock, the ship will ride at anchor and passengers are taken ashore in a tender, one of the small ancillary vessels that travel on board the ship.

Several terms will assist you in finding your way around the ship. The bow is the front of the ship, the aft is the rear, and the center portion is midships, or amidships.

Heading forward, toward the bow, the right side of the ship is known as the starboard side; the left side of the ship is called the port side. Ships have decks, never floors. Decks are named after such things as precious stones (Emerald Deck), activities (Sports Deck), places (Monte Carlo Deck), and planets (Venus Deck).

If you've built up an appetite from all this exploring, you can go to the main seating (or sitting) and eat early, or the second seating and dine late. Some ships have single seating, which means that all passengers eat at the same time for all three meals. Other ships have open seating, in which case you may sit anywhere—at any unoccupied table or join others. By invitation, you may even find yourself at the captain's table.

On board, there are people to help you decode ship lingo. The purser's office is the information center, usually called Purser's Square. The hotel manager is in charge of all passenger-related shipboard services, such as dining, housekeeping, and so on. The chief steward is responsible for cabin services, and cabin stewards or stewardesses take care of cabins; the dining steward is your waiter. The cruise director functions as the emcee, and the cruise staff, who are his assistants, runs all activities and entertainment and makes sure that you are having a good time. Finally, there's the captain, who is in charge of everything.

Cruise lingo is part of the fun, so don't take it too seriously. Here are the most common terms you are likely to encounter.

Add-on A supplementary charge added to the cruise fare, usually applied to correlated airfare and/or postcruise land tours.

Aft Near, toward, or in the rear (stern) of the ship.

Air/Sea A package consisting of the two forms of travel, that is, air to and from the port of embarkation, transfers to/from the port, as well as the cruise itself.

Amidships	In or toward the middle of the ship; the longitudinal center portion of the ship.
Astern	Beyond the ship's stern.
Basis two	A cabin accommodating at least two persons; also referred to as double occupancy.
Batten down	To secure all open hatches or equipment for sea worthiness while the ship is under way.
Beam	Width of the ship (amidships) between its two sides at its widest point.
Berth	Dock, pier, or quay (key); also, the bed in the passenger cabins.
Bow	Front or forward portion of the ship.
Bridge	Navigational and command control center of the ship.
Bulkhead	Upright partition (wall) dividing the ship into cabins or compartments.
Category	The price level of a cabin, based on location on the ship, dimensions, and amenities.
Colors	A national flag or ensign flown from the mast or stern post.
Course	Direction in which the ship is headed, usually expressed in compass degrees.
Crow's nest	Partially enclosed platform at the top of the mast used as a lookout.
Deck plan	An overhead diagram deck by deck illustrating cabin and public room locations in relation to each other.
Disembark	Depart from the ship.
Dock	Berth, pier, or quay (key).
Draft	Measurement in feet from water line to lowest point of ship's keel.
Even keel	The ship in a true vertical position with respect to its vertical axis.
Fathom	Measurement of distance equal to six feet.
First seating	The earlier of two meal times in the ship's main dining rooms.

Fore   The forward mast or the front (bow) of the ship.

Forward   Toward the fore or bow of the ship.

Funnel   The smokestack or "chimney" of the ship.

Galley   The ship's kitchen.

Gangway   The opening through the ship's bulwarks (or through the ship's side) and the ramp by which passengers embark and disembark.

Gross registered ton   A measurement of 100 cubic feet of enclosed revenue-earning space within a ship (see Space ratio).

Hatch   The covering over an opening in a ship's deck, leading to a hold.

Helm   Commonly the ship's steering wheel, but more correctly the entire steering apparatus consisting of the wheel, the rudder, and their connecting cables or hydraulic systems.

Hold   Interior space(s) below the main deck for storage of cargo.

House flag   The flag denoting the company to which the ship belongs.

Hull   The frame and body (shell) of the ship exclusive of masts, superstructure, or rigging.

Knot   A unit of speed equal to 1 nautical mile per hour (6,080.2 feet), as compared to a land mile of 5,280 feet.

League   A measure of distance approximating 3.45 nautical miles.

Leeward   In the direction of that side of the ship opposite from which the wind blows.

Manifest   A list or invoice of a ship's passengers, crew, and cargo.

Midships   (see Amidships)

Nautical mile   6,080.2 feet, as compared to a land mile of 5,280 feet.

Open seating   Seating in the main dining room(s) is not assigned.

Paddlewheel   A wheel with boards around its circumference, and, commonly, the source of propulsion for riverboats.

Pitch   The rocking back and forth (bow to stern) motion of a ship that may be felt in heavy seas when the ship is under way.

Port   The left side of the ship when facing toward the bow.

Port charge   Port taxes, collected by the line and paid to a local government authority; it may include other miscellaneous charges, such as gasoline surcharge and fees.

Port tax   A charge levied by the local government authority to be paid by the passenger.

Prow   The bow or the stem (the front) of the ship.

Purser   A senior management position on board ship. In most cases, the purser is like the general manager of a hotel, but in some cases, he or she is more of the financial or administration officer.

Quay   (pronounced "key") A dock, berth, or pier.

Registry   The country under whose flag the ship is registered and to whose laws the ship and its owners must comply; in addition to compliance with the laws of the countries at which the ship calls and/or embarks/disembarks passengers/cargo.

Rigging   The ropes, chains, and cables that support the ship's masts, spars, kingposts, cranes, and the like.

Roll   The alternate sway of a ship from side to side.

Running lights   Three lights (green on the starboard side, red on the port side, and white at the top of the mast) required by international law to be lighted when the ship is in motion between the times of sunset and sunrise.

Second seating   The later of two meal times in the ship's dining room(s).

Space ratio   A measurement of cubic space per passenger. Gross registered ton divided by the number of passengers (basis two) equals space ratio.

Stabilizer   A gyroscopically operated finlike device extending from both sides of the ship below the water line to provide stability for the ship and reduce its roll.

Stack   The funnel or "chimney" from which the ship's gases of combustion are released into the atmosphere.

Starboard	The right side of the ship when facing toward the bow.
Stateroom	Cabin.
Steward	Personnel on board ship.
Stem	The extreme bow or prow of the ship.
Stern	The extreme rear of the ship.
Superstructure	The structure of the ship above the main deck or water line.
Tender	A small vessel, sometimes the ship's lifeboat, used to move passengers to and from the shore when the ship is at anchor.
Transfers	Conveyances between the ship and other locations, such as airports, hotels, or departure points for shore excursions.
Upper berth	A single-size bed higher from the floor than usual (similar to a bunk bed), usually folded or recessed into the wall or ceiling by day.
Wake	The track of agitated water left behind a ship in motion.
Water line	The line at the side of the ship's hull that corresponds to the surface of the water.
Weigh	To raise, for example, to weigh the anchor.
Windward	Toward the wind, to the direction from which the wind blows.

Time to Go

If you purchase an air/sea package, your cruise begins from the moment you arrive at the airport. Here's how.

CRUISE DOCUMENTS

Normally, you receive your travel documents—including tickets, transfer vouchers, boarding forms, and luggage tags—about two weeks before departure. Some cruise lines, particularly deluxe and smaller ones going to offbeat destinations, begin sending material a month or more in advance, and often include information on ports of call and on shore excursions sold on board ship. A "Welcome Aboard" brochure is intended to familiarize you with your ship. Read it.

Be sure to carry all documents and essential literature you receive from your cruise line or travel agent with you. Do not pack them in your luggage. You must show your cruise ticket when you check in at the dock.

The final documents will include your airline and cruise tickets. Your agent should have checked them before sending them to you. Check them yourself. If you buy your cruise late, documents may come directly to you from the cruise line. Check them, too.

Luggage tags show the cruise line's name and logo. They have spaces for your name and address and the name of your ship, cruise and cabin numbers, and departure date and port. Complete the luggage tags using information contained in your cruise ticket. Attach at least one tag to every piece of your luggage, including your handbags. (An amazing number of people in their excitement leave hand luggage behind on an airplane, in the airport, or on a motorcoach. If it's tagged, airline or port personnel will know immediately what to do with it.)

After you check in at the airport, you won't see your luggage again until you're aboard your ship. Assuming the bags are properly identified, they'll be in your cabin when you reach it or soon afterward. If not, do not panic. Cruise ships, especially large ones, have thousands of bags to load and sort as passengers arrive. In our experience, luggage is moved from the airport to your cabin with amazing speed.

AIRPORT ARRIVAL AND TRANSFERS

As you leave your airplane in Miami, Ft. Lauderdale, San Juan, Vancouver, or any major departure city, you will be met by uniformed cruise line representatives, usually holding a placard showing your ship's name. The representatives gather their charges and escort or direct them to a waiting motorcoach. Keep your transfer voucher handy; you must show it to board the bus.

If you do not spot your cruise line representative, ask airline personnel or other cruise lines' reps for help. Or go to an airport "red" phone and ask that your line's representative be paged. Or proceed to where motorcoaches pick up passengers for transfer to the pier.

You needn't go to the baggage claim area. Your luggage is being transferred directly from the airplane to cruise line trucks for transfer to the appropriate ship. Handling is based on information you wrote on your luggage tags; be sure it's correct.

ADVANCE ARRIVALS OR DELAYED RETURNS

Almost all lines have hotel and sight-seeing packages for people who choose to arrive at their port of departure in advance of their cruise or linger there afterward. Packages are described in your cruise brochure. If your cruise begins after a long flight, lines normally schedule the first day for cruising to give passengers time to overcome jet lag. If the itinerary calls for immediate ports of call, you might consider arriving a day before departure.

Give the most serious consideration to a day-in-advance arrival when you buy the cruise only, are arranging your own transportation to the departure port, or your travel falls during busy travel periods when weather in the northern United States often turns bad and flights are delayed (Thanksgiving, Christmas, New Year's, President's Day weekend).

If you're on an air/sea program, your line has a greater obligation— although not necessarily a legal one—to get you to the ship when you've been delayed, either by postponing the sailing or by arranging a hotel room and transporting you to the first port of call. In such instances, you're likely to be one of many stranded passengers.

Your name is on a passenger list, and the cruise line representative at the airport expects you. They are in touch with the airline and your ship and probably are setting strategy before you arrive. If you're traveling on your own and are delayed, your cruise ship has no record of your flight and no obligation to help, although most will try. If you arrive at least a day early, you can avoid this hassle. Some people advise arriving early to avoid standing in line for check-in. We view this as the least valid reason. Queues at the airport and dockside departure gates are a fact of life in mass-market travel. If you're so impatient that you cannot stand in a check-in line—even if it takes an hour—without having your blood pressure skyrocket, then you're probably on the wrong cruise. Megaships have mega-passengers, and they must be individually processed. (It would speed the process if everyone arrived with all their documents completed properly.)

AT THE PIER

If you're lucky, you will be among the first to arrive from the airport and the first in line for check-in. More likely, you'll be among several hundred others, and, depending on the cruise line, day of the week, size of the ship, and other contingencies, you will stand in line ten minutes to two hours. Pull out a magazine or book and start reading.

Large ships have a check-in system, asking you to line up behind your letter in the alphabet. Despite occasional glitches, this works well. If lines are exceptionally long, you would probably do better to relax in the nearest bar for an hour or so. You have until 30 minutes before departure to board the ship. Some lines let you board until 15 minutes before departure, but we don't suggest cutting it that close.

Normally, lines begin processing passengers at noon or 1 p.m. for a 4 or 5 p.m. departure. But they seldom allow passengers to embark sooner than two or three hours before departure, because time is needed for previous passengers to disembark and the crew to clean the ship and prepare your cabin.

VISITORS

For security reasons, most lines do not allow visitors. If your friends or family want to send you off in style, they can contact your travel agent to arrange a party in your cabin, complete with flowers, wine, and champagne, or a birthday cake or anniversary surprise in the dining room.

Settling In
BOARDING YOUR SHIP

Most ships have uniformed cabin stewards/stewardesses at the gangway to take you to your cabin. Your escort may offer a quick orientation or ask you to wait for your regular steward, whose name is probably on a small tent card on your dresser. Also in your cabin is ship's literature, including an agenda for the day's events, a deck plan, and possibly stationery.

CHECKING OUT YOUR CABIN

Take a quick look around the cabin to be sure everything is working—it usually is on new ships, not necessarily on old ones. Check how to operate air-conditioning, lights, and the hot water faucets—some fancy new ones are tricky, and the water can scald you. Check the location of life preservers, blankets, and pillows—do you have enough? If anything is missing or not as you requested—twin beds instead of a double—report it now. If you cannot locate your steward, go to the purser or front desk. If you do not get satisfaction, work your way up to the *hotel manager.*

HAIR DRYERS/ELECTRIC SHAVERS

Almost all cabins on modern ships have standard 110 AC electrical outlets; your small hair dryer and electric razor won't need an adapter. A few older ships need them. Most new ships have hair dryers. We list this information in the ships' profiles in Part Two, in Standard Features under Cabin Amenities.

LAUNDRY AND DRY CLEANING

Almost all ships have laundry service. Far fewer have dry cleaning facilities. Generally, laundry service is good and reasonable but tends to use lots of bleach. Give your articles to be cleaned or pressed to your steward. They usually are returned in a day, and same-day service is available for an extra fee. Price lists and laundry bags are in your cabin. For safety reasons, ships ask that passengers not use irons in their cabin, but many have public launderettes with an iron and ironing board, as well as coin-operated washers and dryers. The Standard Features section in our cruise line's profile details the availability of launderettes.

TELEPHONES AND OTHER COMMUNICATIONS

All but a few ships have telephones in cabins with instructions for using them. Most phones have direct-dial to the United States 24 hours a day, but be aware of the price. Usually, you are charged $5–15 per minute for a ship-to-shore call. Receiving a call or a fax may cost $3–5 or more per minute. Policies vary. Some allow you to call collect or charge your call to your shipboard account. Celebrity Cruises has technology enabling passengers to dial toll-free numbers in the United States directly from their cabins. The price is $9.50 per minute. Crystal Cruises was among the first to enable passengers to send and receive e-mail with relative ease. Now, many cruise ships have added e-mail facilities. Also, "Internet Stores" in ports of call are becoming available around the world and are usually very inexpensive to use to send and retrieve email.

If someone wants to reach you at sea, they can telephone the ship by calling (800) SEA-CALL, asking for the ship by name and giving its approximate location. Charges for this call will appear on the caller's long-distance telephone bill. Ship-to-shore telephone and fax services are normally available only at sea. When the ship is in port, onshore communications must be used.

CHECKING OUT YOUR SHIP

After you check out your cabin, tour the ship. Deck plan in hand, start at the top and walk the length of each deck. The ship will be your home for a while, and it's nice to feel at home as quickly as possible.

Checking on Your Dining Reservations

When you book your cruise, your travel agent should state your dining preference and request reservations. You may request first or second seating, tables for two, four, six, or eight, and smoking or nonsmoking areas, although most ships departing from U.S. ports now have smokeless dining rooms. Most lines say they honor requests on a first-come, first-served basis, yet few confirm them in advance. Generally, dining reservations are confirmed only by the maître d'hôtel on board.

Royal Caribbean International is among the few lines that print passengers' dining reservations on their cruise tickets. Why, in this computer age, all can't do the same is a mystery—unless it's to allow the maître d'hôtel to control last-minute shuffling and to ensure he gets his tips.

You may receive confirmation of your dining arrangements on check-in, or it may be in your cabin. If not, check on them. Even lines that give you a dining reservation in advance may ask you to confirm it with the maître d'hôtel.

If assigned arrangements are not what you requested, make a beeline for the maître d'hôtel. Most will accommodate you, though not necessarily on the first night. Rest assured, you won't be the only one. No other item causes more consternation than dining room reservations.

If you let the cruise line or maître d'hôtel place you randomly at a table and you are unhappy with your companions, do not hesitate to ask the maître d'hôtel to move you. Nothing is worse than spending a week dining with people with whom you have nothing in common and no basis for conversation. And you don't need to.

Dining Hours

All but the most luxurious or the most informal ships have two seatings for the day's main meals. Generally, they are:

Breakfast
First or Early Seating: 7 or 7:15 to 8 or 8:15 a.m.
Second or Late Seating: 8:15 or 8:30 to 9:15 or 9:30 a.m.

Lunch
First or Early Seating: noon to 1 p.m.
Second or Late Seating: 1:15 or 1:30 to 2:15 or 2:30 p.m.

Dinner
First or Early Seating: 6:15 or 6:30 to 7:30 or 8 p.m.
Second or Late Seating: 8:15 or 8:30 to 9:45 or 10 p.m.

Many ships have open seating for breakfast and lunch and assigned seats for dinner, in which case the hours are likely to be:

Breakfast: 8 to 9:30 a.m.

Lunch: 12:30 to 2 p.m.

Dinner: First Seating: 6:15 or 6:30 to 7:30 or 8 p.m.
Second Seating: 8:15 or 8:30 to 9:45 or 10 p.m.

If you're an early riser, you probably will prefer the early seating. If you close the disco every night, you might choose the late one. You will not be confined to these meals, as there's usually an early-bird coffee, a buffet breakfast, midmorning bouillon, lunch buffet, ice cream on deck, afternoon tea, cocktail canapés, a midnight buffet, an alternative dining venue, and—if you're still hungry—room service and, on some ships, a fruit basket in your cabin.

ESTABLISHING SHIPBOARD CREDIT

Most lines use a cashless system aboard ship. At check-in, you receive a card—like a credit card—which will be your identification card and probably your cabin door key. If you want to establish credit for purchases on board, drinks at the bar, wine in the dining room, and so forth, you must present a major credit card at check-in or the purser's office (you will be told at check-in) to have an imprint made and signed.

On the last night of the cruise, you receive a printout of your charges for review. You can pay the amount with cash or traveler's cheques or have it billed to your credit card. In profiles in Standard Features in Part Two, we list credit cards each cruise line accepts.

Preparing for Time Ashore

PORT TALKS AND SHOPPING GUIDELINES

All ships offer "port talks"—briefings on the country or island and port where the ship will dock. The quality of these talks varies enormously among lines and ships, depending largely on the cruise director's knowledge and the importance the line puts on such programs.

Most mainstream lines with large ships do a lousy job with port talks. On the other hand, adventure and expedition cruises offer superb talks. Small ships generally have a better track record than large ones.

In the Caribbean, particularly, talks on mainstream ships are given by staff with little or no real knowledge of the islands. They do little more than spill trite information and clichés.

The talks often are nothing more than shopping tips, some sponsored by local stores—a practice that has reached scandalous proportions. Cruise directors often receive commissions from local stores, even though they deny it. This vested interest could bias the recommendations.

Avoid being misled. If, during a port talk, the cruise director or anyone else recommends one store over another, shop around before buying. The store recommended may be the best place to buy—or it may not.

Also, be cautious of advice that fabulous buys are available in duty-free shops on board and in ports. Most often, you can do as well or better at discount stores and factory outlets at home. If you are considering sizable purchases of jewelry, cameras, china, or crystal, bring a list of prices from home and comparison shop. Be sure you are comparing similar products. Prices in shipboard shops are a good gauge; they usually are competitive with those in ports.

In the Caribbean, expect to save about 20 percent on such well-known brands as Gucci, Fendi, and Vuitton and on French perfumes, which must be sold at prices set by the makers. Any store caught undercutting the price will be dropped from distribution. The biggest savings are on cigarettes and liquor, not because the price is so much less, but because you save the hefty U.S. taxes imposed on them.

SHORE EXCURSIONS: SOME PITFALLS AND COSTS

"Shore excursions"—the sight-seeing tours passengers take at ports—are often the weakest element of the cruise vacation. That's unfortunate, given their importance to the cruise experience. Shore excursions are available at every stop on a ship's itinerary, almost always at additional cost. The exceptions are adventure and expedition cruises, on which shore visits are an integral part of the experience and one reason these cruises appear to be more costly than mainstream ones. Also, cruises in China usually include the cost of shore excursions, not because cruise lines are altruistic, but because the Chinese want it that way.

With rare exceptions, shore excursions cannot be purchased in advance, which is one reason they're a weak link. Usually, a pamphlet on shore excursions is included in the literature the cruise line sends you. Not all brochures list prices, but you can request them through your travel agent if you need them for budgeting purposes. We are happy to report that more lines are including prices in their literature. Also, more often pamphlets are specific to cruise itineraries, making it easier to select tours of interest.

Shore excursions are sold aboard ship either by a shore excursion office or, rarely, from the purser or cruise director. It has been assumed that people prefer to buy excursions on board because their interests and plans change once the cruise begins. However, that assumption may have no foundation in fact. After you have been subjected to the way shore excursions are sold aboard ships, you might say as we do: There must be a better way.

Often you must choose your excursions on the first night of the cruise. Unless you have done your homework in advance of your cruise, you will be buying blind. The shore excursion office usually has limited hours. For the first few days of a cruise, particularly on large ships, ticket lines are long. Therefore, it really pays to read your cruise literature plus books and magazine articles about your destinations in advance.

Shore excursions normally are operated by local tour companies. Motorcoaches seating 30–50 passengers are used; location and terrain are factors. Most tours assume that passengers are on their first visit to the locale—yet another reason they're a weak link. Shore excursions vary little among cruise lines and are, for the most part, dull, unimaginative, city and/or countryside tours to the best-known sights—a third reason they are a weak link. The few exceptions include excursions on Greek Isles cruises, where escorts are university graduates who must pass stiff examinations to qualify as guides. American Hawaii Cruises' excursions are commendable for their variety of sports and emphasis on nature and culture. Happily, many cruise lines are adding similar selections in an effort to appeal to younger travelers and in response to passengers' requests. The worst are excursions in the Caribbean. However, cruise lines, too, have been working with local operators to improve them and to be more creative with their selections.

As a rule for ordinary tours, expect to pay about $12–15 per hour of touring. For example, a two- to two-and-a-half-hour city tour will cost about $25–35, and a three-hour island tour will be $35–45. Variables include the locale, the number of participants, local costs, and mode of transport.

As you study excursions offered by your line, look for options that keep things simple and reasonably short. Excursions longer than three and a half hours that involve multiple activities, sights, and stops will drive most people nuts. It's on the bus, off the bus, back on the bus, head counts. "Wait, Thelma's still in the rest room!" "Where are Harry and Louise?" "Gertrude's trying on a grass skirt. She'll be here in a minute." "I'll be right back. I left my credit card in the stuffed parrot shop!" With few exceptions you'll spend more time driving among sites and loading and unloading the bus than you will touring or doing something interesting.

When you read descriptions of available excursions, check how long the primary activity or event is. If the written material doesn't say, ask the cruise director. You sometimes discover that the half-day "riverboat excursion" spends only an hour on the water. The remainder of the time is spent commuting and waiting for fellow passengers to shop.

In ports where most attractions you want to see are clustered in a small area, you may save time by taking a cab or walking. Rental cars are an another option. Two people forgoing the $48-per-person half-day excursion save $96, which they can apply toward cab fares, rental cars, and admissions. In most ports, you can see and do a lot for $96.

Ask probing questions about each port. Is it a good and safe place to explore on foot? What are the local people like? At many ports tourists are subjected to swarms of in-your-face hucksters, peddlers, and beggars. In such places, escorted tours, though regimented and inefficient, can be a less stressful way to visit.

When the ship arrives in port, people who have purchased shore excursions are allowed to disembark first and are usually asked to follow a departure schedule to avert a traffic jam at the gangway. This is seldom a problem when the ship docks and passengers can disembark quickly. It can be a problem when the ship must tender, because it cuts an hour or more (depending on ship size) from the time you have in port if you plan to tour on your own.

At the End of Your Cruise

TIPPING

There are no definitive rules about tipping, but because it causes so much consternation for passengers, cruise lines offer guidelines, distributing them aboard ship. Some even publish them in their cruise brochures, which is helpful if you want to budget for them in advance. In Part Two, the cruise ship profiles' Standard Features includes Suggested Tipping. The guidelines are similar: Tip slightly less on budget cruises, slightly more on luxury cruises. Follow guidelines or your inclinations. Ship officers and senior management are never tipped. For all service personnel, tips are their main source of compensation. Only a few deluxe ships include tipping in the cruise cost (noted in the cruise line profiles).

In a session at voyage's end, the cruise director will discuss disembarkation procedures and outline tipping guidelines. There no longer is anything subtle about tipping. On the final cruise day, your cabin steward will leave a supply of envelopes for distributing your tips, possibly with guidelines. Lately, the envelopes are crassly stamped with titles—Cabin Steward, Dining Steward, Waiter—in case you did not know whom to tip!

Normally, tips are given to individuals—your cabin stewards and dining room waiters. On ships with Greek crews and on many small vessels, tips are pooled for distribution to include those behind the scenes, such as kitchen staffs.

Most people distribute tips the last night of the cruise. Some lines, particularly deluxe ones, will arrange prepayment of tips. Check our profiles for these lines.

DEPARTING

To smooth disembarkation, your captain and cruise director will ask you to follow procedures outlined in the cruise director's final talk and repeated on closed-circuit television in your cabin and in the daily agenda. On the last day, your cabin steward will give you luggage tags to be completed and attached to your bags. You are asked to place your bags (except hand luggage) outside your cabin door before you retire. Times vary; some lines want it out by 8 or 10 p.m.—an unreasonable hour for passengers dining at the late seating. Such requests are for the ship's convenience, because no luggage can be unloaded until the ship docks. Do what's convenient for you and tell your cabin steward what to expect.

The last night of a cruise is almost always casual; plan your packing accordingly.

Luggage tags use a color-coded, alphabetic system that enables the ship to disembark passengers by cabin locations and airline departure times for those on air/sea packages. (Passengers on the earliest flights disembark first.) Tags also identify your airline so that your bags will go to the correct place at the airport.

Ships normally dock about 7 or 8 a.m. the last day and require about an hour to unload luggage, meaning no passengers will disembark before 9 a.m. The ship is very eager to unload passengers as quickly as possible. Some people find disembarkation so abrupt that it's unpleasant. Try to remember that the next group of passengers will arrive soon, and staff and crew have only about four hours to prepare the ship and be all smiles for them.

Breakfast is served either at normal hours with the full menu or at abbreviated hours with a short menu. Room service usually isn't available. You will be called to depart by the color of your luggage tags. After leaving the ship, you encounter chaos that varies depending on the port. Usually, you proceed to the baggage holding area, where your luggage has been placed according to the letter of your last name. You are responsible for finding it and taking it to customs. In Miami, for example, baggage handlers help you, and the customs official stands by the exit to take the declaration form you completed aboard ship. They may check your passport, so have it handy.

After clearing customs, give your luggage to the airline representative. It will be trucked to the airport. Then find the motorcoach going to your airline's departure area, show your transfer voucher, and climb aboard. If you aren't on an air/sea package, you may be allowed aboard the motorcoach unless you have lots of luggage. Otherwise, taxis are nearby. Airlines with numerous passengers on their flights may set up desks at the port to enable you to check in at the dock and proceed directly to your gate at the airport. It's so sensible, you wonder why it isn't the norm.

Part Two

Cruise Lines and Their Ships

The Heart of the Matter

This section consists of alphabetical listings of cruise lines and ships serving the U.S. and Canadian markets. In each listing are in-depth cruise line and ship profiles—the heart of this guide. The presentation for each line has three parts: a company profile, standard features, and ship profiles.

Cruise Line Profiles

The first three to four pages focus on the cruise line and the type of cruises it offers. At-a-glance summaries—Type of Ships, Type of Cruises, Cruise Line's Strengths, Cruise Line's Shortcomings, Fellow Passengers, Recommended For, Not Recommended For—help you select cruise lines of potential interest. Some people base their cruise selection on who their fellow passengers are likely to be. Other criteria might be our recommendations or the cruise line's strengths and weaknesses.

Summaries are followed by background on the line, its fleet, and cruise areas to reveal the company behind the cruise. The Style section defines the experience you can expect on any ship of that cruise line. Distinctive Features highlights amenities or facilities that are innovative or may be unavailable on other ships.

Rates

The Rates section explains discounts, special fares, and packages and provides a range of per-person daily (per diem) costs. These figures were derived by averaging cruise-only (no airfare) brochure rates for each cabin class on every ship in the line. Calculations exclude owner's suites, presidential suites, and other extraordinary accommodations. The rate table aims to indicate the most and the least you would pay per day for a cruise if you paid brochure rates. Savvy shoppers almost certainly will be able to chip away 5 to 50 percent of the listed per diem by taking advantage of common discounts. (Note: Our average rate is not calculated by adding the highest and lowest rates in the brochure table and dividing by two. Rather, the average per diem takes into account the number of each type of accommodation available in the line's cabin inventory. The Per Diem Rate Table averages rates for all ships of the line.)

Past Passengers tells what repeat customers can expect, and The Last Word is our summary of the line—the big picture.

Standard Features

Information on elements common to all ships of a line—including officers, staff, dining facilities, dress code, cabin amenities, and electricity—is listed on one page for handy reference.

Cruise Ship Profiles

The cruise line's fleet, starting with its flagship (most representative) vessel, is covered in depth. Sister ships with identical design are clustered. Other ships that vary only in degree receive shorter treatment. We recommend that readers review the entire section for a complete picture of the cruise experience the line offers.

Quality Ratings   To differentiate ships by overall quality of the cruise experience and to allow comparison of ships from different lines, we give ships a rating of 1 to 10, with 10 being the best. The numerical rating (enclosed in a circle) is based on the quality and diversity of the ship's features and service, taking into consideration its state of repair, maintenance, and cleanliness; the design, comfort, decor, and furnishing of public areas; recreational and fitness facilities; meal quality and dining room service; entertainment, activities, and shore excursions; cabin comfort, decor, furnishings, and spaciousness; and hospitality, courtesy, and responsiveness of officers and crew.

We have opted for numerical ratings because some of our colleagues in the travel press have hopelessly muddled the more familiar star ratings. Traditionally, ships have been rated 1 to 5 stars. This system was easily understood by the cruising public and provided a quick way to compare critics' opinions. Recently, however, some writers have changed the scale to 1 to 6 stars, and in one case, 1 to 7 stars, precluding meaningful comparison. We believe a standardized rating system helps consumers. In the absence of such standardization, we have elected to abandon the star business.

Value Ratings   There is no consideration of cost in the quality ratings. If you want the finest cruise available and cost is no issue, look no further than the quality ratings. If, however, you seek both quality *and* value, consult the value rating, expressed in letters. All value ratings are based on brochure rates. Any discount you obtain will improve the value rating for a ship. Value ratings are defined as follows:

A   Exceptional value, a real bargain.
B   Good value.
C   Absolutely fair. You get exactly what you pay for.
D   Somewhat overpriced.
F   Significantly overpriced.

All value ratings are based on brochure rates. Any discount you are able to obtain will improve the value rating for the ship in question.

A Word about New Ships

We do not evaluate or rate new ships until they have been in service for at least one year. This allows the new ship to work out kinks and settle into normal operation. Ratings for new ships will be included in revised editions of the *Unofficial Guide*. If you are considering a cruise on a new ship, check our ratings and descriptions of other ships in the same line for a good idea of what to expect. If a ship has not completed a year of service at press time, it will be marked as a "preview" in the ship's ratings box.

A Matter of Reference

Cruise lines profiled in this section are listed on pages v–vii of the Contents. To find listings of specific ships, refer to Appendix A: Cruise Ships Index, pages 643–655.

Abercrombie & Kent International, Inc.

1520 Kensington Road, Suite 212, Oak Brook, IL 60523-2141
(630) 954-2944; (800) 323-7308; fax (630) 954-3324
www.abercrombiekent.com

Type of Ship   Small expedition vessel.

Type of Cruises   Adventurous, education oriented for sophisticated travelers with avid interest in nature and wildlife.

Cruise Line's Strengths
- superb enrichment program
- highly experienced expedition leaders
- size and maneuverability of ship
- friendliness of staff and crew
- all-inclusive programs
- itineraries

Cruise Line's Shortcomings
- small, spartan cabins and bathrooms
- limited storage space in cabin
- ship subject to vigorous movement in heavy seas

Fellow Passengers   Professional, retired or semiretired, affluent, well-educated, well-traveled, usually age 50 and older, in good health and reasonably fit. Flexible, ecology-minded, intellectually curious. A sizable number are Europeans, especially Germans, and other nationalities.

Recommended For   Adventurous travelers with strong interest in nature, wildlife, geology, history, and photography, who are flexible enough to adapt to weather changes and itinerary changes and fit enough to enjoy hikes in Antarctic snows or in Zodiac rides on the Amazon. Singles make friends easily aboard this vessel.

Not Recommended For   Disabled travelers, young children, or anyone demanding a set routine, entertainment, and luxurious accommodations.

Cruise Areas and Seasons   Antarctica, November–February; Amazon, March–April; North Atlantic, May–August; Transatlantic, October.

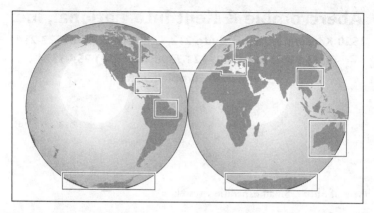

The Line Abercrombie & Kent is a prestigious international tour operator specializing in exotic journeys worldwide for affluent, sophisticated
travelers. Other programs include barge and river cruises in Europe and on
the Amazon, Nile, Yangtze, and Ayeyewaddy Rivers (see Part Three: River
Cruises). In all its programs, the company emphasizes culture and ecologi-
cally sound tourism.

A&K has operated the *Explorer* since 1991. It's the most experienced
vessel sailing Antarctic waters. Built in 1969 in Finland for the late Swedish
travel pioneer Lars-Eric Linblad as the *Linblad Explorer,* it was the world's
first expedition cruise ship. It subsequently sailed as the *Society Explorer* for
Society Expeditions. The *Explorer* has an ice-strengthened hull that allows
it to crunch effortlessly through pack ice. Its small size, shallow draft, and
bow thrusters increase maneuverability among ice floes and icebergs.

The Fleet	Built/Renovated	Tonnage	Passengers
Explorer	1969/92/99	2,398	96

Style High-seas adventure for experienced travelers with a thirst for education and the drive to go beyond the predictable for a rare travel experience, designed for a hardy, affluent few.

Cabins are small, but adequate; what they lack in luxury is balanced by
the travel experience. The international cuisine is good but not gourmet.
Service is friendly and efficient.

Passengers have access to experienced naturalists on the ship's staff, as
well as to guest lecturers, including credentialed zoologists, marine biolo-
gists, geologists, polar explorers, oceanographers, artists, and photographers.

Socializing revolves around lectures. Passengers gather each evening in the lounge for cocktails and a recap of the day's events by the expedition leader and guest lecturers. During Zodiac outings and shore landings, the experts lead small groups, pointing out wildlife, geologic formations, and historical sites.

Distinctive Features   A small but focused library offers books and maps relevant to the cruising area. The navigational bridge is open to passengers at all times. Passengers receive extensive pretrip information covering itinerary, clothing requirements, ecological guidelines, photography tips, and an expedition notebook with reading list. On Antarctic cruises, every passenger is given a parka and backpack. After the cruise, participants are sent a copy of the bridge log and an illustrated voyage diary.

	HIGHEST	LOWEST	AVERAGE
PER DIEM	$1121	$166	$596

The above per diems are calculated from the cruise line's non-discounted *cruise only* fares on standard accommodations. Per diems vary by season, by cabin, and by cruise areas.

Rates   The fare covers all tips, bar drinks, house wines, and shore excursions. Port charges are additional.

Special Fares and Discounts   Early-booking discounts vary; they can be as much as $1,500 per person. Passengers booking consecutive sailings get 20 percent off the second cruise. On some cruises, children traveling with at least one full-paying adult get 50 percent off the adult fare.
• Single Supplement: 150 percent in lower-priced cabin categories; 200 percent for other categories.

Packages
• Air/Sea: Prices include regional transportation within South America; international air is extra.
• Pre/Post: Antarctica programs include a pre- or postcruise stay in the port of embarkation/debarkation with hotel, meals, and sight-seeing.

Past Passengers   Marco Polo is the club for veteran A&K travelers. Small and exclusive, it offers a quarterly newsletter, "members-only" trips, a 5 percent discount on land arrangements on most tours, luggage tags, priority on new destinations, tailored itineraries, a free lending library of A&K videotapes, and eligibility to compete in the annual Marco Polo Photo

Contest. Annual membership is $75, with five-year, lifetime, and children's memberships available.

The Last Word   Cruise ships have flocked to Antarctica in recent years, but the *Explorer* has the longest experience sailing these demanding waters and the most experienced expedition leaders. Weather conditions are very changeable in this remote region; it helps immensely to have staff familiar with alternative landing sites. Antarctic cruises are intended for serious travelers who cherish unusual opportunities. Gadabouts and tourists wanting only to add exotic destinations to their tally should look elsewhere. A&K also markets the deluxe yachts *Clelia II* and *Halcyon* of Classical Cruises as well as the famous *Sea Cloud* and luxury *River Cloud*. For A&K's river cruises, see Part Three.

ABERCROMBIE & KENT STANDARD FEATURES

Officers Northern European and Filipino.

Staff Dining, Cabin/Filipino; Cruise and Entertainment/International.

Dining Facilities One dining room for a single, open seating. Buffet breakfast and lunch, à la carte dinner. Breakfast served in the lounge, mid-morning bouillon, midnight snacks, and coffee and tea throughout the day. Afternoon tea.

Special Diets Vegetarian, low-fat, low-salt. Requests must be made in writing at least three weeks before sailing.

Room Service Light breakfast. In rough seas, passengers may order other meals from the dining room menu.

Dress Code Casual at all times.

Cabin Amenities Hair dryers, radios, toiletries.

Electrical Outlets 220 AC.

Wheelchair Access None.

Recreation and Entertainment Reading, board games, daily quiz; lounge with bar, piano, small dance floor; film/slide shows in lecture hall.

Sports and Fitness Small gym with reclining bicycle, ski machine, free weights; mixed sauna and shower. Small dipping pool (not used during Antarctic cruises). Stretch-and-tone class on deck during sea days.

Other Facilities Gift shop, sun deck, hospital, laundry/pressing service, satellite telecommunications, daily fax news.

Children's Facilities None.

Theme Cruises None.

Smoking Nonsmoking charter flights, dining room, and lounge during lectures and recap sessions.

A&K Suggested Tipping Dining and cabin attendant tips included in cruise cost. Bar/wine waiters tipped at passenger discretion. Extra tips may be contributed to the crew's party and activities fund.

Credit Cards For cruise payment and on-board charges: American Express, Diners Club, Discover, MasterCard, Visa, cash, traveler's cheques, personal checks. On-board shop purchases: Visa and MasterCard only (separate imprint required).

Explorer	Quality ❸	Value C
Registry: Liberia	Length: 239 feet	Beam: 46 feet
Cabins: 53	Draft: 13.7 feet	Speed: 12 knots
Maximum Passengers:	Passenger Decks: 5	Elevators: None
100	Crew: 71	Space Ratio: NA

The Ship   Built expressly for polar waters, the *Explorer* is a jaunty little red ship trimmed in white. Its strong suit is its experience sailing in Antarctica.

A small flotilla of Zodiac boats is available for excursions among ice floes and shore landings. Zodiacs are lowered over the ship's side into the water; passengers descend a stairway to board. Staff members check passengers before they leave the ship to be sure everyone is warmly and safely attired.

The *Explorer*, whose public areas and cabins were refurbished in 1999, is extremely compact but functional, with a main deck with gangway exit, reception desk, fax news and notice board, gift shop, dining room, lounge, bar, and library. E-mail facilities are now available, too.

The lounge is the main socializing area, the site of self-service coffee and tea by day and evening recap sessions. The lecture hall one deck up is used for films and slide shows. Outside the hall is the pool deck, where passengers bundled in wool blankets read, sunbathe, or snooze on deck chairs. Another deck up are the bridge, hospital, and a small gym. A breezy top deck, covered in Astroturf, mainly attracts photographers.

Remarkably, nobody gets cabin keys (there are no locks), and security problems are nil. Nonetheless, leave expensive jewelry at home; you won't need it here. Those who insist are provided safe-deposit boxes at the reception desk.

Itineraries   See Appendix B.

Cabins   Passengers may be surprised initially by the cabins' compactness, but they soon find that all essentials are provided—adequately, if not lavishly. Beds may be short for six-footers. Water-saving bathroom fixtures require getting used to—in the shower, a lever is pressed to deliver 30-second spurts of water. Only the Marco Polo Suite has a bathtub; all other cabins have showers.

Storage space is limited (two narrow closets), especially considering the boots, parkas, and other gear toted along on an Antarctic expedition. But everyone gets a porthole, small vanity/desk and bureau, and nice touches, including extra blankets, hair dryers, toiletries, pitchers of water, writing paper, and postcards. All cabins were given a facelift in 1999.

Specifications 53 outside cabins, including 2 suites. Standard dimensions are 160 square feet. Most cabins have twin lower berths (none convert to doubles); a few have bunks; a few are triples. Suites have queen-size beds. No connecting cabins; no singles.

Dining Meals are casual and lively, with all passengers accommodated in a single, open seating. Tables draped with crisp, white cloths seat four or seven. The international cuisine, recently upgraded, is refreshingly unpretentious.

Breakfast is a large buffet with dishes ranging from muesli and fresh fruit to buttery croissants and sticky Danishes. Also, you can have oatmeal, cold cereals, breakfast meats, and made-to-order eggs. Early risers find coffee and rolls in the lounge, where bouillon is served midmorning.

Everyone's favorite meal is lunch, a buffet table groaning with soup cooked from scratch, imaginative salads, fresh cold seafood, hot fish and meat dishes, pastas, breads and rolls, several desserts, and a cheese tray. Breakfast and lunch offer à la carte menus. Tea time, in the dining room, features cookies and pastries.

Dinner is à la carte, with three or four choices of appetizer, soup, salad, entree, and dessert. Several nights offer theme menus. One evening, weather permitting, a barbecue/buffet with hot mulled wine is served on the sun deck.

At lunch and dinner, wine, beer, and cocktails may be ordered. New this year, all bar drinks and house wines are included without additional costs. Late-night snacks and desserts are served in the lounge.

Service Genuine friendliness is the hallmark of service on this ship. The Filipino dining and cabin staff are very pleasant, well prepared, and eager to please. Although passengers sit at different tables for meals, waiters generally remember preferences, and the two-person bar staff is equally adept. The savvy maître d'hôtel helps passengers mix and is especially considerate of single travelers.

Facilities and Entertainment No formal entertainment or shows are offered; days are packed with intellectual and physical activities. The expedition leader, staff naturalists, and guest lecturers present a recap in the lounge before dinner.

Socializing resumes there after dinner, sometimes continuing into the wee hours. A passenger may tickle the ivories or sing, but guests generally just converse. Slides, a film, or a Hollywood movie may be shown in the lecture hall, which accommodates all passengers. The library is popular at any hour.

Activities and Diversions Lectures are well attended. Most talks are accompanied by audiovisuals. Staff and guest speakers mingle continually with passengers, answering questions or pointing out wildlife. On the bridge, officers show passengers the charts and explain navigational equipment. In the lounge, passengers write postcards, update diaries, and read.

One of the hottest areas aboard is the tiny gift shop, where new items materialize only to be snapped up by passengers with a seemingly insatiable lust for coffee-table books, jewelry, Patagonia jackets, T-shirts, pins, hats, potholders—anything with *Antarctica* on it.

Sports, Fitness, and Beauty   A small gym offers a reclining bicycle, stationary upright bicycle, and a weight machine. There's also a mixed sauna with shower. On days at sea, a stretch-and-tone class is offered on deck (weather permitting). The dipping pool isn't used during Antarctic cruises. There is no beauty salon (the one shown in the brochure has been converted into storage space), but cabins have hair dryers.

Shore Excursions   On the Antarctic, Amazon, and other programs, the cruise price usually includes city tours in pre- and postcruise packages and Zodiac trips and landings.

Postscript   Abercrombie & Kent's precruise literature is excellent for helping you prepare for your cruise. Nevertheless, expect a few rough days at sea, particularly because Antarctic itineraries include a crossing of the unpredictable Drake Passage.

This intimate vessel draws exceptionally interesting, intellectually curious passengers, among whom many lasting friendships are forged. If you don't have a similar thirst for knowledge or the flexibility to deal with frequent changes caused by weather and sea, you could find yourself on the wrong ship a long way from home.

Alaska's Glacier Bay Tours and Cruises/Voyager Cruise Line

226 2nd Avenue West, Seattle, WA 98119
(206) 623-7110; (800) 451-5952; fax (206) 623-7809
www.glacierbaytours.com

Type of Ships   Three small, no-frills coastal ships and one fast, fancier, catamaran-style coastal ship.

Type of Cruises   Casual; active and light adventure; emphasis on nature, wildlife, and local culture.

Cruise Line's Strengths
- small, highly maneuverable ships
- loosely structured itineraries
- Alaska Native culture and off-vessel activities
- all excursions included in cruise price
- friendly shipboard atmosphere
- enthusiastic staff and crew
- naturalists on every cruise

Cruise Line's Shortcomings
- small, spartan cabins with minimal soundproofing
- tiny, head-style bathrooms
- lack of shipboard diversions
- ships not very stable in rough waters

Fellow Passengers   On active-adventure *Wilderness Explorer* and light-adventure *Wilderness Adventurer,* age ranges from 40s to 70s, with 30-somethings and 80-year-olds in the mix. Passengers are uniformly active and interested in nature and wildlife; they are attracted to the ships' itineraries, which favor wilderness areas. Many are veteran hikers and kayakers—two activities central to these cruises. All seek a trip heavy on experience and information and light on formality and glitz. Spartan cabins and lack of diversions suit them fine—in fact, the homey atmosphere draws many passengers. They're happy with the flexible itinerary that frees the captain to sail wherever passengers will get the best Alaska experience, taking into account weather, sea conditions, and wildlife sightings.

On the somewhat upscale (though casual) *Executive Explorer* and *Wilderness Discoverer* (sister ship of *Wilderness Adventurer* but lacking kayaks and other adventure equipment), passengers tend to be older (60 years and up) and less active, though they enjoy the vessels' informality. Both ships offer exploration of Alaska's towns and villages as much as its wilderness.

Recommended For   Outdoors enthusiasts; people interested in Alaska Native culture; those who want to escape television, traffic, and the daily grind; people eager to reach less accessible waterways; those seeking an informal experience in an atmosphere of camaraderie between passengers and crew.

Not Recommended For   People who need entertainment or casinos or would be bored without television or shopping; people wanting to remain anonymous aboard ship; those requiring large cabins and normal bathroom facilities; people taller than 6' 3" (ships' ceilings are low).

Cruise Areas and Seasons   Alaska, May–September; Sea of Cortés (Mexico), January–April.

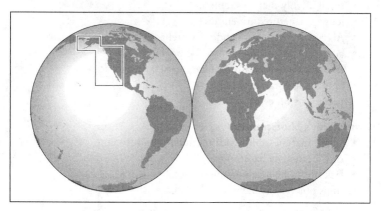

The Line   Formerly owned by Seattle entrepreneur Robert Giersdorf (founder of the America West Steamship Company), Alaska's Glacier Bay Tours and Cruises and its ships, *Wilderness Explorer* and *Executive Explorer,* were purchased in 1996 by Juneau-based Goldbelt, Inc., an Alaska Native corporation set up under the Alaska Native Claims Settlement Act and representing over 3,000 Tlingit and Haida shareholders. Two additional ships, *Wilderness Adventurer* and *Wilderness Discover,* were purchased in 1996 and 1997 from American Canadian Caribbean Line, for which they sailed as *Caribbean Prince* and *Mayan Prince,* respectively. Due to the line's ownership, shipboard programs tend to focus on understanding Alaska Native culture and beliefs, particularly regarding the environment.

In 1997, Glacier Bay Tours and Cruises formed a sister company, Voyager Cruise Line, to offer non-Alaska itineraries. The first, in Mexico's Sea of Cortés, was launched in January 1998. Glacier Bay Tours and Cruises is the official concessionaire for Glacier Bay National Park and provides the only overnight accommodations in the park, at Glacier Bay Lodge.

The Fleet	Built/Renovated	Tonnage	Passengers
Wilderness Adventurer	1984/97/99	89	72
Wilderness Discoverer	1992/99	95	88
Wilderness Explorer	1969/97	98	34

Style   Glacier Bay emphasizes experiences made possible by the small ships' ability to navigate in shallow waters and narrow passages, nose up to shore for wildlife watching, and get closer to whales without frightening them than big ships can.

On their U.S.-registered adventure ships, Glacier Bay places heavier emphasis than other lines on putting passengers in contact with nature. Through kayaking, hikes (often directly from ship, owing to *Adventurer's* and *Discoverer's* bow-landing capabilities), and naturalist lectures, passengers spend much more time enjoying Alaska's natural wonders than shopping in ports or being distracted by shipboard activities.

Naturalists sail with every cruise. One may lead groups no larger than a dozen on an excursion into the rain forest, explaining flora and fauna and pointing out natural features, while another heads a kayaking trip. On a recent Alaska cruise, a Native Aleut naturalist told Tlingit legends in a traditional manner. Other Native storytellers occasionally come aboard to provide cultural background. In the Sea of Cortés, a Mexican naturalist joins American naturalists aboard.

All the line's ships are casual. Meals are never dressy, and the informality of the passenger/crew relationship results in off-duty crew members watching nature videos with passengers and naturalists sitting topside at night with passengers, watching the stars. Most crew members are from Alaska and the Pacific Northwest; a number are Native Alaskans. In fact, some Native crew members are stockholders in the line's parent company, adding noticeable pride of ownership to the way they comport themselves.

The casual atmosphere and small number of passengers allow easy camaraderie. Passengers commonly know one another by name within days and maintain friendships long after the cruise.

Distinctive Features   Shore excursions, kayak, and Zodiac adventures included in cruise price; Native culture–oriented excursions. Dry-launch platforms on *Adventurer* and *Explorer* allow passengers to step directly into their kayaks from the ship. Shallow drafts allow ships to nose up to dockless places; bow ramps let passengers walk out of ship's nose onto dry land. *Executive Explorer's* speed (18 knots, compared to other small ships' 10–13 knots) enables her to visit more ports or spend more time whale watching.

	HIGHEST	LOWEST	AVERAGE
PER DIEM	$540	$200	$325

The above per diems are calculated from the cruise line's non-discounted *cruise only* fares on standard accommodations. Per diems vary by season, by cabin, and by cruise areas.

Rates   All port charges, airport transfers, and shore excursions included.

Special Fares and Discounts
• Single Supplement: 175 percent of twin rate.

Packages
• Air/Sea: Air add-ons available.
• Others: In Alaska, one-, two-, and six-day independent tour packages include high-speed ferry transport from Juneau; Glacier Bay whale-watching cruise; and, with two-day package, overnight at Glacier Bay Lodge. Six-day "Air, Land & Sea" includes air transportation from Juneau to Glacier Bay; day excursions in Glacier Bay, Icy Strait, and Tracy Arm; and overnights in Juneau and Glacier Bay Lodge.
• Pre/Post: Optional four- to nine-day Alaska packages. For example, six-day "Gates of the Arctic" visits Fairbanks, Gates of the Arctic National Park, Athabascan, and Inupik Native village of Evansville, and includes a float trip on the Koyakuk River. In Baja, six-day pre-cruise tour of Mexico's Copper Canyon.

The Last Word   Two words—*adventure* and *informality*—sum up this line's cruise experience. The cruises are for people who want to leave the beaten path and do something really different. When the ship enters wilderness areas, passengers can imagine they are on an expedition into the unknown. Kayaking on a quiet lagoon, hiking through rain forest, or, in the Baja, hiking desert terrain or swimming off of an uninhabited beach will do that to you. There is no better holiday for older children than Alaska, especially for those interested in wildlife and the environment. The *Wilderness Adventurer* and *Wilderness Discoverer*—the fleet's only ships accepting children—are ideal for families, particularly those who hike and camp together.

ALASKA'S GLACIER BAY TOURS AND CRUISES/ VOYAGER CRUISE LINE STANDARD FEATURES

Officers American.

Staff Dining, Cabin, Cruise/American.

Dining Facilities One dining room with open seating, set meal times. Early continental breakfast and cocktail hour with snacks in lounge or on top deck, weather permitting. Coffee, tea, cocoa, fruit, dry snacks throughout day.

Special Diets Notice required at booking. Accommodates vegetarian, low-fat, low-salt.

Room Service None.

Dress Code Casual at all times. Jeans, polos, and flannels the norm in Alaska; shorts and T-shirts in Baja. Many bring dress shirts, chinos, or dresses for the captain's dinner.

Cabin Amenities Upper-deck cabins have windows that open (except *Executive Explorer*). Tiny bathrooms, "head-style" toilet (toilet is in shower stall). Reading lights over beds; small closets, limited drawer space; *Executive Explorer,* large closets.

Electrical Outlets 110 AC.

Wheelchair Access None.

Recreation and Entertainment Lounge with bar, television/VCR with nature, Native-culture videos, films; small library with nature books and field guides; board games. Binoculars available, better to bring your own. Nature and culture talks by naturalists.

Beauty and Fitness None.

Other Facilities No doctor. Crew trained in first aid and CPR.

Children's Facilities None.

Theme Cruises None.

Smoking Prohibited in cabins or public rooms; allowed outside on open decks.

Suggested Tipping $12–15 per person per day. Tips pooled and shared by nonofficer staff and crew.

Credit Cards For cruise payment and on-board charges: American Express, Visa, MasterCard, Diners Club, Discover.

Executive Explorer	Quality ❸	Value C
Registry: United States	Length: 98.5 feet	Beam: 38 feet
Cabins: 25	Draft: 8 feet	Speed: 10 knots
Maximum Passengers:	Passenger Decks: 6	Elevators: None
49	Crew: 18	Space Ratio: NA

The Ship   Though odd-looking with catamaran hulls and three-deck-tall, wedge-shaped superstructure, the *Executive Explorer* is Glacier Bay's most luxurious ship, sailing less adventurous port-to-port itineraries and featuring larger, better-appointed, more inviting cabins and public areas than the line's other ships. She's streamlined, powerful, and able to zip between ports faster than any other small passenger ship on the Alaska scene. But the shallow catamaran draft can make for rough going in open seas. Fortunately, such areas are few on her Inside Passage routes.

Public areas are pleasantly furnished and, like the line's other vessels, decorated with Native Alaskan art. The Vista View Lounge and Vista cabins above it have a wall of windows overlooking the bow. An open top deck and covered area on the middle deck are best for wildlife viewing. An open area at the stern is another option.

Itineraries   See Appendix B.

Cabins   The *Executive Explorer* offers the largest, best-appointed cabins in the line's fleet. All have large windows and are furnished with refrigerator, television/VCR, and considerable closet space. *Executive Explorer* has solid cabin doors; *Wilderness Discoverer* and *Wilderness Explorer* have accordion-style doors.

Bathrooms have doors (aboard *Wilderness Adventurer* and *Wilderness Discoverer,* they're separated from the cabin by a curtain). The bathrooms are small, arranged in the line's space-saving "head style" (toilet is in the shower stall), but the doors alone make bathrooms on this vessel vastly superior. Sinks and vanities are in the main cabin area.

All but Vista Deluxe and B cabins have twin beds that convert to queen size. One B cabin, smaller than the others, has upper and lower berths and accommodates two people but is suggested as a single. The two Vista Deluxe cabins (aft middle deck, below the bridge) face the bow and have a sitting area, queen-size beds, larger closets, and a wall of windows providing a wraparound view.

Specifications   25 outside, including 2 deluxe cabins. No suites. Dimensions, approximately 135 square feet. Two Vista Deluxe with queens; 22 standard with twins (convertible to queens); one with upper/ lower bunks.

Dining   Meals are served in single, open seatings in one dining room. Cuisine, all freshly prepared, tends to be standard American fare with regional specialties, but galley staff often come up with surprising gourmet touches. There are usually two or three entrees for dinner; Alaska salmon is a staple. While food is plentiful (very plentiful!) and well appreciated by passengers, it can be a bit heavy at times.

Between meals there are no dining opportunities save for fruit and coffee/tea in the dining room and dry snacks at the bar. The galley staff bakes fresh cookies at midafternoon and serves a snack (of the nacho and chicken wing variety) at the predinner cocktail hour. One dinner per cruise is designated as the captain's dinner, with lobster and free champagne. With advance notice, the galley staff can accommodate special diets.

Service   Service is one of the line's best features—cordial and warm, capable and professional. Members of the hotel staff, most of them young and mostly from Alaska and the Pacific Northwest, do double and triple duty, cleaning cabins, serving meals, and helping carry luggage on and off the ship. All in all, the service is more like that found at a friendly B&B than at a resort.

Facilities and Entertainment   The ship has only two public rooms— one lounge, which has the vessel's only bar, a small library, board games, and videotapes; and one dining room. It has no exercise or entertainment facilities. A full-time bartender tends bar in the lounge.

Shipboard activities are focused mainly on observing nature and wildlife. On every occasion, naturalists explain the animal's behavior to help make passengers' wildlife viewing more accessible. In the evenings, the naturalists and the ship's cruise director give talks on wildlife, Native culture, and history, and occasionally host participatory games (such as a dice-fueled vegetable "race"). Other than this, entertainment is provided by Alaska itself, and by passenger interaction, sharing stories, and the pleasures of the Alaska encounter.

Postscript   The *Executive Explorer* is a good choice for passengers seeking the kind of relaxed experience at which Glacier Bay Tours and Cruises excels, but who are as interested in visiting the ports as they are in hiking in the wilderness. More comfortable than the line's other ships, she is also a better choice for those with higher expectations regarding their accommodations. With its small number of passengers, you get to enjoy Alaska as part of a very intimate group.

Wilderness Adventurer	Quality ❸	Value **C**
Wilderness Discoverer	Quality ❷	Value **C**
Registry: United States	Length: 157/169 feet	Beam: 38 feet
Cabins: 34/42	Draft: 6.5 feet	Speed: 10 knots
Maximum Passengers:	Passenger Decks: 3	Elevators: None
72/88	Crew: 22	Space Ratio: NA

The Ships   Wide, low-slung, and very shallow in draft, the ships reflect a function-over-form sensibility.

The quiet, maneuverable vessels (formerly *Caribbean Prince* and *Mayan Prince* of American Canadian Caribbean Line) are equipped with innovative features for which ACCL founder Luther Blount is known, including his patented bow ramp, which allows a ship to crawl right up to shores where there is no dock and off-load passengers for hiking and exploration.

Furthermore, the *Wilderness Adventurer* is outfitted with stable, two-person sea kayaks and a dry-launch platform that allows passengers to take their kayaks directly from the ship. Several outside areas—an open bow space, a half-covered top deck, and a small stern area—are ideal for nature watching.

A caution: Due to their shallow drafts, these vessels tend to pitch and roll uncomfortably in rough water, but because they ply the mostly protected waters of Alaska's Inside Passage and Mexico's Sea of Cortés, the going is usually smooth. Also, ceilings are low—only about 6' 4".

In 1999, after *Wilderness Adventurer* ran aground near Juneau, it underwent a quarter-million-dollar repair and renovation, upgrading the comfort level at the same time. All cabins were refitted with new doors and refurbished, and the soundproofing was improved. Public rooms, including the dining room, were also refurbished.

Itineraries   See Appendix B.

Cabins   Very basic, cabins come in three categories (four on *Discoverer*) determined by size and location. All have private bathrooms, and all but those on the lowest deck have picture windows that open—almost as good as having a balcony. Deluxe cabins (*Discoverer* only) and AA cabins on the Sun Deck have twin beds. Some can accommodate a third person. Deluxe cabins have more floor space. A-level cabins on the main deck, aft of the dining room, offer twin beds (double bed in three). B-level cabins, on the lowest deck, have no windows. They are furnished with two twins or one twin and one double bed. Storage in all cabins except deluxe is minimal.

Wilderness Discoverer's bathrooms are "marine heads": Toilet, shower, and sink are in one small space separated from the main cabin area by only a curtain. *Wilderness Adventurer* has solid doors separating the toilet and shower combo from the sink and vanity.

Deluxe cabins on *Discoverer* and cabins 303–306 on *Adventurer* open onto the outside deck, rather than inside corridors, and have real doors. All other cabins have accordion doors. They provide privacy but, with the ship's lack of soundproofing, do little to alleviate noise. Fortunately, night owls are rare. Most passengers are in bed by 9 or 10 p.m., and even light sleepers seem unbothered.

Adventurer *Specifications*   30 outside, 4 inside cabins. No suites. Dimensions, 99 square feet. Eleven cabins with double beds, 23 with twins. Some accommodate third passenger. No singles.

Discoverer *Specifications*   37 outside, 5 inside cabins. No suites. Dimensions, 99 square feet. Six cabins with queen-size beds, 8 with doubles, 28 with twins. Some accommodate third passenger. No singles.

Dining   All meals are served in single, open seatings. Cuisine is basically American, with regional specialties and international touches, all freshly prepared. In Baja, some Mexican specialties are incorporated. Snacks are served during predinner cocktails; cookies are baked fresh daily.

Service   One of the ship's best features, service is friendly, cheerful, and capable. Most staff members are young and come from Alaska and the Pacific Northwest. They do it all: cleaning cabins, serving meals, and toting luggage.

Activities and Diversions   Each ship has a single lounge with a full-time bartender. Entertainment is do-it-yourself, with naturalist lectures and occasional parlor games. Occasionally, a nature video or feature film plays on the lounge VCR, or the crew may challenge passengers to a board game. Passengers spend most shipboard hours reading, conversing, or watching for wildlife. Binoculars are available; most passengers bring their own. The open-bridge policy attracts passengers to the wheelhouse.

On *Wilderness Adventurer* in both Alaska and Baja, activities are hiking, kayaking; add snorkeling in Baja.

Postscript   Small and spartan, these ships nonetheless are wonderful for exploration. *Wilderness Adventurer*'s light adventures offer unique Alaska and Baja experiences, putting passengers directly in touch with nature and local culture on a flexible itinerary that allows time for gaining a sense of place.

Wilderness Discoverer offers a port-to-port Alaska experience comparable to that offered by other small cruise ships in Alaska.

Wilderness Explorer	Quality ❸	Value D
Registry: United States	Length: 112 feet	Beam: 21.1 feet
Cabins: 17	Draft: 7.6 feet	Speed: 9 knots
Maximum Passengers:	Passenger Decks: 3	Elevators: None
34	Crew: 13	Space Ratio: NA

The Ship   The line's oldest ship (another former American Canadian Caribbean Line vessel, built in 1969), *Wilderness Explorer* offers perhaps the most active cruise experience in Alaska.

The ship is tiny, accommodating only 34 passengers in minuscule cabins, but it's the adventure—exploration and the line's respect for the natural environment—that's the big drawing card. Underscoring this concept, the line refers to the ship as its "cruising base camp." It's a means to take passengers into the Alaskan landscape rather than a floating hotel. Nevertheless, interiors are surprisingly bright and cheerful, and the lounge has a piano.

All meals are served in single, open seatings in the dining room on the main deck. Snacks are served during the cocktail hour. Service is consistently friendly and professional.

Itineraries   See Appendix B.

Cabins   Except for one deluxe cabin behind the wheelhouse on the top deck, all cabins are tiny, offering upper and lower bunks, head-style bathrooms, and minimal storage. Tiny "portlights" in A- and B-class cabins admit light but can't be called real windows. AA-class cabins, next to the dining room on the main deck, have slightly more space and real windows. The deluxe cabin is considerably larger than others and has windows on both port and starboard sides. There are no single cabins.

Specifications   17 outside cabins, all with upper and lower berths. No inside cabins, suites, or singles, and none accommodates a third passenger.

Facilities and Entertainment   There is no shipboard entertainment or exercise facility. Passengers amuse themselves with board games, a small library, a television/VCR, and a piano in the lounge. A bar operates on the honor system except during cocktail hour, when it is staffed by a crew member.

Activities and Diversions   Activities center on off-vessel exploration. Passengers who take this cruise through Glacier Bay and Icy Strait should focus on nature exploration and wildlife observation and should be in good physical condition to handle the three- to four-hour kayaking and hiking excursions. The only planned activities aboard are informal nature, culture, and history lectures by the ship's naturalists and the Glacier Bay park naturalist who accompanies the ship within park boundaries.

Postscript A *Wilderness Explorer* cruise is a good choice for those seeking active, ship-based outdoor adventure. The port-free itinerary and small number of passengers mean your Alaska experience will be very personal and completely different from that of a large ship and most small ships. People requiring a lot of personal space should look elsewhere.

American Canadian Caribbean Line
461 Water Street, Warren, RI 02885
(401) 247-0955; (800) 556-7450; fax (401) 247-2350
www.accl-smallships.com

Type of Ships   Small, no frills, budget.

Type of Cruises   Light adventure, destination-oriented, unhurried pace.

Cruise Line's Strengths
- innovative, small ships
- imaginative itineraries
- homey ambience
- friendly, diligent staff
- moderate prices

Cruise Line's Shortcomings
- minimal service
- spartan cabins
- small cabin bathrooms
- limited shipboard facilities
- sparse precruise information

Fellow Passengers   Mature, experienced travelers ages 40–85; retired couples, seniors; water sports enthusiasts. Not all are sporty, but all are good sports; friendly and unpretentious, most with modest means, college-educated, well-traveled. Even affluent passengers care little for luxury and ostentation and are keenly interested in history, wildlife, and ecology. They play bridge and Scrabble and read avidly. Most come from the northeast United States, Florida, and California.

Recommended For   Travelers seeking friendship, companionship, light adventure in unusual destinations, moderate price on small ship with family atmosphere. Those who abhor large ships.

Not Recommended For   Swingers, hyper superachievers, snobs, or night owls.

Cruise Areas and Seasons   Spring–fall, U.S. coastal waterways between Rhode Island and Florida; Hudson River/Erie Canal, New England/ Canada; small mid-America rivers; Mississippi byways from Chicago to New Orleans; Great Lakes/New England via the Erie Canal. Winter, Bahamas; Virgin Islands; Eastern/Southern Caribbean and Orinoco River; Belize, Barrier Reef, Honduras, and Guatemala.

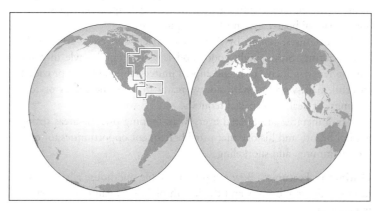

The Line   Shipbuilder and adventurer Luther Blount designed and built his first small ship in 1964 for cruising the Hudson River, Erie Canal, and Canada's inland waterways with his friends. A loyal following developed, and his hobby became a business that pioneered innovative itineraries.

   With slightly larger ships, he expanded to the Bahamas, Virgin Islands, and small islands of the Eastern Caribbean, added "Caribbean" to the line's name, and again pioneered unusual itineraries in Central America, the Southern Caribbean, and other U.S. waterways.

   Each vessel, built at Blount's shipyard in Warren, Rhode Island, has had design improvements, added larger cabins and better public space. But the cruise style is unchanged. ACCL remains a family enterprise. Daughter Nancy Blount is vice president and director of operations, and Luther Blount continues as a hands-on president, designing every aspect of the ships, supervising the building, and scouting new itineraries. His design concepts have been adopted by many small cruise ships.

The Fleet	Built/Renovated	Tonnage	Passengers
Grande Caribe	1997	99	100
Grande Mariner	1998	99	100
Niagara Prince	1994/99	95	84

Style   Adventure at budget prices. Leave your Guccis at home—there's no one who would be impressed. Since its inception, ACCL has maintained an informal, unpretentious atmosphere with limited service and planned entertainment. Passengers receive an intimate look at places they visit. The ships' shallow drafts enable them to cruise small tributaries. Bow ramps, a Blount innovation, allow access to normally inaccessible places, opening secluded beaches for swimming and snorkeling. Ships carry a glass-bottom boat, small sailboats, and snorkeling equipment.

ACCL cruises, staffed by American officers and crew, are run like a family outing. Surprisingly good food is served family-style in a folksy atmosphere conducive to friendships. Limited table service is provided by cheerful, hard-working staff, always ready to bring beverages or second helpings, or deal with special requests.

New itineraries are offered every year, tapping pristine areas strong in natural beauty and history that provide frequent opportunities for exploring, swimming, and snorkeling.

Distinctive Features   Bow ramps; retractable pilothouse allowing vessels to sail under low bridges and the length of Erie Canal; underwater viewing cameras.

	HIGHEST	LOWEST	AVERAGE
PER DIEM	$266	$186	$213

The above per diems are calculated from the cruise line's non-discounted *cruise only* fares on standard accommodations. Per diems vary by season, by cabin, and by cruise areas.

Rates   Port charges are additional. Some shore excursions included.

Special Fares and Discounts   10 percent discount on certain cruises when two cruises are booked back-to-back; up to 30 percent discounts or more periodically on early-bird and special promotions.
- Third Passenger: 15 percent discount for each occupant of cabin.
- Single Supplement: 175 percent for certain cabins, depending on season and time of booking.

Packages
- Air/Sea: On certain Belize, Caribbean, Panama Canal, and Eastern Caribbean sailings.
- Pre/Post: Panama, Belize, Bonaire, Trinidad, New Orleans.

Past Passengers Loyalty is rewarded; after ten cruises, a passenger gets one free. Advanced mailings on new itineraries and special discounts.

The Last Word Up to 68 percent of passengers are repeat, suggesting that ACCL has found the right formula for a certain type of passenger: one who doesn't want or need pampering and appreciates small-ship cruising, preferring conversation and friendship to chorus lines and casinos. New itineraries usually sell out quickly. ACCL reflects the owners' hands-on philosophy and personal touch with customers. Passengers who understand the limitations of a small ship and the nature of these cruises enjoy themselves immensely; those who do not may discover they're on the wrong ship.

ACCL's chief shortcoming is the dearth of information on itineraries, ports of call, and shore excursions sent to passengers before their cruise. Tours are not published in advance, and passengers receive no literature describing places a cruise will visit. ACCL responds that itineraries and tours change, but experience shows they do not change that much. It is difficult to understand why ACCL handles such information haphazardly, particularly when its passengers are destination-focused. It's even more puzzling when you know that ACCL is one of the few cruise lines that does not profit on shore excursions. They're either included in the cruise price or sold at cost—one of many reasons ACCL cruises are a truly good value.

ACCL's chief shortcoming is one that could easily be corrected—namely, the dearth of information on itineraries, ports of call, and shore excursions sent to passengers prior to their cruise. Tours are not published in advance, and passengers receive no supplementary literature describing the places a cruise will visit.

ACCL STANDARD FEATURES

Officers American.

Staff Dining, Cabin, Cruise/American.

Dining Facilities One dining room with open seating; meals served at specific hours: breakfast, 8 a.m.; lunch, noon; dinner, 6 p.m.

Special Diets Cruise line needs notice at booking, but chefs can accommodate basic requests.

Room Service None.

Dress Code Casual at all times; men never need a tie. Gentlemen might bring a jacket and women a dress in case they want to try a fancy place in a port of call.

Cabin Amenities Air-conditioning/heat; upper-deck cabins have windows that can be opened. Very small bathroom with hand-held shower. Reading light; plug for hair dryers. Limited drawer and closet space.

Electrical Outlets 110 AC.

Wheelchair Access No designated cabins; motorized chair between main and sun decks.

Recreation and Entertainment Lounge with bar setup, books, and videos; informal entertainment, occasional lectures; bridge and parlor games. No casino, swimming pool, gym, or theater.

Sports and Other Activities Glass-bottom boat and snorkeling equipment on board for warm weather cruises.

Beauty and Fitness No facilities. On request, cruise director will make appointments with beauty/barber salons in ports.

Other Facilities Ships have no doctors.

Children's Facilities None. Children under age 14 not accepted.

Theme Cruises Fall foliage.

Smoking No smoking inside ships; allowed only in outside open areas.

ACCL Suggested Tipping All tips are pooled and shared; guidelines call for about $12 per person per day.

Credit Cards None.

Niagara Prince	Quality ❷	Value A
Registry: United States	Length: 166 feet	Beam: 40 feet
Cabins: 42	Draft: 6.3 feet	Speed: 12 knots
Maximum Passengers: 84	Passenger Decks: 3	Elevators: None;
	Crew: 15	chairlift
		Space Ratio: NA

The Ship The U.S.-flagged *Niagara Prince,* an innovative small ship with shallow draft, made her debut in 1994. She was designed to navigate the length of the Erie Canal and sail on coastal waters. The comfortable but basic *Niagara Prince* has two passenger decks with homey decor and low ceilings. The lounge and dining room, located forward on the top or sun deck, rather than on the main deck as on earlier ships, has windows at the bow and along the sides, providing enhanced views. The lounge, shaped by the bow, has the ship's only television set, books, and newspapers (updated as available in ports). The dining room is an all-purpose room between meals.

The sun deck also has cabins and a wraparound promenade with small sitting areas at each end.

A flight of steps at the bow accesses the patented bow ramp, used when a site of interest has no dock. Extensions lengthen the ramp and allow for dry shore landings. Stairs from the promenade deck lead to a partially covered rooftop deck with chairs. Also atop is the retractable pilothouse, lowered to pass under bridges by lifting off its roof, folding back its three sides, and disconnecting all the equipment. The captain's chair, console, steering mechanism, and equipment then are lowered to the promenade deck and reconnected so the ship can resume operation. It's quite a scene to watch, leaving you with an I-had-to-see-it-to-believe-it feeling.

Niagara Prince's profile can be made even lower with a hull feature likened by Blount to letting the air out of a tire. It enables the ship to pass under the Erie Canal's lowest bridges and traverse the waterway from Troy to Buffalo, the first boat to do so in over 120 years. (Previous ACCL ships traveled about three-quarters of the way.) The feature also is used to navigate the Chicago River through the heart of the Windy City.

Niagara Prince offers a motorized chairlift for passengers who have difficulty negotiating stairs, and during recent renovations, new hallway railings were added to improve capabilities for handicapped passengers. Other changes included opening the bow area to make it more accessible for passengers, relocating the bar area to increase space in the dining/ lounge area, and refurbishing with new furniture and rugs.

Itineraries   See Appendix B.

Cabins   Small, spartan, but functional cabins have twin beds on metal frames. Storage space is limited to four drawers, about one square foot of counter space, and a four-foot-tall cabinet for hanging clothes; luggage goes under the beds. Accordion doors close tightly, but do not lock.

Bathrooms, ingeniously designed by Blount, are tiny but utilitarian. They're a deluxe version of a "head" on a sailboat or RV. A very small sink with spring taps lets water run for only a few seconds at a time. The hand-held shower is very efficient and can be left in its wall mount when showering; the shower curtain is the "door" to the head. A trap in the floor lets water out. The toilet has a fill-and-flush system that works very well. However, if you do not operate it properly—refilling the water in the bowl after each use—or close the trap in the floor, an unpleasant odor develops.

All but two main-deck cabins are outside. The largest and most desirable cabins are on the sun deck. Six cabins open onto the promenade; others have large sliding windows—a pleasant feature on U.S. waterways when fresh, cool air fills the room.

Cabins are cleaned daily; linens are changed every third day. Bath towels are replaced as needed. (The ship does not have laundry facilities.) There is no room service.

Specifications   40 outside cabins (6 opening onto the promenade); 2 inside; all have private facilities and twin lower beds; some can be converted to doubles. Four cabins have upper and lower berths. Standard dimensions are between 72 and 96 square feet.

Dining   A big advantage on a small ship is its fresh food and homemade bread and pastries. Aboard *Niagara Prince,* well-prepared American fare is much better than expected for the ship's category and better than on more expensive lines.

Menus are posted daily. One of two entrees available is lighter, healthful fare. This reflects past passengers' criticism of the ship's tendency to serve fatty, high-cholesterol foods. New menus are an improvement, but we recommend more salads and green vegetables and less gravy and sauces.

The main course of the hearty breakfast—eggs, pancakes, and so on— varies daily. Lunch usually includes a soup (the best we've had on any ship), salad, and dessert. Dinner features fish, chicken or other meat, vegetables, and dessert. Meals are family-style; staff serves dessert, beverages, and second helpings. Coffee, tea, and cookies are always available in the dining room.

The dining room, which has an open kitchen, has tables for four, six, eight, and ten. The square tables for four are also used for card games. Passengers bring their own liquor and wine, and ACCL provides storage, setups, and ice. For the captain's dinners, ACCL supplies wine and an open bar. Likewise, for Celebration Night, when passengers collectively celebrate birthdays, anniversaries, and so on, the line supplies wine. Make-Your-Own-Sundae, with many varieties of ice cream and toppings, is another popular event.

Service Most crew members—young, energetic, and terrific—are from Rhode Island or neighboring states. The teams that clean the cabins also attend the dining room. They are cheerful, hardworking, unfailingly polite, and particularly accommodating to their mostly older passengers.

Facilities and Entertainment Except for television, videotapes, local talent at some ports, and visiting lecturers, there is no evening entertainment. Most passengers are in bed by 10 p.m. Although the ships have some paperbacks, avid readers should bring their own books.

Passengers gather in the lounge for predinner cocktails. A crew member helps prepare drinks. After dinner, some may linger for a film or bridge and other card and parlor games.

The cruise director's "instant boutique" sells signature shirts, caps, and jackets at least once during each cruise.

Activities and Diversions In addition to games, some cruises have lecturers. Captains are very knowledgeable about places the ships visit and often provide running commentary. Those lucky enough to sail on the Hudson River/Erie Canal with Capt. Robert Gifford will find him a dedicated historian and walking encyclopedia on the region. He acts as a guide while piloting the ship, providing information not available elsewhere. On winter cruises in Belize and the Caribbean, underwater exploration cameras provide live color telecasts of sea life; large-screen monitors are in the lounge, which can accommodate all passengers at one time. The cameras were developed by J. W. Fishers, a leader in underwater exploration equipment. They can be submerged up to 150 feet deep, offering spectacular undersea views—similar to what a scuba diver might see. ACCL is believed to be the first cruise line to offer this feature.

In daytime, the ship can pass slowly over a coral bank or shipwreck or maneuver into a school of fish and, via the camera, view a changing underwater panorama from many angles. At night, with underwater lights, passengers see rare tropical fish.

Sports and Fitness On board, one can walk on the promenade deck.

Ashore, sports activities can include swimming, snorkeling, hiking, and birding, depending on the itinerary.

Beauty On request, the cruise director books appointments with beauty parlors in ports.

Shore Excursions On the cruise's first day, the cruise director distributes descriptions of tours. Excursions vary with itineraries and cost $6–30. ACCL uses local operators specializing in small, special-interest groups. The line says it continuously checks tours and books the most appealing.

Postscript The *Niagara Prince* is a one-of-a-kind ship, sailing unique itineraries through America's most historic waterways. It's both a great value and a great cruise experience.

Grande Caribe	Quality ❷	Value A
Grande Mariner	Quality ❷	Value A
Registry: United States	Length: 183/182 feet	Beam: 40 feet
Cabins: 50	Draft: 6.6 feet	Speed: 12 knots
Maximum Passengers:	Passenger Decks: 3	Elevators: Chairlift
100/96	Crew: 15/17	Space Ratio: NA

The Ships Built at Blount Marine in Warren, Rhode Island, the *Grande Caribe* and her near twin, *Grande Mariner*, are designed for coastal cruises from Labrador to the Amazon. Like other ACCL ships, they have shallow drafts and bow ramps to guarantee access to areas large cruise ships simply cannot reach.

Although the *Grande Caribe* is only slightly larger than her earlier sister ships, her layout varies in several ways. The dining room is on the main deck; the lounge, with wraparound windows, is on the top deck.

The *Grande Caribe,* like her predecessors, has a retractable pilothouse for passage under low bridges and a chairlift for passengers who have trouble negotiating stairs. A new feature is a stern swimming platform. On Caribbean and Central American cruises, the ships carry a Blount-designed glass-bottom boat and Sunfish.

The *Grande Mariner,* which made her debut in 1998, has more comfortable cabins than her sisters do and unique features, including an acoustical "floating deck" between the engine room and main-deck cabins aimed at reducing engine noise, and sound-deadening enclosures for the ship's main generators. (Note: We did not find the ship quieter than her earlier sisters. In fact, our cabin, 44A, was actually noisier from the sound of the generators.) Larger, twin diesel engines give the ship a cruising speed of 12 knots.

In another first for ACCL, the *Grande Mariner* hull is ice-strengthened for cruising in Canadian subarctic waters of Labrador, Newfoundland, and parts of the St. Lawrence River. The ship's 24-passenger glass-bottom boat and shore launch are built with the same foam-based materials found in a life raft.

The *Grande Mariner*'s "vista view" lounge, a multifunctional room located forward on the upper deck, has wraparound windows to showcase passing scenery. The room has a bar, piano, and large projection screen; it can be used for lectures by visiting experts, historians, and naturalists, or for business seminars. A self-service bar has storage shelves for passengers' liquor and a fridge for chilling wine and beer. Nightly, the chef prepares hors d'oeuvres for the cocktail hour.

Itineraries   See Appendix B.

Cabins   The *Grande Caribe* has a third, lower deck (the *Niagara Prince* lacks this) with six cabins fitted with upper and lower berths and no windows. There are three similar, inside cabins on the main deck. These 9 cabins are the least expensive of the *Grande Caribe*'s 50 cabins.

All other cabins are on the main and sun decks and have two beds, either side by side or in an L shape. Two cabins have double beds. Six cabins on the sun deck have doors that open to the outside promenade. The cabins have 80–120 square feet.

On the *Grande Mariner,* each cabin has its own air conditioner with air circulated outside through ducts. Unlike many other ships where air is recirculated, the Blount-designed system supplies fresh air continuously to the cabins, and stale air is removed.

Also, *Grande Mariner*'s cabins are ACCL's most comfortable yet. Bathrooms, particularly, show marked improvement. Gone is the hole in the floor from which odors escaped. Toilets operate on the old principle, but the design is more streamlined. Also new—cabins have doors with locks. However, passengers are not issued keys, and they don't need them.

Specifications   50 cabins (*Caribe* 9, *Mariner* 7 inside/no window; *Caribe* 8, *Mariner* 9 open onto promenade); all have private facilities and twin lower beds (except *Mariner* has 2 cabins with double bed); some converted to doubles. *Caribe* 8, *Mariner* 10 have upper and lower berths; one cabin has 1 double and 1 single. Standard dimensions, 96–110 square feet.

Service   The young and energetic crew members are outstanding. They are hardworking, smiling, and unfailingly polite. The same teams that clean the cabins also attend the dining room. They seem eager to please and are particularly accommodating to their mostly older passengers.

Facilities and Activities   There is no evening entertainment of the usual cruise variety. Passengers gather in the lounge for informal, predinner cocktails. After dinner, some may linger for card or parlor games or to watch a film. The lounge has a television and videotapes, and visiting lecturers or local talent may appear at ports of call. Most passengers are in bed by 10 p.m.

Postscript   ACCL's ships' best features are their staff, itineraries, and the camaraderie among passengers—the latter not found on a large ship. The ships are basic (at times, you feel you're camping), but passengers appear to be happy and having a good time. Clearly they are the type more interested in destinations than in creature comforts.

Our major complaint with ACCL is the lack of adequate precruise information on ports of call and shore excursions. Because ACCL has been doing most of its cruises for many years and local tourist boards usually have plentiful information they're eager to distribute, it is hard to understand why this deficiency persists.

Anyone planning a cruise on the *Grande Caribe* or *Grand Mariner* should read the entire section on ACCL to have a more accurate picture of the cruise experience the line offers.

American Hawaii Cruises/ United States Lines

1380 Port of New Orleans Place, Robin St. Wharf
New Orleans, LA 70130-1890
(800) 765-7000; fax (504) 585-0630
www.cruisehawaii.com

Type of Ship   Modern, classic oceanliners.

Type of Cruise   Destination- and family-oriented, casual and all-American.

Cruise Line's Strengths
- destination
- friendly staff
- kids' program
- shore excursions
- theme cruises

Cruise Line's Shortcomings
- aging ships
- lack of amenities in cabins
- small bathrooms on oldest ship

Fellow Passengers   Families with children during summer; honeymooners, seniors, and retired couples year-round. Most are experienced travelers; 40 percent have visited Hawaii before, and 60 percent have been on a cruise. The average age is 50+ years; 20 percent of passengers are over 70 years old. Median household income is $40,000+. More than a third are celebrating a special event, usually an anniversary.

Recommended For   Families, particularly those with children; first- and second-time visitors to Hawaii; honeymooning couples; seniors and others who want the most convenient way to see the islands; those looking for a cultural experience and a slower pace. Shorter cruises are designed to attract first-timers, younger travelers, and newlyweds.

Not Recommended For Sophisticated travelers who prefer luxury, gourmet cuisine, and independent travel. Singles looking for companionship or persons looking for 24-hour entertainment, gambling, and discos.

Cruise Areas and Seasons Four islands/five ports, Hawaii, year-round.

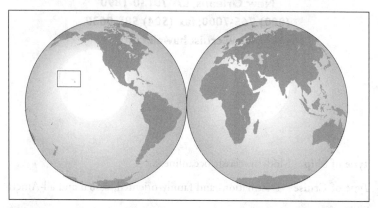

The Line After two multimillion-dollar renovations of the *Independence* by American Classic Voyages Company (parent company of Delta Queen Steamboat Company, which acquired American Hawaii Cruises in July 1993), American Hawaii Cruises turned a liability—its aging ship—into an asset by celebrating her distinguished history, emphasizing the appeal of traditional cruising, and focusing on the Hawaiian aspect of its name.

Sailing into challenges is nothing new for AHC. Created to cruise in Hawaiian waters at a time when U.S. flag operations had all but disappeared, it took an act of Congress (because of the Jones Act) to get AHC's *SS Independence* (in 1979) and *SS Constitution* (in 1982) recommissioned as American flag vessels. (The Jones Act requires that ships cruising solely between two U.S. ports be American-flag vessels, owned by U.S. citizens, built and refurbished in the United States, and staffed with American crew. In 1988, under new ownership, health and fitness centers were added, along with other innovations meant to attract younger people. These included more active, sports-oriented shore excursions; three- and four-day cruises combined with resort vacations; stronger Hawaiian content; and environmental commitment, particularly for protecting the whales that migrate from Alaska to breed in warm Hawaiian waters in winter. Whale-watching cruises accompanied by experts are offered.

American Classic Voyages has begun a major expansion that will double its fleet in Hawaii and will more than quadruple its passenger capacity by 2005. For a start, it is building two privately funded $400 million cruise ships at Litton Industries' Ingalls Shipbuilding division of Pascagoula,

Mississippi. The 72,000-ton, 19,000-passenger vessels are the largest U.S. cruise ships ever built and the first such construction in more than 40 years. Legislation attached to a defense appropriations bill passed by Congress in 1997 gave ACV incentives—a monopoly in the Hawaiian cruise market for 30 years, along with $250,000 toward the design of the vessels—in return for a commitment to build the ships.

ACV has an option for up to four and has created for them a new brand, United States Lines, having bought the famous name from the owners of the now-defunct company. The first ship, scheduled to debut in early 2003, will be able to traverse the Panama Canal. Her twin will join her in 2004. Meanwhile, ACV purchased the 1,214-passenger *Nieuw Amsterdam* from Holland America Lines and renamed her the *Patriot.* After renovations that will add a more Hawaiian theme to her character and AHC's *Independence* moves to her new home port in Kahului, Maui, the *Patriot* will begin weekly cruises from Honolulu in December 2000.

American Classic Voyages trades on the NASDAQ as AMCV and is the parent company of Delta Queen Steamship Company and Delta Queen Coastal Cruises, as well as American Hawaii Cruises and United States Lines.

The Fleet	Built/Renovated	Tonnage	Passengers
Independence (AHC)	1951/94/97	30,090	1,021
Patriot (USL)	1983/99	33,930	1,212

Style Informal, family- and destination-oriented cruises in a congenial atmosphere meant to reflect the traditional *aloha* spirit of Hawaii with a friendly, if not highly polished crew. By the second day, you are likely to be wearing a muumuu or Hawaiian shirt. The Hawaiian experience begins with "Sail Away" festivities featuring native floral arrangements throughout the ship, crew members dressed in Hawaiian attire, and island chants and drums to send cruisers on their way. On boarding, passengers receive a *lei,* the traditional necklace of flowers.

During the cruise, Hawaiian culture is emphasized in activities, entertainment, educational programs, and dining specialties. Atmosphere and dress are casual; there's never a need for a tuxedo and only once—the Captain's Party—for a tie. Life on board is more slowly paced than aboard typical ships on Caribbean and Mexican itineraries. There are no late nights— most people are in bed by midnight or earlier, and the food and activities are geared toward older passengers. At the same time, American Hawaii welcomes kids with its seasonal children's program, which keeps them happy and well occupied, and it recognizes honeymooning couples and about-to-be-newlyweds with its "Romance in Paradise" packages.

Distinctive Features   Cultural displays from the renowned Bishop Museum in Honolulu stimulate interest in Hawaii. A *kumu* (storyteller and teacher of traditions) is on every cruise. Children's rates for most shore excursions.

	HIGHEST	LOWEST	AVERAGE
PER DIEM	$400	$193	$297

The above per diems are calculated from the cruise line's non-discounted *cruise only* fares on standard accommodations. Per diems vary by season, by cabin, and by cruise areas.

Rates   Port charges are additional.

Special Fares and Discounts

• Third/Fourth Passenger: $790.
• Children's Fare: Ages 3–17, sharing cabin with two full-fare passengers, $99. Children under age 3 sail free.
• Standby Fares: Hawaii residents occasionally offered special rates.
• Single Supplement: 160 percent for all categories except suites, which are 200 percent. 24 cabins on the *Independence* (scattered in categories C, D, and F) are designated for singles at the same rate as double occupancy in that category.

Packages

• Air/Sea: Yes.
• Others: Golf, special occasion, honeymoon, anniversary. The "Nani Kai Wedding" package includes the services of a minister or judge, a *lei* and *lei po'o* (floral hairpiece) for the bride, a *lei* or boutonniere for the groom, a chilled bottle of champagne, two dozen 5-by-7 photos in a keepsake album, live music by Hawaiian musicians, and a wedding cake for up to ten people. Cost is $695. A wedding reception costs extra. Weddings are performed on board; only one wedding is scheduled per day, three per cruise. Times for ceremonies are given at the time of the booking. Contact AHC regarding documentation.
• Pre/Post: Any length hotel stays combined with three-, four-, or seven-day cruise.

Past Passengers   Holokai Hui (meaning Seafarer's Club) provides free cabin upgrades, separate check-in, an on-board party, and other features. Passengers are automatically enrolled after their second cruise.

The Last Word   The factors that helped AHC develop its strong niche—American-built/flag vessels with American crew (along with the inherent high costs)—also hampered the line's development. The Jones Act requires that ships cruising solely between two U.S. ports be built in the United States. Yet until the new United States Lines began construction on the new ships, no comparable ship had been built in the United States in 40 years. Added to this, Hawaiian law forbids gambling—a big moneymaker for ships. And there is no duty-free shopping; even on the ship, state sales tax is collected in the gift shop.

AHC's cruises have broad appeal and could be enjoyed by almost anyone visiting Hawaii. They offer the most comfortable way to visit the islands and enjoy local flavor. Shorter cruises, introduced in 1996, are designed to attract younger travelers seeking more variety in a faster-paced vacation, first-time cruisers wishing to sample a cruise without investing in a seven-day trip, and honeymooning couples looking for a midweek departure.

AMERICAN HAWAII/UNITED STATES LINES STANDARD FEATURES

Officers American.

Staff Dining, Cabin, Cruise, and Entertainment/American.

Dining Facilities Two dining rooms (one on *Patriot*) with two seatings/three meals. Breakfast, lunch buffet daily, tea on deck on one afternoon. Cookies, ice cream, popcorn around the clock.

Special Diets Accommodated with advance notice.

Room Service 24 hours with a limited menu through Bell Station, reached by phone. Cabin attendants are on duty from 7:30–11:30 a.m., noon–2 p.m., and 5–9 p.m., and cannot be reached by phone during these times.

Dress Code Casual; tie and jacket requested for captain's gala.

Cabin Amenities Direct cellular telephone service, bathrooms with showers, mirrored vanity. No televisions, except on *Patriot*.

Electrical Outlets 110 AC; shaver and hair dryer outlets in cabins.

Wheelchair Access Two cabins.

Recreation and Entertainment Nightclub, show lounge; three bars, lounges; television screens in top deck bar; movie theater.

Sports and Fitness Two freshwater outside swimming pools, Ping-Pong, fitness center, shuffleboard.

Spa and Beauty Beauty/barber shop, massage.

Other Facilities Boutique, hospital, launderettes/coin-operated machines; conference facilities with audio/visuals.

Children's Facilities Youth center; children's program June–August, enhanced during holidays; children's rates for shore excursions.

Theme Cruises Whale-watching, Big Band, Aloha Festivals, Pearl Harbor.

Smoking No smoking in public rooms. Smoking permitted in cabins and outside decks.

AHC Suggested Tipping Per person, per day: cabin steward, $3.50; waiter, $3.50; busboy, $1.75. 15 percent added to bar bills.

Credit Cards For cruise payment and on-board charges: American Express, Visa, MasterCard, Discover.

Independence	Quality ❹	Value **C**
Registry: United States	Length: 682 feet	Beam: 89 feet
Cabins: 446	Draft: 26.5 feet	Speed: 17 knots
Maximum Passengers: 1,066	Passenger Decks: 9	Elevators: 4
	Crew: 340	Space Ratio: 37

The Ship   Extensive renovations completed in 1994 aimed at creating a more authentic Hawaiian ambience. Even public rooms and decks were given authentic Hawaiian names. Other major improvements include upgraded air-conditioning, electrical, and pollution-control systems and structural repairs. Another multimillion-dollar range of enhancements, particularly for safety, were added in 1997.

The most dramatic changes were in the elegant Kama'aina Lounge and other public areas on the Kama'aina Deck, where, on both sides of the room, 40 feet of windows were added to create an indoor-outdoor "lanai" environment and give passengers better views of the islands and ocean. The lanai effect extends to the aft section, part of which is shaded by canopies. The warmly decorated public rooms display works by local artists. The large open area housing the Bishop Museum display is splendid, as are the updated showroom and lounge.

The ship was originally designed for three classes of passengers, making some public areas difficult to reach. To alleviate this, a grand stairway was added to the aft pool area to connect the ship's three main decks: Kama'aina, Ohana, and the Sun Deck. An additional aft stairway allows access to the pool area from cabins on lower decks. New corridor carpeting with images of dolphins and whales swimming toward the bow is meant to help passengers orient themselves inside the ship.

Itineraries   See Appendix B.

Cabins   The cabins are very comfortable and storage is plentiful. Concealed compartments and beds as well as fold-out tables—created by the ship's designer, Henry Dreyfuss—were retained.

The decor uses brightly colored Hawaiian fabrics from the 1940s and 1950s; bedspreads are in traditional Hawaiian patterns. Although bathrooms were renovated, they remain smaller than those in comparably sized cabins on newer ships, and the fixtures remain 1950s vintage. All baths have showers and a mirrored cabinet, except for three suites on the boat deck and room 258 on Aloha Deck that have tubs; most have a mirrored vanity.

All cabins are equipped with cellular telephone service, enabling passengers to phone the U.S. mainland for considerably less than is charged on other ships. Instructions in the cabin explain the system and fees.

Room service is available through the Bell Station (like a hotel bell captain's desk), reachable by phone around the clock for beverages, light snacks, and ice. (You may have to leave a message.) Cabin attendants are on duty from 7:30–11:30 a.m., noon–2 p.m., and 5–9 p.m.; they are available for cleaning services, towels, and turndowns; delivery of *Tradewinds*, the daily schedule; and maintenance.

The ships' layout for three classes results in 52 cabin configurations, which AHC has grouped in 13 fare categories. Cabins are pictured and described in AHC's easy-to-use brochure. Bed configurations vary—queen, twins convertible to queen, lower and upper Pullman-style berths, or single lower sofabed or settee. The *Independence*'s six solarium suites added on the bridge deck are among the largest, each with 300 square feet, and have high ceilings, skylights, and windows that open. Two cabins designed for the disabled are on the Aloha Deck.

Specifications   240 cabins inside, 206 outside; 37 suites. Standard dimensions are 85–242 square feet. 90 with twin; 126 double/queen; 136 upper and lowers; 24 singles.

Dining   Cuisine received mixed reviews in the past, but lately has had high marks on both quality and variety. To give passengers a taste of the islands, menus include Pacific Rim and Hawaiian regional dishes along with traditional favorites. Local ingredients—fresh fish, fruit, vegetables, and herbs—are used to ensure authenticity. Familiar items may get a new spin, such as Maui mango pasta and roasted rack of lamb with Molokai herbs.

Dinner typically includes a choice of two appetizers, two soups, two salads, six entrees (at least one fish, one pasta, and one vegetarian selection), three desserts, and ice creams and sherbets. California and French wines are featured and cost $16–42.

A wide selection of breakfast and lunch dishes are offered at the expanded buffet on the Ohana Deck (upper deck). The buffet has Hawaiian-style indoor-outdoor cooking, and seating areas extend to the pool area, partially shaded by canopies.

Ice cream and sherbet are a long-standing tradition. *Pu'uwai*, meaning healthy heart, is a low-fat, low-cholesterol program available in the dining room. Daily, a Hawaiian cocktail specialty, such as a Blue Hawaiian or Mai Tai, is featured for $4.75; in the afternoon, a self-service popcorn machine provides snacks.

To accommodate passengers who are ashore during regular meal hours, the ship extended lunch service from 2:30–4:30 p.m., with hot dogs and hamburgers available at the buffet. Coffee and tea, juice, and sodas are available around the clock in the Ohana Buffet.

Service   The young American crew is friendly, courteous, energetic, high-spirited, and attentive. Men and women serve as cabin and dining attendants and receive high marks for efficiency. Particularly noteworthy are the waitresses in the dining room and on the pool deck.

Facilities and Entertainment   Evening entertainment is family-oriented, with local Hawaiian entertainers as standard fare. At the Hoi Hoi Showplace on the Kama'aina Deck, performers celebrate Hawaiian traditions with island entertainment, and the Ray Kennedy Entertainers perform three Broadway-style shows weekly. Next door, the Hapa Haole Bar re-creates the "tourist" Hawaii of the 1930s and 1940s. Headliner vocalists perform "Concerts on the Pacific" nightly in the Kama'aina Lounge.

The very good ship's orchestra has a repertoire ranging from Elvis to traditional Hawaiian music. AHC adds gentlemen hosts to dance with unaccompanied women during Big Band cruises.

The semicircular Constitution Lounge is among the most pleasant areas aboard, offering passengers a 180° view of Hawaii's beautiful scenery. Low-key entertainment is offered in the evening.

Two large television screens are in the poolside Surfrider Bar. (Cabins have no TVs.) The theater shows current movies as many as five times daily; check the daily program for times.

Activities and Diversions   The *kumu,* a teacher of Hawaiian traditions aboard every cruise, brings the spirit of *aloha* and talks about island history, music, crafts, culture, lore, and mythology. He or she meets with passengers at different times throughout the day and evening, choosing settings to enhance and illustrate the stories. Among subjects are native Hawaiian words, the meaning of the *hula* dance, and how to play ancient island games, blow conch shells, make *leis,* and play the ukulele. The *kumu*'s study is by the main lounge on the Kama'aina Deck.

Exhibits by the Bishop Museum teach about Hawaii through displays of ancient games, arts and crafts, traditional garments, and natural artifacts, as well as three-dimensional interactive exhibits on the islands' wildlife and natural history. During whale-watching from January through March, experts from the Pacific Whale Foundation offer seminars on nature and wildlife.

The daily program includes games, line dancing, and such unusual activities as making fabric hibiscus flowers and weaving palm fronds. The ship has a conference center.

Sports and Fitness   Because the ship is in port every day but one and many shore excursions are sports-oriented, shipboard sports are limited. The ship has two small swimming pools and a small fitness room with limited equipment, but no daily fitness programs beyond an early morning walk and stretching program.

On shore, passengers can bike, hike, deep-sea fish, ride horseback, kayak on the Huleia River (where *Raiders of the Lost Ark* was filmed), sail, swim, snorkel, and dive (novices and certified). The newest golf package includes play on leading Hawaiian courses on four islands.

Spa and Beauty   The beauty salon is small; prices are moderate. The massage schedule fills quickly; sign up early.

Children's Facilities   A supervised children's program is available during summer and holidays. Games, talent shows, crafts sessions, parties, and other activities are planned for children in two groups: the *Keiki* (Hawaiian for "kids") program for ages 5–12, and the "Hui O Kau Wela Nalu" (Summer Surf Club) for ages 13–17. The ship has a youth recreation center and a full-time recreation coordinator. Most shore excursions offer kids' rates.

Shore Excursions   American Hawaii shore excursions are among the best offered by any cruise line; plentiful choices suit everyone in the family.

To help in selection, a shore excursion book with photos, descriptions, and prices is placed in cabins, and a display center aboard showcases the more than 60 options available. They include beach picnics; submarine and helicopter rides; and visits to tropical gardens, a macadamia nut farm, working ranch, plantation, the Polynesian Cultural Center, nature parks, craft shops, and local feasts and festivals. Choices also include biking, hiking, kayaking, and snorkeling, not to mention seeing whales, birds, volcanoes, and rain forests. A golf package is priced at $50–145. Shore excursions cannot be purchased before the cruise.

Particularly noteworthy are excursions that enable passengers to enjoy the less explored areas of Hawaii and experience natural attractions. You can explore the Na Pali coast by raft, fly over the 5,000-foot-high rim of Mount Waialeale in a helicopter, or ride horseback along spectacular ocean bluffs. On Hilo, Hawaii Volcanoes National Park is the big attraction; the Old Hawaii: Hilo 100 Years Ago Tour is a quieter look at Hawaii. The Kauai highlight is a helicopter flight, subject to weather conditions. (*Note:* Schedule the Haleakala Crater helicopter flight for morning; afternoons are often cloudy and windy, and aircraft cannot fly.)

If excursions sell out, you can book them on your own from companies offering them. Or, read up on each island in advance, rent a car (your ship will make arrangements), and explore independently.

Theme Cruises   American Hawaii offers theme cruises almost year-round; ask AHC for dates. Whale-watching cruises are January through March, the height of the season when humpback whales are in Hawaiian waters with their young. Naturalists from the Pacific Whale Foundation of Maui, a non-profit educational organization, lecture aboard on breeding, feeding, and migration habits of humpbacks. Optional small-boat excursions to the Hawaiian Islands Humpback Whale National Marine Sanctuary carry passengers closer to the whales while complying with whale-protection regulations. Early-bird savings are available.

Big Band cruises, featuring music of the 1940s, are offered year-round. Aloha Festival sailings, mid-September through mid-October, coincide with Aloha Month, the annual fall festival celebrated throughout Hawaii. Passengers enjoy special presentations on Hawaiian history, art, music, and dance by distinguished local hula schools, storytellers, and artists. Ashore are colorful parades and street celebrations.

Postscript   When the Delta Queen Steamboat Company acquired American Hawaii, Delta Queen made a commitment to do whatever it took to make its ship first class and the cruise the most authentic way to see the islands and experience their culture. The company has invested large sums in the *Independence* to restore and improve her. Even so, she remains typical of oceanliners built when dining rooms and theaters were on lower decks and bathrooms were small. She should be enjoyed as a comfortable classic, offering a great introduction to Hawaii and the easiest way to island hop, especially for first-time visitors wanting to see as much of the islands as possible in a week. With the three- and four-day cruises, it's easy to combine a cruise with a hotel stay in a week's holiday. It also provides a good sampling of cruising for first-timers and ample time in port for those worried about seasickness, claustrophobia, or boredom. The first day of the cruise is at sea—a welcome amenity for those who have traveled long distances.

For old Hawaii hands, the cruise is a new way to see the islands. For experienced cruisers, it's a pleasant and comprehensive visit to the state. But if you are looking for excitement, 24-hour entertainment, gambling, discos, fitness activities, and gourmet cuisine, this is not the cruise for you.

One passenger, impressed with the staff's handling of her partially non-ambulatory husband, told us: "While not wheelchair-bound, my husband was too weak to walk long hallways and gangways or to board the ship. I merely had to phone from the cabin, and, almost instantly, a crew member arrived to push him wherever we needed to go, including to leave the ship. The same was true when we reboarded in port. They were extremely helpful."

Patriot   **(Preview)**

Registry: United States	Length: 704 feet	Beam: 90 feet
Cabins: 606	Draft: 25 feet	Speed: 19 knots
Maximum Passengers:	Passenger Decks: 9	Elevators: 7
1,212	Crew: 542	Space Ratio: 28

The Ship   The *Patriot* (formerly *Nieuw Amsterdam* of Holland America Lines) is scheduled to launch the new United States Lines in December 2000, in advance of the line's first brand-new ship, now under construction. A trendsetter when she made her debut in 1983, many of her innovations have become standard on most cruise ships: doorsills flush with the floor, rather than toe-stubbing raised ones; computerized entry cards instead of door keys; energy-saving, fluorescent light bulbs (9 watts instead of 70 watts); a square stern that provided for 20 percent more outside deck space than was customary for ships of its size.

In preparation for her new role, the ship was renovated with new features added. These include a destination learning center, Graffiti's teen center and video arcade, an Internet lounge, and upgraded conference and meeting facilities. The decor has maintained a tasteful blend of traditional and modern styles with Hawaiian touches added. Most of the public rooms are on the Promenade and Broadway Decks and include many comfortable lounges and cozy bars, arranged asymmetrically along a corridor, which give the interiors a feeling of intimacy.

The *Patriot* has a teak promenade with an unusual 15-foot width that encircles the Upper Promenade Deck. It's wide enough for old-fashioned deck chairs while leaving ample space for two or three people to walk abreast. This feature, often absent on new ships, is greatly appreciated by people who love to cruise the promenade, which is something of a Main Street with passengers strolling, lounging, reading, napping, scanning the water, or watching people.

Itineraries   See Appendix B.

Cabins   The ship has 15 cabin categories of 5 basic types, found on 8 of 9 passenger decks. Rooms are among the largest on any cruise ship in their category. They're homey, with light wooden cabinets and fabrics inspired by Hawaiian motifs. All have phones, closed-circuit television, multichannel music, makeup/writing table, built-in corner or night tables with drawers, light controls at the bed, full-length door mirror, and ample closets.

Walls and floors are insulated for soundproofing. Four cabins accommodate disabled passengers.

Specifications   197 inside cabins, 412 outside cabins; 20 suites with picture window and king-size bed. Standard dimensions 152 square feet inside; 178 square feet outside. 485 cabins with 2 lower beds (87 convert to queen); 50 with queens; 72 with 2 lower/2 upper beds; 142 have bathtubs and showers; no singles; 4 wheelchair-accessible.

Dining   The dining room on the Main Deck has floor-to-ceiling windows overlooking the sea. It's a class act, with many nice touches: fresh flowers, soft lighting, heavy silverware, starched linens, fine china and crystal, a super crew, and dinner music.

The indoor/outdoor Outrigger Cafe overlooks the Broadway Deck pool and offers breakfast and lunch buffets plus alternative dining several nights.

Facilities and Entertainment   With so many lounges, almost everyone finds something to enjoy. One main lounge spans two decks. The balcony has its own bar and overlooks the Broadway Deck. The main showroom, richly appointed with red carpets, looks more like a large cocktail lounge than a theater. The spacious lounge hosts nightly shows and daytime activities. Unfortunately, sight lines aren't great.

There are several lounges, popular late-night gathering spots with floor-to-ceiling windows, live music, small dance floors, and bars.

A favorite room is the Founder's Lounge; another is the Eagle's Watch atop of the Bridge Deck, a daytime observation perch and late-evening rendezvous. The ship's entertainment includes musical revues, jazz, Hawaiian traditional and contemporary music, theme nights, and late-night comedy shows.

Activities and Diversions   Daytime activities include pool games, dance classes, movies in the theater, bridge, horse racing, and bingo. Active travelers will find a fitness program; a jogging track; a health spa with rowing machines, bicycles, weights, and other exercise equipment; and two swimming pools. Supervised children's programs are available year-round.

Shore Excursions   Passengers can select from more than 75 tours of Hawaii's attractions. From January through March, when an estimated 4,000 whales migrate to Hawaii from Alaska, the ship will offer whale-watching cruises accompanied by naturalists.

Carnival Cruise Lines

3655 NW 87th Avenue, Miami, FL 33178-2428
(305) 599-2600; (800) 438-6744; fax (305) 599-8630
www.carnival.com

Type of Ships   New, mod superliners and megaliners.

Type of Cruise   Casual, contemporary mass market. "Fun Ships" hall-mark makes the ship the destination, as central to the cruise as its ports of call.

Cruise Line's Strengths
- lavish recreational and entertainment facilities
- new fleet with unusual, innovative interiors
- larger-than-average cabins for price category
- value
- clear, easy-to-use literature
- variety of dining outlets
- quality of cuisine for price category

Cruise Line's Shortcomings
- megaliner size
- little relief from crowds and glitz
- lack of outdoor promenade deck
- lines for facilities and services

Fellow Passengers   From all walks of life, ages 3 to 93. Although Carnival's image is shiploads of young swingers partying day and night (an image Carnival cultivated to attract young people to cruising), the mix is more likely to range from Joe Sixpack and his Nike-shod kids to Lester and Alice celebrating their fiftieth wedding anniversary. The cruises lend themselves to families with or without kids, honeymooners, married couples, singles, and seniors. Average age: 43. On a typical cruise, 40 percent are ages 35–55; 30 percent younger than 35 (including 250,000 kids annually); 30 percent older than 55. Seventy percent are first-time cruisers. Most have medium income.

Recommended For First-time cruisers who want an active, high-energy, party atmosphere; young singles and couples; young-at-heart of any age; those who enjoy Las Vegas glitz or similar ambience.

Not Recommended For Small-ship devotees; sophisticated travelers who prefer luxury and individual travel; anyone seeking quiet or cerebral travel experience; those who consider Martha's Vineyard their ideal vacation spot.

Cruise Areas and Seasons Bahamas, Caribbean, and West Coast/Mexican Riviera year-round. Panama Canal, Alaska, Hawaii, Bermuda/Canada seasonally.

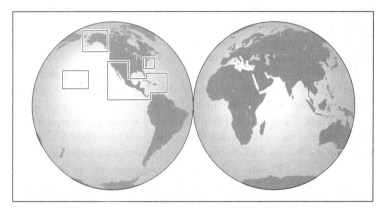

The Line In 25 short years, Carnival Cruise Lines went from one ship that ran aground on its maiden voyage to the largest, most influential company in the cruise business, having revolutionized the nature of cruises along the way. Its story is the stuff of legends.

The late Ted Arison, a cruise executive in Florida, and a maverick travel company in Boston bought the *Mardi Gras* (formerly the *Empress of Canada*) in 1972. After three years of losses and near bankruptcy, Arison took over the company, assumed its $5 million debt, bought the assets— the *Mardi Gras*—for $1, and created the "Fun Ship" concept, turning a profit in his first year and adding two more ships.

Arison's aim was to take the stuffiness out of cruising, abandon the elitist image on which classic oceanliners had thrived, and make cruises fun and available to everyone, particularly to middle America, who never dreamed of a holiday at sea. He hit the right button. Through the 1970s, Carnival ships broke occupancy records while traditional companies were sinking all around.

Carnival continued to defy conventional wisdom. In the late 1970s with spiraling shipbuilding costs and the oil crisis putting the future of cruising in doubt, Carnival ordered a new ship, *Tropicale*, whose technology set new industry standards, changed ship profiles, and enhanced Carnival's "Fun Ship" concept. Then, a decade after its inauspicious beginning, Carnival added three radically new ships—*Holiday, Jubilee*, and *Celebration*—trend-setters of the 1980s and beyond. These 1,800-passenger superliners were not the largest passenger ships ever built, but their design and madcap decor were profoundly different from oceanliners of the past. To prepare for the twenty-first century, Carnival added eight megaliners, each for over 2,600 passengers, and lifted eyebrows with such names as *Fantasy* and *Ecstasy*. They were followed in late 1996 with the 101,000-ton, 3,400-passenger *Carnival Destiny*, the world's largest ship when it was launched. Carnival was so pleased with her performance and passenger response that it ordered four more like her, each costing $450 million.

Along with the *Destiny*-class, Carnival will start a new class of ships with the 84,000-ton *Carnival Spirit*, scheduled to debut in April 2001, and her two sisters, *Carnival Pride*, due late in the year, and *Carnival Legend*, scheduled for 2002. Carnival's new ship investment in the 1990s exceeded $5 billion; those so far for the twenty-first century will add almost $2.2 billion and bring the fleet total to 20 ships. When the new ships for its sister companies—a total of 11—are added in, the expenditure will be $4.5 billion.

Under Arison's son Micky, Carnival's young, aggressive team has marketed cruises as the universal dream vacation for everyone. A publicly held company since 1987, Carnival carries almost two million passengers a year, accounting for 28 percent of all cruise passengers boarding from U.S. ports. In 1989 it broadened its base (and buffed its image) by acquiring the classic Holland America Line and the upscale Windstar Cruises. Later, it acquired partial ownership in ultraluxurious Seabourn Cruise Line. In 1996, Carnival bought part ownership in Airtours, one of Europe's largest tour companies, as a stepping stone into the European market; together, in 1997, Carnival and Airtours bought Costa Cruises, Europe's largest line. The following year, Carnival stunned the cruise world by buying its competitor Cunard from the line's parent company, Kvaerner ASA, for $500 million, and merged the Cunard fleet with Seabourn. Kvaerner, an Anglo-Norwegian conglomerate, owns Kvaerner Masa-Yards in Finland, where six of Carnival's eight *Fantasy*-class ships were built. These acquisitions give Carnival 45 percent of the world cruise market. All operate as separate companies, each with a sharp focus; together, they give Carnival tremendous clout.

In 1999, Carnival became the first major line to launch direct booking on its Web site. In recent years, Carnival has introduced departures from new gateways and expanded its focus on families. Its children's program employs one of cruising's largest staffs of trained personnel, with over 100 child counselors spread over 14 ships on a full-time basis; additional personnel are hired during peak periods. Recently, a second children's playroom was added to all *Fantasy*-class ships.

"Vacation Guarantee," a Carnival innovation, allows a dissatisfied passenger, after notifying the purser's office, to leave a cruise at the first non-U.S. port of call and get a prorated refund. Another Carnival "first": a 24-hour, toll-free hotline—(877) TVL-HTLN—for passengers who encounter a travel emergency (such as severe weather or an airline strike) en route to or returning from their cruise. Passengers outside the United States can call collect (305) 406-4779.

The Fleet	Built/Renovated	Tonnage	Passengers
Carnival Conquest	2002	102,000	2,758
Carnival Destiny	1996	101,353	2,642
Carnival Glory	2003	102,000	2,758
Carnival Legend	2002	84,000	2,112
Carnival Pride	2001	84,000	2,112
Carnival Spirit	2001	84,000	2,112
Carnival Triumph	1999	102,000	2,758
Carnival Victory	2000	101,353	2,642
Celebration	1987	47,262	1,486
Ecstasy	1991	70,367	2,040
Elation	1998	70,367	2,040
Fantasy	1990	70,367	2,040
Fascination	1994	70,367	2,040
Holiday	1985/94/98	46,052	1,452
Imagination	1995	70,367	2,040
Inspiration	1996	70,367	2,040
Jubilee	1986	47,262	1,486
Paradise	1998	70,367	2,040
Sensation	1993	70,367	2,040
Tropicale	1981/89/94	36,674	1,022

Style Youthful and casual, "Fun Ships" have so much action and so many diversions that the ship itself is the cruise experience. An important part of creating Carnival has been Joe Farcus, an interior architect and decorator, unique in his role among the cruise lines. He believes people go on vacation to have fun and his job is to create the surroundings and atmosphere for it. If you accept his flamboyant decor as entertaining, you will find it ingenious. But sometimes, so much bombards the senses that the impact is more exhausting than exhilarating.

The emphasis on fun aims to get people out of their cabins and into public spaces to become part of the action. The variety of activity and entertainment attracts a range of passengers, but the basic appeal is to the young and young at heart—at reasonable prices.

Another characteristic: Perhaps more than any line, Carnival has standardized features on its ships. If you see a water slide on one ship, you can count on its being on the others. A menu with four desserts on one ship will be on others. Even deck names are the same. The uniformity helps keep down costs, and consistency is reassuring to passengers—and to their travel agents.

Distinctive Features Ships' design and decor, children's programs, family packages, two late-night buffets, 24-hour pizzerias, sushi bars on five ships, alternative dining; state-of-the-art fitness centers, areas for topless sunbathing, tuxedo rentals, vacation guarantee, golf program, smoke-free ship, travelers' hotline.

	HIGHEST	LOWEST	AVERAGE
PER DIEM	$337	$152	$201

The above per diems are calculated from the cruise line's non-discounted *cruise only* fares on standard accommodations. Per diems vary by season, by cabin, and by cruise areas.

Rates All include port fees.

Special Fares and Discounts Super Savers early-bird program provides discounts up to $720 per cabin on three- to four-day cruises, $840 on five-day cruises, and up to $1,300 on seven-day cruises.

- Children's Fare: Same as deeply discounted third/fourth person rates. If children are younger than age 12, rates are even lower. Passengers younger than age 21 must be accompanied by a legal guardian in the cabin. Exceptions apply to married couples and to children traveling with parents in a separate cabin.
- Single Supplement: 150 percent or 200 percent, depending on category. Singles matching program, based on questionnaire compatibility.

Packages
- Cruise/Air Add-on with transfers: Yes.

- Pre/Post: Yes. Wedding packages in U.S. home ports and eight Caribbean ports year-round, plus Vancouver in summer.
- Others: Yes.

Past Passengers   No club. After first cruise, passengers receive *Carnival Currents,* the line's on-board magazine, which includes discounts.

The Last Word   Carnival has had an enormous impact on cruises, particularly those aimed at the mass market. The line wrote the book on marketing. Yet, despite its success, a Carnival cruise isn't for everybody. The ships have more glitter than glamour. Some people love them; others think they redefine tacky. For the generation that grew up with shopping malls and Las Vegas–style glitz, Carnival's gargantuan, flashy ships may feel like home. But if big and boisterous is not your style, Carnival is not for you. Yet, everyone should take at least one Carnival cruise to see for themselves. The ships are eye-popping and the atmosphere infectious. Even the most staid, buttoned-down party poopers are often turned on by the Carnival neon and end up having the time of their lives.

CARNIVAL STANDARD FEATURES

Officers Italian.

Staff Dining/International; Cabin/Central American, Asian; Cruise/American and others.

Dining Facilities Two main dining rooms/two seatings for three meals, located on upper decks (*Tropicale,* one dining room). Breakfast and lunch served cafeteria-style on Lido Deck; two late-night buffets. *Destiny*'s lido restaurant is four-in-one: pizzeria, Asian, trattoria, American grill. Seaview Bistro dinner service in lido restaurant.

Special Diets Low-salt, diabetic, vegetarian, bland.

Room Service 24 hours; limited, light menu.

Dress Code Casual; no shorts in evening; two formal nights; tuxedos not required, semiformal dress is acceptable.

Cabin Amenities Closed-circuit television; safe. Bath with shower; international direct-dial phones. Hair dryers on *Destiny, Triumph,* and *Victory*; other ships on request.

Electrical Outlets 110 AC.

Wheelchair Access 11–25 cabins, depending on ship.

Recreation and Entertainment Casino, bingo, disco, library (except *Tropicale*); 10 bar/lounges (17 on *Destiny*; 7 on *Tropicale*); two-deck show lounges (one-deck on *Tropicale*; three-deck on *Destiny*).

Sports and Other Activities Three or four outside swimming pools, shuffleboard, jogging tracks (*Fantasy*-class and *Destiny*), Ping-Pong.

Beauty and Fitness Barber/beauty salon, sauna. Nautica spas on all ships in *Fantasy* and *Holiday* group; full gym, exercise classes, body treatments (small spa on *Tropicale*). Spa fare on menus.

Other Facilities Boutiques, tuxedo rentals, infirmary, drug store, video of cruise souvenir ($50), and coin-operated laundry facilities.

Children's Facilities Camp Carnival, year-round, with supervised activities for toddlers to teens. Video arcades, water slides, playroom, club/disco for teens, children's menus, high chairs. Babysitting arranged for $5 per hour for first child, $3 for each additional child. Passengers under age 21 must be accompanied by adult older than 25.

Smoking Smoke-free dining rooms and main show lounge. *Paradise,* totally smoke free.

Theme Cruises None.

Carnival Suggested Tipping Per person, per day: cabin steward, $3.50; waiter, $3.50; busboy, $2; 15 percent added to wine and bar bill.

Credit Cards Cruise and shipboard charges: American Express, MasterCard, Visa, Discover, Optima.

Fantasy / Ecstasy	Quality ❹	Value B
Elation	Quality ❺	Value A
Fascination / Imagination	Quality ❻	Value A
Inspiration	Quality ❻	Value A
Paradise	Quality ❼	Value A
Sensation	Quality ❹	Value B

Registry: *Fantasy / Ecstasy:* Liberia *Elation / Sensation / Imagination / Fascination / Inspiration*: Panama	Length: 855 feet	Beam: 118 feet
Cabins: 1,022/1,020	Draft: 26 feet	Speed: 21 knots
Maximum Passengers: 2,634/2,594	Passenger Decks: 10 Crew: 920	Elevators: 14 Space Ratio: 34

The Ships   Billed as ships for the twenty-first century, Carnival's eight megaliners have already bedazzled passengers of the 1990s. Their flashy decor and high-energy ambience are Las Vegas, Disneyland, and *Starlight Express* all in one. Atrium lobbies ascend seven decks at the heart of the ship and contain huge, specially commissioned art. Throughout the vessels are so many bars, lounges, and entertainment and recreation outlets—all imaginatively decorated—that they can't be absorbed in one cruise. No one cruises on one of these ships to rest; the senses work overtime.

Except for decor—each ship is themed—the vessels are identical, and as with all Carnival ships, even the deck names are the same. The *Fantasy,* first of the group, is dazzling with its towering atrium awash in lights dominated by a 20-foot-tall kinetic sculpture of rotating cylinders created by Israeli artist Yaacov Agam. Here and in the entertainment areas, 15 miles of computerized lights are programmed to change color—constantly but subtly—from white to cool blue to hot red, altering the ambience with each change. It's awesome!

The second megaliner, *Ecstasy,* is designed as a city at sea. Carnival watchers have declared her the fleet's most elegant and sophisticated vessel, reflecting an effort to upgrade the style. But there's no mistaking this for anything but a Carnival ship, especially when encountering the 24-foot-tall plastic and steel sculpture in the Grand Atrium. Created by kinetic artist Len Janklow, it encompasses 12 huge cubes flooded in light, each holding 8 small cubes that appear to float in space.

Ecstasy's decor takes inspiration from Manhattan's Cafe Society, showcasing exotic woods, Italian marbles, rich carpets, sumptuous fabrics, and a vintage Rolls Royce on the lounge-lined City Lights Boulevard. The promenade's highlights are the Neon Bar, a piano bar with vintage neon signs, and Chinatown Lounge, guarded by huge lion-headed Foo dogs.

Sensation, third in the series, resembles *Ecstasy* with decor slightly more sophisticated than her mates'. Light, sound, and color create a "sensual" environment. Public rooms range from elegant to kitschy. Among them, the Touch of Class Lounge is a "hands-on" experience, with gigantic hands cupping the entrance, hands supporting tables, and chairs and bar stools shaped like hands.

Fascination takes Hollywood of the 1930s, 1940s, and 1950s as its theme, mixing homage and spoofs—and kitsch galore. On the entertainment promenade, Hollywood Boulevard, are Puttin' on the Ritz Lounge, Bogey's Cafe, and the Passage to India Lounge. But the showstoppers are 20 life-sized mannequins of movie legends posed as they might be in real life. At the Stars Bar, you find Gary Cooper and Rita Hayworth, and in the Tara Library, Vivien Leigh and Clark Gable.

Interiors place slightly less emphasis on special effects than those aboard some other Carnival ships. Purple neon dramatically edges each of the seven decks rising from the Grand Atrium's lobby, which is centered by an enormous sculpture, *Nucleus,* by British artist Susanna Holt.

Images of space ships, space stations, and other futuristic technologies are incorporated into four rotating towers of stainless steel and clear plastic that are the centerpiece of *Imagination*'s atrium. The 24-foot sculpture by Len Janklow is among works commissioned from five artists whose imaginations carried them from powerful seascapes to mythical tales of ancient lands.

Architect Joe Farcus's fertile imagination worked overtime creating the decor of the bars and lounges. Most innovative are the ship's 24-hour pizzeria—now a feature on all Carnival ships—and an adjacent bar serving draft and bottled beers from around the world. Favorite nightspots include Shangri-La, for music and dancing, and Mirage, a sing-along piano bar.

Farcus's concept for the *Inspiration* was drawn from the arts. Decor incorporates musical icons, themes, and motifs—from a larger-than-life replica of Elvis's guitar in the disco to the elegant Chopin Lounge with a piano. The ship offers the *Fantasy* group's multideck, glass-domed atrium and dramatic centerpiece, a promenade of lounges and bars, and sports and recreation features.

Elation, which debuted in 1998, boasts significant improvements over her *Fantasy* sisters and incorporates some of the best design elements, including the atrium lobby bar copied from the innovative *Carnival Destiny. Elation* is the first cruise ship with the new Azipod propulsion system, which dramatically reduces engine noise and vibration. The system pulls rather than pushes the ship, eliminating the need for rudders or stern thrusters and increasing maneuverability and fuel efficiency.

Elation is the most sophisticated of the *Fantasy*-class ships and should have a broader appeal than her older, glitzier sisters, although there is still plenty of glitter. *Elation*'s theme is the mythological Muses. The ship's noticeably more elegant decor uses copper tones and inlaid woods. Prisms and fiber-optic lights create subtle lighting and mood changes. Among new features are a sushi bar on the promenade deck, Carnival's largest children's center, a patisserie and coffee bar, a redesigned lido cafe area, a casino bar, and a conference center.

The eighth member of the group, *Paradise,* is the world's first smoke-free cruise ship. A bright red no-smoking emblem is painted on the hull, and a huge white flag with that symbol flies at the bow. Even the staff does not smoke. Carnival takes the no-smoking policy very seriously. Passengers must sign an agreement binding them to the rules; anyone caught smoking is subject to a $250 fine and may be told to leave the ship.

Your first view on boarding *Paradise* is likely to be the atrium, centered by a large circular bar—a feature copied from *Carnival Destiny,* where it has been very popular. *Paradise* immortalizes famous steamships in maritime history and evokes the era when travelers boarded famous vessels and headed to foreign lands.

Immediately, you notice foot-tall Fabergé-like eggs. Used in decor throughout the ship, they have tiny lights to suggest the diamonds and rubies on Fabergé originals. From the bar, a stairway decorated with three kinds of wood winds upward to the Atlantic Deck, where every lounge recalls maritime history.

Itineraries   See Appendix B.

Cabins   As with all Carnival ships, the 12 cabin categories include some of the largest standard cabins and junior suites of any ships in their price category. They are finished in light oak, and although color schemes vary some among ships, the furniture and decor are essentially the same—basic and comfortable.

Almost all cabins have twin beds that convert to king-size ones—a Carnival innovation quickly copied by other cruise lines. Cabins have phones with international direct dial; a desk/dressing table; closed-circuit television with channels for movies, cartoons, and satellite programs (depending on ship's location); stereo music; and wall safes. Outside cabins have picture windows. Bathrooms are well designed and have roomy shower stalls. They have soap and complimentary toiletries; hair dryers are available on request. Closet space is adequate for short, warm-weather cruises. All ships have self-service laundry rooms with washers, dryers, irons, and ironing boards—a big plus for families traveling with children. The *Elation*'s Azipod propulsion system minimizes vibration and engine noise, even in cabins all the way aft or on the lowest passenger decks.

Specifications   383 inside cabins, 564 outside; 54 suites with verandas (28 suites with bathtub Jacuzzi). Standard dimensions, 183–190 square feet; 947 with twins convertible to doubles; 19 inside with upper and lower berths; no singles. All ships have wheelchair-accessible cabins.

Dining   Each ship has two dining rooms with two seatings for three meals. The rooms are on an upper deck and have large windows with good views. Dinners often have themes, such as Caribbean night or French night, with costumed waiters and appropriate music and menus.

Restaurants have round tables for eight people in the center of the room; the sides are lined with rectangular tables, which are sometimes difficult to get in and out of. The *Ecstasy*'s Wind Star and Wind Song and *Elation*'s Imagination and Inspiration dining rooms get more kudos for stylish decor than their older sister. All earn criticism for high noise levels. Also, the ships no longer have wine stewards; wine is served by waiters and busboys unfamiliar with the selections. Breakfast and lunch are served cafeteria-style on the Lido Deck, and there are two late-night buffets. *Fantasy*'s Windows on the Sea is one of the group's most attractive restaurants, with pastel parasols, brass highlights, and etched glass. On the *Ecstasy*, the Panorama Bar and Grill has floor-to-ceiling windows and a playful ambience with signal flags and blue neon lighting. *Fascination*'s Coconut Grove Bar and Grille has imitation palm trees as columns and a bamboo bar and tables.

"Seaview Bistros," alternative casual dining available fleetwide, serve specialty salads, pastas, steaks, and desserts in a cafe setting. They operate each evening from 6 to 9:30 p.m. in the lido restaurant. Tablecloths, preset silverware, and flowers on tables set the tone. Service is buffet-style, but waiters refill drink orders and food requests. The bistros are meant to handle 100–150 people, but twice that number or more can be accommodated. Another winner is the around-the-clock pizzeria, offering delicious pizzas with varied toppings, fresh Caesar salads, and warm garlic rolls. *Paradise,* like *Elation, Imagination, Inspiration, and Jubilee,* has a sushi bar on the Promenade Deck and conference space near the dining room.

Carnival initially was not known for its cuisine, but efforts to upgrade the quality, selection, and variety yielded outstanding results. In 1999, the line introduced new menus fleetwide with lighter, more contemporary cuisine and an expanded wine list. A typical dinner menu offers three juices; four appetizers; three soups; two salads; two fish choices; three entrees of beef, chicken, or turkey; five desserts; and a variety of ice cream and sherbet, cheese, and beverages. At least one item per course is marked as spa fare, which has lower calories, sodium, fat, and cholesterol.

Service   Dining staff generally earn good marks, but cabin attendants get mixed reviews. Cruise directors and their staff are very professional, but the cruise director on ships of this size is in little evidence except when he is on stage. Recent passengers on *Fantasy* reported that contacting their room steward or the purser's desk by phone was nearly impossible. They also complained that they encountered orientation problems on boarding. Rather than being escorted to their cabins, they were handed ship diagrams and directed to find their cabins on their own. The bottom line: Megaliners offer many wonderful facilities and options, but personal service is not among them.

Facilities and Entertainment   One of the *Fantasy* group's most distinctive features is an indoor promenade that serves as an "entertainment boulevard" of bars, lounges, disco, casino, and nightclubs. Called the Century Boulevard on the *Fantasy,* the promenade has the Cats Lounge, with decor inspired by the long-running Broadway show, and Cleopatra's, a piano bar with every conceivable cliché in ancient Egyptian art.

At one end of the boulevard, the spectacular, two-deck Universal show lounge stages nightly entertainment on the scale of a Las Vegas extravaganza. It's outstanding. At the stern is the opulent Majestic Bar, with a king's ransom in marble and onyx. Through the bar is the flamboyant Crystal Lounge, where red and white lights nearly blind you. Here you can catch the naughty cabaret, Midnight Special. The casinos, each with over 200 slot machines, 20 blackjack tables, roulette, and other games, are among the largest afloat.

The most amusing place on the *Fascination's* Hollywood Boulevard is Bar 88, named for the 88 keys on a piano and decorated with huge, neon-lit keys at the door and on the columns between piano-shaped tables. At the Passage to India Lounge, two life-size elephant figures are a prelude to the interior draped with elaborate Indian ceremonial cloth. Furnishings include British colonial-style mahogany chairs, a statue of a multiarmed Hindu deity, a domed shrine holding a Buddha, mosaic ceiling tiles, and floral carpets. The Puttin' on the Ritz Lounge, with decor inspired by Fred Astaire's top hat, offers late-night comedy acts and a vocalist.

Fascination's Palace Lounge, in shimmering golden beige and silvery pink with painted clouds decorating the walls, had the most technologically advanced stage at sea when she was introduced, and her Tribute to Hollywood was among the best shows anywhere. It combined classic Hollywood numbers—such as Marilyn Monroe's "Diamonds Are a Girl's Best Friend" and dancing in the style of Fred Astaire and Ginger Rogers—with contemporary dances to the music of Whitney Houston and Michael Jackson. A takeoff of Madonna raised some eyebrows.

On the *Sensation,* the popular Michelangelo Lounge combines soft gray, yellow, and black in its furnishings and uses classic features, such as Ionic columns, Greek designs, and ceiling frescoes. The bar and dance floor are marble. The Polo Lounge was designed for those a seeking quiet spot—all the ships have at least one such lounge. The *Elation*'s Mikado showroom (named after the Gilbert and Sullivan operetta) strikes a Japanese theme with large fans, rice paper shoji screen walls, Japanese-motif upholstery, and gold-leaf bamboo and chrysanthemum designs sandblasted onto black fossil stone walls and tables.

Duke's piano bar evokes Manhattan in the Jazz Age, paying tribute to Duke Ellington. Entry is via a replica of Washington Square Park's Triumphal Arch. Decor includes replicas of famous New York sights. A bar encircles a white baby grand piano on a turntable. The Jekyll and Hyde Dance Club has eight-foot-tall sculptures of Robert Louis Stevenson's fictional character with split faces, meant to convey benevolence and malice. The heads swivel to the music's tempo, and monitors set into the sculptures show live pictures of dancing guests and music videos.

On the *Paradise* all public rooms are named for oceanliners, and the Blue Riband Library, namesake of the international prize awarded for the fastest transatlantic crossing, pays tribute to them in miniature models and old photographs. It contains a full-scale reproduction of the gold and onyx Hales Trophy, models of ships that won the prize, and memorabilia, including a signed photo of the duke and duchess of Windsor on the *Queen Elizabeth.*

In eye-popping contrast, the America Bar across from the library is named for the *SS America* and all but screams U.S.A. with its red, white, and blue color scheme, starred carpet, and stars and stripes on the walls. At the stern, the 1,300-seat, two-story *Normandie* show lounge carries an Art Deco theme and celebrates the French liner considered by some to be the best ship ever built. Another showroom, the *Queen Mary* Lounge, uses funnels from the great ship as the motif to line the bar and walls, frame the seats, and serve as table bases.

From the Italian liner *Rex,* Farcus took the Latin meaning of *rex* (*king*) and conjured up the king of the jungle, giving the Rex Dance Club a jungle theme.

Activities and Diversions   The ships have the usual array of activities, including bingo, singles party, newlywed game, passenger talent show, horse racing, bridge, ballroom- and country line-dance classes, masquerades, wine and cheese parties, and sing-alongs. There are tours of the galleys and bridge, first-run movies daily, and abundant boutiques. The library/lounge—especially the mahogany-paneled Explorer's Club on *Ecstasy*—is one of the loveliest rooms in the Carnival fleet.

Sports and Fitness   Three swimming pools (one with a slide), Ping-Pong, shuffleboard, and volleyball are available, and pool games are staged almost daily. On Caribbean and Mexican cruises, depending on ports, you can play golf, sail, ride horseback, bike, hike, snorkel, scuba dive, and windsurf.

The 12,000-square-foot Nautica spa on the sports deck is a fully equipped gym with trained instructors. Or one can choose from an array of Jazzercise, exercise, and aerobics classes. The sun deck has a 500-foot outside jogging track; separate locker rooms, dressing rooms, and showers for men and women; and six whirlpools, saunas, and steam rooms—all included in the cruise price. Instructors will also create a fitness regimen for you to follow at home. All Carnival ships have a secluded deck area for topless sunbathing.

In 1998, Carnival added a golf program on *Triumph* for play at more than a dozen courses in the Bahamas, Caribbean, and Mexico. It offers one-on-one, 30- or 60-minute instruction from PGA teaching pros aboard ship and on golf excursions. Shipboard lessons are in a netted driving range where golfers' swings are videotaped and computer analyzed. A take-home video with voice-over instruction and stop-action/slow-motion analysis is provided with each lesson. Golf packages include greens fees, instruction, cart rental or caddie, and transportation to and from courses. Prices range from $40 for on-board lessons to $100 for golf excursions. Equipment rentals include Callaway clubs and Florsheim "soft spike" golf shoes.

Spa and Beauty   The beauty salon and spa, operated by the Steiner Group, a British-based company, has nine private rooms for body and facial treatments—including facials, pedicures, massage, and herbal packs. Services aren't free and can become an expensive indulgence.

Children's Facilities   Camp Carnival, which handles 250,000 kids fleetwide annually, is a year-round program with a wide array of activities supervised by trained counselors for children in four age groups: Toddlers (ages 2–4), Juniors (ages 5–8), Intermediate (ages 9–12), and Teens (ages 13–17). Young children enjoy puppet making, finger painting, and learning the alphabet and numbers; older kids have pizza parties, scavenger hunts, and lip sync contests and play bingo, charades, and Twister. Teens have activities ranging from disco parties and star search contests to evening deck parties. All ships have video arcades, wading pools, water slides, playrooms (two on *Fantasy*-class), teens' club/discos, children's menus, and high chairs.

Recently, Carnival added a second playroom to *Fantasy*-class ships as part of an ongoing fleetwide expansion of Camp Carnival. The new playrooms, designed to accommodate kids ages 5–12, are stocked with age-appropriate toys, games, and puzzles, including such popular pastimes as air hockey, foosball, and "pop-a-shot" basketball, along with the latest high-tech video games. The original playrooms on these ships are now geared toward toddlers.

Both *Elation* and *Paradise* have Carnival's largest children's facility to date, the 2,500-square-foot Children's World. It is divided into three sections. One features an educational computer lab and computer games. The arts and crafts section has spin art, sand art, jewelry-making machines, easels for painting and drawing, and a gallery for display participants' creations. The third is an indoor play area with a climbing maze, toys, games, and a video wall where kids can watch movies, music videos, and cartoons.

The outdoor play area has a schooner-shaped playhouse and a wading pool for toddlers. Teens get special attention, too, with Virtual World, photography workshops, late-night movies, and disco parties on *Elation* and *Paradise*.

Camp Carnival operates from 9 a.m. to 10 p.m. At 10 p.m., babysitting in the form of slumber parties in the children's playrooms becomes available through the purser's office for $5 per hour for the first child, $3 for each additional child. Recently, Carnival added a "Fountain Fun-Card" for those younger than age 21, good for unlimited sodas from the bars (the card is $8 on a 3-day cruise, $28 on an 11-day cruise).

Shore Excursions Recently, Carnival has tried to provide greater variety. Nonetheless, dockside in almost all Caribbean ports are plenty of vans with driver/guides eager for your business and ready to design a tour to your liking. Prices depend on your ability to bargain and the driver's eagerness for your business, but do agree on a fee before the tour begins.

An air/sea package is recommended for cruises departing from Port Canaveral combined with Orlando attractions because the Orlando airport, where most passengers arrive, is about an hour's drive from Port Canaveral, where the ship departs. There is no public transportation between the two; those traveling on their own must hire a taxi or rent a car. Or, those booking "cruise-only" can buy Carnival's transfer package. Also, if you buy the Orlando package, plan to take the Spaceport USA bus tour on the day you sail. That way, the full morning can be spent at Spaceport USA, about 20 minutes from Port Canaveral. A late lunch is available aboard ship until 3:30 p.m. In Alaska, the line offers excursions for teens, along with 60 tours for all ages.

Holiday / Jubilee	Quality ⑤	Value B
Celebration	Quality ⑤	Value B

Registry: *Jubilee, Celebration:* Liberia *Holiday:* Panama	Length: 728/733 feet	Beam: 92 feet
Cabins: 726/743	Draft: 25 feet	Speed: 21 knots
Maximum Passengers: 1,800/1,896	Passenger Decks: 9/10	Elevators: 8
	Crew: 660/67	Space Ratio: 32

The Ships   When the *Holiday* was unveiled in 1985, her decor was called zany. Micky Arison, Carnival's chairman, called it a "Disney World for adults." For those accustomed to the sleek lines of traditional ships, *Holiday*'s boxy look took some getting used to, but it was the innovations inside that revolutionized cruising, making the ship with its four decks for recreation and entertainment as much the destination as its ports of call. The most startling change was the main promenade deck. Instead of circling the ship, as had been typical, the deck runs double-width down only one side—a feature that became standard on all Carnival megaliners. Called Broadway on the *Holiday*, with nearly as much glitter as its namesake, it serves as a meeting place and thoroughfare, with bars, nightclubs, casinos, a disco, and reminders of Broadway: a traffic light, street lamps, an authentic 1934 bus, and Times Square.

A decade later, larger and more flamboyant ships have been added to Carnival's fleet, and the *Holiday* is regarded as traditional. That may be pushing credibility, but it's amazing how quickly passengers became comfortable with the new ideas the *Holiday* introduced. What's more, the innovations continue. A multimillion-dollar renovation in 1998 resulted in cruising's first video simulcasts live via satellite of horse races from top tracks worldwide. The promenade was redesigned, and Doc Holiday's (a country-and-western lounge) was added. A separate section contains Cyber City, a new virtual reality and game center. The fitness center was expanded, the casino renovated, and the lido restaurant remodeled, adding another dinner option and a 24-hour pizzeria.

The *Holiday* was quickly followed by the *Jubilee* and the *Celebration*. The trio are identical in almost all aspects except decor. Each is themed, with the *Jubilee*, inspired by historic, romantic England, having its main promenade called Park Lane, a Victorian gazebo bar, a Trafalgar Square, and Churchill's Library. Generous use of wood throughout the ship makes it more mellow than other Carnival ships. Standouts are the Art Deco Atlantis Lounge showroom and the Sporting Club, a casino with golden slot machines, etched glass, and golden mirrors. In 2000, *Jubilee* was renovated, giving her a sushi bar and an expanded health and fitness facility.

The *Celebration* pays tribute to New Orleans and Mardi Gras, complete with Bourbon Street, an outdoor cafe, bistro, a New Orleans streetcar named (yes) Desire, and a Dixieland band playing nightly on Bourbon Street before dinner. Sculpture by Israeli artist Yaacov Agam greets passengers in the lobby, and his wall pieces decorate public areas. But the most dramatic art is by San Franciscan Helen Webber, whose sculptured aluminum kites hang on wires the full six decks of the stairwells. The *Celebration,* like the other ships, has a quiet corner—Admiral's, a library and writing room dedicated to great oceanliners of the past. On September 30, 2000, she is expected to launch Carnival's first operation from Galveston, Texas—that port's first year-round cruises—with four- and five-day cruises to Mexico.

Itineraries   See Appendix B.

Cabins   For all the unconventional elements on the ships' activity decks, cabins on the *Holiday* trio are downright sane and larger than most on other ships in the same price category. Outside cabins have picture windows; inside have backlit windows of the same size, making the cabin seem larger and less closed in. Cabins are furnished with twin beds that can be converted to kings and have ample closet and drawer space in cabinets of genuine wood. Artwork decorates the walls and adds a touch of class.

Holiday *Specifications*   279 inside cabins, 437 outside; 10 suites with whirlpool bathtubs. Standard dimensions, 180 square feet. 683 with twin beds convertible to kings; 27 inside, 10 outside with upper/lower berths. No singles. 15 wheelchair-accessible.

Jubilee *and* Celebration *Specifications*   290 inside cabins, 443 outside; 10 suites with whirlpool bathtubs. Standard dimensions, 185 square feet. 709 with twin beds convertible to kings; 16 inside, 8 outside with upper/lower berths. No singles.

Dining   The *Holiday* group offers the same menus as aboard *Fantasy*-class ships, with two dining rooms serving three meals. Recently, Carnival upgraded and expanded lido-area food service on all its ships to meet passengers' preference for casual breakfast and lunch choices. At breakfast and lunch, specialties are now offered in addition to standard favorites, such as scrambled eggs, hot dogs, and hamburgers. Particularly popular are the made-to-order pasta stations and expanded salad bars. Cookies, ice cream, and frozen yogurt are available all day in the lido. Staff in the area has been doubled for better service. Wine bars have been added on the promenade decks.

Facilities and Entertainment   The Lido Deck has acres of open space and a swimming pool with a 14-foot-tall spiral water slide, a signature on Carnival ships. A more secluded pool is at the stern; a kids' pool is a deck below. The ships have Nautica spas with separate facilities for men and women. Decks are covered with Burmese teak.

Activities are numerous, ranging from wine tastings and auctions to knobby-knee contests (you would be amazed by how many people join in!).

In the evening, there's barhopping and people-watching on Broadway, Park Lane, or Bourbon Street, and action in the casino or electronic game room. A favorite spot on all three ships is the piano bar, but *Celebration*'s Red Hot Piano Bar wins the award for novelty. Red walls glow under red lights, and the bar is shaped like a red piano with the ivories as the bar counter. Plus, the music is . . . red hot. A spiral staircase leads directly to the casino a deck above.

The ships have huge theaters spanning two decks, where Broadway-style musicals and Las Vegas–type shows are staged twice nightly. Seats are terraced on six levels, giving all 1,000 patrons unobstructed views.

The Camp Carnival year-round children's program offers supervised activities for four age groups. Cyber City incorporates cutting-edge electronic game technology.

Shore Excursions   All Carnival ships offer similar shore excursions at common rates. Most are off-the-shelf tours you usually could take on your own. The main—often only—reason to book excursions through the ships is convenience. Beginning September 30, 2000 *Celebration* launches the first ever year-round cruises from Galveston, Texas. Building on the line's success with four and five day cruises, *Jubilee* moves to Tampa, increasing Carnival's capacity by 45 percent.

Postscript   The *Holiday, Jubilee,* and *Celebration* set the course for Carnival for the decade and had an incalculable impact on cruising. Zany, yes. Successful? You bet. Probably because they were so new and different, passengers took to them enthusiastically—and still do.

Carnival Destiny	Quality ⑧	Value A
Carnival Triumph	(Preview)	
Carnival Victory	(Preview)	

Registry: Panama	Length: 893 feet	Beam: 125 feet
Cabins: 53	Draft: 27 feet	Speed: 22.5 knots
Maximum Passengers: 3,400	Passenger Decks: 12	Elevators: 18
	Crew: 1,070	Space Ratio: 38

The Ships   The *Carnival Destiny* was the largest cruise ship ever built when she made her debut in 1996 and was the first one too wide to transit the Panama Canal. When the ship was being planned six years earlier, Carnival employees were asked to submit their wish lists for enhancing the new vessel. Apparently, they got most of their wishes.

The *Destiny* has Carnival's first double-decked dining room; a show lounge spanning three decks; a double-width promenade lined with lounges and bars; a mall-style shopping area; a 9,000-square-foot casino; 17 bars and lounges; 4 swimming pools and an expansive Nautica spa; a retractable glass dome over the pool area; and sports and recreation facilities similar to the *Fantasy* group of ships. The pool area has a stage for entertainment and teak decks cantilevered in an amphitheater. Virtual World is a high-tech virtual reality game center.

Destiny's configuration is a departure for Carnival. Entertainment and recreation decks are between accommodations decks. The two lowest passenger decks have only cabins, followed by three decks of public rooms, then five decks of cabins and suites with balconies. To avoid big rooms and long corridors that would make the ship's huge size obvious, public rooms span two or three levels. The layout is often confusing, however.

Despite her size—nearly three football fields in length—*Destiny* does not seem as large from the inside as some of her *Fantasy*-class cousins. This is primarily because of the layout and the decor, which is softer and toned down—sometimes even tony—a change from Farcus's flamboyant creations on other Carnival ships.

The Rotunda (Capital Lobby on *Triumph*; Seven Seas Atrium on *Victory*) a nine-deck atrium with four glass elevators and a glass dome, is the ship's focal point. An enormous marble and onyx mural of geometric forms suggesting skyscrapers decorates the walls. But instead of the huge sculptures on *Fantasy*-class ships, *Destiny's* atrium has an attractive lobby bar at its base, creating a meeting place that helps humanize the huge space.

The *Carnival Triumph,* which debuted in 1999, builds on *Destiny*'s success but incorporates new features. Sixty percent of cabins have ocean views with a sitting area, and more than 60 percent of those have verandas. The ship celebrates the world's great cities, with such venues as Underground Tokyo video arcade, the Rome Theater, Vienna Café coffee bar, and Oxford Bar. A huge golden globe dominates the atrium; it's inlaid with glittering fiber optics that mark the world's metropolises. Smaller globes are part of the decor shipwide. The new Panorama Deck, one level above the Lido Deck, has 42 ocean-view cabins, most with verandas, and 24 inside ones, adding capacity for 132 guests. The third ship of the *Destiny* series, *Carnival Victory,* whose theme is the seven seas, arrived in August 2000, beginning on four- and five-day cruises from New York to Canada prior to starting year-round Caribbean cruises. Two more ships in the series, *Carnival Conquest* and *Carnival Glory,* will follow in 2002 and 2003. *Carnival Destiny* will move to a new home port, San Juan, in September, becoming the largest ship based there.

Itineraries   See Appendix B.

Cabins   *Destiny*'s cabins are the largest—220–260 square feet for standard ocean-view—and the most attractively furnished in the Carnival fleet. All have hair dryers, safes, and interactive television. Cabin numbers pinpoint your deck and location (forward, aft, or midship). Each section has its own elevators. Sixty percent of standard outside cabins have small balconies, all with clear panels for unobstructed ocean views. Unfortunately, they do nothing to absorb sound. This and insufficient soundproofing make the cabins noisy. Ocean-view cabins have a sitting area with sofa and coffee table. Veranda cabins create a new category of standard cabins for Carnival that, although larger, are comparable in price to standard outside accommodations on *Fantasy*-class ships. Family cabins are near the children's play facilities.

Note: We have received complaints about inadequate soundproofing between cabins (which may have as much to do with the boisterous nature of *Destiny* passengers as with cabin walls). Particularly to be avoided are cabins on Deck 6 forward, which are directly above lounges that operate most of the night.

Specifications   515 inside cabins, 432 outside with verandas; 48 suites with verandas, some with bathtub Jacuzzi. Standard dimensions, 220–260 square feet; all cabins with twins convertible to double; 4 inside with upper and lower berths; no singles; 25 wheelchair-accessible cabins.

Dining   The Galaxy and Universe restaurants (London and Paris restaurants on *Triumph;* Atlantic and Pacific on *Victory*)—Carnival's first bilevel dining rooms—feel roomy, and the additional space allows wider separation between tables. But the restaurants are noisy. Both dining rooms enjoy ocean views.

The two-deck Sun & Sea (South Beach Club on *Triumph;* Mediterranean on *Victory*), the casual lido restaurant, is dressed in shades of green with yellow, hand-blown Murano glass and hand-painted ceramic tile decorating walls and countertops. Different settings create dining options: Trattoria is the setting for pasta and made-to-order Italian dishes; Happy Valley features Chinese cuisine, stir-fried to order; and The Grille serves hamburgers and hot dogs. Service has also been upgraded; waiters carry dishes and beverages to tables. The "Seaview Bistro" alternative dinner venue offers specialty salads, pastas, steaks, and desserts—plus a daily special—in a cafe setting. The bistro operates each evening from 6 to 9:30 p.m. in a designated area of the lido restaurant. Service is buffet-style, but waiters refill drink orders and food requests. Also open are a 24-hour pizzeria and, on the promenade deck, a patisserie appointed with cherry wood counters and windowed banquettes. The new *Carnival Victory* will have a New York–style deli.

Facilities and Entertainment   In the evening, you are likely to run out of energy before you run out of choices. The flashy Millionaire's Club (Club Monaco on *Triumph;* South China Sea Club on *Victory*), said to be the largest casino afloat, has 321 slot machines and 23 table games. In the lavishly decorated Apollo Bar, the piano revolves, enabling the pianist to shine a spotlight on anyone eager to test the microphone mounted on each table.

At the whimsically decorated Downbeat, where a 20-foot trumpet and French horn are suspended above the bandstand, patrons sit on clarinet-shaped barstools or at glass tables supported by oversized sections of horns.

In the Point After Dance Club, tricolor neon lights snake across the ceiling above a bilevel floor, and over 500 video monitors flash pictures and computer-generated graphics around the room. A staircase by the dance floor leads to the elegant Onyx Room, a more sedate club where backlit alabaster panels glow softly beside a neon and glass dance floor.

The three-deck Palladium show lounge is the most technologically sophisticated afloat, Carnival says. The additional deck below seating levels allows the orchestra pit to be retracted, and the space above enables backdrops, lighting equipment, and performers to be "flown" offstage via cables. A Venetian glass chandelier hangs from the dome; at show time, it goes high-tech with fiber optics.

To achieve the three decks of seats for 1,500 people, some sacrifices were made. The main floor is almost level, making viewing beyond the first few rows difficult for anyone but an NBA player. Also, balcony rails partially block some views. The big production shows—*Formidable,* styled after a French revue, and *Nightclub Express,* which showcases the Cotton Club and other venues—are top-notch.

Yet more entertainment is offered in Virtual World, a game center with virtual reality and electronic games, and All Star Bar, decorated with celebrity memorabilia, including tables bearing autographs of sports stars, and featuring seven big-screen televisions broadcasting sporting events.

Sports, Fitness, and Beauty The *Destiny* has four pools, including a children's pool, and seven whirlpools. Two pools have swim-up bars; another has Carnival's trademark water slide—but here, it is three decks tall and 214 feet long. A retractable dome covers the aft deck and pool.

The 15,000-square-foot Nautica spa and health club has two levels, one with a beauty salon, massage rooms, Jacuzzis, and sauna and steam rooms, the other with an aerobics room and a juice bar. The spa offers hydrotherapy baths, aromatherapy, and other body treatments. There is also a "Nouveau Yu Health Environment Capsule," an egg-shaped, temperature-controlled capsule designed to induce relaxation. The gym has an array of equipment, including bikes, treadmills, step and rowing equipment, and 16 Keiser machines. Instructors lead exercise classes and can be hired as personal trainers. An eighth-mile jogging track is on the sun deck. On the *Triumph,* more open space was provided on the Lido Deck for deck chairs and the fore and aft pools were enlarged and are bordered by "wading" areas by eliminating the swim-up bar found on *Destiny.*

Children's Facilities The two-deck-tall, 1,300-square-foot indoor/ outdoor play center includes a jungle gym and pool. See the *Fantasy* profile for information on Carnival's children's program.

Postscript *Carnival Destiny* is Carnival's most beautiful ship to date, but it's big and noisy, and for now seems to attract people who are eager to party, day and night. That may reflect the excitement generated by its being the first cruise ship over 100,000 tons and will probably diminish when the novelty wears off. Until such time, the ship is definitely not for bookworms, fans of boutique hotels, or travelers seeking a quiet vacation. Also, signage should be improved, because the layout can be confusing. One frustrated passenger remarked at the end of a week's cruise, "I've spent most of my time trying to find my way around."

The bottom line: The *Carnival Destiny* met with such overwhelming passenger enthusiasm that Carnival ordered four more just like her. *Carnival Triumph* debuted in 1999 with Carnival's first cruises from New York; *Carnival Victory* launched in August 2000, also with a series from New York, prior to starting year-round Caribbean cruises.

Tropicale	Quality ❸	Value B
Registry: Liberia	Length: 671 feet	Beam: 85 feet
Cabins: 511	Draft: 23.3 feet	Speed: 22 knots
Maximum Passengers: 1,400	Passenger Decks: 10	Elevators: 8
	Crew: 550	Space Ratio: 36

The Ship   When Carnival launched the *Tropicale* in the 1980s, she was the first new cruise ship in almost a decade, and she offered many new features: all accommodations, except 12 suites, the same size; all cabins with picture windows instead of portholes; expanded deck space for sports and other activities; and twin beds that could be converted to kings—a feature copied throughout the industry.

The forerunner of superliners, yet scaled down in size and activity, *Tropicale* is the right combination for many people. The ship has pioneered new Carnival itineraries. After a multimillion-dollar refurbishment in 1998, the ship launched the line's four- and five-day cruises from Tampa to the Western Caribbean. Carnival also offers land packages in the Tampa/Orlando area that can be combined with the cruise.

Itineraries   See Appendix B.

Cabins   The *Tropicale*'s refurbishing brightened her decor and gave the ship superliner ambience. As with all Carnival ships, *Tropicale* has 12 categories of cabins and similar furnishings.

Specifications   172 inside cabins, 307 outside; 10 suites. Standard dimensions, 150–160 square feet. 479 with twins convertible to kings; upper/lower berths, 15 inside, 5 outside. No singles. 11 wheelchair-accessible cabins.

Dining   The *Tropicale*'s one dining room is on a lower deck. When the ship sails full, the room is crowded and noisy. Theme nights feature music and colorful presentations of the food by the waiters.

Facilities and Entertainment   The *Tropicale* has seven bars and lounges, including a piano bar, but it has neither a cinema nor library. The energy level is low-key compared to Carnival's megaliners, and many shipboard activities generate only mild interest. Although the median age is about 43 years, bingo, country line dancing, and the casino are likely to draw the biggest crowds.

Postscript   The *Tropicale* has a following among Carnival fans who prefer a smaller, low-key ship. Her short cruises are a good sampler for first-timers. However, if you wish to sample the Carnival experience, this ship is the least typical.

Carnival Spirit / Carnival Pride / Carnival Legend
(Preview)

Registry: Panama	Length: 960 feet	Beam: 105.7 feet
Cabins: 1,062	Draft: 25.7 feet	Speed: 24 knots
Maximum Passengers:	Passenger Decks: 12	Elevators: 15
2,124	Crew: 920	Space Ratio: 40

Carnival Spirit, the first of a new class of ships for Carnival under construction at Kvaerner Masa-Yards in Finland, is expected to enter service in April 2001. The $375 million, 84,000-ton cruise ship will be the longest ship in the Carnival fleet, but is still designed to pass through the Panama Canal. It will have the technologically advanced Azipod propulsion system, as well as a number of environmentally-friendly technical enhancements.

The *Carnival Spirit* will boast an exceptional space ratio of 40 (the *Fantasy* class is 34, *Destiny* group 38) with the usual Carnival array of amenities and facilities. The ship will have several levels of suites with private balconies and is expected to set a new standard for outside cabins—80 percent, of which 87 percent will have private balconies.

Carnival Spirit will be the first Carnival ship with a wedding chapel. Other highlights are two consecutive decks of bars, lounges and gathering spots, the upper one with a wraparound outdoor promenade and a unusual alternative restaurant topside, with one end bordering the ship's huge smokestack and the other extending out over the upper-most section of the ship's expansive, multideck atrium. She will also feature a single, two-level main restaurant, large conference center, and an extensive Lido Deck casual eatery.

The ship will have a two-level health and fitness facility, along with a large children's area and huge open decks with several pools, one which will be heated and have a sliding glass roof, known as a magradome. This will be ideal for Alaska, where *Carnival Spirit* will spend her maiden summer on 7-day cruises between Vancouver and Seward/Anchorage, after making her debut on a 16-day Panama Canal cruise departing Miami on April 19. The *Carnival Spirit,* the sixteenth ship in the Carnival fleet, will be followed by two sisters: *Carnival Pride,* in late 2001, and *Carnival Legend,* in 2002.

Celebrity Cruises

1050 Caribbean Way, Miami, FL 33132-2096
(305) 539-6000; (800) 646-1456; fax (800) 437-5111
www.celebrity-cruises.com

Type of Ships   Stylish superliners and megaliners.

Type of Cruise   Moderately priced deluxe; ample activity at comfortable pace; emphasis on quality.

Cruise Line's Strengths
- cuisine
- well-designed, spacious ships
- dining room service
- children's program
- value for money

Cruise Line's Shortcomings
- lack of outside, wraparound promenade deck
- excessive promotion of on-board shopping
- boarding procedures
- loud deck music on some ships

Fellow Passengers   Moderately affluent, ages range from late-30s to 60s in high season; ages lower in off-season. Typical passenger is age 48, married, with household income of $50,000+. He/she tends to be educated, experienced traveler, who understands quality, owns a house in relatively affluent suburb, and has college-age children. Fifty percent cruised before, and of this group, 20–30 percent are repeaters with Celebrity. Due to this line's regular departures from northeast United States in summer, a majority of passengers live on the East Coast; the balance come from Midwest and West Coast.

Recommended For   Middle- to upper-middle-income travelers in their 40s and older, whether first-timers or experienced cruisers, who appreciate good service and cuisine and want recreation and entertainment of a large ship at an easy pace. Those with children during the holidays.

Not Recommended For   Small ship devotees; those seeking adventure travel experience.

Cruise Areas and Seasons   Bahamas, Caribbean year-round; Alaska, Bermuda, in summer; Panama Canal, South America, east and west Mediterranean and Europe, spring, winter, and fall.

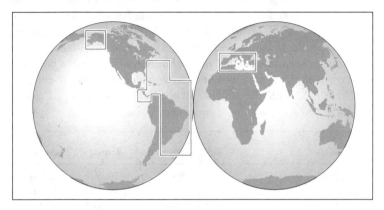

The Line   From its inception in 1989, Celebrity Cruises' objective has been to offer deluxe cruises for experienced travelers at affordable prices. The plan was greeted with skepticism because the new line was being created by the owners of Chandris Cruises, an established company long associated with budget-priced cruises. But in less than three years, Celebrity achieved its goal and did so better than anyone imagined. Almost overnight, word spread that a Celebrity cruise was the best value among cruises, offering as much or more than many higher-priced cruises.

Quickly, too, it became apparent that Celebrity Cruises was more than a new cruise line. It was a completely new product with a new generation of ships designed for 1990s travelers and new standards of service and cuisine in its price category. To their admirers, Celebrity's first vessels define the ideal size of a cruise ship and balanced contemporary design and decor with traditional cruising.

In 1992, Celebrity took up another challenge, teaming with Overseas Shipholding Group, one of the world's largest bulk-shipping companies, to build a new class of cruise ships for the twenty-first century. Once again, Celebrity's ships were winners.

Known as the *Century* series, these ships—*Century, Galaxy,* and *Mercury*—accommodate 26 percent more passengers in 48 percent more space than Celebrity's first generation of ships and have the latest in entertainment and interactive communications systems designed by Sony

Corporation. Even though the new ships are more spacious and deluxe, the mid-level price remains. The addition of these ships enabled Celebrity to expand beyond the Caribbean to Alaska and Europe.

No sooner were these ships in service than Celebrity began building yet another new class of ships, the 91,000-ton *Millennium* group. *Millennium,* the first of the French-built ships, each costing $350 million, made her debut in July 2000, to be followed by *Infinity* in January 2001; *Summit* in August 2001; and the fourth ship in April 2002. Meanwhile, Celebrity merged with Royal Caribbean International in June 1997, but continues to operate as a separate brand. The combination will result in a fleet of 20 ships when all ships of the two lines, some under construction, enter service by 2002. With the addition of the *Millennium* group, Celebrity expects to become a worldwide cruise line.

The Fleet	Built/Renovated	Tonnage	Passengers
Century	1995	70,606	1,750
Galaxy	1996	77,713	1,870
Horizon	1990/98	46,811	1,374
Mercury	1997	74,000	1,870
Zenith	1992/99	47,255	1,374
Millennium	2000	91,000	1,950
Infinity	2001	91,000	1,950
Summit	2001	91,000	1,950
Millennium IV	2002	91,000	1,950

Style   From the handsome, deep blue and white exteriors with their signature stacks to the elegant interiors, Celebrity ships have style, combining the glamour of traditional cruising with a contemporary look. An example: Famous contemporary artists, such as David Hockney and Roy Lichtenstein, are displayed alongside ancient Greek artifacts. On its first ships, introduced when atriums were becoming standard on cruise ships, Celebrity chose instead to make more space for public rooms, giving passengers entertainment and recreation options similar to those on megaliners, but without the glitz. Small lounges, each with its own ambience and entertainment, appeal to a broad range of tastes.

The ships were also designed for passenger comfort and flow. For example, the Rendezvous Lounge amidships provides a place where passengers can mingle before and after dinner, reducing crowds waiting for the restaurant or show lounge to open.

Celebrity distinguished itself from competitors by giving top priority to superior cuisine, hiring as food consultant Michel Roux, an award-winning master French chef who operates a Michelin three-star restaurant, a catering service, and other food enterprises in England. Roux helped design the ships' kitchens, trained its chefs, and works with food suppliers to ensure year-round quality. He's created a sophisticated but unpretentious cuisine for refined palates, emphasized quality over quantity (although quantity is there, too), and established a new standard for competitors. Celebrity has also created a "Gourmet Privileges" program that allows cruisers to dine at gourmet-recommended restaurants in selected cities, either prior to or immediately following their cruise. In 1999, the line added a Customer Service Center (call (800) 529-6918), creating a single point of contact to resolve problems prior to a cruise.

Distinctive Features   Sony communications and entertainment system. Computer room on *Galaxy;* shipboard passenger-service manager. Children's program and specially priced shore excursions. Martini bars; cigar bars. Advance bookings for AquaSpa. Terry robes in all cabins. Alternative restaurant for casual dining. 24-hour room service. Internet cafe and unique restaurant on *Millennium.*

	HIGHEST	LOWEST	AVERAGE
PER DIEM	$643	$200	$402

The above per diems are calculated from the cruise line's non-discounted *cruise only* fares on standard accommodations. Per diems vary by season, by cabin, and by cruise areas.

Rates   All published rates include port fees.

Special Fares and Discounts   Early-bird discounts, called Five Star rates, represent some of cruising's best values. Time-sensitive, capacity-controlled, advance-purchase fares offer up to 50 percent discounts on cruise-only rates (deluxe cabins and suites excluded). Base rates for seven-day cruises offer upgrades for a low fee.

Two itineraries—such as Eastern and Western Caribbean—can be combined at a special rate.

- Third/Fourth Passenger: Yes.
- Children's Fare: Yes.
- Single parents: Seasonally.

- Single Supplement: 150–200 percent, depending on category.
- Guaranteed single rate.

Packages
- Cruise/Air Add-on with transfers: Yes.
- Others: Anniversary, honeymoon, family.
- Pre/Post: Yes.

Past Passengers   The Captain's Club is open to all passengers after their first Celebrity cruise; lifetime membership costs $35 per family. The club offers discounts on cruises, promotional packages, cabin upgrades on specified advance purchases, and other savings. Members receive club baggage tags, pins, newsletter, video of ships or destinations, advance notice on offers, priority check-in and disembarkation, and private cocktail party during the cruise.

The Last Word   Celebrity Cruises has been one of the industry's true success stories. It created the right formula at the right time: classic cruising updated for contemporary lifestyles and available at reasonable prices. Its immediate success resulted from exceeding everyone's expectations and reflected the extensive planning and testing that went into the ships. The line has maintained unusually high standards for its price range. The exception, which we criticized in earlier editions, were *Celebrity*'s shore excursions. We're happy to report that they have improved, particularly in Alaska. There's still room for improvement in the Caribbean. But they do have a redeeming feature: reduced rates for children.

Almost anyone would enjoy a Celebrity cruise, but first-timers with cultivated tastes and experienced cruisers who seek greater comfort and service than is common in this price range will be most appreciative of their value.

CELEBRITY STANDARD FEATURES

Officers   Greek.

Staff   Dining, European; Cabin/International; Cruise/European, American.

Dining Facilities   One main dining room with two seatings for three meals; midnight buffet; indoor/outdoor lido buffet breakfast and lunch. *Century*-class, two-level dining room. Alternative restaurant for casual dining.

Special Diets   Request at time of booking.

Room Service   24-hour menu; butler service in suites.

Dress Code   Casual but not sloppy during the day; informal in evening, with two nights formal or semiformal.

Cabin Amenities   Direct-dial phone; bath with shower; suites with marble bathrooms, Jacuzzi tubs. Terry robes in all cabins. Television with CNN and music channels. Hair dryers on *Century*-class. All *Galaxy, Mercury,* and *Millennium* cabins have mini-bars, safes; upper categories have VCRs.

Electrical Outlets   110 AC.

Wheelchair Access   See Cabin section for each ship.

Recreation and Entertainment   Card room/library, casino, two-deck show lounge, bars/lounges, disco, video game room. Bingo, lotto, horse racing, culinary demonstrations, wine tasting, fashion show, arts and crafts. High-tech entertainment center on *Century*-class.

Sports and Other Activities   Two outside swimming pools; exercise classes, walks, golf putting, dance lessons, Ping-Pong, deck and swimming pool games.

Beauty and Fitness   Barber/beauty salon; health club, gym, and sauna; jogging track on sun deck; elaborate spa with beauty treatments.

Other Facilities   Boutiques, hospital, laundry and dry cleaning services, meeting facilities on *Century*-class. No passenger-operated washers or dryers.

Children's Facilities   Play room; teen disco; babysitters; year-round, age-specific programs with counselors.

Theme Cruises   Occasionally.

Smoking   Not permitted in dining room or theater. Other public rooms have designated areas.

Celebrity Suggested Tipping   Per person per day: cabin steward/butlers, $3.50; dining room waiter, $3.50; busboy, $2. 15 percent service charge added to all beverage checks.

Credit Cards   Cruise/on-board charges: American Express, MasterCard, Visa, Discover.

Horizon	Quality ⑧	Value B
Zenith	Quality ⑧	Value C

Registry: Liberia	Length: 682 feet	Beam: 95 feet
Cabins: 677/687	Draft: 24 feet	Speed: 21.4 knots
Maximum Passengers:	Passenger Decks: 9	Elevators: 7
1,374	Crew: 642/670	Space Ratio: 34.5

The Ships   The *Horizon* launched Celebrity Cruises in 1990, followed the next year by the *Zenith,* her near twin, both German-built. The vessels' similarity aims to facilitate passengers' familiarity and comfort with the fleet and help keep down building costs. The ships incorporate safety features that exceed national and international requirements. These safeguards added about $1 million to the cost of each ship.

Spacious and open, *Horizon*'s ultramodern lines give it an almost futuristic look. Two design teams—from Greece and England—created its distinctive interiors. Original art on walls and displays of ancient artifacts add to the feeling of quality—a characteristic reflected fleetwide.

Public rooms are on four spacious decks. Those on the entertainment deck are connected by a promenade that, in one section, has floor-to-ceiling windows looking out to sea and flooding the area with light.

Building on the success of *Horizon,* Celebrity made a few enhancements on *Zenith,* which was completed in record time using computer-aided design. Michael and Agni Katzourakis, who created interiors for *Horizon* and many other luxury ships, designed the cabins. London-based John McNeece, another veteran of ship interiors, designed the public rooms. In contrast to *Horizon*'s cool sophistication, *Zenith* has a warm, inviting ambience supported by lavish use of fine wood and rich fabrics in soothing colors.

In late 1998, nine public areas of *Horizon* received a $4.5 million makeover to add the signature elements of Celebrity's newer *Century*-class vessels: martini bar, cigar bar, chocolates and coffee cafe, and fancy spa. On Deck 8, the disco was replaced by a new rotunda with alabaster and bronze chandelier and wood flooring inlaid with a marble compass, and Michael's Club, a cigar bar echoing a private English club. Adjoining the club and with similar decor is a new library and card room, available for parties or meetings of up to 70 people. The library offers books plus electronic equipment for audio/visual presentations. Beside high-back chairs are wall units with headsets for listening to audio books and music. The Business Center, also in the library, has two computers and two printers for passenger use.

Under an exclusive agreement with the historic Milan coffeehouse, Pasticceria Confetteria COVA, the Plaza Bar on Deck 5 was transformed to the COVA Café, a coffee and chocolate bar serving cappuccino, espresso, and macchiato; teas; champagne and wine, liqueurs, and chocolates. On Deck 7, the Rendezvous Lounge, the ship's most popular before-dinner area, was enlarged and given an expanded dance floor and redesigned window wall. The lounge has a small bar where a combo plays nightly for dancing and easy listening. Also on Deck 7, in place of the former card room and library are a boutique, art gallery, and Art Deco Martini Bar. The latter serves 26 types of martinis, most costing $5.

In late 1999, *Zenith* was given a similar $9 million upgrading, adding spa treatment rooms, a library and card room, additional buffet lines, and the same signature rooms like a cigar bar and the COVA Café.

Itineraries   See Appendix B.

Cabins   Handsomely fitted in light wood, the spacious, well-designed cabins reflect attention to detail that went into them. For example, all built-in furniture has been finished with rounded corners and edges for safety and durability. Decor is colorful and cheerful; space is generous, with two full-length closets (larger on *Zenith* than on *Horizon*) and plenty of drawers. Bathrooms, large for ships in this price range, have ample counter space. Almost 75 percent are outside cabins. Passengers can dial toll-free numbers in the United States directly from their cabins; fee is $9.50 per minute (most ships charge $15 per minute). All cabins are equipped with the Celebrity Network, enabling you to order meals or wine for dinner, review your account, and request other services directly from your cabin television.

Recent enhancements include in-cabin dining—full breakfast and dinner off the main restaurant menu—and massage. Both are amenities normally found only on luxury ships.

On *Zenith,* lengthening the ninth, tenth, and eleventh decks created space for ten suites and deluxe cabins more than on *Horizon,* and for larger royal suites. Suites have marbled bathrooms with Jacuzzi tubs and excellent showers. Most have a king-size bed and sleeper loveseat. Suites are roomy and have butler service, but unless you can easily afford the higher cost, the true value is in the standard cabins. Stewards can be summoned by phone. Cabins are cleaned and bathroom linens changed twice daily. Missing from these ships are passenger-operated washers and dryers.

In summer and holidays when many children are apt to be aboard *Zenith,* avoid cabins on Europe Deck aft near the playroom—unless some are your own kids.

Horizon *Specifications*   144 inside cabins, 533 outside; 20 suites. Standard dimensions are 172 square feet; 473 with twin (273 convert to doubles); 64 double/king; third/fourth persons available; no singles.

Zenith *Specifications*   146 inside cabins, 541 outside; 21 suites. Standard dimensions are 172 square feet; 462 with twin beds (260 convertible to doubles); 74 double/king; third/fourth persons available; no singles.

Dining   Chef Michel Roux's highly praised cuisine was a major factor in the line's immediate success. Roux's credo is to use the best-quality products and keep menus seasonal. To maintain his high standards, Roux sails on each ship several times a year. Food presentation receives as many accolades as preparation. A typical lunch menu offers a choice of four appetizers, two soups, two salads, two cold and three hot entrees, a selection of vegetables, and four desserts, plus ice creams, sherbet, and cheeses.

Dinners have as many choices plus a special menu by Roux. Every menu includes at least one lean-and-light dish. There is a separate, full week's vegetarian menu. Wines are suggested on menus; prices are moderate to very expensive.

Celebrity eschews themed nights for dinner, common on other lines and often more show than authenticity. Rather, themes are given to the midnight buffets, when chefs are better able to do justice to ethnic cuisine. Another popular nightly feature is the presentation of "Gourmet Bites" in public rooms.

Dining room service is exemplary, and the gracious ambience is enhanced by piano music at lunch and dinner. Although the dining room seats 840, its H layout with raised center lessens the feeling of being in a huge room. Nonetheless, when the ships are full, which they usually are, tables are set close together and the room is crowded. A few tables seat two; most accommodate four, six, or eight.

Alternative casual dinner service is available in the Coral Seas Café on *Horizon* (Windsurf Café on *Zenith*). The limited menu includes an appetizer, soup, salad, pasta, choice of meat, and dessert. Freshly made pizza is also available. A half a million dollars in new equipment, including open rotisseries and large grills, enables diners to see their food being cooked to order.

Breakfast and lunch in the Windsurf Café offer hot and cold selections. When the ships are full, long lines develop, particularly on days at sea when passengers don't need to be up for early excursions. To relieve the problem, waiters at the buffet lines carry your tray to your table. The most informal setting, the outside Grill, serves hamburgers and hot dogs cooked to order.

Service   Particularly in the dining room, service distinguishes Celebrity from other midprice cruise lines. Among their innovations is a passenger service representative, ready to help with problems that crop up and usually found in the main lobby.

Facilities and Entertainment   The ships have lounges for peace or pleasure, with entertainment ranging from a sing-along piano bar and dance music to Broadway-style productions in the two-deck showroom. The popular Rendezvous Lounge, convenient to the dining room and crowded for cocktails, is great for people-watching anytime.

The *Zenith*'s Fleet Bar (America's Cup on the *Horizon*), is among the most attractive rooms afloat. The top-deck, club-like piano bar has a small dance floor and an expanse of windows. It's everyone's favorite spot for drinks and dancing—light and cheerful by day, softly aglow at sunset, and sophisticated at night. The ships also feature champagne and caviar service in the observation lounge and martini bars.

Evening entertainment is balanced between specialty acts (acrobats, comedians, magicians) and big production shows; all are family-appropriate. In the bilevel show lounge, which doubles as a meeting room, most seats have good sight lines. During a week's cruise, two big stage productions are presented. From the upper level, passengers can walk aft to the casino, offering blackjack, roulette, and slot machines, or to the shops. An ATM is nearby, but each transaction costs $5.

Activities and Diversions   Scheduled activities are so numerous that it would be virtually impossible for one person to do them all. But the variety ensures there is enough to suit almost every passenger. Choices range from exercise and dance classes to contests and karaoke. The week's activities might include a singles' party, poolside Island Night, honeymooners' champagne party, a jazz concert, and seminars on cuisine, the stock market, stress management, and estate planning. Art auctions draw mild interest. First-run movies are shown daily in the show lounge, and older films play on cabin television; a week's schedule is provided in your cabin.

Sports and Fitness   Wide, open decks have plenty of space for deck chairs, even when the ships are full, and quiet corners for reading, sunning, or snoozing, but shady areas are limited. At sea, there are swimming pool games, Ping-Pong, trapshooting, darts, shuffleboard, and golf putting. In port, golf, snorkeling, and other sports are offered, depending on location. The ships have large, well-equipped fitness centers and a one-fifth-mile jogging track on their top decks, but no outside, wraparound promenade deck. A full fitness program encompasses four or five activities daily. The cruise price includes use of the facilities, saunas, and exercise classes.

Spa and Beauty   A major addition to *Horizon* in her recent makeover was an AquaSpa on the Sun Deck, replacing the Fantasia bar. Although smaller than those on *Century*-class ships and lacking their thalassotherapy pool, the spa offers many of the same treatments. It houses a beauty salon; six treatment rooms; sauna, fitness, and aerobics area; and separate changing rooms for men and women. All Celebrity ships offer the AquaSpa program designed for the line by Steiner of London, which operates the spa. Services are expensive. *Beware:* Steiner's staff pushes their products aggressively; buy only if you want them. Spas on all Celebrity ships have a barber shop and beauty salon and offer massage, facials, and body treatments for additional fees. Spa programs may be booked in advance.

Children's Facilities   During summer and major holidays, Celebrity ships feature supervised, daily programs for five age groups: Ship Mates (ages 3–6), Celebrity Cadets (ages 7–9), Ensigns (ages 10–12), and Admiral T's (ages 13–15 and 16–17). Younger children enjoy painting, drawing, songs, dances, movies, and other age-appropriate activities. Celebrity Summer Stock lets young thespians participate in theatrical shows with dances and costumes. The Young Mariners' program showcases the operations of the ship and provides the opportunity to meet the captain and learn navigation by the stars.

Junior Olympics offer water volleyball and basketball, golf putting, Ping-Pong, and other games. At meals, kids can join their peers at the Celebrity Breakfast Club and at dinner, order from their own or the regular menu. The program also has family activities and a masquerade parade.

Shore Excursions   In summer, *Horizon* sails weekly from New York to Bermuda, where island tours, glass-bottom boat and snorkel trips, sailing, and nightlife tours are available. Most tours are three hours long and cost $20–70. Children's rates are about 30–40 percent lower. Bermuda is also easy to tour on your own. You can visit historic forts, museums, art galleries, craft shops, duty-free shops, the aquarium, and the lovely botanic gardens. Tennis and golf can be arranged. The National Historic Trust has excellent walking tours. Rental cars are not available, but taxis are. Mopeds or scooters are the most popular modes of transportation.

Century	Quality ⑧	Value B
Galaxy	Quality ⑩	Value B
Mercury	Quality ⑩	Value A

Registry: Liberia	Length: 815/866 feet	Beam: 105/105.62 feet
Cabins: 875/935	Draft: 25/25.5 feet	Speed: 21.5 knots
Maximum Passengers: 1,750/1,870	Passenger Decks: 10	Elevators: 9/10
	Crew: 858/909	Space Ratio: 40

The Ships   Celebrity got a jump on the next millennium with the 1995 debut of the *Century*, first of a new fleet designed for twenty-first-century cruising. The $320 million ship, built at the same German yard as the *Horizon* and *Zenith*, also had the same designers. *Galaxy*, the second of the three sister ships, was launched in 1996, and the third, *Mercury*, in 1997. More than ten design teams worked with *Century*'s builders to achieve a comfortable, inviting, integrated design. With 48 percent more space than their cousin ships but only 26 percent more passengers, this spacious trio has one of cruising's highest passenger-to-space ratios in their category. Public rooms range in style from an elegant wood-paneled bar to a futuristic disco. Sony Corporation of America designed a sophisticated, interactive communications and entertainment system, and the company's music, pictures, and electronic publishing divisions provide products and expertise. Sony Signatures sells the brand's merchandise in *Century*'s boutiques.

Century's focal point is a three-deck Grand Foyer encircled by a staircase and topped with a painted glass dome lit as if by sunlight during the day and as a starlit sky at night. The piazza has marble floors, burled woods, brass trim, suede furniture, and a waterfall with changing fiber-optic images. Nearby are boutiques and Tastings, a wine and coffee piano bar.

The *Galaxy* is essentially *Century*'s twin in layout, but is slightly larger with improvements over her sister ship, including *Galaxy*'s atrium, with a 40-foot-tall video panel projecting changing images and "Sony Wonder," a high-tech center offering free computer classes. The atrium has been improved further on *Mercury* with a spiral staircase leading to the promenade deck, where the port side has the Tastings lounge, and starboard boasts the first floating version of Pasticceria Confetteria COVA, the Milan-based pastry shop famous for its exquisitely packaged chocolates, pastries, and signature coffees.

The *Galaxy*'s best new feature is a retractable glass dome covering a swimming pool and the surrounding deck. The Oasis, one of the ship's most popular areas, has an indoor/outdoor grill and bar that in the evening offers alternative casual dining, introduced fleetwide in 1998.

The ships have multilevel, multipurpose observation lounges that become discos in the evening. One of the ships' two atriums, positioned aft and spanning three decks, opens onto the casino, Rendezvous Lounge, the dining room's foyer, and a champagne bar.

Century-group vessels, like their predecessors, have multimillion-dollar art collections that are virtually contemporary art museums at sea. The focus for *Century* is contemporary masters; for *Galaxy*, the avant garde; and for *Mercury*, recent works by artists who emerged after pop art in the 1960s and 1970s. The collections were assembled by Christina Chandris, the line's curator and fine art advisor, in collaboration with the Marlborough Gallery of New York. The line provides information for a self-guided art tour on all its ships.

Itineraries   See Appendix B.

Cabins   Each deck has its own color scheme, with cabins on each using complementary colors for carpeting and bedspreads. Windows in the spacious cabins are framed in rosewood, conveying luxury and comfort. All *Century* cabins have built-in vanities; generous closet and drawer space; large bathrooms with showers, hair dryers, and terry cloth robes; telephones, safes, and minibars; and radios and televisions. Interactive cabin television enables passengers to order breakfast or room service, book spa appointments, buy shore excursions, gamble (charged to the room), order merchandise from shops, and watch pay-per-view movies (including adult-only selections). Interactive televisions located throughout the ship provide information and entertainment.

Although cabins on *Century* are similar to those on *Zenith* and *Horizon*, they were modified on *Galaxy* to accommodate more features. Some storage space was lost; drawer space, particularly, is inadequate. All have minibars, and upper-category cabins have VCRs. The ships have penthouse and royal suites, and all suites have marble bathrooms, whirlpool tubs, verandas, and butler service.

Century *Specifications*   304 inside cabins, 571 outside; 52 suites, 61 suites and deluxe cabins with verandas. Standard dimensions, 172 square feet; 806 with twin beds, all convertible to doubles; third/fourth persons; no singles. 8 wheelchair-accessible cabins.

Galaxy/Mercury *Specifications*   296 inside cabins, 639 outside; 50 suites and 170 mini-suites with verandas. Standard dimensions, 184 square feet; 877 with twin beds, all convertible to doubles; third/fourth persons; no singles. 8 wheelchair-accessible cabins.

Dining   *Century*'s stylish Grand Restaurant, the main dining room, was Celebrity's first two-tiered dining room; a majestic staircase leads to a colonnaded center aisle reminiscent of the Karnak Temple in Egypt. Each of two galleys prepares food for half of the dining room, thus providing speedier service, consistent temperatures, and freshness. The Orion Restaurant aboard *Galaxy* has a larger second tier to accommodate the ship's greater capacity, and decor is lighter, more contemporary, and less pretentious than on *Century.* The room's focal point is an enormous, backlit ceiling panel of a hemisphere with continents superimposed. The *Mercury*'s Manhattan restaurant, with a backdrop depicting the Big Apple skyline, is completely different from those of its sisters. Food, however, is the same on all three ships and meets the line's high standards.

Other dining areas are the casual Veranda Grill, adjacent to the pool, and Islands Café, with four buffet stations and two bars. The cafe serves an afternoon tea buffet that's in addition to Celebrity's traditional Elegant Tea. *Galaxy*'s Oasis (Palm Springs Grill on *Mercury* and the Sky Bar on *Century*) is a casual dining alternative restaurant. The traditional indoor section, divided into small areas, is very attractive and inviting; the outdoor section has a garden setting, surrounds a small swimming pool, and is covered by a dome (particularly appealing on Alaska itineraries). Among its latest innovations, Celebrity is the first line to offer complimentary pizza delivered to cabins.

Service   European-style service distinguishes Celebrity from other mid-price cruise lines. It's one of the ships' best and most rewarding features.

Facilities and Entertainment   The two-deck Celebrity Theater for Broadway-style revues and cabaret shows has a sloping orchestra section and cantilevered balconies providing unobstructed sight lines. The venue has a revolving stage, the ability to handle multiple backdrops, an orchestra pit with adjustable height, sophisticated lighting, and other special effects.

The Art Deco Crystal Room (The Savoy Nightclub on *Galaxy;* Pavilion on *Mercury*), a low-key night club for evening dancing, has etched-glass panels, luminous alabaster dome ceiling, rotating bronze globe, and chic color scheme of red, black, and gold that recalls 1930s New York. The Savoy employs a jungle motif in its late-night cabaret, and Fortune's Casino has the full roster of games. Rendezvous Square, next to the dining room, is a lively place for cocktails or socializing before and after dinner.

High atop *Century,* Hemisphere (Stratosphere Lounge on the *Galaxy* and Navigator Club on *Mercury*) is an airy, sunlit observation lounge by day transformed into a futuristic "disco under the dome" at night, when window blinds lower automatically, etched-glass room dividers illuminate one by one, and a special table "glows." The hemisphere then rises—cast-

198 Part Two: Cruise Lines and Their Ships

ing light from within—and the dance floor appears. Telescopes are placed around the room's edge for stargazing. On *Galaxy*, the Stratosphere has three sections. The outer one next to the floor-to-ceiling windows is a quiet zone for daytime viewing of scenery and reading. The middle level is ideal for cocktails at sunset, and the innermost can accommodate meetings during the day as pull-down screens separate it from other areas of the lounge. In the evening, the inner room becomes the disco, as sophisticated equipment transforms it and provides a terrific laser light show.

Michael's Club aboard *Century* is an intimate lounge fashioned after a private gentlemen's club, paneled in rich woods and furnished with leather chairs and couches. On *Galaxy*, the room is contemporary in decor and lacks the cachet of the club on *Century*. The clubs (one on *Mercury*, too) have been given over to the cigar smoking fad; craftsmen demonstrate cigar making, an art Columbus learned from the native Indian tribes. The three ships also have martini bars. Flexible walls fold into pillars in a conference center, allowing it also to serve as cinema, meeting room, library, or card room. Keypads in the armchairs can be used for responses to questions or for interactive movies.

Activities and Diversions   Activities are numerous and varied to appeal to a range of passengers and include exercise and dance classes, contests, singles' party, honeymooners' champagne party, and karaoke. Informational seminars also may be scheduled. First-run and adult pay-per-view movies are shown daily on cabin television; a schedule is provided in your cabin. Video game rooms feature Sony equipment.

Sports and Fitness   The spacious ships have 62,000 square feet of open decks and sports, including simulated golf, Ping-Pong, volleyball, basketball, darts, and jogging. The *Century*'s two swimming pools have cylindrical waterfalls and are rimmed with teak benches.

Spa and Beauty   AquaSpa, the ships' health and fitness center, is among the most popular feature on all three ships. It's one of the best-equipped gyms at sea, with a hydropool, saunas, steam rooms, cardiovascular machines, and weight stations. Personal trainers are available to create individualized training programs. Aerobics classes are ongoing. The spa offers a variety of beauty and health treatments. The most unusual is Rasul, based on an Oriental ceremony with a seaweed soap shower, medicinal mud pack, herbal steam bath, and massage.

Not to be missed is the tranquilizing thalassotherapy treatment taken in a 115,000-gallon pool with waterjet massage stations. Spa treatments are expensive; they may be booked in advance of your cruise.

Children's Facilities With every new ship, Celebrity's children's facilities improve. The Fun Factory on *Galaxy* and *Mercury* is a 1,600-square-foot playroom, and there's also a kids' splash pool. As on other Celebrity ships, supervised daily programs are geared to five age groups: Ship Mates (ages 3–6), Celebrity Cadets (ages 7–9), Ensigns (ages 10–12), and Admiral T's (ages 13–15 and 16–17). Junior Olympics offer water volleyball, basketball, Ping-Pong, and other games. Teens have a private lounge with a dance floor, plus a video game room. At meals, kids can join peers at the Celebrity Breakfast Club; at dinner, they order from the regular or a children's menu. The program also offers family activities.

Shore Excursions In summer 1999, when Celebrity launched its European cruises with *Century,* it added "Gourmet Valet," a unique program with *Gourmet* magazine that provides passengers with dining opportunities at *Gourmet*-recommended restaurants in select European ports of call, as well as in the United States and Caribbean, and during the line's pre- and postcruise tours. Passengers can look over the restaurants menus and make reservations through the shore excursion desk.

Postscript Each ship in Celebrity's new class has improved on its predecessor, with the *Mercury* being the best of the trio. Gracious service combines with inviting decor, high-tech wizardry, and glitz to keep the vessels competitive. The sisters will please travelers who prefer large ships for their high-energy entertainment, extensive facilities, state-of-the-art equipment, and elegant restaurants. The vessels' spaciousness is particularly appealing and unusual in their price group.

Millennium	(Preview)	
Registry: Liberia	Length: 964.6 feet	Beam: 105.6 feet
Cabins: 975	Draft: 26.3 feet	Speed: 24 knots
Maximum Passengers: 2,038	Passenger Decks: 11	Elevators: 10
	Crew: 999	Space Ratio: 46.6

The Ship When the *Millennium* debuted in July 2000 in Europe, it launched a new class of ships for Celebrity—somewhat larger than her sister ships and with many of the same facilities, but even more spacious and with contemporary refinements sure to please maturing baby boomers. These include the line's largest spa, a unique specialty restaurant with a dine-in wine cellar, a large boutique of well-known designer fashions, a music library, and extravagantly large suites.

The *Millennium,* the first of four sister ships, launches a new age for Celebrity enabling expansion of its cruise horizons. *Infinity,* to debut in 2001, will offer the line's first cruises to Hawaii. It is also said to be the first cruise ship powered by environmentally friendly gas turbine engines, which reduce exhaust emissions by up to 90 percent and lower noise and vibration levels considerably. That same propulsion system also allows the ship to cruise at 24 knots, thus enabling her to sail to more destinations in shorter time. She is able to transit the Panama Canal. After *Infinity* debuts in January 2001, *Summit* will arrive in late 2001, and a fourth ship in 2002.

Changes in the exterior design—a lean, chiseled profile with a new stack design and hull striping—makes her look like the faster ship that she is. The interiors, created by some of the same design teams that worked on other Celebrity ships, are the line's most sophisticated and elegant to date and have something of a back-to-the-future decor, blending the glamour and grandeur of turn-of-the-century luxury liners with the amenities and state-of-the-art technology that passengers in the new millennium expect. They will also find Celebrity's signature features: museum-quality contemporary art collection throughout the ship, an AquaSpa, COVA Café di Milano, Michael's Club cigar lounge, martini and champagne bars, and cuisine by Michel Roux.

Passengers are introduced to the *Millennium* via the Grand Foyer with a translucent, backlit onyx staircase. Opposite the shore excursion desk is a bank of four glass elevators—the first external-facing ones ever built on a cruise ship—that capture panoramic views as they rise. One passenger, enjoying her elevator ride with Amsterdam views, said, "It was almost as good as a shore excursion." Next to the elevators, a paneled wall of wood and metallic vinyl rises from the entry to the top of the ship through a series of atria.

Itineraries   See Appendix B.

Cabins   Of the 975 cabins, 80 percent are outside, and of those, 74 percent (or 56 percent of the total) have verandas. All cabins have air-conditioning, minibar, safe, telephone with voice mail, shower, hair dryer, multifunction interactive television, and VCR. The standard cabins are furnished with twin beds that are convertible to kings.

All suites have verandas and butler service. The Penthouse suites, measuring 1,432 square feet, plus 1,098 square feet of veranda, have marble floor foyers, separate living and dining rooms; baby grand piano; butler's pantry; master bedroom with generous closets; exercise equipment; dressing room with vanity; marble master bath with twin sinks; whirlpool tub, separate shower, toilet and bidet area; powder room; motorized draperies, lights and security system, two interactive audio/visual entertainment systems with flat-screen television, and a fax machine; veranda with whirlpool, wet bar, and lounges.

Other suites include Royal suites with floor-to-ceiling glass doors; separate living room with dining and sitting area; two entertainment centers with flat-screen TVs and VCRs; walk-in closet; bath with whirlpool tub and stall shower; veranda with whirlpool tub. There are also Celebrity suites, each with themed decor and floor-to-ceiling windows; and Sky suites (including six wheelchair accessible) also with floor-to-ceiling glass doors, sitting area with sofa bed and lounge chair, similar entertainment center, minibar, walk-in closet, and bathroom with whirlpool tub.

Five inside and four outside cabins are wheelchair-accessible and have flat floors, cabin bathroom doorways 35 inches wide. Public elevator doorways are 39 inches wide.

Specifications   639 outside; 296 inside. 2 penthouse suites; 8 Royal suites; 26 Sky suites, plus 6 wheelchair-accessible—all with verandas.

Dining   As on the line's other ships, all of *Millennium*'s dining is under the direction of Michel Roux. The Metropolitan Restaurant, the main dining room, spanning two levels, features bold, geometric motifs in reds, blues, and golds based on French designs from the late 1940s/early 1950s, which the designers describe as "restrained exuberance." At night, panels with dramatic architectural scenes are lowered onto the room's expansive windows with a quintet providing a quiet, elegant accompaniment.

The Olympic, Celebrity's first specialty restaurant, is the ship's showstopper. It takes its name from a rare maritime treasure—a section of the original Edwardian wood-carved paneling from the *Olympic,* the sister ship of the *Titanic.* First discovered in a private English residence, the exquisite French walnut paneling ornamented with gold lead in Louis XVI style, was bought at auction at Sotheby's. Seating only 134 people, the intimate dining room uses an Edwardian theme for its decor, to convey a nostalgic ambience of the elegant golden days of steamship travel. The Olympic restaurant also has the cruise industry's first demonstration galley (an open kitchen where guests can see their meals being prepared). The restaurant has its own menu of gourmet cuisine, and to make the dining experience even more memorable, some dishes are presented and finished table side. One treat is Waldorf pudding—a recreation of an original dessert from the Olympic. There is a piano/violin duo entertaining. Memorabilia from the Olympic includes White Star Line china and the ship's bell, which is on exhibit in the foyer. Adjoining the room is a separate wine cellar, which can be used as private dining room for small groups of eight persons or so. The fee for dining in the Olympic is $12 per person and worth every penny. Michael Roux's cuisine is delicious; the decor and ambience are fabulous; the service impeccable.

The Ocean Café, an indoor/outdoor restaurant designed to resemble a Portuguese outdoor cafe, is the casual dining venue for breakfast and lunch buffet, while the Ocean Grill, with a separate entrance, is an alternative dining venue featuring steak, fish, rotisserie chicken, pizza, and pasta. There is no fee for this by-reservation, partial-waiter-service restaurant.

Service Service in the Metropolitan Restaurant is very attentive and up to Celebrity's high standards. In the buffet-style Ocean Café, we never had to carry our trays; waiters would instantly leap to assist us. In the Olympic, we experienced the highest level of service we ever had on a ship of this category and price range. Orchestrated corps of waiters attended to every detail and dishes were presented to diners in unison.

Facilities and Entertainment The Celebrity Theater is the line's first three-tiered show lounge, seating 900 passengers in a classical-inspired but contemporary setting with a full circular balcony. Designed by premier theater designers, the stage, orchestra pits, and lighting can accommodate most any Broadway-style show at sea. Sightlines are excellent.

The ever-popular Rendezvous Lounge, an elegant cocktail lounge that leads to the dining room, has music for dancing and The Platinum Club, on a balcony overlooking the lounge, there is a martini bar and a champagne bar. Michael's Club, another Celebrity tradition, is a richly appointed cigar lounge with traditional English Georgian decor and natural cherry paneling. Extremes, at the top of the ship overlooking the pool deck, is Celebrity's first sports bar.

Also high above the ship is the Cosmos, a three-level, glass-sheathed observation lounge for panoramic viewing by day and transformed into an early evening cabaret and piano bar with a dance floor and a late night disco. The Fortunes Casino, designed in turn of the nineteenth century Belle Epoch decor, has 228 slot machines and 23 game tables.

Overlooking the Grand Foyer is a card room; Words, a two-story library; and nearby, Notes, a music library that has private listening stations with personal CD players and headsets and offers 1,500 selections of music in varying styles. Online@CelebrityCruises is the line's first Internet cafe, with 18 individual stations, enabling passengers to check their e-mail and other services. The charge is 95 cents per minute. Computer classes are available for $59 an hour.

During Baltic cruises, the ship's entertainment is enhanced with lectures and folkloric presentations from groups at ports of call.

The ship's conference/cinema is designed to hold more than 300 people in auditorium-style seating and offers the latest audiovisual technology including seat voting/interactive system and full control booth. The center also can double as the ship's cinema. Five flexible rooms, each offering television, monitors, computers, teleconferencing, Internet connections, fax machines, and private satellite telephones, are available for meetings and other functions.

At The Emporium, the *Millennium*'s European-styled shopping arcade, which Celebrity claims offers the largest selection of shopping of any ship afloat, has designer boutiques, an art gallery, and signature Celebrity shops.

Sports and Fitness   The Resort Deck with the pool area has the Riviera pool with four freshwater whirlpools and plenty of areas for sunbathing as well as shaded spots. The deck also houses an entertainment area with a canopied stage and bandstand, a teakwood dance floor, and two outdoor bars. Forward is the AquaSpa, Aqua Dome, and the fitness area. The Sunrise Deck overlooks the pool area has a running track and golf simulator, and the Sports Deck has refreshment areas, a full-size basketball court, paddle tennis, volleyball, and quoits, a game similar to horseshoes. The promenade does not completely circle the ship, as the lower level of the Metropolitan Restaurant takes up the aft portion of Promenade Deck. Also, there are no self-service launderettes; particularly missed on long sailings.

Spa and Beauty   The 25,000-square-foot AquaSpa, which Celebrity says is the largest and most extensive spa of any cruise ship, is an impressive facility that includes a fitness area; a gym with upper- and lower-body equipment, 3 benches with bell racks, 2 semi-private matted areas, 2 rowers, 4 exercise bikes, 4 recumbent bikes, 4 upright bikes, 14 treadmills, 6 steppers, aerobics area, indoor hydropool with 2 air beds, 2 whirlpools, sauna, steam, tropical showers, and a cafe serving delicious light breakfast and lunch in a conservatory setting with piped-in New Age music. The AquaSpa has a beauty parlor and 16 treatment rooms, including a dry float room with shower, 8 treatment rooms with shower, 3 dry treatment rooms, one disabled-accessible full-body treatment room, and other specialty rooms. The spa offers Celebrity's water-oriented treatments of Middle Eastern, Asian, and European origin and specialties such as thalassotherapy, hydrotherapy, thermal baths, a new aromatic bath, seawater whirlpool, and first-at-sea treatments such as hot stone therapy. Under the Aqua Dome (a glass roof over the hydropool) passengers can enjoy light, healthy cuisine from a buffet and juice bars as they relax.

Children's Facilities   The Fun Factory for children ages 3–12 offers a variety of activities under a theme of ocean travel and exploration. A puzzle wall, movie room, colorful play area, and separate arts-and-crafts room are available for younger children, whereas the older children have their own broadcast room and video game arcade. The teen's room, next to the Fun Factory, includes a broadcast room with a dance floor, CD jukebox, and a video game room.

Shore Excursion   A good variety of tours is available. For example, on the Russia and the Baltic voyage, a three-hour visit to the Hermitage Museum in St. Petersburg is $52 (with entrance prior to its opening to the general public); and an evening at the ballet at Alexandrinsky Theater is $65. A 13-hour excursion by train to Berlin from Rostock is $295 and includes highlights of East and West Berlin, breakfast snack on the train, buffet lunch at a Berlin hotel restaurant, and dinner snack on the return trip. An Oslo city tour including the Viking Ship and Kon Tiki Museums is $46.

Clipper Cruise Line

7711 Bonhomme Avenue, St. Louis, MO 63105
(314) 727-2929; (800) 325-0010; fax (314) 727-6576
www.clippercruise.com

Type of Ships   Deluxe and first-class small ships.

Type of Cruise   Destination-oriented, light adventure, low-key, intellectually stimulating cruises for nature- and culture-oriented travelers on the byways of the Americas and exotic, off-beat destinations.

Cruise Line's Strengths
- itineraries
- small ship experience
- cuisine
- accompanying naturalists and experts
- maneuverability of small ships

Cruise Line's Shortcomings
- lack of cabin amenities and service on oldest ships
- limited shipboard activities
- shallow-draft older vessels in turbulent waters
- lack of discounts for advance purchase

Fellow Passengers   Relatively affluent, educated, usually professionals, often retired or semiretired and part of a university alumni group. They come from throughout the United States and prefer small ships—often after trying a larger vessel—for the camaraderie, ambience, and small number of passengers.

They are not looking for last-minute specials. They are mature, well-traveled, low-key, and, often, seasoned cruisers and Clipper repeaters. Most are environmentally minded and intellectually curious. Some prefer remote, relatively unknown areas; others seek destinations closer to home with strong cultural and natural history appeal, particularly places where small ships have access but large ships must pass by.

Recommended For   Experienced travelers who like the coziness of a country inn where people are called by name; big-ship refugees turned off by mainstream cruises and seeking quieter, more substantial travel experience; inquisitive minds who travel to learn.

Not Recommended For   Night owls, swingers, party seekers, unsophisticated travelers, people who want to be entertained, those with marginal interest in history and nature; and people who like to wear finery.

Cruise Areas and Seasons   Caribbean, South and Central America, Panama Canal, Antarctica in winter; Europe, eastern seaboard, New England/Canada, Great Lakes, West Coast, Mexico, Alaska in spring, summer, fall; Asia, year-round.

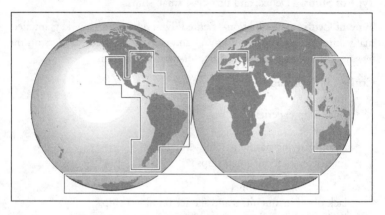

The Line   Clipper Cruise Line was created in 1982 to provide culture- and nature-oriented cruises on small coastal ships along historic byways of the United States and the Caribbean. Central and South America, Antarctica, and Asia were added as ocean-going ships joined the fleet.

The *Nantucket Clipper* and *Yorktown Clipper* are United States built and registered and have American crews. Their shallow drafts and turn-on-a-dime maneuverability enable them to sail into places where larger ships cannot go. Destinations are as diverse as the Alaskan fjords and the Antebellum South.

In 1997, Clipper Cruises was acquired by INTRAV, a long-established, St. Louis–based group tour operator, and acquired another vessel, the 121-passenger *Clipper Adventure*. The ship's ice-hardened hull enables her to sail from the Arctic to Antarctica. The following year, the deluxe, 120-passenger *Clipper Odyssey* joined the fleet. The ship has added a completely new dimension to the cruise line, both in her style, offering more amenities, and in her destinations, sailing in Asia and Australia for the first time.

In 1999, Kuoni, a prominent Swiss tour company, acquired INTRAV and Clipper Cruises.

The Fleet	Built/Renovated	Tonnage	Passengers
Clipper Adventurer	1975/97	4,364	122
Clipper Odyssey	1989	5,200	120
Nantucket Clipper	1984	1,471	102
Yorktown Clipper	1988	2,354	138

Style   Clipper cruises emphasize destinations rather than shipboard fun and games. Their size provides intimacy and sense of place often missing on large ships. The ships cruise mostly during the day, stopping for passengers to tour an island, hike in a rain forest, enjoy a secluded beach, or snorkel in reef-filled waters. Absent but not missed are casinos, discos, staged entertainment, and organized diversions of large ships. The ships' size provides for cordiality resembling that in a country inn. There are passengers enough to ensure an interesting mix. It's easy to meet everyone in the course of a week and for camaraderie to develop effortlessly. The convivial crew members bolsters the friendly atmosphere.

Life aboard is casual, unregimented, and leisurely. The experience is enhanced by naturalists and experts who, in addition to presenting seminars, talk informally with passengers during shore excursions and cocktail hour.

Clipper is proud of its role in providing environmentally responsible travel, saying that ship size and the nature of the cruises have a minimal impact on destinations. A consumer protection plan, pioneered by Clipper, places passenger funds in an escrow account monitored by the Federal Maritime Commission.

Distinctive Features   Historians, naturalists, and other experts travel as guides on ships; Zodiac landing craft aboard. Excellent precruise literature. Consumer protection plan.

	HIGHEST	LOWEST	AVERAGE
PER DIEM	$539	$261	$392

The above per diems are calculated from the cruise line's non-discounted *cruise only* fares on standard accommodations. Per diems vary by season, by cabin, and by cruise areas.

Rates   All published rates include port fees and most shore excursions.

Special Fares and Discounts   Available for special promotions.
- Third Passenger: Specific to each cruise, quoted in brochure.
- Single Supplement: Specific for each category, quoted in brochure; otherwise, 150 percent of brochure rate on other cabins, when available.

Packages
- Air/Sea: For some departures.
- Others: No.
- Pre/Post: Alaska; train tours combined with Sea of Cortés, northern California, and Pacific Northwest; Asia, among others.

Past Passengers   Clipper calls its many repeaters Clipper Alumni. They are the first to receive information on new itineraries and may exceed 70 percent of passengers on such cruises. Alumni are acknowledged on every cruise at the captain's party. Second- to eighth-time cruisers receive gifts (wine, flowers); those beyond get discounts of $200–400 per cabin.

The Last Word   Clipper has been transformed from a coastal cruise line to a worldwide one since obtaining its new ships. Nonetheless, it continues to attract people who recoil at the notion of today's megaships. Yet, anyone who does not fit into Clipper's country-club, somewhat academic atmosphere could quickly feel out of place. To compare Clipper's small ship cruise experience with that of large ships is comparing apples to oranges. In terms of the published prices, however, they are comparable. The difference is that Clipper does not discount its prices, even for early-bird bookings—a practice almost standard elsewhere. Prices, particularly for cruises on the two older ships, seem high given their lack of some shipboard services and facilities—no swimming pool, elevator, beauty shop, laundry room or laundry service, or cabin telephone and television. Clipper's two latest acquisitions with their amenities come closer to the mark. Precruise information sent by Clipper is thorough, some papers are the length of a book. These excellent reference materials reflect the line's commitment to making its cruises stimulating, enriching, and memorable.

CLIPPER STANDARD FEATURES

Officers   American; *Clipper Adventurer*, European; *Clipper Odyssey*, Australian and European.

Staff   *Nantucket, Yorktown*, dining, cabin/American; *Adventurer, Odyssey*, dining, cabin/Filipino; Cruise/American, all ships.

Dining Facilities   Single-seating dining room for three meals with open seating, buffet breakfast and lunch in lounge, and occasional lunch buffet on sun deck or picnic on shore. Self-service juice, coffee, and tea in lounge.

Special Diets   Accommodated with advance notice.

Room Service   None.

Dress Code   Casual but smart; coat and tie recommended for special occasions or going to fashionable restaurants in ports of call.

Cabin Amenities   Radio, but no television or phones; bathrooms with showers; no other amenities. *Odyssey*, television for movies only, safe, minibar, music system; bathroom with small tub and shower. *Adventurer, Odyssey*, hair dryer.

Electrical Outlets   110 AC, except *Adventurer;* 220 AC.

Wheelchair Access   One cabin and elevator, on *Odyssey* only.

Recreation and Entertainment   Seminars by naturalists, historians and other experts; movies; occasional local entertainers. *Adventurer, Odyssey*, two lounges, bars, library.

Sports and Other Activities   Swimming, snorkeling, beach walks, wilderness and rain forest hiking. Swimming pool on *Odyssey* only.

Beauty and Fitness   *Nantucket, Yorktown*, no beauty/barber shop; services generally available in port.

Other Facilities   *Adventurer, Odyssey*, infirmary with doctor, gift shop, laundry service. *Nantucket, Yorktown*, no laundry service; no doctor aboard except Costa Rica, Sea of Cortés, and Orinoco cruises.

Children's Facilities   None.

Theme Cruises   None.

Smoking   No smoking allowed in any interior areas, including cabins, at any time. Smoking permitted only on outside decks.

Clipper Suggested Tipping   Tips pooled. $9 per passenger per day, deposited in a box at cruise's end. No service charge added to wine or bar bill.

Credit Cards   For cruise payment: American Express, Diner's Club, Discover, MasterCard, Visa; for on-board charges: American Express, MasterCard, Visa.

Nantucket Clipper	Quality ⑤	Value C
Yorktown Clipper	Quality ⑤	Value C

Registry: United States	Length: 207/257 feet	Beam: 37/43 feet
Cabins: 51/69	Draft: 8 feet	Speed: 9.5 knots
Maximum Passengers:	Passenger Decks: 3/4	Elevators: None
102/138	Crew: 32/40	Space Ratio: NA

The Ships   United States–built and flying the American flag, the *Nantucket Clipper* and the slightly larger *Yorktown Clipper* are almost identical. With their shallow drafts, the ships glide into small places as easily as they tie up in small ports, sailboat-filled harbors, and coves.

The *Nantucket Clipper* has three passenger decks and the *Yorktown Clipper* four decks, including a spacious top sun deck aft of the bridge—a comfortable place for watching the passing scene. Cabins and lounges are decorated with quality furnishings. No glitter, no glitz.

Both ships have a single forward observation lounge and bar on the center deck that serves as a social center. Three sides of the cheerful room have large windows trimmed with light wood. Textured fabric and neutral colors give the lounge a warm, contemporary look. During cruises, the room has the air of a club, with passengers conversing, reading, writing postcards, or simply watching scenery. It is also the scene for lectures, early breakfast buffet, afternoon cookies, and hors d'oeuvres at cocktail time.

Itineraries   See Appendix B.

Cabins   All six categories of cabins are outside, and all but the lowest category have picture windows. Cabins on the promenade deck open onto an outdoor, wraparound deck (as on river steamboats). Although these have an airy feel, some passengers might prefer cabins that open onto a central corridor. On the *Yorktown,* four cabins on the sun deck are the largest and most private.

The cabins are small but adequate, well lighted, offer ample storage, and appear more spacious because of a large wall mirror. Beds are parallel or at right angles; the latter provides more floor space. The furnishings have a clean, modern look, with pastel curtains and bedcovers, closets and dressers in light wood, and landscape paintings on the wall. The bathrooms have showers only and are small, with limited shelf space. In a bid to let passengers get away from it all, cabins have neither telephones nor televisions. Radios, however, provide wake-up calls, ship information, and music. Some cabins get noise from the hydraulic lift that raises and lowers the gangplank in port. Also, there is no convenient place to dry wet clothes.

There is no room service. Laundry, beauty shop, and barber shop are available in port. The ships carry no nurses or doctors. However, the vessels are almost always near shore in case of medical emergency. Lack of medical staff and the difficulty of walking on steep gangways make the ships unsuitable for physically disabled persons.

Specifications   All outside cabins; no suites. Standard dimensions range from 122–139 square feet on *Yorktown Clipper;* 106–123 square feet on *Nantucket Clipper.* All have two lower beds, some with pull-down third bunk; no singles. None are wheelchair-accessible.

Dining   The dining room, on the lower deck, has large windows and pleasant decor reflecting quality. Passengers dine at a single, open seating at round or square marble-topped tables, which are covered with cloths for dinner. The food is American cuisine overseen by a chef trained at either the prestigious Culinary Institute of America or at Johnson and Wales. Meals features excellent soups, good-quality beef, fresh seafood, vegetables, and fruit. They're presented in a straightforward manner by the young, cheerful staff. Selections are not as extensive as on larger ships—dinner menus offer two entrees—but all menus feature a regional specialty. A small but moderately priced selection of wines is available.

An early light breakfast is served in the lounge; lunch buffets are offered on the sun deck, weather permitting. Snacks, including fresh fruit, are available throughout the day. In the afternoon, freshly baked chocolate chip cookies are set out in the lounge, welcomed by passengers who have gathered in anticipation. The bar is open from 11 a.m. to midnight.

Service   The clean-cut staff of young American men and women are cheerful, attentive, friendly, and unfailingly polite. Most are college students from the U.S. heartland, where Clipper is based, who sign on for a year of employment. They take care of the restaurant, bar, and cabins, working 12 hours a day, 6 days a week, and smiling through it all.

Facilities and Entertainment   Daily seminars by naturalists, historians, or other experts on places visited on the cruise precede follow-up discussions after the visits. The naturalist also acts as guide for nature walks, bird-watching, and study of the local environment. Afternoons at sea, a movie plays in the dining room.

A local folklorist or other interesting character may come on board for a lecture, discussion, or entertainment. The cruise director briefs passengers daily about upcoming adventures. Evenings in port enable passengers to explore local night life. Otherwise, passengers gather in the lounge after dinner to visit, or they retire to the dining room to watch videos. Most are in their cabins by 10 p.m.

Activities and Diversions Deck space is adequate for a destination-oriented ship, and most people use it to sunbathe, read, or watch the scenery—often through binoculars. Activity centers around the destination, whether it's a tour of a historic town, a golf game, or a forest hike. There are no organized fun and games.

Sports and Fitness Walkers can circumnavigate the promenade deck, and when the ships tie up at night, as they often do, passengers walk into town. Depending on itinerary and weather, snorkeling directly from the ship is available, and scuba diving, windsurfing, deep-sea fishing, golf, or tennis can be arranged. The ships have no pools, whirlpools, exercise equipment, or fitness centers.

Shore Excursions Cruises usually call at ports seldom visited by other ships and often tie up at small, out-of-the-way marinas and yacht harbors, enabling passengers to explore remote islands and coastlines on foot. Where *Nantucket Clipper* cannot dock, passengers go ashore by Zodiac boat; *Yorktown Clipper* has dib launches. Generally, such excursions are included in the cruise price. In urban areas, ships often tie up within walking distance of cultural attractions and offer above-average tours at reasonable costs.

Postscript Although the adventures are light and seldom far from civilization, many itineraries entail walking, wet landings, and climbing in and out of Zodiac boats in remote areas. Some involve traversing open sea, and with the ships' shallow drafts, passengers may have a bumpy ride for several hours. Because the ships do not carry doctors and do not have elevators, they are not able to handle passengers with health or physical limitations.

Clipper Adventurer	Quality ❽	Value C
Registry: Bahamas	Length: 330 feet	Beam: 53.5 feet
Cabins: 61	Draft: 16 feet	Speed: 14 knots
Maximum Passengers:	Passenger Decks: 4	Elevators: None
122	Crew: 122	Space Ratio: NA

The Ship The *Clipper Adventurer* is the former *Alla Tarasova*, a Russian expedition vessel with an A-1 Super Ice-class rating. Her itinerary is designed by Hasse Nilsson, the widely known former master of the *Linblad Explorer* and the first captain to take passengers through the Northwest Passage.

Built in 1975 in Yugoslavia, the ship received a $15 million renovation before joining Clipper's fleet in 1998. As a result, she is one of the most comfortable and stylish expedition ships afloat, designed to be more elegant than Clipper's older craft while retaining the feeling of an adventure ship. The renovations added a window-lined observation lounge, library/card room and bar, small gym, beauty salon, covered promenade, and observation platform directly below the bridge. To ensure comfort even further, stabilizers were added in 1998. The ship's public rooms are mahogany-paneled and the furnishings upholstered in handsome colors of deep blue, red, and aquamarine.

The handsome vessel with its refined decor and upgraded amenities helps the line merge the more upscale passengers of INTRAV with Clipper's eclectic mix. The ship is well suited for exploration with her ice-class hull, great maneuverability, and shallow draft that enable her to sail near shorelines, in polar waters, or along scenic riverbanks.

Itineraries   See Appendix B.

Cabins   The ship has 61 all-new, all-outside cabins averaging 130 square feet, including four suites. All have large windows or portholes. There are seven categories. Cabins are designed to be comfortable rather than posh. Twin lower beds are in an L shape or parallel (no queens). Bathrooms are tiled, with showers. Closet and storage space is ample. The suites on Boat Deck have separate seating areas with desks and chairs.

Dining   A window-lined dining room accommodates all passengers at one leisurely seating at tables for two to seven. American and regional dishes are prepared by trained chefs. Service is provided by a Filipino staff who are as cheerful and pleasant as they are attentive and accommodating.

Activities and Diversions   The main lounge and bar of the cozy, club-like ship is the center for informal talks by staff naturalists, historians, and other specialists. Also in the lounge are breakfast and lunch buffets, before-dinner hors d'oeuvres, and musical performances. The Clipper Club lounge near the dining room is the favorite spot for cocktails. One level up, the small library offers books on wildlife and literature. The quiet retreat, furnished with silk-covered armchairs, doubles as a card room, with board games and puzzles.

One of the ship's best features is a large observation platform directly below the bridge. It's ideal for viewing wildlife or scenery. (Also, the captain maintains a 24-hour open bridge.) Promenades on two decks provide additional viewing venues. The wide Boat Deck promenade has a partially covered area aft and provides teak benches perfect for scene-watching or conversation. The Promenade Deck has a wide, enclosed deck, allowing exercise out of the elements.

Other facilities and amenities include a small gym, beauty shop, a full-time physician, gift shop, and laundry service—the first time such amenities have been available on a Clipper ship. *Adventurer* is equipped with ten Zodiac landing craft for exploring hard-to-reach places.

Clipper Odyssey	Quality ⑨	Value B
Registry: Bahamas	Length: 340 feet	Beam: 51 feet
Cabins: 60	Draft: 14 feet	Speed: 15 knots
Maximum Passengers:	Passenger Decks: 5	Elevators: 1
120	Crew: 15	Space Ratio: 83

The Ship   In September 1998, less than seven months after launching the *Clipper Adventurer,* the cruise line acquired a fourth ship, the 120-passenger deluxe vessel *Oceanic Odyssey,* from Spice Islands Cruises. When Clipper took over operations in November 1999, the ship was renamed the *Clipper Odyssey.*

Designed in Holland and constructed in 1989 by Japanese craftsmen, the ship is beautifully built with quality furnishings and the detail of a deluxe yacht with an intimate and casual ambience. The decor is warm and comfortable with traces of its Japanese origins in the pictures and other art.

The center of activity is the main lounge and bar on deck four, which is used for most activities, whether for lectures, socializing, or waiting for the warm chocolate chips cookies served in the afternoon. At cocktail time, when most passengers gather in the lounge, the dining staff lays out generous hot and cold hors d'oeuvres. Usually, the expedition staff gives a briefing on the day's activity ashore and preparations for the following day. After dinner, passengers usually return to the lounge for a lecture by one of the expert guides accompanying the cruise. Adjacent to the lounge is a library with good collections of reference books for each of the areas the ship visits.

One deck up, the Day Lounge, when not in use for light meals, becomes the card and reading room. Here, a self-service counter has coffee, tea, and juices around the clock. Directly outside is an outdoor deck and swimming pool. In good weather, the outdoor deck is used for informal parties. All five passenger decks are served by a central elevator.

Itineraries   See Appendix B.

Cabins   Accommodations, spread over four decks, are spacious, all-outside cabins with sitting areas. All standard cabins are the same size—approximately 180 square feet—and have large windows, except for a few on the lower deck, which have portholes. Each cabin provides a high degree of comfort, with television for videos and movies, a safe, mini-fridge, music system, and hair dryer—amenities lacking from Clipper's older ships. Bathrooms have a small, Japanese-style tub and shower. The rooms are furnished with a blonde wood, built-in dresser/desk with shallow drawers, a refrigerator, and two small hanging closets, plus bedside night tables with drawers. Beds can be configured as twin or queen size. One cabin is designed for disabled travelers. The nine suites on the uppermost accommodations deck have verandas. *Instant News* from London (faxed news) is available daily.

Specifications   60 outside cabins; 9 suites with verandas. Standard dimensions, 180 square feet. All have two lower twin or queen beds; no singles. One wheelchair-accessible.

Dining   The attractive Main Dining Room offers open, single seating at set hours for three meals and serves high-quality, well-prepared cuisine with regional accents using fresh ingredients, often bought from local markets on the ship's route. As with other Clipper ships, the chef is a graduate of the Culinary Institute of America or another reputable culinary school.

Breakfast in the dining room is a buffet feast of fruits, cereals, breads, eggs cooked to order, and a specialty of the day. Lunch and dinner menus are varied and creative and offer a choice of two soups, fish, chicken, meat, or vegetarian entree, and dessert. Dinner has similar selections with even more choices. In addition, there is a daily healthy menu. Passengers may order half-portions of any course. A wine is suggested for each course of dinner; wine is available by the glass for an additional charge. Continental breakfast and light lunch are also served indoors in the sunny Day Lounge or poolside. Dress is casual throughout the day and only slightly more fashionable in the evening.

Service   The service rendered by the ship's Filipino staff in the dining room, bar, decks, and cabins ranks at the top of the list of the ship's best features and is the equal of some of the most luxurious ships afloat. They are smiling, pleasant, thoughtful, hardworking, and gracious at every hour of the day. Dining room waiters make a point of learning passengers' names from the first day, and even though passengers sit where they choose, the waiters seem to remember their individual likes and needs.

Facilities   The ship has a swimming pool and Jacuzzi; a small, well-stocked reading room, and a boutique. The ship's band plays dance music in the main lounge. The ship's INMARSAT telecommunications system permits worldwide, 24-hour telephone and fax communication, and there is a computer station for passengers to send e-mail.

Sport, Fitness, and Beauty   The small gym on the Bridge Deck has a treadmill, stairmaster, bicycle, and free weights. There is a jogging track on the top deck. *Odyssey* has ample teak-covered deck space and the broad upper deck for sunbathing.

At the beginning of the cruise, passengers are issued snorkel gear to keep for their entire trip. Depending on the area of the cruise, the expedition staff takes passengers in Zodiac landing craft on shore excursions in remote areas and for swimming and snorkeling. The staff will arrange scuba diving where it is available for an additional charge.

The tiny hair salon on deck three has two chairs; the attendant, who also manages the ship's tiny boutique, does simple wash and set or blow dry. Next door is the small doctor's clinic staffed by a registered physician.

Postscript   Acquisition of *Clipper Odyssey* is part of the line's ambitious five-year growth plan, reflecting management's confidence in the future of small ships, despite ever-larger, entertainment-driven ships entering the market. Clipper, perceiving a demographic shift in its favor, views itself as the antidote to big-ship cruising and says affluent, discerning travelers want an intimate, substantive cruise experience. We agree.

Club Med

75 Valencia Avenue, Coral Gables, FL 33134
(800) CLUB MED; (800) 258-2633; fax (305) 443-0562
www.clubmed.com

Type of Ship   One of the world's largest cruise ships with sails.

Type of Cruise   Casual, sports-oriented, all-inclusive vacations with easy lifestyle for active, upscale vacationers.

Cruise Line's Strengths
- cabins
- unlimited water sports
- itineraries
- carefree, international ambience

Cruise Line's Shortcomings
- language and cultural collisions
- cuisine
- entertainment
- limited use of sails

Fellow Passengers   *Club Med 2* attracts a range of passengers that changes with the cruise, season, and location. Typically, passengers are 30–60 years old. The majority are couples. Forty percent have been on other cruises, 20 percent are Club Med repeaters, and 20 percent are first-timers who chose Club Med because they view its cruises as more active and adventurous than standard offerings, which they shun.

The *Club Med 2* sails in the Caribbean from January through March, when approximately 15 percent of passengers are American, but this number can be as low as 10 percent. Summer sailings in the Mediterranean have more Americans, sometimes as high as 50 percent. The Americans are mostly active, urban professionals from Northeast cities, ages 27–50. They are not shopping for the lowest price. They weekend in the Hamptons, dine at little restaurants, and belong to tennis or squash clubs. They are more interested in water sports and visiting less traveled islands than in lavish eating or shopping.

Recommended For Francophiles and those at ease with French ambience, sailing buffs but not hard-core sailors, Club Med village alumni or those who like the concept but want more luxury, and those who want to improve their French.

Not Recommended For Anyone uncomfortable in a French milieu or who prefers American atmosphere and large ships.

Cruise Areas and Seasons Seven days, Caribbean in winter, Mediterranean in summer; transatlantic cruises, spring and fall.

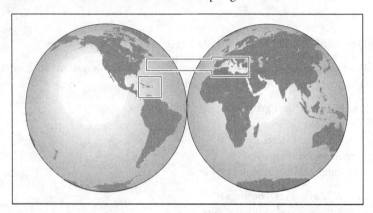

The Line In 1990, after two decades of spreading the gospel of all-inclusive resort vacations and their easy lifestyle, Club Med applied its formula to the world's largest sailboats equipped as cruise ships. (In 1997, *Club Med 1* was purchased by Windstar Cruises and renamed *Wind Surf.*)

As long as two football fields and rigged with five 164-foot masts and seven computer-monitored sails, the ship marries twentieth-century technology to yesteryear's seafaring. She sails like a dream, with no listing or heeling—and no officers on deck. They're on the bridge monitoring computers.

The Fleet	Built/Renovated	Tonnage	Passengers
Club Med 2	1992	14,000	392

Style Cruises are basically a French product, an all-inclusive vacation with the same informal, carefree ambience of Club Med villages, but in deluxe surroundings with cruise ship amenities. Unique to both operations are GOs—*gentils organisateurs*—the social hosts and hostesses who keep the action and smiles going day and night. Most GOs are French, other

Europeans or Americans who speak very good French. Their first task on your boarding is to familiarize you with the ship and answer questions. They organize shipboard activities and can usually give valuable tips on the best bars and restaurants in ports of call.

Spacious rooms, understated nautical decor, and easy camaraderie with staff create a relaxed ambience that makes it easy to imagine you're on your own yacht, a feeling Club Med encourages. But promotional brochures notwithstanding, there are no yachts for 390 people. People who normally go to resorts or on scuba diving trips, or who would like a leisurely holiday in the sun, get just about all this—sports, destinations, sun, relaxation, and French ambience—in one package when they sail with Club Med.

The dress code is as varied as the passengers. At the two gala dinners during a week's cruise, guests who prefer beaded dresses and tuxedos wear them; others may wear ethnic fashions, including turbans and caftans. In general, days are casual and nights are casual chic.

Club Med 2 has the same design as the Windstar vessel, but it's a third larger and carries more than twice as many passengers. Those who have experienced both recognize that even among small ships, size makes a big difference. The Club Med ship has an open, nautical feeling and is glitz-free, but with more than 300 passengers, it loses much of the intimacy that makes the smaller version so appealing.

Distinctive Features   All outside cabins; sports platform at the stern becomes private marina. Mauritian stewards.

	HIGHEST	LOWEST	AVERAGE
PER DIEM	$385	$130	$219

The above per diems are calculated from the cruise line's non-discounted *cruise only* fares on standard accommodations. Per diems vary by season, by cabin, and by cruise areas.

Rates   Tips, wine and beer at lunch and dinner, and most water sports are included in the cruise fare; port charges are additional.

Special Fares and Discounts   Club Med occasionally offers specially priced cruises, but it does not discount prices.
- Single Supplement: 130 percent additional, subject to availability.

Packages
- Air/Sea: Yes.
- Others: Honeymoon; golf; cruise/Club Med village combinations.
- Pre/Post: Yes.

Past Passengers   No club or promotions.

The Last Word   Most passengers like the informality and sociability of the GO concept, garnering a deeper sense of involvement in the cruise and memories of people as much as places. The camaraderie also encourages some reluctant passengers to participate more in activities. On the other hand, the constant interaction between the young and bouncy GOs and passengers creates a summer camp atmosphere that is not for everyone and can easily annoy some.

The GO team is bilingual in English and French, but French is the ship's primary language. That could be a problem for English speakers who aren't up to the language challenge, don't like to depend on gestures to communicate with fellow travelers, or who might feel the balance is unequal between English and French spoken during shows, activities, and excursions.

The language problem can vary with the staff—some are more careful to translate during shows and activities. And the amount of English—or any language—spoken during a voyage may depend on the number of non–French-speaking guests on that cruise.

Club Med says it's addressing the language issue, but its attitude basically is: This is a French-European product, and passengers should be aware of that fact before they come aboard. The cruise is, after all, an experience where Americans might lunch with people from Normandy, snorkel with Italians, and have cocktails with Austrians. That's meant to be part of the attraction. Whether this taste of Europe works for you depends on you and, perhaps, the passengers from the other side of the Atlantic. But when half the passengers are middle-aged French whom one person described as "solid, *vin ordinaire* bourgeoisie," and the other half are an equally unsophisticated Americans and other nationals, the twain, alas, seem never to meet. A them-versus-us situation can develop. Obviously, that isn't what Club Med intended.

If you go with realistic expectations and not romanticized illusions, you probably will have a wonderful time, and, indeed, it might be like being on your own yacht.

CLUB MED STANDARD FEATURES

Officers French and International.

Staff Dining/French, Mauritian; Cabin/Filipino, Mauritian; Cruise/ French, other European GOs (*gentils organisateurs*).

Dining Facilities Two ocean-viewing dining rooms with single seating, unassigned at dinner. One à la carte; one buffet for breakfast, lunch, and dinner. Open-air cafe and one bar serves continental breakfast; another bar serves afternoon tea with French pastries.

Special Diets Request at time of booking.

Room Service 24-hour with limited menu.

Dress Code Relaxed, casual attire, such as Bermuda shorts, deck shoes, polo shirt, and blazer; formal gala night dinner.

Cabin Amenities Bath with shower, television with remote control, radio, minibar, safe, ship-to-shore telephone, terry cloth robes, hair dryer.

Electrical Outlets 110/220 AC.

Wheelchair Access None.

Recreation and Entertainment Three bars and lounges, nightclub, casino, piano bar, disco.

Sports and Other Activities Two swimming pools; aerobics and exercise classes daily; water sports platform with snorkeling, windsurfing, and water skiing. Boats for diving excursions for certified divers.

Beauty and Fitness Beauty salon, fitness center, sauna, tanning salon, spa treatments, whirlpools.

Other Facilities Boutique, observation deck, laundry, no dry cleaning service.

Children's Facilities Younger than age 12 not accepted; no youth programs.

Theme Cruises Golf.

Smoking Nonsmoking sections in restaurants; smoking allowed in public areas.

Club Med Suggested Tipping Tips not permitted.

Credit Cards For cruise payment and on-board charges: American Express, MasterCard, Visa.

Club Med 2	Quality ❷	Value B
Registry: Bahamas	Length: 613 feet	Beam: 66 feet
Cabins: 191	Draft: 16 feet	Speed: 15 knots
Maximum Passengers:	Passenger Decks: 6	Elevators: 2
392	Crew: 181	Space Ratio: 36

The Ship   Under combined sail and diesel power, rigged with computer-monitored sails, this ship cuts quite a picture on the water. Shallow drafts allow her to enter small harbors and protected waters where larger ships cannot go.

Built at a French shipyard by French naval architects, the Club Med vessel, like Windstar vessels, has American computers that limit heeling to less than two degrees. Electric engines provide quiet auxiliary power. Handling appears to be effortless.

The ship is spacious and has eight Burmese teak decks. Interiors by the well-known European designer Albert Pinto evoke understated luxury through meticulous craftsmanship and the use of fine mahogany, quality fabrics, and leather, reminiscent of classic sailing ships. Crisp, simple, white and blue decor predominates, with brass, chrome, glass, and mirror accents.

Even inside, the ship is open to her surroundings. A glass roof covers half the main lounge, bathing the area in light. Walls of windows, plus open-air sections in two aft bars, afford refreshing sea and shore views. The light and openness add a special touch.

Language problems aside, the cruises' most appealing features are their international atmosphere and the extras, such as wine with lunch and dinner and a lobster bake on the beach. These plus water sports and gratuities are covered in the cost.

In the Caribbean, the ship visits a port each day and sails at night. Unfortunately, passengers get very little opportunity to experience the pleasure of sailing under canvas. They disembark daily for shore excursions, snorkeling and sunbathing, or sight-seeing.

Itineraries   See Appendix B.

Cabins   Large, comfortable, and handsomely decorated in navy blue and white with hand-rubbed mahogany cabinetwork, all cabins are on the outside and have twin portholes. They're fitted with twin or queen-size beds, a mahogany desk, large mirrors, ample closets, closed-circuit television, radio, safe, refrigerator, minibar, and satellite telephone, which is also used to order room service. The teak-floored baths have showers, hair dryers, and fluffy bathrobes.

Six large, top-deck suites are next to the captain's quarters. They have sitting areas and large baths with circular showers, toiletries, hair dryers, and color-coded towels for each occupant.

The television has four channels—one in French, one in English, one giving information on the day's port, and one in whatever language predominates among passengers. Movie selections are modest.

Guests are welcomed aboard with a fruit basket in their cabin, along with complimentary champagne, fresh flowers, and bottled water. (*Note:* Only the first bottle of water is free.) Unlike at Club Med villages, breakfast can be enjoyed in your room. There is 24-hour room service, and laundry service is available for an extra charge. Cabins and public areas are very quiet.

The choice cabins are on D (Desirade) Deck; those below on C (Caraibes) share the deck with the water sports platform. The rooms with three and four bunks are on B (Borneo) Deck.

Specifications 191 outside cabins; 6 suites; 124 twin (31 kings, 55 convertible to doubles); 23 cabins accommodate 3 passengers; 4 have 4 beds. Standard dimensions are 188 square feet. No singles.

Dining Dinner is a serious affair lasting up to three hours. The ship has two ocean-view dining rooms, each with a different menu. Le Grand Bleu, an open-air veranda cafe on the top deck, serves casual breakfast, luncheon buffets, and theme dinners featuring cuisines from around the world. Deauville is a more intimate, formal dining room. The à la carte menu offers several choices for each course (Club Med villages have only buffets).

Both restaurants have waiters and unreserved, unassigned seating at tables for two or more, with continuous service during dining hours. Officers and staff dine with passengers. Americans, unaccustomed to lengthy meals, say they would prefer the option of a more casual restaurant for dinner.

French cuisine is featured. The sometimes uninspired food is not what one might expect of a deluxe French ship. On the other hand, Club Med villages have never been gourmet havens.

Buffets include freshly baked breads and croissants. Salads and entrees at lunch—fish, veal, pasta, curries—are good but not gourmet. European touches include cheese carts and café au lait.

Complimentary wine from Club Med's private label, beer, and bottled water accompany lunch and dinner. Selections from an extensive wine list cost extra. Most seven-night Caribbean itineraries offer a lobster beach picnic.

Although continental breakfast from room service costs nothing extra, room-service lunch, dinner, and snacks are pricey. The food quality is not always comparable to that served in the dining rooms. Tea with French pastries is served every afternoon with music in the navy-and-white-checked piano bar.

Service   The Club Med imprint is obvious. Officers are French and the crew, Filipino. The staff, dressed in impeccable white shirts, shorts, and socks, handle dining and hotel duties and earn praise for their friendly, professional service. The energetic, tanned, attractive GOs are managed by the Chef du Village, the cruise director. They're easily recognized by their striped French sailor blouses. These cheery camp counselors do it all: work the reception desk, run activities, teach sports, and entertain. During their off hours, they hang out with passengers.

Facilities and Entertainment   The Topkapi Piano Bar, one of five bars, is the most popular for afternoon tea or after-dinner drinks (prices are higher than average). Happily, waiters do not push to sell drinks, as occurs on many other ships.

A small but fully equipped casino with English female croupiers offers roulette, blackjack, and slot machines. Blackjack and roulette are taught in the afternoon.

A lounge that doubles as a theater has a bar, stage, bandstand, and dance floor. A different show or program is presented here each evening by GOs—some more entertaining than others and all amateur. Because passengers become friends with GOs during the cruise, watching them dance and mouth the words to taped songs can be fun, but you may feel like the audience during parents' weekend at a junior college, one person said. Some passengers believe that luxury prices they paid merit more professional entertainers.

Party-seekers make their way to the chrome and glass disco with its lighted dance floor, or the Fantasia nightclub, hidden on the bottom deck next to the engine room behind an unmarked door. Perhaps because of its location, the only evening it seems to be crowded is for the weekly GO show. At least one night will be Carnival Night in the Caribbean. That's the time to unpack your costumes or your ingenuity, or both. You don't have to participate, but most passengers do and seem to enjoy it.

Activities and Diversions   Sight-seeing, sports, Scrabble, bridge, Trivial Pursuit, dance contests, and karaoke are among organized daytime diversions. A small, multilanguage library and card tables with leather chairs are in a lounge. The boutique sells cruise wear, perfumes, accessories from European fashion names, and Club Med gear.

Sports, Fitness, and Beauty   The Nautical Hall is a teak sports platform at the stern that unfolds into the sea to become a marina when the ship is anchored. The vessel carries sailboards, sailboats, snorkel fins, and masks and provides free lessons in water skiing, windsurfing, sailing, and snorkeling. Two ski boats with scuba equipment take certified divers on diving trips. The scuba program is one of the line's best values.

The less ambitious can retire to chaise longues around the two outdoor swimming pools—one fresh, one saltwater. Deck chairs are set about over three decks. Even when the ship is full, space to lounge is ample. The supervised fitness center has a treadmill, stationary bicycles, and weight training equipment. Passengers exercise while enjoying a panoramic view from the top deck. Aerobics, stretching on Astroturf, and water exercise in the pool are offered daily. Several decks below is a pine sauna and massage room. Skeet and Ping-Pong are also available.

Club Med 2 has a golf simulator (additional cost) that enables passengers to "play" world-famous courses. Spa options include licensed massage therapists, mineral and moisturizing whirlpools, jet hydrotherapy, seaweed baths, back and leg treatments, and tanning tables. A beauty salon offers hair and facial services. Beauty services and treatments cost extra.

Shore Excursions   Half-day and daylong excursions are offered at most ports and are accompanied by a GO and local guide. Some ports are reached by tender. Shore walks, beach trips, and the weekly lobster fest are included in the fare; port excursions are not and can be costly.

Theme Cruises   Six-night golf cruise from Martinique.

Postscript   Smokers are in the majority on *Club Med 2* and have the run of the ship. Restaurants have nonsmoking sections, but smoking is allowed in all public areas. The ship's ventilation system seems to combat the smoke effectively. Don't forget to pack a French-English dictionary, unless you're fluent in French.

Commodore Cruise Line

4000 Hollywood Blvd., Suite 385 South Tower
Hollywood, FL 33021
(954) 967-2100; (800) 237-5361; fax (954) 967-2147
www.commodorecruise.com

Type of Ships   Classic, midsize oceanliners.

Type of Cruise   Casual, unpretentious, budget priced; a cruise for all ages.

Cruise Line's Strengths
  * high value for low price
  * outstanding staff
  * family cabins
  * varied entertainment

Cruise Line's Shortcomings
  * age of ships
  * noise level
  * rushed port visits

Fellow Passengers   First-timers, newlyweds, families, older couples, singles, young retirees, senior citizens, and experienced cruisers of all ages. With New Orleans as the home port, the majority are likely to come from Louisiana and neighboring Texas, Mississippi, and Alabama, and others from the Midwest and California. The median age is about 49 in spring and fall; it's the mid-40s in summer and winter holidays, when passengers with children and younger couples increase.

The majority of passengers are professionals or in management; 58 percent are college graduates. Average household income is $52,000 per year; the male-to-female ratio is almost equal. About 25 percent are retired; about a quarter are senior citizens. Groups account for approximately 40 percent of passengers. Fifty-four percent have cruised before; 46 percent are first-timers; 98 percent say they would cruise again.

Recommended For Budget-conscious first-timers, families, and others seeking an easy, laid-back vacation with dependable service and plentiful activity in a friendly, informal atmosphere.

Not Recommended For Passengers seeking a sophisticated or intellectual experience or the resort facilities of a superliner.

Cruise Areas and Seasons Western Caribbean and Central America, year-round.

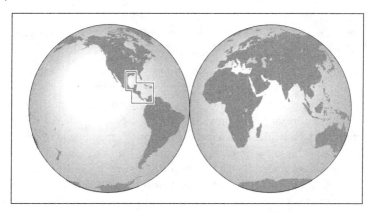

The Line Begun in 1966, Commodore Cruise Line was a trailblazer in offering weekly cruises from Miami to the Caribbean. Building a fleet of three vessels dubbed "Happy Ships," it sailed these routes for more than two decades, developing a solid reputation for tried-and-true cruises. The line became known for theme cruises—Oktoberfest, Mayfest, Country and Western—an idea it pioneered.

In 1987, Commodore was acquired by Effjohn International, a Scandinavian company that operates one of the world's largest passenger fleets. Commodore was merged first with Bermuda Star Line and later with Crown Cruise Lines, a company in which Effjohn had ownership. Through it all, Commodore maintained its identity, leaving behind the stiff competition among megaliners in Florida and moving to New Orleans, where, until recently, it had the only Caribbean cruises departing weekly year-round. In 2000, for the first time, the line introduced longer cruises of 10 to 14 days on selected itineraries.

In 1995, Commodore was acquired by a group of Miami investors headed by travel industry veteran Fred A. Mayer, a founder of Regency Cruises and former head of Exprinter, a tour and cruise wholesaler. One of Commodore's ships, *Enchanted Seas,* is on long-term lease to World

Explorer Cruises. In 1998, Commodore's parent, Commodore Holdings, Ltd., concluded a five-year lease on the 500-passenger *Island Holiday,* which it renamed *Enchanted Capri,* and arranged for Casino America to operate the ship's casinos.

Commodore Holdings acquired the *Crown Dynasty* (formerly *Norwegian Dynasty*) from Norwegian Cruise Line in late 1999. It is the first of three ships planned for Commodore's new sister division, Crown Cruise Line, which is catering to a more upscale market than Commodore's.

The Fleet	Built/Renovated	Tonnage	Passengers
Enchanted Isle	1958/94/97	23,395	725
Enchanted Capri	1996/97/98	15,410	468

Style Some passengers describe a Commodore cruise as comfortable like a pair of favorite slippers. It provides a relaxing vacation at affordable prices with plentiful activities in a congenial atmosphere, appealing to Americans of all ages who know and want good value. Many repeaters have tried larger ships but prefer the warm, restful atmosphere of Commodore.

Except for theme cruises, when the passenger mix and ambience might vary, Commodore aims to provide dependable, satisfying cruises for a broad spectrum of vacationers. Clientele have become younger as cruising has reached wider audiences. At the same time, the over-60 age group seems to have a swell time, although some opt to remain aboard at ports requiring a tender.

Distinctive Features Elaborate theme nights on all cruises. On Key West/Western Caribbean itinerary, ship remains overnight in Cozumel.

	HIGHEST	LOWEST	AVERAGE
PER DIEM	$225	$154	$202

The above per diems are calculated from the cruise line's non-discounted *cruise only* fares on standard accommodations. Per diems vary by season, by cabin, and by cruise areas.

Rates Port charges are included.

Special Fares and Discounts Early-booking discounts of up to $150 per cabin are available on reservations 90 days before sailing.
- Third/Fourth Person: $350.
- Single Supplement: From 150 percent to 200 percent, depending on cabin category; includes air transportation.

Packages
- Air/Sea: Yes.
- Others: Honeymoon package includes cabin with double bed, welcome cocktail, champagne, wine with dinner, photograph, and flowers; all $50 extra.
- Pre/Post: Yes, plus four-day Mardi Gras/New Orleans package.

Past Passengers   Club Repeaters are offered special sailings with discounted rates and special events on board.

The Last Word   If you know what to expect, Commodore's cruises are among the industry's best values and a good choice for first-time cruisers. They're an affordable option for honeymooning couples. Seniors who like plenty of daytime activity and nighttime entertainment find Commodore a comfortable choice. *Enchanted Isle* shows its age, but the line must be doing something right. Cruises sail almost full year-round, with loyal fans returning time and again and newcomers attracted by the price. They get what they pay for; there are no surprises.

COMMODORE STANDARD FEATURES

Officers *Enchanted Isle,* European, Scandinavian, and others; *Enchanted Capri,* Ukrainian.

Staff *Isle,* dining, cabin/international; cruise/American. *Capri,* Caribbean and others.

Dining Facilities One dining room, two seatings for three meals; open seating breakfast and lunch; breakfast, lunch, and midnight buffet.

Special Diets Requests three weeks in advance of sailing.

Room Service 24 hours, limited menu.

Dress Code Casual by day; casual or informal in evening; formal suggested but not required for captain's welcome and farewell dinners. Shorts not allowed in dining room for dinner; no tank tops or caps in dining room at any time.

Cabin Amenities *Isle,* phone; closed-circuit television has two channels with first-run movies, multi-channel music system; baths with shower, most superiors also have tub. *Capri,* no phone or television.

Electrical Outlets *Isle,* 110 AC; *Capri,* 220 AC.

Wheelchair Access *Isle,* public areas ramped; cabins modified.

Recreation and Entertainment Casino, disco, nightclub, show lounge, cinema and theater, observation lounge, library, card and meeting room. Bingo, bridge, dancing classes, horse racing, arts and crafts classes. *Isle,* video game room.

Sports and Other Activities One outdoor swimming pool; Ping-Pong, pool games, trapshooting, exercise, aerobics. No wraparound deck.

Beauty and Fitness Small exercise room. *Isle,* massage, beauty/barber shop; *Capri,* none.

Other Facilities Boutiques, medical facilities, laundry service.

Children's Facilities *Isle,* youth counselors summer and holidays. Small video/game room. Commodore Cuddly mascot.

Theme Cruises Music, Big Band, comedy, and Cajun cooking.

Smoking Smoke-free dining room; public rooms have smoking and nonsmoking sections.

Commodore Suggested Tipping Per person per day: cabin steward, $3; dining room waiter, $3; busboy, $2. Per week: head waiter, $4. 15 percent of check is added to wine and bar bills.

Credit Cards For cruise payment and onboard charges: American Express, Discover, MasterCard, Visa. No cash used during cruise; instead, passengers are billed and the tab is settled at end of cruise.

Enchanted Isle	Quality ❸	Value B
Registry: Panama	Length: 617 feet	Beam: 88 feet
Cabins: 361	Draft: 28 feet	Speed: 20 knots
Maximum Passengers:	Passenger Decks: 9	Elevators: 3
792	Crew: 350	Space Ratio: 33

The Ship   The spacious ship has a warm ambience set by the congenial staff, starting with the captain. Passengers enjoy more personalized service than is found on larger ships. Cabins are large; some hold up to five people and are popular with families, especially when coupled with the low prices.

Enchanted Isle (formerly the *Bermuda Star* and *Veendam*) is almost a twin of the *Enchanted Seas,* now under lease by World Explorer Cruises. The ships were built in 1957 by Ingalls Shipbuilding Corporation of Pascagoula, Mississippi. After a year as a floating hotel in St. Petersburg, Russia, and a facelift in Poland, the *Enchanted Isle* returned to Caribbean service in 1994. In 1997, she received another $3.5 million in updating and upgrading of public areas, cabins, exteriors, and operating systems.

The ship has a variety of public rooms and lounges and ample deck space. Public rooms are in good shape, and the air-conditioning functions well. On the other hand, passengers seem to have a good time and aren't too concerned about decor.

The promenade deck contains most of the public rooms and runs the length of the ship, from the casino at the fore to the main pool at the stern. Side decks are teak and spacious, but they don't encircle the ship. The limited number of elevators means long walks from some cabins.

Itineraries   See Appendix B.

Cabins   Comfortable and spacious, depending on category, the cabins have ample closets and storage space for two, perhaps three people, but are cramped for four. More than 75 percent are outside. Most top-priced cabins have bathtubs; others have showers. Some bathrooms have a bidet. Water is steaming hot, and recently retiled bathrooms are spotless. All cabins were refurbished in 1997.

Desk and bathroom amenities, such as stationery and shampoo, are not provided. Electrical outlets are few; one accommodates a hair dryer. Reading lights beside the bed provide plenty of light.

Lifeboats partially obstruct views from some cabins on the boat and navigation and sun decks; this is noted in the Commodore brochure. Cabins on the lowest deck have no elevator access.

In renovations, 9 suites were added and 40 cabins were fitted with double beds. Two suites are wheelchair-accessible; two have private balconies.

Specifications 72 inside cabins, 286 outside; 72 for third/fourth persons; 3 singles; 9 suites. Standard dimensions, inside or outside, 152 square feet; deluxe and superior, 191–293 square feet. Many configurations: some twins with upper and lower berths; some with double and some with twin beds convertible to doubles; some connecting cabins.

Dining Cuisine in the Riviera Dining Room has received mixed reviews, mainly for its lack of consistency. However, a new chef seems to be performing miracles; many passengers say they are repeaters because of the good food.

Selections are fewer than aboard more expensive ships, but are certainly adequate. A typical dinner menu offers two juices, two appetizers, three soups, three pasta choices, three salads, four entrees with vegetables, cheese, three desserts, and beverages. Second helpings are available on request. Vegetarian and low-fat "spa cuisine" is offered at every meal.

Most seating is at round tables for eight in close proximity to one another; some banquettes and smaller seats are in corners. The noise is uncomfortably loud. No smoking is allowed in the dining room.

Service, though sometimes rushed, gets as high marks as the food. The maître d'hôtel and the dining staff seem genuinely eager to offer a pleasant dining experience, but the noise and crowding complicate their task.

The Bistro, an informal dining area on the promenade deck, has a Caribbean feeling, with decor in a festive, teal-colored palette. The facility offers indoor/outdoor dining for breakfast and lunch buffets in a cheerful and comfortable atmosphere. The inside bar features happy-hour hot snacks. Outside in the evening are a full-service bar, covered entertainment area, and poolside grill.

A stage and sound and lighting systems were added during renovation. The Bistro now has nighttime entertainment from 9 to 11 p.m. The new Bistro Espresso Bar, open from 8 a.m. to 1 a.m. daily, serves a variety of beverages, including espresso, cappuccino, and specialty variations of these drinks. Cost is $1.50–2.50 each.

Burgers and hot dogs are prepared on deck daily at lunch. In the afternoon, tea and snacks are offered. During the summer and holidays, pizza, tacos, burgers, and a child's plate are served. Midnight buffets are attractive, but ordinary. Room service offers continental breakfast and a limited menu of beverages and sandwiches.

Service Without question, Commodore's staff is its biggest asset. Passengers lavish praise on the staff and service—among the best of any ship offering weekly Caribbean cruises.

The crew is efficient, thorough, pleasant, and accommodating. They have an average of ten years' service experience. It is not uncommon for repeat passengers to request a specific room steward or waiter. Bar service is excellent, and bartenders are willing to accommodate unusual requests.

You get the impression that they like their jobs and employer. (The staff and crew are allowed to invite family members to cruise with them after being with the company three months.) The positive attitude is reflected in the excellent way the staff and passengers interact. By cruise's end, most staffers are able to call passengers by name.

Land personnel are also applauded. In addition to transferring passengers who book flights through the cruise lines, uniformed representatives at the New Orleans airport are praised for their courtesy and help for those who make their own arrangements, giving them clear directions regarding transportation to the dock.

Facilities and Entertainment   Each day and evening reflect the place being visited. Theme nights are extremely popular, and some passengers pack with them in mind, carrying costumes for Mardi Gras night and poodle skirts and bobby socks for the 1950s hop. The ship's orchestra is excellent; entertainment by singers, magicians, and comedians is well done, keeping passengers coming back each night.

The lip sync show, games with audience participation, and horse races draw the biggest crowds. Unlike most ships, the *Enchanted Isle* lets passengers "purchase" horses for the week and the "owners" are given materials to decorate them—some take their decorated horses to dinner! The casino, with an adjacent bar, offers slots, blackjack, and roulette.

Each lounge has its own personality—one quiet and intimate; another open and loud—with enough variety to suit all. Seating in the Grand Lounge, the main showroom, gradually declines toward the center floor, somewhat like a theater. Pillars block some seats; sight lines otherwise are good. The sides, on higher levels, have a full-service bar and large windows offering spectacular daytime views. During renovation, the lounge received upgraded light and sound equipment, and new upholstering, carpeting, and wall coverings in gold and brown tones.

The Spyglass Lounge piano bar on the sun deck, a quiet retreat with the best view of the front of the ship, is popular with older passengers who enjoy the quiet piano/cocktail music, but it seems to take first-timers a few days to find it. Its bar opens in late afternoon, and there's music before dinner. Gentlemen hosts are available as dance partners for women passengers.

The Deck Disco party begins at 11 p.m., and passengers dance into the wee hours in Neptune's Lounge with state-of-the art light and sound equipment. It's supposed to close at 2 a.m., but most nights it remains open until after 4 a.m. for dancing to current rock and rap hits. Bartenders and waiters stay until the last passenger is ready to call it a night.

Activities and Diversions   During days at sea, there is usually a talk by a guest expert or a special feature on topics as varied as wine tasting, napkin folding, and finances. Game show addicts flock to Commodore's versions of Liar's Club, Family Feud, Newlywed/Not-so-Newlywed Game, and Jeopardy. Ice carving is also popular and includes a photo session.

Television movies, changed daily, are usually first-run, Academy Award winners. The ship has a pleasant card room with four tables, a small video game room, and a theater (always cold) where movies are shown when the ship is in port. The theater is a gathering place for shore-excursion participants.

The library has a very limited selection of books and odd checkout hours. Passengers should bring their own reading material. The boutique offers a 50 percent discount on liquor and daily specials on souvenir T-shirts and similar gifts.

Sports, Fitness, and Beauty   One outside swimming pool on the promenade deck has received a much-needed retiling. Deck chairs are supplied only on the promenade deck; however, no one seems to mind if passengers take their own chairs to quiet spots.

A beauty salon, barber shop, and massage room are tucked away on the Theatre Deck. Massages are popular and should be booked early. The fitness center has two stationary bicycles, a treadmill, free weights, and weight resistance machines. Morning toning, stretching, and aerobics classes and guided jogging around the ship are offered. There's neither a sauna nor a spa.

Children's Facilities   There are no facilities exclusively for children. Games and activities are held in the library, card room, outside decks, swimming areas, and theater. Up to 4 youth counselors are aboard to coordinate activities when there are at least 15 children on a cruise. Commodore Cuddly, a bear mascot that entertains young passengers, has three outfits: a Commodore outfit for greeting guests; a T-shirt with epaulets for shipboard activities; and a nightshirt for a tuck-in service for junior passengers.

Shore Excursions   Cannot be booked in advance. Tours and sports are offered at prices typical for the Caribbean, ranging from $30 for a 2-hour Cayman Island tour to $80 for a 7.5-hour visit to Tulum from Playa del Carmen with return by ferry to Cozumel. Passengers complain that some excursions are rushed. Port talks vary in substance. The presentation on Cozumel is very helpful, with good tips on shopping and restaurants. For

Grand Cayman and Jamaica, the talks push jewelry shopping so strongly that it's obvious someone receives a hefty commission to promote specific stores.

In Grand Cayman, tenders are used to convey passengers to shore. In Cozumel, on/off boarding is quick and easy. There, horseback riding, an introductory scuba course, and excursions for certified divers are available.

Theme Cruises   Commodore has expanded theme cruises. Zydeco and Country and Western are standards; occasional others include Women in Jazz, Esplanade, Rock 'n' Roll, Arts and Crafts, and Stop Smoking.

Postscript   A word of caution: During embarkation, black soot from smokestacks may cover the ship's open decks and soil your clothes. Newly installed stacks may have eliminated this problem. Also, officers and staff are somewhat lax about attendance at the compulsory lifeboat drill.

Commodore ships aren't megaliners. They are a good, solid value; first-time and budget cruisers get their money's worth. Some cabins require considerable walking to stairs and elevators. Some passengers complain about the lack of religious services. But overall, the ships can be recommended as long as people know what to expect: superior service, good (not great) food, entertainment, and plenty of activities. Furthermore, the ships visit some of the Caribbean's most popular ports.

Enchanted Capri	Quality ❸	Value C
Registry: Bahamas	Length: 515 feet	Beam: 71 feet
Cabins: 248	Draft: 20 feet	Speed: 18 knots
Maximum Passengers:	Passenger Decks: 8	Elevators: 1
468	Crew: 27	Space Ratio: NA

The Ship   In 1998, as the first step in its expansion plans, Commodore acquired this vessel and introduced her on two- and five-day cruises from New Orleans year-round.

Built in 1975 in Turku, Finland, as a ferry for the Baltic Sea and later sailing as the Soviet cruise ship *Azerbaydzhan,* the *Enchanted Capri* was refurbished in 1984 in Bremerhaven, Germany, and again in 1997 in Freeport, Grand Bahama.

Currently, the *Enchanted Capri* exhibits a split personality, mirroring the psychological state of the former Soviet Union: on the outside, she's geared up to party in the sun, but on the inside, she still has the heart of a Russian bear.

Make no mistake: Commodore's approach—overwhelming passengers with activities, entertainment, food, and drink, all at bargain prices—is foremost here. This is a fun ship from the moment you step aboard to the minute you disembark. There are all the goofy pool games ever invented for cruise ships. There's a proportionately huge 24-hour casino. There's a stern pool always buzzing with music and drink. And there's some surprisingly good entertainment.

Balancing this are clear reminders of the ship's past: the Ukrainian crew, signs in Russian (with English subtitles), artwork depicting Russian and Azerbaijani folk scenes, and life jackets stamped with the Soviet hammer and sickle. A surreal moment: watching passengers frolic around the pool while next to them an engineer wearing dark coveralls and carrying a battered toolbox trudges up the stairs, looking for all the world like he's headed to his factory job in Irkutsk.

With a sense of humor, you'll find this appealing. Also appealing is the fact that *Enchanted Capri* is smaller and more truly shiplike than the huge vessels built today—you'll never feel you're in a land-based hotel. She's a classic oceangoer with well-trodden wooden decks, machinery more in evidence than glitz, and a deep draught that gives a stable ride even on the sometimes choppy Gulf of Mexico.

Itineraries   See Appendix B.

Cabins   No matter the category, your cabin will be spacious; almost all can comfortably accommodate a third passenger, and some a fourth. Two of the 8 suites—the Royal Suites—are extraordinary, with a very large sitting room and bedroom, 4 phone-booth–sized closets, 19 (19!) drawers, 6 large storage cabinets, a couch, a full-sized refrigerator, writing and makeup tables, and a 7-hook coatrack strong enough to hold your Siberian parka. It's easy to speculate that these suites were reserved for communist officials or military officers in the ship's Soviet days.

Standard inside and outside cabins have twin beds arranged either at right angles or in upper and lower berths. Decor tends toward Brady Bunch–era patterns and textures. Bathrooms are big enough that you won't bump into fixtures. Each has a shower; suites have bathtubs.

Specifications   113 inside cabins, 131 outside including 8 suites; 138 for third/fourth persons. Standard cabins range from 120 square feet for upper/lower berths and 125–155 square feet for inside cabins, to 140–145 square feet for outside cabins and 285 square feet for junior suites. Some cabins have upper and lower berths, some, twin beds, but none convert to a double.

Dining All meals are served in the ship's Tradewinds Dining Room. The food is filling but unremarkable. Expect standard budget-cruise fare: beef, chicken, pastas, drab salads. Midnight buffets, however, are another matter, the best culinary experiences aboard. Although not gourmet, they're a sight to behold: mountains of chocolate-covered strawberries and bonbons, platters of caviar and toast, mounds of pasta and vegetables, a carving table of beef, and tray after tray of cheese, breads, and cold cuts, all presided over by birds and animals carved from cheeses and fruits.

Service As with Commodore's *Enchanted Isle,* service aboard the *Capri* balances any drawbacks and makes the experience shine. Though not the white-gloved attention you'll find on upscale cruise lines, it's friendly and caring and gives passengers the sense that the service staff—mostly Caribbean islanders—really enjoy their jobs and want passengers to enjoy their stay.

Waiters' and bartenders' light camaraderie puts most passengers at ease, and cabin stewards are solicitous, friendly, and efficient. Cabins—in fact, the entire ship—are kept remarkably clean and tidy.

Facilities and Entertainment Public facilities are limited: main show lounge, casino, sunny library/sitting room at the ship's highest point, piano bar/lounge, small disco, and an almost retro (without trying to be) cinema that shows recent films several times a day.

The casino is the central element—so much so that the lease on the ship is held jointly by Commodore and Biloxi's Isle of Capri casinos. It's a sizable room, and it's open around the clock once the ship reaches international waters.

Entertainment includes three musical acts that perform throughout the day at the ship's various venues. The Caribbean dance band uses real steel drums instead of synthesized ones. A pianist is usually performing in the Rendezvous Lounge, and the *Enchanted Capri* Orchestra—a surprise with its snappy Big Band sound and jazzy arrangements—performs at night in the show lounge.

Each evening also offers at least one show. On a recent sailing, comedian/impressionist Cliff Lawrence and a "Lullabies of Broadway" revue topped the bill.

Activities and Diversions Although the *Capri* is casino-oriented, it offers distractions for nongamblers and those too young to wager. These include bingo, horse racing, art auctions, team trivia matches, and Ping-Pong tournaments—standard cruise favorites. Deck games also include staples: beer-drinking contests, break-the-balloon-with-your-butt contests, and—always the showstopper—competition to determine which female passenger can stuff the most Ping-Pong balls into her bathing suit while floating in the pool. Most five-day voyages feature theme nights of various kinds.

Sports, Fitness, and Beauty   Limited gym, sauna, and beauty salon facilities are available. Determined souls can jog on this ship, though it takes some doing—running up a ladder, reversing course, climbing stairways to the deck above, and weaving past passengers who are drinking around the pool.

Children's Activities   There's a small children's center. Programs are divided by age, with age-appropriate activities chosen by counselors. Generally, one counselor is aboard per 10 children.

Costa Cruise Lines

80 SW Eighth Street, Miami, FL 33130-3097
(305) 358-7325; (800) 462-6782; fax (305) 375-0676
www.costacruises.com

Type of Ships   New, modern superliners and traditional oceanliners.

Type of Cruise   Mass market, designed for Europeans as much as North Americans—hence, more European in service and ambience.

Cruise Line's Strengths
- cabins on most ships
- Italian style and service
- friendly crew
- itineraries

Cruise Line's Shortcomings
- noise level in dining rooms
- excessive announcements
- language problems
- lack of consistency

Fellow Passengers   Costa has two seasons: Caribbean from late fall to early spring; and Northern Europe, Mediterranean, and Norwegian fjords from spring through fall. As a result, it has two sets of passengers. In the Caribbean, up to 80 percent of passengers are North Americans, depending on the cruise; average age is 54 years, with annual household income of $50,000+. A bevy of Italian-American fans and newlyweds are attracted by the line's Italian style. Most have cruised before.

In Europe, 80 percent or more are Europeans likely to have traveled abroad, perhaps have even cruised before. Among the North Americans, average age is about the same as Caribbean cruisers', but those on a European cruise would be inclined to rent a car and drive through Europe on their own instead of taking an escorted tour. They enjoy traveling with and meeting people from other countries.

Recommended For   Italophiles; first-time cruisers and less experienced travelers who want to sample European ambience, but with facilities typical of a large ship; and repeat cruisers who want to try something different.

Not Recommended For   Those who like small ships and an all-American atmosphere or prefer to travel with Americans.

Cruise Areas and Seasons   Caribbean, Mediterranean, Greek islands, the Holy Land, Black Sea, Northern Europe, Norwegian fjords, the Baltic, Russia, South America, and transatlantic cruises.

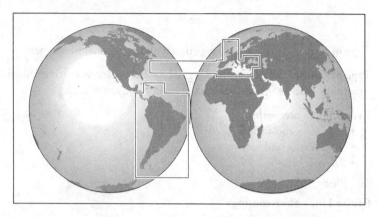

The Line   Genoa-based Costa Crociere, parent company of Costa Cruise Lines, had been in the shipping business for over 100 years and in the passenger business for almost 50 years when it was bought by Carnival Cruises and Airtour, its European partner, in 1997. Costa, Europe's largest cruise line, was among the earliest lines to offer one-week Caribbean cruises from Miami (1959) and the first to introduce an air/sea program (late 1960s). Despite its long Florida-Caribbean association, Costa changed course in 1993 to become more Europe-focused. Of its seven ships, only two sail from U.S. ports, and they sail only in winter. The others are positioned in Europe, the Caribbean, and South America.

Costa launched the 1990s with four new ships costing more than $1 billion and intended to serve a broad spectrum of passengers. The ships are a marked departure from the classic oceanliners of Costa's older fleet. They combine modern and classic qualities with new design features. Already, two ships of the group are being stretched, adding 20 percent to their capacity. The 76,000-ton *CostaVictoria,* added in 1996 as the line's largest ship at the time, is being supplanted by even larger ships, costing an estimated $400 million each. *CostaAtlantica,* the first of the 84,000-ton vessels, debuted in July 2000.

The Fleet	Built/Renovated	Tonnage	Passengers
CostaAllegra	1992	28,500	820
CostaAtlantica	2000	84,000	2,112
CostaClassica	1991/2000	53,000/77,000	1,308/2,058
CostaMarina	1969/90	25,500	776
CostaRiviera	1963/94/98	31,500	974
CostaRomantica	1993	53,000	1,356
CostaVictoria	1996	76,000	1,928

Style   In the early 1980s, Costa coined the phrase "cruising Italian style" to celebrate its Italian basis in everything from design to cuisine. Despite its success, Costa replaced the concept with "Euroluxe" when it introduced its new ships at the beginning of the 1990s. Perhaps this helped them establish their dominant position in Europe, but it was neither understood nor well received by North Americans. Costa quickly returned to saluting its Italian connection.

The new ships are designed and built in Italy by Italians, with floors and walls of Italian marble, splendid wood cabinetry, designer fabrics and linens, and Italian art throughout. They reflect the sophisticated architecture and decor of modern Italian designers rather than the classic Italian look. The newest ships, the German-built *CostaVictoria* and the Finnish-built *CostaAtlantica,* remain true to the Italian style. Life on board is made to seem *molto Italiano,* from the pasta and espresso to Italian language lessons, Italian cooking classes, Italian ice cream, pizzas in the pizzerias, and toga parties. Theme nights, such as "Festa Italiana," feature an Italian street festival with bocce ball games, tarantella dance lessons, pizza dough–tossing contests, Venetian mask making, and more. Yet for all the trimmings, the Italian ambience has been diluted, mainly because Costa ships no longer have all-Italian crews.

The ships are very much "today" with gyms, spas, and fitness programs, and Costa's Caribbean shore excursions emphasize outdoor activities. One of Costa's most popular innovations is its "private" beach on Isla Catalina off the Dominican Republic, where passengers on Eastern Caribbean cruises spend the day. The island is near the sprawling resort of Casa de Campo, which, among its many facilities, has a tennis village and three of the Caribbean's best golf courses.

Distinctive Features   Pizzerias serve free, hot pizza throughout the day. On Caribbean cruises, couples can renew their wedding vows in a shipboard ceremony.

	HIGHEST	LOWEST	AVERAGE
PER DIEM	$467	$150	$275

The above per diems are calculated from the cruise line's non-discounted *cruise only* fares on standard accommodations. Per diems vary by season, by cabin, and by cruise areas.

Rates   Port charges are included.

Special Fares and Discounts   Andiamo Fares provide 10–20 percent discounts, depending on category, for bookings 120 days in advance in the Caribbean and 90 days in Europe. Additional discounts on Andiamo Fares are available in some categories for seniors. Combining Eastern and Western Caribbean or two Mediterranean cruises into 14-nighters offers savings, too.

- Children's Fare: Same as third/fourth passenger fares (works for single parents, too); also $199 for children age 17 and younger on some cruises.
- Single Supplement: 150–200 percent.

Packages
- Air/Sea: Yes, for Europe; mostly as add-ons for Caribbean.
- Others: Spa, seniors, honeymoon, family.
- Pre/Post: Yes, in Amsterdam, Copenhagen, Genoa, London, Nice/Monte Carlo, Paris, Rome, Venice, Ft. Lauderdale, or Orlando, depending on cruise.

Past Passengers   No repeat passenger club. Past passengers receive mailings announcing new itineraries and offering discounts.

The Last Word   Costa's expansion has been bumpy, and the avalanche of criticism regarding quality, Euroluxe, and the radical look of the *Costa-Classica* didn't help. The worst seems to be behind them now, but work is still needed, particularly in establishing product consistency. To its credit, Costa has dared to be different in style and the markets it pursues, preferring to be number one in Europe, where it has a strong base and years of experience, rather than struggling in the fierce competition of the Caribbean. The strategy virtually guarantees that when you take a Costa cruise, the experience will be European rather than catering to American tastes.

Some Americans welcome the opportunity to take a European vacation with Europeans. Others are turned off by cliques in lounges and bars and the steady stream of announcements—for bingo, shopping talks, shore excursions—in five languages, even though English-speaking hostesses are aboard to cater to North Americans.

Areas are designated as smoking or nonsmoking on Costa ships, but some European smokers flout the restriction—defiantly.

COSTA CRUISE LINES STANDARD FEATURES

Officers Italian.

Staff Dining/Italian, other European, Asian, Central Americans; Cabin/International; Cruise and Entertainment/International.

Dining Facilities One main dining room (two on *Costa Victoria*), two seatings for three meals, midnight buffet featuring Italian cuisine; indoor/outdoor buffet breakfast and lunch. Alternative dining; *Victoria, Atlantica* extra charge. Pizzerias and pastry cafes on most ships.

Special Diets Should be requested four weeks in advance.

Room Service 24 hours, limited menu; butler service in suites with full service for meals from dining room menus.

Dress Code Casual; informal evenings; two nights formal/semi-formal.

Cabin Amenities Phone, radio, private shower, hair dryer, safe, television; suites have whirlpool bath, minibar, and veranda (except *Marina*).

Electrical Outlets 110/220 AC; adapters available on board.

Wheelchair Access Six cabins on *Classica, Romantica,* and *Victoria;* eight on *Allegra.*

Recreation and Entertainment Casino, bars and lounges with nightly entertainment, showrooms, disco, dance and Italian language lessons, bingo, bridge, horse racing, library, card room.

Sports and Other Activities Three swimming pools, *Atlantica* (one for children); two, *Classica, Romantica, Victoria* (plus one inside); one, *Allegra, Marina, Riviera.* Exercise classes, snorkeling lessons, paddle tennis, Ping-Pong, deck and pool games. *Victoria,* tennis/basketball.

Beauty and Fitness Barber shop and beauty salon, spa, sauna, European beauty treatments, fitness centers, jogging track, whirlpools.

Other Facilities Boutiques, medical facility, laundry and dry cleaning services, meeting room, chapel.

Children's Facilities Costa Kids year-round; babysitters.

Theme Cruises Yes.

Smoking Smoking in designated public areas.

Costa Suggested Tipping Per person per day: cabin steward, $3; waiter, $3; busboy, $1.50; head waiter, $1 for Caribbean; 50¢ less for each in Europe. 15 percent gratuity added to all beverage bills (including mineral water in the dining room).

Credit Cards For cruise payment and on-board charges: American Express, Carte Blanche, Diners Club, Discover, MasterCard, Visa.

CostaRomantica	Quality ❼	Value B
CostaClassica	Quality ❸	Value C

Registry: Italian	Length: 722/722(865) feet	Beam: 102 feet
Cabins: 678/654 (1,029)	Draft: 24 feet	Speed: 18.5 knots
Maximum Passengers:	Passenger Decks: 3	Elevators: 8
1,356/1,308 (2,058)	Crew: 610	Space Ratio: 40/41.5

The Ships   *CostaRomantica* and *CostaClassica* are almost identical. These spacious ships with public rooms on the upper four decks have ultramodern Italian interiors using a king's ransom in marble, dramatic window walls, futuristic sculptures, clean lines, angular shapes, and fine art to create a new look that reflects modern Italian design and a radical departure from traditional European oceanliners.

Perhaps because *Classica* was so different, initial reaction to her was unfavorable. Some called the decor harsh, saying the marble and severe lines rendered some interiors cold, whereas elsewhere the furnishings were too ornate. Others said the white marble stairways with metal trim looked more like a hospital than a cruise ship. Costa took heed and on the *Romantica* used more wood paneling, particularly by elevators and stairwells, warmer fabrics, and other refinements that made the interiors more approachable.

In November 2000, *CostaClassica* is to be stretched by the insertion of a 147-foot section that will add 375 cabins (of which 102 will have verandas) and an additional deck running the entire length of the ship, increasing her overall size from 53,000 to 77,000 tons. The $100 million project, to be done at Cammell Laird in England, is expected to be completed by March 2001. Similar alterations are planned for *CostaRomantica* in 2001.

Passengers are introduced to the ship in its dramatic Grand Lobby, set low on the Copenhagen Deck, which is dedicated entirely to cabins, as are the deck below and the two decks above. White-gloved room stewards escort passengers to their cabins. The background music of Vivaldi and other Italian composers is meant to underscore the start of a week of "cruising Italian style." The ships' layouts are easy to follow, with one lounge or public space flowing to the next, creating openness and harmony. Decks are named after European cities.

The dramatic centerpiece of *Romantica*'s lobby is a moving sculpture by Japanese artist Susumu Shingu. Installed in 1992 to commemorate the Columbus quincentennial, it's a mobile whose panels move continuously and change color against the area's Cararra marble walls and floors.

Romantica's heart and social center is the Piazza Italia on the Verona Deck—an atrium furnished as a lounge, with a small bandstand and dance floor on one side and a bar on the other. The lounge is the favorite gathering spot for prelunch and predinner drinks, as it's a short walk from the dining room. Encased in soft green Venetian stucco walls, the lounge offers a quietly elegant setting with jacquard fabrics in greens and blues enhanced with fresh greenery.

Forward are meeting rooms, the library, chapel, card room, and the ground floor of L'Opera, the bilevel show lounge. From the Piazza, a double stairway leads up to the Vienna Deck and the popular Romeo's Pizzeria and Juliet's Patisserie. Forward are shops on the Via Condetti, named for Rome's fashionable shopping street.

Itineraries   See Appendix B.

Cabins   Spacious and well-designed, cabins are these ships' best feature. Standard cabins are fitted in cherry wood furnishings, including a dresser/desk unit with large mirror, bedside tables, a control panel for lights by the bed, ample closet space, and two chairs, one of which opens into a bed suitable for a child.

Elegant touches are the white curtain spanning the room, which can be raised and lowered to cover the oversized porthole; designer amenities; and high-quality bed and bath linens. All cabins have television, radio, safe, direct-dial satellite phone, and hair dryer. The 24-hour room service offers sandwiches and beverages.

Romantica's top deck has a group of suites over the bridge in the area occupied by the spa on the *Classica*. The six largest suites—all named for famous operas—have floor-to-ceiling window walls. Another group of ten large suites are amidships on the Madrid Deck and have verandas large enough for chaise longues. *Classica*'s ten suites also have verandas. All suites have bathroom phone, whirlpool bath, separate shower, double vanity, spacious sitting area with minibar (there's a charge), and daily fresh fruit. Furnishings include authentic tapestries, handwoven bedspreads, and Renaissance art. Butler service and room service for any meal from dining room menus, complete with table, are available.

CostaRomantica *Specifications*   216 inside cabins, 428 outside; 16 suites, 18 minisuites. Standard dimensions are 175 square feet inside, 200 square feet outside. 340 with twin beds; 56 with queen. 126 inside cabins, 116 outside take third and fourth persons; no singles.(Specifications will change following the addition of 375 cabins—102 with verandas—in November 2000.)

CostaClassica *Specifications*   216 inside cabins, 428 outside; 10 suites with verandas. Standard dimensions are 150–200 square feet. 158 with twin beds (152 convertible to double), 121 queen. 359 cabins take third and fourth persons; no singles. (The new section to be inserted in November 2000 will add 375 cabins, including 10 suites, 14 minisuites with verandas, and 102 outside cabins with verandas.)

Dining   *Romantica*'s Botticelli Restaurant, similar to *Classica*'s counterpart, Tivoli, is beautifully laid out almost entirely in off-white and brown Carrara marble with coffered ceilings. Elegantly designed wicker-backed chairs encircle round tables, most seating eight, dressed in starched white cloths, fine china, glassware, and flowers.

The room is lovely, but the lack of carpeting or wall coverings causes an extraordinarily high noise level that hinders conversation. Acoustical material was added, particularly in the ceiling, which helped—but not enough. Side tables toward the back of the room get less noise. Two wings at the entrance are smoking areas.

The restaurants on both ships have movable side panels faced with a variety of scenes—a European city, landscapes, or Italian gardens—that change each evening. They were designed by Giorgio Cristini, set designer for Milan's famous La Scala opera house.

Dinner menus have fewer selections than offered on some ships in Costa's price group, but choices are ample and of good quality, balancing Italian and European dishes with American favorites. A different pasta is featured at lunch and dinner; American audiences rave over them.

A typical dinner menu offers three appetizers, two soups, two salads, three pastas, four entrees (one vegetarian), three or more desserts, ice cream, sherbet, cheese, and fresh fruit. The presentation is always attractive. (For those considering two consecutive cruises, for example, the one-week Eastern Caribbean cruise followed by a Western Caribbean trip, the menus and entertainment are rotated every seven days, repeating the second week.)

Il Giardino, the lido cafe for indoor breakfast and lunch buffets, was redesigned to improve serving problems encountered in the *Classica*'s La Trattoria. Unfortunately, that didn't help the food. Breakfast and lunch selections in the dining room are far superior. Il Giardino, however, is among the ship's prettiest informal settings, its rattan chairs dressed in English country fabrics against aquamarine glass walls and wood floors. At least two evenings per cruise, a dinner buffet is offered. The midnight buffet's setting changes depending on weather and the theme.

Adjacent to the lido cafe, the Terrazza Cafe reproduces the *Classica*'s popular Alfresco Cafe, the ship's most pleasant location from dawn to dusk. Set with wicker chairs and tables under a high-peaked canvas canopy, it provides a cool, inviting outdoor setting for breakfast and lunch.

The other big hit is Romeo's Pizzeria, where pizza is served throughout the day. It's free, but you might want to buy a glass of wine or beer to wash it down. Romeo's neighbor, Juliet's Patisserie/Bar, open from 9 a.m. to midnight, serves pastries, without charge, and espresso. It's also the Martini Bar.

Afternoon tea, with fabulous desserts, is served daily, and a cart dispenses Italian ice cream from 10 p.m. to midnight. In 1998, Costa introduced "Notte Tropical," an outdoor tropical buffet.

Service   In recent years Costa has changed its crews' makeup, with major impact. The ships no longer are all Italian. They're now multinational, as are most other cruise lines. As a result, Costa lost an edge that distinguished it from the pack. Italian officers still command the ships, and Italians supervise the restaurants, but the flair and fun that Italian waiters can create is often missing.

The hotel and dining staff come from India, Asia, the Caribbean, Europe, and Central and South America. A few speak some English. Service is attentive, friendly, and good—often, very good—but for those who knew Costa before, the *ambiente* isn't the same. The cruise staff cheerfully runs daily activities, but you're unlikely to see the cruise director except to open the nightly show.

Facilities and Entertainment   Evening entertainment is planned to appeal to the multinational passenger mix. *Romantica*'s main show lounge, the L'Opera Theater (Coloseo on *Classica*), is a modern interpretation of a classic, horseshoe-shaped concert hall. Creating a glamorous setting are red and royal blue carpets, blue velvet seats against a wall of blue mosaics, and brass accents. Most seats have good sight lines, and back sufferers will like the hard, stiff balcony seats. L'Opera has shows nightly.

Romantica's casino is spectacular, with stucco walls inlaid with gold accents and a large crystal chandelier. Columns covered in mosaics complement a large mosaic mural by artist Sambonet entitled *Amazonia*. A rounded bar set against a blue marble backdrop is stunning. The casino offers blackjack, roulette tables, and slot machines.

The Tango Ballroom, a multipurpose lounge with large dance floor, becomes a high-energy nightclub with live music. The room has window walls and is a lovely daytime retreat.

The Diva Disco, atop the ship, is a daytime observation and cocktail lounge and late-night hot spot. Mirrored walls reflect panoramas admitted by floor-to-ceiling windows, creating almost funhouse scenes of sea and ports.

Everyone's favorite is the toga party, when passengers create Roman garb from sheets provided by the ship. It's remarkable how many ways passengers find to make togas, and almost all passengers join in and have a great time.

Activities and Diversions Daytime diversions include lessons in dance, Italian language, and gaming; bingo; bridge; backgammon; culinary demonstrations; port and shopping talks; horse racing; and the Not-So-Newlywed Game. The teen center has a video game room, and there's a library and card room. Movies are shown on cabin television.

The full-service conference center offers meeting space, audiovisual equipment, movable leather chairs equipped with flip-top desks, and a board room for 20. The center has its own front desk, which meeting planners applaud.

Sports, Fitness, and Beauty The ships have two outdoor pools separated by Costa's distinctive yellow stacks. One has four Jacuzzis and is surrounded by three terraces of teak decks with lounge chairs. The second is inlaid with ceramic tiles; suspended above it is a Susumu sculpture in red metal, which changes shape in the wind.

The Caracalla Spa on the *Classica* has floor-to-ceiling windows. *Romantica*'s smaller spa is beside the stack. In addition to weights, life cycles, and treadmills, the spa has sauna, steam, and massage rooms, plus a beauty salon offering personalized hair and body treatments.

A partial deck above the swimming pools has a jogging track and sunbathing space. Beneath the Diva Disco is an area cantilevered above the deck; it's a great hideaway—for those who find it—for sunning or snoozing in stylish cabana chairs.

Children's Facilities Costa Kids, a year-round program available on Caribbean and European cruises, offers daily activities geared to two age groups: Costa Kids Club, 3–12 years; and Costa Teens Club, 13–17 years. Two youth counselors are aboard each ship year-round; counselors are added when there are more than 12 children on a cruise. Youth Center activities include Nintendo competitions, bridge and galley tours, arts and crafts, a treasure hunt, Italian lessons, bingo, board games, karaoke contests, pizza parties, ice cream socials, face painting, cartoons, and movies. The *Classica* also has a teen center. At sea, Kids Club hours generally are 9–11:30 a.m., 2–5:30 p.m., and 8–11 p.m.

European cruises have three clubs: Baby Club, ages 3–6; Junior Club, ages 7–12; and Teens Club, ages 13–17. Baby Club offers a story hour, crafts, games, and ice cream parties. Junior Club has aerobics, puppet theater, mini-Olympics, and team treasure hunts. Teens Club offers sports and fitness programs, guitar lessons, video productions, and a rock and roll hour. In Europe, free babysitting for ages 3–6 is available, subject to staff availability.

Postscript After heavy criticism for seemingly endless shipboard announcements in five languages beginning at 8 a.m., Costa says it has trimmed the intrusion; however, we still hear complaints. Since most of this information is in the daily agenda, the broadcasts would seem unnecessary.

CostaAllegra	**(South America)**	
CostaMarina	**(South America)**	
Registry: Italian	Length: 616/572 feet	Beam: 84 feet
Cabins: 410/383	Draft: 24 feet	Speed: 21.5/19 knots
Maximum Passengers:	Passenger Decks: 8	Elevators: 4
820/1,005	Crew: 430/385	Space Ratio: 37/32.3

The Ships Built from a freighter hull, *CostaAllegra* is an unusual-looking cruise ship from its bow to its cutaway stern which is almost all glass. The elaborate use of glass—from floor-to-ceiling windows of the dining room to the glass walls and transparent dome over the disco and spa—allows natural light to stream through the ship, giving it an airy feeling.

Not the smallest of the fleet, but smaller than Costa's newest ships and with a more intimate ambience, *CostaAllegra* is distinctively contemporary Italian in design and decor, though not as radical as the *CostaClassica*. Glass, mirrors, and water combine to create visual effects that enliven the ship.

For example, the pool deck has a glass-bottom "canal" in which water flows from the whirlpool to the swimming pool. A deck below, refracted light ripples through the glass ceiling of the elegant Murano Bar and the glass atrium.

Art has been integrated in the ship's layout. The eight passenger decks are named for Impressionist artists—Manet, Rousseau, Degas, Modigliani, Toulouse-Lautrec, Gauguin, and Van Gogh. Each level has reproductions and stylized murals taken from the artists' work. Marble is used, but more sparingly than on the *Classica* or *Romantica*.

The *CostaMarina,* built in 1969, is similar to the *Allegra,* starting with its odd profile. A dome caps her glass-walled stern, and the cluster of yellow stacks bearing a big "C" on them is easily recognized as Costa's. Rebuilt in 1990, *CostaMarina* was designed by the *Allegra*'s architect, Guido Canali, and has his signature use of glass and water to flood the ship with light.

CostaMarina also has a three-deck, glass-walled atrium and a glass-domed roof above the Galaxy nightclub. Its waterfall cascades over slanted glass from the sports deck to the Laguna Deck, emptying into a small swimming pool. Portholes in the Casino Lounge on the Marina Deck offer underwater views of the pool.

The ships' layouts are easy to navigate. Most public rooms are on the top three decks. Cabins are on the lower three and the center deck, which they share with the dining room. Unlike the *Allegra, CostaMarina* has an escalator, the first on a cruise ship. It links the Marina Deck to the dining room, one flight below.

On the *Allegra,* passengers arrive in a three-deck atrium lobby on the Lautrec Deck that is dominated by an ultramodern glass sculpture. Atrium walls are covered with hand-painted watercolors depicting the history of Italian theater.

The *Allegra's* modest size allows for fewer lounges and bars than her bigger sisters have, but they're enough to provide the entertainment and activities of a modern cruise. On the Degas Deck, a show lounge anchors the forward end; a nightclub, the stern. Between are the casino, elegant shops around the Piazzetta Allegra, a patisserie, the light-filled Murano Bar, a card room, and a handsome, little-used library with few books.

One flight up, the Rousseau Deck has suites at the bow, a swimming pool with waterfall, the Yacht Club Buffet, and the Crystal Club under the dramatic glass dome easily spotted in the ship's profile. Floor-to-ceiling windows make it a popular observation lounge by day; at night it's a lively disco.

The top deck accommodates a greenery-filled spa, a second level with a solarium, spa treatment rooms, children's center, and a jogging track. The ship also has a chapel and meeting room.

Itineraries   See Appendix B.

Cabins   The *CostaAllegra* has 12 categories of cabins, almost as many inside as outside. *CostaMarina* has eight categories, with more inside than outside cabins—unusual for new ships. All cabins are on the lower four decks, except for eight suites and eight inside cabins on a higher deck. The *Allegra* has eight wheelchair-accessible cabins with ramp access, and wide doors and grab bars in the bathrooms.

Cabins on Costa's newer ships are larger, but these are well designed and comfortable, with ample drawer and closet space. All have twin beds, desk and dresser, phone, safe, television/radio, hair dryer, bathroom with shower, and oversized portholes.

Allegra's three grand suites are just under the bridge, offering the same view the captain sees. They have separate living rooms and bedrooms, second bedrooms, marble baths with Jacuzzi tubs, and separate showers. The ten smaller suites have sitting areas with sofa and chairs, Jacuzzi tubs and showers, and verandas. *Marina*'s eight suites have bathrooms with tubs and verandas and are tastefully furnished in deep blue with white walls and contemporary art.

Cabin service repeatedly gets high marks for being efficient and attentive. The room service menu has pizza in the evening.

CostaAllegra *Specifications* 192 inside cabins, 205 outside; 13 suites. Standard dimensions are 146–156 square feet. Grand suites with sitting area and bar. 378 with twin beds (268 convertible to doubles); 116 third and fourth persons; 6 singles; 8 equipped for disabled.

CostaMarina *Specifications* 205 inside cabins, 175 outside. Standard dimensions are 140–170 square feet. 283 with twin beds, most convert to double; 8 suites; 204 three/four persons; 14 singles.

Dining *CostaAllegra*'s Montmarte Restaurant, dressed in gray and burgundy, resembles an elegant European restaurant. Huge portholes frame side walls, and glass panels at the stern flood the room with light. Tables seating four to eight are separated by glass panels and live greenery. A baby grand piano provides music. The *CostaMarina*'s spacious, attractive Crystal Restaurant has windows on three sides to showcase the sea and scenery. Both ships' restaurants offer two seatings and a midnight buffet.

The predominantly Italian cuisine is served in European style, with frequent tableside preparations and beautiful presentation. Always a favorite, freshly prepared pasta is on every lunch and dinner menu, along with a variety of continental selections. The poolside Pasta Festival on a day at sea is an all-you-can-eat pasta lover's dream with a half-dozen or more pastas made continuously. Dinner menus offer about the same number of choices—ample but not extravagant—as aboard other Costa ships.

Breakfast and lunch buffets in the *Allegra*'s indoor/outdoor Yacht Club appear to have the right mix of good food and variety, avoiding the criticism suffered by the *Classica* and *Romantica* spreads. The attractive facility has wicker chairs with blue-striped cushions, wooden tables inlaid with blue panels, and miniatures of sailing ships. Afternoon tea is served, and cabin service is available from a limited menu.

Service The *CostaAllegra* has Italian officers, dining room supervisors, and head waiters. Other staff represents a mix of nationalities. All get good reviews for friendly, attentive, efficient service.

Facilities and Entertainment Activities, sports, and entertainment are not as elaborate on the *CostaAllegra* and *CostaMarina* in Europe as on Costa's ships in the Caribbean. They don't need to be. European itineraries are port-intensive, and European passengers are more attuned to friendship and conversation.

But there's no shortage of possibilities for those who enjoy moderately paced shipboard activity. Standards include bingo, a fashion show, card and parlor games, poolside fun by day, and low-key shows and dancing in several lounges in the evening. Quality varies, but individual performers and the ship's cruise staff generally are most popular.

Also available are supervised children's activities, shops, meeting rooms, a library, and a card room.

Sports, Fitness, and Beauty   In addition to the pool and whirlpool, *Allegra* has a jogging track on the top deck and the spa has exercise equipment (no charge)—each item in its own garden environment with light streaming from the glass ceiling. Also offered are sauna, steam room, massage, beauty salon, barber shop, and rooms for beauty treatments (additional cost). The *Marina*'s spa and fitness center has similar facilities, but it lacks a jogging track and has less deck space.

Postscript   When *CostaAllegra* was introduced, the line was finding its way back from the wrong turn it took with the "Euroluxe" idea and the less-than-successful introduction of *CostaClassica*. The *CostaAllegra,* perhaps because she is smaller with a friendly and lively *ambiente,* helped the line's reputation. *CostaAllegra* gets consistently good reviews for food and service.

Readers considering any Costa cruise should read the entire section on the line to become familiar with its services and facilities.

CostaVictoria	Quality ⑤	Value D
Registry: Italian	Length: 828 feet	Beam: 105 feet
Cabins: 964	Draft: 24 feet	Speed: 23 knots
Maximum Passengers:	Passenger Decks: 3	Elevators: 12
1,928	Crew: 800	Space Ratio: 38.9

The Ship   Costa's first megaship made her debut in 1996. Designed by well-known naval architect Robert Tillberg, she was the largest passenger liner built in Germany when she was launched. Despite her size, her shallow draft provides exceptional maneuverability and gives the ship access to smaller ports and the Panama and Suez Canals.

Ultramodern and sophisticated, *CostaVictoria* emulates the style of *CostaClassica* and *CostaRomantica,* though she carries almost a third more passengers. The larger size makes possible more choices in dining and entertainment.

The main entrance, the circular Planetarium Atrium, spans seven decks and has four glass elevators connecting the lobby with the pool deck above. It's capped by a large glass dome admitting sunlight that reflects off a colored glass sculpture by Milanese artist Gianfranco Pardi on the lowest level (Deck 5). Deck 5 also has the purser's office, shore excursion desk, and a piano bar. All but one of the ten passenger decks are named after Italian operas.

The most dramatic room is the Concorde Plaza observation lounge at the bow. It spans four decks; a floor-to-ceiling glass wall provides spectacular ocean views. The area is designed as an Italian piazza, a signature feature of Costa ships. Opposite the windows is a marble dance floor adjoining a center stage; its backdrop is a waterfall inspired by Leonardo Da Vinci's drawings of the moon eclipsing the sun. The plaza is decorated in blues, silver, and gold. The lounge serves as an elegant area for socializing, special events, and evening entertainment, including cabaret shows, games, bingo, and port lectures.

Other public rooms include a disco, children's playroom, teen club, shopping arcade, library, card room, and chapel, plus three conference rooms equipped with audio and video, overhead, and computer projection systems.

Itineraries   See Appendix B.

Cabins   The majority of cabins are on the upper decks. Sixty percent are outside cabins with a porthole or large, square window. Cabins are small compared to those on the *Classica* and *Romantica,* and none has a private balcony. *CostaVictoria* was the line's first ship to have a minibar, safe, hair dryer, and interactive television in every cabin. All cabins have direct-dial telephones and sliding doors that separate the living area and bathroom. Circular bathrooms have rounded showers and vanity areas.

The 6 top suites and 14 minisuites, forward on the pool and sports decks, are decorated with Laura Ashley fabrics and trimmed with pearwood. They have sitting areas, whirlpool baths, walk-in closets, and queen beds, plus one upper berth and a Murphy bed, thus accommodating up to four people. Butler service is provided.

The *CostaVictoria*'s unique "fan coil" system allows each cabin to be refreshed with its own recycled air or outside air. Thus, nonsmokers' air isn't mixed with smokers'. The ship does not have self-service laundromats for passsenger use.

Specifications   391 inside, 553 outside; 20 suites; 6 wheelchair-accessible. Standard cabins range from 120 to 150 square feet.

Dining   *CostaVictoria* was the first Costa vessel to have two dining rooms: Sinfonia Restaurant aft and Fantasia Restaurant amidships. Both are decorated with marble and pine walls and glass chandeliers from Murano. Both restaurants have picture windows. Murals transform the windows from ocean views by day to Italian scenes by night. Unfortunately, the food isn't up to the standard of the *Romantica* and *Classica,* despite recent efforts to improve it. The glass-enclosed Tavernetta Lounge has a bar, lively entertainment, and dancing, and it doubles as an alternative dining venue, Ristorante Magnifico by Zefferino, modeled after the famous Zefferino's in Genoa. Passengers must make reservations and pay an extra charge of $18.75 per person, but given the uneven quality of the dining rooms' fare, it's worth it and has proven to be a popular alternative. Walls are hung with ten paintings of earlier Costa passenger ships by artist Stephen Card and contribute to the cozy atmosphere created by the addition of candlelight, flowers, soft music, and excellent service.

Passengers dine informally at an indoor/outdoor buffet serving breakfast and lunch. Bolero, the indoor buffet, is surrounded by glass windows and furnished with rattan chairs and marble tables. The outdoor Terraza Café, similar to ones on *Classica* and *Romantica* but much larger, is protected by a large white canopy made by Canobbio, an Italian firm specializing in circus tents and sports arena coverings. Other dining options include two buffets, a pizzeria, ice cream bar, and grill.

Facilities and Entertainment   The two-deck Festival Show Lounge is decorated in rich reds with Tivoli lights twinkling in the ceiling. The stage can be raised for variety and production shows or lowered for dancing.

The Grand Bar Orpheus, with a bar trimmed in rare, blue Brazilian marble, is popular for cocktails and after-dinner espresso. It's connected by a curved glass stairway to the big, bright Monte Carlo Casino. Just outside the casino is Capriccio Lounge, an intimate piano bar decorated with floor-to-ceiling mosaics by Italian painter Emilio Tadini.

Theme nights may include Notte Tropical, the lively Festa Italiana, and the rollicking Roman Bacchanal.

Sports, Fitness, and Beauty   The Solarium, a top-deck viewing and sunning area, has pipes that continuously emit mists of cool water. The two outdoor pools are surrounded by six whirlpools and two shuffleboard courts. Nearby is the Wimbledon Tennis Court, a miniature court using smaller racquets and balls. It can be converted to a basketball or volleyball court.

The Pompei Spa has an indoor swimming pool centered with a large mosaic and surrounded by Roman columns and teakwood lounge chairs. The spa also offers a Turkish bath, saunas, massage, thalassotherapy, hydrotherapy, and other beauty treatment rooms. Unfortunately, the rooms lack hooks for hanging your towel or clothes when all the lockers are taken, which seems to be a common event. A 1,312-foot jogging track connects the spa to the gymnasium, which is equipped with weight-training equipment and an aerobics room. This is the first ship to carry products from Tuscany's chic Terme di Saturnia. There is a beauty salon.

Costa's Golf Academy-at-Sea on Caribbean cruises offers on-board golf clinics, private lessons with a PGA pro, and play in port. Video swing analysis and lessons range from a 15-minute swing-check for $25 to a 60-minute golf lesson for $60. Other activities include golf seminars, putting competitions, tournaments, and range practice. Golfers can rent top-of-the-line clubs and shoes. Courses available are Mahogany Run, St. Thomas; Teeth of the Dog, Casa de Campo, Dominican Republic; Runaway Bay and Sandals Golf Resort, Jamaica; and The Links at Safe Haven, Grand Cayman, among others. Fees vary. The PGA instructor accompanies participants when they play in port.

Children's Facilities   Peter Pan's Children's Club is the center of youth activities. A disco and teen club offer a dance floor, video games, four computer stations, and a large television monitor.

Shore Excursions   On her Eastern Caribbean cruises, the ship stops at Isla Catalina, where Costa developed facilities for a fun day at the beach with games and water sports. The ship also offers tours to Casa de Campo, one of the Caribbean's largest resorts, for tennis, horseback riding, and golf on world-famous Pete Dye courses. You must buy the ship's shore excursion to go to Casa de Campo; cruise passengers are not allowed to go there on their own. The ship also offers diving and snorkeling at selected ports.

In Europe, shore excursions generally are as varied as the cruises and range from a glacier walk in Norway to a visit to Egyptian pyramids. For most locations, brochures describe only one or two tours, without prices, making planning difficult. Itineraries are port-intensive, rarely including more than one or two days at sea during a week.

Postscript   *CostaVictoria* is in the style of Costa's newest fleet, and the promise of "Cruising Italian Style" seems to be halfhearted when so many opportunities are missed. For example, each deck is named for an Italian opera, yet it is impossible to get Italian opera—or even Pavarotti—on the cabin radio, nor are any Italian movies (with or without English subtitles) shown on the disappointing cabin movie channel where the run-of-the-mill film menu is about as inspiring as the pasta and pizza. Cabins are small compared to the line's older ships and lack verandas—a strong trend on new ships. Longtime Costa fans who expect this ship to be like the

CostaRomantica or to have the *ambiente* of the *CostaRiviera* will be disappointed. It's a different product.

CostaAtlantica	**(Preview)**	
Registry: Italian	Length: 960 feet	Beam: 106 feet
Cabins: 1,057	Draft: 19.5 feet	Speed: 24 knots
Maximum Passengers:	Passenger Decks: 12	Elevators: 12
2,680	Crew: NA	Space Ratio: NA

The Ship   Costa's newest ship, *CostaAtlantica,* which made her debut in July 2000 on a European series, is the largest ship in the fleet. The ship has 1,057 cabins, of which 78 percent are outside. There are 678 cabins (including 58 suites) with verandas; 68 accommodations have French verandas—a marked improvement over her sister ship, *CostaVictoria,* which has no verandas.

Facilities include three swimming pools, one with a retractable magrodome to convert the pool deck into an 11,000-square-foot solarium, providing all-weather swimming. Another pool, dedicated to children, has a water slide.

CostaAtlantica features a replica of "Caffe Florian," the famous eighteenth-century landmark in St. Mark's Square in Venice. This indoor/outdoor cafe serves drinks and aperitifs with background music meant to evoke the romance of this Venetian legend that captivated such luminaries as Vivaldi, Dickens, and Stravinsky, among others.

Estimated to cost $400 million, the *CostaAtlantica* is meant to combine European elegance with American comforts. She has 12 passenger decks, all named after films directed by the great Italian director Federico Fellini. The Caruso Theatre, the main show lounge, is an impressive three-level room with a capacity of 1,167. There is a Madame Butterfly Grand Lounge, complete with waitresses dressed in geisha style, and several other lounges and bars.

The ship has several dining venues. The two-level Tiziano Restaurant is the main dining room. The Botticelli Buffet serves breakfast and lunch in an informal sitting; the Napoli Pizzeria serves fresh hot pizza, and the alternative dining venue, Ristorante Magnifico by Zefferino, similar to the one on the *CostaVictoria,* is modeled after its namesake in Genoa and has an extra charge of $18.75.

The new ship also has a fitness center and full-service spa set on two levels; a children's area with a video arcade; shops; and conference facilities.

CostaAtlantica is equipped with a dual Azipod propulsion system, new technology introduced in 1997 on the *Carnival Destiny* that contributes to the ship's smooth sailing. With a cruising speed of 22 knots and a maximum speed of 24 knots, the *CostaAtlantica* is the fastest ship in the Costa fleet.

Itineraries   See Appendix B.

Costa Cruise Lines European Fleet

CostaRiviera   Costa Cruise Lines' oldest vessel is marketed primarily in Europe. A popular ship familiar to Costa's North American fans, she helped define "cruising Italian style." The vessel was seconded to American Family Cruises. When that line failed, the ship was returned to Costa service in Europe. She now sails year-round from Savona on Eastern and Western Mediterranean itineraries.

The ship was renovated after it returned to Costa in 1994. Some facilities added for children by American Family Cruises were retained, enhancing the ship's attractiveness for families. More recent renovations added a two-deck atrium lobby and new bathrooms in cabins on three decks. All public rooms and cabins where refurbished with new carpeting, wall coverings, bedding, full-length mirrors, and television. Areas on the Riviera Deck, the beauty salon, and shops have been remodeled; the casino was expanded; and winter garden promenades were added to each side of the ship.

Crown Cruise Line

4000 Hollywood Blvd., Suite 385 South Tower
Hollywood, FL 33021
(954) 967-2100; (800) 237-5361; fax (954) 967-2148
www.crowncruiseline.com

Type of Ships   Modern, midsize oceanliners.

Type of Cruise   Upscale, moderately priced.

Cruise Line's Strengths
- friendly, conscientious staff
- value for money
- cabins
- southwestern Caribbean itineraries
- program for certified divers
- ship size
- dining room cuisine
- plentiful shaded space on deck

Cruise Line's Shortcomings
- buffets & casual dining
- complex travel itineraries occassioned by Caribbean port of departure
- transfers from airport to ship in Aruba

Fellow Passengers   Mid- to upper-mid-income people ($60,000+ household income) from mid-30s to early 60s who appreciate and can afford a higher quality and somewhat more sophisticated cruise experience than offered by larger, mass market ships.

Recommended For   Those who seek a more upscale cruise experience than that provided by contemporary, mass-market cruise lines. Cruises designed for successful baby boomers and younger folks with some prior experience traveling in the Caribbean, as the itinerary offers a balance of options for beach and water sports, scenic and historic sight-seeing, and shopping and visits to some less frequented ports.

Not Recommended For Wheelchair-bound people due to limited availability of staterooms and access to most public areas.

Cruise Areas and Seasons Southern Caribbean, November–April; Bermuda, May–October.

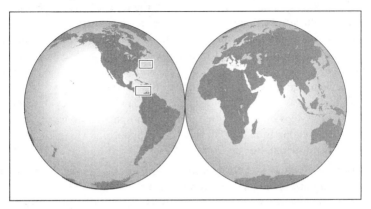

The Line Crown Cruise Line represents the new, upscale product of Commodore Cruise Line, a New Orleans based company specializing in budget cruises to the western Caribbean. The original Crown Cruise Line was based in Florida and operated a single ship out of Palm Beach. Commodore acquired Crown in 1992 specifically to develop an upmarket brand with a new ship. Plans were frustrated, however, when Effjohn International, Commodore's Scandinavian parent company, chartered the newly completed *Crown Dynasty* to Cunard to operate under the Cunard Crown banner. Cunard, struggling with the charter, turned the *Crown Dynasty* over to Norwegian Cruise Lines in 1997. NCL managed the *Dynasty* until the charter expired in 1999. Meanwhile, Effjohn sold Commodore to the new Commodore Cruise Lines, which picked up the *Dynasty* from NCL and launched Crown Cruise Line, finally making good on the upscale product envisioned eight years earlier

The *Crown Dynasty,* following a $5 million renovation kicked off it's first cruise season in December 1999, offering a deluxe, small-ship-feel cruise experience at prices comparable to or below those of mid-market lines. During its first year with the *Dynasty,* Crown Cruise Line operated cruises in the southeastern Caribbean, originating in Aruba during the winter, and in spring, repositioning the ship to Baltimore and Philadelphia for cruises to Bermuda and Canada in the summer and fall.

The Fleet	Built/Renovated	Tonnage	Passengers
Crown Dynasty	1993/99	20,000	820

Style Elegant but not stuffy, the decor of the *Crown Dynasty* communicates a sophistication that is apparent the moment you step on board, with a welcoming atmosphere where formality is gratefully absent. Expansive glass windows throughout the ship, large open decks and terraces, and a five-story atrium create a feeling of space and openness. Polished woods, gentle lighting, and soft hues contribute to the stylish comfort.

The ship was designed to provide the features and amenities of the new, large cruise ships but in a more intimate atmosphere. The result is more personal attention from the staff and a better opportunity for passengers to make friends with fellow travelers.

Distinctive Features Ship's unusual design (see ship's profile); itineraries; Bermuda hotel stays and cruise combination.

	HIGHEST	LOWEST	AVERAGE
PER DIEM	$302	$202	$251

The above per diems are calculated from the cruise line's non-discounted *cruise only* fares on standard accommodations. Per diems vary by season, by cabin, and by cruise areas.

Special Fares and Discounts
- Second person in cabin free with 150 day advance booking
- Third/Fourth Person: Yes
- Single Supplement: 150 percent for cabins; 200 percent for suites.

Packages
- Air/Sea: Yes
- Others: Yes
- Pre/Post: Aruba season—3-night hotel package at La Cabana Beach Resort & Casino, Aruba from $349 per person double. Bermuda Season, additional packages available through Apple Vacations.

The Last Word In a world of global acquisitions and mergers, it's tough for a small cruise line to hold its own. Crown, like its parent Commodore, provides a tremendous bang for the buck on one of the nicest and most livable of the luxury liners built in the '90s. For a line this small, every passenger is important, and that's exactly they way they make you feel. Crown is set to chip away at the big players in the industry, sailing into 2001 with interesting itineraries, unique ports of call, and prices that are hard to beat.

CROWN STANDARD FEATURES

Officers European/International

Staff European/International

Dining Facilities One dining room for two seatings with open seating for breakfast and lunch and assigned seating for dinner. Casual cafe for breakfast and light lunch buffet, afternoon snacks, late-night buffet.

Special Diets Vegetarian and light entrees for lunch and dinner with cholesterol, caloric, and sodium values noted. Other special dietary needs accommodated with advance notice.

Room Service 24 hours. Butler service in deluxe suites.

Dress Code Stylish resort wear during day. For evening, three nights casual, no shorts; two nights semiformal (tie optional; jacket required for men); two nights formal.

Cabin Amenities Bathrobes, hair dryers, safes, radios, telephones, television with cable and movie channels, and deluxe toiletries.

Electrical Outlets 110 AC.

Wheelchair Access Four cabins; four elevators.

Recreation and Entertainment Piano bar; show lounge with nightly Broadway-style shows; casino; club with nightly vocal entertainment; disco.

Sports and Other Activities Fitness center, walking/jogging track, swimming pool, Jacuzzi, deck games.

Beauty and Fitness Spa with exercise facilities; beauty salon.

Other Facilities Library, card room.

Children's Facilities Room available throughout the year, offering games, toys, and play structures. "Shipmates," a children's program with youth counselors to supervise activities, available during summer and holidays.

Theme Cruises None.

Smoking Permitted in cabins and public areas; dining room and show lounge have smoking sections.

Crown Suggested Tipping Per person, per day: cabin steward, $3.50; dining waiter, $3.50; bus boy: $2; maître d'hôtel $0.75; 15 percent service charge added on bar checks.

Credit Cards For cruise payment and on-board charges: American Express, Discover, MasterCard, Visa.

Crown Dynasty	Quality ⑤	Value A
Registry: Panama	Length: 537 feet	Beam: 74 feet
Cabins: 419	Draft: 18 feet	Speed: 21 knots
Maximum Passengers:	Passenger Decks: 8	Elevators: 4
820	Crew: 310	Space Ratio: 24

The Ship In October 1999, the *Crown Dynasty* (formerly *Norwegian Dynasty* of Norwegian Cruise Lines), became the first ship of the reconstituted Crown Cruise Line, catering to a more upscale market than its sister company, Commodore Cruise Line.

During the winter months, the *Crown Dynasty* is based in Aruba, sailing on seven-day cruises in the Southern and Eastern Caribbean. In May, she heads to Philadelphia for the summer for cruises to Bermuda's West End with six of the series departing from Baltimore. Apple Vacations, a major Caribbean tour company, packages the cruises with hotel stays, giving passengers the option of flying one way and cruising the other.

Built in 1993 in Spain, *Crown Dynasty* was one of the prettiest ships of the decade, with a sleek, contemporary profile and an unusual interior. Designed by Scandinavian architect Petter Yran, who has created the interiors of the *Sea Goddess* and other luxury ships, the *Crown Dynasty* has a cheerful, open ambience with walls of glass, plentiful deck space, and expansive sea views.

The contemporary interiors, with muted colors in some contexts and vibrant colors in others, was given a Bermuda theme during her most recent renovation, and all the public rooms and decks were renamed using Bermuda locations. All are enriched with teak and other fine wood, marble, murals, and paintings. The warm interiors and quality furnishings convey a deluxe, small-ship feeling. The ship's primary attraction is that it's small enough to be cozy, but large enough to offer modern cruise ship amenities and facilities.

The layout of the ship is unusual, if not unique. The greenery-filled, five-deck atrium lobby is aft, rather than amidships. Also, it's on the starboard side rather than at the center, permitting a nearly solid bank of windows to tower from Decks 4–8. The walls of glass admit natural light and spectacular sea views, helping connect passengers with the sea.

From the atrium's base on Deck 4 (actually, the third of seven passenger decks), music from a baby grand piano fills the lobby and helps set the tone. Deck 5 one flight up is devoted to public rooms. It's anchored at both ends by lounges oriented to the port side horizontally and facing large windows (rather than the usual arrangement of lounges facing the bow or stern). The multilevel Gombey show lounge, for example, is semicircular, with the stage and dance floor on the port side. Between the lounges are shops, a casino, and a bar.

In another innovation, four of the main public rooms are stacked vertically at the stern, allowing for large windows in virtually every area. The decks are connected by outdoor stairways and open decks. The result is a bright, open atmosphere, sea panoramas, and plentiful deck space.

Itineraries   See Appendix B.

Cabins   The ship has ten categories of cabins on five decks; about two thirds are outside. Cabins are nicely appointed in pastels with light wood furniture and brass fixtures. All have televisions, phones, safes, and card-key door locks. Closet space is good, but drawer space is minimal. Many cabins are fitted with twin beds that can be converted to a queen. Bathrooms are small but have large medicine cabinets, mirrored doors, and vanities and are provided with quality lotions and soaps and fluffy bathrobes.

Deluxe cabins and suites have refrigerators and sitting areas with large windows. Ten suites have private balconies. Four wheelchair-accessible cabins have large bathrooms with grab bars and wide doorways.

Specifications   124 inside cabins, 233 outside, including 31 junior suites (most with partially obstructed views) and 12 deluxe suites (10 with verandas). Standard dimensions are 130 square feet for inside cabins, 140 square feet for outside cabins and 160–350 square feet for suites. 354 cabins with 2 lower beds convert to double; 36 with 2 lower and 2 upper berths; 1 with 1 lower and 1 upper berth; no singles; 4 wheelchair-accessible.

Service   Service is professional, friendly, and attentive without being obtrusive. The only glitch, curiously, is in the Hamilton Dining Room, where an insufficient number of wine stewards makes wine service spotty.

Dining   The nonsmoking, 420-seat Hamilton Dining Room has a skylight and panoramic windows on three sides, providing natural light and sea views for all diners. Although tables are close, noise is low. The room, decorated in muted colors with lively, contemporary art, has a variety of table configurations separated from service areas by frosted glass. Wine stewards serve from an extensive wine list.

Cuisine in the main dining room is varied, creative, and attractively presented. Locally available ingredients, including seafood, and Caribbean specialties are regularly featured. Meat is offered at every meal and cooked to order. Light cuisine and vegetarian meals are also provided at every meal. Portions are ample.

Above the dining room on Deck 6 is a casual indoor/outdoor Dockyard Cafe, where breakfast and lunch buffets, afternoon tea, and late-night buffets are served. The 276-seat cafe, more elegantly decorated than usual for a lido cafe, opens onto a two-deck outdoor lounge area where passengers may eat (and smoke). The 24-hour room service has a limited menu. Meals in the Dockyard Cafe are decidedly less compelling than the Hamilton Dining Room, and rank below average in general for cruise ship buffet service. Breakfast is better than lunch, featuring a cook-to-order omelet station. Lunches in the Dockyard Cafe, as well as many of the late evening buffets, are long on bulk and short on creativity and taste. It's not that you can't find something to enjoy, but among the selections offered, there seem to be more misses than hits.

Facilities and Entertainment   Above the cafe is the Port Royal Pub, which is used for informal gatherings, games, and movies; it has a full-service bar and is the disco at night.

The Queen of Bermuda Bar, a quiet retreat adjacent to the casino, is favored for early evening cocktails and after-dinner drinks. Tastefully decorated, it's separated from the main thoroughfare by frosted glass and wood paneling. Next door, the Atlantic Casino offers slot machines, blackjack, Caribbean stud poker, and roulette.

The Gombey show lounge offers various performers—a comic, ventriloquist, singer, dancer—and Broadway-style revues. Aft on the St. George's Deck (5) is the Southampton Club, a large lounge with a bar and dance floor. Directly above on Warwick Deck is the Dockyard Café; and above it, the Port Royal Pub. The ship also has a cozy library with good sea views and a card room. Additional facilities include a photo processing lab, laundry service, and medical center.

Activities and Diversions   Activities aboard *Crown Dynasty* start with morning exercise sessions. Port talks, games, various tournaments, bingo, art auctions, wine tastings, lectures, and even snorkel clinics draw a crowd in the afternoon.

Sports, Fitness, and Beauty   Sandys, the top deck, has a swimming pool, Jacuzzis, and the Horseshoe Bay Bar. Forward, the Royal Bermuda Spa has large windows facing the bow and is equipped with state-of-the-art exercise equipment, stationary bicycles, treadmills, Stairmasters, rowing machines, an aerobics area, and a juice bar. It also has a beauty salon with hair and body treatments, two saunas, and steam and massage rooms. A jogging track rims the pool on an overhang, and windscreens line the deck's perimeter.

A wide outside promenade dotted with lounge chairs circles Deck 5, providing an uninterrupted track for walking or jogging.

Children's Facilities   The Rainbow Room is near the swimming pool on Deck 8 and is available throughout the year, offering children's games, toys, and play structures. "Shipmates" is a full children's program available in the summer and during holidays with youth counselors on board to supervise activities. Babysitting services are not formally available, but can be arranged between passengers and interested crewmembers.

Shore Excursions   Aruba season (November–April), the five-port itinerary offers a balance of options for beach and water sports, scenic and historic sight-seeing, and shopping at several ports that are not typically visited by the larger ships.

The Bermuda season ship (May–October) departs the U.S. on Wednesday afternoon and arrives in Bermuda on Friday afternoon, docking at the King's Wharf Marina on Ireland Island until noon on Monday. The return voyage departs Bermuda at noon Monday and docks in Philadelphia or Baltimore shortly after breakfast. While in port, the Crown Dynasty serves as a resort hotel, helping passengers to coordinate favorite activities as well as offering off-the-shelf sightseeing tours.

Postscript   Despite the increase in seasoned cruisers who prefer smaller ships, their choices in the midprice range are limited. As one of the few midsize ships built this decade, *Crown Dynasty* helps fill the void. She offers an attractive, modern alternative not only to big ships but also to older ships that predominate in her size and price range, and to expensive boutique ships, which account for most of the new small ships.

Cruise West

(Alaska Sightseeing/Cruise West)
2401 Fourth Avenue, Suite 700, Seattle, WA 98121
(206) 441-8687; (800) 888-9378; fax (206) 441-4757
www.ascw.com

Type of Ships Six small, informal, cabin-equipped, minicoastal cruising vessels and one day-touring boat.

Type of Cruises Casual, close-up, light adventure, with emphasis on scenery and wildlife in coastal areas, seasonally.

Cruise Line's Strengths
- innovative itineraries
- enthusiastic crew
- itinerary flexibility allows extra time for wildlife viewing
- small ships
- cuisine

Cruise Line's Shortcomings
- small cabins; noisy lower-deck cabins
- small bathrooms with handheld showers on some ships
- limited shipboard facilities
- lack of evening activities
- lack of discounts on cruises

Fellow Passengers Mature, physically active; mid-40s to mid-80s. Retired couples and seniors. Passengers somewhat older on Columbia River cruises; younger on Alaskan cruises. Day cruises attract growing number of 30-somethings. Up to 70 percent have college degrees or some college education; passengers are well traveled and more curious about nature, history, and ecology than typical passengers on mainstream cruise ships.

Passengers are outgoing; most would rather rise early to catch the sunrise than party late. Most are from California, Florida, New York, Great Lakes region, Pacific Northwest, and Texas; some from Canada. About 24 percent are repeaters. Regardless of age, they like the intimacy of a casual cruise to places larger liners cannot reach.

Recommended For Small-ship devotees; people looking for light adventure, to experience a region up-close; those preferring wildlife to nightlife and who like to travel in jeans.

Not Recommended For Travelers who need to be entertained; seek a lavish, resortlike experience with emphasis on nightlife; prefer facilities and activities of large ships; gamblers.

Cruise Areas and Seasons Alaska and western Canada, April–October; Pacific Northwest and California, March–November; Sea of Cortés, December–April.

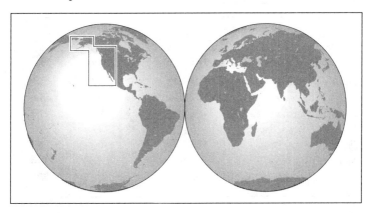

The Line After flying "The Hump" in the China-Burma-India theater in World War II, Charles B. "Chuck" West moved to Alaska to become a bush pilot. Flying over the northern wilderness, he recognized Alaska's great tourism potential. In 1946, he organized, sold, and piloted the first all-tourist air excursion north of the Arctic Circle. From that, he built the largest tour company in Alaska—Westours—which he sold to Holland America Line in 1973.

Starting over again at age 60, West built the tour company that became Alaska Sightseeing/Cruise West. In 1986, he built a luxury cruiser for day tours on Prince William Sound. Two years later, he purchased a second motor-yacht for day cruises on the Inside Passage.

In 1990, the company acquired its first overnight coastal cruising vessels and began service from Juneau to Glacier Bay. Other ships followed as the company expanded its operations. In 1997, *Spirit of Endeavour* was added, the line's most luxurious ship to date. She offers a more upscale level of cruises. The fast-growing line, adding six vessels in seven years, has become North America's largest small-ship cruise company. In 1998, it took another major step, sending two ships to cruise Mexico's Sea of Cortés for the winter, thus becoming a year-round operator. In early 1999, the company separated Alaska Sightseeing from Cruise West—the tours from the cruises—naming the cruise sector Cruise West. The line's American-built and -flagged vessels are subject to Federal Maritime Commission bonding and strict U.S. Coast Guard inspections.

Cruise West's latest move—the addition of *Spirit of Oceanus* in spring 2001—will launch a new era for the line, enabling it to develop new worldwide itineraries and attract new audiences. The all-suite ship, formerly *Renaissance V,* is the line's first ocean-going vessel and the most luxurious ship in the fleet by far.

The Fleet	Built/Renovated	Tonnage	Passengers
Spirit of Alaska	1980/1995	97	78
Spirit of Columbia	1979/1995	98	78
Spirit of Discovery	1976/1992	94	84
Spirit of Endeavour	1985/1996	95	102
Spirit of Glacier Bay	1971/1994	97	52
Spirit of '98	1984/1995	96	96
Spirit of Oceanus	1991	1,263	114
Sheltered Seas (day-cruiser)	1986/1994	95	70

Style Cruise West believes that responsible travel means having enriching experiences that cause minimal impact on the environment. The company encourages environmental education and understanding through unusual, up-close experiences, while respecting wildlife and natural habitats.

The small, shallow-draft vessels can nose into shore for close views of scenery and wildlife and navigate intricate waterways, narrow locks, and small marinas inaccessible to larger ships. Their size and casual atmosphere inspire instant friendships not always possible on larger ships.

Three of the seven vessels have bow-landing capabilities, enabling them to pull up to wilderness beaches or shore-side parks. En route, narration and occasional talks by park rangers, historians, and other specialists inform passengers of the history, geology, and wildlife of areas they're visiting. Otherwise, on-board style is unstructured.

Passengers entertain themselves by immersing themselves in the scenery and wildlife, reading, playing cards and games, or socializing with other passengers and the crew.

Cruise West's young, mostly college-age crew is recruited primarily from the Pacific Northwest and Alaska. Their caring attitude and enthusiasm are one of the line's strengths. Also notable is the cuisine, which is more sophisticated than is normally associated with small-ship, light-adventure cruising.

Distinctive Features   Bow-ramp on *Spirit of Columbia;* bow stairs on *Spirit of Glacier Bay* and *Spirit of Alaska.* Open bridge. Dib launches (inflatable, Zodiac-like motorized launches with covers, seats, and railings) on *Spirit of '98* and *Spirit of Endeavour* provide shore access in Sea of Cortés.

	HIGHEST	LOWEST	AVERAGE
PER DIEM	$628	$114	$342

The above per diems are calculated from the cruise line's non-discounted *cruise only* fares on standard accommodations. Per diems vary by season, by cabin, and by cruise areas.

Rates   Port charges additional, except Sea of Cortés cruises.

Special Fares and Discounts
• Single Supplement: 175 percent of twin rate; single cabins on *Spirit of Glacier Bay* and *Spirit of Discovery.*

Packages
• Air/Sea: Air add-ons available from up to 75 gateways.
• Pre/Post: Variety of cruise-tour Alaska packages with up to nine days of land touring.

Past Passengers   The Quyana Club (name means "thank you" in Tu'pik Eskimo) offers passengers newsletters, shipboard credits, and seasonal savings on cruises and pre/post packages.

The Last Word   The company remains faithful to its founder's vision that small groups maximize travelers' enjoyment without overwhelming villages, small ports, and wilderness areas they visit, and that the focus should be outward, on nature and culture, rather than inward, on nightclubs and gambling. By focusing on wildlife, passengers are likely to see whales, bears, seals, and eagles—and the wilderness, Cruise West says it is increasing awareness and support for protection of natural treasures.

Most passengers try an Alaskan cruise first. If they like it, they graduate to cruises elsewhere. Baja California gives Cruise West alumni a complete contrast to Alaska or the Northwest. Yet the Sea of Cortés offers similar attractions—wildlife, beautiful scenery, and interesting culture—and much the same appeal.

CRUISE WEST STANDARD FEATURES

Officers American.

Staff Dining, Cabin, Cruise/American.

Dining Facilities One dining room with open seating; meals served at specific hours. Early continental breakfast and 6 p.m. appetizers in forward lounge. Coffee, tea, fresh fruit available throughout day.

Special Diets Vegetarian, low-fat, low-salt, and other heart-healthy requests accommodated; notice required at time of booking;

Room Service None, except for owner's suite on the *Spirit of '98*.

Dress Code Casual at all times. Most passengers wear jeans, chinos, and layer with shirts, sweaters, and windbreakers in cooler climates.

Cabin Amenities Air-conditioning/thermostat; upper-deck cabins have windows that open. Most bathrooms are small, some with hand-held showers. Reading lights over bed; limited closets, storage. Some cabins have sink and vanity in room, separate from bathroom. *Spirit of Endeavour, Spirit of '98,* television, phone.

Electrical Outlets 110 AC.

Wheelchair Access *Spirit of '98* has elevator; two cabins accessible for disabled passengers.

Recreation and Entertainment Forward lounge with bar setup, television, small library with reference books of area, informational videos, movies; informal entertainment by crew; occasional talks by historians, park rangers, and other experts. Bridge, other card and board games. Ships stock binoculars, but it's wise to bring your own. Musical entertainment on Sea of Cortés cruises.

Beauty and Fitness Some fitness equipment, such as stair steps and exercise bicycles. No beauty/barber shop.

Other Facilities Doctor on Sea of Cortés cruises only; at least one crew member on each vessel is trained in "First Response."

Children's Facilities None.

Theme Cruises None.

Smoking Not allowed in public rooms or cabins; smoking allowed only on outside, open deck areas.

Cruise West Suggested Tipping $10 per passenger per day. All tips are pooled and shared by nonofficer staff.

Credit Cards For cruise payment and on-board charges: American Express, Visa, MasterCard.

Spirit of '98	Quality ❷	Value C
Registry: United States	Length: 192 feet	Beam: 40 feet
Cabins: 49	Draft: 9.3 feet	Speed: 13 knots
Maximum Passengers:	Passenger Decks: 3	Elevators: 1
96	Crew: 26	Space Ratio: NA

The Ship   Added in 1993, *Spirit of '98* was built in 1984 by previous owners and sailed as the *Pilgrim Belle, Colonial Explorer,* and *Victorian Empress.* The handsome vessel has the profile and interior of a turn-of-the-century riverboat. In 1994, she had a role in Kevin Costner's movie *Wyatt Earp.*

The decor recalls a Victorian country hotel. Accenting a handsome mahogany and mirrored bar in the forward observation lounge are fanciful wall lamps and wood columns trimmed with strip mirrors. Continuing the theme on her four decks are extensive use of wood, wingback chairs, leaded glass, and old-fashioned brass lamps.

Itineraries   See Appendix B.

Cabins   All cabins are outside and have varied arrangements. They're roomy, with closet and storage space adequate for a casual cruise. All are decorated in rich Victorian-style colors and fabrics. All are air-conditioned but have windows that open—a welcome feature. Cabins on lounge and upper decks open onto promenades. Main-deck, lower-priced cabins have windows on the outside hull, a benefit for those who like privacy but want to keep their curtains open.

The ship has an amazingly large, two-room owner's suite on the top deck with picture windows on both sides. The only cabin on the deck, just behind the bridge, it has a sitting area, a game and meeting area, complimentary bar, television, VCR, king-size bed, and bath with full-size tub. Occupants may have their meals served en suite.

Specifications   48 outside cabins; 1 suite. Dimensions range from 100–120 square feet. 40 with twins; 2 with upper/lower bunks; 6 with queen. No singles.

Dining   The Klondike Dining Room provides seating at a variety of table configurations, including booths next to the picture windows. One open seating is offered at each of three meals.

The cuisine is better than expected for this type of cruise. In most destinations, it's Pacific Northwest fare encompassing fresh seafood, local produce, and Northwest wines and local specialty beers. In Mexico, meals have Mexican choices. Bread and pastries are baked on board. Coffee, tea, cocoa, and fruit are available all day.

An early continental breakfast is available in the forward lounge; full breakfast is at 7:30 a.m. in the dining room. Lunch features soups, salads, and sandwiches. Appetizers served between 6 and 7 p.m. may include Alaskan Dungeness crab and artichoke dip or baked Brie.

Entrees at dinner are attractively presented and surprisingly sophisticated. They may include fresh halibut in Dijon sauce, veal piccata with white wine and capers, or Oregon razor clams grilled with garlic aioli.

Service   The young, enthusiastic crew are friendly, caring, and especially considerate of older passengers. These "customer service representatives" perform a variety of duties, including cleaning cabins and serving in the dining room.

Facilities and Entertainment   Most entertainment is provided by the passengers interacting with each other in conversation, cards, or board games in the lounge or dining room. Absent are a pool, casino, aerobics class, bingo, midnight buffet, or napkin-folding classes. The crew provides informal talent and lively entertainment on Crew and Casino nights. Vegetable races are amusing—and can be lucrative for those who wager correctly on such entries as Percy Potato or the Lemon Sisters. A television shows evening movies. Occasional guest lectures, talks by the cruise coordinator/naturalist, and entertainment from the old-style player piano are offered.

Activities and Diversions   Unusual in coastal cruise ships, Soapy's Parlor is a second, quiet lounge with wraparound windows at the stern, a good spot for watching the vessel's wake. Tea is served in the afternoon.

The bridge deck has ample space for sunning, viewing scenery, or lounging. A barbecue lunch is offered in good weather. The forward lounge is the ship's social center at night. A small area serves as a gift shop, where caps, mugs, and similar items are sold. A shuffleboard and huge checkerboard are on the bridge deck, along with two exercise machines.

Spirit of Discovery	Quality ❷	Value D
Registry: United States	Length: 166 feet	Beam: 37 feet
Cabins: 43	Draft: 7.5 feet	Speed: 13 knots
Maximum Passengers: 84	Passenger Decks: 3	Elevators: None
	Crew: 21	Space Ratio: NA

The Ship   Built in 1976 as the *Independence* and renamed *Columbia,* this handsome vessel cruised the East Coast and Puget Sound before being acquired by Cruise West in 1992 and renamed *Spirit of Discovery*. The forward lounge of this three-deck vessel is the ship's social center and cool-weather retreat. Nicely decorated in blue, soft grays, teals, and mauves, it has a bar with standard spirits plus Pacific Northwest wines and specialty brews. Furniture is arranged in conversational groupings. These, along with mirrored ceiling and chrome accents, give it the look of a private yacht or small, European-style hotel.

The lounge offers good views to both sides and over the bow through vertical windows at the front. Passengers at the bow can almost touch the vegetation when the ship noses up to shore. The bridge has a wraparound viewing area and is open to passengers at most times.

Itineraries   See Appendix B.

Cabins   Cabins on all three decks are outside with large windows. Most are small but adequate and furnished with a vanity, desk, and chair. Bathrooms have showers. Closets could use more hangers. Two sought-after smaller cabins, sold as singles, are amidships on the bridge deck.

Four spacious, deluxe cabins on the top level have a queen-size bed, desk and chair, television/VCR unit, and fridge/minibar. All bridge deck and most lounge deck cabins open onto a promenade. The two lowest-priced cabins are on the lower main deck forward, reduced in size to fit the hull's curvature.

Specifications   43 outside cabins; no suites. Dimensions range from 64 square feet (single cabin) to 127 square feet. 34 with twins, 1 with double, 4 queens, 2 with upper/lower berths, 2 singles.

Dining   The Grand Pacific Dining Room, aft on the main deck, is pleasant and airy, but a bit noisy because it's over the engine room. The food is imaginative and quite good, encompassing Pacific Northwest versions of classic American fare with fresh local produce and seafood. All passengers dine in one open seating; table configurations vary.

A continental breakfast is available for early risers. Sit-down breakfast, lunch, and 6 p.m. appetizers are served. Two entrees are offered at dinner; they may include lingcod baked in parchment or a superb rack of Ellensburg lamb roasted with Dijon rosemary crust.

Service   Customer service, galley and engine crew, and deck hands are young Americans, most from the Pacific Northwest. They're attentive, enthusiastic, and outgoing. Friendships form between crew and passengers, and many crew members receive holiday greetings from passengers for years after they meet.

Sports, Beauty, and Fitness   A stair stepper, exercise bicycle, and rowing machine are available.

Spirit of Alaska	Quality ❷	Value D
Spirit of Columbia	Quality ❷	Value D
Registry: United States	Length: 143 feet	Beam: 28 feet
Cabins: 39/38	Draft: 7.5/6.5 feet	Speed: 12/10 knots
Maximum Passengers:	Passenger Decks: 4	Elevators: None
78	Crew: 21	Space Ratio: NA

The Ships   *Spirit of Alaska* and *Spirit of Columbia* are identical in size, similar in layout, and smaller versions of their sister ships. *Spirit of Alaska,* built in 1980 as the *Pacific Northwest Explorer,* was extensively renovated when she was acquired by Cruise West in 1991 and renovated again in 1995. *Spirit of Columbia* (formerly *New Shoreham II* of American Canadian Caribbean Line) joined in 1994 after being refitted in a "Western National Park Lodge" theme.

Both ships have four decks, with most cabins on the lower and upper decks and a forward lounge and dining room amidships on the main deck. The lounge is the center of social life and site of briefings. It has a small bar, gift shop, reference library focused on the cruise area, television, and movie videos. The upper deck has an unobstructed walking/jogging circuit and several exercise machines.

On *Spirit of Alaska,* the bridge deck provides open and covered seating and a good-weather venue for buffet lunches. Bow ramp stairs enable passengers to walk directly onto shore; some complain the stairs are steep and difficult to negotiate.

Besides decor, *Spirit of Columbia* differs in having a large owner's suite with windows overlooking the bow, three additional suites, a raised wheelhouse with 360-degree viewing, and a unique bow ramp. A hinged, V-shaped segment of the bow can be lowered to form a ramp, giving direct access to shore from the forward lounge.

Itineraries   See Appendix B.

Cabins   Cabins on both ships range from roomy—for ships of this size— to very small. *Spirit of Alaska*'s suites and deluxe cabins have small sitting areas and open onto promenades. Three bridge-deck suites have oversized double beds and windows on two sides; each accommodates a third person.

Spirit of Columbia's 11 suites and deluxe cabins have a television/VCR, refrigerator, side tables, and a chair. Suites have a double bed; deluxe rooms, twins. The owner's suite has a queen-size bed, bathtub/shower, and complimentary bar. Upper- and bridge-deck cabins open directly onto promenades.

On both ships, main-deck cabins are on the short passage between the dining room and forward lounge, a high-traffic area, but convenient for those who want easy access to activities and facilities. Windows in these cabins are on the outside hull, ensuring privacy. Lower-deck cabins have portlights high on the bulkhead and not for viewing. Baths are small units with handheld showers and curtains on tracks. Most cabins have twin beds; all have reading lights, closets, and under-bed storage. They're just above the engine room and can be noisy when the ship is under way, but are a good buy for budget-watchers.

Alaska *Specifications*   12 inside; 24 outside; 3 suites. Dimensions range from 81–130.5 square feet. 26 with twins; 13 with doubles; 7 cabins accommodate third persons; no singles.

Columbia *Specifications*   12 inside; 20 outside; 7 suites. Dimensions range from 73.5–176 square feet.

Dining   Meals are served at a single, open seating. Cuisine is good American fare emphasizing fresh Pacific Northwest and Alaskan seafood and local produce. The *Spirit of Alaska*'s Grand Pacific Dining Room was upgraded in 1994; long, family-style tables were scrapped for more intimate round and square ones. Upholstered banquettes run bow to stern underneath side windows.

Service   The young American staff helps set the friendly ambience and, despite the considerable workload, remains courteous, enthusiastic, and helpful, especially to seniors. Most retain a sense of awe about the magnificent region the vessel sails, often sharing passengers' excitement for wildlife sightings or glacier calvings.

Postscript   *Spirit of Alaska* itineraries are designed for adventurous travelers who want a slice of authentic Alaska—seldom-visited areas, unspoiled wilderness, and small ports and villages inaccessible to large cruise ships. *Spirit of Columbia*'s cruises are filled with historical references to the Lewis and Clark expedition of 1804–06, cultural and adventurous aspects, and diverse scenery—from the crashing Pacific headlands to thick forests, rolling wheat fields, barren hills, and deep canyons.

Readers considering booking either ship should review the *Spirit of '98* or *Spirit of Discovery* section for more details on Cruise West facilities and services.

Spirit of Glacier Bay	Quality ❷	Value D
Registry: United States	Length: 125 feet	Beam: 28 feet
Cabins: 27	Draft: 6.5 feet	Speed: 11 knots
Maximum Passengers: 52	Passenger Decks: 3	Elevators: None
	Crew: 16	Space Ratio: NA

The Ship   The smallest of the fleet, this coastal cruiser was Cruise West's first cabin-equipped, overnight vessel. Built in 1971 by the American ship-yard that produced *Spirit of Alaska,* the *Spirit of Glacier Bay* was extensively renovated in 1990 and 1994. She's similar to *Spirit of Alaska,* but has one less deck and two upper-deck, freestanding cabins called "The Condos." Each has picture windows to the side and aft and are quite private.

The *Spirit of Glacier Bay* has a forward lounge with picture windows above banquettes and a small bar. Cocktail tables and upholstered chairs in the center of the room accommodate conversation groups. A television and VCR show informational videos and movies. The upper deck has an unob-structed walking circuit and exercise equipment.

The Snug Harbor Dining Room lies amidships near a block of four larger cabins with windows on the outside hull. Bow and stern observation areas are on the top deck; a covered area is amidships.

The homey little vessel with her relaxed ambience, casual dress, and low-key social life is suited to short cruises to off-the-beaten-track places.

Itineraries   See Appendix B.

Cabins   Half of the *Spirit of Glacier Bay*'s cabins have picture windows; they sell quickly. The 13 more economical cabins below deck are smaller, with high portlight windows unsuited to viewing. These cabins are above the engine room and can be noisy when the ship is under way. Nonethe-less, they're far more economical than outside picture-window cabins, offering hundreds of dollars in savings. All cabins are simply decorated and have private bathrooms with showers, air-conditioning, and heat control. Two popular single cabins are far forward on the upper deck.

Specifications   13 inside; 14 outside; no suites. Dimensions, 63–90 square feet. 23 with twins; 2 double; 2 with upper/lowers; 2 singles. 2 cab-ins accommodate third persons.

Dining   All passengers eat at one open seating. Tables include the below-window upholstered banquettes. Passengers are pleasantly surprised at the sophisticated Pacific Northwest fare prepared in the small galley. The menu, similar to *Spirit of Alaska*'s, offers meat dishes, but many passengers favor the seafood from local waters.

Service   The young American crew has a friendly, eager-to-please attitude. Friendships grow quickly between the staff and older passengers. Officers are older professionals with the same outgoing manner. They keep the wheelhouse open to passengers.

Spirit of Endeavor	Quality ❸	Value C
Registry: United States	Length: 217 feet	Beam: 37 feet
Cabins: 51	Draft: 8.5 feet	Speed: 13 knots
Maximum Passengers:	Passenger Decks: 4	Elevators: None
102	Crew: 28	Space Ratio: NA

The Ship   Built in 1983 in Jeffersonville, Indiana, *Spirit of Endeavour* (formerly *Newport Clipper* of Clipper Cruise Lines) was launched in 1996 after a $5 million refurbishing, as Cruise West's most luxurious ship and flagship. One of the more deluxe small vessels sailing in Alaska, she added a new level of comfort to the line's fleet. She has teak decks, a wide companionway, and comfortable lounges.

Cabins are large compared to her sister ships' and have wide picture windows. They're equipped with phone, television, VCR, and tiled baths. Refurbishing in 1999 added new closets, lighting and window treatments, wall coverings, artwork and furniture, and upgrading of the bathrooms. The dining room, which accommodates all passengers at a single open seating, has new furniture. The ship does not have an elevator.

In the renovations, all cabins and public areas were refurbished, safety features were updated, and new engines and bridge electronics were installed. New bow and stern designs increase the ship's fuel efficiency by more than 22 percent. A "bulbous" underwater bow extension splits the water, reducing the bow wake and water resistance. A stern ferring forces water to flow closer to the surface, reducing drag.

Among Cruise West ships, the *Spirit of Endeavour*'s clean lines and raked bow make it look most like a small cruise ship. Viewing breathtaking scenery is a major activity on this ship, which appeals to persons looking for quiet social life and a relaxed itinerary. Passengers give high marks to the ship's educational programs, and they appreciate finding binoculars and umbrellas in their cabins.

Itineraries   See Appendix B.

Postscript   Readers interested in sailing on *Spirit of Endeavor* should review all of the Cruise West section.

Spirit of Oceanus	(preview)	
Registry: Bahamas	Length: 295 feet	Beam: 50 feet
Cabins: 57	Draft: 13.25 feet	Speed: 14.5 knots
Maximum Passengers:	Passenger Decks: 5	Elevators: 1
114	Crew: 65	Space Ratio: NA

The Ship   Cruise West will take possession of its new ship, *Spirit of Oceanus,* in April 2001 in Singapore. After some cosmetic refurbishing in a Singapore shipyard, the ship will sail on a 32-day voyage from Singapore to Whittier, entering Alaska service on June 9, 2001—at which time she will become the line's flagship, taking over that honor from *Spirit of Endeavour.*

Built in 1991 as the *Renaissance V,* the ship was renamed *Sun Vista* when she was purchased by Sun Cruises, and later became *MegaStar Sagittarius* under Star Cruises, from whom Cruise West purchased her in June 2000.

The luxurious *Spirit of Oceanus* is Cruise West's first oceangoing vessel, and as such, opens up new horizons for the line, from new destinations worldwide to newer, more upscale cruises that would appeal to a completely new market.

Registered in the Bahamas—another first for Cruise West—the ship will have American officers and an on-board naturalist guide, along with an English-speaking crew whose numbers will constitute the highest crew-to-guests ratio in the line's fleet.

Cabins   *Spirit of Oceanus* has spacious, all-outside suites, each with a large picture window or porthole, and ranging in size from 215 to 353 square feet. The 12 suites on Sun and Bridge Decks have private teak balconies—yet another first for Cruise West's fleet. Other cabin amenities include a walk-in closet, marble-topped vanity, and a lounge area separated from the bedroom by a curtain. All suites can be configured with two twin beds or a full queen size bed and have a television/VCR, safe, minibar, satellite telephone, and private bathroom with a marble sink and shower.

Facilities   The handsomely-appointed *Spirit of Oceanus* has marble and polished hardwood interiors, sumptuous fabrics, and fine art. There are two large lounges (one with a grand piano) and several elegant bars, providing havens for conversation, reading, or playing board games. Among other new features passengers will enjoy on a Cruise West ship for the first time are a hot tub on the aft Bridge Deck, a health facility, and a patio bar.

The ship also has a library, an elevator providing access to all five passenger decks, and spacious outside viewing areas and walkways on four of the five guest decks. The elegant dining room accommodates all guests at a single seating.

Day Cruises   *Sheltered Seas*, a day cruiser, is not covered here because her type of cruises are outside the scope of this book. For more information, contact the cruise line.

Crystal Cruises

2049 Century Park East, Suite 1400, Los Angeles, CA 90067
(310) 785-9300; fax (310) 785-3891
www.crystalcruises.com

Type of Ships   Modern, luxury superliners.

Type of Cruise   Modern version of glamorous, traditional cruising with a touch of California glitz, for upscale, sophisticated travelers.

Cruise Line's Strengths
- service
- beautifully designed ships
- large number of cabins with verandas
- alternative restaurants
- globe-roaming itineraries

Cruise Line's Shortcomings
- two seatings in main dining room
- some cabins with restricted views
- limited closet space; some small bathrooms
- inadequate seating capacity in alternative restaurants

Fellow Passengers   Professional, retired or semiretired, experienced travelers; likely to be business owners, entrepreneurs, and executives rather than staff; ages 45–70. Typical passenger is affluent, active, fashion-conscious, friendly 55–60-year-old couple or mature single.

Recommended For   Quality-conscious travelers who appreciate style with flash and want large-ship facilities; urbane first-time cruisers who can afford it.

Not Recommended For   Anyone uncomfortable in sophisticated ambience.

Cruise Areas and Seasons   Caribbean, Mexico, Panama Canal in fall, winter, and spring; South America, China/Orient, and Asia in fall, winter;

World Cruise in winter; Europe and Alaska in summer; and South Pacific in autumn.

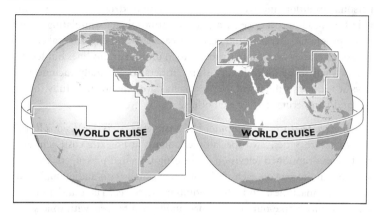

The Line Two years before her first ship debuted in 1990, Crystal Cruises promised it would return grand oceanliners' elegance and personalized service to modern cruises for the "upscale mass" market—an apparently inconsistent term. The line not only delivered on its promise but *Crystal Harmony,* its first ship, was even better than its advanced billing. It quickly became the ship by which others in her class—or aspiring to be in her class—were measured.

And therein lies the tale. There *were* no other ships in her class. Crystal Cruises created a niche all its own: *Crystal Harmony* is the size of most superliners but carries a third fewer passengers. (Some comparably sized ships carry twice as many passengers.) As a result, *Crystal Harmony* offers the best of all worlds: the facilities of a large ship with the personalized service of a small vessel and with spaciousness even some luxurious ships cannot match.

The *Crystal Harmony* was built in Japan by Mitsubishi Heavy Industries, a subsidiary of Nippon Yusen Kaisha, the Japanese shipbuilding giant known for its technologically advanced ships and the owner of California-based Crystal Cruises. The ship incorporates state-of-the-art engines, radar, and navigational equipment. Comfort and amenities go far beyond the norm. Ironically, *Crystal Symphony,* twin of *Crystal Harmony,* was built in Finland, for cost-saving reasons. In early 2000, Crystal announced its intention to build a third ship.

The Fleet	Built/Renovated	Tonnage	Passengers
Crystal Harmony	1990	49,400	940
Crystal Symphony	1995	51,044	940

Style   Exceptionally spacious ships with superliner facilities and Rodeo Drive style are designed for affluent travelers willing to pay for luxury and personal attention and who appreciate quality in details. The cruises provide fine food and service in a gracious atmosphere; stimulating enrichment programs, a year-round roster of celebrity and expert speakers, and varied itineraries with more structure than ultraluxurious lines but less formality than some older luxury ships. Itineraries generally include more days at sea than is the norm, so passengers have time to enjoy fully the luxury and pampering that Crystal offers.

Distinctive Features   Computer University@Sea. Crystal Visions Enrichment Lecture Series. Two specialty restaurants at no extra cost; gentlemen hosts; close-captioned television for hearing-impaired passengers; free, self-service laundromat on each deck; business center with audiovisual equipment, fax machines, and office equipment; secretarial, translation, and e-mail services; take-out laptops; air-conditioned tenders with toilets.

	HIGHEST	LOWEST	AVERAGE
PER DIEM	$825	$374	$587

The above per diems are calculated from the cruise line's non-discounted *cruise only* fares on standard accommodations. Per diems vary by season, by cabin, and by cruise areas.

Rates   Port charges additional.

Special Fares and Discounts   Crystal has advance-purchase discounts ranging from 10 to 30 percent and more, depending on the cruise; they may be used with other promotional rates and Crystal Society savings. Another group marked with a V in Crystal's brochure offers two-for-one savings.
- Third Passenger: Minimum fare for cruise.
- Children's Fare: Younger than age 12, half fare with two full-paying adults.
- Single Supplement: Crystal's single's fare begins at 125 percent of the double occupancy rate for the lowest categories and is applicable to advance-purchase discount rates.

Packages
- Air/Sea: Yes.
- Others: Honeymoon.
- Pre/Post: Yes.

Past Passengers   Crystal Society past-passenger club offers amenities that increase with the number of cruises. These include business- and first-class air upgrades, confirmed stateroom and penthouse upgrades, shipboard credits from $200 to $800 per couple, free cruises in staterooms and penthouses, limousine transfers, prepaid gratuities, and private luncheon and dinner parties.

Passengers are automatically enrolled after their first Crystal cruise and receive financial bonuses with every subsequent cruise. The higher reward levels are 5–30 cruises, 50, 70, and 100 cruises, but all members receive a 5 percent cruise discount, an additional 5 percent savings for reservations made while on a cruise, priority check-in, a Crystal Society travel bag, membership card, recognition pin, quarterly newsletter, and, beginning with the tenth cruise, a complimentary bottle of wine and fresh flowers on every cruise. Several cruises, including the annual president's cruise, are Crystal Society Sailings (marked with a C in the compendium) and feature a personal escort, exclusive events, and special gifts.

The Last Word   Crystal Cruises identified a market of experienced travelers (but not necessarily experienced cruise passengers) who weren't being served by other cruise lines and created a product that set new standards of luxury for large ships. Those who can afford the cruises get quality all the way. Compare Crystal's quality and extra amenities with those of other lines in the same price bracket, and you find Crystal's cruises are among cruising's best values.

CRYSTAL CRUISES STANDARD FEATURES

Officers Norwegian and Japanese.

Staff Dining/European; Cabin/International; Cruise/American.

Dining Facilities One main dining room, two seatings for three meals with open seating for breakfast and lunch; buffet breakfast and lunch on Lido Deck; alternative dinner restaurants; midnight buffet; tea.

Special Diets Requests should be made when reservations are confirmed.

Room Service 24-hour menu; butler service on penthouse deck.

Dress Code Casual by day; casually elegant in the evening, with two formal evenings per week of cruising.

Cabin Amenities Direct-dial phone with voicemail; television with CNN and ESPN, VCR; stocked minibar; safe; bathroom with tub, two hair dryers, robes; suites with marble bathrooms and whirlpool tubs.

Electrical Outlets 110/220 AC.

Wheelchair Access Four cabins on *Harmony;* seven on *Symphony.*

Recreation and Entertainment Casino, disco, nightclub, show lounge, piano bar, coffee/wine bar, cinema/theater, six lounges, observation lounge, card/meeting room, video game room, smoking room. Guest lecturers, area specialists, celebrities. Bingo, bridge, dancing, and crafts classes. Computer classes.

Sports and Other Activities Two outdoor swimming pools, one with retractable roof; two Jacuzzis; teak deck for walking/jogging; paddle tennis; golf clinics and practice corner; deck and pool games.

Beauty and Fitness See text.

Other Facilities Boutiques, concierge, hospital, laundry/dry cleaning, valet service, launderettes, video camera rentals, meeting facilities, business service center, e-mail facilities.

Children's Facilities Playroom, babysitters, youth programs.

Theme Cruises Yes.

Smoking Dining rooms nonsmoking; public rooms smoking in designated areas.

Crystal Suggested Tipping Per person per day, cabin stewardess, $4; waiter, $4; assistant waiter, $2.50; $6 per person per meal in alternative restaurants; 15 percent added to bar bills.

Credit Cards For cruise payment and on-board charges: all major credit cards. Aboard ship uses a charge system with the bill settled at the end of the cruise.

| *Crystal Harmony* | Quality ⑨ | Value B |
| *Crystal Symphony* | Quality ⑩ | Value B |

Registry: Bahamas	Length: 781/791 feet	Beam: 97/99 feet
Cabins: 408	Draft: 25 feet	Speed: 22 knots
Maximum Passengers:	Passenger Decks: 8	Elevators: 9
1,010	Crew: 545	Space Ratio: 52.6/54.3

The Ships Gleaming white inside and out, *Crystal Harmony* is a symphony of Japanese technology and artistry, European service and tradition, and American flair for fun and entertainment. The elegance is in its simplicity, clean lines, and extraordinary attention to details. Its quality, luxury, and spaciousness—one of the highest ratios of passenger-to-space of any ship—are immediately evident. The decor has a bit of glitz, but is always in good taste. It was created by Swedish, Italian, and British designers influenced by Japanese artistic understatement. Quiet colors and quality furnishings harmonize. Fine fabrics and textures are set against marble and woods accented with brass and stainless steel. The generous use of glass gives interiors an airy ambience.

Passengers' introduction to the ship is the Crystal Plaza, an atrium lobby with cascades of lucite lights, stairways, and railings that appear to float in space. They're outlined with brass fixtures against white marble walls. Deep green suede, fresh greenery, hand-cut glass sculpture, and a waterfall provide accents. Summing up the feeling of opulence is a—what else?—crystal piano. The beautiful vessel has lounges for many purposes and moods, and most have been refurbished. The Palm Court, one of the most handsome lounges afloat, is an airy space in white and mint green with graceful palms under skylights. It wears the atmosphere of a traditional palm court in the afternoon when tables are set for tea with crisp linens and gleaming silver and a harpist strums. Forward of the Palm Court is the fabulous Vista Lounge, a trilevel observation room with white leather chairs on sky blue carpets and floor-to-ceiling windows that frame a 270-degree view.

Crystal Symphony, introduced in 1995, is essentially a twin of *Crystal Harmony,* with improvements on the latter. Among enhancements, the Crystal Cove Lounge, Crystal Plaza, and Lido Cafe were doubled in size; the casino and shopping arcade expanded; and a video room added. Also, a spiral waterfall highlights *Symphony*'s atrium, and its color scheme is beige and light green, rather than *Harmony*'s blue.

One of the most noticeable—but least successful—alterations is the combining of the popular Palm Court with the Observation Lounge.

Other important changes are in the cabins—all outside, about a third more having verandas than on the *Harmony,* and all with larger, better-designed bathrooms. The two alternative restaurants were enlarged and moved.

Itineraries   See Appendix B.

Cabins   Large, comfortable, and handsomely appointed with fine fabrics and quality furnishings, the well-equipped cabins have sitting areas. In 1997, all cabins on Decks 8, 9, and 10—more than half of *Crystal Harmony*'s cabins and all penthouse suites—were refurbished. Quality European fabrics by Italian designer Lorenzo Rubelli provide a warm combination of textured wheat colors. Mediterranean blue and yellow appear in Deck 8 cabins; coral and blue in Deck 9 cabins with verandas. Standard cabins have adequate closet and storage space, although some complain that hanging space is limited for long voyages. Drawer space and bathtub size have been corrected. Large down pillows and comforters on beds, plush robes, fluffy towels, fine toiletries, and voicemail on the direct-dial telephone reflect attention to detail. All cabins have fresh flowers, two hair dryers, and television with CNN and ESPN.

More than half of all cabins have private verandas. Lifeboats obstruct views from some cabins (Categories G, Horizon, and promenade decks). Crystal's literature notes "limited" or "extremely limited" views and prices the cabins accordingly.

The ship's ultimate luxury is on the all-suite, concierge-attended Penthouse Deck. Suites have large bedrooms, large sitting areas, and luxurious marble bathrooms with Jacuzzi bathtubs. The four most extravagant suites encompass 948 square feet. All were completely renovated and outfitted with new appointments in May 2000.

The suites are attended by four European-trained, white-gloved butlers and six Scandinavian stewardesses. The young men, dressed in formal attire (some find this pretentious) are as competent as they are eager to serve. They will unpack your bags (and repack them at cruise end), arrange a party or a dinner in your suite, and attend to other special requests. Nightly at cocktail time, they serve hors d'oeuvres and pour drinks from your fully stocked bar.

During a day at sea, passengers are given a ship tour on which they visit all cabin categories—a useful sales gimmick! And should the impulse seize you to book your next Crystal voyage right there, a "cruise consultant" is aboard to make the arrangements—at a discount.

Symphony's standard cabins are roomier than *Harmony*'s. All are outside, and 278—about a third more—have verandas and overall dimensions of 246 square feet. Other standard cabins cover 202 square feet and have large windows. All have a sitting area with love seat. Some Penthouse Deck suites are arranged to allow larger closets. Standard-cabin bathrooms have been enlarged. All have two sinks in a six-foot counter, bathtubs plus showers, and larger closets with more hanging space. All Penthouse Deck suites have verandas.

Harmony *Specifications*   19 inside cabins, 461 outside; 198 with veranda. Standard dimensions, 196 square feet. 62 penthouse suites with verandas measuring 360 or 492 square feet. No singles. All twins convert to queens or kings. 4 wheelchair-accessible.

Symphony *Specifications*   480 outside cabins, including 64 penthouse suites with verandas and 278 deluxe cabins (246 square feet) with verandas; 138 deluxe (202 square feet) without verandas; 7 wheelchair accessible.

Dining   Super in quality and stunning in presentation, cuisine is one of *Crystal Harmony*'s best features, on par with good restaurants in New York and Los Angeles. Food is served on fine china by waiters who are as polished as the silver. The spacious peach and blue dining room with floor-to-ceiling windows and modern chandeliers is elegant and well designed. More space than usual is allowed between tables—helping keep noise down. Tables for two are more numerous than usual. *Symphony*'s dining room is slightly more subdued than *Harmony*'s.

Dinner menus, placed in cabins in advance, are greatly varied during a cruise. Typically, they include a choice of four appetizers; three soups; two salads; pasta; five entrees of fish, poultry, and meat; vegetables; and an array of desserts. Low-salt, low-fat, and low-sugar choices are available. The maître d'hôtel often asks passengers for their favorite dishes, which the kitchen will prepare with advance notice. The wine list has over 170 varieties. The ships' most innovative features—and the first for cruising—are the intimate, alternative dinner restaurants, available at no extra cost to all passengers. On *Harmony,* they are Kyoto, which serves Japanese specialties and other Asian cuisine, and Prego, featuring Italian dishes. Each restaurant has its own kitchen; dishes are cooked to order. Reservations are required; make yours early because both are enormously popular.

The *Symphony*'s alternative restaurants—Prego, offering Italian cuisine, and Jade Garden, serving Chinese fare—are on Deck 6 instead of Deck 11 as on the *Harmony,* giving passengers easier access to the restaurants and entertainment areas on the same deck. Each has a separate entrance.

Symphony's Prego, twice as large as its *Harmony* counterpart, has a waiting list almost every night and probably ranks as the ship's main attraction. Decorated to suggest Venice, the room has banquettes and high-backed chairs around tables seating four or six. Dishes are outstanding. The Jade Garden, with a tiny water garden at the entrance, doesn't equal *Harmony*'s Kyoto in decor, ambience, or cuisine. Decor with a white, hard finish and bright lighting seems more appropriate for a computer room. The cuisine, heavier and more oily than Americans expect in Chinese food, cannot compare to the Kyoto's Japanese specialties.

The level of service and cuisine in the dining room and alternative restaurants is meant to compensate for the lack of the single-sitting dining room traditional on luxury ships. (Die-hards consider this Crystal's unforgivable sin.)

The alternative restaurants have a hidden charm: Dining in the same surroundings on a long cruise can sometimes become boring. The two additional restaurants offer a change of ambience and cuisine—a great bonus.

The indoor/outdoor Lido Cafe serves breakfast, midmorning bouillon, and lunch. Luncheon and themed buffets set up around the pool are very popular. The Trident Bar, an extension of the Neptune Pool swim-up bar, offers hot dogs, hamburgers, and other snacks, and there's a bar for ice cream and frozen yogurt. By moving the *Symphony*'s alternative restaurants to Deck 6, the Lido Cafe's size was doubled, a second buffet counter was added, and the cafe was connected to indoor/outdoor seating for breakfast and lunch.

A sumptuous tea is served daily in the Palm Court, and the Crystal Plaza is the setting for a weekly dessert extravaganza set to the music of Mozart. Should you still suffer hunger pangs, the fruit basket in your cabin will have been replenished, or your cabin attendant will bring any item on the extensive room service menu. You also may dine in your cabin, with courses served one by one.

The attractive Bistro Cafe serves coffee and pastries for late risers and wine and cheese, coffees, teas, and desserts during the day. Charming French prints that decorate the wall are reproduced on the cafe's pottery. On several sailings, a wine and food festival features guest chefs and wine experts. Crystal's Director of Culinary Operations, Toni Neumeister, formerly with Royal Viking Lines, is among cruising's most celebrated chefs.

Service   Both ships have among the highest crew-to-passenger ratios in cruising. The well-trained staff is young, cheerful, and eager to please; service is thoroughly professional and consistently excellent. Dining room staff primarily are Italian, Spanish, and Portuguese; cabin attendants, Filipino; and the cruise and entertainment staff, American. A European-style concierge and purser service is available round-the-clock.

Facilities and Entertainment   Predinner options include cocktails in the Vista Lounge or wood-paneled Avenue Saloon (enlarged on the *Symphony*), or a classical concert by a harpist or trio. A cabaret show in Club 2100 and two full-scale, high-quality, Broadway-style productions in the Galaxy show lounge are offered at night. Local entertainers may perform at ports of call. One evening is a masquerade party.

The Starlite Club, *Symphony*'s Art Deco replacement for *Harmony*'s Club 2100 and disco, is one of the ship's most attractive lounges. It's used for the captain's cocktail and past-passenger parties, pre- and postdinner cocktails, and dancing. In late evening, it becomes the disco, depending on passenger preference during each sailing.

Galaxy Lounge, the main show lounge, offers an array of first-rate productions that might range from classical ballet to a Broadway revue. Crystal has its own production team, Gretchen Goertz and Kathy Orme, who create all the production shows and are very original and very good. The talented show troupe includes former dancers from the Bolshoi Ballet and London's West End. The shows usually have spectacular costumes—some valued at $10,000 apiece—and sets by award-winning designers.

Crystal Harmony boasts the only casino at sea operated by Caesars Palace of Las Vegas. The casino (enlarged on *Symphony*) has Roman columns at the entrance and toga-clad dealers, and offers blackjack, slots, and roulette. Before sailing, passengers receive an application for credit at the casino.

Activities and Diversions   Cultural and destination-oriented lectures by experts, political figures, and diplomats are a regular afternoon or after-dinner feature. Daytime pursuits include card and other games, dancing classes, golf clinics, and arts and crafts. The well-stocked library has added videos, books, and periodicals.

Crystal has expanded its Computer University@Sea. Depending on cruise length, classes range from *PC Basics* to *How to Create Your Own Home Page*. The classroom aboard *Symphony* has 22 computer work stations and hands-on lab sessions. Passengers may also schedule private instruction in their cabins. Rental laptop computers are available. A similar room has been added in the Compass Room/Business Center on the *Harmony*.

Crystal was among the first to introduce e-mail service on its ships. The cost is $3 per message up to 20,000 bytes (about eight typed pages). That's a bargain compared to a satellite phone call, which costs $9–15 per minute. Passengers have their own e-mail address (e.g., JaneDoe@HARMONY.CUatSea.com), which they receive with their cruise ticket. E-mail is downloaded and distributed four times daily.

The Hollywood Theatre, with high-definition video projection and hearing-aid headsets, runs films each afternoon and evening. Films and other programs also are available on cabin televisions.

For further diversion, pricey temptations with designer names are sold in the pretty shops on Avenue of the Stars.

Sports, Fitness, and Beauty   A lap pool has adjacent whirlpools, and an indoor/outdoor swimming pool has a swim-up bar and a retractable roof. There's generous sunning space on deck, plus Ping-Pong, shuffleboard, pool games, golf, and the only full-scale paddle tennis court at sea. Deck 7 offers a wraparound, unobstructed route for walking or jogging.

The large salon/spa on the top deck has health club facilities with exercise equipment, aerobics and exercise classes, and separate steam rooms and saunas for men and women at no charge. Personalized cuisine programs are available. The salon offers an array of pricey body and facial treatments, including a 35-minute massage for $75, a half-day of treatments for $250, and a customized "weight loss" package of ten hours in three sessions for $500. The latest addition is a massage therapy session for couples. During *Harmony*'s most recent renovations, spa facilities were improved and exercise equipment increased. In association with Callaway Golf, Crystal offers a program on some sailings that enables participants to play historic courses worldwide. Callaway equipment includes right-handed or left-handed clubs for men and women.

Children's Facilities   Supervised youth programs are provided only when the line knows in advance that a sizable number of children will be aboard. Fantasia, a children's playroom, is more of an entertainment center, with video games for children ages 3–16. Babysitting can be arranged with crew members for about $5 per hour.

Shore Excursions   Shore excursions are sold on board, but some may be available in advance. Details are in the shore excursion brochure passengers receive before their cruise.

Efficient service in air-conditioned tenders, as needed, is a much-appreciated amenity. The concierge and excursion desk are helpful in suggesting and arranging independent port programs. Crystal provides good maps and information about each port.

Crystal continues to add interesting and ambitious excursions, particularly on Alaska cruises. They range from hiking, kayaking, rafting, and horseback riding to wildlife viewing. One exotic option is a 70-mile float-plane ride from Ketchikan to Anan Creek, where only 48 people each day are permitted to watch black and brown bears feeding from the creek. Another is a wildlife tour in dugout canoes on a Botswana safari offered on Southern Africa cruises.

Cunard Line, Ltd.

6100 Blue Lagoon Drive, Suite 400, Miami, FL 33126
(305) 463-3000; (800) 7-cunard (728-6273); fax (305) 463-3010
www.cunard.com

Type of Ships   Large superliner and midsize traditional ship.

Type of Cruises   Wide range of destinations and durations, from warm-weather vacations to transatlantic summer service for affluent, demanding travelers; distinctively British pedigree.

Cruise Line's Strengths
- name recognition
- distinctive ships
- itineraries
- accommodations and service
- large number of single cabins

Cruise Line's Shortcomings
- vintage fleet
- mixed products on *QE2*

Fellow Passengers   Cunard attracts a broad spectrum of passengers—from first-timers eager to visit many ports to veterans who seldom leave the ship—but most are affluent, mature, experienced travelers. Depending on time of year, the makeup is American and British, with large contingents of Europeans and repeaters. *QE2*'s world cruises attract a crowd—affluent and older, taking long winter vacations—very different from that on summer, transatlantic service when passengers may be all ages, incomes, and professions, many families with children, and people eager to take an ocean voyage on the famous ship.

Recommended For   Those who enjoy a certain amount of formality and tradition, abhor glitz, and are accustomed to luxury and willing to pay for it.

Not Recommended For   Those uncomfortable in elegance who prefer a casual or nonstop party atmosphere.

Cruise Areas and Seasons   Around the world in winter; transatlantic, April–December; Europe, spring–fall; Caribbean, South America, Orient, Bermuda, South Pacific, New England/Canada, Panama Canal, and Africa seasonally.

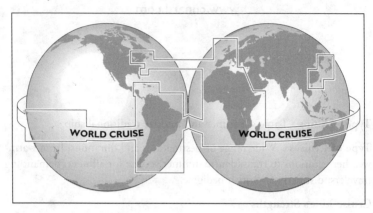

The Line   Cunard Line, with a history stretching back to 1840, sailed into the new millennium with new owners, new management, a new organization, and a new direction. Yet reinventing itself is nothing new for Cunard. With the postwar birth of the jet age and the demise of transatlantic passenger service, traditional steamship companies like Cunard had to adapt to the new realities to survive. Some converted their ships for modern cruising, some built new ships, and some bought or merged with other cruise lines. Cunard took all these steps and more.

During the era of the grand oceanliners, Cunard Lines was best known for its queens—the *Queen Mary* and *Queen Elizabeth*—which set the standard of elegance at sea for decades. *Queen Elizabeth 2* made her debut in 1969, when the future of transatlantic service was uncertain.

In 1971, Cunard was acquired by Trafalgar House, a multinational conglomerate headquartered in London, but doubts persisted throughout the decade on whether the line would survive. Having the only oceanliner on regular transatlantic service helped keep her going. In 1982, the *QE2* was pressed into Her Majesty's service during the Falkland Islands War. For Cunard and the *QE2,* it was a blessing in disguise, giving the ship a new lease on life with the publicity and a much-needed refurbishing by the British government before her return to passenger service.

In the 1980s, Cunard moved to corner the luxury market, first by acquiring the *Sagafjord* and *Vistafjord,* traditional oceanliners epitomizing luxury cruising, and in 1986, the ultradeluxe *Sea Goddess* twins, the first "boutique" ships built to provide the world's most exclusive, elegant cruises. Then, in 1994, Cunard purchased the highly acclaimed *Royal Viking Sun* and the prestigious Royal Viking name. But two years later, Trafalgar House was taken over by the Norwegian company Kvaerner ASA, and in 1998, Cunard was sold to Carnival Corporation and merged with Seabourn Cruise Line, in which Carnival has a 50 percent equity. The acquisition made Carnival a major player in the luxury market. In late 1999, the *Royal Viking Sun* and *Sea Goddess I* and *II* were moved to the Seabourn group and renamed accordingly, leaving only the *QE2* and *Vistafjord,* renamed *Caronia,* under the Cunard brand. The new owners spent $38 million renovating the *QE2, Caronia,* and *Seabourn Sun* to ready them for the new millennium.

From the outset Carnival told stockholders it plans to rebuild Cunard with new ships. The first, dubbed Project Queen Mary and scheduled to debut in 2003, will be the "grandest and largest passenger liner ever built," evoking the bygone era of seagoing luxury while representing the next era of oceanliner evolution with elegance, style, and grace to create "a new golden age of sea travel for those who missed the first."

The Fleet	Built/Renovated	Tonnage	Passengers
Queen Elizabeth 2	1969/87/94/96/99	70,327	1,700
Caronia	1973/83/94/97/99	24,492	665

Style The legendary *Queen Elizabeth 2* has a style all her own. She is the only passenger ship sailing the Atlantic on a regular schedule, from April to December, with three levels of service. She also sails on an annual world cruise from January to April, while shorter cruises, usually in the Caribbean and Europe, fill the weeks between.

To many the *QE2* is the ultimate cruise experience. A city at sea, she dwarfs all but the newest megaliners. She is proud, elegant, formal, and as British as—well, yes—the queen. Throughout its history, Cunard has been an innovator in response to changing lifestyles. *QE2* was the first ship to have a full-fledged spa. Recognizing the impact of the electronic revolution, Cunard installed the first computer learning center, satellite edition of world news delivered daily to passengers, and a CD-ROM library on the *QE2.* The spacious and graceful *Caronia* maintains the ambience of traditional cruising.

Distinctive Features Gentlemen hosts dance and dine with unaccompanied women year-round.• *QE2* computer learning center, 18-car garage, golf driving range and putting green, florist, kennel, tuxedo rental, CD-ROM library, and book shop.

	HIGHEST	LOWEST	AVERAGE
PER DIEM			
QE2	$1133	$237	$649
Caronia	$751	$225	$455

The above per diems are calculated from the cruise line's non-discounted *cruise only* fares on standard accommodations. Per diems vary by season, by cabin, and by cruise areas.

Rates Most port charges are included.

Special Fares and Discounts
- Early-booking discounts: A variety of time-sensitive discounts are available, ranging from 20 percent for booking and deposit a year in advance, 30 percent for payment in full a year in advance; 10 percent for Cunard World Club members; 15 percent for World Cruise Society members; and others when two or more cruises are combined.
- Third/Fourth persons: Specific fares listed in chart in brochure
- Single Fares: Single occupancy cabins listed in brochure. Supplement for single occupancy of double cabin is 175–200 percent, depending on cabin.

Packages
- Air/Sea: Yes.
- Other Packages: Yes.
- Pre/Post: Yes.

Past Passengers Passengers are enrolled into the Cunard World Club, the past passenger program. Levels are: Bronze, two to four cruises; Silver, five to seven; and Gold, eight or more cruises or more than 100 days of cruising. Benefits include on-board credits and social events and discounts on published fares that may be combined with the 5 percent on-board discount. On-board credits are issued per cabin: Bronze, $100; Silver, $150; Gold, $200. They may be applied toward the purchase of goods and services, including spa treatments, shore excursions, and boutique items. Space-available upgrades are offered to Silver and Gold members before sailing.

The Last Word   Cunard is known for luxury, but if you don't understand the differences in the levels of luxury, it can be somewhat misleading. For example, the popular image of the *QE2* is glamour, grand luxury, and haute cuisine. For those who buy the highest-priced suites and deluxe cabins and dine in the grills, this picture is accurate—but that's less than 30 percent of passengers. On her transatlantic run, *QE2* has three levels of service determined by cabin category, which is a polite way of saying three classes based on price. Each of three categories is assigned specific restaurants, and entry to the others is restricted accordingly. Try to dine or drink in the Queen's Grill or Bar, which is reserved for the top categories only, and you quickly learn what class distinction means. The redeeming factor is that all entertainment, sports, recreational facilities, and shops are available to everyone, regardless of class.

CUNARD STANDARD FEATURES

Officers British.

Staff *QE2,* Dining, Cabin, Cruise/British and International. *Caronia,* Scandinavian and International.

Dining Facilities *QE2,* single seating in five dining rooms for three meals, except *Mauretania,* two seatings on transatlantic; informal lido cafe for three meals and midnight buffet; snack bar. *Caronia,* one dining room, single seating for three meals. Casual indoor/outdoor cafe for lunch buffets. Alternative Italian restaurant.

Special Diets Diabetic, low-calorie, low-cholesterol, low-salt, and vegetarian.

Room Service 24-hour room service. *Caronia,* full menus.

Dress Code Formal/informal, casual for dining, depending on evening.

Cabin Amenities Radio, direct-dial telephones, 20-channel television with CNN. Bathroom with tub and shower in mid and top categories. Refrigerators, walk-in closets, verandas. Caronia, VCR, hair dryer.

Electrical Outlets 110 AC.

Wheelchair Access *QE2,* ramps; four cabins; bathtubs with grab bars, wide doors, low sills. *Caronia,* four cabins.

Recreation and Entertainment Casino, cabaret, revues. Life-enrichment seminars, guest lectures. Lounges, bars, disco, bingo, dance lessons, gentlemen hosts, computer learning center.

Sports and Other Activities Indoor/outdoor pools, deck sports, golf putting and driving net, jogging track, paddle tennis, Ping-Pong. *Caronia,* golf simulator.

Beauty and Fitness Spa, fitness center, gym, barber/beauty salon, exercise class. See text for more details. *Caronia,* saunas, walking/jogging deck.

Other Facilities Cinema/theater, launderette, laundry/dry cleaning service, library, shops, hospital. *QE2,* tuxedo rental shop, foreign exchange; Harrods; 18-car garage, florist, board room, synagogue, kennel (transatlantic only). *Caronia,* concierge, bookstore, library.

Children's Facilities *QE2,* teen center, video, supervised children's playrooms, nursery, nannies, babysitting. *Caronia,* counselors seasonally.

Theme Cruises Year-round selection.

Smoking Designated areas in public rooms.

Cunard Suggested Tipping *QE2,* $10–13 per day added to bill, depending on cabin category; *Caronia,* $11 per day. Gratuities included in fare for cruises of 90 days or more.

Credit Cards For cruise payment and on-board charges: American Express, Diners Club, Discover, MasterCard, Visa.

Queen Elizabeth 2	Quality **7**	Value C
Registry: England	Length: 963 feet	Beam: 105 feet
Cabins: 950	Draft: 32.75 feet	Speed: 28.5 knots
Maximum Passengers: 1,778	Passenger Decks: 12	Elevators: 13
	Crew: 921	Space Ratio: 36

The Ship   *Queen Elizabeth 2,* Cunard's flagship, is the lone survivor of a long, rich history of ocean travel. After extensive face-lifts in 1995, 1996, and 1999, her new look emphasizes her uniqueness: a grand oceanliner with the flexibility to provide a modern cruise experience. It is said that 50 coats of paint were stripped from her exteriors.

Renovations included major remodeling of most public areas. Interiors were created by John McNeece, Britain's leading cruise-ship interior designer, and MET Studio, an architectural and design firm that worked with James Gardner, the *QE2*'s original designer. They improved passenger flow and added new decor, facilities, and ambience that address today's lifestyle while retaining the ship's distinctive character. By integrating *QE2* and Cunard history into the decor, the designers created a ship as modern as the twenty-first century along with a floating museum named Heritage Trail. Escorted tours of the 24 exhibits underscoring her traditions are available. The most recent renovations include a complete redesign on one restaurant and further refurbishing of cabins and public rooms.

Public rooms are on three decks—Quarter, Upper, and Boat—with new links and stairways to let traffic flow naturally and to reflect passengers' activities at different times of day. Promenades echo the earlier Queens. Passengers enter the *QE2* through the Midships Lobby, a two-story atrium on Deck 2 elegantly decorated in mulberry and green against honey-colored cherry wood trimmed in bronze, where a harpist is usually in residence during embarkation. A four-part mural by Peter Sutton depicting the history of Cunard and the *QE2* covers the atrium's circular walls. The bell from the first *Queen Elizabeth* and the *Spirit of Atlantic* statuette are displayed.

Itineraries   See Appendix B.

Cabins   Comfortable and convenient, all cabins were refurbished, their bathrooms retiled and given new fixtures in the recent renovations, and two new Grand suites (QS category), including one wheelchair-accessible, and another enlarged, and two cabins in Princess Grill were added.

The *QE2*'s complex arrangement of cabin categories is different for the world cruise and the transatlantic service. Because dining assignments are determined by cabin category, it's important to understand precisely what you're buying. In principle, when you pay more, you get more.

For the world cruise, the top 8 among 22 categories—plus the 5 named suites—dine in the Queens Grill. On transatlantic and short cruises, there are fewer categories; the top four, one deluxe single, and the named suites dine in the Queens Grill. The next group, ultradeluxe, is split between the Princess and Britannia Grills. Assignments continue on down the line.

Categories don't completely reflect the variety of configurations. The top two decks, Signal and Sun Boat, have the largest, most luxurious suites with verandas and penthouse service, which includes butlers whose duties range from planning parties to arranging priority disembarkation and customs preclearance.

Ultradeluxe cabins are amidships on Sun Deck, Deck 1, and Deck 2; other categories are fore and aft on Decks 2 and 3 as well as the two lower decks. All cabins have television with 24-hour CNN, information, and movies. Cabins in grill and deluxe class have refrigerators, VCRs, and bathrooms with tub and shower; premium class has bathrooms with shower only. Bathrooms of 55 penthouse suites are in marble. *QE2* has a total of 151 single cabins, covering a variety of categories.

Specifications   107 single and 239 double inside cabins; 43 singles and 592 doubles outside; 700 with 2 lower beds. 7 ultra-luxury suites. Some wheelchair-accessible cabins available. Standard dimensions not available.

Dining   All five dining rooms have single seating for each meal. The Mauretania Restaurant, named for an early Cunard ship, has vintage photographs, a 1907 telegraph from the vessel, and as the centerpiece, White Horses, a sculpture by Althea Wynne, depicts four horses riding waves, emblematic of the British sailors' term for whitecaps. At the entrance is a 15-foot model of the *Mauretania* (one of the Heritage Trail's largest items) on display. On transatlantic service, this restaurant has two seatings.

The Caronia Restaurant, named for another Cunard ship of legendary opulence, got a complete makeover in the most recent renovations and is now one of the ship's most attractive rooms. In the style of a English country house, it has rich mahogany-paneled walls and columns and a white-painted ceiling with Murano glass chandeliers in a spreading leaf design. On the back wall behind the captain's table is a lovely Italian hill country scene. It has a new stereo system and air-conditioning intended to eliminate drafts.

The Princess and Britannia Grills, both recently renovated, have their own separate entrances from the Crystal Bar. The latter's name honors Cunard's first ship, *Britannia,* a model of which is displayed in the Heritage

Trail group entitled "Samuel Cunard and the Paddle Steamers." The Queens Grill is reserved for passengers booked in Queens Grill class only. Among its latest renovations are etched glass doors and a completely new galley.

Menus are identical in all restaurants, but the Queens Grill is where cuisine is meant to be of the highest gourmet standard, and patrons enjoy tableside preparations. The rooms' sizes and ambience differ more than the food. Fare includes hors d'oeuvres, three soups, sorbet, five entrees, two salads, four or five desserts, cheese, ice cream, sherbet, and fruit. A spa menu is available.

The Lido is the ship's most obvious bow to current lifestyles. It was transformed into a buffet-style restaurant, providing an informal setting for breakfast, lunch, dinner, and the midnight buffet. Coffee and drinks are served all day. From our experience, with the exception of the Queens Grill, the food—and certainly the service—are the best aboard, surpassing even the Princess Grill. Floor-to-ceiling windows open to the outside deck, making the room light and airy. White, beige, and mint decor is set off by two murals by Italian artist Giancarlo Impiglia depicting the *QE2* cruise experience. Stairs lead from the cafe to the Deck 1 lido area and the Pavilion bar and grill.

Service   Officers are British, but most hotel and cabin staff are European, many of them women. The level of dining room service rises with the dining room and price. In grill class, service is meant to be luxurious. For other passengers, it's, well, British. Most passengers say it's friendly and attentive. Unless you're in a top suite, do not expect cabin and dining service will be any different or better than most mainstream ships.

Facilities and Entertainment   Lifestyle updates have been central to the ship's renovations, evidenced in the Golden Lion near the Upper Deck theater and casino. The large, classic English pub is decorated in mahogany and plaid. It's the ship's informal social center, offering an upright piano, television, karaoke, and darts. Many lagers, stouts, and draught beers, plus local brews in port, are served. The classy Grand Lounge showroom has a fully equipped, curtained stage, dance floor, a new audio system and improved sight lines. The latest addition brings fledgling Broadway and West End shows for development aboard the *QE2*. Passengers may enjoy segments of the shows or attend rehearsals, workshops, and improvisation sessions performed by the actual cast that may appear on opening night.

The popular Yacht Club, aft, with handsome nautical decor and America's Cup memorabilia, was expanded to become a lounge and bar by day and a sophisticated nightclub in the evening. Outside the club on Deck 3 are sunning space and deck sports.

The Chart Room on Quarter Deck showcases Cunard's nautical antiques.

An electronic world map behind the bar tracks the ship's course. A piano from the *Queen Mary* plays for cocktails and after dinner. A bust of Queen Elizabeth II decorates the blue and gold Queens Room, which retains its dignified best with new furniture and new royal blue carpeting interwoven with gold Tudor roses. The royal connection is showcased in exhibits of the Queen's Standards, presented to the ship by Queen Elizabeth. Included are photographs and portraits of the queen and queen mother.

The room is the setting for former afternoon tea with live music and evening ballroom dancing. (Gentlemen who forget their formal attire may visit the *QE2* tuxedo rental shop, and unescorted ladies may dance with gentlemen hosts.) Lounges offer varied dance music and celebrity performers, who in the past have included Bill Cosby, Peter Duchin and his orchestra, and Dick Clark, among others.

Activities and Diversions   Varied lounges and public rooms provide an array of activities. A day could begin with exercise in the fitness center or jogging, progress to a lesson in the computer center, and move to a seminar or workshop in the theater. The latter also functions as a lecture hall, conference room, and cinema. There is also a new business center.

The Life Enrichment Program, part of every cruise, offers seminars, workshops, and lectures by experts. Also available are bingo, horse racing, arts and crafts, and beauty demonstrations. Theme cruises add such attractions as jazz or classical concerts. In addition to attending classes in the Computer Learning Center, passengers can send and receive e-mail and faxes at more than a dozen computer stations.

The *QE2*'s is the only library at sea with a full-time professional librarian. Now doubled in size with a book shop, it has more than 6,000 books, hundreds of videos, and a multimedia reference library that includes material on CD-ROM. Red leather seats and desks are provided, but the library is so popular there's often no place to sit. Another *QE2* exclusive is Harrods, the famous London department store, which has rejoined the shops of the Royal Promenade with a more prominent location.

Sports, Fitness, and Beauty   The ship has indoor and outdoor pools. Deck sports include golf (putting and driving area), shuffleboard, Ping-Pong, and jogging on a track. Exercise classes are available daily in the fitness center and gym on Deck 7. The European-style spa on Deck 6 offers a sauna, massage, and beauty and body treatments. Steiner of London operates the barber shop and beauty salon on Deck 1. Among her extensive facilities, the *QE2* has one of the largest, best-equipped hospitals afloat.

Children's Facilities   Club 2000 teen center is on Quarter Deck, and a supervised children's playroom and nursery are available high up on Sun Deck.

Shore Excursions   Booklets sent to passengers are cruise-specific, with thumbnail sketches of each port of call.

Theme Cruises   Run from spring to fall, theme cruises vary from year to year. They're likely to spotlight art and antiques, big band and nostalgia, Broadway, classical music, gardening, jazz, murder mystery, natural history, opera, and theater. A schedule is available.

Postscript   Although the *QE2* looks contemporary, she seems more a traditional oceanliner than when she first appeared in her 1960s Formica gloss. Despite updates, she remains the same: a unique ship with a mystique no other vessel can duplicate. Given her reputation and aura, passenger expectations run higher for the *QE2* than for any other ship. That virtually ensures that some passengers with inflated fantasies will be dissatisfied. Skeptics may be surprised, if not thrilled, and most aboard will be happy they sailed on the *Queen.*

Caronia	Quality **7**	Value C
Registry: Great Britain	Length: 628 feet	Beam: 82 feet
Cabins: 375	Draft: 27 feet	Speed: 20 knots
Maximum Passengers: 665	Passenger Decks: 9	Elevators: 6
	Crew: 379	Space Ratio: 35

The Ship   A spacious vessel designed for long cruises and gracious living, the *Caronia* (formerly *Vistafjord*) was launched by the now-vanished Norwegian American Cruises in 1973, and acquired by Cunard in 1983. She's a classic luxury liner, with the tasteful look of quiet grace and beautiful, distinctive interiors created when expensive hardwoods were used lavishly.

The ship is known for excellent European-style service and friendly officers and crew. Its consistent quality attracts discerning, well-heeled passengers, among them an unusually high number of repeaters. Americans and Britons predominate, but there are also many Germans—enough that the ship is bilingual. Announcements and printed materials are in English and German. Depending on the itinerary, other Europeans might be aboard, creating a cosmopolitan ambience. The majority of passengers are older than 60, and activities are geared toward them.

A renovation in 1994 gave *Caronia* 11 luxurious suites, a cozy Italian restaurant, a new public address system, a new purser's office with interactive scan map to help you find your way, and other improvements. Further updates were made in 1997 and in 1999, adding more shops, a ten-station computer center, bookstore, and remaking the North Cape Bar into the paneled White Star Bar.

Itineraries   See Appendix B.

Cabins   *Caronia's* large, tastefully decorated cabins encompass 17 categories and 10 configurations. Some with connecting doors can combine to create a two-room suite with separate sitting area. Most cabins have twin beds (some convert to king), one or two chairs and a cocktail table, large mirrored dresser with locking drawers, minifridge, and generous closets. The ship has a significantly large number of singles.

All have television, radio, and soundproof walls and are equipped with safes, refrigerators, hair dryers, and VCRs. Telephones have caller recognition, a beeper system for calling stewards, an automatic wake-up-call system, and a 911 call button for emergencies. All cabins have new bathrooms, and 90 percent of them have tubs as well as showers. Terry robes are supplied, and your basket of fresh fruit is replenished daily.

Each of the 11 deluxe suites on the Bridge Deck has a private balcony. Two of the suites are duplexes with huge living rooms, as well as private Jacuzzis, saunas, and exercise rooms. Four cabins on the main and upper decks accommodate handicapped passengers. Cabins are attended by Scandinavian stewardesses who are as amiable as they are capable.

Specifications   17 singles and 34 double inside cabins; 34 single and 267 double outside; 17 suites with private balcony. Standard dimensions, 175 square feet. 71 single cabins. Four for disabled.

Dining   The bright, cheerful dining room easily holds all passengers at one seating. Its sea-foam green decor is complemented with gold-trimmed white china. All meals have open seating.

The sophisticated international cuisine consistently receives high marks for variety, preparation, and presentation. The highest-quality products—fresh when possible—are used. Fish is a feature; delicate pastries, a highlight. A typical menu has three appetizers, two soups, two salads, four entrees, four desserts plus a diabetic dessert, cheese, and fruit. Vegetarian and spa menus are available. American and European wines are stocked.

Waiters are excellent, but, surprisingly, no busboys help them. This may result in slow service, but on this type of ship, service is never rushed. Dining is a main activity of the day and is meant to be leisurely.

The popular, glass-enclosed Lido Cafe serves early-morning coffee and freshly baked rolls, as well as buffet breakfast and lunch, and there's an ice cream parlor. Midday buffets, frequently themed, feature hot and cold dishes, hot dogs, and hamburgers. Tivoli, an alternative restaurant serving fine Italian cuisine is located on the top level of Club Piccadilly, a bilevel lounge and nightclub, decorated in elegant black, red, and beige. In ocean-liner tradition, hot bouillon is served on deck at daily 11 a.m. Afternoon tea is offered in the ballroom, often with a fashion show, and at the Lido Cafe. A late snack is laid out at 11 p.m. in the dining room. Around-the-clock room service offers selections from dining room menus during meal hours and light fare at other times.

Facilities and Entertainment Evening entertainment belies *Caronia*'s somewhat staid image. The ballroom is the main showroom; nightly entertainment might be a Broadway-style revue or variety show, an updated version of a Gilbert and Sullivan operetta, or a guest performer. One night may bring a presentation of sea chanteys by the crew; another, a folkloric group from the port of call. The room's dance floor draws a crowd when big band music plays before dinner and after the show. A small casino next door offers blackjack and slot machines.

On the same deck, the Garden Lounge frequently hosts classical concerts, special parties and dancing. The room has been refurbished to enhance its garden ambience. One flight up, the cozy Club Piccadilly offers piano music at noon, the ship's trio at cocktails, and a nightly cabaret. After the show, it becomes the disco.

Activities and Diversions The ship offers full days of activities. Gentlemen hosts are available for dance classes and afternoon teas, as well as for dining and ballroom dancing. Bridge instructors organize games. Other options include arts and crafts sessions, bingo, chess, Scrabble, backgammon, discussions on wines, astrology sessions, daily lectures by guest experts, a bridge tour, and recorded music on your cabin radio and television.

The residential-style library, furnished with leather seats, has a video library, a CD-ROM search system, and a small business center with a credit card–operated fax machine and word processors. The theater, near the library, shows current films or hosts guest lecturers.

Sports, Fitness, and Beauty *Caronia* has one outdoor and one indoor swimming pool, Jacuzzis, shuffleboard, Ping-Pong, and a golf putting area. A wraparound deck invites walking and jogging (seven laps per mile), and the Sports Deck was recently roofed to expand activities. The spa organizes daily exercises. The beauty salon and barber shop offer mud wraps, massage, and other beauty treatments.

Theme Cruises Thirteen cruises were given themes as different as Eco Issue of the New Century to a Taste of the Bayou. A schedule is available from the cruise line.

Postscript *Caronia* offers cruising at its most traditional, catering to older, seasoned cruisers. Anyone unaccustomed to formality might easily be bored. Although the ship isn't a mecca for swingers, singles, or couples younger than age 40, those who find an itinerary they like and who want low-key luxury and top-notch service without pretension would be suitable passengers. Shipboard activity is ample, and you will be in the company of others who are well read and well traveled. There's a lot to be said for that, too.

THE QUEEN MARY PROJECT

Preliminary sketches from the Queen Mary Project indicate that Cunard's new owners plan to build an oceanliner reminiscent of great transatlantic steamships and, in their words, "relaunch the golden age of travel for those who missed the first one." The yet-unnamed dream ship, costing upward of $700 million, is expected to debut in 2003.

The 146,000-ton vessel with a 1,100-foot-long slick hull will carry 2,800 passengers in a "quasi-class system" similar to that on *QE2*. Cabin category will determine assignments in each of three restaurants. One large dining room will have a grand staircase similar to one moviegoers saw in *Titanic*. The new ship will boast the largest spa afloat. Seventy-five percent of the cabins will have balconies.

The vessel will be the world's largest marine museum and will have historic areas open to visitors in port. A floating microbrewery will produce Cunard-brand beer.

Plans call for the liner to sail regularly between Europe and the United States on six-day crossings between New York and Southampton. Additional ports include Boston, Cherbourg, and Hamburg. Pre- and postcruise land packages will be offered for both continents.

Delta Queen Steamboat Company/
Delta Coastal Cruises

Robin Street Wharf, 1380 Port of New Orleans Place
New Orleans, LA 70130-1890
(504) 586-0631; (800) 543-1949; fax (504) 585-0630
www.deltaqueen.com

Type of Ships   Classic steamboats and coastal cruises.

Type of Cruises   River cruises through America's heartland and Pacific Northwest.

Cruise Line's Strengths
- the steamboats
- the setting
- turn-of-the-century atmosphere

Cruise Line's Shortcomings
- limited shipboard activities
- small cabins on the *Delta Queen*

Fellow Passengers   Mix of ages, nationalities, families, couples, singles, and grandparents traveling with grandchildren. Group is likely to be cosmopolitan: Norwegians, Dutch, British, Germans, Canadians, and Americans. Average age is 62 years; it drops on shorter trips, which usually include more families. Most passengers are retired, with annual incomes over $35,000. There are young and middle-aged honeymooners and repeaters who have sailed on the steamboats many times. A surprising number of passengers live near the river and cruise to enjoy it in a different way. Fifty-five percent have been to Alaska; about 70 percent have cruised on an upscale, traditional line.

Recommended For   Anyone interested in American history, culture, and literature or just good, old-fashioned values regardless of age. Those who enjoy the relaxed pace and shoreline visibility that river cruises offer. Dixieland jazz fans. The paddle wheel's gentle motion and the cruises' locale appeal most to seniors, but those elements also attract anyone uneasy about ocean voyages or straying far from home.

Not Recommended For   Travelers expecting European-style elegance, elaborate cuisine, and polished service. Those who don't enjoy a certain amount of hokum. Families with young children (for lack of children's facilities). Those requiring large-ship amenities, such as cabin television.

Cruise Areas and Seasons   Mississippi, Atchafalaya (Louisiana), Red (Louisiana), Cumberland, Tennessee, Ohio, Kanawha (West Virginia) rivers, year-round.

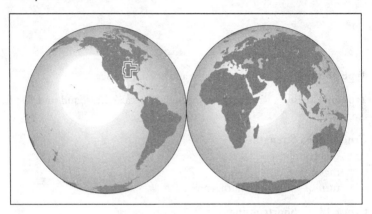

The Line   The Delta Queen Steamboat Company is the oldest American flag line. Of the five authentic, steam-powered paddle wheelers in the United States, Delta Queen's are the only ones offering overnight accommodations and traveling the length of inland rivers.

The forerunner of the cruise line was founded in 1890 by Capt. Gordon C. Greene, who pioneered riverboat vacations, and his wife, Mary, also an accomplished river pilot and steamboat captain. The couple and their sons owned and operated 28 steamers over the years. After World War II, Tom Greene purchased the *Delta Queen* in California, remodeled her, and inaugurated her with Mississippi River cruises in 1948. A decade later, he sold the company. In 1973, new owners renamed the line *Delta Queen* Steamboat Company. In 1976, they built the Mississippi Queen, which is twice as large as her sister steamer.

The line's owner now, American Classic Voyages, also owns American Hawaii Cruises and the newly created United States Lines. In 1995, ACV added *American Queen,* the largest steamboat ever built, celebrating her debut with the 125th annual Great Steamboat Race in New Orleans.

In the next decade, ACV is expanding in a big way. The *Columbia Queen* debuted in summer 2000 and sails the Northwest from her base in Portland, Oregon. Under construction are the first two of five 226-passenger coastal ships to sail the Eastern Seaboard from Halifax to Miami as well as northern California and the Pacific Northwest. The 300-foot diesel-driven vessels, costing about $35 million each, are being built in turn-of-the-century steamer style with period decor, but will offer four-star amenities and state-of-the-art technology. Guido Perla and Associates of Seattle designed the vessels, and Andrea Piacentini Design of Seattle is creating the interiors. The first two ships, *Cape May Light* and *Cape Cod Light,* will enter service in 2001. The cruises will be destination-oriented, with shore excursions focusing on historical and scenic places.

The Fleet	Built/Renovated	Tonnage	Passengers
American Queen	1995	3,707	436
Delta Queen	1927/84/98	3,360	174
Mississippi Queen	1976/96	3,364	420
Columbia Queen	1999	n.a.	162
Cape May Light	2001	1,580	226
Cape Cod Light	2001	1,580	226

Style   A cruise on one of the Queens differs from an ocean voyage. Delta Queen calls the experience "Steamboatin'," a unique visit with the American soul and character. While floating down the Mississippi on one of these "wedding cakes" at a lazy nine knots per hour, visions of Huck Finn and Tom Sawyer are sure to arise—as they have for thousands of folks who have come before you. Nostalgia is thick when a morning mist hangs over the shoreline and the only sounds are the low hum of engines and the red paddle wheel churning the river's muddy water. Mark Twain wrote that the Mississippi at morning has a "haunting sense of loneliness, isolation, remoteness from the worry and bustle of the world. The dawn creeps in stealthily, the tranquillity is profound and infinitely satisfying."

After breakfast, the cruise "Riverlorian" relates colorful bits of river history. Later, your boat, festooned in red, white, and blue flags, arrives in a port with its calliope (an organlike instrument with whistles sounded by steam or compressed air) in full song. Most likely, you'll be met by the mayor and other townfolk, who personally offer passengers directions. It's an experience not likely found on standard cruises.

Distinctive Features   Paddle wheel, calliope, *Delta Queen*'s authentic interiors, Dixieland jazz, Southern specialties, immersion in nineteenth-century life on the Mississippi.

Rates   Port charges included.

	HIGHEST	LOWEST	AVERAGE
PER DIEM	$499	$282	$386

The above per diems are calculated from the cruise line's non-discounted *cruise only* fares on standard accommodations. Per diems vary by season, by cabin, and by cruise areas.

Special Fares and Discounts   Early-booking bonus and instant-purchase incentives available on most cruises.

- Children's Fares: One child age 16 or younger cruises free in some cabins on the Mississippi Queen and American Queen when sharing a cabin with two full-fare adults.
- Single Supplement: 150–175 percent, depending on vessel and cabin category.

Packages
- Air/Sea: Yes.
- Others: Theme cruises, such as Kentucky Derby.
- Pre/Post: Packages in New Orleans, Memphis, St. Louis, Minneapolis/St. Paul, and other main ports.

Past Passengers   Members of the Paddlewheel Steamboat Society of America receive a newsletter, champagne reception aboard ship; advance notice of schedules; and discounts in the ships' gift shops.

The Last Word   For most passengers, the real destination of these cruises is the steamboats. Most people love this homespun, star-spangled slice of Americana, from the Huck Finn picnic to the foot-stomping Dixieland jazz. The riverboats have universal appeal and transcend age barriers. Aboard a recent cruise was an under-40 couple with sons 8 and 12 years old. The boys got a daily lesson in American history on the boat and in ports, but they also enjoyed romping on the Mississippi shoreline, à la Huck Finn. Then, one night in the lounge, the older boy was seen playing chess with a 96-year-old passenger.

DELTA QUEEN STANDARD FEATURES

Officers American.

Staff Dining, Cabin, Cruise/American.

Dining Facilities One dining room with two seatings for three meals daily, plus tea and moonlight buffet; open seating breakfast.

Special Diets Diabetic, kosher, low-calorie/cholesterol, low-salt, and vegetarian. Request with cruise reservations.

Room Service Continental breakfast served in cabins on request.

Dress Code Casual but neat during the day; fashionable dress for evening—jacket and tie for men, dress or stylish suit for women.

Cabin Amenities Some cabins with brass beds, Tiffany-style windows, veranda, sitting area, baths with shower, writing area. *American Queen,* emergency call buttons by bed; suites and deluxe cabins have tubs.

Electrical Outlets 110 AC.

Wheelchair Access Companion recommended. See text.

Recreation and Entertainment Jazz, big bands, cabaret, and Broadway stage revues in lounges; riverboat shows; bridge; bingo; calliope concerts; crafts and cooking demonstrations; sing-alongs.

Sports and Other Activities Jogging on deck, shuffleboard *(Mississippi Queen),* kite flying, Ping-Pong.

Beauty and Fitness Small exercise room, whirlpool, aerobics, beauty salon on *American Queen* and *Mississippi Queen.*

Other Facilities Gift shop; *American Queen* and *Mississippi Queen* conference centers, fax service, library; theater on *American Queen* and *Mississippi Queen.*

Children's Facilities None.

Theme Cruises See specific ships.

Smoking *Delta Queen,* smoking on outside decks only; *American Queen* and *Mississippi Queen,* smoking section in lounges.

Delta Queen Suggested Tipping Per person per night, waiter/waitress, $3.75; busboy, $2.50; cabin attendant, $3.75; dining room captain, $2.50; 15 percent of bill for wine steward; $3.50 per bag for porter.

Credit Cards For cruise payment and on-board charges: American Express, Diner's Club, Discover, MasterCard, Visa. Only gift shops accept cash. Traveler's and personal checks can be cashed at purser's office.

Delta Queen   Quality ❸   Value D

Registry: United States	Length: 285 feet	Beam: 60 feet
Cabins: 87	Draft: 9 feet	Speed: 9 knots
Maximum Passengers: 174	Passenger Decks: 3	Elevators: None
	Crew: 79	Space Ratio: 19

The Ship   The *Delta Queen* is the only remaining authentic example of the thousands of overnight paddle-wheel steamers that once plied the nation's rivers. She has the warmth of a bed-and-breakfast inn, and her small-town friendliness mirrors the heartland ports she visits.

From the outside, this waterborne piece of history looks rather ordinary, except for her paddle wheel. Inside, however, she enchants with Tiffany-style stained glass, brass fittings, and rich, polished woods from another era. Simply knowing the *Delta Queen* is the real thing makes you appreciate every ceiling molding and creak in the floor. There's no other cruise vessel like her, and there never will be, because passenger vessels no longer can be built of wood. Indeed, *Delta Queen*'s elaborate superstructure, which adds so much to her character, was almost her undoing.

In the 1920s, the ship was one of two steamers commissioned by the California Transportation Company for luxury overnight travel on the Sacramento River between Sacramento and San Francisco. Their steel hulls were fabricated in Scotland, then dismantled and shipped to California for reassembly. The wheel shafts and cranks were forged in Germany. Her American-built superstructure was crafted from pine, oak, teak, mahogany, and Oregon cedar.

The *Delta Queen* and her twin, *Delta King,* were launched in 1927 at the astounding cost of $875,000 each and became famous for their deluxe appointments. The *Delta Queen* might have died as other steamships did, but at the outbreak of World War II, the navy commandeered her, painted her battleship gray, and used her to ferry troops across San Francisco Bay.

At war's end, the U.S. Maritime Commission auctioned the boat. Tom Greene, president of Cincinnati-based Greene Line Steamers, forerunner of the Delta Queen company, bought her for just $46,250. Greene had the vessel towed 5,378 miles in a 37-day trip to New Orleans via the Panama Canal. From Louisiana, she steamed on her own up the Mississippi and Ohio Rivers to Pittsburgh, where she was refitted to her original state. She made her Mississippi River debut in June 1948.

By 1962, the ship's demise seemed imminent, but publicist Betty Blake revived the tradition of steamboat races to draw attention to the venerable steamer. It worked. Then, in 1969, the *Delta Queen* returned to death's door when the federal safety standards banned wooden vessels as fire hazards. Blake organized a letter and petition campaign that won a congressional exemption the ship still enjoys. The riverboat was made fire-resistant, but in November 1970 again faced demise. Another act of Congress, however, saved the *Delta Queen,* placing her on the National Register of Historic Places. More than a million dollars was spent to enhance fire resistance. In 1989, she was designated a National Historic Landmark.

To ocean veterans, a cruise on the *Delta Queen* requires reorientation. Large cruise ships take at least a day to figure out; *Delta Queen* requires under an hour. The small, intimate boat is like an inn. Arriving passengers are greeted by riverboat dandies and Southern belles in hoop gowns, the reception setting the cruise's tone.

At the speed of 6–8 miles per hour, the ship averages 100 miles a day (an automobile covers that distance in 90 minutes), but after a day, distance and speed become irrelevant. Life aboard is a tonic for stress. Seasickness is no issue. The steamboat's hush—scarcely a murmur—is immediately apparent.

Passengers settle in to watch the passing scenery—forested banks, marshy coves, and high bluffs—and a lively parade of barges and towboats heaped with grain, coal, scrap iron, and fuel. (Binoculars are helpful.)

Approaching port becomes a major event. The *Delta Queen*'s throaty whistle and cheerful tunes from her 93-year-old calliope announce her arrival and draw people to the river. During docking, people ashore and passengers at the rails chat.

The engine room, open to passengers at all hours, is a marvel—immense pistons pushing huge beams that cause the giant red paddle wheel to turn. Engineers keep fresh coffee ready to welcome visitors.

Itineraries   See Appendix B.

Cabins   Cabins fall into eight categories, all outside with private showers. Hair dryers are allowed. Four of six suites have picture windows framed by stained glass, a conversation area, queen-size bed, bathtub, and shower; the other two have smaller sitting areas and shower only. Suites are furnished with antiques, while the homey furnishings in standard cabins range from good reproductions to collectibles and include patchwork quilts and wooden shutters. A few standard cabins have double beds; the remainder have twins.

The lowest-priced cabins have upper and lower berths. All are small but comfortable and clean. They range from 44 square feet for the smallest quarters to 68 square feet for mid-priced cabins to 135 and 156 square feet for top accommodations.

Cabins on two of the three decks face wide promenades dubbed the "front porch of America." Rooms on cabin deck open inside onto the quiet Betty Blake Lounge, but they have outside-facing windows.

Bathrooms are small but functional; many have sinks outside the bathroom door. There's a dresser and, instead of a closet, an open rack with brass rods.

Specifications   87 outside cabins; 6 suites. Standard dimensions, 100 square feet. 56 with twin beds; 4 with double; 8 queens; 19 with upper and lower berths.

Dining   The Orleans Dining Room offers two seatings. Most tables accommodate four, although some seat two or six. Wide windows on two sides frame a river panorama. A pianist entertains throughout dinner.

A continental breakfast is served in the Forward Cabin Lounge. All other meals are in the dining room, with choices from the menu or buffet at breakfast and lunch. The breakfast buffet offers oatmeal, grits, fruit, ham, eggs Benedict Cajun (with crawfish sauce), and flavored pancakes. Southern specialties like biscuits and gravy can be ordered.

Menus feature American favorites—steak, stew, ribs, catfish, fried chicken, roast duck, and roast lamb—and Southern recipes. Portions are relatively small, yet sensible for those who sample all five courses. Preparation ranges from good to excellent. One of the four entrees at each meal is labeled Traditional River Fare. Possibilities include creamy red beans, rice with Cajun sausage and ham chunks, and crawfish pie. The Forward Cabin Lounge has coffee and iced tea available all day, afternoon tea, and a moonlight buffet at 10:30 p.m.—not as elaborate as aboard seagoing cruise ships, but offering desserts, fruits, and several hot items.

Service   Fresh-faced young Midwesterners provide cheerful service. The staff seems to be a well-integrated, clean-cut, happy family. Their attitude is infectious and genuinely appreciated by passengers. Cabin stewardesses keep everything neat as a pin.

Facilities and Entertainment   The laid-back *Delta Queen* offers simple pleasures. Televisions are absent, and the only telephone is for ship-to-shore communication. Despite images of riverboat gamblers, there's no casino; passengers must settle for bingo.

The Forward Cabin Lounge, distinguished by mirrors and wooden pillars, is a popular place to prop your feet and watch the passing scenery through the windows. The lounge also has tables for card games and dining. Loaner binoculars are available free from the shore excursion desk.

The *Delta Queen*'s centerpiece is the Grand Staircase, which links the

Forward Cabin Lounge to the Texas Lounge upstairs. An ornate bronze fili-gree railing, scrolled latticework, and hardwood paneling accent this impressive stairway which is crowned by a Tiffany chandelier. The ship is casual, but a lady in flowing skirts could make a grand entrance on the staircase.

At the Texas Lounge entrance is plaque recognizing the *Delta Queen*'s landmark status. The wood-paneled lounge's piano bar is a magnet for the sing-along crowd. Passengers come here for popcorn, hot dogs, or hors d'oeuvres at cocktail hour. Wide windows provide the ideal setting for watching the river and sunsets.

The Orleans Dining Room, the boat's largest room, doubles as the entertainment lounge after the second-seating dinner. Tables are rearranged to accommodate a stage. Entertainers dazzle audiences with ragtime piano, Dixieland jazz, or banjo artistry. After the show, many pas-sengers retire to the Texas Lounge for dancing and music. The wholesome entertainment is in keeping with the boat's character, and passengers get involved in festivities and hokey contests. By 11 p.m., most of the crowd has turned in.

Activities and Diversions   Days aren't packed with activities, but there's enough to do, including some things you'd never encounter on an ocean-liner: flying kites from the deck, for example. The musically inclined—or curious—can try their hand at the calliope. Everyone who tries the key-board gets a commemorative certificate.

Other daytime activities include card tournaments, lessons on *Delta Queen* history, radio trivia games, pilothouse tours, wine and cheese par-ties, sing-alongs, a Mardi Gras costume party, champagne receptions, and walking and jogging to calliope music. Riverlorian talks are well attended.

The softly lighted Betty Blake Lounge, furnished with armchairs, sofas, desks, and bookcases, is fine for reading, board games, or writing postcards (a Delta Queen postmark is available in the adjacent purser's office).

Sign the purser's blackboard to receive a morning wake-up: a rap on your door. Next to the purser's office is a gift shop and shore excursion office.

Shore Excursions   Rural and urban ports offer visits to an array of heart-land attractions, including Antebellum Southern plantations, Mark Twain's boyhood home, Gateway Arch in St. Louis, Civil War sites, and many museums.

Theme Cruises   Perennial themes are the Kentucky Derby in May, Great Steamboat Race in June, Good Old Summertime in July and August, and Fall Foliage in October and November. Cruises with educational themes have been increased to appeal to travelers seeking a learning vacation.

Postscript The *Delta Queen* has been called a romantic anachronism; there is nothing like her. To cruise on her is to experience another time. Her small size and leisurely pace are conducive to meeting and chatting with fellow passengers. It's a small-town atmosphere that might not suit everyone.

Mississippi Queen	Quality ❹	Value D
Registry: United States	Length: 382 feet	Beam: 68 feet
Cabins: 208	Draft: 9 feet	Speed: 10 knots
Maximum Passengers: 422	Passenger Decks: 3	Elevators: 2
	Crew: 157	Space Ratio: 8

The Ship If the *Delta Queen* is a floating country inn, her larger sister, *Mississippi Queen,* is a stately Victorian showboat. Proud and pretty, she rolls down the river like the grandest float in a parade. On board, it's the Fourth of July—a red, white, and blue celebration of Americana amid Victoriana. And for good measure, one day's lunch is always an old-fashioned barbecue picnic with all the trimmings.

Polished brass railings, beveled mirrors, crystal chandeliers, and white wicker chairs evoke the turn of the century, yet the *Mississippi Queen* offers six decks of comfort and many modern cruise ship amenities, including bathing pool, six lounges and bars, a small gym, library, gift shop, elevators, cabin telephones, some private verandas, and a beauty salon.

Modern comforts aside, this ship is a true steamboat, powered by an authentic steam engine. Her huge paddle wheel is not just for show. Visit the Paddle Wheel Bar on Texas Deck and watch through floor-to-ceiling windows as the paddle wheel's bucket planks churn to drive the vessel.

Itineraries See Appendix B.

Cabins The *Mississippi Queen's* modern side is best appreciated in her cabins. All accommodations have air-conditioning, wall-to-wall carpeting, telephones, and private bathrooms. Standard cabins are compact and have tiny bathrooms with showers. Suites and outside deluxe cabins have private verandas, but only suites have bathrooms with tubs and showers. Each cabin displays historical art pertaining to its name. Cabin staff attend rooms twice daily to replenish towels and ice.

Specifications 73 inside cabins, 135 outside; 26 suites (68 with verandas). Standard dimensions are 123 square feet. 167 with twins; 20 with double; 20 with upper and lower berths; 1 wheelchair-accessible.

Dining   Two seatings are offered at each of three meals. Menu choices are similar to the *Delta Queen*'s and change daily. Five-course dinners include appetizers, soup, salad, entree, and dessert. Grazers find a light lunch buffet in the Grand Saloon, a late-night buffet in the Upper Paddlewheel Lounge, and hot dogs and ice cream all day at the open-air Calliope Bar. A room service continental breakfast may be ordered the previous night, although delivery may not be prompt.

Facilities and Entertainment   Entertainment is G-rated and genuine, emphasizing big band hits of the 1940s and 1950s, Broadway favorites, ragtime, and Dixieland jazz. The band plays nightly for dancing in the Grand Saloon. The *Mississippi Queen* features, as do her sister ships, a Riverlorian who regales passengers with tales from the past, historic tidbits about the river, and explanations of river activity.

Shore Excursions   Land tours cost extra and are purchased on board unless arranged beforehand by a tour group. Tours in port last about three hours and cost from $5 to $30 per person per excursion.

Theme Cruises   Topics are listed in the line's literature. They're similar to those aboard sister ships.

Postscript   For those who prefer more amenities and a larger ship, the *Mississippi Queen*'s Victorian style, modern comforts, and additional activities are probably an acceptable trade-off for the charm and singularity of the *Delta Queen*. Readers planning to book the *Mississippi Queen* should review all the Delta Queen Steamboat Company profile.

American Queen	Quality ⑧	Value C
Registry: United States	Length: 418 feet	Beam: 89.4 feet
Cabins: 222	Draft: 8.6 feet	Speed: 10 knots
Maximum Passengers:	Passenger Decks: 6	Elevators: 2
436	Crew: 165	Space Ratio: NA

The Ship   On her debut in 1995, this paddle wheeler retraced the route of the first steamboat to travel from Pittsburgh to New Orleans (1811). The inauguration increased the line's capacity 70 percent.

Constructed in Amelia, Louisiana, *American Queen* was the largest passenger vessel built in a U.S. shipyard in more than four decades. Building required three years. No expense was spared in re-creating the luxurious setting of yesteryear. The new vessel merges the best features of the *Delta Queen* and the Victoriana of the *Mississippi Queen,* both of which are smaller, and the grand style of nineteenth-century steamboats with modern shipbuilding technology and selected cruise ship amenities. Her white exterior is laden with gingerbread filigree, and a 50-ton, red paddle wheel turns at the stern. Inside are a swimming pool, gym, conference center, movie theater, and elevators.

The vessel is powered by two 1930s Nordberg steam engines salvaged from the Kennedy, a dredge belonging to the U.S. Army Corps of Engineers. Each of the rebuilt engines generates 750 horsepower.

The *American Queen* rises 97 feet from the water line to the top of its fluted stacks, making quite a show. The stacks and pilothouse, which has a six-foot-tall rooster weathervane, can be lowered to enable the vessel to pass under low bridges.

Itineraries   See Appendix B.

Cabins   A Victorian theme employs period wallpaper, floral carpets and fabrics, brass fixtures, etched glass, and antiques or good reproductions. Even modern plumbing and electrical fixtures are disguised as antiques. Each cabin is named after a river town or historic steamboat.

Seven categories are distributed on all but the lowest passenger deck. Some cabins have bay windows; 98 have verandas. Three-fourths are outside; some have windows or private verandas, but most have French doors. Mid-range standard cabins are considerably larger than on her sister ships.

Cabins are more "senior friendly," with larger bathrooms, emergency call buttons by each bed, and levers (rather than handles) on doors. As on *Delta Queen,* several cabins open onto promenade decks. Although *American Queen* is much larger, such touches provide a sense of community and make it easy for passengers to meet.

Specifications   54 inside cabins, 168 outside; 29 suites and cabins with veranda. Standard dimensions are 141 and 190 square feet. 208 with twin beds; 2 with doubles; 4 queens; 8 singles; 9 wheelchair-accessible.

Dining   Interior designers borrowed liberally from historic steamboats, particularly the 1878 *J. M. White,* called the most graceful and spacious steamboat of her time. Her dining saloon—which Mark Twain described as "dainty as a drawing room; when I looked down her long, gilded saloon, it was like gazing through a splendid tunnel"—has been copied and named the J. M. White Dining Room.

Located on main deck, the lowest passenger deck, the dining room spans two decks. Tall windows have ornate fretwork arches. A dropped ceiling divides the room and gives each half a soaring appearance. Each side has a vaulted space with huge mirrors in spectacular gilt frames dating from the 1880s. Providing music is a 1895 rosewood grand piano—one of 200 antiques accenting the vessel's Victorian decor.

Service   Staff is traditionally attired, and the all-American crew is unfailingly cheerful, hardworking, and eager to please.

Facilities and Entertainment   A lounge and bar at the dining room entrance links the lobby and Grand Saloon below, where entertainment is staged nightly and a dance band plays. Designed as an idealized 1880 opera house, the theater has a proscenium stage and is ringed with private boxes on the second-story balcony.

The Mark Twain Gallery around the upper level of the dining room honors the author whose *Life on the Mississippi* captures the essence of steamboating. Books and curio cases contain exhibits on regional wildlife and steamboat history and river memorabilia. Furnishings include Tiffany-style lamps and writing tables. Window areas provide cozy nooks for reading, writing, or watching the scenery.

Forward from the gallery to starboard is the Gentlemen's Card Room, a masculine room meant to resemble Teddy Roosevelt's library. Cases are filled with books typical of late-nineteenth-century homes, with many first-person accounts of exploration and vintage how-to books. One of the ship's two television sets is tucked behind cabinet doors.

To port is the Ladies Parlor, a Victorian drawing room where afternoon tea is served. From the gallery to amidships is the purser's lobby and grand, gilded staircase under a spectacular filigreed ceiling, also harking to the *J. M. White*. Beyond is the Grand Saloon's upper level and the lively Engine Room Bar overlooking the paddle wheel. The engine room viewing area is open to passengers around the clock, and engineers, proud of the vessel, seem never to tire of answering questions.

Forward on Texas Deck is the cruise line's signature "Front Porch of America," complete with swings and rockers. Above, the Promenade Deck has a full-circuit walkway and the Calliope Bar. Stairs behind the bar lead to the topmost sun deck and Crow's Nest observation platform, small exercise room, and bathing pool (essentially a large hot tub). The Observation Deck also has a full-circuit promenade (seven laps equal a mile). Loaner binoculars are available.

A Riverlorian holds court in the Chart Room on Observation Deck, where passengers find authentic old piloting instruments and navigational charts as well as the boat's 1,500-pound bronze bell. At the end of her first season, names of all inaugural passengers were engraved on the bell.

Theme Cruises　Topics, described in the line's large brochure, range from jazz to the Civil War to Gardens of the River.

Postscript　The company's brochure has easy-to-read deck plans for all three ships, accompanied by detailed descriptions of cabin layout, furnishings, and facilities.

Readers planning to cruise on the *American Queen* should review the entire section on the Delta Queen Steamboat Company for comparison.

Columbia Queen　(Preview)

Registry: United States	Length: 215 feet	Beam: 60 feet
Cabins: 81	Draft: 12 feet	Speed: 11 knots
Maximum Passengers:	Passenger Decks: 124	Elevators: 1
161	Crew: NA	Space Ratio: NA

The Ship　*Columbia Queen,* which debuted in summer 2000, marked the company's first venture in cruising beyond the Mississippi River region. The new riverboat sails year-round in the Pacific Northwest on the Columbia, Snake, and Willamette Rivers from her home port of Portland, Oregon.

Designed by naval architects Rodney E. Lay and Associates of Jacksonville, Florida, who also designed the *American Queen,* the new vessel is similar in appearance to her sister ship but without the paddle wheel. Her decor reflects the heritage of the Pacific Northwest.

To underscore that heritage, the ship was christened by Randy'L Hedow Teton, who was the model for Sacagawea on the new U.S. golden dollar. Sacagawea was the Shoshone woman who guided the Lewis and Clark expedition along much of the route *Columbia Queen* sails today.

Itineraries　See Appendix B.

Cabins　The Northwestern riverboat decor is carried out in the cabins as well. All cabins are furnished with full-size twin beds that convert to a king-size bed, satellite television, radio with one vessel channel, hair dryer, iron, and ironing board.

Specifications　69 percent are outside cabins. Four "AAA" category have 235 square feet; two open on to the deck and two open on to French balconies; 15 "AA" category have, 220 square feet and all open on to French balconies. The 37 "A" or standard cabins measure 165 square feet, and 24 "B" cabins have 143 square feet. There is one single room of 91 square feet The entire vessel is wheelchair-accessible, including one "A" category cabin.

Facilities   The ship's lounges do double duty. Astoria Room, the main dining room, is an elegant two-tiered space on the Main Deck, the lower passenger deck, designed for dining and entertainment. The room is large enough to seat all passengers at one time and can be transformed into the main show lounge and theater. Next to it, the Lewis & Clark Lounge is a cozy room for drinks and hors d'oeuvres before dinner or for relaxing any time of day. Two decks up on Explorer Deck, the Explorer Bar is an elegantly appointed piano bar with wood paneling, an oak bar, and a grand piano. The room is lined with tall windows that open on to panoramic views.

Forward on Cabin Deck is the Purser's Lobby, a lounge with the purser's desk and a gift shop. It functions as a cozy meeting place and a library with bookcases and plenty of comfortable chairs.

The Back Porch, a bright area on the Observation Deck aft offers continental breakfast, coffee around the clock, and a small bar. The deck is enclosed by French doors and windows that remain open on fair weather days.

Shore Excursions   *Columbia Queen:* 18 shore excursions for the cruise, which it calls "Journey of Discovery," to reflect the Pacific Northwest's history from four perspectives: Native Americans; The Explorer and the Pioneer; The Wild West; and The River as the Highway of History. As is traditional with the line, a Riverlorian gives talks on the region's history and culture and is available to passengers for questions and discussions throughout the cruise.

DELTA QUEEN COASTAL VOYAGES

Cape May Light/Cape Cod Light

Registry: United States	Length: 300 feet	Beam: 50 feet
Cabins: 114	Draft: 12.5 feet	Speed: 13 knots
Maximum Passengers: 226	Passenger Decks: 5	Elevators: 1
	Crew: 75	Space Ratio: 19

The Ships   The new Delta Queen Coastal Voyages, a sister company to Delta Queen Steamship Company, is scheduled to begin operations in spring of 2001 with two new ships. *Cape May Light* arrives first, with the second, *Cape Cod Light,* to follow later in the year. The idea and design of the ships, which are being built at Atlantic Marine, Inc. of Jacksonville, Florida, were inspired by the historic coastal vessels of Fall River Line, which served overnight passengers on northeastern U.S. coastal routes for nearly a century, beginning in the mid-1800s. The decor will feature classic nautical and Federal styles with modern amenities and state-of-the-art safety technology.

Initially, the new vessels will sail along the Eastern Seaboard, Great Lakes, Caribbean, and Central America, and later, they will cruise in Alaska and on the West Coast. The ships have been specially designed for their coastal itineraries, enabling them to reach destinations not easily accessible to larger ships—from cozy coves to picturesque fishing harbors. The ships' size and layout are meant to create an intimate onboard ambience, enhanced by the friendly service of their American crew for which the Delta Queen Steamships are known.

Itineraries   See Appendix B.

Cabins   Out of the ship's 114 cabins, 100 have coastal views. Categories "A" and "B" cabins offer expansive views from double windows. All cabins have classic, New England Federal and nautical decor reminiscent of turn-of-the-century coastal ships and are furnished with a queen bed or two lower twin beds; television with satellite service, VCR, radio, ship-to-shore telephone with data port; cherry wood dresser and nightstand, storage space, and wall-to-wall carpeting. The two Owner's Suites, measuring 328 square feet, have a sofa bed, a game table and a 180-degree view of the coastal scenery from panoramic windows.

Specifications   100 outside cabins, 14 inside. 2 Owner's Suites, 38 category "A" outside, measuring 155–165 square feet; 61 category "B" outside, 136–148 square feet; 13 category "C" inside, 145 square feet, except 2 singles, 107 square feet, and 2 wheelchair-accessible, 188 square feet.

Facilities   Public rooms include the Foyer and Purser's Lobby, accented with warm wood tones to enhance the decor. Corinthian columns similar to those of stately New England mansions flank the Foyer's Grand Staircase with its custom wrought-iron grillwork and polished brass railings.

The Grand Saloon, the main venue for evening entertainment on the Saloon Deck mid-ship, is furnished with overstuffed chairs and richly upholstered banquettes along the perimeter. Large crystal chandeliers brighten the stamped metal ceiling; gold, green, and red accents add warmth to the room. At each corner are game tables for poker, bridge or backgammon.

The Chart Room Bar, with access to the Grand Saloon and the outside deck, is an intimate gathering spot for cocktails before dinner or in the evening. The room has Tiffany-style stained-glass window accents and an oak bar, representative of *Delta Queen*'s signature heavy wooden bar. It is lined with bookshelves with volumes on American history, coastal destinations, and routes of old ships. The gift shop, also on Saloon Deck, stocks nautical themed gifts and souvenirs, the ship's logo apparel, books, jewelry, disposable cameras, and limited sundries.

The dining room, with two seatings for three meals, is edged with large picture windows and decorated in a palette of gold, cream, and blue, highlighted by a custom-made chandelier from Tiffany Stained Glass of Chicago. Tables are with ecru damask linens.

The Canopy Bar, a casual outdoor lounge on the Observation Deck—the top deck—is the setting for sunrise breakfast buffets and evening happy hour. Heaters and fold-down awnings provide comfort year-round.

Disney Cruise Line

210 Celebration Place, Suite 400, Celebration, FL 34747-4600
(407) 566-3500; (800) 951-3532; fax: (407) 566-7739
www.disneycruise.com

Type of Ships   New megaliners.

Type of Cruises   Family-oriented mainstream cruises combined with a Walt Disney World vacation, designed for all ages.

Cruise Line's Strengths
- Disney name recognition
- new, innovative ships
- dining venue variety and presentation
- friendly, conscientious staff
- outstanding private island
- precruise and in-cabin literature
- children's facilities
- family cabins

Cruise Line's Shortcomings
- intrusive, loud public announcements
- Disney overdose
- over-regimentation of children's programs
- uneven cuisine
- unnecessary pressure to vacate ship on disembarkation

Fellow Passengers   A cross section of the nation, ages 3–93—similar to patrons at Disney theme parks.

Recommended For   Families with children or grandchildren. But, like the Disney parks, a Disney product for kids of all ages.

Not Recommended For   Anyone who isn't enraptured by Disney.

Cruise Areas and Seasons   Bahamas, year-round.

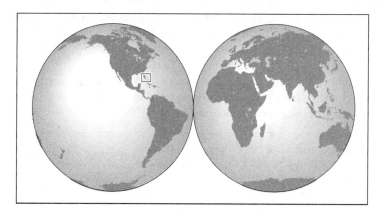

The Line   When Disney does something, it does it big, in a spare-no-expenses way. So, we were ready for the Disney Cruise Line to make a huge splash when its first ship, *Disney Magic,* was launched in 1998. What you see now—with the arrival of her twin, *Disney Wonder*—is the result of three years of intensive planning by cruise industry veterans, Disney creative talent, and dozens of the world's best-known ship designers.

Their task was to design a product that makes every adult feel the vacation is intended for them, while at the same time giving every child the same impression. The results may surprise people; whether they please everyone, particularly adults without children, remains to be seen.

The ships are both classic and innovative. Exteriors have traditional lines, reminiscent of great oceanliners. Inside, they're up to the minute technologically and full of novel ideas in dining, entertainment, cabin design, and entertainment facilities. Even Disney's exclusive cruise terminal at Port Canaveral is part of the overall strategy, aiming to make enjoyable even embarkation and disembarkation.

Disney created a "seamless vacation package," combining a three- or four-day stay at Walt Disney World with a three- or four-day cruise. Disney Cruise Line passengers are met at the airport by Disney staff and transported to the terminal in easily identifiable buses. During the hour's ride, they watch a cruise video. When your cruise is packaged with a stay at a Disney hotel, you check in once. The key that unlocks your hotel room door opens the door to your cruise cabin.

The major innovation is in dining. Each evening on board, you dine in a different restaurant with a different motif, but your waiters and dining companions move with you.

To cater to varied constituencies, some facilities, services, activities, and programs were designed specifically for adults without children, seniors, and honeymooning couples. For example, in addition to the themed restaurants, each ship has an alternative restaurant, swimming pool, and nightclub for use by adults only, and entertainment ranges from family musicals to adults-only comedy.

Overcoming the hassle of tendering passengers was an important consideration when Disney selected its private Bahamian island visited on all cruises; deep water enables ships to pull dockside. In August 2000, the line started a new seven-day Caribbean itinerary for the first time.

The Fleet	Built/Renovated	Tonnage	Passengers
Disney Magic	1998	83,000	1,750
Disney Wonder	1999	83,000	1,750

Distinctive Features   Three themed restaurants with "rotation" dining, sports bar in a funnel, children's facilities, cabin design, port terminal, cruise literature. Pagers allow adults to stay in touch with their kids when the children are participating in programs.

	HIGHEST	LOWEST	AVERAGE
PER DIEM	$583	$119	$306

The above per diems are calculated from the cruise line's non-discounted *cruise only* fares on standard accommodations. Per diems vary by season, by cabin, and by cruise areas.

Rates   Price includes port charges.

Special Fares and Discounts   Early booking can save $500–700 per cabin on a seven-night package; $200–550 on three- and four-day ones.
- Children's fares: Prices start at $179 per child.

Packages   Weeklong packages pair a visit to Walt Disney World in Orlando with unlimited admission to the theme parks, and a three- or four-night cruise. A seven-day, cruise-only package is available. Most people buy the cruise/park package. Consult the Disney brochure for these prices.
- Air/Sea: Yes.
- Others: Honeymoon.
- Pre/Post: Yes.

The Last Word   Cruise experts questioned whether Disney could fill its ships when kids are in school, but Disney estimated that if 1–2 percent of the 30 million plus annual visitors to Disney's resorts and parks bought a Disney cruise vacation, the ships would sell out. The vessels are complex and innovative, breaking the mold of traditional cruise ships.

DISNEY CRUISE LINE STANDARD FEATURES

Officers European.

Staff Cabin, Dining/European, Cruise/American.

Dining Facilities Three themed family restaurants with "rotation" dining; alternative adults-only restaurant; indoor/outdoor cafe for breakfast, lunch, snacks, and buffet dinner for children; pool bar/grill for burgers, pizza, and sandwiches; ice cream bar.

Special Diets On request; health-conscious cuisine program.

Room Service 24 hours.

Dress Code Casual by day; casual and informal in the evenings.

Cabin Amenities Direct-dial telephone with voicemail; tub and shower, two-in-one bathrooms; television, safe, hair dryer, minibar stocked for fee. In-room massage for Deck 8 suites; beachside massages all for a fee.

Electrical Outlets 110 AC.

Wheelchair Access Yes.

Recreation and Entertainment Showroom, theater, nightclub, comedy club, family nightclub, adult nightclub, sports bar, lounges.

Sports and Other Activities Sports deck, basketball, paddle tennis, family sports, adult pool, Ping-Pong, shuffleboard, biking and water sports on Castaway Cay (extra charge).

Beauty and Fitness Spa with sauna, steam rooms; beauty salon.

Other Facilities Self-service launderettes; digital photographic services and camera and video recorder rentals; dry cleaning, valet services; satellite phone services; medical facilities; guest services desk; 24-hour front desk service; fax and secretarial services; conference facilities.

Children's Facilities Age-specific supervised children's program, year-round youth counselors; children's drop-off service in evenings; private babysitting ($11 per hour for first child, $1 each for others); teen club; nursery for ages 12 weeks to 3 years.

Smoking Smoking not allowed except in designated areas.

Disney Suggested Tipping Waiter: three-night cruise, $10.50; four-night, $14; assistant waiter, $7.50 and $10. Cabin steward: three-night cruise, $10.50; four-night, $14; 15 percent service charge added to bar bills.

Credit Cards For cruise payment and on-board charges: all major credit cards.

Disney Magic	Quality ⑧	Value C
Disney Wonder	Quality ⑧	Value C

Registry: Bahamas	Length: 964 feet	Beam: 106 feet
Cabins: 875	Draft: 25.3 feet	Speed: 21.5 knots
Maximum Passengers:	Passenger Decks: 11	Elevators: 1248
2,400	Crew: 945	Space Ratio: NA

The Ships   *Disney Magic* and *Disney Wonder* are modern cruise ships with long, sleek lines, twin smokestacks, and styling that recalls classic liners but with instantly recognizable Disney signatures. Colors—black, white, red, and yellow—and the face-and-ears silhouette on the stacks are clearly those of Mickey Mouse. Look closely and you'll see that *Magic*'s figurehead is a 15-foot Goofy (Donald Duck on *Wonder*) swinging upside down from a boatswain's chair, "painting" the stern.

Interiors combine nautical themes and Art Deco inspiration, but Disney images are everywhere, from Mickey's profile in the wrought iron balustrades to the bronze statue of Helmsman Mickey at the center of the three-deck Grand Atrium. Disney art is on every wall, stairwell, and corridor. Some works are valuable old prints of Disney cartoon characters. A grand staircase sweeps from the atrium lobby to shops selling Disney Cruise–themed clothing, collectibles, jewelry, and sundries; classic Disney toys; and souvenirs. (The shops are always full of buyers; some people speculate that the cruise line derives as much revenue here as other lines do from their casinos, which the Disney ships do not have.)

The ships have two lower decks with cabins, three decks with dining rooms and showrooms, then three decks of cabins, and two sports and sun decks with separate pools and facilities for families and for adults without kids. Signs with arrows point the way to lounges and facilities, and all elevators are clearly marked forward, aft, or amidships. (More deck plans mounted on walls would help newcomers get their bearings.) Passengers receive a Disney Passport, a purse-size booklet covering just about everything you need to know for your cruise. Daily in your cabin, you receive "Your Personal Navigator," listing on-board entertainment and activities separated into options for teens, children, adults, and families, plus shore excursions.

Itineraries   See Appendix B.

Cabins   Cabins and suites are spacious with generous wood paneling throughout. About three fourths are outside, almost half with verandas.

The 12 cabin categories range from standard to deluxe, deluxe with veranda, family suite, one- and two-bedroom suite, and royal suite. Categories are similar to those at Walt Disney World hotels. Passengers who spend three or four days at a Disney hotel are matched with a cruise cabin in a comparable category.

Note: If you're staying at a Disney resort before your cruise, be sure to complete and return your cruise forms at the hotel. By showing your shore-side room key card at the cruise terminal, you can bypass lines and board directly. Cruise-only passengers may encounter a wait at check-in.

Cabin design reveals Disney's finely tuned understanding of the needs of families and children and offers a cruise-industry first: a split bathroom with bathtub/shower and sink in one room, and toilet, sink, and vanity in another. This configuration, found in all but standard inside cabins, allows any member of the family to use the bathroom without monopolizing it entirely. All bathrooms have both tub and shower.

Note: For added convenience, couple or families should pack two of essentials like toothpaste, providing one for each sink.

All cabins sleep at least three; many accommodate up to six. In some, pull-down Murphy beds provide additional daytime floor space. Storage space is generous. Bureaus are designed to look like steamer trunks. Cabins have direct-dial telephone with voicemail messaging; television; hair dryer; and minibar (stocked for a fee). The room key also opens the minibar and safe. Keys are marked Adult or Child. The latter cannot open the minibar or safe.

Specifications   186 inside, 689 outside; 385 suites with verandas, 82 family suites, 16 one-bedroom suites, 2 two-bedroom suites, 2 royal suites; 14 wheelchair-accessible. All cabins accommodate 3; inside up to 4; deluxe with verandas up to 4; family and 1-bedroom suites up to 5; 2-bedroom suites up to 7; royal suites up to 8.

Dining   Disney's most innovative area is dining. Ships have three different family restaurants, plus an alternative restaurant for adults only. Each night passengers move to a different family restaurant, each with a different theme and menu, taking along their table companions and wait staff. In each restaurant, tableware, linens, menu covers, and waiters' uniforms fit the theme.

On *Magic,* Lumiere's—named for the candlestick character in *Beauty and the Beast*—is a handsome, Art Deco venue serving continental cuisine. A mural depicts Beauty and the Beast (the equivalent restaurant on *Wonder* is called Triton, themed after The Little Mermaid). Parrot Cay dishes up Caribbean-accented food in a fun, tropical setting and is proving to be the most popular for breakfast. But it's Animator's Palate that reflects the creative genius of Disney animation. Diners are given the impression they have entered a black-and-white sketchbook. Over the course of the meal, the sketches on the walls are transformed through fiber optics into a full-color extravaganza. Waiters change their costumes from black and white to color. The first course is a montage of appetizers served on a palette-shaped plate, and dessert—a tasteless mousse in the shape of Mickey—comes with a parade by waiters bearing trays of colorful syrups—mango, chocolate, and strawberry—used to decorate it. It's entertaining, but the food is less than inspired, and hot dishes are likely to arrive cold, but no ones seems to care—they are too absorbed in watching Disney perform its magic.

Palo, the casual Italian restaurant named for the pole gondoliers use to navigate Venetian canals, is the intimate, adults-only restaurant. It's the best on board. The lovely, semicircular room has a sophisticated ambience with soft lighting, Venetian glass, inlaid wood, and a backlit bar. Northern Italian cuisine is featured. Food and presentation are excellent. More than two dozen kinds of wines are available by the glass ($5.50–25). There's a $5-per-person cover charge. Reservations are required; make them as soon as you board or risk being shut out. (Disney underestimated demand for this venue.) Other dining options include Topsiders (Beach Blanket Buffet on *Wonder*), an indoor/outdoor cafe serving breakfast, lunch, snacks, and a buffet dinner for children; a pool bar and grill for hamburgers, hot dogs, and sandwiches; Pinocchio's Pizzeria; an ice cream and frozen yogurt bar; and 24-hour room service.

Service Passengers lavishly praise Disney cast members, as cruise and park staffs are called. Staffs are among the most accommodating you will encounter in travel, and they try hard to smooth your way. More than once when I stopped to get my bearings, a staff member was beside me in seconds to help.

Facilities and Entertainment Nightly entertainment is unlike any other cruise line's and features quality, Disney-produced shows. The 1,000-seat Walt Disney Theater stages a different musical production each night, with talented actors, singers, and dancers. These family musicals are on the level of Disney theme parks' live entertainment rather than Broadway and may appeal more to children than to adults.

Disney Dreams has about every Disney character and song ever heard and offers a light plot wherein Peter Pan visits a girl who dreams of Disney's famous characters. It's pure schmaltz, but audiences give it a standing ovation.

Another night offers *Hercules, The MUSE-ical,* a comedy that's the least saccharine of the lot. *Voyage of the Ghost Ship* is an original musical with a story line, great staging, and special effects; songs and dances show the talented singers and dancers at their best. In the smaller Buena Vista Theater with full-screen cinema, passengers watch first-run movies and classic Disney films.

Studio Sea, modeled after a television- or film-production set, is a family-oriented nightclub offering dance music, cabaret acts, passenger game shows, and multimedia entertainment. The Art Deco Promenade Lounge is a daytime haven for reading and relaxation and a nightspot for cocktails and piano music. ESPN Skybox, a sports bar in the ship's forward, decorative funnel, has a big screen for viewing sporting events and a small viewing area with stadium seating.

Beat Street is an adult-oriented evening entertainment district with shops and three themed nightclubs: Rockin' Bar D, with live bands playing rock and roll, Top 40, and country music; Off Beat, an improv comedy club; and Sessions, a casual yet sophisticated place to enjoy easy music. Disney ships have no casinos. (Research showed its target markets weren't interested in gambling at sea, Disney says.) They also don't have a library or offer afternoon tea (a highlight on many cruise ships).

Activities and Diversions   Disney diversions are geared to children, families, and adults. A day at Castaway Cay, Disney's 1,000-acre private island, is meant to be the ultimate escape. The natural environment has been preserved. Miles of white sand beaches are surrounded by beautiful water. A pier allows access without tendering. A four-car, open tram (like those at Disney World) conveys passengers from the ship to Scuttle's Cove family beach. The shuttle runs every five minutes. You could walk the quarter-mile to the beach, but it's inadvisable in the blistering heat. (Bring sunblock and wear a hat.) Strollers are available, as are rental bikes, floats, and kayaks. Lounge chairs under pastel umbrellas are plentiful, and some hammocks swing under the palms, but otherwise there's very little shade.

Disney Imagineers have created shops, rest rooms, and pavilions that give the impression they have been there for years. A supervised children's area includes a "dig" at a half-buried whale skeleton. Water sports are offered in a protected lagoon. One snorkeling course is near shore; the other, farther out, requires more endurance. On the distant course, snorkelers see a variety of fish they identify from a waterproof card provided with rental equipment. Lifeguards watch snorkelers all around the courses. The cruise line has also planted several "shipwrecks." On one in about ten feet of water, snorkelers can see Mickey Mouse riding the bow of the ship. There's also a treasure chest, its contents guarded by large fish.

Rental equipment costs a pricey $27 for adults and $19.50 for children. Nature trails and bike paths are provided. The main beach offers kids' activities, live Bahamian music, and shops. Cookie's Bar-B-Cue serves a buffet lunch of burgers, pork ribs, hot dogs, baked beans, slaw, corn on the cob, fruit, and potato chips.

A second tram connects to Serenity Bay, the adult beach on the island's opposite side. The adult beach is a long sweep of sugary sand. A bar serves drinks, and passengers can enjoy a massage in one of the private cabanas with shuttered doors opening on the sea. Passengers must be back on the ship by 3:15 p.m. Most say they would have liked more time on the island.

Sports, Fitness, and Beauty   Of three top-deck pools, one has a Mickey Mouse motif and water slide and is intended for families. Another is set aside for team sports; the third is for adults. At night, the pool area can be transformed for deck parties and dancing.

The 8,500-square-foot, ocean-view Vista Spa and salon above the bridge offers Cybex exercise equipment, an aerobics room, exercise instruction, thermal-bath area, saunas, and steam rooms. It's supervised by a qualified fitness director. The spa, run by the British-based Steiner group, offers pricey beauty treatments along with a sales pitch for Steiner products. Despite high prices, the spa has proved to be very popular; it's generally booked for the entire cruise within hours of embarkation. New for 2000, passengers in Deck 8 concierge level suites can have a private massage in their suite or veranda. A 50-minute massage costs $105.

The Sports Deck has a paddle tennis court, Ping-Pong, basketball court, and shuffleboard. A full promenade deck lures walkers and joggers, but has no lounge chairs.

Children's Facilities   Playrooms and other kids' facilities occupy more than 15,000 square feet. Programs of age-specific activities are among the most extensive in cruising. They include challenging interactive activities and play areas supervised by trained counselors. Also offered are a children's drop-off service in the evening and private, in-room babysitting ($11 per hour for the first child and $1 for each additional child in the same family). Even at these prices, babysitters are booked up almost immediately after passengers board. Recently added is babysitting for tots in a nursery for ages 12 weeks to 3 years old; it operates from 2 to 4 p.m. and 7 p.m. to midnight, nightly. Cost is $6 per child, per hour; $5 per hour for each additional child.

The Oceaneer's Adventure program encompasses Oceaneer's Club (ages 3–8), themed to resemble Captain Hook's pirate ship, with plenty of places for activity; and Oceaneer's Lab (ages 9–12), with high-tech play, including video games, computers, lab equipment, and a small room for listening to CDs. Kids wear ID bracelets, and parents receive pagers for staying in touch with their playing children. Both parents and children give the youth programs high marks. Children in the drop-off program are taken to dinner at Topsiders.

Common Grounds (Deck 9) is a teen area themed after a coffee bar. It has a game arcade and organized activities, including nighttime volleyball. The program is a hit, as teens enjoy having a large part of the upper deck to themselves in the evenings.

Shore Excursions   The ships dock in Nassau for 18 hours, ample time to explore the island, enjoy a sport, visit Atlantis resort on Paradise Island, and take in a show and casino. The ship offers 12 excursions for Nassau, most of them fairly standard tours. Among choices are the Historical Harbor Cruise ($20 for adults; $14.50 for children), the Blue Lagoon Beach Day ($25/$17.50), Crystal Cay Marine Park ($23/$16.50), the Island World Exuma Adventure ($150 per person), and deep-sea fishing ($700 per person for a half-day). Children's prices apply to ages 3 through 9.

Postscript   Disney Cruise Line attracts a high percentage of first-time cruisers, thanks to Disney's reputation for quality, service, and entertainment, which helps dispel doubts about cruise vacations. At the same time, great effort was made to ensure that the ships appeal to adults—with or without children—as much as to families. Indeed, Disney issued a separate brochure on adult vacations. Early indications were that the line needed to make some changes to satisfy the adult market. On our follow-up sailing, adults without children were catered to in myriad ways and presented with an extensive menu of adult activities. The presence of hundreds of children on board did not diminish the adult experience.

More difficult to escape than children, however, is Disney's sugary, cuter-than-a-billion-Beanie-babies entertainment, which permeates every cruise. Expressed differently, you don't need to adore children to enjoy a Disney cruise, but you'd better love Disney. At departure, arrival in port, and other times throughout the cruise, instead of the usual ship's horn, you hear the first seven notes of "When You Wish Upon a Star."

Our main criticism of the ships' design is that all outdoor public areas focus inward—toward the pools rather than seaward, as if Disney wants you to forget you're on a ship. There's no public place on any deck where you can relax in the shade and watch the ocean (at least not without a plexiglass wall separating you). If this quintessential cruise pleasure ranks high with you, book a cabin with private veranda.

A second characteristic, expected but nonetheless irritating, is the extent to which the ship is childproofed. There's enough plexiglass on *Disney Magic* to build a subdivision of transparent houses. The pool deck (Deck 9) feels as if it's hermetically sealed. Some bothersome areas could quickly be improved. Examples: Public announcements are too loud and intrusive. *Magic* bar bills include a 15 percent gratuity, then have an empty space marked "gratuity" below the total. This amounts to a second tip. Guest Services says the space enables passengers to reward "extraordinary" service with something "extra." But most passengers, especially first-timers, won't know that or may be too shy to ask and will add a second tip.

Food and service is uneven. Two examples: At Palo, food is excellent, but service is very slow. At Topsiders, food is mediocre, the selections limited, and the tables very crowded, but the service is outstanding.

Disembarkation is a mixed bag. On the plus side, passengers booked on airline flights can check in for them shoreside. (Too bad all cruise lines can't provide this service.)

Holland America Line / Westours, Inc.

300 Elliott Avenue West, Seattle, WA 98119
(206) 281-3535; (877) SAIL HAL; fax (206) 281-7110
(800) 628-4855
www.hollandamerica.com

Type of Ships   Modern superliners.

Type of Cruises   Essence of traditional yet modern, high-quality mainstream cruises.

Cruise Line's Strengths
- tradition and experience
- easy-to-like ships
- consistent quality and style
- worldwide itineraries
- impeccable condition of ships

Cruise Line's Shortcomings
- show lounge entertainment
- shore excursion cancellation policy
- dining staff service and communication problems on new ships due to language

Fellow Passengers   Experienced travelers and families who seek comfort and consistency, appreciate quality and a high level of service, prefer a refined environment, and choose cruises by their destinations. Many are retired business owners with some college education, executives, and professionals, but the range includes young nurses and secretaries on their first cruise, affluent seniors who cruise often, honeymooners, young families, and some disabled travelers. They're social-minded, well mannered, and outgoing, but not loud. They enjoy traveling with old friends and making new friends. They're conservative, careful with money, and seek good value. They often cruise to celebrate a special occasion, such as an anniversary, or to hold a family reunion.

The average age is mid-50s in winter, younger in summer, but varies by cruise length and itinerary. A seven-day Alaska and seven-day Caribbean

334 Part Two: Cruise Lines and Their Ships

cruise on the same ship, for example, attract different ages and incomes. More than 55 percent are couples; 50 percent are groups—as different as business or tour groups, or square dancing and stamp collecting clubs.

Recommended For   Those who enjoy cruise traditions and want a quality experience in a refined environment, but like facilities and choices available on superliners. Small-ship devotees open to trying a large ship. Budget cruisers able to move up to higher quality.

Not Recommended For   Swingers, party seekers, late-night revelers, trend seekers, or pacesetters.

Cruise Areas and Seasons   Caribbean, year-round; Panama Canal, fall to spring; Alaska, Europe, Eastern Canada, New England, transatlantic, summer; Mexico, Hawaii, spring and fall; South America, world cruise, winter.

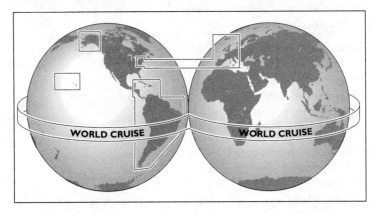

The Line   Holland America has carried passengers since 1871. It's among the few lines to make a successful transition from classic steamship company to modern cruise line, and it did so better than most, managing to keep its identity and traditions intact while developing a fine mainstream product.

The turning point came in the early 1980s when the line introduced the *Nieuw Amsterdam* (sold in 2000) and *Noordam,* forerunners of today's superliners. They were considered revolutionary because of such features as a square stern that provided 20 percent more open deck; two outdoor heated pools; a fully equipped gym, spa, and whirlpool; coded cards rather than keys for cabins; and television for in-cabin movies—all features that have become standard on new ships.

Holland America took its next big step in 1988, buying the beautiful *Homeric* (from the now-defunct Home Lines), renaming it *Westerdam,* and giving it an $84 million stretch job. The line also acquired the unusual Windstar Cruises. The following year, Holland America, Windstar, and

Seattle-based Westours, which pioneered Alaska tours and cruises, were acquired by Carnival Cruise Lines. The marriage proved to be brilliant, enabling Holland America to continue its expansion (four stunning new ships introduced in the 1990s) and allowing the line to expand in Alaska, return to Europe after nearly two decades, and increase its number of longer cruises. All were factors critical to HAL's retaining its many loyal fans.

The new ships, *Maasdam, Ryndam, Veendam,* and *Statendam,* resulted from a wish list drawn up by their designers and Holland America staff. The vessels combine classic elegance with state-of-the-art technology, offering such features as multideck atriums, fountains, Jacuzzis, jogging tracks, and theaters Broadway would envy. They were the first HAL ships to have private verandas. The *Rotterdam,* introduced in 1997 with a top cruising speed of 25 knots—20 percent faster than average—gave the line new flexibility in creating itineraries. A sister ship, *Amsterdam,* is scheduled to follow in fall 2000. Meanwhile, slightly larger twins were delivered in 1999 and 2000, and a brand-new class of 84,000-ton cruise ships are expected in 2002 and 2003, with options on three more.

In 1998, HAL introduced University at Sea, an enrichment program with seminars as diverse as Caribbean Art and Strategic Investing. Developed with Eckerd College in St. Petersburg, Florida, and operated by Continuing Education, Inc., the courses are available on Caribbean, Panama Canal, and Alaska cruises. No degrees or prerequisites are required. In an effort to widen its audience and meet the market's demand for short vacations, in 2000, HAL for the first time offered 25 short cruises of five days or less.

The Fleet	Built/Renovated	Tonnage	Passengers
Amsterdam	2000	61,000	1,380
Maasdam	1994	50,000	1,266
Noordam	1984	33,930	1,214
Rotterdam	1997	59,652	1,316
Ryndam	1994	50,000	1,266
Statendam	1993	55,451	1,266
Veendam	1996	50,000	1,266
Volendam	1999	63,000	1,440
Westerdam	1986/90	53,872	1,494
Zaandam	2000	63,000	1,440
Unnamed	2002	84,000	2,000
Unnamed	2003	84,000	2,000

Style   HAL cruises are classic but contemporary, blending Old World traditions with modern lifestyles. They offer the full range of activities expected on large, mass-market ships. Outstanding service by a friendly staff is the line's hallmark. The pace is leisurely, designed for experienced, mature travelers and families.

To attract younger passengers, the line expanded on-board sports and fitness facilities, added sports bars and ESPN programming, beefed up its children's program, and offered alternative dining. The line has added sports and adventure shore excursions for active passengers on Alaska and Caribbean cruises and "Just for Kids" adventure and learning excursions in Alaska.

In January 1997, Holland America bought the uninhabited 2,400-acre Bahamian island of Little San Salvador, renamed it Half Moon Cay, and developed it as HAL's private island destination on Caribbean itineraries. Located between Eleuthera and Cat Island, less than 100 miles southeast of Nassau, the 45-acre facility fronts a gorgeous white sand beach. Three areas, connected by walkways and a tram, are an arrival marina and plaza built to resemble ruins of a Spanish fort, a shopping area styled as a West Indian village, and a food pavilion. The market has shops, an ice cream parlor, coffee shop, bar, and art gallery. There is a children's playground, wedding chapel, and post office selling Bahamian stamps. Passengers can sign the cost of all services and sports to their cabins; cash is required for commemorative island stamps. Passengers get a barbecue lunch of West Indian selections. The sports center offers snorkeling and diving on nearby reefs, Sunfish sailing, other water sports, volleyball, and basketball. Nature trails feature a bird sanctuary designated by the Bahaman National Trust.

Holland America's vessels feel like ships, not floating hotels. The fleet shares characteristics that reinforce the line's traditions: art and antiques reflecting Holland's association with trade and exploration in the Americas; Dutch officers and Indonesian crews, linking Holland's historical ties to Asia; and the Crow's Nest, an observation bar inspired by the lookout on the main mast of the company's old sailing ships.

Distinctive Features   Escalators on newest ships, self-service laundry, good libraries, fresh flowers shipwide, fruit basket in cabins, hot hors d'oeuvres at cocktails, chimes played by a uniformed steward to announce dinner, private Bahamian island, alternative dining, Internet centers; world cruise specials: robes and personalized stationery.

	HIGHEST	LOWEST	AVERAGE
PER DIEM	$618	$154	$351

The above per diems are calculated from the cruise line's non-discounted *cruise only* fares on standard accommodations. Per diems vary by season, by cabin, and by cruise areas.

Rates Port charges are included. *Note:* HAL advertises "tipping not required." Yet, tips are not included in the fare. Hence, tipping is permitted—and has come to be expected.

Special Fares and Discounts Save up to 45 percent for early booking under the Caribbean Savings program. A similar Alaska program offers 25 percent. Membership Miles, a program with American Express, offers mileage redeemable for upgrades and discount dollars.
- Third/Fourth Passenger: Low rates.
- Children's Fare: Reduced rates for ages 2–18; specific rates for younger than age 2. Age 19 and older are billed as third/fourth persons sharing parents' room.
- Single Supplement: 135–200 percent of double rate or specific rate on certain cruises; guaranteed share program.

Packages
- Air/Sea: Yes.
- Pre/Post: Yes.
- Others: Renewal of vows and other pricey packages for special occasions—Total Indulgence, $395, includes Sevruga caviar and chilled Dom Perignon champagne at embarkation, a VIP cocktail party hosted by the captain, "Behind the Scenes" ship tour preceding lunch at chef's table, private card lesson with $25 in chips, chocolate truffle dessert after farewell dinner, and spa day for one.

Past Passengers Mariner Club members receive discount and upgrade offers about five times a year, amenities, recognition, theme cruises, and occasional cruises with HAL's president. New enhancements include baggage tags, separate check-in, party hosted by the captain, certificates for third to tenth cruise, and medallions for 40,000 miles to 250,000 miles.

The Last Word Holland America puts itself in the premium category, between luxury and economy, but it's at the high end of premium, a hair's breadth from luxury, and deluxe by any standard. Refinements and thoughtful touches it offers are unavailable on most comparably priced ships.

HAL's consistency—even the names of most public rooms are the same fleetwide—has built a large, loyal following that doesn't find the predictability boring; rather, reassuring.

We continue to be dismayed by Holland America's ambiguous tipping policy. HAL says the crew is not allowed to solicit tips, yet, they *are* allowed to accept them—and they expect them. In all my years of cruising, I have never had a cabin steward or waiter ask (i.e., solicit) me for a tip. Is HAL implying that when other cruise lines publish a "suggested tipping" scale and print envelopes that appear in your cabin for each person whom passengers are expected to tip, it's done by the crew?

HOLLAND AMERICA LINE STANDARD FEATURES

Officers Dutch; *Veendam,* British.

Staff Dining/Dutch supervisors, Indonesian and Filipino staff; Cabin/Indonesian and Filipino; Cruise/American and others. Bar, deck, some entertainment/Filipino.

Dining Facilities One dining room, two seatings. Indoor/outdoor lido restaurants for casual buffet breakfast, lunch, and alternative dining; taco, pasta, and ice cream bars.

Special Diets Kosher; low-sodium, low-cholesterol, low-fat; vegetarian; sugar-free desserts; baby foods. Request 30 days in advance.

Room Service 24 hours.

Dress Code Casual or informal with two formal/semiformal nights per week of cruise. Tuxedo rental service available.

Cabin Amenities Television with CNN, TNT; multichannel music system; hair dryers, direct-dial telephone. Suites and deluxe cabins have VCR, whirlpool bath, and minibar.

Electrical Outlets 110 AC.

Wheelchair Access 23 cabins on *Rotterdam;* 21, *Volendam/Zaandam;* 4–6 on others.

Recreation and Entertainment Theater for movies and lectures; show lounge; nightclub; casino, bars, and lounges; karaoke; masquerades; crew show; culinary demonstrations; kitchen tours; bingo, card games, bridge; pool games; dance classes; library. Sports bars with ESPN.

Sports and Other Activities Two outdoor pools, tennis, golf putting, volleyball, Ping-Pong, shuffleboard.

Beauty and Fitness Beauty/barber shop, saunas, massage, fitness program, gym with professional instructors, jogging track, practice tennis.

Other Facilities Religious services, medical facilities, laundry/dry cleaning service, laundry rooms, meeting room. Credit card phones. Wedding ceremony and amenity packages for vows renewal, honeymoons, and anniversaries at additional charge. Internet centers.

Children's Facilities Club HAL year-round youth program with counselors and age-specific activities for three age groups; "Just for Kids" adventure and learning shore excursions.

Theme Cruises See specific ships.

Smoking Designated smoking areas in public rooms; some, such as card room, library, and theater, are designated no smoking.

Holland America Suggested Tipping Not required; crew cannot solicit tips, but allowed to accept them. No gratuity added to bar bills.

Credit Cards Cruise and on-board charges: American Express, Discover, MasterCard, Visa; no cash.

Maasdam	Quality ⑨	Value B
Ryndam	Quality ⑦	Value C
Statendam	Quality ⑧	Value B
Veendam	Quality ⑧	Value B

Registry: *Maasdam / Ryndam /*	Length: 157/169 feet	Beam: 101 feet
Statendam: United States	Draft: 24.6 feet	Speed: 21 knots
Veendam: Bahamas	Passenger Decks: 10	Elevators: 8
Cabins: 663	Crew: 602	Space Ratio: 43.4
Maximum Passengers: 1,266		

The Ships   The *Statendam* and her sisters introduced a new class of ships in the 1990s that set the style and standard for Holland America into the next century. They combine Old World tradition with state-of-the-art technology and provide an imposing yet inviting ambience. The spacious ships differ in decor but are identical in layout and offer almost identical facilities and activities.

Interiors of the Italian-built ships were designed by De Vlaming, Fenns, and Dingemans, the Dutch firm that was responsible for earlier HAL ships and helped establish the line's signature look and layout.

In the new group's public areas, designers drew from Holland America's history to capture the golden age of Dutch shipping, but in a contemporary context. Multimillion-dollar collections of art and artifacts from the seventeenth to nineteenth centuries are integrated in decor. These combine with contemporary art to enhance the ships' modern image. Together, they make the ships floating art galleries.

In materials, the world was VFD's emporium. Designers used whatever was interesting: woolen fabrics from Holland; leathers from Germany, France, and England; glass from Italy. Cabins were made in Finland, a Danish company supplied teak, and furniture was built in Slovenia. Galley equipment came from the United States.

Public rooms span two decks on the Promenade and Upper Promenade in an asymmetrical pattern, allowing for bars and lounges of different sizes.

The *Maasdam,* fifth ship in the company's history with that name, is a far cry from the first *Maasdam*— a double-masted iron steamship that carried 8 first-class and 288 steerage passengers. It sailed the Atlantic monthly from 1872 to 1884 at a speed of ten knots. Today's computer-piloted *Maasdam* has only one class and moves at more than twice that speed.

Passengers are introduced to the *Maasdam* by a three-deck atrium on the Lower Promenade Deck. Under a ceiling of mirrors and fiber-optic lights, the atrium sparkles with a 30-foot glass sculpture, *Totem*, by Italian artist Luciano Vistosi. The sculpture contains thousands of pieces of glass that catch the light and cast specks of color on nearby surfaces. The best place to see it is from the stairs that rim the atrium.

To one side of the atrium are the Java Cafe for espresso and cappuccino, and the Wajang Movie Theatre for movies, lectures, and religious services. Adjacent meeting rooms offer audiovisual facilities.

Atrium sculptures on *Statendam* and *Ryndam* are classic in style but out of scale with their setting. On *Statendam*, it's a huge fountain with a bronze statue of three enormous mermaids rising from the sea. On *Ryndam*, it's a tribute in marble (five tons!) to sea legends. An oversized sea dragon twines around the sculpture's top and an undersized boat at the bottom, an improbable mermaid on its bow. The *Statendam,* also the fifth HAL ship to bear the name, is more baroque than the other ships and often eclectic. Interiors range from conservative to bizarre, blending textures and earth tones with classic European and exotic Indonesian motifs.

The *Veendam,* most stylish of the group, has the same layout as *Maasdam* but with different color schemes, furnishings, and art. The atrium features a glass sculpture, as on *Maasdam,* but of different design. Adjacent is the Crystal Terrace.

Itineraries   See Appendix B.

Cabins   Comfortable, contemporary furnishings in light wood are combined with continental touches. Standard cabins are almost 30 percent larger than comparable ones on ships of similar category. Large mirrors lighten the rooms, and in many, curtains separate the sleeping and sitting areas. Seventy-seven percent are outside cabins.

The decor uses two color schemes: peach and blue. Customized patterns reminiscent of Indonesian batik fabrics are used for curtains and bedspreads. Original art portraying Dutch themes accents standard rooms. Suites have original paintings and serigraphs depicting Dutch scenes.

All cabins have hair dryers, direct-dial telephone with computerized wake-up service, multichannel music system, and closed-circuit television. Full-length double closets and deep chests of drawers—nice features for long cruises—provide ample storage.

Standard cabins have sofas; 70 percent have sofa beds. All outside cabins have a bathtub and shower. Suites and deluxe cabins have a veranda, minibar, VCR, and whirlpool bath. Each suite also has a small private dining area; laundry and dry cleaning service is free.

Specifications   148 inside cabins, 485 outside (including 120 deluxe cabins and 29 suites with verandas). All with twin beds convertible to queen. Standard dimensions are 186 square feet, inside cabin; 196 square feet, outside cabin. 16 deluxe/36 standard outside have connecting doors for family suites. Some upper/lower berths and single cabins; 6 wheelchair-accessible cabins.

Dining The ships' crowning glories are their dazzling Rotterdam Dining Rooms. Surrounded on three sides by floor-to-ceiling windows that embrace the scenery and span the Promenade and Upper Promenade Decks, the rooms are a harmony of elegant tradition and modern technology. An impressive curved staircase connects the two levels, inviting grand entrances.

On the *Maasdam,* a fountain of antique Argentine marble is the lower level's centerpiece. A ceiling canopy of a thousand morning glories is made of blown glass from Murano, Italy. Between the decks is a border of fiber-optic "florets" programmed to change color, altering the room's mood.

One recent passenger's verdict: "The room is so beautiful it takes your breath away." The room is large but remarkably quiet; diners can converse in normal voices and hear chamber music playing on the balcony. The secret: Glass ceilings look spectacular—and absorb sound.

Many tables have either window or balcony seats. A microphone at the captain's table on the main floor allows him or other speakers to address the room; upper-level guests view the speaker on television monitors. Small, upper-level dining rooms—the King's and Queen's Rooms—are available for private parties.

Maasdam's dining room is decorated in red accented by blue. Four large, colorful linen screens depicting day and night cover the walls on both decks.

Dining here and on all Holland America ships is more elegant, and menu choices more extensive, than on most of mainstream cruise ships. Tables are set with white Rosenthal china bearing a gold HAL logo, silver tableware, wine coolers, and fresh flowers on starched tablecloths.

A typical dinner menu offers a choice of seven appetizers (six cold, one hot); three soups (two hot, one cold), three salads (five dressings); six entrees, including a vegetarian selection and a light and healthy one, plus selections of cheese and fruit; six desserts; pastries; ice cream; and light and sugar-free desserts.

Responding to passengers' preference for casual, flexibly timed breakfast and lunch—and the recently added alternative dining in the evening—Holland America has worked to perfect the lido buffet, outdoing competitors in quality, choice, and presentation. The best example is the *Maasdam*'s Lido Restaurant with its floor-to-ceiling windows and warm teal and coral interiors. Buffets offer hot selections, prepared to order, and cold treats. *Ryndam*'s Lido Restaurant has a cheerful setting with colorful abstract ceramic paintings and a ceiling stripe of whimsical yellow neon.

More lunch choices—hot dogs, hamburgers, pasta, satay, and tacos—are available by the lido pool. A free ice cream bar is open daily. Sandwiches, desserts, coffee, and tea are available here around the clock. On port days, food is available by the pool, often with extended hours (up to 5 p.m.), for returning passengers. Hot hors d'oeuvres with Indonesian tidbits are served in public rooms before dinner, and a weekly Indonesian lido buffet is popular.

Should you still be hungry, the 24-hour room service menu has been expanded, and your cabin's fruit basket is freshened daily.

Service HAL's efficient Dutch officers and friendly Indonesian and Filipino crew are a winning combination. Unobtrusive service by an unfailingly gracious and attentive staff is a hallmark and a primary reason the line has so many loyal fans. Dining room supervisory personnel are officers, and many crew members have been with Holland America for many years.

Unlike aboard most cruise ships, a uniformed steward passes through the ship playing chimes to summon passengers to dine. (Older passengers will be reminded of the pageboy in Philip Morris cigarette ads.)

It grieves us to report that HAL's service slipped as the introduction of four ships in less than three years required an army of new employees who need more training. We hope this situation will improve as they settle in. Some employees' limited knowledge of English is a problem, particularly in the dining room.

Facilities and Entertainment The *Maasdam* and her sisters each have five lounges, often with the same names and similar entertainment. The Promenade Deck is anchored by the two-deck main show lounge and designed by Joe Farcus, who is known for his innovative, flamboyant ship interiors for Carnival Cruise Lines.

In the *Maasdam*'s Rembrandt Show Lounge, Delft ceramic tiles are set against brocade, gold-tinted mirrors and mahogany paneling to recall the seventeenth-century Dutch master whose portrait is etched into glass doors at the entrance. The Vermeer Lounge on the *Ryndam* honors the seventeenth-century Dutch master Jan Vermeer. It's Art Nouveau in style, reminiscent of great movie palaces of the 1930s, with lacy mahogany woodwork and silver columns amid dozens of luminescent tulips.

For the Van Gogh Lounge on the *Statendam,* the artist's *Starry Night* is the inspiration in computerized special effects, fiber-optic lighting, and curtain drawing. Staircases frame the stage, whose revolving platform facilitates set changes. The *Veendam*'s Rubens Lounge is named after the celebrated sixteenth-century Flemish painter Peter Paul Rubens and features glass sculptures in the style of Rubens.

The lounges offer Broadway-style shows similar to entertainment on other mainstream cruise ships. Big production shows had never been Holland America's strong point until 1998, when the line introduced *Barry Manilow's Copacabana,* a production based on Manilow's popular song "Copacabana." Staged originally at Caesars Atlantic City, the show, set in 1948 at the famous New York nightclub, Copacabana, and in Havana, told the tragic love story of Lola, Tony, Rico, and Conchita. It played for two years in London's West End and was made into a television movie. HAL's version was given a happy ending. The $1.3 million production debuted in December 1998 on *Ryndam,* in February 1999 on *Statendam,* and November on *Volendam.* Every cruise has two performances, one for each dinner seating.

The Ocean Bar on the Upper Promenade showcases music by a combo. Here Matthys Roling, one of Holland's best-known artists, created her signature "drapery" art, decorating ceilings and walls in beige and red fabric. The oddly shaped Piano Bar, adjacent to the casino and popular for sing-alongs, is designed around a piano, with two semicircles of tables and curving sofas. Lights are programmed to change, altering the cozy room's ambience.

The casino offers blackjack, Caribbean poker, roulette, dice, and slot machines. Outside it, kinetic artist Yaacov Agam created a computer display wall that shows thousands of constantly changing images. The Explorer's Lounge farther aft is a pleasant spot for an after-dinner drink accompanied by the Rosario Strings—a Holland American tradition. The *Ryndam*'s lounge displays a stunning mural of a seventeenth-century Dutch harbor filled with ships. The cigar ceremony—a long-time HAL exclusive—is no more. The irony is that it was extinguished just as cigar bars became the newest fad.

By day, the Crow's Nest is an observation lounge, its angled windows overlooking the bow. It's ideal for viewing a Panama Canal transit or Alaskan scenery. At night, the lounge becomes the disco. Joe Farcus designed this room on the *Maasdam, Ryndam,* and *Statendam.* On the *Maasdam,* his interiors reflect the Pacific Northwest and Alaska scenery. Dark green "ubatuba" granite on walls is capped by white marble with jagged edges simulating snowcapped mountains; triangular lighting resembles evergreen trees. Large sections of the floor are made of slices of oak trees pieced together like a mosaic; the pattern is repeated in tabletops. A wavelike ceiling pattern suggests the northern lights and gives the evening disco a fantasy atmosphere.

Light fixtures have a sketch of the *Halve Maen,* (*Half Moon*), the sailing ship of Dutch explorer Henry Hudson and Holland America Line's corporate symbol.

On the *Veendam,* the Crow's Nest was designed by Dutch architect Frans Dingemans as a multipurpose area divided into three spaces—a gardenlike room with rattan chairs and greenery, for afternoon tea; the nautical Captain's Area with leather armchairs, which can be partitioned off for private parties; and the disco.

Activities and Diversions   Throughout the day and evening are activities including lectures, bridge tournaments, dance lessons, bingo, golf putting contests, kite flying, movies (with popcorn), and religious services. The most unusual diversions are guided tours of the ship's art and antiquities.

University at Sea, a series of personal and professional enrichment seminars, spotlight topics including nursing issues, memoir writing, and Caribbean culture and history. The programs are offered (extra fee) on Caribbean, Panama Canal, and Alaska cruises. Ask HAL for specifics on programs and costs.

The ships have large, comfortable card and puzzle rooms, a shopping arcade, and libraries with floor-to-ceiling windows. The *Maasdam*'s library displays paintings of the five *Maasdams* in Holland America's history. In the *Ryndam*'s forward staircase, paintings of the three previous *Ryndams* are hung. The ships hold auctions of contemporary art. Be wary of the sales pitch. If the bargain sounds too good to be true, it probably is.

Sports, Fitness, and Beauty   The new ships' upper decks cater to active passengers. At the center of a teak expanse on Navigation Deck is one of two outdoor swimming pools. On the lido, a second swimming pool, with whirlpools and wading pool, has a retractable glass roof for use in cool weather—a great asset on Alaskan cruises. A tiled wall with a bronze sculpture of dolphins frames the area.

The topside Sports Deck has two practice tennis courts (on *Statendam,* the space is a jogging track). A teak deck encircling the Lower Promenade Deck has space for deck chairs, walkers, and joggers (four laps equal one mile). The fleetwide Passport to Fitness program awards points for daily exercises and activities that can be redeemed for prizes, such as a belt pack or T-shirt.

The Ocean Spa has a beauty salon and fitness center with steam rooms, saunas, rooms for massages and facials, and a juice bar. The ocean-view gym is equipped with treadmills, step machines, rowing machines, Lifecycles, and a Hydra fitness circuit with ten resistance machines. In front of the spa is an outside deck for exercise classes.

Children's Facilities   All ships have year-round, full-time youth coordinators (one for every 30 children, more during holidays and summer). They organize and supervise programs for three age groups: 5–8 years, 9–12 years, and teens.

Daily activities for children ages 5–8 may include storytelling, candy bar bingo, games, arts and crafts, charades, and ice cream parties. Those age 9–12 might learn golf putting, have dance lessons or theme parties, or participate in deck sports or scavenger hunts, Ping-Pong, or karaoke. Older children have a teen disco, dance lessons, arcade games, sports, card games, trivia contests, bingo, and movies.

All have pizza and Coketail parties and ship tours. The ships have wading pools, activity rooms with video games, and children's menus listing such favorites as hamburgers, hot dogs, fish-n-chips, chicken fingers, and pizza.

On the first night of each cruise, kids and their parents meet the youth coordinator, who outlines the program. At sea, there is at least one activity in the morning, afternoon, and evening; none are scheduled on port days. Babysitting by staff volunteers (availability isn't guaranteed) costs $7 per hour for the first child and $5 more per hour for additional children from the same family.

Shore Excursions   Holland America/Westours has been a leader in Alaska travel and offers programs ranging from cruising near glaciers on dayboats to rail travel on the domed McKinley Explorer. In Ketchikan, you can have a 4½-hour sight-seeing/flight-seeing combination, or you can kayak, fish, or pan for gold. Alaskan cruises that include the Inside Passage are highlighted by a visit to Glacier Bay National Park. Every Glacier Route cruise offers visits to Sitka's Alaska Raptor Rehabilitation Center, dedicated to returning injured bald eagles to the wild. Holland America Line/Westours recently donated $1.2 million to help the center buy 17 acres of land, and it leased the building from the University of Alaska.

In the Caribbean, the line offers 175 shore excursions at 30 Caribbean ports. Most are standard offerings with moderate to moderately expensive rates. Flight-seeing is available frequently, and certified divers are offered scuba excursions. Twenty tours designated "environmentally sensitive" are eco-tours focusing on the islands' nature, history, and culture. These tours, designed to help passengers understand the islands better, range from guided rain forest hikes to air tours to view the archaeological sites. European shore excursions can be expensive on any line, but HAL's seem to cost more than its closest competitor. Save money by taking standard city tours on your own and buying only those excursions that are unique or that visit attractions difficult to reach on your own.

Note: Be very sure of your tour choices before you buy. In addition to the industry's standard policy of no refunds for cancellations 24 hours before a tour, Holland America charges a 10 percent fee for any cancellation.

Postscript   HAL has a tipping-not-required policy, but so many passengers leave tips that it calls the policy into question. If you want to tip, use the guidelines for other ships in its category ($3–3.50 per day for your dining steward and a similar amount for your cabin attendant).

Westerdam	Quality ⑧	Value B
Registry: Netherlands	Length: 798 feet	Beam: 95 feet
Cabins: 747	Draft: 75.5 feet	Speed: 22 knots
Maximum Passengers:	Passenger Decks: 9	Elevators: 7
1,494	Crew: 642	Space Ratio: 36.4

The Ship   The *Westerdam,* the largest ship in Holland America's fleet, is not one of the new superliners, but she fits well with them. Longer by 78 feet and slightly narrower, she has 114 more cabins but fewer decks and a lower space-to-passenger ratio, although she's a spacious ship. (Moviegoers saw this in *Out to Sea,* the 1997 comedy starring Jack Lemmon and Walter Matthau.)

When Holland America bought the *Westerdam* in 1989, she was only three years old and had been hailed as one of the decade's most magnificent ships. She combines the style and refinement of great liners with state-of-the-art facilities.

To increase her capacity from 1,000 to 1,494 passengers and fit her with standard HAL facilities, the company spent $84 million to have the ship stretched. A 130-foot section was added, providing space for a two-tiered show lounge, more bars, a sports deck, fitness facilities, library, larger restaurant, and second buffet.

Comfortable, classy, and contemporary, the *Westerdam* is dressed in pastel blues, greens, lilac, and peach with lovely woods and large flower arrangements. Art and antiques relate to Holland's seventeenth- and eighteenth-century trading tradition. Most public rooms are on the Promenade Deck, anchored by the casino and several lounges forward and the bilevel Admiral's Lounge aft. The Amsterdam Dining Room is on the lowest passenger deck. The main section has an interesting wood and plexiglass dome. Although the room isn't as spectacular as those on HAL's new quartet, dining on the *Westerdam* is just as much a treat and consistently praised by passengers. Dining is elegant and menu choices extensive; linen-covered tables are set with Rosenthal china bearing HAL's gold logo, silver tableware, and fresh flowers.

The *Westerdam* has two lido restaurants, and Holland America makes the most of its superior buffets. You can have breakfast and lunch—and alternative dining several nights—in the pleasant settings of the veranda by the Sun Deck pool or the Lido Restaurant by the Upper Promenade pool.

Itineraries   See Appendix B.

Cabins   The *Westerdam* has 21 cabin categories and boasts some of the largest standard cabins afloat—most with comfortable sitting areas. Minimum cabins are only slightly smaller, and suites are more than double average size. Most are fitted with twin beds; more than a third can be converted to queens. All have ample drawer and closet space. The comfortable decor employs the same soothing colors of public rooms. All cabins have telephone, closed-circuit television, multichannel music system, and fine toiletries; all outside cabins (except a few lower-priced ones) have bathrooms with a tub and shower.

Specifications   252 inside cabins, 495 outside. Standard dimensions, 200 square feet for outside cabins. Some upper/lower berths; no singles; 4 wheelchair-accessible.

Facilities and Entertainment   *Westerdam's* entertainment and activities are similar to those on sister ships. The Promenade Deck has a cluster of lounges and bars. In the Peartree Club, an orchestra plays for predinner cocktails. Later, the space becomes a disco. The Saloon next door is sports bar, and across the way, the Big Apple has a small dance floor.

The Explorer's Lounge, with private-club ambience, is popular for afternoon tea, predinner cocktails, or after-dinner coffee and liqueur sipped to the music of the Rosario Strings. Next door, the Book Chest is a delightful spot for those reading in quiet comfort.

The nearby Ocean Bar, where every table has a sea view, is the best for people-watching because everyone passes en route to the Queen's Lounge, a multipurpose room with evening entertainment, and Admiral's Lounge, the main showroom.

Guided tours of the ship's art and antiquities are always crowded. The ship holds auctions of contemporary art; be wary of the sales pitch—it's very unlikely you're getting a bargain.

Activities and Diversions   The theater on Sun Deck is particularly pretty, with gray velour seats and deep blue carpets and walls. Current films are shown daily (with popcorn). The space is also used for religious services, meetings, and lectures.

Other daytime activities include bridge tournaments, dance lessons, karaoke, and bingo. The ship occasionally hosts music festivals and photography cruises. *Westerdam* has a year-round children's program.

Sports, Fitness, and Beauty   The Sports Deck has an unobstructed 40-by-40-foot jogging track, glass windbreaker walls, and two tennis practice courts. A retractable roof protects the Sun Deck swimming pool, two Jacuzzis, and bar. The fitness center on Navigation Deck offers exercise equipment, saunas, and massage rooms. The beauty salon and barber shop are on Promenade Deck.

Noordam	Quality ❻	Value C
Registry: Netherlands	Length: 704 feet	Beam: 89 feet
Cabins: 607	Draft: 26 feet	Speed: 19 knots
Maximum Passengers:	Passenger Decks: 9	Elevators: 7
1,214	Crew: 22542	Space Ratio: 28

The Ship   The *Noordam* was the forerunner of the *Maasdam* group and is similar to them, particularly in features for which Holland America is known. (Her twin, *Nieuw Amsterdam,* was sold recently to the new United States Lines.) The spacious trendsetter had square sterns and 20 percent more outside deck space than was customary for ships of her size and introduced many features now common on today's cruise ships. The ship offered doorsills flush with the floor, rather than the then-common toe-stubbing raised ones and was the first to use energy-saving, fluorescent light bulbs (9 watts instead of 70 watts).

The decor, created by the Dutch design firm responsible for the *Maasdam* group, laid the basis for the Holland America look, tastefully blending traditional and modern styles and using museum-quality art and artifacts to underline Holland and Holland America's history. The theme of *Noordam*'s art collection is the Dutch East India Company. Huge floral displays add class.

A great deal was borrowed from the *Rotterdam V*—HAL's flagship until her retirement in 1997. Notable is the teak promenade with the unusual 15-foot width that encircles the Upper Promenade Deck. It's wide enough for old-fashioned, cushioned deck chairs while leaving ample space for two or three people abreast or joggers to pass. Often absent on new ships, this feature is thoroughly appreciated by people who love to cruise. The promenade, particularly in nice weather, is something of a Main Street with passengers strolling, lounging, reading, napping, scanning the water, or watching people.

Most public rooms are on the Promenade and Upper Promenade decks. They're always as spotless and efficient as they are comfortable and inviting. To give the interiors intimacy, designers created many lounges and bars and arranged them asymmetrically. In spring 2000, the ship was renovated from stern to stern.

Itineraries   See Appendix B.

Cabins   The *Noordam* has 15 cabin categories of 5 basic types, found on eight of nine passenger decks. Rooms are among the largest on any cruise ship in their category. They're homey, with light wooden cabinets and fabrics inspired by Indonesian batik.

All have phones, closed-circuit television, multichannel music, combination makeup/writing table, built-in corner or night tables with drawers, light controls at the bed, full-length door mirror, and ample closets. Walls and floors are insulated for soundproofing. Four cabins accommodate disabled passengers.

Specifications   194 inside cabins, 411 outside cabins; 20 suites with picture window and king-size bed. Standard dimensions are 152 square feet inside and 178 square feet outside. 485 cabins with 2 lower beds (87 convert to queen); 50 with queens; 72 with 2 lower/2 upper beds; 142 have bathtubs and showers; no singles; 4 handicapped-accessible.

Dining   The Amsterdam Dining Room on the Main Deck with floor-to-ceiling windows overlooking the sea, is a class act, with many HAL touches: fresh flowers, soft lighting, heavy silverware, starched linens, fine china and crystal, a super Indonesian crew, and dinner music by the Rosario Strings. The dining room generally has one seating at breakfast and lunch and two at dinner with elaborate menus.

The indoor/outdoor Lido Restaurant overlooks the Promenade Deck pool and offers breakfast and lunch buffets plus alternative dining several nights. Lido Terrace outside serves hamburgers, hot dogs, and tacos, and offers do-it-yourself sundaes—all at no additional charge. The lido also hosts the midnight buffet and weekly Indonesian buffet. Lest you worry about feeling hungry, a Royal Dutch Tea is served in the afternoons, 24-hour cabin service is available, and your steward freshens your cabin's fruit basket daily.

Service Indonesians form most of the dining room and cabin crew, whereas Filipinos—generally more outgoing—provide musical entertainment and bar service. Many have long years of service, and all are unfailingly polite and efficient. They are HAL's biggest asset.

Facilities and Entertainment With so many lounges, almost everyone finds something to enjoy. In the stunning Admiral Lounge, a replica of the stern of a seventeenth-century Dutch East India Company ship forms the stage's backdrop. The spacious lounge hosts nightly shows and many daytime activities. Unfortunately, sight lines aren't great.

Canal Street, named for a well-known street in New York, leads to Henry's Bar and the Hudson Lounge, popular late-night gathering spots with floor-to-ceiling windows, live music, small dance floors, and bars. As on all HAL ships, a favorite room is the Explorer's Lounge, where passengers enjoy afternoon tea and after-dinner coffee to the music of the Rosario Strings. Crow's Nest Lounge atop of the Sun Deck is a daytime observation perch and late-evening rendezvous. The Hornpipe Club, adjacent the casino, doubles as a disco.

Activities and Diversions Daytime activities include pool games, dance classes, movies in the Princess Theatre, bridge, horse racing, and bingo. Active travelers find the Passport to Fitness program; a jogging track; and a health spa with rowing machines, bicycles, weights, and other exercise equipment. Supervised children's programs are available year-round.

Rotterdam	Quality ⑨	Value C
Amsterdam	(Preview)	
Registry: Netherlands	Length: 778/780 feet	Beam: 103.5/105.8 feet
Cabins: 658/690	Draft: 29.8 feet	Speed: 23 knots
Maximum Passengers:	Passenger Decks: 10	Elevators: 12
1,316/1,440	Crew: 647	Space Ratio: 47/44.2

The Ships The *Rotterdam,* the line's sixth ship bearing that name, upholds Holland America's tradition in contemporary style but little resembles *Rotterdam V.* She's more like the *Statendam* quartet, with almost the same layout and with many of their most popular features. Passengers recognize immediately that they are on a Holland America ship. Her slightly larger sister, *Amsterdam,* is scheduled to make her debut in autumn 2000.

When the new *Rotterdam* debuted in late 1997, she was designated the line's flagship and introduced new features. She is intended to be the fastest cruise ship afloat, giving HAL new flexibility in itineraries. She also has more deluxe cabins with verandas, an alternative restaurant, extensive facilities for the handicapped, and a private lounge and concierge desk for suite passengers.

F. C. J. Dingemans, principal architect of the *Rotterdam* and *Statendam* group, describes the *Rotterdam*'s interiors as an evolution from the other four ships. There are a three-story atrium (oval instead of octagonal); a larger lido restaurant; and a dome over the lido pool. But *Rotterdam* differs from *Statendam*-class ships: She's faster, longer, wider, and more spacious. Because she's designed to be speedier, the hull is longer and more tapered. Like *Rotterdam V,* she has two funnels aft. Passenger capacity is higher— 1,316 versus 1,266 passengers. Three staircases instead of two put passengers never farther than about 125 feet from access to the public rooms.

The interior was inspired by her predecessor, not replicated, though some of her namesake's rich interiors and 1930s Art Deco style have been incorporated. The new ship uses more woods and darker colors to achieve a classic ambience. Artworks commissioned for the new vessel and museum-quality antiques evoke the Dutch maritime tradition.

A huge sculpture fills the three-deck atrium. More a curiosity than a work of art, it represents a Flemish clock tower with 14 timepieces. It's embellished with mermaids, dolphins, and snakes.

All HAL ships have valuable art collections, but this ship's is the most varied. Works include glass wall sculptures, an eighteenth-century French oil painting, seventeenth-century Japanese armor, eighteenth-century Chinese silk scrolls, and antique furniture. The most memorable are life-sized replicas of the terra-cotta warriors found at Xi'an, China.

HAL invested $1 million to add a closed-loop system for the hearing impaired, Braille directories and directional buttons in the elevators, and large-print menus for the visually impaired. In cabins, light-flashing telephones and bed-shaker alarm systems are available. The ship has 23 wheelchair-accessible cabins; 4 have connecting doors for accompanying companions. The *Rotterdam* was the second ship of the fleet to install an Internet center. Plans call for them to be added fleetwide.

The *Amsterdam,* a near-sister of the *Rotterdam,* has distinctive features of her own. The atrium centerpiece is an ornate "Astrolabe" clock tower with a carillon in its base and four different faces: an astrolabe, world clock, planetary clock, and astrological clock. On display near the Crow's Nest Lounge is "Four Seasons," a gold-plated sculpture of four pieces, originally created for the *Nieuw Amsterdam* of 1938 and bought from a private collector. At the Lido pool, passengers will see a trio by British sculptor Susanna Holt—two brown bears fishing and their cub nearby.

The *Amsterdam* has 15 more suites than her sibling; and The Web Site, an Internet center, is in an accessible location adjacent to the Java Café©, off the atrium.

Itineraries   See Appendix B.

Cabins   Standard cabins, a roomy 185–195 square feet, are similar to those in the *Statendam* group. Another 120 deluxe cabins with 245 square feet, have verandas with chaise longues, whirlpool bathtubs, VCRs, mini-bars, and refrigerators.

Navigation Deck 7 has 40 suites, all with verandas and concierge and a private lounge accessed by key card. At the concierge desk, passengers may settle accounts, book shore excursions, and make special requests. The area's glass walls overlook the corridor, but when privacy is wanted, an electric current makes the high-tech glass opaque. Each of four penthouse suites offers living room, dining area and kitchen, bedroom and dressing areas, and steward's entrance. Two suites are wheelchair-accessible.

Specifications   117 inside cabins, 541 outside; 40 suites; 160 cabins with verandas; some adjoining cabins. 498 standard cabins with twin beds; 618 with convertible twins or queen beds; 284 with third and fourth berths. No singles. 23 cabins for disabled passengers. The *Amsterdam* has 133 inside cabins, 557 outside, and 52 suites.

Dining   The elegant, two-level La Fontaine Dining Room spans the Promenade and Upper Promenade Decks. Decor mingles Venetian, contemporary, and baroque designs. Panoramic windows overlook the stern. The ceiling represents a star-filled night sky broken by circles of colored glass. Around the balcony are hundreds of individually lighted Venetian-glass morning glories. On the back wall are two giant murals of waterbirds, recalling *Rotterdam V*'s famous Ritz Carlton room.

At Odyssey, a specialty Italian restaurant, passengers dine by reservation at no extra charge. The opulent room is reminiscent of a Venetian villa. The room is dressed in black with gold-framed mirrors in the ceiling, black and gold columns along the walls, and glass candelabras in alcoves. About 90 people can be seated in three intimate areas. Tables have a movable top that slides forward to ease access to banquettes. The restaurant also serves lunch on days at sea.

In the large, informal Lido Restaurant, passengers can enjoy a full breakfast and lunch or have hot dogs and hamburgers grilled to order and make-it-yourself tacos. An ice cream sundae bar, tea, and coffee are available all day. Alternative evening dining is offered several days of every cruise.

Facilities and Entertainment The Ambassador Lounge and Tropic Bar (Upper Promenade Deck) has a movable wall allowing different configurations. After dinner, the lounge is a large room for dancing; in late evening, it's an intimate piano bar with the piano on a turntable.

Repeat passengers will recognize a collection of small public rooms. The adjoining Half Moon and Hudson Rooms accommodate up to 115 people for meetings or parties. Ocean Bar has replicas of items from the old Holland America building in Rotterdam; a copy of the sculpture of Henry Hudson's ship, *Half Moon,* crowns the roof. The larger Explorers' Lounge focuses on maritime heritage of Italy and Holland in a large mural of Renaissance Venice. The dance floor is made of Italian marble in a floral pattern.

The Crow's Nest Lounge is on all Holland America ships, but this by far is the most successful. Floor-to-ceiling windows wrap around three quarters of this delightful daytime observation lounge. The room has three sections. To one side is a "Tea Area" decorated with porcelain and silver. To the other is a "Captain's Area," with leather chairs and old ship models. At center is a circular bar and dance floor that become the nighttime disco.

Queens Lounge, the two-level main show lounge, has state-of-the-art sound and lighting equipment, a rotating stage, hydraulic lifts, and a dance floor. Deep red, burgundy, and orange in decor reflect the opulent age of sea travel. Huge, gold-etched Murano glass chandeliers resemble upside-down umbrellas. Along the room's sides, statues of Moorish guards holding large candelabra. The theater curtain is hand-painted satin in maroon, gold, and black.

Children's Facilities The Sports Deck has a children's playroom with craft-making areas, video games, and a teen disco. When only a few youngsters are aboard, the space can be used for morning coffee or afternoon snacks.

Postscript Like her predecessor, *Rotterdam* appeals most to traditionalists who remember—and those who imagine—the era of grand ocean travel. Her cruises are fairly dressy. Men are asked to wear jackets in public areas after 6 p.m., and there are usually two formal evenings a week, more during long cruises. Readers considering a cruise on *Rotterdam* should review the entire HAL section for a full picture of the cruise experience it offers.

Volendam	(Preview)	
Zaandam	(Preview)	
Registry: Nehterlands	Length: 780 feet	Beam: 105.8 feet
Cabins: 690	Draft: 24 feet	Speed: 23 knots
Maximum Passengers:	Passenger Decks: 10	Elevators: 12
1,440	Crew: NA	Space Ratio: NA

The Ships   Sister ships *Volendam* and *Zaandam,* built at the Fincantieri in Italy, are a new generation of luxury cruise ships. The *Volendam,* delivered in November 1999, and *Zaandam,* delivered in May 2000, combine features from the *Statendam*-class vessels and the *Rotterdam.* The new ships are about as long and wide as *Rotterdam,* but their tonnage is greater because they have more passenger cabins—1,440 compared to *Rotterdam*'s 1,316 passengers.

The principal architect, Frans Dingemans, who has worked on most of the HAL fleet, has created interiors in keeping with HAL's tradition and passenger preferences. The theme of *Volendam*'s decor is flowers—from the seventeenth to twenty-first centuries—and are featured in public rooms' fabrics, art, doors, and other design elements throughout the ship. Music is the *Zaandam*'s theme, with music-related decor throughout.

Layout of the new ships' public rooms is the same as that of *Rotterdam,* including three staircases, an alternative restaurant, a lounge with additional dance floor, and a children's room on Sports Deck that can be used for meetings or receptions.

In the *Volendam*'s three-deck-tall atrium is a monumental crystal sculpture by Luciano Vistosi, one of Italy's leading contemporary glass artists. He also created the towering atrium sculptures of the *Maasdam* and *Veendam.* Centerpiece of the *Zaandam*'s atrium is an impressive pipe organ with mechanical figures of dancing musicians. The organ may be played by hand or operated automatically. Both ships showcase multimillion-dollar art collections, including works created specifically for the vessels by world-class artists.

Cabins   The new ships have more deluxe veranda cabins than their sister ship. The penthouse, 28 deluxe suites, and 168 minisuites and deluxe cabins have large verandas, VCR, whirlpool bath, and minibar. All cabins have a sofa, hair dryer, telephone with voicemail and computerized wake-up service, music system, and television. They are furnished with twin beds, convertible to a queen size.

Specifications 1 penthouse and 28 suites with verandas; 168 deluxe cabins (120 deluxe minisuites) with verandas, 384 standard outside; 139 standard inside; 21 wheelchair-accessible cabins.

Dining The *Volendam*'s impressive bilevel Rotterdam Dining Room, located at the stern, has huge windows and an elegant staircase connected the two levels. Overhead, six large wrought-iron chandeliers designed by Italian artist Gilbert Lebigre hang from the ceiling; they are lighted by fiber optics. The Marco Polo, the *Volendam*'s alternative restaurant, evokes a California-style "artists' bistro." Italian fare, including pastas and pizzas, is served in a relaxed setting. Its beechwood walls hold the drawings and etchings—reproductions and originals—of artists ranging from old masters to new talent. The restaurant has its own kitchen and staff and serves lunch and dinner daily; there is no extra charge.

Facilities Art Deco design of the two-level Frans Hals Lounge, the *Volendam*'s main show lounge, was inspired by Amsterdam's famous Tuschinski Theater. The multicolored ceiling and colonnades contrast with dark wood walls and huge, colorful ceramic vases. The Casino Bar is the ship's sports bar, showcasing cinematic memorabilia. On *Zaandam,* the Casino Bar spotlights music memorabilia.

There are HAL's traditional Explorer's Lounge, Ocean Bar, Piano Bar, Library, Half Moon and Hudson Room, which serves as a card or meeting room; Wajang Theater, which is equipped with writing tables and headphones to be used for meetings; Java Café, where complimentary espresso drinks are available; and Crow's Nest, which doubles as an observation lounge and nightclub.

The Navigation Deck was extended aft to accommodate additional cabins, and the outdoor swimming pool moved to the Lido Deck. The arrangement provides direct access between indoor and outdoor swimming pools and the Lido Restaurant. For *Volendam*'s lido pool area, British artist Susanna Holt created a bronze sculpture of arcing dolphins, similar to those found on other HAL ships.

Another change on the new ships that frequent HAL passengers will notice is the funnel design that resembles more closely those of the *Noordam* rather than the *Rotterdam* or the *Statendam* group.

The *Volendam* was also the first of the fleet to have "The Web Site," an Internet center with eight computer terminals and a printer where passengers can send and receive e-mail. Open 24 hours, it is staffed from 9 a.m. to noon, 2 to 6 p.m., and 9 p.m. to midnight. The basic charge is $0.75 per minute with a five-minute minimum. Instructions for use are posted on each computer terminal.

Beauty and Fitness   The ships have a large Steiner-operated spa and fitness center with beauty salon/barber shop, dual saunas and steam rooms, six treatment rooms, juice bar, and a glass-walled exercise room with the latest equipment. The Lower Promenade Deck is a wraparound teak deck, ideal for walking or cooling off in the line's traditional wooden deck chairs.

Norwegian Cruise Line

7665 Corporate Center Drive, Miami, FL 33126
(305) 436-4000; (800) 327-7030; fax (305) 436-4120
www.ncl.com

Type of Ships   Modern superliners, unique oceanliner.

Type of Cruises   Contemporary, mainstream, emphasizing sports and fitness, themes, and special interests.

Cruise Line's Strengths
- sports activities
- dining options
- theme cruises
- 50 percent nonsmoking cabins
- innovative ships

Cruise Line's Shortcomings
- uneven cuisine
- loud deck music
- small bathrooms on some ships
- disparate fleet

Fellow Passengers   Norwegian Cruise Line is everyman's cruise line, with attractive ships where anyone can feel comfortable. Passengers, most from the United States and Canada, represent all walks of life, including young professionals, families, seniors, and special-interest groups. They are often attracted by NCL's theme and special-interest cruises and sports programs. Annual per-person income is about $35,000.

Recommended For   First-time cruisers, active travelers of all ages who want a fun vacation and like the facilities of a large ship—but not as large as a megaliner. Joiners. Repeaters and middle-income travelers. People interested in sports and music. Those who vacation with their children.

Not Recommended For   Gourmands. Snobs or seasoned travelers with five-star expectations. Sedentary travelers.

Cruise Areas and Seasons   Bahamas, Caribbean, Australia, New Zealand, year-round; Asia, Australia, South America, winter; Bermuda, Alaska, Europe, spring and summer; New England/Canada, Hawaii, Mexico, Mediterranean, fall; Panama Canal, May and September.

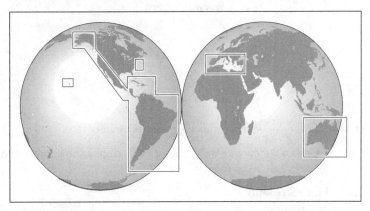

The Line   On December 19, 1966, the *Sunward* sailed from Miami with 540 passengers on the first of three- and four-day cruises to be offered year-round by Norwegian Caribbean Line between Miami and the Bahamas. With this trip, NCL was born. Those cruises—the first packaged for the mass market—are credited with launching modern cruising. Since then, NCL, renamed Norwegian Cruise Line, has played a major role in shaping today's cruises. Within five years of start-up, NCL had acquired three brand-new ships, pioneered weekly cruises to many Caribbean destinations, and introduced a day on a private island in its itineraries—a feature quickly copied by most competitors.

Yet for all these innovations, nothing equaled in excitement and impact NCL's purchase of the *Norway* in 1980. After buying her as the *France* for $18 million, NCL spent $100 million to transform her from a great ocean-liner to a Caribbean cruise ship, setting in motion trends that transformed cruising completely. At the time, the *Norway* was the largest passenger ship afloat—the first megaliner—carrying up to 2,000 passengers. Her size enabled NCL to create a completely new environment, converting the ship from a transportation vessel to a floating resort. Restaurants, bars, lounges, entertainment, and sports facilities were added to keep passengers busy almost round the clock.

Later in the decade, a series of costly expansion decisions, including the acquisition of Royal Viking Line and Royal Cruise Line, weakened NCL's debt-encumbered parent company, opening the way for more aggressive lines to take over its pacesetting role. But by the 1990s, NCL was re-creating itself with a fleet of new ships, introducing superliners, with innovations that had made NCL a trendsetter. Among the most notable were alternative dining; sports bars with broadcasts of CNN, ESPN, and major sporting events; and separate sitting areas in standard cabins, an amenity usually reserved for deluxe accommodations—all innovations that have become standard on new large ships.

In 1997, NCL became the first line to base a ship in Houston for year-round cruises to the Western Caribbean. The following year, it became the first major, mainstream cruise line to base a ship in southern South America—which NCL dubbed Alaska South—for the winter season. The vessel sails 14-day cruises between Chile and Argentina. NCL also took over two ships of the defunct Majesty Cruise Line; ordered a 2,000-passenger ship; bought an unfinished hull intended for Costa Cruises (since completed as the *Norwegian Sky*); stretched two ships, increasing their capacity 40 percent; streamlined the fleet with new names for all except *Norway;* and launched a promotion with *Sports Illustrated* that includes an annual sports-oriented cruise and *SI* bars on the fleet, starting with *Norway.* As part of its strategy to become a worldwide cruise line, NCL bought Orient Lines; the next year, they stretched a third ship and launched the new *Norwegian Sky.*

At the dawn of the millennium, in a move that stunned all cruise watchers, a bidding war between Carnival Cruises and Star Cruises, Asia's major cruise line, ended with Star Cruises as the sole owner of NCL. Among the first announcements by NCL's new president were the new owners' intention to build a series of megaships for the line and to launch "Freestyle Cruising," an innovative concept challenging many cruise traditions.

The Fleet	Built/Renovated	Tonnage	Passengers
Norway	1960/79/93	76,049	2,032
Norwegian Dream	1992/98	50,760	1,748
Norwegian Majesty	1992/99	38,000	1,460
Norwegian Sea	1988	42,000	1,504
Norwegian Sky	1999	77,104	2,002
Norwegian Sun	2000	77,000	2,000
Norwegian Wind	1993/98	50,760	1,748

Style   NCL has always been at the heart of mainstream cruising. Attractive ships reflect contemporary lifestyles and offer a variety of activities for all ages almost around the clock, emphasizing sports, music, and entertainment. Theme cruises are year-round. NCL ships have thoughtful amenities and "signature" items, including a full luncheon buffet served on embarkation, expanded room service menus, and ice cream parlors and alternative restaurant at no extra charge; the Chocoholic Buffet, a weekly dessert extravaganza; wine stewards (some of NCL's competitors have eliminated them); and pool and beach attendants to provide chilled towels. All dining rooms are nonsmoking. In some casinos, some blackjack tables are reserved for nonsmokers. On the newest ships, cabins are equipped for the hearing-impaired. An extensive, year-round children's program includes supervised activities.

Sports Afloat is among cruising's most comprehensive year-round sports and fitness programs. It became more high-profile with the introduction of *Sports Illustrated* bars in the NCL fleet in 1998. Fitness centers—now opened 24 hours/7 days a week fleetwide—offer fully equipped exercise facilities, aerobics classes, basketball/volleyball courts, golf practice facilities, NCL Olympics, an incentive program that rewards participants, and SuperSport theme cruises focusing on a single sport with celebrities and specialists aboard. Water sports instruction is combined with experience in ports. All ships have a "Dive-In" snorkeling program and can arrange scuba excursions for certified divers—even in Alaska. Great Stirrup Cay, NCL's private Bahamian island, offers varied activities.

Under its new owners, NCL has introduced "Freestyle Cruising" to replace some of cruising's time-honored traditions with flexibility and options. The goal is to broaden cruising's appeal. Gone are rigid dining hours, assigned seating, and dress codes. Instead, NCL's ships' dining venues will have open seating and open dining with continuous service like in a restaurant. Passengers dine when they want, where they want, and with whom they want. NCL's newest ships will have nine restaurants from which to choose. The dress code is also optional, from casual to formal, depending on the venue. Other elements of Freestyle Cruising include increased service with a ratio of almost one crew member per cabin; upgraded cabins; more relaxed disembarkation; enhanced enrichment from computer classes to yoga and mountain biking; and a simplified gratuity system. The new program, being phased in gradually through the fleet, has been introduced first on *Norwegian Sky* and *Norwegian Majesty; Norwegian Sun,* under construction, will be the first to incorporate specific facilities for it during the building.

Distinctive Features Chocoholic buffets, dive program and offbeat excursions in Alaska, single/open seating for many meals; alternative dining; official cruise line of the Miami Dolphins football team; full-scale Broadway shows; sports bars, music and sports theme cruises. Nonsmoking cabins, cabins for hearing-impaired. 24/7 fitness centers, Internet centers.

	HIGHEST	LOWEST	AVERAGE
PER DIEM	$508	$157	$279

The above per diems are calculated from the cruise line's non-discounted *cruise only* fares on standard accommodations. Per diems vary by season, by cabin, and by cruise areas.

Rates   Port charges are included.

Special Fares and Discounts   NCL's LeaderShip fares, available through travel agents, are capacity-controlled. Discounts are up to 50 percent. Via the EuropePlus program, booking 180 days or more in advance gets you a free two-night pre- or post-cruise stay in a first-class hotel. Other early-booking fares are available. NCL's Premium Air Service handles requests for upgrades, stopovers, and flights on specific airlines, and air/sea bookings. Requests for deviations must be written or faxed 60 days in advance. A nonrefundable $50-per-person service fee, plus fare differential (if applicable) is assessed.
- Children's Fare: Third/fourth person's fares.
- Single Supplement: Guaranteed singles rate, subject to availability.

Packages
- Air/Sea: Yes.
- Pre/Post: Yes.
- Others: Yes.

Past Passengers   Latitudes past passenger club provides expedited check-in and embarkation at selected ports, captain's reception, *New York Times* news by fax, bridge and galley tours, special cruises with $200 on-board credit, members' events, gifts, upgrades, discounts on selected cruises, newsletter, and customer service phone line. Members-only promotions are listed on NCL's Web site.

The Last Word   In recent years, NCL had a litany of problems and financial woes that caused its quality to slip and its competitors to outpace it in expansion and innovations. After steps to improve its bottom line, NCL's outlook brightened. Now, with its new owners, which have very deep pockets, its future should be radiant. Meanwhile, NCL continues to be a work in progress.

NORWEGIAN CRUISE LINE STANDARD FEATURES

Officers Norwegian.

Staff Dining and Cabin/International; Cruise/American.

Dining Facilities *Crown, Star,* one dining room; *Norway, Sea, Majesty, Sky,* two; *Wind, Dream,* four—all with open seating for breakfast and two open seatings for lunch. Embarkation lunch; Chocoholic, midnight buffets; Le Bistro, Sport Bar & Grill; ice cream parlors; pizzerias.

Special Diets Vegetarian, low-salt/calorie, kosher; must be requested 30 days in advance.

Room Service 24 hours.

Dress Code Casual for day, informal in evening. One formal night on short cruises, two on seven-day with formal/semiformal attire.

Cabin Amenities Phone, refrigerator in suites, some bathrooms with tub, sitting areas in standard cabins on newest ships, television with CNN and ESPN. Hair dryers. *Crown,* suites; *Norway, Sun/Sky,* suites; *Dream, Wind, Majesty, Sea,* all cabins. *Majesty,* ironing board.

Electrical Outlets 110 AC. *Majesty,* 110/220 AC.

Wheelchair Access All have cabins, bathtubs with grab bars. *Norway,* 10 cabins; *Dream, Wind,* 11; *Majesty,* 4; *Sky,* 5; *Star,* 4.

Recreation and Entertainment Six or seven lounges, sports bars; Broadway shows, Las Vegas–style revues, comedy; nightclub; disco; casino; library (except *Sea*). Wine tastings; singles, honeymooner parties; video arcade (except *Norway*). Gentlemen hosts on long voyages.

Sports and Other Activities Sports Afloat program with golf practice, basketball, volleyball, Ping-Pong. Snorkeling; scuba for certified divers. Private island with rental equipment. Two swimming pools (one on *Star*); jogging track.

Beauty and Fitness Aerobics, fitness center, sauna, jogging track, barber/beauty salon. Spa on *Norway, Dream, Wind, Sky.*

Other Facilitie Medical, dry cleaning/laundry. Conference.

Children's Facilities Year-round program with youth counselors. Children's menus. Babysitting; private $8, group $4 for first child, $2 second. *Majesty, Sky,* kids' splash pool; play room; *Dream, Majesty, Wind, Sky,* new children's facilities. Soda packages, $8–16; backpacks with souvenirs, $28–40.

Theme Cruises Refer to text.

Smoking Nonsmoking dining room. Public rooms have nonsmoking sections.

NCL Suggested Tipping Per person per day, maître d', $1.50; waiter and cabin steward, $3.50; busboy, $2; 15 percent added to bar tabs.

Credit Cards For cruise payment and on-board charges: American Express, Visa, MasterCard, Discover.

Norway	Quality ❹	Value C
Registry: Bahamas	Length: 1,035 feet	Beam: 110 feet
Cabins: 1,016	Draft: 35 feet	Speed: 20 knots
Maximum Passengers:	Passenger Decks: 12	Elevators: 11
2,370	Crew: 920	Space Ratio: 38

The Ship   The *Norway* is one of a kind, a great lady with classic lines and lots of character. When NCL bought the *France* in 1979, she had been mothballed for five years. But at $18 million, she was a bargain. Her high-quality equipment and workmanship were unrivaled. To build such a vessel today would cost $1 billion.

NCL spent $100 million to transform her into the *Norway*—a city at sea. She has more staff than many ships have passengers. A $63 million update for the 1990s restored much of the beauty that made her legendary as the *France*. Two glass-enclosed top decks, a forward observation deck, 124 luxurious cabins, a huge spa, fitness center, and jogging track were added. The work preserved her classic features, including irreplaceable bronze murals, gold and silver wall treatments, and art from the *France*. Only the Monte Carlo Casino shows contemporary glitz.

Itineraries   See Appendix B.

Cabins   Most cabins are roomy with ample storage. Twenty categories spread across ten decks. The top six categories, most on the top three decks, offer concierge service. All port-side cabins are nonsmoking.

Cabins on original passenger decks have been restored to graceful charm and appeal to traditionalists. Art Deco vanities with three-sided movable mirrors were retained. Many rooms have exquisite, glass-inlaid armoires from the original first-class cabins. All cabins display posters issued in 1994 to celebrate the ship's heritage. Some of *France*'s original cabins with gold leaf and bronze fixtures were left intact.

Of the two decks added in 1990, the Sun Deck houses 32 penthouse suites, and Sky Deck has 84 deluxe cabins and suites with floor-to-ceiling windows; almost half have verandas. Two owner's suites and two grand deluxe suites decorated in royal blue and white are at the bow. They differ; some have floor-to-ceiling windows and wraparound balconies, others have a Jacuzzi; all have living room, bedroom, dressing room, and refrigerator. The owner's suites on the Viking Deck are original; they have two bedrooms and two full bathrooms. All cabins have television with CNN and ESPN.

Specifications   371 inside cabins, 475 outside; 170 suites. Standard dimensions, 150 square feet; 503 cabins with 2 lower beds; 369 with double/queen bed; 124 with upper and lower berths; 10 wheelchair-accessible.

Dining *Norway* has two beautiful dining rooms. The Windward was the first-class Chambord restaurant on *France,* noted for its unobstructed expanse. Patrons descend a glamorous staircase and are seated amid gold and bronze murals. The former golden dome was redesigned into a star-filled night sky.

The contemporary Leeward Restaurant is more dramatic. A spiral staircase leads to a mezzanine, reopened in 1990 renovations. Service and food are the same in both rooms; seating is based on cabin location rather than category. Forward-cabin passengers eat at Windward; aft, in Leeward.

The Great Outdoor Restaurant overlooking the stern has a country-club look, with teak ceiling and overhead fans. It's the setting for breakfast and lunch buffets and deck parties during some theme cruises. The food isn't up to the dining room's level.

The Art Deco Le Bistro alternative restaurant serves dinner at no additional charge; $5 tip is suggested. The restaurant, open to all passengers, accommodates 140 on a first-come, first-served basis. Wines are available by the glass.

Theme evenings include the popular Viking Night, when costumed staff in elaborately decorated dining rooms offer Scandinavian specialties. A Viking ship replica is the midnight buffet's centerpiece. SS France Night evokes the grand style of cruising's past.

The *Norway* was the first to offer NCL's expanded room service menus and the wildly popular chocoholic dessert buffet. High tea is served in the Art Deco Club Internationale lounge. Late-night snackers may find a Caribbean deck party.

Passengers do not seem to agree on the *Norway's* cuisine. Some say the food is excellent; others say it's good but not exceptional. Still others express disappointment.

Service There's no agreement on service, either. Some say it's wonderful; others call it NCL's weakest link, particularly in the dining room. Most praise cabin attendants. On a ship this large, varying opinions aren't unusual. People come with their own experiences and expectations. One waiter or bartender can make all the difference. However, the bottom line is that the service is uneven.

Facilities and Entertainment *Norway* has facilities to handle big-time entertainment, such as Broadway shows and Las Vegas–style revues. There's also music for dancing, disco, a piano bar, and comedy.

Most of the action, except for the spa and sports, is on the central International and Pool Decks. Saga Theatre hosts blockbuster shows. The *Sports Illustrated* Bar is the first aboard NCL ships. The stylish Club

Internationale best reflects the *France*'s splendor. The lounge windows soaring from floor to high ceiling, plush sofas, and fabulous Art Deco touches are carefully preserved. It's ideal for afternoon tea. At other times, it's a sophisticated jazz bar.

The million-dollar Monte Carlo Casino has black granite floors, mirrored walls, and a palette of magenta, hot pink, crimson, and royal blue accents. Ten replicas of antique slot machines by the entrance join 236 of the latest models. Nearby is North Cape Lounge and bar, popular all-hours for entertainment. The disco Dazzles (downstairs where the indoor touristclass swimming pool was) parties into the wee hours.

Activities and Diversions   *Norway* is said to offer 80 or more activities. That's likely, considering the schedule of art auctions, bingo, dance classes, culinary demonstrations, word puzzles, trapshooting, parlor games, fashion shows, bridge, and more.

Sports and Fitness   Facilities are outstanding. The ship has more than 65,000 square feet of outdoor decks—a mecca for sun worshippers. Shade-seekers find a covered lounging area behind the bridge on Fjord Deck. Also, lounge chairs have hoods for blocking the sun.

The fitness center, basketball and volleyball courts, and one-sixth-mile jogging track are on the Olympic Deck. The ocean-view fitness center— open 24 hours, 7 days a week—provides workout equipment and daily exercise classes. Topside between the stacks is a tremendous open deck and pool with bar. The year-round Sports Afloat program is tied to shipboard fitness programs and activities in port. SuperSports theme cruises spotlight popular sports and feature specialists and celebrities who offer performance tips and participate in events with passengers at no extra cost. In Motion On The Ocean incentive program offers participants prizes such as waist packs and T-shirts for sports activity, including exercise classes.

Spa and Beauty   The luxurious Roman Spa has 16 treatment rooms for body wraps, aromatherapy, and other beauty treatments; 8 massage rooms; 4 herbal therapy baths (cruising's first); cardiovascular exercise equipment; 2 steam rooms; 2 saunas; 7 showers and 4 body-jet showers; a Jacuzzi for 8 people; gym; beauty salon; shallow pool for water aerobics; and juice bar. Dining rooms offer a spa menu.

Designed and managed by Steiner of London, the spa has a Europeantrained staff. Evoking a luxurious Roman bath—the Romans never had it so good!—the spa has a large central area where white columns support high-arched ceilings. Leather lounges line the sides. The Gladiators training room offers Stairmasters, bikes, rowing machines, a Jacuzzi, and a computerized fitness analysis machine. Clients don plush robes in oh-so-clever dressing rooms. Spa experiences range from an hour to all day or week—none of it cheap.

Children's Facilities   Coordinators plan and supervise daily activities in the year-round children's program. An NCL brochure lists activities for four age groups: Junior Sailors (ages 3–5), First Mates (6–8), Navigators (9–12), and Teens (13–17). It also describes the Kids Soda package; unlimited soda fountain access costs $8 for a three-day cruise or $16 for seven days. A Kids Backpack provides baseball cap, luggage tags, T-shirt, and more and costs $28–39.50, depending on cruise length.

Kids meet the captain at a Coketail party; for the masquerade ball, they receive help in making costumes. A Norwegian officer conducts their bridge tour, and races, treasure hunts, and games are planned for the day at the beach. A children's playroom called "Trolland" is located on the International Deck. The ship publishes Kids' Cruise News and Teen Cruise News daily. Also available are a children's playroom, ice cream bar, and children's menus.

Guaranteed private babysitting is available from noon to 2 a.m. Fee is $8 per hour for the first child, $2 each additional child from the same family; two-hour minimum (surcharge on Christmas and New Year's cruises). Group babysitting for "potty-trained" children is $4 per hour for first child and $2 for each additional child from the same family. Kids younger than age two sail free.

Shore Excursions   Overall prices range from $20 for a two-hour tour of St. John to $79 for a flight over the Virgin Islands; some have reduced prices for children. Great Stirrup Cay, NCL's private Bahamian island, is among the ship's most popular stops. (Bring insect repellent.) Activities and equipment include glass-bottom paddleboats, kayaks, sailboats, and "vu" boards (like boogie boards with a viewing port). The Dive-In snorkeling program offers instruction. A scuba program for certified divers is offered in St. John and St. Thomas. Golf can be arranged in St. Thomas.

Because of its size, *Norway* often anchors at sea and tenders passengers ashore in large, swift boats. They're 80 feet long and weigh 55 tons each but can be raised and lowered in minutes by giant cranes. Each carries 400 people. At Great Stirrup Cay, passengers disembark directly onto the sand through lowered front doors.

Theme Cruises   NCL's cruise book lists *Norway*'s theme cruises with dates.

Postscript   *Norway* is a ship for all ages, but her age is showing. No matter how much money NCL spends, we wonder how long she will last with so many new ships crowding her seas. She has numerous loyal fans, many of whom have sailed on her 20 times or more.

Norwegian Dream	Quality ⑤	Value C
Norwegian Wind	Quality ⑤	Value C
Registry: Bahamas	Length: 754 feet	Beam: 94 feet
Cabins: 874	Draft: 22 feet	Speed: 18 knots
Maximum Passengers: 1,748	Passenger Decks: 10	Elevators: 10
	Crew: 614	Space Ratio: 29

The Ships   The twin ships *Norwegian Dream* and *Norwegian Wind* were designed for people who want to know they're on a ship at sea. At almost every turn, glass walls frame the ocean and connect with the outdoors. Many modern cruise ships have lost this link. But these ships, breaking the mold on design, have unusual features inside and out. All five upper decks are open and slant downward to create a profile more sleek than those of most large new ships.

In early 1998 at a cost of $138 million, both ships were stretched 130 feet, and all cabins and most public rooms were refurbished. Lengthening resulted in a sleeker, more hydrodynamic profile, the captain says. The new section increased the ship's length to 754 feet and its passenger capacity by 40 percent (from 1,246 to 1,748). Added were 251 cabins, but the space ratio decreased, surrendering some of the ship's spaciousness.

Lengthening resulted in a new entrance and lobby and 12 new owner's suites; expansion of the Four Seasons Dining Room; a larger casino and nightclub; an enlarged fitness center and spa; new children's playroom; new coffee bar and lounge; splash pool, wet bar, and two Jacuzzis; outdoor cafe and pizzeria; and three new passenger elevators. Show lounges and bars received additional seating, and the shopping arcade nearly doubled.

The striking new entrance, on the Promenade Deck, has a Nordic motif in blue and gray with wood blinds, marble accents, and Art Deco lighting. Here are a 24-hour reception desk, information and concierge desks, the purser's office, and shore excursion and "Dive In" desks. Most innovative are the dining rooms—four instead of the traditional one or two. The rooms have multiple tiers, creating more intimate settings and enabling all diners to enjoy panoramas through acres of windows.

Topside, the tiered Sun Deck becomes an amphitheater for evening entertainment. *Norwegian Dream* was the first ship to have a Sports Bar and Grill with live satellite broadcasts of ESPN, NBA, and NFL programs.

The ships have identical interiors; even names of decks, public rooms, and suites are the same. The comfortable, contemporary settings are the work of well-known Norwegian designers Petter Yran and Bjorn Storbraaten. Quality fabrics, fine woods, marble, and brass trim translate to casual elegance. Windows and use of glass make the outdoors part of indoor decor. Light floods the interiors, giving them a lively atmosphere.

Itineraries See Appendix B.

Cabins The ships offer 15 categories; almost all are on the lower five of the vessels' ten decks. All port-side cabins are nonsmoking; 16 cabins are equipped for the hearing-impaired, and 11 are wheelchair-accessible.

All cabins and suites are decorated in blue, teal, beige, and rose, with new carpeting, curtains, bedspreads, and furnishings. Passengers in International Deck cabins added when the ships were lengthened must access them through the Four Seasons Restaurant, which was expanded across the ship's girth. Or, these passengers must detour up or down a deck.

Unusual in the mid-price ships, 85 percent of cabins are outside with large windows; standard cabins are larger than average; all have a sitting area with table and sofa chair or love seat that converts to a third bed; and a curtain separates sleeping and living areas.

There are some trade-offs. Bathrooms are small, particularly the shower stall, and storage space is insufficient. Space around beds is tight, but separate sitting and sleeping areas compensate. Almost all cabins have twin beds that convert into a queen; remote-control, multichannel television with CNN and ESPN; radio; telephone; and hair dryer. Cabin stewards provide twice-daily service.

Each new owner's suite measures 385 square feet and accommodates up to five people. Located on the Sun Deck, they're decorated in rose and blues. Each has a separate bedroom and living room with convertible double sofa, television, stereo system, refrigerator, and balcony. Bathrooms have a tub and shower and entrances from both hall and bedroom. Other top-category suites also have balconies; most have refrigerators and floor-to-ceiling windows. They're served by an attentive concierge who provides complimentary amenities, including wine and hors d'oeuvres.

Specifications 142 inside cabins, 600 outside; 18 owner's suites; 52 penthouse suites with balcony; 62 suites. Standard outside dimensions, 160 square feet. Most cabins have 2 lower beds convertible to queen; some have third and fourth berths. 1 single; 11 wheelchair-accessible; 16 hearing-impaired.

Dining Each of the three main dining rooms has its own personality and setting; the fourth is an informal dinner cafe. All have the same menus, and food comes from a central kitchen.

Tables and dining rooms are assigned for dinner (two seatings); other meals are open seating. Thus, passengers can choose any of the three rooms for breakfast and lunch. Having these choices makes the cruise more personal. The diverse, distinctive settings make dining more fun and interesting, and open seating enables passengers to meet.

The three levels of Terraces are separated by greenery and connected by twin stairways. Some passengers say the arrangement suggests a supper club in vintage Hollywood movies. A mural covers the back wall, and a wall of glass admits splendid views.

The Four Seasons Dining Room, extending side-to-side of the ship, is the largest dining room. Floor-to-ceiling bay windows extend over the water and offer spectacular views. Four terraced areas provide excellent sight lines. Glass walls brighten the room and draw eyes to the sea.

Sun Terraces, the smallest dining room, is casually appointed in light wood and wicker. It's set on three narrow terraces with walls of glass on three sides that extend overhead. Shades protect diners when the sun is above. The view is across the aft swimming pool to the sea.

Le Bistro, the alternative restaurant, serves dinner from 7 p.m. to midnight and is open to all passengers on a first-come, first-served basis (no additional charge). The cozy, informal cafe offers a daily pasta dish prepared tableside and other light fare. Wine by the glass is available.

The Coffee Bar and Lounge is designed as a "coffee house," with memorabilia such as antique coffee machines on display. Coffee and coffee-flavored drinks are served. The area, with curved walls and quiet niches, incorporates the ship's library and card room.

The Sports Bar and Grill, decorated with sports photos and memorabilia, serves popcorn to passengers watching sports events on the bank of television monitors. Free ice cream and frozen yogurt are available poolside each afternoon. If you aren't watching calories and are willing to stand in long lines, you can pig out at the one-night Chocoholic Buffet.

The Sun Deck splash pool has a semicircular "wet bar." Nearby, the casual Outdoor Cafe and Pizzeria serves breakfast and lunch buffets and snacks.

Service The ships are praised for good cabin service, but complaints about service in dining areas are common. After stretching, the ships increased crew from 483 to 617, and the ratio of passengers to crew became 2.8—a negative sign for a line seeking more upscale passengers.

Facilities and Entertainment Fabulous entertainment is the cruise highlight. Passengers often give the shows standing ovations. *Dreamgirls* was the opener for the *Norwegian Dream,* and the ship has featured *42nd Street* in the Stardust Lounge, the main showroom. On alternate nights there are Las Vegas–style variety shows. The room is well laid out in four tiers, providing comfortable seats and clear sight lines. The lounge has a dance floor, and dance music may be provided.

The Art Deco casino is much larger than its predecessor. Dressed in hot magenta and black, it offers blackjack, Caribbean stud poker, craps, roulette, "Let It Ride," and 158 slot machines. Adjacent to the casino is Dazzles nightclub, which has a circular granite bar, a circular dance floor, and curved sofas in velvet Harlequin patterns. Lucky's piano bar has a dance floor and is popular after the show.

Other nighttime action spots are the Sports Deck, anchored by the Sports Bar and the Observatory Lounge. The fun and lively Sports Bar attracts fans for ESPN broadcasts. The Observatory, with floor-to-ceiling windows, is ideal for viewing Caribbean sunsets on the *Norwegian Dream* or Alaskan wilderness on the *Norwegian Wind.* Open decks are sometimes used for outdoor parties. The informal Rendezvous Lounge, next to Four Seasons Dining Room, is a good meeting spot.

Activities and Diversions   Daytime activities include art auctions, bingo, dance classes, bridge tours, culinary demonstrations, and pool and parlor games. We repeat our warning: At art auctions, know what you're buying. Bargains are rare, despite the sales pitch.

A conference center on Sun Deck accommodates 60 people and can be divided into two spaces.

Sports, Fitness, and Beauty   Sports and fitness programs are offered year-round. The Sports Deck is mecca for active passengers. Golf instruction and a driving range, plus two outdoor pools, are available. Upstairs on Sky Deck is the basketball and volleyball court. The International Deck offers a small pool.

The Health Spa and Fitness Center on Sports Deck has been enlarged to a full-service spa with eight private treatment rooms for massage therapy, herbal wraps, and facials. A weight room has Cybex training equipment. Aerobics and other exercise classes balance excesses at the Chocoholic Buffet. A wide walking/jogging track wraps around Promenade Deck. The beauty salon is next to the observation lounge.

Tiered teak decks, separated by decorative greenery are a sunbathers' and people-watchers' delight at the forward pool. It's an innovative design, but it's noisy. On some evenings the area hosts outdoor events and dancing.

Snorkeling instruction is offered while ships are at sea, and hands-on experience is available in ports of call. The Alaskan dive program is a hit. Sports theme cruises—among them golf, tennis, baseball, and running—

offer specialists and sports celebrities. An active or retired NFL player is aboard most seven-day cruises.

Children's Facilities   An enlarged Kids Korner play room is the base for NCL's year-round "Kid's Crew" program. The supervised program focuses on four age groups. Details are in an NCL brochure. Activities include visiting the bridge, dances, arts and crafts, and "Circus at Sea," in which children learn circus routines. The Youth Center Video Arcade on the Sports Deck has a dozen video simulators. (See Children's Facilities in the *Norway* profile for more details.)

Shore Excursions   In Alaska, *Norwegian Wind* offers some of mainstream cruising's best offbeat excursions. Among the most popular is Dive Into Adventure, for snorkeling and scuba diving. It's active and attracts a variety of passengers. Plus, few people can say they have been diving in Alaska. At excursion's end, participants shiver out of wet suits and jump into the heated pool on Sun Deck.

Other programs available are glacier hiking, mountain biking, forest trekking, a six-hour hike outside Skagway, and three hours of sea-kayaking from Juneau (you're likely to see a whale close enough to feel its spray). Flight-seeing from Juneau to a remote lodge showcases vast ice fields.

The more exotic tours have few slots; book early. Alaska shore excursions are expensive on every cruise line. Operators must make their money in a very short season. Sample prices (per person) include: six-hour hike to Denver Falls at Skagway, $79; sea-kayaking in Juneau, $68; flight-seeing with Juneau Taku Lodge, $168.

Norwegian Sea	Quality ❹	Value C
Registry: Bahamas	Length: 700 feet	Beam: 93 feet
Cabins: 763	Draft: 22 feet	Speed: 20 knots
Maximum Passengers:	Passenger Decks: 9	Elevators: 6
1,518	Crew: 630	Space Ratio: 27

The Ship   NCL's preparation for the 1990s began in 1988 with the debut of *Seaward,* renamed *Norwegian Sea,* the line's first brand-new ship in two decades. The vessel was a class act from her unveiling. Glass, chrome, and Formica, with an almost total absence of wood, gave her a contemporary look fashionable at the time. A decade later, the interiors seem dated.

Designers Robert Tillberg and Petter Yran created spaciousness by employing floor-to-ceiling windows to open the ship and provide splendid seascapes in lounges and four novel, glass-enclosed stairways. Also appealing are the small lounges—pleasant corners for drinks, conversation, and relaxation. Pastels accented by brass and mirrored walls are used shipwide.

Itineraries   See Appendix B.

Cabins   The ship offers 16 categories, with the 6 pricier ones on three upper decks and the others on the three lower decks. Compared to NCL's newer ships, *Norwegian Sea*'s cabins are small. Standard cabins don't have a sitting area. Most are fitted with twin beds in an L shape; all have hair dryers and television for movies and 24-hour CNN and ESPN. Storage includes two closets and lots of drawers. Bathrooms are small, with meager counter space and small showers. Stewards service cabins twice daily. Port-side cabins are nonsmoking. Views from most cabins on Deck 7 are obstructed by lifeboats; windows of those on Deck 6 overlook the Promenade Deck (the one-way glass doesn't work well when cabin lights are on). Some "J" category inside cabins with two lowers and two uppers are small—suitable as a quad only for those really watching their pennies.

Specifications   243 inside cabins, 513 outside; 7 suites. Standard dimensions, 122 and 140 square feet. 462 with 2 lower beds (convertible to queen); 290 with 2 lowers and third/fourth berths; no singles; 4 wheelchair-accessible.

Dining   The dining rooms—Four Seasons and Seven Seas—have open seating for breakfast and lunch on port days, assigned seating for lunch on sea days, and two seatings nightly for dinner. Most tables are set for four, six, or eight; very few tables seat two. Menu selections are varied, with two to four options per course, but the food generally is unremarkable. The best choices are lamb and steaks, which are consistently high quality. Espresso and cappuccino are available without charge.

The Big Apple Cafe, the small lido restaurant sporting marble-top tables and garden awnings, has panoramic sea views. It's open almost around the clock, serving informal buffets at breakfast and lunch, pizza, afternoon snacks, and light suppers. Neither the food nor ambience is as inviting as the dining rooms'.

The alternative restaurant Le Bistro at the Palm Tree serves gourmet fare—the best aboard—at no additional charge ($5 tip suggested). The no-reservations cafe, open from 6 to 11 p.m., has its own kitchen and offers an eclectic menu with a daily specialty. It only seats 82, so arrive early or very late.

Service   *Norwegian Sea*'s best feature is service—warm, friendly, and efficient. Staff for dining rooms, Le Bistro, and cabins, in particular, is outstanding. Some information desk staff with "attitude" clouds the picture.

Facilities and Entertainment   At the stern are the little-used Observatory Lounge (curtains were drawn every time we looked in, defeating the room's purpose), Gatsby's wine bar, and Boomer's disco.

The International Deck is entertainment central. Focus is the two-deck Crystal Court dominated by a crystal and marble water sculpture. To one side is Oscar's, a stylish piano bar that's frequently the scene of art auctions. At center deck is Everything Under the Sun, the large shopping arcade; bargains are few despite daily promotions. Forward is the Cabaret Lounge showroom. Except for the Broadway show, entertainment is disappointing and dated, especially the *Sea Legs* revue. Seats are very comfortable, but sight lines are hampered by the room's many columns and uniform elevation.

The Stardust Lounge, for dancing and entertainment, has concentric circles radiating from the large dance floor. Some are reminded of old-time movie nightclubs. It's used during the day for lectures, port talks, and bingo (pricey). The large Monte Carlo Casino has much less glitz than gaming rooms on other cruise ships. Slot machines line the room's side promenade.

Activities and Diversions   An unobstructed, quarter-mile deck circles the Promenade Deck. Its nonslip metal surface, instead of teak, is assumed to be a compromise that kept the ship's construction price low. Overall, the daily agenda has fewer options than usually are found on a cruise ship.

Sports and Fitness   Topside, the ship has a large sunning area with a 42-foot pool, one of the longest on any cruise ship. A second pool has overhead sprinklers, shallows for lounging, and twin hot tubs. Nearby is Lickety Splits which serves ice cream in early afternoon. One flight up, a sun deck forms a balcony on the pools' periphery. Forward is a small fitness center and sauna, golf driving range, and another bar.

Children's Facilities   The Porthole playroom is open some hours when the ship is at sea, but it's mostly closed when the ship is in port. Group babysitting is available; arrange private babysitting through the purser's desk. Age-specific children's programs are available.

Shore Excursions   All are rated for the degree of fitness required, but many shore excursions are overpriced and can be done on your own less expensively.

Postscript   Readers planning a cruise on *Norwegian Sea* should review the entire NCL section to have a full picture of the line's cruise experience.

Norwegian Majesty   Quality ⑤   Value C

Registry: Panama	Length: 680 feet	Beam: 91 feet
Cabins: 731	Draft: 20 feet	Speed: 21 knots
Maximum Passengers:	Passenger Decks: 9	Elevators: 6
1,460	Crew: 550	Space Ratio: 28

The Ship   *Norwegian Majesty* was lengthened in 1999 by 112 feet through insertion of a prefabricated midsection that added 203 new cabins plus new public areas and facilities, increasing the ship's capacity 40 percent (or from 1,056 to 1,460 passengers). Interiors throughout were refurbished. *Majesty* was the third NCL ship to be lengthened in less than two years. The work added a second pool, second dining room, new casino, another outdoor bar, Le Bistro restaurant, coffee bar, and substantially more deck space. Crew cabins were expanded to accommodate increased staff. Two new elevators and a third stair tower were incorporated. Corridors and stair towers received new carpets shipwide. All decks and most public rooms were renamed.

The lengthening also gave *Norwegian Majesty* a sleeker, more hydrodynamic profile, enabling the ship to maintain its 20-knot speed with the same power plant, despite increased size. New buoyancy reduced the ship's draft, allowing her to call on all current ports and at some that were previously inaccessible because of shallower waters.

Norwegian Majesty debuted in 1992 as Majesty Cruises' *Royal Majesty* and was intended to appeal to affluent passengers with understated elegance. Stylish interiors create a refined, harmonious environment of simplicity and clean lines. Contemporary decor employs soft colors, natural wood, leather sofas, glass, mirrors, and fresh foliage. Models of old sailing vessels bow to tradition. The ship is well laid out, with many quiet corners. Characteristic of NCL, forward lounges have walls of sloped windows.

Passengers step almost directly into the two-deck atrium that serves as the main lobby and contains the front desk and shore excursion office. Called Crossroads, the circular area has white marble floors and stairs to a white marble island centered with a baby grand piano and furnished with banquettes.

The Atlantic Deck is devoted entirely to public areas. Off the lobby is the new Four Seasons Dining Room; beyond, the Seven Seas Dining Room. Forward are boutiques, a small library, card room, and meeting room. Small lounges border Rendezvous, a large, V-shaped piano bar connecting to Royal Fireworks, a multipurpose lounge with panoramic windows.

Itineraries   See Appendix B.

Cabins   Ten categories range from royal suites to inside cabins with lower and upper berths. About 71 percent are outside, and a high percentage are nonsmoking. Standard cabins are modest in size. They have clean, uncluttered lines and are finished in natural wood. Most have twin beds separated by a chest of drawers. A desk unit has drawer space and a dressing mirror, and three closets add to storage. Each cabin has a television carrying CNN, cable sports, shipboard notices, and movies. Bathrooms have showers and a large sink, with ample counter and shelf space and a hair dryer. All cabins have a built-in ironing board.

New cabins have beige, rose, green, or blue decor. When existing cabins are restyled, these colors will be used. Upper category suites and cabins have a minibar, queen beds, and large windows. Forward on Majesty Deck, a group of cabins spans an unusual half-moon contour overlooking the bow. The two Royal Suites on Norway Deck have marble baths and 24-hour butler service.

Specifications   731 total cabins. The 203 new ones are in deluxe or standard outside and standard inside categories. 185 inside cabins, 451 outside; 22 suites. Standard cabins have 125–140 square feet. 487 cabins with 2 lowers (134 convert to doubles); 41 with double beds; 193 with 3 berths; 177 with 4 berths; 22 suites accommodate 3 persons; 4 wheelchair-accessible.

Dining   The impressive Seven Seas Dining Room has wraparound, full-length windows. A white baby grand plays on a small island at the center. Most tables are set for four or six, contributing to the room's intimate feeling. Seven Seas, the first smoke-free dining room on a major cruise ship, has new chairs and carpeting in soothing blues.

The new Four Seasons Dining Room also offers ocean panoramas through floor-to-ceiling windows. Adjacent is the 58-seat Le Bistro alternative restaurant, which serves light Italian and continental cuisine in flexible dining hours. A new galley will serve both restaurants.

Breakfast and lunch buffets are served inside the casual Cafe Royale on Sun Deck; outside space overlooks two pools. The room is attractively furnished in light wood and wicker chairs. It's tight for buffet lines. Buffets are average, offering a range of hot and cold dishes, daily specialties, and cakes, pastries, muffins, and breads. The cafe is connected to the Royal Observatory, a handsome observation lounge/bar below that doubles as a sports bar.

Piazza San Marco Grill, a second Sun Deck serving area, is partially covered. Burgers, hot dogs, pizza, ice cream, snacks, and late-night buffets (different from the nightly midnight buffet) are offered.

Service   The crew encompasses 34 nationalities, and except for the dining room, service shipwide has received generally good reviews.

Facilities and Entertainment   The Palace Theater show lounge is on one level with a steeply tiered floor. Sight lines to the circular stage are excellent from almost every seat. Decor is in gold, rust, and blue tones.

In the new midsection is Monte Carlo Casino, offering 6 blackjack tables, 2 Caribbean Stud Poker tables, 1 roulette table, 1 dice table, and 131 slot machines. Next door, the attractive Polo Bar provides piano music nightly. One deck below, a small coffee bar and lounge offers coffees, teas, and coffee-flavored drinks, plus bar service.

Royal Fireworks is a quiet area or meeting space by day and a dance lounge before and after dinner.

When the ship is in Bermuda, she isn't allowed to stage big productions or open the casino. Instead, the ship offers excursions to local nightclubs. An evening cocktail cruise along Bermuda's pretty shores is another option.

Activities and Diversions   Daytime offerings include bridge tours, Ping-Pong tournaments, bridge and Scrabble games, fruit- and vegetable-carving demonstrations, poolside fashion show, and classes in napkin-folding, wine tasting, and dance. The ship has a card room, well-stocked library, and small board room.

Sports, Fitness, and Beauty   Fitness fans pair workouts and ocean views in the gym. Equipment includes Life Circuit machines and a Nordic Track. Exercise and dance classes are held in a mirrored studio. The spa on Promenade Deck has saunas for men and women and offers massage. A small beauty parlor also offers facials and spa treatments. A jogging track circles Promenade Deck.

Top decks have been transformed by the addition of a second swimming pool and the Topsider's Bar, a second open-air bar. Sky Deck, a new space above the Sun Deck, provides more sunning area while shading the two pools and whirlpools below. It has lounge chairs, rest rooms, and showers.

Children's Facilities   Supervised activities include movies, bridge tours, treasure hunts, and magic tricks. A children's menu is available. Kids Korner play area has a kiddies' pool, playground rides, ball slide, and puppet theater. Bathrooms have lowered kiddies' sinks. Older children have a video arcade with a dozen game machines. (See the Children's Facilities in the *Norway* profile for details.)

Shore Excursions   On Bahamas cruises, standard tours are offered, but opportunities abound for passengers to explore the island leisurely on their own. The ship spends four full days in St. George's, in front of King's Square. Nearby are shops, historic St. Peter's church, and motor-scooter rentals (the island's most popular transport; no car rentals are available). The picturesque town is ideal for a walking and convenient to beaches, but not to Hamilton, a town at the island's opposite end. Among excursions available is a visit to the Bermuda Aquarium Museum and Zoo. The ship's sports program offers sailing, snorkeling, scuba diving, and deep-sea fishing.

Norwegian Sky	(Preview)	
Norwegian Sun	(Preview)	
Registry: Bahamas	Length: 853 feet	Beam: 108 feet/ 105.8 feet
Cabins: 900/1,000	Draft: 26 feet	Speed: 23 knots
Maximum Passengers: 2,002/2,400	Passenger Decks: 11	Elevators: 12
	Crew: 800/960	Space Ratio: 38

The Ship The unfinished hull intended as Costa Cruises' *CostaOlympia* was completed by NCL as the *Norwegian Sky*. She debuted in August 1999 as the first of a new generation of NCL vessels, with a sister ship arriving in 2001. Swedish marine architects Tillberg Design created the handsome interiors of the $300 million vessel, the line's largest new ship to date. They are a rhapsody in blue, romanticizing the ship's name, with sky-blue and sea-blue decor throughout the ship.

The initial impression one has upon entering the glass-domed, eight-deck atrium is one of cool elegance. There is no glitz or bright lights but rather, an airy, refined setting with a multimillion-dollar art collection integrated into the decor.

The operative word on this ship is *options*—with three dining rooms, an outdoor buffet, an indoor garden buffet, pizzeria, and wine bar, and the NCL signature Sports Bar & Grill, Le Bistro, and an ice cream bar. There are also champagne and cigar bars.

The reception and purser's desks, concierge, and shore excursion offices are on Atlantic Deck. Neptune's Court, a second atrium, has a grand staircase just outside the Seven Seas Dining Room, connecting Atlantic deck to Promenade and International Decks with the main show lounge.

The *Sky* debuted NCL's first Internet Café, where passengers can go online 24 hours a day, an enhancement soon to be added to all NCL ships. Ship's photographers have digital cameras, enabling passengers to e-mail photos home (additional fee). A "Skycam" on the bridge is downloaded onto a Web site so family ashore can track the voyage. Other facilities include the Atrium Room, available for small private functions, and a medical center.

In a joint venture, dutyfree.com and Colombian Emeralds International manage *Norwegian Sky* gift shops. Passengers view patterns and designs at a kiosk, with home delivery available. Liquor selections, displayed in the shopping arcade, can be ordered through room service.

The *Norwegian Sun,* the *Sky's* sister ship to be launched in September 2001, will be the first of the fleet to have NCL's new Freestyle Cruising elements included during the building. Among them are more dining options—nine distinctive restaurants—the most of any ship departing from North American ports; several pay-as-you-go.

Among other new features, *Norwegian Sun* will have a "lifestyle area" for classes in computers, financial planning, yoga, etc.; a larger Internet cafe with 30 terminals, instead of the Sun's 18; a wedding chapel; a significantly larger gym and spa; larger cabins, and a new cabin category—minisuites with balconies.

Itineraries   See Appendix B.

Cabins   The *Sky* cabins are similar but smaller than those on *Norwegian Dream* and are furnished with two lower beds that convert to a queen, a sitting area, dressing table, refrigerator, safe, remote control television, radio, telephone, large circular windows, and private bathroom with duvet. Other than the penthouses and owner suites, all cabins are uniform in size and efficiently laid out, but smaller than average. The glaring shortcoming is insufficient storage space—a leftover because the ship was already under construction when NCL took over the project. Most have only three shallow drawers. To compensate, NCL recently installed more shelf and drawer space in all cabins. Closet space is adequate. About 20 percent of the cabins have teak-floored balconies; all have Internet hookups. Fourteen penthouses with teakwood furnished balconies have butler service and an exclusive room service menu for breakfast, lunch and dinner.

Some of the *Sky's* shortcomings are being corrected on the *Sun* with more than 100 additional outside cabins (67 percent in total), larger cabins, and 30 minisuites with balconies, measuring 267 square feet. Outside cabins with balconies have nearly 20 square feet more than in the same category on the *Sky.* Four Owner's Suites, located forward above the ship's bridge, have 502 square feet each. All cabins have extra closet and drawer space.

Norwegian Sky *Specifications*   1,000 cabins. 14 penthouse suites; 258 cabins, including 21 junior suites, have balconies. 8 owner's suites have balconies with Jacuzzis. Standard cabins measure about 150 square feet; 6 wheelchair-accessible.

Norwegian Sun *Specifications*   30 minisuites with balconies; outside cabins with balconies measure 172 square feet, inside cabins, 176 square feet.

Dining   The ship's two main dining rooms, Four Seasons and Seven Seas, have two seatings and are connected by the intimate Horizons, a third, small dining room. The latter has a dozen or so roomy gold banquettes along large windows looking on to panoramic ocean views on one side of the room. Suite passengers are given first preference at Horizons' banquettes and window seats.

Other dining options include the richly furnished Le Bistro, with floor-to-ceiling windows, serving French/Mediterranean cuisine with tableside cooking, and Ciao Chow, a funky Italian/Chinese eatery. Le Bistro, which serves dinner until 11 p.m., and Horizons require reservations; they are very popular, so book early in the cruise.

The casual Great Outdoor Restaurant and Garden Cafe have "food action stations" serving up paella, sushi, Norwegian waffles, pasta, and more, intended to eliminate long buffet lines. Both cafes offer breakfast, lunch, and snack specialties that vary daily. There is a pizzeria and Sprinkles Ice Cream Bar. The 24-hour room-service menu offers pizza, too.

Passengers give the ship's cuisine, especially the alternative dining options, good reviews. The only dining disappointment is breakfast and lunch in the pool deck cafe for their lack of variety.

While the *Sky* was NCL's first ship to offer Freestyle Cruising, the *Sun* will reflect the concept with its dining options. On a seven-day cruise, passengers will never need to eat dinner in the same restaurant more than once, unless they want to. Rather, they can chose from two main dining rooms with open seating and open from 5:30 p.m. to midnight every evening; a formal Italian restaurant by reservation; French fare at Le Bistro; a Pacific Rim restaurant complex with a sushi bar and teppanyaki room; a California/Hawaii/Asian fusion restaurant; a tapas bar with entertainment; a 24-hour indoor/outdoor cafe with food stations serving hamburgers, hot dogs, soups and salads; and a "healthy living" restaurant with Cooking Light dishes and spa menus.

Facilities and Entertainment   Gatsby's, a wine and tapas bar, is one of the best-looking lounges on the ship, with deep burgundy carpets, plush gold chairs, and leopard-print ottomans set against lush foliage, wood paneling, and floor-to-ceiling windows. The Atrium Bar, another piano bar with large glass windows and a view of the white and gold lobby area, serves champagne and premium vodkas along with caviar and pâté de foie gras. A modest but respectable half-bottle of Veuve Clicquot accompanied by pâté de foie gras is a mere $38; if you go for the works, a bottle of Dom Perignon with Sevruga caviar and pâté will set you back $150.

Nonsmoking guests can select from the martini menu in the Wind-jammer Bar on starboard side, while cigar connoisseurs enjoy their freshly hand-rolled stogie and premium cigars and brandy selections behind the glass walls of the adjoining but segregated Churchill's Cigar Club with humidor and seating for 35, on port side. The Coffee Bar has a great selection of coffees and liqueurs at fair prices.

Monte Carlo Casino offers blackjack, roulette, Caribbean poker, and slot machines. Now playing in the golden, two-deck Stardust Lounge with a proscenium stage is *Hey Mr. Producer: The Musical World of Cameron Mackintosh,* which highlights legendary musicals Mackintosh produced in the last 30 years, including *Cats, Miss Saigon, Les Miserables,* and *The Phantom of the Opera*. With its sound, lighting, and audiovisual facilities, it's possible to transform the lounge into a disco.

Checkers Lounge in black, white, gold, and red colors and a checkerboard pattern floor has what NCL claims is the longest bar at sea. Passengers may choose cabaret acts, illusionists, comedians, and on some cruises, the wildly popular jazz and pop show of Jane L. Powell & Company. The entertainment is uniformly of high standard in keeping with the NCL tradition.

The *Sky* also has a wedding chapel for ceremonies in port, a library, and the Victoria Conference Center, which seats 100 and can be divided into three smaller rooms.

On the Pool Deck, the Topsider's Bar is a long poolside bar with stools and outdoor tables; on the Sports Deck, the Sports Bar offers televisions with videotaped and live broadcasts of sporting events. It combines with The Zone, the teen disco. The Observatory Lounge has floor-to-ceiling windows overlooking the bow.

Roaming the decks is a "Skymobile" beverage cart making drink deliveries to passengers. When *Norwegian Sky* sails in the Caribbean, pool attendants provide Evian water, suntan lotion, cold face towels, and fresh fruit.

Sports, Fitness, and Beauty   The two swimming pools are connected by steps and a central wading platform to four hot tubs and set off by dark wood decks and dark green lounge chairs. Also on the enormous Sun Deck is Body Waves, a full-service spa operated by British-based Steiner, with ten therapists trained in a wide range of spa treatments, including some exotic ones such as Reiki, an ancient Japanese art of hands healing. It has a uni-sex beauty salon and a gym/aerobics area with Lifecycles and Lifesteps equipment to be used while enjoying ocean views through floor-to-ceiling glass walls.

On Sports Deck, passengers will find two golf driving nets, a full-size basketball/volleyball court, a batting cage, and shuffleboard. A jogging/walking track circles the Promenade Deck (3.5 laps equal 1 mile).

Children's Facilities Kids Korner playroom on International Deck offers "Kid's Crew," a year-round, supervised program divided into four age groups: Junior Sailors (ages 3–5), First Mates (6–8), Navigators (9–12), and Teens (13–17). The Crew has its own center and video arcade. A children's splash pool is on Sports Deck. Baby sitting is available for a fee from noon to 2 a.m.

Orient Lines

1510 SE Seventeenth Street, Suite 400
Ft. Lauderdale, FL 33316-1716
(954) 527-6660; (800) 333-7300; fax (954) 527-6657
www.orientlines.com

Type of Ships   Updated, midsize oceanliners.

Type of Cruise   Affordable, destination-intensive, light adventure with first-class amenities, fine cuisine, and refined ambience.

Cruise Line's Strengths
- stylish ships
- attentive crew
- alternative dining venues
- itineraries
- singles policy
- price
- dock-level gangway door on Marco Polo
- expert lecturers on longer voyages
- precruise information

Cruise Line's Shortcomings
- limited room service
- entertainment
- limited on-board shopping

Fellow Passengers   In the short time Orient Lines has operated, it has attracted mature, experienced, inquisitive passengers who are friendly and interested in the line's off-the-beaten-track itineraries. On longer cruises, passengers range in age from 50 to 70, with average annual incomes of about $75,000, and are retired or semiretired, business owners, managers, or professionals. Most are North Americans, but some cruises might include Brits and other Europeans, Australians, and South Africans, depending on the itinerary. Many are veteran cruisers, but several are first-timers who have traveled frequently and are drawn to an Orient cruise by its strong destination focus. After the line introduced summer Mediterranean cruises, however, the age of passengers dropped from an average of 55 to 35–54, and passengers from the Midwest and Northeast nearly tripled.

Recommended For   Orient Lines has two seasons, each with a different appeal. On longer, winter cruises, passengers tend to be seasoned travelers, not necessarily experienced cruisers, who have the curiosity to appreciate exotic destinations, seek a learning experience but like to travel in comfort. Also, small-ship devotees wanting to sample a cruise on a larger ship but not a megaliner. From May–October, passengers tend to be first-time cruisers, families, honeymooners; those wanting a land and sea vacation in Europe.

Not Recommended For   Unsophisticated or inexperienced travelers and those seeking a high-energy, holiday-at-sea, party atmosphere.

Cruise Areas and Seasons   In winter, Antarctica, New Zealand, Australia, Southeast Asia, India, Indian Ocean, Egypt, Africa, and South America, including the Amazon. In summer, Mediterranean, Greek Isles, Black Sea, Northern Europe, Scandinavia, and Russia.

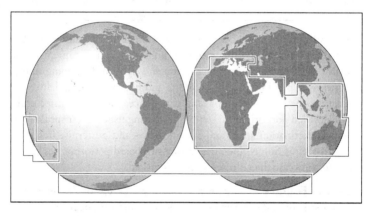

The Line   Orient Lines originated in 1991 when its former CEO, Gerry Herrod, a British entrepreneur and tour and cruise line veteran, bought the Russian liner *Alexander Pushkin* for about $25 million, when it had been in a Singapore yard for minor repairs and the Soviets couldn't pay their bills. The ship, built in East Germany in 1965 for the Soviets—who hoped to generate hard currency by cashing in on the growing cruise market—was one of four sister ships with ice-strengthened hulls. They served as Soviet troop ships.

At the cost of $75 million, Orient Lines transformed the vessel into a luxury liner and named her *Marco Polo*. At the same time, the cruise line was launched to offer upscale voyages for experienced travelers to exotic destinations at reasonable prices. In its second year, the mission changed somewhat when the line found great success in a summer Mediterranean program.

Orient Lines was purchased by Norwegian Cruise Line in 1998, but continues to operate as a separate entity. Meanwhile, NCL, including Orient Lines, was purchased by Asian-based Star Cruises. In 2000, NCL's former *Norwegian Crown* joined Orient Lines after extensive renovation and was renamed *Crown Odyssey,* the ship's original name. The *Crown Odyssey* is expected to offer the same shipboard experience as the *Marco Polo.* Her addition more than doubled Orient Lines' passenger capacity and has enabled it to expand its worldwide offerings. *Crown Odyssey*'s hull and superstructure were designed for long-distance cruising, making her an ideal fit for Orient Lines.

The Fleet	Built/Renovated	Tonnage	Passengers
Marco Polo	1965/1993	22,080	848
Crown Odyssey	1988/2000	34,250	1,050

Style   "Adventure in elegance" is one way Orient Lines' cruises have been described. From the start, Orient differed from most mainstream cruise lines by focusing on destinations, giving as much weight to developing unusual itineraries as to providing all the comforts and fine cuisine of a deluxe ship.

Meant to be an all-encompassing experience, the line's winter cruises include detailed port briefings, lectures by distinguished guest speakers and experts on destination areas, and extended pre- and postcruise hotel stays with sight-seeing. Some itineraries feature shipboard performances by local groups to showcase the culture of regions visited.

Distinctive Features   Gentlemen social hosts (except on Mediterranean cruises); local cultural performances; helicopter and topside helipad; videotaping of lectures for replay on ship's television; low single supplement. One of only two luxury ships permitted to cruise Antarctica.

	HIGHEST	LOWEST	AVERAGE
PER DIEM	$700	$123	$288

The above per diems are calculated from the cruise line's non-discounted *cruise only* fares on standard accommodations. Per diems vary by season, by cabin, and by cruise areas.

Rates Port charges are additional.

Special Fares and Discounts Advance-purchase 10 percent discounts, 120 days before departure, depending on itinerary and cabin. Savings up to 28 percent for two or more cruises in sequence.

- Single Supplement: 25 percent on all cabin categories except A and suites. For Mediterranean sailings, 50 percent for categories D–K, 75 percent for B and C, 100 percent for A and suites. The line frequently waives the supplement in special promotions.
- Guaranteed share program in specific cabin categories.

Packages
- Air/Sea: Yes.
- Pre/Post: Cruises are designed as cruise/tours with one- to three-day pre- and/or postcruise hotel stays in gateway cities. Several Mediterranean itineraries also include two- to six-day escorted motorcoach tours.
- Others: Yes.

Past Passengers After their first cruise, passengers are enrolled in the Polo Club and receive information on new itineraries, the club magazine, cruise discounts, a travel bag, $25–75 on-board credit (depending on cruise length), a bottle of wine in their cabin, and a VIP party with the captain.

The Last Word The ships are midsize by today's standards; yet among the largest ships cruising to exotic destinations regularly. Their size enables them to provide upscale comforts and a full range of facilities, while their capacity provides a larger passenger base over which to spread costs. Hence, the line can offer cruises at prices considerably lower than its competitors with smaller deluxe ships.

Orient Lines cares about single travelers. In addition to having gentlemen hosts to dine and dance with unaccompanied women passengers, the line offers one of cruising's lowest single supplements as well as occasional singles promotions. Also, it's fastidious in matching participants in its guaranteed-share program.

Children are rare aboard the ships but are treated like royalty. On a recent cruise, a precocious 12-year-old—the only child on board—toured the engine room; was given a ship's uniform with officer's hat, name tag, and commander's stripes; had free run of the bridge; and was allowed to steer the ship.

ORIENT LINES STANDARD FEATURES

Officers Scandinavian, European.

Staff Dining, Cabin/Filipino; Cruise/American and British.

Dining Facilities One dining room with open seating for breakfast and lunch and two seatings for dinner with assigned tables; Lido restaurant for buffet breakfast, lunch, tea and specialty dinners. *Crown,* alternative dining.

Special Diets 30 days' advance notice.

Room Servic Continental breakfast, cabin attendants on call.

Dress Code Casual by day; several formal/semiformal nights.

Cabin Amenities Direct-dial telephone, safe, television with CNN, movies and ship programs, radio, hair dryer, toiletries. Bathrobes and slippers in upper-category cabins; small refrigerators in suites. Deluxe suites with sitting room, marble bathroom with tub and shower, and stocked minibars.

Electrical Outlet 110 AC.

Wheelchair Access *Marco Polo,* two cabins; *Crown,* four cabins.

Recreation and Entertainment Four lounges, port/country lectures by experts, piano and/or string trio at cocktails and after dinner, folkloric dancers in port; library, card room.

Sports and Other Activities Small outdoor swimming pool on *Marco Polo;* one indoor, one outdoor pool on *Crown;* Ping-Pong.

Beauty and Fitness Beauty salon/spa, massage, aerobics studio, exercise equipment, Jacuzzis, saunas.

Other Facilities Medical unit. Zodiacs; helicopter and landing pad; meeting room.

Children's Facilities No special facilities.

Smoking None in dining room; smoking permitted in designated wing of main lounge bar during shows, but not during lectures and briefings.

Orient Suggested Tipping Per day per person, cabin steward, $3; waiter, $3.75; busboy, $2; 15 percent of bar bill.

Credit Cards For cruise payment and on-board charges: American Express, MasterCard, Visa, Diner's Club, Discover.

Marco Polo	Quality **8**	Value A
Registry: Bahamas	Length: 578 feet	Beam: 77 feet
Cabins: 425	Draft: 27 feet	Speed: 19.5 knots
Maximum Passengers:	Passenger Decks: 8	Elevators: 4
848	Crew: 350	Space Ratio: 27.6

The Ship   A lovely vessel with classic lines, *Marco Polo* has been enhanced by handsome Art Deco interiors created by A. and M. Katzourakis of Athens. Reminiscent of grand liners of the 1920s, pastel furnishings are set against etched and beveled glass, brass, chrome, and rich wood and accented by Thai and Burmese antiques and prints, plus modern paintings. *Marco Polo* is a comfortable ship designed for long cruises. Built for Arctic service, her hull is strengthened for icy waters and ice floes, with many extra frames added. A gangway door enables passengers to enter the ship at the same level as most docks and piers, averting a long walk up a steep gangway. A significant advantage is *Marco Polo*'s superior stability. Twelve-foot waves and rough seas, particularly in such notorious waters as Drake Passage on an Antarctica cruise, are hardly noticeable.

Most cabins are on the main deck, one level below Belvedere Deck, which accommodates most public rooms and includes the lobby, three of four entertainment lounges and bars, the casino, and a library with over 1,000 volumes.

Outside vantage points—especially on the upper deck forward and Promenade Deck aft—are numerous for viewing scenery and wildlife or watching sunsets.

Itineraries   See Appendix B.

Cabins   Being an older vessel, *Marco Polo* has a variety of cabin sizes and configurations. Almost 70 percent are outside; those in upper A–D categories have picture windows.

Cabins are light and handsomely appointed with light wood furniture and pastel bedspreads, curtains, and carpeting. Most are comfortably sized for long cruises, with ample storage space, dressing table with pullout writing desk, and good reading lights. All have a telephone with international direct-dialing; radio; television with CNN, two channels for movies, and one for ship programs; safe; and a bathroom with shower, built-in hair dryer, and complimentary toiletries. Upper-category cabins provide bathrobes, slippers, and safes. Deluxe suites have a large sitting room, separate bedroom, large marble bathroom with tub and shower, and stocked minibar, replenished without charge. Junior suites and some deluxe cabins have a sitting area and bath with tub and shower. Family cabins have curtain-divided sleeping areas.

Views from accommodations on Sky Deck, including junior suites and deluxe cabins, and ten cabins on the upper deck, are partially obstructed by lifeboats. These are noted on the deck plan in the line's brochure. Two deluxe suites and some upper-deck and Promenade Deck cabins have windows facing deck areas; however, one-way glass prevents outsiders from seeing in.

Specifications   131 inside cabins, 288 outside; 6 suites. Standard dimensions 140–180 square feet. 388 cabins with 2 lower beds (42 convertible to double beds); 28 accommodate third passenger; 10 accommodate 4 passengers. Suites and some upper-category cabins have double/queen-size beds, some have twin beds convertible to doubles. 2 cabins wheelchair-accessible.

Dining   Fine cuisine and exemplary service in elegant surroundings with tables set in fine china, crystal, and fresh flowers make dining one of the ship's best features. Seven Seas Restaurant is a large, formal room dressed in mauves and grays. Breakfast and lunch have open seating, but the two dinner seatings have assigned tables seating four, six, or eight.

Entry is from the central foyer graced with large abstract paintings and Oriental statues. A central, raised area with Art Deco circular ceiling is separated from lower sides by etched glass partitions. Booths and tables for two to ten people are by windows at either side of the room. Floor-to-ceiling mirrors on inside walls help create a spacious feeling. The room is designated nonsmoking.

Dinner menus offer three appetizers, two soups, four entrees, and two or three desserts, cheeses, and fruits. Lighter, vegetarian, low-fat, or low-salt selections are indicated. Wines from South Africa, Australia, Argentina, Chile, California, and Europe are offered at reasonable prices. Raffles serves casual breakfast and lunch buffets, plus Asian food on some evenings; at lunch its aft corners have cooked-to-order pasta and specialty stations, and outside, there's a deck grill and an ice cream and dessert bar. Its large windows overlook the pool deck. Chairs and tables with umbrellas are set around the pool. Afternoon tea is served here and in the small Palm Court.

Twice weekly in the evenings, Raffles becomes an elegant, very popular bistro for 90 passengers (reservations required) with a changing menu of Chinese, Thai, and other Asian cuisine. A $15 charge per person includes wine and gratuities. On more casual Mediterranean sailings, Raffles' capacity increases to 370, and Italian and regional specialties are served all but one night of the cruise, when the Asian menu is featured.

Surprising for a deluxe ship, room service is unavailable, except for continental breakfast and in case of illness. The line maintains that the ship's fine-dining experience is best enjoyed in the dining room. Some passengers might disagree after a long, tiring day on tour. Despite the official policy, most cabin stewards will bring food to the cabin on request. Another point: On tour days, dress for dinner is casual, and the dining room atmosphere more relaxed.

Service *Marco Polo*'s tone is set by its friendly, service-oriented officers; lively British and American cruise staff; and most of all, its well-trained, hard working Filipino crew, who win high praise for their attentiveness and cheerful dispositions. The dining staff seems to anticipate your every need, and the restaurant managers must have eyes in the back of their heads, always observing and rushing to correct eve the simplest error. Cabin staff know passengers' names minutes after their arrival, and address them by name throughout the cruise. This courtesy makes an indelible impression. Overall, the service on the *Marco Polo* is as fine as any we've had on a cruise ship, including the most luxurious ships at triple the price.

Facilities and Entertainment The Ambassador Lounge showroom features local entertainment brought on board in various ports. These presentations and Filipino crew show are highlights of the cruise and much better than mediocre musical revues and variety shows staged on other nights. Other entertainment might include a classical concert, piano recital.

The lounge, divided into three curved sections, slopes gently toward the stage. Sight lines are good except behind pillars or when the room is completely full. Large windows span both sides of the room, and a marble-topped bar flanked by mirrors is at the rear. Diamond-shaped lighting fixtures, blue carpets and curtains, and pink decor give the room a 1930s look.

Between the show lounge and lobby, the Polo Lounge piano bar with a cream-colored baby grand piano encircled by a bar, is popular for predinner cocktails and late-evening relaxing and sing-alongs. It's also used for afternoon bridge games. Le Casino offers roulette, blackjack, and slot and video-poker machines. To one side is an elegant white marble bar, black leather swivel chairs, and photos of famous entertainers. Off the casino are a small card room and a well-stocked library with comfortable leather armchairs and big windows. Guidebooks for the many countries visited by *Marco Polo* are provided.

Between the lobby and casino is the Palm Court, a small room with marble-topped tables and wicker chairs. It's a pleasurable retreat for afternoon tea or quiet conversation. Opposite are two small boutiques. Tucked away in a small area is the Internet service.

The Charleston Club is one of several multipurpose lounges. It's used for bingo, painting lessons, cocktails, late-evening music and dancing, and midnight pizza. Glass doors open onto a lounge with a white baby grand piano and small bandstand, marble-topped bar, and dance floor. The lounge is a popular late-night gathering spot, though most passengers retire early.

Activities and Diversions   Lectures by experts on the cruise region are well attended. Speakers might include such famous people as mountaineer Sir Edmund Hillary, wildlife expert Peter Alden, and anthropologist Donna Pido. Lectures are not presented on Mediterranean cruises because of itineraries' port-intensive nature.

Among other diversions are bridge tours; origami (Japanese paper-folding); art classes, bridge and backgammon lessons and tournaments; workshops on magic; white-elephant sales; passenger talent shows; service club meetings (including Lions, Kiwanis, and Rotary); fashion shows; and joke contests.

Sports, Fitness, and Beauty   On the Pool Deck is a 15-foot-long swimming pool with teak benches on three sides. Ping-Pong and shuffleboard are available. A fitness center on the upper deck has a mirrored exercise room with treadmills, stationary bicycles, rowing machine, stair steppers, weight machines, and free weights. Aerobics and exercise classes are offered. Separate saunas for men and women and three outside Jacuzzis are available.

The beauty salon, operated by the Steiner group of London, offers a full range of services, including facials, massage, and hydrotherapy. Most are expensive indulgences.

An upper-deck jogging track ringing the ship consists mostly of a narrow, rubberized path behind the lifeboats. For walkers, Promenade Deck has a one-fifth-mile course between the Charleston Club and bridge gangway. It's all on teak decks with sea views.

Shore Excursions   All cruises feature pre- or postcruise packages and are particularly popular given the distances most passengers travel to the ship. Most cruises also include an unusual highlight ashore. For example, a cruise/safari in Kenya visits the home of Isak Dinesen (Karen Blixen), the author of *Out of Africa,* and wildlife-rich Amboseli National Park.

Typical short shore excursions might include a snorkeling trip to a protected reef in the Seychelles or a visit to see the Komodo dragons of Indonesia. Having the helipad is reassuring in case of an emergency in remote areas and for scouting ice conditions in Antarctica.

Note: Shore transport in some remote/primitive locations is not top of the line. Because of this, some shore excursions are inappropriate for passengers with limited mobility. Also, a fee may be charged for upgraded shore accommodations, but it is worth the cost in some out-of-the-way locations.

Postscript   Orient Lines publishes excellent cruise brochures. The most important features, special events, and workshops for every cruise are highlighted in an easy-to-spot format. Literature detailing trip planning, sent to passengers before sailing, is good.

Writing in 1298, Marco Polo opened his famous *Travels* with the words: "Ye kings, princes, nobles, townsfolk and all who wish to know the marvels of the world, have this book read unto you." If he were writing today, he might say, "All ye who wish to know the marvels of the world, take a cruise on the *Marco Polo.*"

Crown Odyssey	(Preview)	
Registry: Bahamas	Length: 614 feet	Beam: 92.5 feet
Cabins: 51	Draft: 24 feet	Speed: 20 knots
Maximum Passengers:	Passenger Decks: 10	Elevators: 4
1,050	Crew: 470	Space Ratio: 32.6

The Ship   In April 2000, Norwegian Cruise Line transferred *Norwegian Crown* to Orient Lines, its sister company, and renamed her *Crown Odyssey* (the ship's original name). From May to October, she sails the Mediterranean between Barcelona and Istanbul; in winter, she's cruising in Asia on a variety of itineraries from the Indian Ocean to the South Pacific, including Tahiti and Hawaii, new destinations for Orient Lines. Her transiting of the Panama Canal on a cruise from Los Angeles will also mark Orient Lines' first sailing in North American waters.

Built in 1988, the spacious ship was widely acclaimed for her quality decor by A. and M. Katzourakis. It is a modern interpretation of classic architectural elements with stunning Art Deco design. Used generously in public rooms are marble, fine woods, original art, antiques, chrome, mirrors, stained glass, smoked glass, reflective ceilings, and brass finishes.

Renovations made prior to her new role include a redesigned and expansion of the Yacht Club to double as a daytime lido cafe and an evening bistro for alternative dining; a new al fresco lunch venue on Penthouse Deck; and a redesigned Lido Deck with a new lounge, bar, Internet and e-mail center, library, and card room; as well as renovations of the main lobby, dining room, and Top of the Crown lounge.

On Marina Deck, a central foyer houses the reception desk, shore excursion office, sundries shop, and a small gallery with fine antique reproductions leading to Seven Continents Restaurant.

At the foot of a circular grand staircase connecting the reception area and Odyssey Deck is a six-foot spherical sculpture in bronze by Italian artist Arnaldo Pomodoro and access Monte Carlo Court, a large piano bar. It's the ship's social hub, where passengers gather for cocktails and conversation. A mosaic of backlighted stained-glass panels in geometric patterns extends the height of all the ship's stairwells.

Itineraries   See Appendix B.

Cabins   *Crown* offers 18 categories on seven decks. About 78 percent are outside cabins, and more than half of the bathrooms have tubs. Most cabins are large; even the smallest have 154 square feet and the same basic amenities. All have full vanities, two mirrored closets, tie and shoe racks, safe, hardwood furniture and cabinetry, locked drawers, good lighting, and contemporary art. Bathrooms are marble or tiled and have large mirrors, recessed shelves, and hair dryers. Many bathtubs are midsize. All cabins have direct-dial phones and television with CNN and satellite channels.

Each of the 16 penthouse suites has a private veranda, sitting room with a convertible sofa bed, refrigerator, walk-in closet, queen or convertible twin beds; marble bathroom with whirlpool tub, and butler service. Four apartments can be combined with adjacent units to provide more than 1,000 square feet.

Suites are named for exotic destinations, echoed in decor through original paintings and antiques. Glass partitions separate sitting and sleeping areas. Beds in the Superior AB Suite category fold into the wall to create a meeting room.

Specifications   107 inside cabins, 319 outside; 16 penthouse suites with verandas; 20 deluxe suites; 34 junior suites. Standard dimensions, 165 square feet. 284 double cabins; 150 triples; 82 quads; no singles; 32 connecting outside cabins. 4 cabins wheelchair-accessible.

Dining   The elegantly appointed Seven Continents Restaurant, the main dining room, is a two-level room with a sunken central section under Tiffany-style glass domes. It's trimmed with lacquered woods, glass panels, and picture windows. There are two seatings, with open seating for breakfast and lunch and assigned for dinner. Spa cuisine is available.

The Yacht Club Café has been renovated to serve as a dining venue for buffet breakfast and lunch with both indoor and outdoor dining. In the evenings, it is transformed into an alternative bistro restaurant with dining indoor and al fresco. The cafe opens onto the swimming pool. Cafe d'Italia is a new al fresco dining venue for lunch on Penthouse Deck, aft, serving pizza and grilled specialties.

Facilities and Entertainment Evening entertainment is offered in the multitiered, Art Deco Stardust Lounge, where smoky gray mirrors create a sound-wave design in the tiered ceiling. Opaque crystals in Lalique-style glass panels continues the effect on the back wall. A sloping floor gives almost every seat good sight lines. The stage can be lowered to become a dance floor.

The intimate Rendezvous Bar next door is popular for cocktails, and the casino offers blackjack, roulette, Caribbean poker, and slot machines. Adjacent to the casino is the Monte Carlo Piano Bar.

The ship's crowning glory, you might say, is the Top of the Crown, a circular observation lounge and bar with glass domes and floor-to-ceiling windows that offer sweeping views in three directions. A daytime retreat for reading and viewing scenery, it becomes a nighttime disco with an illuminated glass dance floor. Gentlemen hosts are on board to dance and socialize with unaccompanied women.

Activities and Diversions Daily activities include the Discovery Lecture Series (except on European cruises) deck sports, bingo, bridge, dance classes, art, cooking demonstrations, and wine-tasting classes. The Coronet Theatre, which spans two decks, shows current films on a full-size screen. The theater also has writing tables and simultaneous-translation equipment for use in seminars, conferences, and religious services. The renovated Lido Deck aft area has a new Palm Court lounge, bar, and Internet and e-mail center.

Sports, Fitness, and Beauty The Penthouse Deck has a pleasant teak sunning area, a splash pool, and two whirlpools. An abstract stainless steel sculpture dominates the center of the pools. There ship has a basketball and volleyball court, shuffleboard, and Ping-Pong.

On the ship's lowest level is an indoor pool—unusual on modern ships and a great asset when the ship is sailing in cold climes. There also is a fitness center and spa with a full-time director. It has two whirlpools, gym with Universal exercise equipment, men's and women's saunas and massage rooms, and a juice bar. The beauty salon offers herbal therapy and other beauty treatments.

P&O Cruises

10100 Santa Monica Boulevard
Los Angeles, CA 90067

(310) 553-1770; (800) PRINCESS (774-6237)
fax (310) 284-2857

www.pocruises.com

Type of Ships   New superliners and classic oceanliner.

Type of Cruises   Very British; moderately priced and deluxe with world-wide itineraries.

Cruise Line's Strengths
- well-organized ships, aboard and ashore
- nonrepeating itineraries with vast number of ports
- distinctively British character
- excellent daytime programs and nighttime entertainment

Cruise Line's Shortcomings
- small serving portions
- limited fresh salads and pastas
- limited buffet selections

Fellow Passengers   Most are British, all ages and incomes, many cruising together for years. Americans, Australians, and New Zealanders are sizable minority on around-the-world voyages.

Recommended For   Anglophiles who like British humor, food, interests. On the around-the-world voyage, the well-traveled who like journeying with the well-traveled.

Not Recommended For   Americans not enamored of all things British; those who might not appreciate fiercely loyal passengers, who in turn might not appreciate Americans who don't conform to British ways.

Cruise Areas and Seasons   England to Northern Europe, Iberian peninsula, Atlantic islands, and Mediterranean in summer; some Caribbean in winter before annual around-the-world voyages: one eastbound via Africa to Orient; one westbound via Panama Canal to Pacific, Australia, New Zealand; return via Southeast Asia, Suez Canal, Mediterranean or South Africa.

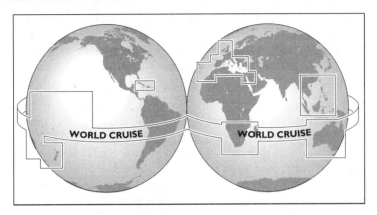

The Line   British-based P&O Cruises' official name is Peninsular and Oriental Steam Navigation Company, a link to the original company founded in 1837 whose principal routes served the empire from India to New Zealand. After World War II, new North American and transpacific routes were opened, and by 1960, P&O had merged with the Orient Line to form P&O Orient Lines and finally P&O Cruises. Princess Cruises, in Los Angeles, is the company's North American subsidiary. In 2000, P&O Cruises and Princess Cruises, along with the company's two other cruise lines, were being split off from the shipping company to form a new entity, which will be operated as an independent company listed on the New York and London stock exchanges.

In April 1995, when P&O Cruises introduced the *Oriana,* its first brand-new ship in more than two decades, it signal the start of a modern cruise line for today's market, adding air-sea cruises in the Mediterranean, replacing her old ships with newer ones, and building new ships. The *Aurora,* a sister to *Oriana,* was scheduled for delivery in 2000. The 1,850-passenger vessel, built in Germany, is designed for British passengers. Almost half of her cabins have balconies, and dining alternatives have been added.

P&O focuses on three programs: cruises departing from Southampton, those based in the Caribbean in winter, and annual around-the-world voyages. The latter retain a colonial flavor because many older passengers had connections with the British colonies, and some staff and crew have years of service with the line. Many Australians, retired or on long leave, travel to and from Britain via P&O.

The Fleet	Built/Renovated	Tonnage	Passengers
Arcadia	1989/1997	63,524	1,475
Aurora	2000	76,000	1,850
Oriana	1995	69,000	1,806
Victoria	1966/86/97	28,000	746

Style   The British style cannot be overemphasized, and it's what most passengers want. The atmosphere is very social, helped by friendly British officers who mingle with passengers and host tables at dinner time—a popular feature.

Unless a non–English-speaking group is aboard, English is the only language used by the crew. Apart from Indian crew members and the purser's staff, most staff members know only English. British traits aboard ship include very British cooking, some passengers' reserved nature, precise timing for activities, fondness for a "pint" (of beer or lager) before lunch, afternoon tea, British humor, cricket matches, and fascination with sports and politics. Because passengers generally don't like change, little has changed aboard P&O ships.

Distinctive Features   British ambience, afternoon teas, excellent lecturers on ports' history and culture, classical pianists, social interaction with the British officers, Sunday religious services (Anglican) with a passenger/staff choir.

	HIGHEST	LOWEST	AVERAGE
PER DIEM	$633	$362	$447

The above per diems are calculated from the cruise line's non-discounted *cruise only* fares on standard accommodations. Per diems vary by season, by cabin, and by cruise areas.

Rates   Port charges are included.

Special Fares and Discounts
- Third/Fourth Passenger: 50 percent of minimum rate, based on inside upper/lower berth, on *Victoria*.

Packages
- Air/Sea: Yes.
- Pre/Post: Yes.

Past Passengers   You must take a P&O cruise to qualify for The Posh Club. Membership is £30 a year. Members receive information about cruises and discounts, plus recognition aboard ship.

The Last Word   With its new ships, P&O has more to offer American passengers, but its appeal is still to Anglophiles. P&O summer cruises in Northern Europe and around-the-world voyages (or segments) in winter attract serious destination cruisers. Shorter cruises from England to warm destinations attract sun worshippers escaping Britain's climate.

P&O Cruises, represented in the United States by Princess Cruises, is headquartered at 77 New Oxford Street, London WC1A1PP; phone 071-800-2222.

P&O CRUISES STANDARD FEATURES

Officers British.

Staff Dining, Cabin/Indian, also British, European. Cruise/British.

Dining Facilities One dining room with two assigned seatings. Two restaurants on *Oriana, Aurora.* Indoor/outdoor buffet breakfast and lunch; *Oriana, Arcadia,* buffet dinner sometimes in evening; *Aurora,* 24-hour bistro.

Special Diets Request at time of booking.

Room Service Early a.m. coffee, tea, and biscuits; sandwiches/snacks.

Dress Code Jacket and tie on most nights at sea; some formal evenings when most men wear tuxedos or dinner jackets and women don cocktail and long dresses.

Cabin Amenities Television, radio, safes; BBC news; phones; high percentage of bathtubs on *Oriana* and *Victoria. Oriana* cabins have refrigerators.

Electrical Outlets 220 AC.

Wheelchair Access 10 cabins on *Arcadia,* 8 on *Victoria* and *Oriana* in various price categories; 22 on *Aurora.*

Recreation and Entertainment Card room, library, casinos, many bars, show lounge and cabarets, classical pianists, disco, dance classes, bingo, whist (similar to bingo), bridge, evening quiz games, arts, crafts, lecturers. *Aurora,* 5 lounges, 12 bars, concert hall/cinema. Virtual reality center.

Sports and Other Activities One outdoor pool, one inside on *Victoria;* two on *Arcadia;* three on *Oriana, Aurora* (one for children); exercise classes; deck tennis; cricket matches; Ping-Pong; deck and pool games. *Aurora,* golf simulator.

Beauty and Fitness Barber/hair stylist; gym and sauna; wraparound deck, mostly for walkers—and there are lots of them. *Aurora,* four Jacuzzis, health spa.

Other Facilities Shops, well-equipped hospital, self-service laundries, laundry/dry cleaning services, meeting rooms, cinema. *Aurora,* business center, medical center.

Children's Facilities Excellent children's programs; programs for teenagers. *Aurora,* children's and teenagers' rooms, night nursery.

Theme Cruises Astronomy, bridge, bird-watching, classical music.

Smoking Designated areas, but not strict.

P&O Suggested Tipping Per person per day, cabin steward, $1.50; dining steward, $1; assistant steward on *Victoria,* $0.50; section wine stewards, $1; 10 percent added to bar bills.

Credit Cards Currency on board is British pound; for on-board charges: American Express, Diners Club, MasterCard, Visa.

Oriana	Quality ⑧	Value C
Registry: Britain	Length: 855 feet	Beam: 106 feet
Cabins: 914	Draft: 26 feet	Speed: 24 knots
Maximum Passengers:	Passenger Decks: 11	Elevators: 10
1,806	Crew: 760	Space Ratio: 38.4

The Ship   The *Oriana,* which made her debut in April 1995, is big but beautiful. New and modern, she nonetheless has the design and decor of a classic liner. No flashy neon or glitz here. Interiors are as fine and refined as tea in a British parlor. On walls are classic oil paintings, watercolors, historic documents, and ship models. And the ship has aspects many ships catering to the American market lack: an inviting calm and numerous nooks where it's easy to relax, read, sip a beverage, write postcards, and let the world go by. It's cruising as it should be.

To hold its loyal passengers, P&O mirrored many of the old *Canberra*'s distinctive features in the new ship. For instance, the *Oriana* has many singles and four-berth cabins, known as "friendly fours," for economical cruising and for families. *Oriana* even resembles *Canberra,* right up to the aft twin funnels.

The variety of public rooms—17 in all—allows all types of passengers to find comfortable and familiar surroundings. Vast amounts of open deck call to British sun worshippers and those who take a daily "constitutional." Two main dining rooms and outstanding children's facilities are also offered.

Itineraries   See Appendix B.

Cabins   *Oriana*'s cabins are more luxurious than in P&O's tradition. They are spacious, with ample storage space and private facilities. Some have bathtubs, hair dryers, minibars, safes, telephones, televisions, and refrigerators. Suites have large bathrooms with bathtubs.

The *Oriana* has 11 categories of cabins and an especially wide range of configurations, including numerous single cabins—rare on today's megaliners. Almost all cabins, including suites, are on the three middle decks.

Specifications   8 suites, 16 deluxe cabins, 628 doubles, 114 singles, 6 three-berth, 40 four-berth cabins; 94 cabins with balconies; 8 wheelchair-accessible.

Dining   The two main restaurants, Peninsula and Oriental, offer two sittings for three meals. They're deep in the hull but have large windows. Servers are mainly Indian, with some British and Europeans.

The cuisine is very British: lots of meat and potatoes and sauces, but few salads. Soups are excellent; but an English breakfast, with kippers and such, takes some getting used to. On occasion you see strange items on the menu. For example, for the annual Robert Burns Night honoring the famous Scottish poet, only a Scotsman could understand the fare: "Royal highland haggis with champit tatties 'n' bashed neeps and wee drap o' the cratur." (Translation: sausage with mashed potatoes and turnips in a sauce with a drop of whiskey—scotch, of course.) But rest assured, most nights the menus are easy to understand, if a little boring.

The Conservatory alternative restaurant on Lido Deck has indoor/outdoor seating and serves an informal buffet breakfast and lunch. The area can become very crowded at peak lunch hours; plan to eat after 1:30 p.m. Ultra-simple fare is also available at the aptly named Alfresco Pizzaria.

Service   Throughout the ship, service by Indian stewards is very good. The Indian staff with more forthcoming personalities and better command of English has replaced the former predominating Goanese.

Facilities and Entertainment   Public rooms spread over two main decks offer a variety of atmospheres catering to class-conscious Britons. Many reflect in style and name the company's 163-year history. Entertainment includes classical music in the elegant Curzon Room, cabaret shows in the Pacific Lounge, the large production show in Theatre Royal, and Harlequins, the disco.

In addition, there is the Lord's Tavern, the cricket-themed on-board "pub"; the living room–like Anderson Lounge (named for a P&O founder), for after-dinner coffee and drinks; a cinema for films and lectures; and the spacious Crow's Nest observation bar and lounge, with wraparound windows and a trio playing dance music before and after dinner. The Monte Carlo Casino is very small compared with those on big ships sailing the Caribbean.

Activities and Diversions   The elaborate program of activities ranges from games such as bingo to arts, crafts, bridge, and dance classes; classical music; quizzes; elaborate shows; and cabaret. Port lecturers are excellent—very knowledgeable, but generally with a dry, British sense of humor. They wouldn't dream of giving the shopping sales pitches typical on many Caribbean cruise ships. The comfortable library is supplied by Ocean Books, supplier to the *QE2,* among others.

Sports, Fitness, and Beauty   The *Oriana* has acres of open deck and activities for enjoying it, including deck tennis, deck quoits, shuffleboard, golf nets, and trapshooting. Cricket matches between passengers and officers are popular. Adult and children's pool games are a major spectacle, watched by passengers on the wraparound mezzanine. One of two adult pools is a generous 42 feet long. Passengers take daily walks on a wide promenade sprinkled with deck chairs shaded by lifeboats. A large spa offers aerobics, a gym, Jacuzzis, sauna, massage, beauty and therapy rooms, and a hair salon.

Children's Facilities P&O's children's program is highly praised. Youngsters and teens have separate, supervised spaces with well-designed programs. Children have their own pool and lido area, and they eat at an early sitting, with or without their parents. A staffed night nursery is available.

Postscript Although *Oriana* is new, she operates in the P&O tradition. But Americans who like the British style or are turned off by the glitz, loud music, and constant commotion of today's megaliners will enjoy this ship. They're likely to find that about 10 percent of passengers are Americans of similar sentiment.

Victoria	Quality ⑤	Value B
Registry: Britain	Length: 660 feet	Beam: 87 feet
Cabins: 379	Draft: 28 feet	Speed: 21.5 knots
Maximum Passengers:	Passenger Decks: 7	Elevators: 4
746	Crew: 436	Space Ratio: 38.2

The Ship The *Victoria* (formerly *Sea Princess*) was the last liner built for the now-defunct Swedish American Line. When P&O bought her in 1978, more cabins were added to help revenues, and one funnel was removed, spoiling her handsome profile. After several years of making an annual around-the-world cruise from Southampton, the *Victoria* was moved to the Mediterranean when *Oriana* arrived in 1995.

The *Victoria* is lovely, inside and out. She retained much of her fine Scandinavian design and Scottish workmanship in public rooms, which also display maritime artwork spotlighting P&O's history. Wood paneling is used all over the ship.

Itineraries See Appendix B.

Cabins Her original cabins are spacious and nearly all outside. Newer cabins are more functional; some are inside. In a $6 million face-lift in 1997, all cabins received new furnishings, televisions, and personal safes, and bathrooms were renovated.

All cabins have televisions, radios, and phones. Original cabins are much better designed and appointed than newer ones. For instance, they have small foyers and sitting areas. Many cabins, including some singles, have bathtubs. The premier AA category cabins on A Deck are named after famous P&O liners.

Specifications   370 cabins, 84 inside, 286 outside; 22 singles (inside and outside). Cabin size 138–467 square feet. Beds aren't movable. Cabins A17, A96, A97, B16, B17, B68, B117, and B118 are wheelchair-accessible.

Dining   In the recent renovations, the Coral Dining Room, the main venue, was reconfigured to accommodate more passengers and offer more tables for two. The room's glass panels featuring classic ships were re-engraved. The lido buffet received a sail-like canopy reminiscent of *Oriana*'s Lords Tavern, and all-new buffet areas were installed to improve passenger flow and service.

The dining room has two sittings for three meals. The food is mostly British fare. The best choices are soups, roasts, lunchtime curry, cheese board, and desserts. Americans will find the portions smaller than on most ships, but the British often choose five to seven courses. Salads and vegetables are only fair, and pasta variety is lacking.

Service   Stewards are British, European (many living in Britain), or Indians, and service is formal and generally quite good. Britons don't demand much extra service; your requests may be met with reserve. Nearly all passengers take morning coffee or tea; that means being awakened at 7–7:30 a.m. The service, by Indians, is good. Many officers host tables at dinner.

Facilities and Entertainment   The ship has several good dance bands, good lounge entertainment, excellent classical pianists, and cabaret acts. Starlight Lounge is a wonderful split-level nightclub. The casino has blackjack, roulette, slots, and a craps table.

The Carib Lounge has been refurbished, and the adjoining pool area was redecked and given an improved stage area. Other changes include new carpets in all corridors, redesign of the beauty salon, galley and air-conditioning renovations, and an environmentally friendly dry cleaning machine.

Activities and Diversions   Daytime entertainment runs from bingo to some of cruising's best port lectures. Excellent instruction in bridge, arts, crafts, and dance is offered. On longer voyages, passengers' artwork is displayed. Theaters show full-length films, travel documentaries, and slides. The passengers-officers cricket match is *the* sporting event of the voyage.

Sports, Fitness, and Beauty   Adult and children's games are offered at the outdoor pool. Deck quoits are popular, as are Ping-Pong and shuffleboard. All have organized competitions. Deck chairs go fast on days of warm-weather cruising.

Beauty salons are professionally operated. Exercise classes are popular, but the gym lacks the sophistication of those on newer ships. Britons love to walk, and they do so in droves after breakfast. *Victoria,* designed for North Atlantic sailings, also has an indoor pool and sauna.

Children's Facilities   Excellent facilities, activities, and supervision by matrons are provided for children. The more children, the more fun it is at playroom activities, the pool, the deck games, and Coketail parties, one of which the captain hosts. An early dinner sitting is available. A children's tea and teen programs are offered.

Shore Excursions   Excursions are well organized and include both standard and unusual activities. Highly informed port lecturers are not shopping promoters. Several have been with the company for many years. Local guides vary. Excursions are fairly priced.

Theme Cruises   Theme cruises are offered occasionally. Bridge is probably the most popular, although a noted astronomer or show personality may appear.

Arcadia	Quality ❺	Value C
Registry: Liberia	Length: 811 feet	Beam: 105 feet
Cabins: 748	Draft: 27 feet	Speed: 21.5 knots
Maximum Passengers:	Passenger Decks: 11	Elevators: 9
1,475	Crew: 650	Space Ratio: 43

The Ship   After Princess and Sitmar cruise lines merged in 1988, Sitmar's *Fair Majesty,* then under construction, was renamed *Star Princess* and launched as a Princess ship. In late 1997, she moved to P&O Cruises and was renamed *Arcadia* and given some features to give her more the ambience of a classic oceanliner than the dazzle of superliners of the 1980s.

Passengers are introduced to the spacious lady in the Garden Court, a three-story balconied atrium with a kinetic, stainless-steel mobile by California artist George Baker. The enormous, computer-controlled sculpture is only part of the ship's million-dollar, museum-quality contemporary art collection.

From the Garden Court's lower deck, a wide spiral stairway with brass-trimmed glass balustrades ascends to decks offering bars, cafes, lounges, a casino, a glittering shopping arcade, and the Century bar. Music from a white grand piano on the first landing of the stairs sets the tone.

Equally dazzling is the circular Windows on the World observation and entertainment lounge above the bridge. Eighty feet in diameter, the room has floor-to-ceiling windows with 270-degree panoramas. In the evening, it becomes a nightclub, with cabaret entertainment and dancing

Itineraries   See Appendix B.

Cabins   *Arcadia*'s standard cabins are among the largest on any ship in its price range. Two thirds are outside. They are on 6 of the 11 decks in 17 categories and 4 types: inside and outside doubles (with large windows), minisuites with veranda, and suites with verandas.

All have direct-dial telephone, safe, refrigerator, hair dryer, walk-in closet, separate dressing area, key card for door, color television with CNN, and four-channel radio. Twin beds convert to queens.

Specifications   165 inside, 560 outside cabins (including 38 mini-suites and 12 suites with private balconies). Standard dimensions, 188 square feet. 598 cabins with 2 twins that convert to queens; 64 singles; 36 cabins with third and fourth berths; 8 wheelchair-accessible.

Dining   The main dining room, decorated in rich reds and wood, has a waterfall at its entrance. It's divided into nooks, with tables for two to ten, and offers two seatings for three meals.

Menus are similar to those on other P&O vessels. They're posted in bars and around the ship. Course selections are ample. Portion size will seem small to some Americans; Britons eat more courses, but less in each.

Other options include a casual indoor/outdoor buffet restaurant for breakfast and lunch and a pizzeria serving made-to-order pizzas all day; both are on the Lido Deck, convenient to swimming pools. The patisserie on a lower deck has fresh pastries and specialty coffees; in the evening, it's a bar with a dance band.

Facilities and Entertainment   Revues are presented in a two-level show-room on the Promenade Deck. The casino has blackjack, craps, roulette, and slot machines. The Oval, a small cricket-themed pub, offers live music and dancing. A lounge on Sun Deck hosts daytime activities and late-night disco. Bridge and other games are played in the card and game rooms, and readers gravitate to the library. One flight down, the shopping arcade opens onto the atrium's third deck. The theater screens current and classic films and functions as a conference center.

Of the two pools on Lido Deck, one has a swim-up bar, and the other has a waterfall and four whirlpools. On Sun Deck are an outdoor running track (one sixth of a mile), paddle tennis, deck cricket, and deck quoits. The fitness center below has a gym with exercise equipment, an aerobics area, a beauty/barber shop, and sauna and massage rooms.

Children's Facilities The youth and teen activities centers, open daily, include a play room, small swimming pool, video games, jukebox, television, game tables, nursery, and teen room.

Postscript Readers planning a cruise on *Arcadia* should review the entire P&O Cruises section for a full picture of the cruise experience the line offers.

Aurora	**(Preview)**	
Registry: Britain	Length: 886 feet	Beam: 106 feet
Cabins: 934	Draft: 26 feet	Speed: 24 knots
Maximum Passengers:	Passenger Decks: 10	Elevators: 10
1,850	Crew: 417	Space Ratio: 41.1

The Ship *Oriana*'s near twin, *Aurora*, made her debut in early 2000, sailing from the United Kingdom. *Aurora* has new features, modifications, and some "firsts" for a ship dedicated primarily to the British market, including two-deck penthouse suites, four decks of cabins with balconies, and interconnecting family cabins.

Aurora also has P&O's first 24-hour bistro-style restaurant, coffee and chocolate bar, champagne bar, tea- and coffee-making facilities in all cabins, retractable dome over one swimming pool, and a virtual reality center. The ship's size and spaciousness allows for a range of public rooms and entertainment facilities, as well as some larger public rooms, such as restaurants, a cinema, and shops. Nonetheless, the vessel retains the intimacy of smaller ships.

Among the ship's best assets are around-the-clock dining—a first for P&O—in the bistro-style restaurant, and fast-food availability—another P&O first—in the poolside Deck Cafe.

Itineraries See Appendix B.

Cabins *Aurora* offers P&O's widest choice of cabins. They range from two-deck penthouse suites to interconnecting cabins suitable for families. Over 40 percent of cabins have a balcony, among them standard cabins. There are 120 cabins with two additional upper berths, and sofa beds are available in 50 percent of cabins, minisuites, and suites. Half of the cabins have both bathtub and shower, and all cabins have tea- and coffee-making facilities. Cabins also have a refrigerator, safe, television, direct-dial telephone, individually controlled air-conditioning, and music system. Twin beds can be converted to a queen-size bed. One two-deck penthouse has a grand piano; the other, a library. Both have upper and lower balconies; spiral staircases connect sleeping and living decks.

Specifications   934 cabins; 272 standard, 96 deluxe, 18 minisuites, 10 suites, 2 two-deck penthouse suites—all with balconies. 225 standard outside, 273 standard inside, 16 larger outside interconnecting pairs. 22 cabins for disabled passengers; some have balconies, 8 outside, 8 inside.

Dining   One of the two main restaurants has a Moorish theme, the other Egyptian. Both have grand staircase entrances and more tables for two than on P&O's other ships.

Facilities and Entertainment   Available are a West End–style theater supported by the latest production technology, a casino, and the new-concept main show lounge offering a spacious bar, large dance floor, and retractable stage. Amidships is an intimate, futuristic nightclub with small dance floor and stage. One deck above is a large concert hall/cinema showing first-run films and staging classical concerts; card and writing rooms; a library; and a business center with personal computers.

Aurora has 12 bars, including a sports bar with wide-screen television monitors, a champagne bar, and a specialty coffee and chocolate bar. The latter two are firsts on a ship designed for British passengers. A club-style bar has mahogany paneling and a fireplace. The Crow's Nest on Deck 13 is the highest bar on board and has live dance music. Other bars are near swimming pools and in lounge areas.

The focus of the ship's four-deck atrium is a waterfall and Lalique glass–style sculpture. Surrounding are shops and a Tour Office enlarged to provide a greater range of travel services. The ship also has a medical center.

Sports, Fitness, and Beauty   A pool between decks 11 and 12 has a waterfall and is surrounded by tiered decks. Another pool can be covered by a dome in inclement weather; still another is reserved for families at certain times of year. The ship has four Jacuzzis and ample deck space for sunbathing.

A netted deck area is adaptable for cricket, soccer, and tennis, and golfers can practice on the golf simulator. Deck quoits and shuffleboard also are provided.

A well-equipped gym and aerobics studio overlooks the forward pool and waterfall. The spacious area is linked by stairs to health and beauty facilities (hair salon, treatment rooms, sauna, and steam rooms).

Children's Facilities Four age-specific areas are offered. An under-age-5 playroom has an enclosed deck area with a paddling pool; 6- to 9-year olds have their own deck space, plus indoor play area; 10- to 13-year-olds area have a "den" environment with disco; and teenagers set their pace in Decibels. The virtual-reality center is for children of all ages. Cabins have baby "listening" facilities, and a night nursery is available for children under age five.

Premier Cruises

400 Challenger Road, Cape Canaveral, FL 32920
(407) 783-5061; (800) 990-7770; fax (407) 784-3138
www.premiercruises.com

Type of Ships   Renovated, midsize, classic oceanliners.

Type of Cruises   Casual, low-key family-oriented in homey surroundings on less traveled routes. Short, Bahamas cruises combined with Orlando attractions.

Cruise Line's Strengths
- itineraries
- service and crew
- friendly ambience
- children's programs
- large family cabins on some ships

Cruise Line's Shortcomings
- aging ships
- noise level on deck
- evening entertainment
- lack or limited fitness facilities on some ships

Fellow Passengers   Varies according to ship and itinerary but generally experienced travelers, seasoned cruisers, and families, ranging in age from 40s to 70s, motivated by low-key style and good value. Honeymooners, retirees or semiretired, business owners with some college education, and professionals, older couples, and loyal fans of specific ships. Moderately active, modest income, salt-of-the-earth types. Cruise ship nostalgia buffs. Typical passengers on *Big Red Boat I* are a vacationing family (adults ages 30–44) with a household income of $35,000 or more. Because "family" has several meanings, passengers range from traditional families with two children to single parents, grandparents with grandkids, and blended families with stepchildren. During school holidays, children are more numerous, but they rarely exceed 30 percent of passengers. Many passengers have

408

no children with them, and more than 5 percent are honeymooners! There are also passengers from around the world—probably the result of packaging the cruise with a Walt Disney World or Universal Studios vacation and benefiting from the worldwide fame of Orlando attractions. Other ships are on new itineraries, too new to characterize but they are meant to appeal to a family market.

Recommended For Families, couples, singles, honeymooners, retirees who want a basic, informal cruise. Those who like to cruise often, aren't highly sophisticated travelers, and prefer an unpretentious atmosphere and easy pace. First-time cruisers of modest means who want port-intensive cruises; others who have tired of crowded Caribbean ports.

Not Recommended For Swingers; party-seekers; those seeking glamorous, "in" spot ambience, luxury, exclusivity, intellectual travel, or megaliner glitter.

Cruise Areas and Seasons Bahamas, Caribbean, Mexico, year-round; New England/Canada, Alaska, summer.

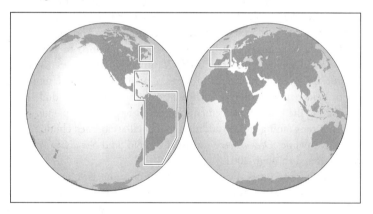

The Line Premier has been a work-in-progress for several years. Formed in 1983, pioneering family cruising with Disney World and other Orlando attractions packages, Premier, along with Seawind Cruise Line and Dolphin Cruise Line, was bought in 1997 by an investment group of Norwegian shipping executives and financial institutions, who merged the lines and their five ships under one banner, Premier Cruises. Later that year, they added Holland America Line's venerable *Rotterdam,* renaming her *Rembrandt.*

After financial woes in 1998, Premier's assets were taken over by its bondholders and the company was restructured, with Bruce Nierenberg—

one of the line's founders—in charge. His first move was to create two distinct cruise experiences—identified by ship colors: The blue fleet representing Premier's traditional cruises and offering a more adult-oriented experience; and the red fleet, easily recognized by the much-publicized *Big Red Boat,* signifying family cruising. All the ships included activities and amenities appealing to both audiences.

Then, in 2000, he moved Premier closer to its roots—the family market—by expanding its Big Red Boat brand and repositioning the ships in: New York for the Northeast, Port Canaveral and Tampa for the Southeast, and Houston for the Southwest. In addition to its traditional home in Port Canaveral, Premier says its strategy of using some relatively untested home ports is to bring the ships to where the people live, reducing air transportation costs, to generate business from new areas of the country, and to get away from the intense competition from new ships and new cruise lines in Florida.

The three vessels under the Big Red Boat brand include *BRB I* (formerly *Oceanic*), which continues her three- and four-night Bahamas itineraries from Port Canaveral with cruise/land packages for Universal Studios and Walt Disney World. *BRB II* (the newly acquired *Edinburgh Castle,* formerly the *Enrico Costa*) sails on seven-night cruises from New York to New England/Canada in summer and from Port Canaveral/Tampa to the Eastern and Western Caribbean in winter. *BRB III* (formerly *IslandBreeze*) sails from Houston on seven-night cruises to Mexico, pioneering a new cruise destination, Veracruz, and offering such pre/post excursions and a dude ranch stay. Among the ships' enhancements for family appeal is a separate, supervised children's dining area, in addition to its well-established children's program. Meanwhile, *OceanBreeze* was recently sold, and *Seawind Crown* has been chartered through 2001.

Premier Cruise Lines was the first line to position itself in Port Canaveral to tap the enormous reservoir of potential passengers among visitors to Disney World, the nation's biggest tourist attraction. The line created quality packages combining its three- and four-night cruises with Disney, painted the ship's hull bright red to present a youthful image, and ensured cruises' appeal by including something for everyone: a full-time children's program divided into five supervised, age-specific programs from tots to teens; SeaSports for fitness enthusiasts; top-notch entertainment, a casino, piano bar, and disco for night owls; champagne and double beds for newlyweds; and plenty of good food. More recently, Premier has spent millions refurbishing its ships, upgrading food and beverage services and amenities, and adding deluxe features, such as terry robes (which passengers can keep!) in suites.

The Fleet	Built/Renovated	Tonnage	Passengers
Big Red Boat I (Oceanic)	1965/1993	38,772	1,116
Big Red Boat II (Edinburgh Castle)	1966/2000	35,000	1,500
Big Red Boat III (IslandBreeze)	1961/97	31,793	1,146
SeaBreeze	1958/91	21,000	840
Rembrandt	1959/97	38,645	1,074
Seawind Crown	1961/94	24,000	764

Style   Premier offers classic cruises on vessels that feel like ships, not floating hotels. Cruise traditions blend with modern lifestyles. Although Premier's ships had different origins, most are close in size and capacity—large enough to offer a range of facilities and activities, yet small enough to create an amicable ambience.

The ships have teak decks, wide promenades, spacious cabins (but few suites), and public rooms with mellowed woods and brass. Some have partially enclosed promenade decks—refuges from bad weather or tropical sun. The dining room is on a lower deck, and a theater, health club, or disco is deep in the ship—features typical of older vessels. Most have small gyms with basic equipment and outdoor pools (*Rembrandt* has one indoors).

The ships' size helps in creating the congenial atmosphere in which passengers recognize almost everyone aboard within a few days. The pace is leisurely, the staff warm and friendly, and entertainment varied, from classical music and cabaret shows to country and western nights. (Cruise staff members double as entertainers.) Passengers can learn snorkeling and diving, participate in a fitness program, and enjoy afternoon tea.

Families with children set the rhythm on the *Big Red Boats,* cramming in as much as possible and taking full advantage of the ship's activities and facilities. The atmosphere is cheerful and fun-filled, and well after a family's normal bedtime, the energy remains high, with show lounges still buzzing and cruisers of all ages piling their plates at the midnight buffet.

Distinctive Features   Children's programs, special prices on shore excursions; single-parent, grandparent, family-reunion packages; snorkeling/diving programs. Precruise purchase of shore excursions.

	HIGHEST	LOWEST	AVERAGE
PER DIEM	$329	$143	$226

The above per diems are calculated from the cruise line's non-discounted *cruise only* fares on standard accommodations. Per diems vary by season, by cabin, and by cruise areas.

412   Part Two: Cruise Lines and Their Ships

Rates   Port charges included in fares.

Special Fares and Discounts   Early-bird discounts; savings on two consecutive cruises. Senior discounts for age 55 and older and one companion in cabin categories C–H. Family-reunion discounts for five or more people.

- Children's Fare: Third/fourth person rates. Kids Vacation Free allows two children, ages 2–17, to sail free when accompanied by two full-fare adults. Packages also include free hotel stay and theme park admissions. Children ages 2–9 receive special low fare.
- Single Supplement: 125–200 percent of double-occupancy rates, depending on cabin category.

Packages
- Air/Sea: Yes.
- Others: Honeymoon, wedding, anniversary.
- Pre/Post: *Big Red Boat* has packages combining the cruise with Walt Disney World Resort; airfare; admission to the Disney parks; Spaceport USA tour, Astronaut Hall of Fame, or Splendid China admission; rental car with unlimited mileage; discounts at Disney Village hotels and marketplace; and kids 12 and younger eat free with one paying adult per child at participating restaurants. Other land packages combine Central Florida attractions with cruises.

Past Passengers   The newly created Encore Club rewards past passengers based on the number of sailing nights accrued with the line on four levels: Bronze, 2–29 sailing nights; Silver, 30–59 nights; Gold, 60–99 nights; and Platinum, 100 or more nights. Members of all levels receive a $50 On-Board coupon booklet, one per cabin, and an invitation to a members-only cocktail party. Rewards range from fruit baskets and wine to two-category cabin upgrades and VIP seating at the officers' table for dinner.

The Last Word   Since 1997, Premier has gone from one ship sailing to the Bahamas to a fleet of seven ships and is sailing out of six ports coast to coast. The line's main task has been to clarify its image. Its main focus is now family travel. Its cruises—comfortable, easy-paced, and economical—are suitable for all ages. There are no pretensions, no surprises. Nonetheless, the ships are showing their age, and to promote them requires constant vigilance. So long as you understand these are not deluxe cruises and you do not have unrealistic expectations, you will get value for your money and a pleasant cruise.

Seawind Crown is under charter through 2001 and has not been included in this edition.

PREMIER CRUISES STANDARD FEATURES

Officers Mostly Greek; *Rembrandt,* international

Staff Dining, Cabin/International; Cruise/American and European.

Dining Facilities One main dining room, two seatings for breakfast, lunch, and dinner; assigned tables for dinner; midnight buffet; lido restaurant for breakfast, lunch, and some late buffets. *Rembrandt* two dining rooms. *BRB I,* adults-only options; children's menu.

Special Diets Low-fat, low-cholesterol entrees available; low-salt, kosher, vegetarian on request one month in advance.

Room Service 24 hours, limited menu; *Rembrandt,* 10 a.m.–10 p.m.

Dress Code Casual by day; casual or informal in evenings; jacket and tie for some evenings; formal suggested (not required) for captain's gala.

Cabin Amenities Telephone, radio, television, hair dryers, small refrigerators, robes in suites.

Electrical Outlets 110 AC; *BRB I,* 220 AC; passengers must bring adapters to use hair curlers and curling irons.

Wheelchair Access Some cabins available. *Rembrandt, BRB I* provide ramps. *BRB I* cabins with wide bathroom doors, bathtubs with grab bar. *BRB II,* 4 cabins.

Recreation and Entertainment Casino, disco, nightclub, bars, show lounge with nightly entertainment, dance classes, horse racing, games, arts and crafts, bingo, singles parties, wine tasting, library, cinema, card room, video game rooms, masquerades.

Sports and Other Activities Outdoor pool (three on *BRB III*), *BRB I,* retractable glass dome; *Rembrandt,* one indoor and one outdoor; wraparound promenade, whirlpools (except *BRB III*); shuffleboard, skeet shooting, Ping-Pong; snorkel/scuba program.

Beauty and Fitness Beauty/barber shop, massage, sauna, exercise room with equipment, exercise classes.

Other Facilities Boutique, medical, laundry services. Conference room (*BRB I, Rembrandt*); chapel on some ships.

Children's Facilities Year-round youth counselors and age-specific programs on four ships; children's menu. See text for more information.

Theme Cruises Jazz, country and western, 1950s on some ships.

Smoking Designated public areas; no smoking in dining room.

Premier Suggested Tipping Per person per day, cabin steward, $3.50; waiter, $3.50; busboy, $1.75; maitre d'hôtel, $5 per cruise.

Credit Cards For cruise payment, cruise/package, and on board: American Express, MasterCard, Discover, Visa.

Rembrandt	Quality ❼	Value A
Registry: Bahamas	Length: 748 feet	Beam: 94 feet
Cabins: 575	Draft: 29.8 feet	Speed: 20 knots
Maximum Passengers: 1,074	Passenger Decks: 10	Elevators: 8
	Crew: 550	Space Ratio: 35

The Ship   Completed in 1959, toward the sunset of the transatlantic golden era, *Rembrandt* was rebuilt in 1969 and renovated in 1989. After Premier acquired the *Rotterdam* in autumn 1997, it renamed her *Rembrandt* in recognition of the ship's Dutch heritage. She embodies the elegance of a grand oceanliner with rich interiors, big public rooms, sweeping staircases, cozy bars, and multimillion-dollar art.

Public rooms are essentially the same as the day the ship was launched. Recent renovations freshened the original Art Deco designs while keeping the style and character intact. Improvements include upgrading of many bathrooms and systems for telephone and public address, plumbing, and air-conditioning.

One of the most interesting holdovers from her oceanliner days is the central stairway—two parallel flights of stairs with baffles—designed to segregate the ship's first and tourist classes. The stairway remains, although it hasn't been used since 1971. The design does give the ship a spacious main stairway and more than the usual number of elevators amidships.

Itineraries   See Appendix B.

Cabins   *Rembrandt* has 11 categories of cabins, ranging from small to spacious with varied layouts—typical of ships built in the age of two-class vessels. Cabins retain their built-in dressing tables with lighted mirrors and other wood furnishings, such as teak and mahogany paneling and cabinetry. Some cabins have a flip-down tray on the wall beside the bed to hold drinks or food while you watch television. In the most recent renovations, cabins were brightened with new floral fabrics, and double beds replaced upper and lower berths in 61 cabins. Storage space is generous.

Almost every cabin has a full-size bathtub. Nicer-than-average amenities include full-size bottles of shampoo, conditioner, and plenty of soap, presented in a souvenir case. Cabin television includes CNN and three first-run movies daily. Air-conditioning doesn't seem to work properly in cabins or most public areas. In fact, the only really cool room is the casino. The deck plan notes cabins on Sun and Boat Decks with partially obstructed views.

Specifications 268 inside, 295 outside cabins, 12 suites; and some adjoining cabins. Dimensions range from 112 to 379 square feet. Standard cabins have twin or double beds; some have third and fourth berths. 32 singles (28 outside).

Dining The two spacious dining rooms, Odyssey and LaFontaine, have domed ceilings that span two decks. The setting is elegant. Colorful Delft ceramic plaques line the walls—in Odyssey, they depict Greek myths, and in LaFontaine, they're scenes from Aesop's *Fables*. Table separation damps conversation spillover, and the room's acoustics allow you to hear the person across from you without straining.

Menus offer varied dinner choices, including two appetizers, two soups, salad, five entrees, three desserts, and ice cream, along with light fare, vegetarian, and sugar-free dessert selections. Food ranged from mediocre to above average and bland to tasty. Nothing was exotic. Some food was overcooked and the portions small, but if a passenger complained about quality or quantity of food, it was quickly replaced. Presentation does get high marks.

Breakfast and lunch buffets in the light and bright Lido Restaurant feature a variety of food, from salads to lamb chops. A nice feature is the outdoor grill serving burgers, hot dogs, steak, pork chops, fries, and baked potatoes every afternoon. A midnight buffet is offered nightly. Continental breakfast is available en suite from 7 to 10 a.m. Room service is available from 10 a.m. to 10 p.m. The menus offer sandwiches, salads, and soups. Afternoon tea is a favorite; formal and informal versions are scheduled. At the informal tea, a variety of teas—hot and cold—plus sandwiches and cookies are served. The twice-weekly formal tea is not to be missed. Held in the luxurious Ritz Carlton Lounge with music playing softly in the background, it's possibly the most elegant tea service on a ship. White-gloved waiters serve teas, canapés, and desserts. Passengers wearing shorts will be turned away from the formal tea, but slacks are acceptable.

Service *Rembrandt* excels in service. Dining rooms were set to perfection, and an efficient and cheery wait staff never failed to greet passengers. Each server quickly learned passengers' preferences; many subsequently were met without asking. Cabin service is above average. In addition to twice-daily attending, stewards check throughout the day to see if more ice or fresh towels are needed. Room service, lax on some ships, was delivered in 10 to 15 minutes. Salads were crisp, soups piping hot, and sandwiches freshly made. Guests marvel at the staff's and crew's performance. On a recent cruise, a couple mentioned at the purser's desk that their cabin was smaller than they expected, though they were sailing at a deeply discounted rate. He noted their stateroom number and within an hour moved them to a much larger cabin.

Facilities and Entertainment   The Queen's Lounge showroom is the largest of the ship's seven lounges. The Ritz Carlton Lounge, with a balcony and bar, is an elegant setting for dancing and late-night cabaret. Painstakingly restored in 1989, it has a dramatic, 90-foot-high wraparound mural depicting an Aegean seascape in cool blues. Another dramatic setting for after dinner is the top-deck Sky Room, dressed in sophisticated lavenders and blues, where a pianist plays nightly. Entertainment includes music in lounges and on deck at times throughout the day and a Las Vegas–style revue at night in the theater. Acts are likely to be a dance troupe, a comedian, an illusionist, and singers. The disco operates from 11 p.m. to the wee hours.

Activities and Diversions   The cruise starts with a minitour of the ship offered every half hour by cruise staff. The day's program might include karaoke, bridge tours, arts and crafts, parlor games, bridge, pool games, bingo, trivia, golf lessons, shuffleboard, dance lessons, an art auction, a talent show, a Ping-Pong or darts tournament, a wine seminar, makeup tips, horse races, a singles party, a repeaters party, ice carving demonstrations, a scavenger hunt, lectures on art and other topics, and movies. Shops sell items ranging from duty-free liquor to logo gifts.

Sports, Fitness, and Beauty   Fitness and beauty programs are a priority, and many are available. A full-service beauty salon is available. The small fitness area has treadmills, bicycles, stair climbers, and saunas. The staff includes a personal trainer who will organize a personal fitness program for you to take home. Prices are reasonable and, in some cases, much less then you might pay elsewhere. For example, a one-hour session with a personal trainer is $35; a full-body massage, $70; and a foot-and-ankle massage, $20. The "Sea Fit" program offers group exercise. Participation in low-impact activities, such as water aerobics, stretching, or walking, earns tokens redeemable for gifts at cruise's end. The ship has a large outdoor pool and a huge indoor one, originally used by first-class passengers. The favorite place to stroll or snooze is the wide, wraparound Promenade Deck, lined with old-fashioned wooden steamer chairs. Part of the deck rounding the bow is enclosed with glass windows that open. Practice tennis and shuffleboard courts are topside.

Children's Facilities   "Cruisin' Kids" offers supervised activities daily, 9 a.m.–10 p.m. A list is provided during boarding. There's a "Kids Room." Group babysitting is available from 9 p.m. to 2 a.m. for a fee.

Postscript   *Rembrandt* appeals most to traditionalists who remember—
and those who imagine—the era of grand oceanliners. Yet, anyone who
appreciates style and nostalgia will enjoy her. The ship epitomizes tradition, and even at her age, she remains outstanding, proving timeless grace
and reason for Premier to name her its flagship.

Big Red Boat I (Oceanic) Quality ❹   Value A

Registry: Bahamas	Length: 782 feet	Beam: 96 feet
Cabins: 590	Draft: 28 feet	Speed: 28 knots
Maximum Passengers:	Passenger Decks: 3	Elevators: None
1,609	Crew: 565	Space Ratio: 25

The Ship   The *Big Red Boat I* has the sleek lines of a classic liner and
structural solidness absent from many of today's glitzy ships. Reminders of
the past include traditional round portholes, mosaic art in stairwells, and
teak decks. Doors to public rest rooms are so heavy that children need help
opening them. The *BRB I* was given a major face-lift in 1994. Decor—
colorful, but not garish—is accented by mirrors and twinkling lights. The
Lounge Deck, the setting for most entertainment, often swarms with people en route to a show, the gift shop, the tour desk, or the casino. Unfortunately, passengers must transit the noisy, crowded Lucky Star Casino to
other public areas. Bars and lounges offer quiet nooks. Public rooms are
comfortable, well appointed, and generally large enough to handle the
crowds. But evening shows in the Broadway Showroom fill quickly on
capacity cruises.

The four-night *BRB I* cruise includes a day at sea, allowing passengers
to enjoy the ship. The more hectic three-night itinerary spends a high percentage of time in port.

Itineraries   See Appendix B.

Cabins   Premier has the largest cabins available on three- and four-night
Bahamas cruises. Because it targets families, the *BRB I* has an unusual
number of cabins suitable for four or five passengers. A cabin sleeping five
has a double bed, a convertible bed, and two upper berths. All cabins have
a television with nine channels, including current movies. Upper-grade
cabins are unusually roomy. Apartment suites (for up to five people) on the
exclusive top deck offer balconies and king-size beds.

Specifications 329 inside cabins, 261 outside; 65 suites, 8 with verandas. Dimensions 140–455 square feet. 337 cabins with 2 lower beds (59 triples; 99 quads); 1 cabin with double bed; 2 cabins with queen and 101 with double take third; 68 cabins take up to four; 73 cabins take up to five; 8 suites with king accommodate third and fourth persons.

Dining Food generally compares with a shore-side family restaurant, but is served with cruise ship flair. Menus brim with turkey, chicken, prime rib, and burgers. French Night offers escargots, lobster bisque, roast duckling in orange sauce, and Châteaubriand. Caribbean Night brings out Jamaican jerked pork with black beans and plantains, lobster tail served with lime butter, and cream of coconut soup. America the Beautiful and Italian theme nights also lend festive notes to the Seven Continents Restaurant.

Mighty Healthy Platter options include broiled chicken, fresh fruit and vegetables, yogurt, and a bran muffin. Youngsters can order from the main menu or a children's menu with peanut butter and jelly, pizza, and hot dogs. Waiters are especially attentive to children. Because children are numerous, the dining room is noisy, particularly at the 6 p.m. seating. Once each cruise, a kids-only dinner with entertainment is served in the Riviera Pool area, leaving parents free to dine alone.

Pool Deck breakfast and lunch buffets are a casual alternative to the main dining room. Coffee, lemonade, and juice machines are available all day. Make your own sundae every afternoon in Big Dipper Ice Cream Parlor, or chase hunger with afternoon tea, cocktail-hour and late-night snacks in some lounges, and a lavish midnight buffet in the dining room.

Service The staff is friendly, professional, and geared to helping families enjoy their vacation. The smooth-running operation is blessed with top-notch personnel, from American and British youth counselors to European, Asian, and Caribbean waiters.

Facilities and Entertainment The Broadway Showroom presents musical revues, comedy, and magic suitable for the entire family. Posts and people's heads interrupt sight lines in many sections. Late-night shows in the cabaret invite audience participation. Performers also appear in the intimate Tropicana Piano Bar, Heroes and Legends Pub, and Lucky Star Lounge. The Star Fighter Arcade offers video games, and Lucky Star Casino has blackjack, roulette, and slot machines. (Children younger than age 18 aren't allowed to gamble.) Next to the casino are the Milky Way Shops, selling beachwear, souvenirs, and duty-free goods. The bilevel Hollywood Theater presents first-run movies and the innovative Voyages of Discovery, multimedia educational presentations on underwater life, astronomy, Caribbean history, and great ships.

Activities and Diversions   Although the ship is known for its ambitious children's program, activities for adults abound. Choices might include a wine-tasting seminar, trivia quiz, art auction, nutrition lecture, poker lessons, bingo, horse racing, trapshooting, or Family Feud tune-guessing game. A party is held for singles, including single parents. Passengers can perform at karaoke sessions and a talent show.

Sports, Fitness, and Beauty   A sliding glass roof shelters the Sun Deck pool area on overcast days and at night. (On some days, the enclosure can be hot and stuffy.) The ship offers an outdoor whirlpool, supervised children's pool, and jogging track overlooking the Pool Deck. SeaSport fitness program offers aerobics classes, water aerobics, and a gym with Nautilus, Universal, and Lifecycle equipment. In conjunction with Premier's popular Splashdown scuba diving outings in the Bahamas, passengers can take on-board scuba classes with trained instructors. The pricey Steiner Beauty and Fitness Salon offers hair styling, facials, massages, and slimming and toning treatments.

Children's Facilities   *BRB I* goes all out to keep young cruisers busy from morning to bedtime. On embarkation, children receive an agenda of planned activities in five age groups. Full-time counselors are augmented by interns during summer. All full-time counselors have degrees in education, nursing, or related fields; a few are certified British nannies. Kids spend much of their time in Pluto's Playhouse, a supervised recreational center; a kids-only pool is outside the door. Children from two to four years old are enrolled in the First Mates program, which often meets in the Astro Room play area. Those ages five to ten stay in the Children's Center, where activities include stories, sing-alongs, treasure hunts, cartoons, and magic shows. Parents must sign their children in and out of the center.

Activities for two older groups take place in Star Fighter Arcade and the Space Station Teen Center, where video games line one wall. Navigators (ages 11–13) participate in Ping-Pong tournaments, pool games, autograph hunts, and such games as Pictionary and Outburst. Teen Cruisers (ages 14–17) enjoy dances, karaoke, a Midnight Madness party, and the Dating Game. A party featuring a juggler, magician, and comic characters is arranged for younger children.

Child care for ages 2–12 is available after supervised activities end. Between 10 p.m. and 2 a.m., the cost is $5 per hour for one child and an additional $3 per hour for each additional child. Thus, 24-hour child care is available. After the cruise, children can remain in touch with favorite counselors by e-mailing kids@premiercruises.com.

Shore Excursions The line's cruise brochure describes shore excursions and prices. Premier is among the few cruise lines that enable passengers to buy shore excursions before the cruise through their travel agent. During the overnight call in Nassau, Dolphin Encounter is available on Salt Cay, an uninhabited island also known as Blue Lagoon. Buffet lunch is served, and up to five hours are allowed for water sports or snoozing in hammocks strung between the palms. Youth counselors organize games.

Postscript A *Big Red Boat* cruise, combined with a visit to Walt Disney World, may be the perfect family vacation. The children's programs keep kids entertained while mom and dad relax or participate in adult activities. The schedule also gives parents quality time with their children. On the other hand, plenty of people without children enjoy these cruises thoroughly. The ship is showing its age and the food is only average, but as one passenger said, "My kids were having such a great time, it hardly mattered."

Big Red Boat II (Preview)
(Edinburgh Castle)

Registry: Bahamas	Length: 713 feet	Beam: 96 feet
Cabins: 484	Draft: 29 feet	Speed: 24 knots
Maximum Passengers:	Passenger Decks: 9	Elevators: 4
1,500	Crew: 568	Space Ratio: NA

The Ship Built in 1966 as the *Eugenio C,* the flagship of Costa Cruises, she was extensively renovated in 1988. After she was sold to a British company in the mid 1990s, she became the *Edinburgh Castle,* and had a brief run for Manhattan Cruises, a short-lived effort in 1998 to bring shipboard gambling to New York City. More recently, she sailed from Britain for Direct Cruises, a local company. Prior to her entering service for Premier Cruises, she was renovated and given her new name.

The ship has many lounges, large and small, and often with floor to ceiling windows providing a sunny and airy atmosphere and sea views throughout the ship. It has one of the largest dining rooms of any ship its size, but its layout, in effect, divides it into three sections.

There is a showroom for nightly entertainment, theater for showing movies, casino, and an Internet cafe. The ship has a beauty salon, sundry shop, gift shop, and medical facility. There are two swimming pools and a fitness center.

The cabins cover a wide range; most are roomy, including some for up to six people, with ample storage space. There are six suites and four wheelchair-designated cabins; there are also some singles. All cabins have television and telephones and are furnished with either two lower beds or double bed, two lowers and two upper berths, queens, and kings.

The children's facilities include play rooms divided by age and the same program for five separate age groups as available on *Big Red Boat I.*

Big Red Boat III (Island Breeze)

Quality ⑤ **Value A**

Registry: Bahamas	Length: 760 feet	Beam: 90 feet
Cabins: 580	Draft: 32 feet	Speed: 22 knots
Maximum Passengers:	Passenger Decks: 8	Elevators: 4
1,146	Crew: 612	Space Ratio: 33

The Ship   At one time, the *Big Red Boat III* was the world's sixth-largest passenger ship. Now, megaliners dwarf it. But many people prefer the ship's smaller size and feeling of a real ship.

Completed in 1961 by Union-Castle Line as a one-class mail ship that ran between England and South Africa, she was bought by Carnival in 1977 and rebuilt for Caribbean cruising. In 1996, she was acquired by Dolphin Cruise Line and renamed. Despite her age, the ship is in good condition after a $10 million refurbishing in 1997.

BRB III has one dining room, five bars and lounges, a show lounge, a cinema, and a spa.

Itineraries   See Appendix B.

Cabins   Eleven categories range from suites to upper/lower berth cabins. Most have twin beds, bedside lights, chair, two large chests of drawers, two full-size closets, telephone, and radio, but no television. Bathrooms have showers.

Specifications   308 inside cabins, 272 outside. Standard dimensions, 132 square feet. 352 with twins; 146 queens; 39 inside, 5 outside, upper/lower berths; 14 singles. No wheelchair-accessible.

Dining   Columns and partitions divide the expansive Grand Dining Room into a series of rooms. Breakfast and lunch are usually open seatings; dinner has assigned seating at tables for two to eight persons. Food gets mixed reviews, but service is lauded. Dinner menus are typical of Premier, offering three appetizers; three soups; two salads; four fish, meat, pasta, and game entrees; three desserts (including one diabetic); and assorted cheese, ice creams, and sherbets. Spa selections and a children's menu are available.

Buffet breakfast and lunch—not elaborate, but adequate—are available at the Capri Bar and Grill by the top-deck swimming pool, and the midnight buffet served at 11 p.m. in the Cordoba Lounge is fancy and extensive. Afternoon tea is served in the Capri Bar.

Service   The hardworking, helpful, and cheerful international crew consistently receives high marks for service and eagerness to please.

Facilities and Entertainment   All entertainment facilities are on the Promenade Deck, which in spite of its name, doesn't encircle the ship. The Piccadilly Theatre showroom stages shows nightly. Lounges and the disco offer entertainment and dance music. Wooden panels separate The Pub from the casino, giving the lounge the air of a cozy club—a great place for late-night beverages and sing-alongs. A theater shows movies.

Activities and Diversions   Passengers relax in solitude or join games on the plentiful deck space. The daily program offers the usual aerobics, contests, port talks, swimming pool games, bingo, Ping-Pong, and shuffleboard. A video arcade is available. The homey library and larger Portofino Lounge are sometimes used for meetings.

Sports, Fitness, and Beauty   The ship has three swimming pools, a massage room, a sauna, and a beauty salon. The gym, with four treadmills and other equipment, looks into the bottom half of the swimming pool.

Children's Facilities   The supervised children's program is billed as both learning and play experience. Youth counselors are aboard for every cruise; their ranks increase during summer and holidays. There's no babysitting service.

SeaBreeze	Quality ❸	Value A
Registry: Panama	Length: 605 feet	Beam: 79 feet
Cabins: 423	Draft: 29 feet	Speed: 21 knots
Maximum Passengers:	Passenger Decks: 9	Elevators: 42
1,150	Crew: 400	Space Ratio: 26

The Ship   Extensively renovated and well maintained, *SeaBreeze* belies its age. Built in 1958 as Costa's transatlantic flagship *Federico C, SeaBreeze* was Premier's *Star/Ship Royale* before being acquired by Dolphin in 1989. The ship's appeal starts with its sleek silhouette. At the stern, four sun decks rise successively to offer ample sunning space. Happily, outdoor dining is offered on two of the decks. Inside, public rooms have tasteful decor in eye-catching colors with reflective metal ceilings, mirrored pillars, and plants. On both ships, elevators access all but the top deck and lowest, which houses the disco. The atmosphere is casual, except for two gala nights when formal attire is requested.

Itineraries   See Appendix B.

Cabins   *SeaBreeze* has 11 categories of cabins—all comfortable, with modern decor in pastels and colorful prints. Standard rooms are compact with functional storage space. Spacious upper-level cabins have sitting areas, extra storage, queen beds, and tubs. On both ships, standard cabins have phones, radios, and baths with showers, but no television.

   Specifications   161 inside cabins, 263 outside; 7 suites. Standard dimensions unavailable. 93 inside, 154 outside with twin beds; 53 inside, 90 outside with double bed; 32 family cabins; 24 upper/ lower berths; 2 singles. No wheelchair-accessible cabins.

Dining   The ship's main dining room is on a lower deck. Breakfast and lunch seatings are mostly open; dinner is assigned. Tables accommodate two to ten people. Food is good, sometimes very good, and well presented—features outstanding in this price range. Dinner is accompanied by live piano music and occasional performances by a singing maître d'hôtel and dancing waiters. Themed dinners—French Night, Italian Night, and Caribbean Night—offer appropriate menus and costumed waiters. Breakfast and lunch buffets are in an indoor-outdoor setting and a midnight buffet in *SeaBreeze*'s Bacchanalia Restaurant. Room service is limited to continental breakfast.

Service   Service is the ship's best feature. Cruise staff creates a convivial atmosphere, and the friendly, courteous international crew delivers very good to excellent service, despite occasional language lapses.

Facilities and Entertainment   *SeaBreeze* offers Las Vegas–style entertainment and variety shows in its dazzling Carmen Lounge. By day, the room has good natural light and is usually a quiet corner for relaxing indoors. The piano bar, photo gallery, and gift shops, separate the show lounge from the lively casino, which offers slots, blackjack, craps, and roulette. A small disco plus other lounge/bars provide music nightly.

Activities and Diversions   Daily activities are cruise-ship standards: quizzes and games, dance classes, bridge tournaments, fashion show, perfume seminar, mileage pool, bridge tours, skeet shooting, basketball, horse racing, bingo, service club meetings, golf driving, passenger talent shows, masquerade parties, ice-carving and food demonstrations, and occasional concerts.

During a week's cruise, seven films are shown, each usually four times per day, in the large theater (available as a meeting room). The library is limited; if you plan to read, bring your own books. There are video game and card rooms. Boutiques offer daily specials.

Sports, Fitness, and Beauty   *SeaBreeze* offers four decks for sitting and sunning and a pool, but its best feature is a wide promenade encircling the ship (six laps equal one mile). Shaded deck chairs provide an alternative to sunbathing. Basketball, shuffleboard, Ping-Pong, and pool games are offered.

The ship has a beauty/barber shop, massage rooms, whirlpools, morning toning, stretch and aerobic sessions, and small gym with stationary bikes, rowing machines, and weights.

SeaBreeze, along with other *Big Red Boats* has a Discover Scuba Diving program, a noncertification package developed by PADI (Professional Association of Diving Instructors). Included are three hours of classroom instruction, introductory dives in pools, and a one-hour PADI instructor–led dive on a coral reef in about 15–35 feet of water.

Children's Facilities   The year-round, supervised children's program, includes special menus, games, and activities. *SeaBreeze* has family cabins.

Shore Excursions   Choices are similar to those offered by most other cruise ships, but prices are often more moderate, and the line offers low prices for children.

Princess Cruises

10100 Santa Monica Boulevard, Los Angeles, CA 90067
(310) 553-1770; (800) PRINCESS (774-6237); fax (310) 277-6175
www.princesscruises.com

Type of Ships   Large and midsize traditional ships, superliners, and megaliners.

Type of Cruises   Modern, mainstream, worldwide, moderately upscale.

Cruise Line's Strengths
- worldwide itineraries
- extensive shore excursions
- Caribbean "private" island
- "The Love Boat" name recognition
- spacious cabins (many with verandas on most ships)
- 24-hour restaurant on most ships

Cruise Line's Shortcomings
- dissimilar ships
- uneven cuisine
- weak production shows on some ships

Fellow Passengers   Princess passengers are difficult to characterize because their ages and incomes vary with the ships, seasons, and destinations. Basically, passengers are age 45 and older with annual incomes of $40,000 and more. They tend to be experienced travelers who cruise frequently and enjoy Princess's mainstream vacation, but they can range from a California schoolteacher or a Midwestern computer systems analyst on a first cruise to affluent retirees on their twentieth cruise. On one-week Caribbean cruises, the average age is about 35 years. On longer cruises and those to "exotic" destinations, the average age is 55 or older.

Recommended For   Modestly affluent first-timers, frequent cruisers who want easy-paced travel and prefer a balance between sea and land time, and those who understand *The Love Boat* was only a television show.

Not Recommended For   Swingers or first-time cruisers in search of "The Love Boat"; small-ship devotees.

Cruise Areas and Seasons   Caribbean, Bermuda, Panama Canal, Mexico, Amazon, Orient, Holy Land, Australia/South Pacific, Hawaii/Tahiti, Southeast Asia, Africa, winter; Alaska, Europe, Scandinavia, Mediterranean, Baltic, Canada/New England, summer.

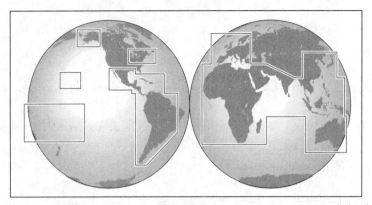

The Line   From its inception three decades ago, Princess Cruises helped create the relaxed, casual atmosphere that typifies today's cruises. The line continues to benefit from its involvement in *The Love Boat* television series, which had an incalculable impact on modern cruising, popularizing it for a generation of television viewers—those who make up most of cruise passengers today—and helping dispel cruising's elitist image.

P&O, Peninsular and Orient Steam Navigation Company, a British firm and one of the world's oldest and largest steamship companies, entered the cruise business in August 1844. In 1974, it bought Princess Cruises, which had been an American company, acquired the *Island Princess* (recently sold to an Asian cruise line) and added the first *Sun Princess*. The following year, P&O bought *Island Princess*'s sister, *Sea Venture,* and renamed her *Pacific Princess,* better known to TV viewers as "The Love Boat."

In the early 1980s, Princess became a trendsetter for modern mainstream cruising when it launched the *Royal Princess.* Still the Princess flagship, she was hailed as the most stylish ship of the day, setting new standards in comfort and amenities.

In 1988, Princess almost doubled its capacity when it acquired Los Angeles–based Sitmar Cruises, another cruise pioneer. The move wasn't as wonderful as it first seemed. Instead of creating two separate brands, Princess integrated the Sitmar ships—three Sitmar ships in service and three on the way—into its fleet. Yet, the styles of the two companies—one British, one Italian—were so different that merging them was difficult. Two ships, *Crown Princess* and *Regal Princess,* with radically different profiles and interiors were a major break with tradition. No one has rushed to copy them.

Princess's latest ventures—$3 billion in megaships—are the most dazzling ever. *Sun Princess,* dubbed the "Super Love Boat," was the first of the Grand Class series and the line's largest vessel when it entered service in 1995. She was followed by triples over the following four years. The quartet had the same architect, Njal Eide, as the *Royal Princess,* and like her, came with significant new features, including cruising's first 24-hour restaurant, two atrium lobbies, and two show lounges.

In 1998, Princess unveiled the 109,000-ton, $400 million *Grand Princess,* the largest cruise ship ever built at the time and the first of the Princess fleet too large to transit the Panama Canal. The expansion tripled the line's capacity. Two copies of *Grand Princess* are scheduled for delivery in 2001 and 2002.

And this would seem to be only the beginning. In 1999, Princess ordered two 113,000-ton vessels and two 88,000-ton ships, which will join the fleet between 2002 and 2004, doubling Princess's capacity once again. The four ships plus one for P&O Cruises will cost $2 billion. At the same time, P&O has split Princess Cruises along with its other cruise lines, P&O Cruises, P&O Australia, and Aida Cruises, from the parent company under one umbrella and will offer the new company on the London and New York stock exchanges in late 2000.

Already a major player in Alaska and the Panama Canal, Princess has increased its Caribbean presence, added itineraries throughout Asia and the Pacific, expanded in Europe, and added a safari in Kenya and South Africa. Princess calls at over 200 ports on six continents.

Princess's Alaska role was enhanced in 1997 with the opening of the $20 million Mount McKinley Princess Lodge, featured on the line's cruise tours. The lodge, on 146 acres inside Denali State Park, has a spectacular view of 20,320-foot Mount McKinley and the Alaska Range. On Caribbean cruises, the line offers Princess Cay, its "private island," in the Bahamas. Princess has one of the industry's best and most extensive selections of shore excursions. Almost all can be booked in advance of your cruise. Princess is also a leader in seasonal savings, deeply discounted advance-purchase fares, and two-for-one promotions. Just about everything you ever wanted to know about Princess is available on its thousand-page Web site.

The Fleet	Built/Renovated	Tonnage	Passengers
Crown Princess	1990/97/2000	70,000	1,590
Dawn Princess	1997	77,000	1,950
Golden Princess	2001	109,000	2,600
Grand Princess	1998	109,000	2,600
Ocean Princess	2000	77,000	1,950
Pacific Princess	1972/85/93	20,000	640
Regal Princess	1991/97/99	70,000	1,590
Royal Princess	1984/94	45,000	1,200
Sea Princess	1998	77,000	1,950
Sun Princess	1995	77,000	1,950
Unnamed I	2002	109,000	2,600
Unnamed II	2002	113,000	2,700
Unnamed III	2003	88,000	2,000
Unnamed IV	2004	113,000	2,700
Unnamed V	2004	88,000	2,000

Style   California modern in the mainstream, sedate but not staid, a Princess cruise is the essence of mass-market cruising: warm, inviting, and comfortable, suitable for a broad spectrum of people. The fleet has British officers, with their steamship tradition; Italian officers, with their natural charm; and a multicultural dining and hotel staff. Often trendsetters in facilities and amenities, the ships have the look of a well-bred, middle- to upper-middle-class environment—nothing flashy or exaggerated—where almost anyone can feel at home. The line has worked hard to improve its entertainment and food with menus featuring fresh, contemporary selections that had been missing in the past. Shipboard activities are varied and many. Ships fleetwide have gyms, saunas, and spa services and offer fitness and sports programs aboard and in port. Recently, Princess introduced telemedicine technology, giving ships' doctors worldwide access to medical specialists.

The noteworthy New Waves scuba diving program, associated with PADI (Professional Association of Diving Instructors), offers snorkeling and scuba certification. Princess remains the only mainstream line to offer passengers the opportunity to become certified divers during a cruise.

Distinctive Features   Scuba certification; 24-hour restaurants; terry robes in all cabins; fresh fruit in cabins; fresh flowers in suites. CNN, ESPN, Discovery and Learning Channels fleetwide. Shore excursions literature; self-service laundromats, pizzerias on eight ships, many cabins with verandas and refrigerators, Valentine's Day–Love Boat promotion, private Bahamian island.

	HIGHEST	LOWEST	AVERAGE
PER DIEM	$852	$182	$408

The above per diems are calculated from the cruise line's non-discounted *cruise only* fares on standard accommodations. Per diems vary by season, by cabin, and by cruise areas.

Rates   Port charges included.

Special Fares and Discounts   Frequent two-for-one fares; savings and upgrades on combining consecutive cruises.
- Third/Fourth Berth: 50 percent of fare.
- Children's Fare: Same as Third/Fourth Berth.
- Single Supplement: 160–200 percent, Love Boat Savers discounts apply.

Packages
- Air/Sea: Yes.
- Others: Yes.
- Pre/Post: Yes.

Past Passengers   Captain's Circle past-passenger club members are invited to captain-hosted cocktail party and participate in activities including a club photo contest with prizes. Each receives a membership number to use when booking a cruise or corresponding with Princess, ensuring they receive club benefits. Recognition pins are given, from the First Officer's pin for third and fourth cruises to a Commodore pin for ten or more. Quality gifts, such as Tiffany crystal, are presented at on-board parties to passengers who have sailed the most days with Princess. Members receive newsletters reporting new itineraries, new ship plans, staff profiles, chef's recipes, special discounts, and coupons for specific sailings and members-only sailings.

The Last Word   For millions of Americans, the popular image of cruising is a Princess cruise. It's perhaps not as luxurious or glamorous as the television image, but apparently close enough for the line to attract more than 750,000 passengers a year. At the same time, Princess's fleet is a mixed bag with ships differing in size, layout, and caliber. Some see the diversity as good, with each ship being a new Princess for passengers to meet. Others say the variety is unimportant; you're buying a cruise, not a ship.

Princess's strength is in its itineraries and well-executed shore excursions, and those should be your criteria for choosing a Princess cruise. Very little changes from ship to ship. Your ship will be comfortable, your cruise enjoyable, and you will get a lot for your money, if you have realistic expectations and plan ahead to take advantage of the line's heavily discounted fares.

PRINCESS CRUISES STANDARD FEATURES

Officers British and Italian.

Staff Dining/Italian, European; Cabin, Filipino; Cruise/American, British, Filipino.

Dining Facilities One main dining room, two seatings for three meals (*Sun* group, two dining rooms; *Grand,* three); informal buffet breakfast, lunch on Lido Deck; pizzeria; patisserie. *Grand, Royal,* and *Sun* group, 24-hour dining; *Grand,* Italian, Southwestern restaurants.

Special Diets Diabetic, low-calorie/cholesterol/salt, vegetarian.

Room Service 24-hour room service with light menu.

Dress Code Casual during day; evenings vary, usually there are two casual, three informal, and two formal in week's cruise.

Cabin Amenities CNN, ESPN, Discovery/Learning Channels and movies on television; fresh fruit daily in cabins; terry robes; direct-dial telephone; minifridges on *Royal, Crown, Regal, Sun* group; in suites and deluxe cabins on *Pacific.* Hair dryers on *Sun* group; *Grand* suites, butler service.

Electrical Outlets 220/110 AC.

Wheelchair Access 29 cabins on *Grand;* 19 on *Sun* group; 10 on *Crown* and *Regal;* 4 on *Pacific* and *Royal.*

Recreation and Entertainment Las Vegas– and Broadway-style revues, music and dancing, casino, disco, wine and caviar bar, karaoke, theater, dance classes, bingo, bridge. *Grand,* virtual reality center, three show lounges.

Sports and Other Activities Two/three outdoor pools on all ships; *Grand,* five; paddle tennis (except *Pacific*); jogging; scuba program; golf practice. *Grand,* swim-against-current lap pool.

Beauty and Fitness Saunas, beauty/barber salon, spa, fitness program.

Other Facilities Library, hospital, boutiques; self-service laundry (except *Pacific*); meeting facilities; religious services; *Grand,* wedding chapel.

Children's Facilities Love Boat Kids, Princess's youth program on all ships; special facilities and full-time youth coordinators: *Crown, Grand, Regal,* and *Sun* group. Babysitting available 10 p.m.–1 a.m. See text.

Theme Cruises Love Boat National Holiday, Valentine's-themed cruises.

Smoking No smoking in dining rooms and main showrooms; other public rooms have designated areas.

Princess Suggested Tipping Per person, per day: cabin steward and waiter, $3 each; busboy, $1.75; 15 percent of bar bill.

Credit Cards For cruise payment and on-board charges: American Express/Optima, Carte Blanche, Diners Club, MasterCard, Visa, Discover.

Royal Princess	Quality ❽	Value C
Registry: Great Britain	Length: 750 feet	Beam: 106 feet
Cabins: 600	Draft: 26 feet	Speed: 21.5 knots
Maximum Passengers:	Passenger Decks: 9	Elevators: 6
1,200	Crew: 500	Space Ratio: 38

The Ship The ship was so beautiful, people couldn't stop talking about her—or her godmother, the Princess of Wales, who christened her. Both made an indelible mark on the 1980s.

Launched in 1984, *Royal Princess* was at the time the most expensive passenger ship ever built. Her sleek lines and tapered bow looked traditional, but she had so many innovations inside that she was called revolutionary and set new standards in passenger comfort for the cruise ships that followed.

Royal Princess was the first cruise ship to have all outside cabins (she still holds this distinction for her size class); she also was first to have television with remote control, minirefrigerators, and full bathrooms with tub and shower in all cabins. She was first to have verandas in all suites, deluxe cabins, and some lesser categories, and large windows instead of portholes in every category. The biggest Princess ship when she debuted (but hardly a superliner by today's standards), she has two acres of open teak decks, three swimming pools, and a fully equipped spa. She remains the apex of Princess style, with refined, easy-to-like decor. Interiors are defined less by walls than by art, sculpture, glass with brass railings, and live plants. Muted colors and abundant windows create openness throughout the ship.

Royal Princess's layout is unusual. Most public rooms are on the two lower levels, and virtually all cabins are on upper decks. A large foyer on the lower Plaza Deck spans two decks—the first shipboard atrium, perhaps. The greenery-filled area is dominated by a large sculpture by David Norris consisting of a bronze spiral with seagulls rising over rocks and a splashing fountain. A dramatic staircase with glass balustrade curves in two wings upward to the Princess Court on Riviera Deck, where a portrait of Princess Diana hangs. The court, actually a balcony with piano lounge overlooking the foyer, is a gathering spot where passengers enjoy prelunch or predinner drinks, entertained by a pianist/vocalist. Riviera Deck also holds the main showroom, cabaret-style lounge, casino, boutique, card room, and a theater offering current and classic movies daily.

Itineraries See Appendix B.

Cabins   *Royal Princess* has 20 categories of cabins—all outside and spacious, and each with picture windows, a tiled bathroom with tub and shower, retractable clothesline, mirrored medicine cabinet door, and deluxe amenities, including terry robes. All cabins have minirefrigerator, safe, multifunction phone, four-channel music radio, remote-control television with CNN and other cable channels, and key cards for the door. Quality interiors and attention to detail are reflected in a large dressing table with makeup lights and mirrors, an easy-to-reach hair dryer plug, ample drawers, and three large closets. In many cabins, a twin bed folds into a wall, providing extra sitting space by day. Some cabins on the Baja, Caribe, and Dolphin Decks have obstructed views, indicated on the deck plan.

Suites and cabins with verandas are very roomy; the outside deck accommodates a chaise longue, small table, and chair. If you can afford a veranda, it's worth the additional cost. Thoroughly enjoyable, it's your private corner to enjoy breakfast, the peace and serenity of days at sea, and the fresh sea air day or night. The two largest suites have separate sitting and dining rooms, Jacuzzi bathtub, separate bedroom with queen-size bed, and large veranda. Minisuites are similar, but don't have walls between bedrooms and sitting areas. Self-service launderettes offer dryers, irons, and ironing boards. You pay for soap and use of machines.

Specifications   600 outside cabins (150 with verandas, including 52 minisuites, 12 suites, 2 deluxe suites). Standard dimensions, 168 square feet. All cabins and suites with twin beds (convertible to queen); some cabins accommodate third person. 10 wheelchair-accessible.

Dining   The warm, pleasant Continental Dining Room has a raised perimeter level delineated with brass railings. Small islands of round tables break up the space, provide privacy, and help lower the noise level and allow easy conversation. Three meals are served in two seatings, usually with open seating on port days for breakfast and lunch and assigned seats for dinner. Most tables seat four to eight people; a few "twos" are available. The food is consistently high quality and a cut above that aboard other Princess ships.

Senior dining staff is Italian and very attentive. Count on the maître d'hôtel or senior staff member to prepare fresh pasta tableside every evening. Don't be shy if your favorite pasta isn't on the menu. Ask for it. The staff loves showing how well they can make it. Menus are posted at bars and elsewhere shipwide. They list six courses for lunch and seven for dinner. One dinner, for example, offered four appetizers, three soups, salad, pasta special, six entrees (at least one low-calorie), four desserts, and assorted cheeses and fresh fruits.

After the successful introduction of cruising's first 24-hour restaurant on *Sun Princess,* a 24-hour Lido Cafe was introduced on *Royal Princess,* followed by a pizzeria. The indoor/outdoor cafe with tile-topped tables is cheerful at any time. Smokers and nonsmokers sit in separate enclosures. Also available are sheltered tables outdoors on Lido Deck and the stern's breezy deck. Afternoon tea is served in the Riviera Club, and a late-night buffet, often themed, is served in Princess Court.

Service   The dining room staff is the ship's most service-oriented group. They go out of their way for passengers. The British officers socialize in the bars and at meals, where they host tables.

Facilities and Entertainment   The International Lounge used by day for concerts, such as the Regimental Band of the Royal Welsh Fusiliers before departure from Southampton on the Baltic cruise. At night, the lounge presents Broadway- and Las Vegas–style shows. The predictable fare of song and dance isn't up to Princess's reputation for outstanding shows. Seats are tiered; sight lines are good, except from the back. Two new shows debuted recently. The Riviera Club and Bar and adjacent Terrace Room are the ship's most elegant lounges. They offer cabaret-style entertainment. Also available is the Crown Casino.

Floor-to-ceiling windows in the Horizon Lounge provide a 280-degree panorama. The large room is quiet except during morning exercise class or evening karaoke. It's popular for afternoon wine tastings or cocktail hour (daily drink at a special price). After-dinner coffees and liqueurs are served here, and around midnight, the room becomes a disco.

Activities and Diversions   You might start your day's activities with bridge or dance lessons, a craft demonstration, or having your handwriting analyzed. In the afternoon you might play golf or Ping-Pong, take a lesson in the casino, join a word or trivia game, or watch a culinary demonstration or horse races. Movie are shown three times daily in the comfortable Princess Theatre. And then, there's bingo.

Books are available any hour from the well-stocked library, but reading there is tough. The area, between two lounges, has comfortable sofas and chairs that make it a popular place for passengers to stop and chat.

Sports, Fitness, and Beauty   A cluster of five small pools is the centerpiece of the Lido Deck, the main outdoor recreation area. On Sun Deck, passengers sunbathe on a raised platform, play table tennis and shuffleboard, swim in one of cruising's largest lap pools, and exercise in the spa. The fitness complex has a gym with Nautilus and other equipment, sauna and massage rooms, and a large Jacuzzi. Programmed daily exercise starts with a walk-a-mile, stretch, and aerobics. Joggers and walkers circle the wraparound teak promenade on Dolphin Deck (three and a half laps equal one mile). The beauty salon offers hair and body treatments.

Shore Excursions   Separate brochures describe each cruise's shore excursions, and videos are available for purchase. For *Royal Princess*'s Baltic cruise alone, 40 tours are available, ranging in price from $20 for a half-day outing to over $1,000 for a full day of sight-seeing by private van. The lineup is fairly standard but varied, and trips are well organized, the guides first-rate. Princess offers hotel and tour packages that can be combined with European cruises.

Postscript   From launch, this classy ship was admired by competitors as much as her owners, and it's one vessel passengers request by name, rather than by itinerary. Like fine wine, she has mellowed nicely. Her passengers are older, more affluent, and less active than those on Princess's newer Caribbean fleet. Most are Americans. Her itineraries—most two to three weeks—appeal to travelers with time and money for extended cruises. Those weary of glitzy megaliners will appreciate her most.

Crown Princess	Quality ➏	Value C
Regal Princess	Quality ➐	Value C
Registry: Liberia	Length: 811 feet	Beam: 105 feet
Cabins: 798	Draft: 26 feet	Speed: 22.5 knots
Maximum Passengers:	Passenger Decks: 11	Elevators: 9
1,590	Crew: 630	Space Ratio: 44

The Ships   Anyone familiar with the *Crown Princess* and *Regal Princess* may not recognize them after their recent interior renovation and redesign that added a new 24-hour cafe, a children's center, and a remodeled atrium. The goal of the project, which comprised the largest refurbishment ever done on Princess ships, was to bring these twins in line with the newer *Grand* group, often using design, decor and color schemes from them.

The *Crown Princess* was christened in 1990 by actress Sophia Loren during Princess Cruises' twenty-fifth anniversary; *Regal Princess,* whose godmother is former British prime minister Margaret Thatcher, was added the following year. Part of the inventory Princess received from its Sitmar purchase, the twin ships were very different from any other vessel. Designed by Renzo Piano, architect of Paris's Pompidou Center, these Italian-built superliners have sleek lines that Piano says were inspired by the shape of a dolphin. Even now, the unorthodox design garners mixed reviews.

The good news: space and comfort. *Crown* and *Regal* are superliners, but they carry 25–30 percent fewer passengers than their counterparts. The spaciousness is apparent in wide corridors, lounges with high ceilings, and large cabins. Even standard cabins are the size of some other ships' suites. The ships' appointments range from elegant, with top-quality fabrics and well-made furnishings and museum-quality works by renowned artists (including Frank Stella, Robert Motherwell, and David Hockney) to the eclectic. Some bars display pop art, and eighteenth-century romantic landscapes hang in dining rooms. The result is an interesting, stimulating, and entertaining environment.

The main drawback of the interiors is that they look and feel like a hotel. Outside decks are few, and corridors with no ocean view border promenades and lounges. Unless your cabin has a veranda, you must go to the top deck or small, upper aft areas to see the seascape. The forward section, particularly, is closed off from the sea. And the Dome atop of the ship, meant to be a quiet observation lounge, is frenetic: Slot machines buzz in the casino, dance music spills from bars, and the area is thronged. The cavernous space might have been better used for outdoor decks.

The ship's new look is most evident in the three-deck atrium, The Plaza, which serves as the lobby and gathering place. Overall, it has been given a warmer, more inviting look. The backdrop of the main staircase is a large vertical water sculpture and a series of small, marble pools intended to create a restful atmosphere with the sound of water. Columns and railings are now covered with cherry wood, and greenery-filled marble planters at their base add warmth. There is a new marble floor at the base of the main staircase, and a large glass chandelier hangs above it. In the Patisserie on the first level, windows were added, helping give the space an airy appearance. Behind the newly paneled reception desk is a dramatic three-dimensional sculpture of swimming dolphins. On the upper decks, rich wood paneling was also added to the facades of the shops and bars around the atrium.

Actually, the most extensive aspect of the recent renovations is not seen. New stern thrusters were installed, increasing the ships' maneuvering capability and allowing them to visit ports without tug facilities.

Itineraries   See Appendix B.

Cabins   Spacious cabins are one of the ships' best features. They come in 26 categories and four basic arrangements: inside or outside standard doubles; outside double with a tiny balcony; outside minisuites with small veranda; and full suites with veranda. The 6 top categories plus the largest of the inside group are on three upper decks; the other 11 categories are spread across four lower decks. All have five-channel television with CNN, ESPN, and Discovery Channel; four-channel radio; direct-dial telephone; refrigerator; safe; walk-in closets, separate dressing area, and generous drawer space; and key card for door locks. Terry robes and fresh fruit are provided in all cabins. Standard outside cabins without balcony have oversized windows. Lifeboats are midway down the sides of the ship; 26 cabins on Dolphin Deck have obstructed views (they are indicated on the deck plan).

Specifications   171 inside, 430 outside cabins (134 with verandas); 36 minisuites, 14 suites with verandas. Standard dimensions, 190 square feet. All with 2 lower beds, convertible to queen; some have third/fourth berths; no singles. 10 wheelchair-accessible.

Dining   The main dining room, which has two seatings for three meals, was extensively redesigned from floor to ceiling with new decorative touches, including new carpets and wall coverings, lighting and dimmer system, artwork, and treatment to the stainless steel surfaces to soften the room's appearance. Also changing the look is a new table arrangement, adapted from the *Grand*-Class ships, that provides for greater privacy and better service.

Dinner menus are posted at bars and elsewhere aboard the ships. They're similar fleetwide, offering six courses for lunch and seven for dinner, with numerous selections for each course. Pizza lovers will enjoy the poolside pizzeria, complete with checkered tablecloths and Chianti bottles. It's open for lunch and in the evening, serving made-to-order pizzas at no extra cost. The patisserie has excellent espresso and cappuccino and assorted fresh pastries.

Crown's Café Cabana and *Regal*'s Cafe del Sol have been transformed into 24-hour restaurants with increased seating capacity by an extension at the aft end of the cafes. They were remodeled with new seating arrangements and serving lines and given new decor; a new galley was added for bistro service in the evening. The extension also provided space for a dance floor and stage. On the open deck, there's a new salad bar and a hamburger bar.

Service   Reports indicate that service and food on both ships have improved as Princess has worked to correct past flaws.

Facilities and Entertainment   Another of the ships' best features are their lounges—greatly varied in size, decor, ambience, and entertainment. The largest is the handsome International Lounge, a bilevel show lounge with a horseshoe-shaped stage. Bacchus on *Regal* and Chianti on *Crown* are small wine-by-the-glass and caviar bars that were given a more intimate setting with lowered ceilings and glass partitions, along with new murals and other decorative accents. Kipling's has a stage for a piano, a dance floor, and a mirrored bar. The room sparkles with brass and glass and has ceiling fans suggesting the days of the raj. On *Regal,* it's called The Bengal Bar, complete with a brass statue of a Bengal tiger. To complete the fantasy, liquor bottles are stacked to the ceiling and the bartender must use a ladder to retrieve them.

Next door, the intimate Intermezzo piano bar displays murals of fashionably dressed revelers from the 1920s. The Adagio, as it's called on the *Regal,* also has an espresso machine. One flight up, The Stage Door cabaret and late-night disco offers a sunken dance floor. Characters on the Lido Deck is a colorful poolside bar serving innovative drinks. The huge, top-deck Dome with 19-foot ceilings is largely occupied by the casino. It has a dance floor, bar, and 100 trees! A cinema, library, and card room are available.

Sports, Fitness, and Beauty   The Sun Deck has two outdoor pools, one with a swim-up bar and the other with waterfalls and whirlpools; a paddle tennis/volleyball court; and a one-sixth-mile jogging track. There's no wraparound deck. Images, a beauty and fitness center, has an aerobics area, weight machines, exercise bikes, and a steam room.

Children's Facilities   During the latest renovations, a brand-new, 2,000-square-foot children's center was added to the top deck sports, directly above the cafe extension, replacing the basketball court. The center was prefabricated at the shipyard and lifted into place on the ship in one piece and secured. The multipurpose center can be divided into separate areas for children and teens or converted into a meeting or conference room.

"Love Boat Kids," Princess's youth program, provides supervised activities and facilities for children ages 2–17 (evening activities while the ship is at sea). Activities may be available in port, but youth coordinators don't tend youngsters while parents are ashore. Children younger than age 18 must be accompanied by an adult and have written consent from both parents or legal guardians to cruise.

Pacific Princess	Quality ⑤	Value C
Registry: Great Britain	Length: 553 feet	Beam: 82 feet
Cabins: 326	Draft: 25 feet	Speed: 20 knots
Maximum Passengers:	Passenger Decks: 7	Elevators: 4
640	Crew: 350	Space Ratio: 33

The Ship   A leisurely pace and friendliness are hallmarks of the ship, the original Love Boat, that changed the face of cruising three decades ago. (Her sister ship, *Island Princess,* was sold to an Asian line in 1999.) The smallest of the fleet—almost considered a small ship compared with Princess's mega-liners—*Pacific* launched Princess cruises and set its style. Built in the early 1970s, the ship is a classic with traditional lines and abundant wood and brass. Instead of the hotel ambience and nightclub look of some Princess competitors, this vessel is homey, more like your living room.

Now, after a multimillion-dollar face-lift, *Pacific Princess* is better than ever. The extensive renovations added tiered floors in the main lounge to improve sight lines and a larger dance floor. State-of-the-art equipment was added to the gym, space for the casino and video arcade was increased, and the ship received a new air-conditioning system and radar equipment. New fabrics and furnishings were installed, but the ship retains the comfortable style typical of Princess. *Pacific Princess* is appreciated by her many loyal fans for her warmth and intimacy. She's designed to appeal to American tastes, but she attracts British passengers, too. The ship is well laid out and easy to learn—that's an advantage of her size. Passengers board at Purser's Square, a bilevel lobby on Fiesta Deck. A hospitable space with a spiral staircase—not quite as broad as the version seen on television's *The Love Boat*—curves up to the Aloha Deck. Both the Fiesta and Aloha Decks are devoted almost entirely to cabins. Most public rooms are on the Riviera Deck, and the topside Sun—or Lido—Deck is the sports center. (Princess calls the pool the world's most photographed.)

Itineraries   See Appendix B.

Cabins   Rooms are small by Princess standards and nothing like the TV version, but they're adequate and comfortable. In addition to all-new furnishings, the renovations brought satellite television with CNN, ESPN, and a new telephone system. Outside cabins outnumber inside ones by more than three to one among the ship's 18 categories. All cabins have twin beds, usually in L shape; one may fold into the wall to provide more daytime space. Most bathrooms have shower only; suites and mini-suites have refrigerators and bathrooms with tubs. All have four-channel radios. Two deluxe outside singles on Promenade Deck are always the first to sell. No cabins or suites have verandas. No cabins are wheelchair-accessible; disabled passengers are limited to four per cruise.

Specifications 67 inside, 223 outside; 9 minisuites; 4 suites; 2 deluxe outside single cabins. Standard dimensions, 126 square feet. All cabins with twins except 2 singles.

Dining The attractive Coral Dining Room serves three meals in two seatings. Menus follow the Princess standard. For example, dinner offers four appetizers, three soups, a salad, a pasta special, six entrees (with one or more low-calorie), four desserts, and assorted cheeses and fresh fruits. Pasta dishes draw generous praise. (Most chefs are Italian.)

Buffet breakfast and lunch are served on Lido Deck. New buffet stations offer made-to-order omelets and waffles for breakfast and a salad bar at lunch. Also added are poolside tables and lounge chairs for al fresco dining. Afternoon tea is served in the dining room.

Service Other than senior Italian dining room staff, the crew is a British affair. Officers, purser, office staff, cabin attendants, cruise director, and staff are British. The officers participate in ship social life, hosting tables at dinner and mingling in the disco. Overall, service and food on the *Pacific* are considered among the fleet's best.

Facilities and Entertainment You could start your mornings at the putting green, walk the Sun Deck (18 laps equal a mile), or join exercise classes. (The Promenade Deck doesn't circle the ship.) The Sun Deck pool has a retractable roof for use in inclement weather. Sunbathing space is plentiful. Also available are sauna and massage facilities, beauty salon, barber shop, and gym.

During days at sea, bridge and backgammon are played in the card and game room on Riviera Deck; lounges offer dance classes, bingo, horse racing, crafts, cooking demonstrations, and other diversions. Readers gravitate to the library and the Terrace Lounge for quiet corners.

Nightlife is anchored on the Riviera Deck by Las Vegas–style production shows nightly in the newly tiered Carousel Lounge. The cruise director and staff are part of the entertainment some nights, and passenger participation is high in most events.

The popular Pacific Lounge and its adjoining bar are good people-watching spots. The nicely appointed lounge has a small stage and dance floor, and a spectacular wall of windows spanning two decks and overlooking the Riviera pool and sea. Bright and cheerful by day, it becomes an intimate setting with subdued lighting at night. Stairs access the Terrace Room. Another daytime observation spot, the Starlight Lounge, is popular for cocktails and after-dinner drinks.

Movies play daily in the Princess Theatre, which is arranged like a nightclub, with comfortable chairs and cocktail tables. The theater also is used as a meeting room and for interdenominational Sunday worship services. Behind the theater is Pirate's Cove, a small disco that becomes lively after 10 or 11 p.m. when the British officers arrive. Next door is a neon-lighted casino with blackjack and slot machines.

Postscript   Newer Princess ships may have overtaken *Pacific Princess* in size and elegance, but this midsize lady remains the choice of many of Princess's most loyal fans. Already a favorite on the West Coast, the original Love Boat will have an opportunity to collect East Coast admirers now that she has launched Princess Cruises' first New York–Bermuda series.

Sun Princess	Quality ⑩	Value B
Dawn Princess	Quality ⑨	Value C
Sea Princess	Quality ⑧	Value C
Ocean Princess	(Preview)	
Registry: Liberia	Length: 865 feet	Beam: 106 feet
Cabins: 1,030	Draft: 26 feet	Speed: 21 knots
Maximum Passengers:	Passenger Decks: 14	Elevators: 9
1,950	Crew: 830	Space Ratio: 39

The Ships   Before its launch, *Sun Princess*—at the time, the largest cruise ship ever built—was described by Princess as offering an intimate feeling. Skeptics scoffed.

But guess what? Princess did it. Well, "intimate" is perhaps a stretch, but it certainly managed to diminish the interiors of this big ship to a human scale. The Italian-built ship made her debut in December 1995, the first of Princess's *Grand*-Class series. Her mates, *Dawn Princess,* arrived in 1997; *Sea Princess,* in 1998; and *Ocean Princess,* in 2000. From the outside, the gleaming white liners look colossal, towering 14 decks and stretching nearly three football fields in length. But inside, clever design has created a welcoming, accessible ambience. The ships are spacious without being overwhelming. Warm colors and refined decor enhance the inviting atmosphere.

The group sets new criteria for megaliners. Their layout is innovative in many ways. Small spaces capture the intimacy of a small ship while creating new options. Rather than one cavernous atrium, these ships offer two. Instead of one enormous show lounge, there are two main show lounges. Two dining rooms are on different decks, and their layout, decor, and table arrangements help create an intimate ambience. Five dining outlets, including cruising's first 24-hour restaurant, provide options. Small lounges offer an array of entertainment. Although other ships offer multiple lounges and dining alternatives, none has developed the concept to the extent that Princess's *Grand*-Class ships have. Whatever you choose to do, you *can* do, and whatever you miss one night, you can catch the next night.

The four-deck Grand Plaza is the ships' main atrium and social hub. It's a showcase of the exquisite Italian craftsmanship evident throughout the vessels and sets the tone for each ship. On the *Sun Princess,* in the elegant space, golden marble suggests the sun, and beige, bronze, and brown accents hint at shade. Sunbursts are set in the marble floors at every level of the atrium, and a backlit stained-glass dome overhead conveys an abstract underwater scene in aqua and turquoise. Glass elevators and a circular, floating staircase connect the decks and provide a stunning setting for the captains' parties.

Among the amenities are five swimming pools; a huge health center and spa; children's and teen rooms; a shopping arcade; computerized golf simulator; library and reading room with "audio chairs," each with its own bay window looking out to sea; and a business and conference center for up to 300 people. Each ship has a $2.5 million collection of paintings, sculptures, ceramic tiles, and Murano glass.

Another significant feature of the ships is their connection with the sea. A wraparound teak promenade lined with canopied steamer chairs provides a peaceful setting where passengers can read, daydream, or snooze.

Itineraries   See Appendix B.

Cabins   About two-thirds of cabins are outside; 70 percent of those have private balconies. There are 20 cabin categories. Nineteen cabins—among the most on any cruise ship—were designed to Americans With Disabilities Act specifications. Lifeboats obstruct views from 28 outside cabins on Promenade Deck. All standard cabins have a queen-size bed convertible to two singles, refrigerator, safe, ample closet, and bath with shower, terry robes, and hair dryers. All are well appointed and decorated in light, eye-pleasing colors.

Category A minisuites with private balcony are lavish in comfort, decor, and size—almost 400 square feet, plus the balcony. A marble-floored foyer with a mirror gives the illusion of a large apartment. Tastefully decorated in beige and butter tones accented by light woods and fine fabrics, each has a separate sitting area with leather chairs and a sofa that converts to a queen-size bed, and an entertainment console with television and music channels. A bar includes refrigerator.

The bedroom, separated by a curtained archway, has a queen-size bed, vanity/desk, and second television. Drawer space is ample, and the small walk-in closet has a safe. Sliding doors in the sitting area and bedroom lead to a balcony extending the length of the suite. Two lounge chairs and a table make it ideal for breakfast or napping. Etched glass divides the whirlpool tub from a shower stall, and a door separates the toilet and wash basin.

Specifications 372 inside, 603 outside cabins (411 with verandas); 32 minisuites and 6 suites with verandas. Standard dimensions, 135–173 square feet. All with 2 lower beds, convertible to queen; 300 with third berths; no singles. 19 wheelchair-accessible.

Dining Here are the choices: two dining rooms, a food court (cruising's first 24-hour restaurant) pizzeria, grill, patisserie, ice cream bar (there's a charge), and 24-hour room service.

The two main dining rooms are on Emerald Deck and Plaza Deck. They have an asymmetrical seating layout and small table groups in various sizes separated by etched-glass dividers. The design gives each group of tables a certain privacy. Separate galleys and service stations in every corner reduce traffic and help ensure that food reaches tables at the proper temperature. The walls are decorated with lovely scenic murals, adding to the gracious surroundings. Lunch and dinner menus offer a selection of appetizers, soups, salads, entrees, and desserts. A pasta special is offered every evening, although it is no longer prepared tableside. Healthy Choice selections, included on the regular menu, provide low-cholesterol, low-fat, and low-sodium alternatives. Wine list choices are reasonably priced, some under $20. Wines are also available by the glass.

Horizon Court on Lido Deck is an innovative 24-hour cafe with 270-degree ocean views through floor-to-ceiling windows, with seating on a trio of terraces. By day, buffets are served at two stations; at night, the center of the room becomes a restaurant with table service and a dance band. Reservations aren't needed, and there's no extra charge.

Breakfast choices range from fresh fruit to hot dishes, with a different special daily. At noon, entrees include ravioli, roast beef, and a salad bar, but selection and preparation do not match the quality or variety in the dining room. Overall, the 24-hour concept is great, but it still needs improvement.

The pizzeria offers a sidewalk cafe setting with marble-top tables and wrought-iron chairs on the balcony overlooking the atrium. Open for lunch and from 6 p.m. to 2 a.m., it serves pizza hot from the ovens, which are in plain sight. Waiters take orders for drinks and pizzas. There's no charge for the pizza, but diners tip the waiters. The outdoor Grill offers cooked-to-order hamburgers and hot dogs; the patisserie on the Plaza Deck offers espresso, cappuccino, and pastries. Sundaes, the poolside ice cream parlor, is a Haagen-Dazs concession, and there's a charge per scoop.

Service Officers are Italian, dining staff European, bar and cabin stewards Filipino, and reception and cruise staff American and British. Most of the crew are friendly and well trained, especially the dining staff, which consistently garners high praise. Service at the reception desk is uneven, and individual cabin stewards, ever smiling and eager to please, have received mixed reviews, often the result of insufficient training.

Facilities and Entertainment The Grand Plaza is the ships' hub. The Promenade Deck contains only public rooms and is anchored by the two showrooms. Forward is the Princess Theatre, with an enormous stage for Broadway-style productions. Graduated theater seating and an absence of pillars ensure fine sight lines.

Aft is the marble-walled Vista Lounge with tiered seating and floor-to-ceiling ocean views. Dancing and cabaret-style entertainment are offered. To one side, a large, free-form bar encourages mingling.

Shows in both lounges are repeated—four performances each for early and late seating over consecutive days. The ship's program suggests that passengers attend according to their dining room seating, but some passengers prefer to return to one show for an encore. This hasn't created seating problems because not all passengers attend all performances.

The Grand Casino offers slot machines, video poker, blackjack, roulette, and craps. The stained-glass ceiling, lighted to simulate a spinning roulette wheel, is visible on the deck below, from where passengers access the casino via a staircase in the second atrium. On the *Sun,* a bronze tubular sculpture by Arizonan Lyle London decorates the lower level.

Flanking the ship's second atrium are the disco and the romantic Rendezvous Lounge. The disco's entrance glitters with fiber-optic lights and a video dance floor, rather than video wall. Rendezvous Lounge, an elegant refuge across from the disco, serves caviar, imported wines, and champagnes by the glass. The Atrium Lounge, with a white baby grand piano and dance floor, is particularly popular for predinner cocktails and late-night sing-alongs. Afternoon tea is also served there as well as in the Horizon.

The Wheelhouse Bar near the Princess Theatre is one of the ship's most attractive, inviting rooms. Resembling a British men's club, it's decorated in rosewood and dark burgundy with sumptuous, spruce-green leather chairs. Ship models and P&O memorabilia adorn the walls. Live dance music seems a jarring note in this room that could be ideal for quiet conversation. Yet, passengers seem to enjoy the lively atmosphere, packing the dance floor before dinner and late into the night. On the *Sun*, a gallery outside the bar displays of costumes worn by opera diva Dame Joan Sutherland.

Activities and Diversions The wood-paneled library has a large selection of books, plus "audio chairs" with built-in headsets that are set by large bay windows for watching the water while listening. The Card Room is also used as a meeting room or for private parties. The ships offers a full schedule of daytime diversions from art auctions and dance lessons to bridge tournaments and bingo. A tiny, computer-equipped Business Center with Internet access is next to the beauty parlor.

Note: Art auctions have become ubiquitous on major cruise ships. Most of the art is terrible and terribly overpriced, despite claims to the contrary. One *Sea Princess* passenger recently wrote to Princess management: "the tacky, in-your-face display of art for auction [is] everywhere on the ship from embarkation to disembarkation—and it grew day by day . . . on easels, hanging on walls, and even stacked up around the casino lobby, Atrium piano bar, and Wheelhouse and Horizon Court. Tacked on to many were auction announcements with the time and location highlighted in thick orange magic marker. Flyers also appeared in cabin mailboxes almost daily, and, after the 'final' auction, another notice appeared announcing the 'requested FINAL 'Rocky IV, Death Wish' absolutely final auction.' Frankly, Princess has too much class to be using this sort of revenue-generating scheme in the first place, but the carnival hawker's atmosphere and the total lack of knowledge or finesse exhibited by the auctioneer were almost comical. *Sea Princess,* like her sisters, is an elegant ship with lovely decor, but even the 'legitimate' artwork in many passageways and some elevator lobbies was obscured by the easels and announcements of art for sale."

We couldn't agree more.

Sports, Fitness, and Beauty Some of the most innovative architectural designs benefit sports and fitness. One of the ship's pools is open to the sky, though set between two decks. On Riviera Deck are the main pools and the ocean-view spa. Half of this large area is a well-equipped gym; the other half is a mirrored room where aerobics classes are held. The spa has 11 massage and beauty treatment rooms, saunas, showers, changing facilities, and an ocean-view beauty salon. Next door, a computerized golf center simulates play on a half-dozen top courses ($30 per half-hour).

Sunbathing areas are spread across three top decks with a pool and bar (live band during daytime) on one; another pool, whirlpool, and grill on another; and a splash pool, bar, and paddle tennis/volleyball/basketball court on the third. A one-sixth-mile jogging track girdles the top deck; a broad teak promenade encircles the ship. (Three times around equals a mile.)

Children's Facilities "Love Boat Kids," Princess's fleetwide youth program, offers supervised, age-appropriate activities. *Sun Princess's* Fun Zone is one of the most enchanting children's playrooms at sea. There, kids ages 2–12 romp in a splash pool, play in a castle and big-as-life doll's house, and perform in a little theater. Next door, Cyberspace (Wired on *Sea*), the teens' gathering place, offers organized activities, video games, a disco, and refreshments.

Postscript Of all the megaliners launched since the mid-1990s, *Sun Princess* and her siblings have best reduced behemoth interiors to human scale. They also prove that big can be beautiful, in large part through their fine Italian craftsmanship. With choices 24 hours a day—in dining, activities, entertainment, and relaxing—anyone seeking less regimented cruising should find happiness on these ships.

Grand Princess	Quality ⑨	Value B
Golden Princess	(Preview)	
Registry: Liberia	Length: 951 feet	Beam: 118 feet
Cabins: 1,296	Draft: 26 feet	Speed: 22 knots
Maximum Passengers:	Passenger Decks: 16	Elevators: 12
2,600	Crew: 1,110	Space Ratio: 42

The Ship Saying the 109,000-ton, $450 million *Grand Princess* is the largest, most expensive cruise ship built doesn't say much. But comparisons clarify the image: *Grand Princess* is about four times the length of New York's Grand Central Station. She's 28 feet taller than Niagara Falls, 49 feet taller than the Statue of Liberty, and too wide by 43 feet to transit the Panama Canal.

And what does "most expensive" mean? *Grand Princess's* price tag was almost twice the cost of the Pathfinder mission to Mars. Happily, there's plenty on the grandest cruise ship at sea to suggest that Princess got its money's worth. Of the ship's 936 outside cabins, 710 have balconies— more than on any other cruise ship. She was the first with three main dining rooms and three main show lounges, each with a different show nightly. Her 13,500-square-foot casino is the largest afloat.

Get the picture? She's big, expensive, and has plenty of wow! But *Grand Princess* also comes with innovations even more exciting than those of the *Sun Princess* group. For starters, she has cruising's first wedding chapel (Princess is, after all, the company of *The Love Boat*); the first virtual-reality arcade with a motion-based ride for up to 18 people, car races, and skiing; a blue-screen video production facility that lets passengers star in their own videos; and the first swim-against-the-current lap pool at sea. She's the first cruise ship with a Southwestern-style restaurant—one of three alternative restaurants—and the first to have 28 wheelchair-accessible cabins. She also is the only cruise ship with duplicate operational and technical systems to ensure continued operation in emergencies.

Grand Princess's most unusual and noticeable design feature is the Skywalk, an aluminum structure suspended 15 decks above the water at the stern like a skybox at a stadium. Accessed by a glass-enclosed moving walkway, it's an observation lounge by day and a disco by night.

The ship's enormous interior is diminished by being divided into many small spaces offering dozens of activities—so many choices that a week of cruising still isn't enough time to try them all. The myriad options should be a comfort to first-time cruisers fearful of feeling confined or having nothing to do.

Among other distinctive features is the bridge, which extends beyond both sides of the ship. It's glass-enclosed to protect the computerized navigational instruments. A bow observation area gives passengers nearly the same view that officers have from the bridge. Balconies, outlined in blue glass, are built out from the ship's body of the ship in stair-stepped tiers. The design opens all balconies to the sun, but the negatives are a loss of privacy (cabins above overlook lower spaces) and noise traveling upward.

Itineraries   See Appendix B.

Cabins   *Grand Princess* has 35 cabin categories! Most cabins are on Decks 8–12, with a few on Deck 5; 70 percent are outside cabins. Of 710 outside cabins, 80 percent have verandas, and the majority range from 215– 255 square feet, a spaciousness generally available only in deluxe suites. Decor uses pastels and renders a pleasant ambience. Closet and shelf space is generous; drawers are limited but adequate.

Grand Princess balconies offer several benefits. First, they entice passengers to spend more time in their cabins, reducing crowds in public areas. Second, frequent cruisers like them. Third, with so many available in standard cabins, the amenity is affordable for a wider audience. The ship also has cruising's most numerous wheelchair-accessible cabins, and they're available in all main categories.

Cabins are more traditional in layout than those on the *Sun* group. Suites have tiled (not marbled) bathrooms and do not have Jacuzzi tubs. Suites and minisuites have butlers to augment regular cabin stewards and provide amenities commonly associated with luxury hotels. (Our experience on an early cruise suggests that the butlers need much more training to make their services noteworthy. In theory, they're available to polish golf clubs, serve in-suite afternoon tea, arrange for film developing, post mail, book excursions, and provide valet services such as pressing, dry cleaning, and shoe shines.) The two 800-square-foot Grand Suites are aptly named. Each has a large balcony with whirlpool, a living room with fireplace, wet bar, three televisions, and walk-in closets.

Specifications 928 outside; 372 inside. 208 suites with balconies (325–800 square feet); 502 outside cabins with balconies (215–255 square feet); 218 standard outside (165–210 square feet); 372 inside (160 square feet); 28 wheelchair-accessible including 18 outside/10 inside (240–385 square feet); 609 with upper berths.

Dining *Grand Princess* has eight dining venues. Based on cabin location, you're assigned to one of three main dining rooms where all three meals are served. Named for famous Italian artists—Botticelli, Da Vinci, and Michelangelo—the rooms have low ceilings and clusters of tables in a serpentine layout that breaks the space so guests don't feel they're dining in a large room with many people.

Horizon Court, the 24-hour lido cafe, has its own galley and a terrace for outdoor dining. The layout is different from that on *Sun Princess* and less inviting. The food needs attention, too.

Open for lunch and dinner by reservation are Sabatini's Trattoria, an Italian specialty restaurant, and the Painted Desert, serving Tex-Mex fare. (Princess has experimented with several menus to gauge passenger preference.) Outdoors is Poseidon's Pizza, where pizza is served all day; Trident Grill, providing hot dogs and burgers; and I Scream Ice Cream bar, a Häagen-Dazs concession where servings cost $3.95. The Promenade Bar overlooking the atrium on Deck 7 doubles as a patisserie, serving a light breakfast of croissants and espresso. Room service is available 24 hours.

Because dining is available at all times, passengers do not need to plan shore time around mealtimes. The many dining options also reduce lines and crowds.

Facilities and Entertainment   The ship offers a great variety of entertainment. Each of three showrooms has its own shows nightly. Vista Show Lounge, the midsize theater, presents cabaret-style entertainment that's quite varied. Princess Theatre, a two-deck showroom, stages large-scale production shows and revues and has the best sight lines and most comfortable seats of any shipboard theater we have experienced. The shows, all produced by Princess's production department, are outstanding. The Explorer's Lounge nightclub features soloists and bands playing a variety of music. Atlantis Casino, designed by the architects who created Caesars Palace Forum in Las Vegas, has one of the world's largest examples of holographic art. It also has 260 slot machines, 17 blackjack/poker tables, roulette, and craps.

The ship has many other small entertainment places, some with music and dancing. The Wheelhouse Bar, with the ambience of a private club, offers music for dancing; Snookers sports bar has a bank of television monitors that broadcasts sports programs, also available in cabins (the system can show events on Princess Theatre's big screen, too). Calypso Bar and Oasis Bar, outdoors and poolside, are frequently the scene of special events, including the Captain's Party. A retractable dome can be closed in bad weather. Center Court Bar is near the sports facilities; Sea Breeze and the Mermaid's Tail are mid-deck bars. Alfresco's bar overlooks the aft pool, which can be covered and converted into a stage for live concerts.

Activities and Diversions   Voyage of Discovery, the $2.5 million virtual-reality center, is an eye-popper. The room has interactive games and a cyberbar, but its main attraction is a wild, motion-based virtual-reality ride that seats 18 people. Passengers buy a Voyager card for $20, which they use to start machines, and the cost of play (50 cents to $3) is deducted.

At the blue-screen Limelight Studio, passengers can star in their own video, inserted into an existing scene from a popular movie or historical event. Standard diversions also are plentiful: bingo, karaoke, cards, board games, and writing room. The small business center has phone, fax, and computer facilities. (There's a charge to use business center equipment.) In the 36-seat wedding chapel, couples can be married or renew their vows with the captain presiding.

Shops sell sundries, clothing, jewelry, perfumes, and souvenirs. All are convenient to the Grand Atrium, the heart of the ship. In the Art Gallery, reproduction and original prints are for sale, and the ubiquitous auctions are held almost daily and often obscure the ship's $3 million museum-quality collection of contemporary art. The ship's library, A Quiet Corner, boasts an extensive book collection. Just outside are ever-popular private reading/listening chairs.

Sports, Fitness, and Beauty   *Grand Princess* has five swimming pools—including one for children and one for crew—and nine whirlpools. The Princess Links computerized golf simulator lets passengers try some of the world's top courses. A landscaped putting green is available, as are paddle tennis, basketball, and volleyball courts. A swim-against-the-current lap pool is the centerpiece of the Plantation Spa. The gym has treadmills, Stairmasters, Lifecycles, weight machines, an area for exercise and aerobics classes, a juice bar, and an outside jogging track. There are changing rooms and saunas (no charge) for men and women. The beauty spa, operated by Steiner, has 11 massage rooms offering a range of pricey treatments, such as aromatherapy massage, mud and seaweed wraps, and reflexology. A teak promenade encircles the ship; five and a half laps is just shy of a mile.

Children's Facilities   The two-level Fun Zone Children's Center offers a whale-shaped splash pool, life-sized doll's house, children's theater, ball jump, games, and more. Programs are age-specific and supervised. The Off Limits Teen Center, also bilevel, has a video disco, refreshment bar, video games, and private whirlpool.

Shore Excursions   Passengers receive a 64-page *Adventures Ashore* booklet describing shore excursions for their cruise. Most half-day trips cost $35–55; full-day outings range from $90 to $125. Our experience is that Princess shore excursions are well organized, particularly given the size of ship and number of people touring. Excursions on Mediterranean cruises cover the most important attractions; we recommend them, especially for first-timers. Passengers familiar with the ports may want to arrange their own activities.

Postscript   The *Grand Princess* is meant to be *Grand*-Class cruising at its best. Certainly with 16 decks, she reaches dizzying heights. But even with her many innovations and attractions, passengers who have sailed with the line before will recognize she's very much a Princess ship. *Grand Princess* will appeal most to those who see her size as a positive thing, providing options every hour of the day. She's sure to be popular with first-time cruisers, fulfilling their images of cruising from television's *The Love Boat.*

A big dividend of her size is a smooth ride. Those concerned about sea-sickness will be happy aboard *Grand Princess.* Those with health problems will be comforted to know she has a two-way video system (the first cruise ship to have it) that allows the ship's doctors to confer live with medical specialists at Mount Sinai Hospital in New York and other top U.S. hospitals.

Her sister ship, *Golden Princess,* is scheduled to debut in May 2001 and a third copy, yet unnamed, in January 2002. They, along with the four-member *Sun* group, are part of the line's *Grand*-Class series—a six-year project begun in 1995 and costing P&O almost $3 billion. Integrating seven enormous ships in six years is a gigantic job. So far, Princess seems to be taking it in stride and has been able to maintain the high standards, particularly of service, that has gained it its loyal following.

Radisson Seven Seas Cruises

600 Corporate Drive, Suite 410, Fort Lauderdale, FL 33334
(954) 776-6123; (800) 477-7500
(800) 285-1835; fax (954) 772-3763
www.rssc.com

Type of Ships   Unusual small ships with big-ship facilities.

Type of Cruises   Quiet, luxury, destination-oriented cruises with personal service, intimate ambience and sophisticated amenities.

Cruise Line's Strengths
- service
- itineraries
- cuisine
- single, flex-time/open-seating dining
- all-inclusive prices
- alternative dining
- all-outside deluxe accommodations and amenities

Cruise Line's Shortcomings
- lack of promenade or outdoor wraparound deck
- limited lounges and public rooms
- limited entertainment and shipboard activities
- disparate fleet

Fellow Passengers   Three distinct ships were brought under one umbrella in 1995 and joined by a fourth in 1997. Among their similarities is the type of passengers they attract: affluent, well-educated, well-traveled, 45 years and older, $100,000+ annual income. They cherish their individuality and shun group travel. There are subtle differences. *Diamond*'s passengers are slightly more affluent, senior executives, professionals, and high-end resort vacationers. Typical age is 50+; over 75 percent are Americans. They usually have cruised before on luxury liners, have sophisticated tastes, and care about elegance and service. Some are likely to be special-occasion celebrators and incentive awards winners. *Song of Flower*'s passengers are active, CEOs and other successful types, retired or semiretired. Average age is 62.

They travel extensively and are interested in foreign cultures. Those on Asia cruises tend to be even more seasoned travelers than those on Europe trips. They are involved with the world and are interesting individuals with refined tastes. They care about service, but prefer slightly homier surroundings than *Diamond*'s passengers do. Some are first-time cruisers; many are repeaters. *Paul Gauguin*'s romantic destination, Tahiti, is an important factor in which passengers the ship attracts, particularly honeymooners and divers. The vessel also is popular with incentive groups. The typical *Navigator* passenger is well traveled, 50+, with $125,000 average income; most own their company. Many are veterans of other upscale cruise lines.

Recommended For   Upscale, independent, active, seasoned travelers accustomed to luxury and quality. Small-ship devotees who appreciate the advantages and accept the limitations of such vessels. Pacesetters, trendmakers, and those who dare to be different for *Diamond;* intellectually curious, culturally inclined for *Song of Flower;* romantics for *Paul Gauguin.*

Not Recommended For   Joiners; people who need to be entertained or want a full day of shipboard activity; those seeking social action of a large, mainstream ship or who thrive in a Las Vegas atmosphere.

Cruise Areas and Seasons   Asia, Caribbean, Transcanal, South America in winter; Mediterranean, Northern Europe, Norwegian fjords in summer; Tahiti year-round.

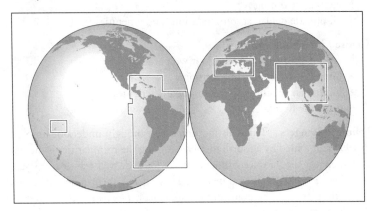

The Line   In 1995, Radisson Diamond Cruises and Seven Seas Cruise Line merged to form Radisson Seven Seas Cruises. The deal represented an expansion into cruising by Radisson Hotels International, while the new line brought three market segments—contemporary, traditional, and light adventure—in the luxury cruise market under one umbrella.

The futuristic *Radisson Diamond,* planned primarily for the corporate meeting and incentive market, combines the amenities of a larger ship with the intimacy of a smaller one. The unusual ship offers short cruises in the Caribbean, Panama Canal, and Mediterranean in a contemporary setting. When sufficient corporate market failed to materialize, the line changed course and sought affluent, seasoned travelers accustomed to luxury and fine cuisine who like to travel in a quiet, sophisticated environment.

Song of Flower, recognized as one of luxury cruising's best values, offers traditional, personalized voyages to some of the most interesting European and Asian ports. Begun in 1990 by a wealthy Japanese businesswoman who established its high standards, Seven Seas Cruise Line quickly made its mark by offering deluxe cruises at rates considerably lower than its competitors and winning accolades and awards after only its first year. The vessel is now owned by K Line, one of Japan's largest shipping companies. *Song of Flower* cruises are designed for American and European travelers; Japanese passengers are few.

Radisson Seven Seas introduced the *Paul Gauguin* in 1998 and in a joint venture with Monte Carlo–based V. Ships, it debuted the all-suite luxury *Seven Seas Navigator* in 1999. The ships are part of a plan for Radisson Seven Seas to add one new vessel each year for the next five years. The next ship, *Seven Seas Mariner,* a 708-passenger, all-suite, all-balcony vessel, is scheduled for delivery in March 2001, and her sister ship in 2002. Each ship boasts some of cruising's highest space-to-passenger and crew-to-passenger ratios. Together, they equal a group of compatible, yet different and distinctive, deluxe cruise experiences.

The Fleet	Built/Renovated	Tonnage	Passengers
Paul Gauguin	1998	18,800	320
Radisson Diamond	1992	20,295	350
Seven Seas Mariner	2001	50,000	700
Seven Seas Navigator	1999	30,000	490
Song of Flower	1986/90	8,282	180
Seven Seas Voyager	2002	46,000	708

Style   The ship size, small number of passengers, and price ensure the cruises a certain exclusivity. They also help define the high level of service and personal attention passengers expect—and receive.

Shipboard life on *Diamond* is informal during the day but formal in style (though not necessarily in dress) in the evening. Surroundings are spacious and luxurious, the service pampering, the ambience sophisticated. The ship has loyal fans.

Classy but unpretentious, *Song of Flower* has been described as having the confidence and calm of "old money" at an exclusive club. Its small size, shallow draft, and maneuverability enable it to go where large ships cannot. *Paul Gauguin* and the slightly larger *Navigator* fit the group well.

Distinctive Features   No-tipping policy. Water sports platform/marina. Extensive book and video libraries. Open bridge policy. *Diamond*'s design. *Song of Flower*'s inclusive prices cover even cigarettes and postage stamps.

	HIGHEST	LOWEST	AVERAGE
PER DIEM	$882	$245	$499

The above per diems are calculated from the cruise line's non-discounted *cruise only* fares on standard accommodations. Per diems vary by season, by cabin, and by cruise areas.

Rates   Gratuities and wines with lunch and dinner included. All beverages or room bar initial setup included, depending on ship. Most shore excursions are included on *Song of Flower*. Port charges are additional.

Special Fares and Discounts
- Early booking, 120 days in advance, saves up to $1,300 per person, depending on cruise, and on combined cruises.
- Third Person: 50 percent of fare on *Song of Flower*.
- Single Supplement: Specific amounts per cruise listed in brochure

Packages
- Air/Sea: Yes.
- Pre/Post: Yes.

Past Passengers   Radisson Seven Seas Society, for repeat passengers, publishes a newsletter and offers members sailings with incentives and special prices. Some sailings are hosted by the line's president. Members receive quality gifts based on the number of days they cruise.

The Last Word   The *Diamond* is so different, it's difficult to compare it with other cruise ships. Does the design provide advantages over conventional cruise ships? On balance, no. Choosing *Diamond* means selecting something really different. Alternatively, *Song of Flower* offers value and a traditional cruise experience. *Paul Gauguin* focuses on one destination; *Navigator* roams the world.

RADISSON SEVEN SEAS CRUISES
STANDARD FEATURES

Officers *Diamond*/Finnish; *Song of Flower*/Norwegian; *Paul Gauguin, Seven Seas Mariner*/French; *Seven Sea Navigator,* Italian.

Staff Dining and Cabin/European. *Diamond:* Cruise/American. *Paul Gauguin* and *Song of Flower:* Dining/European and Filipino; Cruise/American and British.

Dining Facilities One dining room (*Paul Gauguin,* two) with open seating for three meals; informal indoor/outdoor cafe for buffet breakfast and lunch. Reservations-only alternative dining on *Diamond, Navigator,* and *Mariner.*

Special Diets Accommodated with advance notice.

Room Service 24-hour service with full-meal, in-cabin dining.

Dress Code Casual by day; most evenings, jackets required for men. Formal/semiformal for captain's parties. Visits in some ports of call may require women to cover heads, legs, and arms.

Cabin Amenities Direct-dial telephone, hair dryer, television, VCR, radio, stocked minibar (*Paul Gauguin* with nonalcoholic beverages); marble bathroom with tub and shower (except *Song of Flower,* lowest category with showers only). *Diamond,* CNN, safe. *Song of Flower,* flowers and fruit, bathrobes. *Diamond, Navigator,* all suites; *Paul Gauguin,* verandas, terry robes, safe.

Electrical Outlets 110 AC.

Wheelchair Access Two cabins, except *Song of Flower,* limited facilities.

Recreation and Entertainment Nightclub, cabaret, and piano entertainment in two lounges, small casino, dancing, card games, backgammon, book/video library, lecture program.

Sports and Other Activities One outside pool. See text.

Beauty and Fitness Beauty salon. Small gym. See text.

Other Facilities Business center on *Diamond;* boutique; hospital.

Children's Facilities None.

Theme Cruises Yes

Smoking Sections designated in public areas; no cigar or pipe smoking in dining room; nonsmoking cabins on *Song of Flower.*

Radisson Seven Seas Suggested Tipping No-tipping policy; tips for special service on *Diamond;* none accepted on *Song of Flower.*

Credit Cards For cruise payment and on-board charges: American Express, Diners Club, MasterCard, Visa, plus Discover on *Diamond.*

Radisson Diamond   Quality ❼   Value C

Registry: Bahamas	Length: 420 feet	Beam: 103 feet
Cabins: 177	Draft: 26 feet	Speed: 12.5 knots
Maximum Passengers:	Passenger Decks: 3	Elevators: 4
350	Crew: 191	Space Ratio: 58

The Ship   If you were the first to fly the Concorde or are on a list to go to the moon, you may want to try the *Diamond,* which has the most revolutionary design of any cruise ship built in this century. Sitting high above the water on twin hulls, this extraordinary ship is a traffic-stopper.

Diamond's design uses SWATH (small waterplane area twin hull) technology intended to provide less motion, engine noise, and propeller vibration, plus greater stability than conventional ships. Does it? Maybe. The design has trade-offs. Top cruising speed is slightly over 12 knots per hour, about 40 percent slower than most cruise ships. This limits the range and flexibility of *Diamond*'s itineraries. Moreover, both hulls contain machinery, and there's no underwater connection between them. To reach one from the other, staff must climb stairs to the main structure, cross over, and descend the other side.

The good news is that *Diamond* is unusually spacious and its cabins among the largest and most elegant at sea. Indeed, the interior is more like a luxury hotel, complete with meeting center and boardroom. Interiors combine contemporary and Art Deco styles with fine fabrics. A five-story atrium at the ship's entrance contains the reception desk, two glass-enclosed elevators, and an ebony-and-brass staircase leading to all decks, including the spa and jogging track at the top.

Itineraries   See Appendix B.

Cabins   *Diamond* has six categories of cabins. All are large outside suites, either with a veranda or a larger sitting area. During recent renovations, four balcony suites have been connected to create a pair of new, two-room master suites. Most accommodations have twin beds convertible to queen size. The lounging area has a sofa, chairs, and large bay windows. Quietly elegant decor incorporates high-quality fabrics. Suites are very comfortable and have the amenities of a luxury hotel, including refrigerator stocked with beverages and complimentary initial minibar. Storage space is generous, and bathrooms have a marble vanity, hair dryer, retractable clothesline, bathtub, and shower, but are small for this price range. All suites have entertainment systems with closed-circuit, remote-controlled, five-channel television with CNN and VCR, stereo/radio, CD player, dressing table, international direct-dial telephone, and safe. Two executive suites, which were recently renovated, offer a king-size bed, whirlpool tub, balcony, and bay window. Two wheelchair-accessible suites have been relocated to Deck 7 and refurbished. Room service, available 24 hours daily, is prompt and efficient. The extensive menu lists hot and cold items, including freshly baked pizza, and full-course meals during regular meal hours.

Specifications   177 outside cabins (123 with verandas); 2 executive suites. Standard dimensions are 245 square feet including veranda or sitting area. All with twin beds, most convertible to queens. None accommodates third/fourth person; no singles. 2 wheelchair-accessible.

Dining   The spacious Grand Dining Room, with floor-to-ceiling windows embracing the sea, is one of the most elegant rooms afloat. Fine service, gracious ambience, and generous space between tables add to the luxury. Seating is open; neither times nor tables are assigned. Gourmet cuisine is the ship's most outstanding feature. Selections change daily and include fresh seafood and prime meats. Preparation and presentation are varied and sophisticated. Fresh pasta dishes are offered at lunch and dinner. Wine is included with dinner. The informal Grill on the top deck offers indoor/outdoor dining from full menus and elaborate breakfast and lunch buffets. In the evening, it's a 50-seat Italian restaurant, complete with red tablecloths and singing waiters. Reservations are required (by noon), but there's no extra charge. The Grill is very good, very popular, and very noisy. The menu changes daily; delectable pastas are featured.

Service   The ship's senior hotel and dining staff, many of them Italians, have years of luxury-ship experience. Most cabin and dining attendants are women from Austria, Germany, and Sweden; most are working on a ship for the first time. They are courteous and eager to please but lack polish.

Facilities and Entertainment   Space that might have accommodated public lounges was used in meeting rooms, but bars and lounges are ample. The largest lounge, Windows, takes its name from a wall of windows—a waste because the room is used mostly at night. The lounge has an upper-level bar overlooking a small dance floor and orchestra, and they recently added a new stage and sound system. It's popular for cocktails when a combo plays and for after-dinner cabaret entertainment. Aerobics are offered in daytime, and late at night, it's the disco.

The Club piano bar and lounge features a singer/ pianist on most nights and is a comfortable rendezvous for conversation almost any time. The small Chips Casino offers roulette, blackjack, and slots.

Activities and Diversions   Some people like the lack of organized recreation; others could be bored. Depending on itinerary, offerings include educational and cultural lectures by guest experts, bridge instruction, card games, and backgammon.

The library has a good selection of books and videotapes available 24 hours a day with no check-in/out required. The meeting/business center has audiovisual equipment, publishing facilities, fax and communications services, satellite communication facilities, computer hookups, desk facilities, and staff support.

Sports, Fitness, and Beauty   A European-style spa provides herbal wraps, massages, and beauty treatments for additional fees. There's no charge for the sauna and steam room, aerobics, yoga, and other exercise. The gym has exercise equipment, an outdoor jogging track, swimming pool, and Jacuzzi. Also available are shuffleboard and table tennis.

Diamond has a retractable, free-floating marina platform used for water sports, weather permitting. Options include water skiing, sailing, windsurfing, and diving (for certified enthusiasts).

Radisson Seven Seas is the Professional Golfers' Association's official cruise line. A "Golf Academy" and PGA-designated cruises in Europe are offered and include play at famous courses, a private lesson, and clinics with a PGA-certified pro. *Diamond* has a driving range, putting green, and computerized swing analyzer. In the Caribbean, golf packages are available at 12 ports and can be booked before you cruise.

Shore Excursions   *Diamond* offers a wide selection of sight-seeing and sports options.

Song of Flower	Quality ⑨	Value B
Registry: Norway	Length: 408 feet	Beam: 52.5 feet
Cabins: 80	Draft: 15 feet	Speed: 17 knots
Maximum Passengers:	Passenger Decks: 6	Elevators: 2
180	Crew: 144	Space Ratio: 48

The Ship   *Song of Flower* has proved that good things come in small packages. This small, low-key ship offers outstanding cuisine and superb service that is never ostentatious. Its diverse itineraries combine popular and less traveled routes. Everything is included, down to tips, brand-choice liquors, fine wine, and even postage stamps.

Launched in 1986 as the *Explorer Starship, Song of Flower* was refurbished when she was acquired in 1989 by Seven Seas. Recent reports indicate that she needs another refurbishing. Now owned by K Line America Inc., she's large enough to offer a variety of public rooms and activities, but small enough to convey small ships' friendly, easy-to-approach ambience. Perhaps that and the high staff-to-passenger ratio account for passengers' astonishment when the ship delivers the pampering they dream about at prices, though not cheap, that make people feel they have gotten their money's worth.

Handsome but understated, *Song of Flower* has pleasing appointments enhanced by beautiful arrangements of fresh flowers. Public rooms and cabins are on five of the ship's six decks. The attractive Main Lounge on Promenade Deck is the largest room. It's used for most functions and evening entertainment. With its size and shallow draft, the vessel can sail in areas where large ships can't. She also carries a large tender for ferrying passengers to shore when necessary.

Itineraries   See Appendix B.

Cabins   *Song of Flower* offers six categories of cabins and price levels— enabling her to attract an audience wider than those aboard all-suite, one-price competitors. Choices include twins with shower, veranda suites, and cabins with two baths. All are outside and forward from engine noise, and all have the same amenities: television with CNN and other cable access, VCR, direct-dial telephone, hair dryer, and bar-refrigerator replenished daily at no additional charge. There's ample drawer and closet space, good lighting, mirrors, and such thoughtful additions as umbrellas, slippers, robes, hats and sun visors, fine toiletries, fresh fruit, and flowers (replenished daily).

The spacious cabins are dressed in pastels and blond furniture, giving them a light, airy look. The ten two-room suites have a sitting room and two baths, one with a bathtub and the other a half-bath with shower. Ten veranda suites have bathrooms with full bathtub and shower; sliding glass doors open onto private terraces. Standard cabins have picture windows and bathtubs; those in the lower category have showers and portholes.

Specifications   100 outside cabins (including 10 suites with private veranda; 10 suites with sitting area and 2 baths). Standard dimensions, 200 square feet. 80 with twin beds (30 convertible to doubles); some cabins with convertible sofa bed for third person. No singles.

Dining   The Galaxy Dining Room is quiet and inviting. The single, open seating with flexible hours enables passengers to dine whenever and with whomever they please. Piano music accompanies lunch and dinner. Tables are set with fine china and silver on white linens and brightened with fresh flowers. Most tables accommodate four or six; a few seat two. Angelo's, a small, 30-seat Italian trattoria serving Tuscan and Florentine specialties, is the ship's alternative restaurant.

The cuisine is excellent and splendidly presented. Widely varied menus feature local products bought daily, when practical. Quality rather than quantity is emphasized, though there's no shortage of choices. Dinner typically offers three appetizers, three soups, two salads, a sorbet, four main entrees, three or four desserts, plus ice creams and petit fours. Special requests can be accommodated; ask in advance.

Quality wines (included in the cruise price) are served at lunch and dinner, and the sommelier willingly explains the choices for each meal. The dining room has a cappuccino/espresso machine.

The same selections offered in the dining room are served at breakfast and lunch in an outdoor cafe on Sun Deck, weather permitting. Lunch also includes pasta and a main course, changed daily. An elegant tea is served in the afternoon, and midnight buffets may feature pizza or sushi. Room service has an extensive menu, available 24 hours.

Service   Most passengers rank service as *Song of Flower*'s most outstanding feature. Dining and bar staff is primarily European and Filipino. Scandinavian stewardesses attend cabins. Crew members are polished and professional—most having served on other prestigious ships or private yachts. Yet it's their friendly, caring manner that endears them. They're attentive but never intrusive, anticipating needs and handling requests quickly. Gratuities are included in the cruise fare, and staff doesn't accept tips. When they're gracious, it's because they take pride in their work, like their job, and want to please—not because they're angling for tips.

Facilities and Entertainment   The Main Lounge showroom can accommodate all passengers at once. By day, expansive windows make it a pleasant place to relax. Staged nightly are cabaret shows featuring dancers, vocalists, magicians, puppeteers, comedians, and others. The entertainment isn't brilliant, but it's adequate. The Night Club piano bar and lounge is popular for cocktails and after-dinner drinks; it doubles as the late-night disco. The casino offers roulette, blackjack, and slot machines. In daytime, the Observation Lounge is the most popular perch for viewing scenery. It's especially pleasant for afternoon tea when light from windows on three sides bathes the room.

Activities and Diversions   The vessel is in port most days; shipboard activities are few. Also, passengers on this small ship tend to socialize with one another and need little organized activity to keep busy. Depending on itinerary, experts lecture on destinations. The library is well stocked with books and videos; it's open around the clock. Also available are a card and reading room and a boutique.

Sports, Fitness, and Beauty   A heated swimming pool and large whirlpool are on Sun Deck. To one side is a bar; to the other, a small health club with Lifecycles, Stairmaster, weights, and a sauna. The ship also has a golf driving range. In warmer climates, a water sports platform equipped with jet skis, windsurfing boards, snorkeling equipment, and a Zodiac is lowered from the ship's stern. There's no walk-around promenade. The beauty salon, operated by the London-based Steiner group, offers hair and beauty care and Shiatsu, Swedish, and deep-tissue massage—at additional cost.

Shore Excursions   All Asia and Northern Australia cruises include airfare, all shore excursions, and pre- and postcruise hotel stays—making them exceptional values. In Europe, shore excursions are extra but more moderately priced than those of other luxury cruise lines. Guides are uniformly good. Excursions cannot be booked in advance. The concierge will arrange tours for passengers to take on their own.

Paul Gaugin	Quality ⑨	Value B
Registry: France	Length: 513 feet	Beam: 71 feet
Cabins: 160	Draft: 16.9 feet	Speed: 18 knots
Maximum Passengers: 320	Passenger Decks: 7	Elevators: 4
	Crew: 206	Space Ratio: 59

The Ship   Named for the French artist whose life and work embodied the romance of French Polynesia, the *Paul Gauguin* is meant to be the most deluxe ship ever to cruise the South Seas year-round. Its space ratio is among cruising's highest. Shallow draft allows access to small, rarely frequented ports.

The French-built vessel is owned by French investors and operated by Radisson Seven Seas. *Gauguin*'s clean lines, understated elegance, and attention to detail are immediately apparent. The yachtlike ship has an airy ambience with stylish touches, such as blond paneling and gray carpets.

Itineraries   See Appendix B.

Cabins   All accommodations are outside suites with separate sitting area; 50 percent have verandas. Each is furnished with a queen- or twin-size beds (convertible to queen), closed-circuit television and VCR, safe, direct-dial telephone, and refrigerator stocked with soft drinks, mineral water, and complimentary liquor on arrival. Interiors are enriched by crown moldings and wood accents. Finely crafted furnishings include a love seat and vanity/desk. Storage space includes two closets and built-in drawers. Marble bathrooms have a full-size bathtub and shower, plush towels and cotton robes, hair dryer, and assorted toiletries. Some passengers report being able to hear conversations next door. Cabins above the engine are noisy.

Specifications   160 outside cabins and suites; 80 with balconies. Cabins range from 202 square feet with picture window or portholes and 249 square feet with 56-square-foot veranda, to the 457-square-foot owner's suite with 77-square-foot veranda. 1 wheelchair-accessible.

Dining   Two restaurants offer single, open seating. Both have ocean views on three sides. An outdoor bistro provides casual dining throughout the day and evening. An espresso bar and 24-hour room service are other options. Restaurant L'Etoile, the main dining room, features French and continental cuisine. The smaller La Veranda is a reservations-only dinner restaurant offering two menus per cruise. Taste of Italy and a Taste of France are "theme" evenings. Passengers say Taste of France is far superior in food quality and service. Complimentary wine is served at lunch and dinner; the ship has an excellent wine list. Guests with reservations enjoy predinner cocktails and hors d'oeuvres in the Connoisseur Club (open after dinner for drinks and cigars). Evening attire is "country club elegant" (no ties).

Service   The crew generally succeeds in its quest to provide outstanding service. There are a few glitches in the dining room and in cabin maintenance, but the overall experience is fine.

Facilities and Entertainment   Le Grand Salon is the main lounge for early-evening dancing, entertainment, and daily lectures. Indoor/outdoor La Palette Lounge is used for afternoon tea, cocktails, and late-night disco. The small casino has blackjack, roulette, and slot machines, but local regulations bar use of the slots. Other public rooms include a reception area, card room, and boutique stocked with Polynesian gifts.

In tribute to Gauguin and French Polynesia, the Fare (pronounced *faray*) Tahiti Gallery is a library well-stocked with books, videos, and other materials on the artist and region. A guest lecturer on every cruise discusses regional history and attractions.

Nighttime entertainment is minimal. Three movies are shown daily on the closed-circuit cabin system; the reception desk lends videos. A pianist/singer performs in La Palette before dinner, and the ship's Filipino band plays for dancing before dinner in Le Grand Salon and afterward in La Palette until 11:30 p.m., when the disco starts up.

Sports, Fitness, and Beauty   The fitness center offers free weights and exercise machines that are in use constantly. Aerobics, hydro-calisthenics, and a walkathon are held daily. A separate Carita of Paris salon and spa offers a steam room, massage, facials, and beauty treatments such as aromatherapy. Three- to six-day spa packages are available.

Paul Gauguin has an outdoor pool and splash bar on an upper deck and a retractable marina at sea level where passengers indulge in sports, including diving and snorkeling. Windsurfing and kayaking equipment is available. Snorkeling gear can be signed out at the cruise's start. Diving is a major attraction. The ship provides PADI-certified instructors and dive boats, as well as courses for novices (PADI certification available) and excursions for certified divers.

Shore Excursions   Many shore excursions are water-oriented. Outings include a jet-ski tour of Bora Bora, outrigger/jeep combination tours, shark feeding, and helicopter tours. Weather permitting, a beach party is held on the line's private *motu,* a small islet.

Postscript   Passengers concerned about seasickness should know that rough sailing isn't unusual for this ship, owing to her shallow draft and the sometimes rough Pacific waters.

Seven Seas Navigator   (Preview)

Registry: Italy	Length: 560 feet	Beam: 81 feet
Cabins: 250	Draft: 21 feet	Speed: 20 knots
Maximum Passengers:	Passenger Decks: 5	Elevators: 5
490	Crew: 325	Space Ratio: 67.3

The Ship   In a joint venture with Monte Carlo–based V. Ships, Radisson Seven Seas Cruises launched its all-suite luxury ship, *Seven Seas Navigator,* in August 1999. The Italian-built, $200 million vessel is the fastest and largest in the Radisson fleet to date and has an ice-strengthened hull, giving her the ability to operate virtually anywhere in the world. *Navigator* is the second of five ships—one each year—that Radisson Seven Seas plans to add. V. Ships, established in 1984, is a company of the Vlasov Group, one of the world's largest providers of ship management and related services.

Described as a small ship with a big-ship feel, the spacious *Navigator* has half a dozen lounges, superbly appointed outside suites (90 percent with balconies, walk-in closets, and well-appointed bathrooms), a single-seating dining room and an alternative restaurant, one of the industry's highest space ratios, a wide teak deck surrounding the pool, and world-wide, port-intensive itineraries.

Designed by Norwegian architects Yran & Storbraaten, *Navigator's* public rooms are strikingly contemporary and minimalist. Yet unusual lamps, exotic chairs, and varied materials and textures provide visual interest. The entire ship is well integrated, with light blue carpeting throughout and bold oil paintings (all for sale) decorating the corridors. A bank of glass elevators, however, seems out of place on a small luxury vessel, and the exposed machinery provides a jarring note.

The Italian-flagged ship has an Italian captain and Italian and European senior officers. In her maiden year, she was the line's first venture to South America, where she spent part of the winter, and Alaska, where she cruised in summer prior to heading for Australia for the Olympics.

Cabins   Particular attention was lavished on the accommodations. They range from a roomy standard suites of 301 square feet plus veranda to Master Suites with 1,067 square feet plus a 106 square-foot balcony. All standard suites are identical; price varies by location. Ten suites are interconnected. Four suites are wheelchair-accessible with extra-wide doors and large, shower-only bathrooms.

The suites, like the rest of the elegant ship, are decorated in subdued colors with cherry wood accents. They have sitting areas, twin beds convertible to a queen, marble bathrooms with separate tub and shower, and walk-in closet with safe. Other amenities include a minibar with premium liquor set-up, bathrobes, hair dryer, television with VCR, and Judith Jackson bath products.

In standard suites a coffee table rises to dining table height with the touch of a button, and upper-level suites have proper dining room tables. Passengers can dine en suite, ordering from the dining room menu during meal hours, with dishes served course by course. The ship offers 24-hour room service.

Master and Grand Suites, which come with butler service, have a foyer with a powder room, living/dining area, and a separate bedroom with bath that has a bidet.

Specifications   245 suites. Standard suites measure 301 square feet plus balconies; 10 Grand Suites are 538 square feet plus balconies; 4 Master Suites measure 1,238 square feet plus balconies. 4 wheelchair-accessible.

Dining   The open, single-seating Compass Rose Restaurant provides a gracious setting, with a small dance floor for occasional dinner dances. An alabaster compass rose skylight looks down on the pale yellow walls;

draperies in soft pastels frame the picture windows; and potted plants are interspersed among the widely spaced tables.

Passengers stroll across a parquet floor to enter the Portofino Grill, the alternative restaurant located on an upper deck with its own galley. It provides a gorgeous setting of linen-draped tables, blue cushioned chairs, and filmy white curtains, imparting a true Mediterranean flavor. At breakfast and lunch, the indoor/outdoor Portofino provides buffet dining; at night a wing of the spacious room is transformed into an à la carte restaurant featuring Northern Italian specialties. Tables must be reserved for dinner, but there is no service charge here or elsewhere on this gratuities-included ship. Complimentary dinner wine is poured here and in the main dining room.

Facilities and Entertainment   The two-tiered Seven Seas show lounge hosts varied entertainment, ranging from Broadway revues to concert pianists. The Stars Lounge is the disco/after-hours club where sleek, deep-blue leather chairs backed in wood line up along a glass-topped bar.

A few steps away, cigar lovers gather in the Connoisseur Club's tobacco-colored leather armchairs near a granite topped faux fireplace. Next door, the small Navigator Lounge serves cocktails throughout the day. At the large library stocked with books, periodicals, and 800 videos, there are three computers where passengers can check their e-mail. Two boutiques sell designer wares.

A dark, rich-looking casino sports tables for blackjack, stud poker, roulette, and craps; slots and poker machines are found in a separate room. High on Deck 12, passengers walk through a hall of marble and carpet to emerge in the light, attractive Galileo's, a piano bar and lounge with indoor/outdoor seating and a dance floor. One deck higher, forward, the Vista Lounge provides a hideaway of tambour chairs with thick yellow-and-green striped cushions. It can be use for private party.

Beauty, Sports, and Fitness   Adjacent to the Vista Lounge are the spa, gym, and aerobics rooms, managed by noted aromatherapy practitioner Judith Jackson, whose programs are featured at resorts such as the Breakers and the Greenbriar.

The large amidships pool area offers a grill and two Jacuzzis, plus a venue for moonlight barbecues and dancing. Golfers get two driving cages and a putting green.

Seven Seas Mariner	(Preview)	
Registry: France	Length: 670 feet	Beam: 90 feet
Cabins: 354	Draft: 21.4 feet	Speed: 20 knots
Maximum Passengers: 700	Passenger Decks: NA	Elevators: NA
	Crew: 445	Space Ratio: 71.4

The Ship   In another joint venture, Monte Carlo–based V. Ships and Radisson Seven Seas are building cruising's first all-balcony, all-suite luxury cruise ship. Scheduled for delivery in March 2001, the *Seven Seas Mariner* has the same architects and interior designer, Petter Yran and Bjorn Storbraaten of Norway, who designed *Song of Flower* and other luxury cruise ships. *Mariner* will be the largest ship in the Radisson fleet and will have 280 standard ocean-view suites of 301 square feet including balconies, and 80 suites ranging from 390 to 1,110 square feet. In addition to 24-hour room service, *Mariner* will have four dining venues, including a main dining room able to accommodate all passengers in one open seating, an international grill, and an Asian specialty restaurant. She will also feature a deluxe spa.

The French-flagged ship will have a French captain and French and European senior officers. She is expected to offer itineraries worldwide.

The vessel's innovative pod propulsion system eliminates the traditional shaft-and-rudder system, making the vessel 10–15 percent more efficient and reducing noise and vibration. The pods have forward-facing propellers that can be turned 360 degrees, which optimizes maneuverability, fuel efficiency, and speed.

The new *Mariner* will continue the line's plan to add a new ship annually for five years. Her sister ship, *Seven Seas Voyager* (the working name) is expected to be delivered in 2002.

Royal Caribbean International

1050 Caribbean Way, Miami, FL 33132
(305) 539-6000; (800) 659-7225; fax (800) 722-5329
www.royalcaribbean.com

Type of Ships   Superliners and megaliners.

Type of Cruises   Mainstream, mass market, modestly upscale, wholesome ambience.

Cruise Line's Strengths
- outstanding facilities and activities
- entertainment
- product consistency

Cruise Line's Shortcomings
- small cabins on older fleet
- limited storage in cabins on older fleet
- impersonal nature of big ships

Fellow Passengers   Moderately upscale couples and singles. Families with household income of $40,000+. They're fun-seekers looking for wide variety in shipboard activities and destinations. Average age is early 40s, slightly lower on three- and four-night cruises and slightly higher on ten-night or longer trips. In summer, the age drops because of numerous families traveling with children. Under 25 percent are age 60 or older. About half of the passengers have cruised at least once, and a quarter are Royal Caribbean repeaters. They're almost evenly divided between men and women, and nine in ten are North American. Up to 73 percent of men and 65 percent of women are married; 16 percent are retired; 36 percent are professional, managerial, or proprietors; 9 percent are homemakers. About 50 percent vacation twice or more annually. Educational level, occupations, and age change when three- and four-night cruisers are factored in. Less expensive, shorter cruises appeal to younger people because they're affordable and allow first-timers to sample cruising with minimal commitment.

Recommended For   Almost anyone taking a first cruise. Those who like large ships, want an array of options, want to be active, sociable, and don't mind large crowds and lines. Ideal for families with several generations traveling together because there's something for every age.

Not Recommended For   Small-ship devotees; those who seek a quiet or intellectual milieu, hate crowds, and have no patience for long lines; those who expect a luxury cruise with five-star amenities.

Cruise Areas and Seasons   Caribbean, Bahamas, Mexico, year-round. Bermuda, Europe, Alaska, in summer. Hawaii, spring and fall. Panama Canal, winter, May, and fall. Asia, Australia, fall and winter.

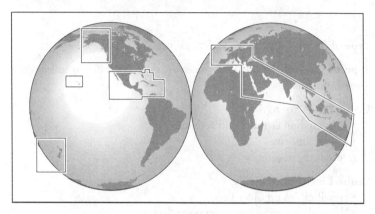

The Line   Founded in 1969 as a partnership of three prominent Norwegian shipping companies, Royal Caribbean Cruises Ltd. (the new marketing name is Royal Caribbean International) was the first line to launch ships designed for year-round Caribbean cruising. The vessels proved to be so popular that within five years more capacity was needed. To provide it, two vessels were "stretched"—cut in half, then lengthened by inserting prefabricated midsections.

For the 1980s, RCCL added superliners with unique designs. Introduction in 1988 of the *Sovereign of the Seas*—first in a new generation of megaliners and the largest cruise ship ever built at the time—got a head start on the 1990s. Few ships in history have received so much attention. On *Sovereign*'s arrival in Miami, traffic backed up for miles as people on shore tried to glimpse her. That year, RCCL merged with Admiral Cruises and for the first time began offering short cruises, Admiral's forte.

To get a jump on the twenty-first century, the line launched Project Vision for a new generation of six megaliners. *Legend of the Seas,* first in the group, debuted in 1995 with acres of glass and cruising's first 18-hole miniature golf course. By 1998, all six ships had joined the fleet. The following year, RCCL launched *Voyager of the Seas,* the first of a new class of ships and the industry's first 142,000-ton cruise ship. Two more, *Explorer of the Seas* and *Adventure of the Seas,* are scheduled to enter service in October 2000 and spring 2002. RCCL will also introduce Vantage, another new class—2,000-passenger, 85,000-ton ships—with *Radiance of the Seas* in 2001 and *Brilliance of the Seas* in 2002.

After two decades of focusing solely on the Caribbean, the line branched out, first to Bermuda and then to the West Coast, Mexico, Alaska, Europe, and Asia, and in 2000, added Africa and South America. To reflect its growth, the line changed its marketing name to Royal Caribbean International (the corporate name remains Royal Caribbean Cruises Ltd.) and created a new logo that retains the crown (of its Norwegian origins). It also created a new product, Cruise Hyatt, combining a three- or four-night hotel stay with a cruise departing from Puerto Rico or other locations where Hyatt has hotels.

In a surprise move in 1997, RCCL bought Celebrity Cruises—a deal worth $1.3 billion that has resulted in a fleet of 20 ships when all vessels of the two lines enter service by 2001. Celebrity operates as a separate brand.

For all its firsts and innovative designs, RCCL is still a conservative company that built its success on a solid, consistent product. Royal Caribbean is a public company, traded on the New York Stock Exchange. Majority ownership is held, however, by one of its founders, Anders Wilhelmsen and Co., and the Pritzker family of Chicago, who also hold controlling interest in Hyatt Hotels.

The Fleet	Built/Renovated	Tonnage	Passengers
Adventure of the Seas	2001	142,000	3,114
Brilliance of the Seas	2002	85,000	2,000
Enchantment of the Seas	1997/99	74,000	1,950
Explorer of the Seas	2000	142,000	3,114
Grandeur of the Seas	1996/98	74,000	1,950
Legend of the Seas	1995	69,130	1,804
Majesty of the Seas	1992/97	73,941	2,354
Monarch of the Seas	1991/99	73,941	2,766
Nordic Empress	1990/98	48,563	1,600
Radiance of the Seas	2001	88,000	2,100
Rhapsody of the Seas	1997	78,491	2,000
Sovereign of the Seas	1988/96	73,192	2,274
Splendour of the Seas	1996/98	70,950	1,804
Viking Serenade	1982/91	40,132	1,840
Vision of the Seas	1998	78,491	2,000
Voyager of the Seas	1999	142,000	3,114

Style   RCCL ships are designed for high-volume, year-round, warm-weather cruises of the Caribbean, Bahamas, and Mexico. More recently, the line has sailed seasonally in Alaska, Bermuda, and Europe.

With its new global vision, Royal Caribbean now says the "Caribbean" in its name represents a style of cruising, not just a place to cruise. And the "C" in RCCL could just as well stand for consistency. Whether you take a Royal Caribbean cruise in Europe, Asia, or the Caribbean, the atmosphere is friendly and relaxed, and activities are many and varied. But understand, these are big ships that hum with activities almost around the clock. They have acres of sun decks, large pools, and lots of outdoor activity: games, competitions, the ShipShape fitness program, and sports that often combine with sports in port. For example, Golf Ahoy! participants play at courses throughout the cruise line's network. RCCL is the official cruise line of the Professional Golfers' Association and Senior PGA Tour. The ships have cheerful, contemporary decor with themes related to Broadway hits, operas, and the circus. Cabins are small but functional on all but the newest ships. All vessels have programs for children.

Distinctive Features   Viking Crown Lounge; Golf Ahoy! program; *Legend* and *Splendour*'s miniature golf courses; *Voyager*'s rock climbing wall and ice skating rink; Labadee, RCCL's private beach; Crown & Anchor lounges in San Juan and St. Thomas. Room service from dining room menus during lunch and dinner; children's program. Passenger Internet centers.

	HIGHEST	LOWEST	AVERAGE
PER DIEM	$505	$150	$291

The above per diems are calculated from the cruise line's non-discounted *cruise only* fares on standard accommodations. Per diems vary by season, by cabin, and by cruise areas.

Rates   Port charges are included.

Special Fares and Discounts
- Breakthrough Fares are capacity-controlled discounts (up to 40 percent) that change daily. The earlier you buy, the better the discount.
- Third/Fourth Person: Yes.
- Children's Fare: Third/fourth person rates, and promotional fares for free travel or as low as $49 or $99 for a child age 11 or younger.
- Single Supplement: From 150 percent when specific cabin requested.

- Single Guarantee: Category and cabin assigned by RCCL.
- Share Fare: RCCL matches persons of same gender and smoking preference.

Packages
- Air/Sea: Yes.
- Cruise-only/air add-ons with transfers: Yes
- Others: Honeymoon, golf, family, wedding. Crowning Touches and Royal Occasions packages (extra charge) designed for honeymooners or special occasion.
- Pre/Post: In departure ports and some vacation spots. Cruise Hyatt combines three/four-night hotel with cruise.

Past Passengers   The four membership levels of the Crown and Anchor Society for repeat passengers are based on how many cruises you take: Silver membership, after one cruise; Gold, two cruises; Platinum, five; and Diamond, ten or more. The biggest benefit is personalized attention by shipboard personnel. Members also get *Crown & Anchor,* a quarterly magazine with information on new programs, itineraries, and ships; special offers and coupons; a color-coded landing card sticker; and on cruises of seven or more nights, a cocktail party. Gold members also receive special offers on future cruises; Platinum, terry robes for use during the cruise; and Diamond, exclusive coupons, boarding privileges, and a bottle of champagne on boarding.

The Last Word   Royal Caribbean is a pacesetter among cruise lines, respected by friends and competitors for its weight and wisdom. For example, to end the discounting chaos, RCCL created Breakthrough Fares, a capacity-controlled advance-booking discount system that the entire industry embraced instantly. A smaller or less respected line could not have had the same impact.

RCCL is a cruise line of megaliners. It targets 80 percent of people buying cruises; only budget and luxury customers are excluded. RCCL's vision may not be shared by its more affluent fans of the past who have seen the product's service and quality change. There's no denying that the big ships are big and impersonal, and they have blurred and narrowed the quality that once separated RCCL from the pack. If you don't like big ships, this isn't the line for you. But, if you want a cruise vacation on ships that have everything, RCCL offers value that's hard to beat.

ROYAL CARIBBEAN INT'L. STANDARD FEATURES

Officers Norwegian, International.

Staff Dining, Cabin/International; Cruise/American and British.

Dining Facilities Two seatings for three meals plus midnight buffet; indoor/outdoor cafe with breakfast and lunch buffet; alternative dining for dinner with table service on all ships. *Voyager*-Class, three-level dining room, five alternative venues.

Special Diets Low-fat, low-cholesterol, lean cuisine. Full vegetarian menus. Request kosher at time of booking.

Room Service 24 hours with light menu; dining room menus for lunch and dinner.

Dress Code Casual but neat by day; informal in evening; one or two nights formal/semiformal. Tuxedo rental available.

Cabin Amenities Direct-dial telephone; radio; television; daily world news update; bathtubs in suites; suites with marble baths on *Majesty, Monarch.*

Electrical Outlets 110 AC.

Wheelchair Access Ramp on all ships; 4 cabins on *Majesty, Monarch, Nordic Empress, Viking Serenade;* 10 cabins on *Sovereign;* 17 on *Legend/Splendour,* 14 on other *Vision* ships; 26 on *Voyager*-Class.

Recreation and Entertainment Show lounge with entertainment nightly; disco, bingo, horse racing, movies, wine tastings, dance lessons. Viking Crown Lounge, bars/lounges, card room, library.

Sports and Other Activities Two outdoor pools; *Viking Serenade,* indoor/outdoor pool. Sports deck with basketball, Ping-Pong, shuffleboard, skeet shooting. Miniature golf course on *Legend* and *Splendour* and *Voyager*-Class.

Beauty and Fitness Beauty/barber shop; massage; sauna; Ship-Shape fitness program; jogging track; health club/gym. Solarium, elaborate spa on *Vision* and *Voyager* ships.

Other Facilities Boutiques; medical facilities; laundry/dry cleaning services; meeting rooms; cinema/theater on *Majesty, Monarch, Sovereign.*

Children's Facilities Youth programs year-round on all. Playrooms and teen centers on *Sovereign, Vision,* and *Voyager* ships, *Nordic Empress, Viking Serenade;* teen nightclub on *Majesty, Monarch, Viking Serenade,* and *Vision* and *Voyager* ships.

Theme Cruises Jazz, country music, variety of sports.

Smoking Public rooms are nonsmoking except in designated areas.

RCCL Suggested Tipping Per person per day, cabin steward, $3.50; dining room waiter, $3.50; busboy, $2; 15 percent to bar waiters.

Credit Cards For cruise payment and on-board charges: American Express, Carte Blanche, Diners Club, Discover, MasterCard, Visa.

Sovereign of the Seas	Quality ⑤	Value C
Majesty / Monarch	Quality ⑤	Value C
Registry: Norway	Length: 880 feet	Beam: 106 feet
Cabins: 1,140	Draft: 25 feet	Speed: 19 knots
Maximum Passengers:	Passenger Decks: 14	Elevators: 11
2,852/2,744	Crew: 825/827	Space Ratio: 30.8/32.3

The Ships First, try to grasp the size: three football fields laid end to end. From a lounge 14 decks above the water, you could look the Statue of Liberty in the eyes. At the pier, a double berth is necessary, and almost every ship in sight is smaller. When the *Sovereign of the Seas* was introduced in 1988, she was the largest cruise ship ever built and stirred unprecedented excitement and publicity. More important, she came with innovations that have influenced the design of all superliners and megaliners that followed.

Her dramatic atrium, the Centrum, was a cruise ship first and was quickly copied. Located amidships and spanning five decks, the atrium opens the space to create a light and inviting environment. Stairs and balconies around the atrium and its glass-enclosed elevators seem suspended in air. A white piano set amid tropical foliage at the atrium's base plays soft music that carries to upper decks and sets the harmonious tone found ship-wide. The atrium, similar to a hotel's lobby, provides a friendly focal point. Passengers are dazzled, but not intimidated, and the notion of entering a behemoth dissipates. The atrium also separates the forward section of the ship, which contains the cabins, from the aft with all public rooms and dining, sports, entertainment, and recreation facilities. The arrangement has several advantages: Cabins are quieter; distances among public areas are shorter; and the ship doesn't seem so enormous.

Another element: The ship looks outward—few areas lack natural light or a view to the outdoors—a feature absent on many new ships. Superb design features downplay the *Sovereign*'s gigantic size. Together with an incredible array of facilities, they explain passengers' immediate acceptance of the megaliner. *Sovereign*'s twins, *Monarch of the Seas* and *Majesty of the Seas,* arrived with few changes—a few more cabins, a family suite, and a redesigned Windjammer Cafe. Many public rooms carry the same names. Throughout, contemporary elegance creates a warm, inviting ambience.

The three ships are floating resorts, making the most of their size by providing spaces for varying tastes. These include the signature Viking Crown Lounge perched high on the stack; wide, outdoor promenades encircling the vessels; and sunny and shaded areas on three decks. They offer so many facilities and activities that even the most frantically active person can't participate in all of the options.

Regardless of ship or itinerary, the real experience is on board the *Sovereign* sisters, where you can live the good life in megadoses, as one friend put it. In one day, you could start with breakfast in bed, exercise in the gym, have a massage, buy diamonds or duty-free perfume, relax on deck, take in a movie, and savor champagne and caviar in the wine bar before dinner. After a seven-course meal in the dining room, you could two-step, line-dance, disco, or limbo; watch the revue in the show lounge; listen to late-night comedy; or try your luck in the casino until it's time for the midnight buffet. Robin Leach, eat your heart out.

Itineraries   See Appendix B.

Cabins   Each of the trio has 16 categories of cabins. *Monarch* and *Majesty* cabins are similar to *Sovereign*'s in size and decor, but have major enhancements. Verandas were added to 50 deluxe outside cabins, and suites and family suites sleeping up to six were created. The latter have two bedrooms, sitting room, two bathrooms, and veranda. *Majesty* has 146 cabins in the larger outside category, which are considerably more comfortable than those on *Sovereign,* and the Bridge Deck contains only suites and deluxe staterooms with private verandas.

Bathrooms, though not large, are well designed. They have plenty of shelves for toiletries, thick towels, hair dryers, and excellent water pressure. Light decor helps compensate for standard cabins' smallness. Designed to make the most out of every inch of space, they're fitted with a vanity table, chair, and twin beds convertible to daytime couches.

Sovereign *Specifications*   418 inside cabins, 710 outside; 12 suites. Standard dimensions, inside cabins 119 square feet, outside 122 square feet. 945 with twin beds (convertible to doubles); 196 third/fourth persons; no singles. 6 wheelchair-accessible.

Majesty *and* Monarch *Specifications*   444 inside cabins, 721 outside; 12 suites; 62 deluxe cabins and suites with verandas. Standard dimensions, 120 square feet. 917 with twin beds (convertible to queen); 260 third/fourth persons; no singles. 4 wheelchair-accessible.

Dining   RCCL ships don't serve gourmet fare and don't aim to. Rather, galleys produce tasty food that's plentiful but not excessive, with ample variety. All ships have the same menus (consistency at work), although longer European cruises may feature dishes of the locale. A typical menu offers seven juices and appetizers; three soups; two salads; five entrees with a choice of pasta, fish, chicken, veal, and beef; three desserts; and a selection of cheeses and ice cream.

In keeping with its ShipShape program, all menus have light selections annotated with nutritional information. You can also select vegetarian dishes or request the full vegetarian menu for an entire cruise. Wine lists include California, French, other European, and South American vintages. Prices are moderate.

Each ship has two dining rooms serving three meals, all with assigned seating. The *Sovereign*'s Kismet Dining Room has elaborate columns and lighting fixtures; its twin, Gigi Dining Room, has columns styled after palm trees. *Majesty*'s Mikado Dining Room has a Japanese theme, whereas the springtime theme of its twin, Maytime, is expressed in a mural of apple trees in bloom. *Monarch*'s two dining rooms offer greater contrast. The Brigadoon Dining Room has a Scottish tartan motif; frosted glass dividers and gothic arches divide the space. In the Flower Drum Song Dining Room, a mural of Chinese fans enhances the sophisticated, Oriental decor. Backlighted panels between fluted columns divide the room. Lunch and dinner can be ordered from room service from dining room menus.

One of the most noticeable differences between *Sovereign* and her sisters is the two-deck, indoor-outdoor Windjammer Cafe, the place for casual breakfasts and lunches and alternative dinner venue. Breakfast and lunch buffets offer a variety of hot and cold dishes. Quality of the food is equal to that in the dining room, but selections are more limited. Dinner offers full table service, and menus change daily. The Windjammer Cafe, wrapped on three sides by windows and spanning the ship's width, was redesigned, expanded, and lightened on the *Monarch* and *Majesty*. In place of *Sovereign*'s centerpiece—a two-story, mahogany-framed tree with crystal bubbles—*Monarch* and *Majesty* have a mini-atrium with winter garden, waterfalls, and skylight.

Service   RCCL's crews, from the Norwegian captains to mini–United Nations of the cabin and dining room staff, are courteous and eager to please. An affable, largely Caribbean group of stewards serve the *Sovereign* group. They tidy rooms twice daily and provide evening turndown service. Dining staffs have many Europeans and provide attentive, efficient service. Indeed, the staff is so conscious of the constant evaluation of their work, as reflected in passengers' comment cards, that they sometimes overdo their attention. And it's likely that your waiter, when his supervisors aren't around, will all but beg you to praise him in your comment cards—his job may depend on it.

Facilities and Entertainment   Almost 24 hours a day, there's music to suit every mood—including big band, steel band, Latin, country, rock, strolling violins, and classical concerts. The Follies Lounge, *Sovereign*'s richly decorated bilevel showroom, stages two shows nightly. Other entertainment may include such headliners as Diahann Carroll or Phyllis Diller. The rooms have video walls with 50 television monitors on movable banks of 25 screens each. Comfortable seats have excellent sight lines, with a few exceptions. Smoking isn't permitted in these lounges. Other large lounges—Finian's Rainbow and the Music Man—have late-night entertainers and music. Anything Goes is the late-into-the night disco. *Monarch*'s disco, Ain't Misbehavin', has a glass sculpture of Fats Waller.

Cantilevered from the funnel and encircling it is the extraordinary Viking Crown Lounge. The room, 12 stories above the water, provides a fabulous 360-degree view of the sea and sunset.

Among small lounges is the nautical-motif Schooner Bar, a favorite casual bar by day and a lively piano bar at night. Casino Royale next door offers blackjack, 170 slot machines, and American roulette. On *Monarch*, fiber-optic lights sparkle in the casino's carpeting. Touch of Class is a chic champagne bar where 50 people can clink flutes and scoop caviar. Decor lives up to the lounge's name and includes two lifelike bronze statues of 1920s flappers. Other options include Flashes teen nightclub, karaoke, a shopping boulevard, and a theater showing films daily.

Activities and Diversions   Among activities may be bingo; napkin folding; wine tasting; parlor games; dance classes; bridge; ice carving; parties for singles, children, and teens; a costume party; religious services; and a passenger talent show. The wood-paneled library resembles an English club; it can also be used for meetings. Two levels of sun decks provide peace, privacy, and a place to read.

Sports, Fitness, and Beauty   Fitness enthusiasts have a one-third-mile outside deck encircling the vessel and a second jogging track. The well-equipped health clubs offers a large exercise room with ballet barres, stair-steppers, bicycles, rowing machines, weight-training equipment, and a high-energy staff. The sports deck has twin swimming pools, two whirlpools, and a basketball court. Saunas and locker rooms are available at no extra cost.

ShipShape Fitness activities start with a sunrise stretch class or water exercises, and low-impact aerobics and other programs are timed not to interfere with shore visits. Walkathons, basketball, and Ping-Pong tournaments round out the program. Participants earn "dollars" for each activity, redeemable for T-shirts and visors. Vitality Unlimited class is designed for senior citizens. All exercise classes are led by experienced fitness personnel, and all menus offer two low-fat, low-calorie entrees, prepared to American Heart Association guidelines. The beauty salon/barber shop offers massage and beauty treatments at additional cost.

Children's Facilities   RCCL was among the first lines to create a children's program with youth centers, play rooms, and counselors. The *Sovereign* group offers the program year-round. They also have video arcades and teen centers. *Majesty* and *Monarch* have teen nightclubs.

Youngsters have their own daily agenda, slipped under the cabin door each night. Among the activities are ice cream and pizza parties, dance classes, golf putting, face painting, midnight basketball, autograph hunts, talent shows, and shore tours. Babysitters (extra cost), cribs, and high chairs are available. Captain Sealy's Kids' Gallery, a menu for children ages 4–12, offers such favorites as peanut butter sandwiches, hamburgers, and pizzas, along with salads, fruit, and alphabet soup.

Shore Excursions Descriptive booklets are included with documents mailed to passengers. Excursions target many interests, but essentially they're standard programs. Except for its golf programs and cruises that include Labadee in their itinerary, RCCL's shore excursions are similar to those of other lines cruising the Caribbean. They include island tours, beach trips, and snorkeling and diving. Created in 1987, RCCL's private resort, Labadee, on the north coast of Haiti, offers the best day at the beach of any line. Its setting is beautiful—lush mountains rise behind a lovely cove with a series of crescent-shaped beaches. There are pavilions for dining, entertainment, water sports equipment, and a marketplace with Haitian crafts, which are the Caribbean's best. Music, dancing, and performances by a local folklore group are provided. In spring 2000, *Sovereign* began year-round Bahamas cruises from Port Canaveral, her new home port, catering especially to the family market. Her itinerary calls for a day at Coco Cay, a small Bahamian island. Diversions for a range of ages include beach games, pedal boats, shopping, steel-band music, visits to a shipwreck led by snorkeling instructors, a barbecue, palm-shaded trails, six sandy beaches for swimming, and hammocks and beach chairs for lounging. The island is large enough to provide secluded spots. Children's programs are available.

Nordic Empress	Quality ❺	Value C
Registry: Liberia	Length: 692 feet	Beam: 100 feet
Cabins: 801	Draft: 25 feet	Speed: 19.5 knots
Maximum Passengers:	Passenger Decks: 12	Elevators: 7
2,020	Crew: 685	Space Ratio: 30.4

The Ship Created for the short-cruise market, *Nordic Empress* dazzles with its design—from light that streams in by day to nighttime glitter. Passengers board at the nine-deck-tall atrium called the Centrum. Two of four elevators are glass and overlook a waterfall and greenery. Most public rooms flow from here. Two center decks contain the dining room, show-room, casino, and lounges. The Sun Deck topside is an all-day center of activities—from sunning and swimming to entertainment and dancing under the stars. It also contains the fitness and kids' centers.

The *Nordic Empress* continues RCCL's consistency. There are no surprises except the ship itself, which has a very different look from other members of the fleet. The vessel offers a good sampler for those wanting to try a high-energy, activity-filled cruise and for busy people seeking weekend getaways.

Itineraries   See Appendix B.

Cabins   The dozen categories include many inside and lower-priced out-side cabins. All are designed to be light and tropical in feeling. All have two lower beds, color television, three-channel radio, telephone, and private bath. Sixty percent are outside cabins with large windows. All suites and deluxe cabins have balconies.

Specifications   318 inside cabins, 483 outside; 6 suites; 69 deluxe cab-ins with verandas. Standard dimensions, 194 square feet. 495 with twin beds (all convertible to double); 358 with upper/lower berths accommo-dating third and fourth persons; no singles; 4 wheelchair-accessible.

Dining   The two-level Carmen Dining Room has walls of floor-to-ceiling windows spanning two decks and providing panoramic views. There are two seatings for the three meals. Menus are the same as offered on other RCCL ships and include theme dinners.

Meals and snacks are served around the clock, starting with early-riser's breakfast at 6:30 a.m. and ending with the midnight buffet. A typical seven-course menu lists a wide choice of juices and appetizers; soups; sal-ads; pasta; entrees with fish, chicken, veal, and beef; desserts; cheese; and ice cream. All menus have health-conscious selections.

Breakfast and lunch buffets are served in the glass-domed Windjammer Cafe. It's also the alternative dinner restaurant, offering full table service between 6:30 and 10:30 p.m., and a midnight buffet. A Sun Worshipper's lunch and afternoon tea are served poolside. The full dining room menu is available for room service at lunch and dinner.

Service   *Nordic Empress*'s crew are eager to please. Stewards, most Caribbean, make up rooms twice a day and provide evening turndown ser-vice. The friendly dining staff quickly learn your preferences. As on all other RCCL ships, they will encourage good reviews on your passenger comment cards.

Facilities and Entertainment   Nighttime entertainment is some of RCCL's best, with good shows, music, and dancing for many tastes. Even a three-day cruise fits in the captain's cocktail party and a passenger talent show. Big, Broadway-style productions are staged in the impressive, tiered Strike Up The Band lounge. Sight lines are good from almost any seat. The lounge also has a dance floor.

The ship's most dazzling feature is the trilevel Casino Royale, offering 220 slot machines, 9 blackjack tables, roulette, craps, and wheel of fortune. Between the casino and Centrum is the festive Carousel Pub, designed with a merry-go-round theme. Under the tented ceiling is a mural with carousel paraphernalia. The larger, Art Deco High Society lounge features entertainment and dance music from the 1950s to '90s.

Viking Crown Lounge is at the stern on Sun Deck, rather than cantilevered from the stack as on other RCCL ships. Nonetheless, with three walls of windows, it's a fine observation area. Late night, it's a disco.

Note: When the ship is in Bermuda during summer, much of this entertainment won't be available. Bermudan regulations don't allow ships to open their casinos or stage shows while they're in port. However, the ship offers Bermuda-by-Night shore excursions, or you can explore local night life independently.

Activities and Diversions   Passengers on short cruises usually pack in as many activities as possible. *Nordic Empress* provides abundant choices. Topside by day are outdoor games and entertainment; by night are music and dancing. Elsewhere are dance classes, cards, crafts, bingo, and karaoke.

Sports, Fitness, and Beauty   The large ShipShape Fitness Center has a glass-enclosed exercise area and an array of equipment, plus saunas, showers, and massage rooms. On deck are three whirlpools and two fountains that cascade into two pools (one for children). The beauty salon offers hair, facial, and beauty treatments (additional charge). Video golf in the Golf Ahoy! Center enables participants to try their skill at world-famous courses projected on the screen. A computer analyzes the stroke and scores the game. ShipShape activities range from aquadynamics to basketball free throws. "Dollars" earned for participation can be redeemed for T-shirts and visors.

Children's Facilities   Kids' Konnection is a multipurpose, 95-square-foot play room for children ages 5–12. Designed with a space-station theme, the room has an 11-foot ceiling, making room for the Tubular Time labyrinth of suspended tubes that are lighted and carpeted inside. Children can crawl through the tubes to a slide and clubhouse platform.

The youth program provides participants with a daily agenda, slipped under the cabin door at night. It's packed with activities, including ice cream and pizza parties, face painting, midnight basketball, talent shows, and shore tours. Menus designed for children ages 4–12 offer such favorites as peanut butter sandwiches, hot dogs, and pizzas, plus salads and fruit. Babysitters (extra cost), cribs, and high chairs are available.

Shore Excursions   Descriptive booklets accompany documents mailed to passengers. Excursions target varied interests but essentially are off-the-shelf programs, among them island tours, beach trips, snorkeling, and diving.

Viking Serenade	Quality ❹	Value C
Registry: Liberia	Length: 620 feet	Beam: 89 feet
Cabins: 756	Draft: 24 feet	Speed: 21 knots
Maximum Passengers:	Passenger Decks: 11	Elevators: 5
1,863	Crew: 610	Space Ratio: 26.5

The Ship   Unlike Royal Caribbean's fleet in design, the *Viking Serenade*'s beginning as a car ferry explains her boxy silhouette. Built in 1982, she was rebuilt in 1991 after RCCL obtained her in the Admiral Cruises acquisition. The $75 million conversion added cabins, the Viking Crown Lounge, a second dining room, a conference center, and a children's playroom. Existing cabins and public rooms were renovated, and in 1994, public rooms and the Teen Center were again refurbished.

Of 11 passenger decks, all but the lower 2 have public rooms. Entertainment options include Hello Dolly, the main lounge, staging Las Vegas–type revues; Bali Hai, for entertainment and dancing; and Schooner Bar, the popular piano bar. Three meals in two seatings are served in the Magic Flute Dining Room and smaller Aida Dining Room. Theme dinners and buffets are scheduled.

Decor blends California casual and contemporary Scandinavian designs. Very much identified with the upbeat, active California scene, the ship attracts a mix of passengers. Action centers on the Sun Deck, which contains a fitness center (exercise equipment and the ShipShape program), sauna and massage rooms, the pool (with a retractable dome), open jogging track, teen center, and the Windjammer Cafe. The indoor/outdoor eatery serves breakfast and lunch buffets and afternoon ice cream, and is the alternative dining area, offering table service between 6:30 and 10:30 p.m. Upgraded room service provides lunch and dinner from the full dining room menu. Above is the Viking Crown Lounge with floor-to-ceiling windows on three sides. It's a daytime observation lounge and a late-night disco. The ship has a shopping arcade, beauty salon, and barber shop.

Itineraries   See Appendix B.

Cabins   In general, cabins, in 16 categories, are larger than those on RCCL's older ships. They have television, radios, curtained closets, large dressing tables, and two sofa-style beds (convert to queen). Five deluxe suites have private balconies. The Royal Suite has a sitting area, wet bar, whirlpool tub, and walk-in closet.

Specifications   278 inside cabins, 478 outside; 8 suites. Standard dimensions, 162 square feet. 511 with twin beds (499 convertible to double); 358 third/fourth persons; no singles. 4 wheelchair-accessible.

Postscript   *Viking Serenade*'s different look and feel results in part from its West Coast location, but she still delivers the line's consistency. Readers considering a cruise on this ship should review the entire RCCL section for a better understanding of the cruise experience the line offers.

Legend of the Seas	Quality ❼	Value B
Splendour / Rhapsody	Quality ❼	Value A
Enchantment / Grandeur	Quality ❼	Value A
Vision of the Seas	Quality ❽	Value A

Registry: *Legend / Grandeur / Vision:* Liberia; *Splendour / Enchantment / Rhapsody:* Norway	Length: 867/916/915 feet	
	Beam: 105/105.6 feet	
Cabins: 902/975/1,000	Draft: 25/24 feet	Speed: 24/22 knots
Maximum Passengers: 2,076/2,446/2,435	Passenger Decks: 11	Elevators: 11/9
	Crew: 724/760/765	Space Ratio: 38.32

The Ships   *Legend of the Seas* arrived in 1995, the first of six megaliners in the Project Vision series. Her twin, *Splendour of the Seas,* and sister, *Grandeur of the Seas,* followed in 1996. *Grandeur*'s twin, *Enchantment of the Seas,* was launched in 1997, as was *Rhapsody of the Seas,* which was followed a year later by her twin, *Vision of the Seas.* Each has distinguishing features. Constructed in France and Finland, the megaliners were quickly labeled "the ships of glass." Each has two acres of windows, glass windbreaks, skylights, and walls of windows in public spaces. The Centrum, the centerpiece atrium, rises seven decks—two more than on *Sovereign*-Class vessels—and is topped by the Viking Crown Lounge. Bubble elevators whisk passengers to the lounge.

At the Centrum's base is the Champagne Terrace and Bar, where fine wines and champagne are served by the glass. The elegant setting sets the tone for the ships. *Grandeur*'s Champagne Bar covers the Centrum's entire lower level. A white baby grand piano stands next to a stairway to the second level. Decorative screens create conversation corners.

Works of art on *Splendour* were created by more than 50 artists and studios. The ship's atrium sculpture is the fleet's most dramatic. The work consists of three elements symbolizing the solar system. The dominant component, an 18-foot gilded disc representing the sun, hangs on a diagonal, silhouetted by rays from the skylight. Iridescent bulbs around the disc transmit and reflect colored light throughout the atrium. Hundreds of steel cords attached to the upper, outer rim of the disc gather at the top of the atrium and are illuminated, creating a glow. The ships embrace the sea and vistas through windows and glass. Natural light sparkles, and open space is abundant.

On the Sun Deck is the Solarium, a landscaped indoor/outdoor area with a second swimming pool, whirlpools, and a cafe. Its Crystal Canopy provides cover in inclement weather. Unlike glass roofs on other ships, this one doesn't fold onto itself; instead it moves intact. The design uses much more glass, admitting maximum light into the Solarium when the roof is closed. The most celebrated new features on *Legend* and *Splendour* are the world's first floating 18-hole miniature golf courses. A station, where equipment and tee times can be obtained, resembles a miniature clubhouse.

Itineraries   See Appendix B.

Cabins   A major improvement in the *Legend*-Class is the size of standard cabins—153 square feet compared to 122 square feet in comparable *Sovereign*-group cabins, For two decades Royal Caribbean said cabin size was unimportant because passengers spend so little time in their rooms, but in the *Vision* series, cabins are larger and more comfortable, with sitting areas and, for the first time, many balconies—one in four. There are many more have bathrooms with tubs and showers, too. Pastels and light woods are used in decor. The Royal Suite has a baby grand piano, whirlpool tub, and veranda.

Legend/Splendour *Specifications*   327 inside cabins, 575 outside; 83 suites; 4 family suites; 231 with balconies; 388 third/fourth persons; no singles; 17 wheelchair-accessible.

Grandeur/Enchantment *Specifications*   399 inside cabins, 576 outside, 18 suites; 4 family suites; 72 deluxe outside; 212 with balconies; 403 third/fourth persons; no singles; 14 wheelchair-accessible.

Rhapsody/Vision *Specifications*   407 inside cabins, 593 outside; 18 suites; 72 deluxe; 4 family suites; 229 with balconies; 287 third/fourth persons; no singles; 14 wheelchair-accessible.

Dining *Legend*'s Romeo and Juliet Dining Room (the King and I on *Splendour* and Great Gatsby on *Grandeur*) spans two decks and has 20-foot-tall glass walls on each side—offering spectacular views from every table. Because the dining room is in the ship's superstructure rather than the hull, walls can be virtually all glass—the load-bearing function handled by interior columns. A revolving platform with a grand piano on the first level is framed by curving stairways to the balcony.

Decor in *Splendour*'s King and I is noteworthy. A Thai temple facade has been replicated, and 16 historical paintings plus 2 epic murals were created by artists of Thailand's royal family. Each painting tells a story.

The nautical-motif Windjammer Cafe on Sun Deck is the indoor/outdoor area for breakfast and lunch buffets and alternative evening dining. Floor-to-ceiling glass walls on three sides and a sloping skylight brighten the room. Each lunch has a theme, and ethnic food joins the regular array of hot dishes, salads, and sandwiches. Dinner, served between 6:30 and 10:30 p.m., offers full table service. The cafe also is a popular spot for reading, playing cards, and watching the water.

Service Dining room service meets RCCL's high standards, but room stewards are getting mixed reviews. Many workers know little English, and they lack training, the latter probably resulting from the line's adding so many large ships in a short time.

Facilities and Entertainment *Vision* ships are state-of-the-art at every turn. Computers helped design the bilevel That's Entertainment Theatre on *Legend* (Palladium Theater on *Grandeur* and 42nd Street Theatre on *Splendour*) to ensure good sight lines for nightly, full-scale Broadway productions. The venue has a computerized system to move scenery, a device commonly used on Broadway, and an orchestra pit that can be raised and lowered.

The Schooner Bar is a piano lounge popular for its sing-along sessions. Decor includes authentic rigging and an aroma of tar. Casino Royale is next door. On *Grandeur,* passengers enter across a glass floor strewn with "sunken treasure" of jewels and gold coins. The casino offers blackjack, Caribbean poker, roulette, craps, and 178 slot machines.

The spacious Anchor's Away Lounge on *Legend* (South Pacific Lounge on *Grandeur* and Top Hat Lounge on *Splendour*) spans the ship's stern. It's a second showroom, used for parlor games, art auctions, daytime dance activities, and late-night shows and dancing. Topside, the glass-sheathed Viking Crown Lounge is an observation lounge by day and a nightclub and disco at night. Nightclub action is away from the room's quieter piano bar. On all the ships, the lounge is accessible from the atrium by glass elevators. Aft of the show lounge (to entice you coming and going!) is a mall with varied shops in attractive settings. For example, the Harbour Shop, selling liquor and sundries, recalls an old English vintner's shop through aged timber, antique barrels, and stone floors.

The conference center can be divided into four rooms, each with a full audio/visual support. Adjoining is an attractive lounge that also can be divided. A card room can be divided into two sections, and a 2,000-volume library that on the *Grandeur* has an amusing lifelike sculpture titled *Snoozin.* Explorers Court, off the Centrum on the port side of Deck 8, is the place to relax, read, or converse. Starboard is the Crown & Anchor Study (named after the RCCL logo), a more formal gathering place.

Sports, Fitness, and Beauty   The Sun Deck has an outdoor pool. Contrasting is the quiet Solarium, the second pool area. When the Windjammer and main dining room are closed, the Solarium's cafe serves snacks, alcoholic beverages, sodas, and juices. The area can be covered by a glass canopy. Beyond the Solarium, the ShipShape Fitness Center and spa contain a beauty salon, aerobics area, gym, changing rooms, saunas, steam baths, and seven massage rooms (treatments are pricey). A sports deck is at the stern. Each ship has a padded promenade circling most of the ship.

Legend's much-publicized golf course, Legend of the Links (Splendour of the Greens on *Splendour*), is above the spa. It was designed by Adventure Golf Services, whose other miniature courses include one at the Mall of America in Bloomington, Minnesota. RCCL, official cruise line of the Professional Golfers' Association and the Senior PGA Tour, also is a member of the Miniature Golf Association of America. Each hole of the 6,000-square-foot Links is surrounded by rough to simulate a shore-side layout. The 18 holes range in size from 155 to 230 square feet, tees are 5 feet wide, and the longest hole is 32 feet. Each game costs $5; $30 buys unlimited play. The glass dome over the aft swimming pool can slide to the golf course, where it can be raised to provide almost ten feet of vertical clearance for golfers. A walkway along one edge of the course has benches to encourage spectators. Halogen lights illuminate nighttime play, and baffles redirect wind generated by the motion. A jogging track surrounds the course. Tournaments and children's tee times are available.

Children's Facilities   Outstanding *Vision* facilities for children complement RCCL's free, supervised youth program, Adventure Ocean, available year-round, day and evening, and in port. Activities target ages 3–17. Daily schedules are delivered to cabins. Among the most original activities is teacher-led Mad Science, which aims to make science entertaining and amusing. Group babysitting ($4 an hour per child) is available in the afternoon when the ship is in port and in late evening. Family suites have separate bedrooms for children.

Club Ocean is the children's center. On *Grandeur,* it's submarine-themed and includes a tunnel, slide, pool of colored balls, and writing wall.

Nearby is Fanta-SEAS (Optix on the *Legend*) , the space-themed teen center. The ships also have video arcades.

Note: If you or your children consume a lot of soft drinks, consider buying the "Coke Deal." For $1 per person per day plus $1, participants get all the fountain (not canned) drinks they want.

Postscript   Royal Caribbean's reputation for delivering consistent service and quality holds up on these ships. But these are megaliners; you need patience for crowds and long lines, no matter how smoothly the ships operate. At the same time, their size and array of facilities and activities are treats in themselves and fuel the action-packed, high-energy atmosphere aboard.

In summer, *Vision* offers two- to four-night itineraries in the Pacific Northwest and provides shorter cruises from Seattle to Vancouver and Victoria, British Colombia. *Legend,* which introduced the line's Royal Journeys in Asia and the Middle East in 1999, continues the exotic cruises, adding an African safari in 2000. Some itineraries offer overland excursions, disembarking the ship in one port and rejoining it in another. In December 2000, *Splendour* introduces RCCL's first South American cruises.

Voyager of the Seas (Preview)		
Explorer of the Seas (Preview)		
Adventurer of the Seas (Preview)		
Registry: Norway	Length: 1,109 feet	Beam: 157.5 feet
Cabins: 1,900	Draft: 29 feet	Speed: 22 knots
Maximum Passengers:	Passenger Decks: 15	Elevators: 14
3,114	Crew: 1,181	Space Ratio: NA

The Ships   The $500 million *Voyager of the Seas,* the largest cruise ship ever built—142,000-tons—and the first of three, made her maiden voyage in November 1999. Her sister ship, *Explorer of the Seas,* is expected in autumn 2000; the third, *Adventure of the Seas,* in 2001.

Voyager is awesome. She's twice the size of the largest aircraft carrier ever built, twice as wide as Broadway in New York, and taller than a 20-story building. She has six diesel engines, each the size of a locomotive, and they produce 15,000 horsepower—the equivalent of 150 cars.

Twenty-one million hours worked by a crew of 10,000 people were needed to cut, shape, bend, and weld over 300,000 pieces of steel into the vessel's hull. Her 14 passenger decks cover 646,000 square feet. Furnishings include 538,000 square feet of carpeting, 15,000 chairs, and a $12 million art collection.

The *Voyager* is cruise ship as entertainment. In contrast to other mega-liners, where the goal has been to reduce the behemoth to human scale, RCCL has made a virtue of *Voyager*'s enormous size, touting her many options and features that only a ship of its size could offer. These include an ice rink, rock-climbing wall, inline skating track, five-story theater, and trilevel dining room.

Voyager also has a television studio, wedding chapel, and the largest youth facilities and largest spa and fitness center afloat. Fifty percent of cabins have balconies. Food and entertainment options and conference facilities rival those at major resorts.

At the heart of the ship, the Royal Promenade stretches the length of one and a half football fields between a 10-story atrium at one end and an 11-story grand atrium at the other. Stores, an ice cream parlor, champagne bar, and pub border the tree-lined boulevard. Around-the-clock entertainment—including jugglers, magicians, and mimes—brings a street fair atmosphere to the Promenade. Overhead lighting simulates day-to-night conditions outside. Three decks of inside cabins "with a view" overlook the boulevard. The rooms have window seats to watch the scene below, but the idea has not worked as RCCL planned because the line failed to put one-way glass on the windows; hence, passengers in these cabins can see and be seen. To avoid being part of the peep show, they must keep their curtains closed.

Studio B is *Voyager*'s pièce de résistance. It has a 40-by-60-foot ice-skating rink with arena-style seating for 900 spectators and is available for passenger use during the day (skates may be rented) and for ice shows at night. Well, it's different. Fifty television monitors and a broadcast studio are adjacent to the area, which can also serve as a show lounge or conference facility, or be used for game and variety shows and musical concerts.

When I first heard about the ice-skating rink for a ship cruising the Caribbean, I was puzzled, to say the least. But I was pleasantly surprised when I saw it in action. The entertainment is wholesome and high-quality and is certainly a welcome alternative, particularly for families, to the stale Las Vegas shows that have become the staple of most cruise ships.

Explorer of the Seas will have the same unusual attractions as *Voyager*, including the Royal Promenade, ice-skating rink, inline skating track, and rock-climbing wall, plus she will be the first ship to boast a state-of-the-art atmospheric and marine laboratory with an interactive environmental classroom. She will also be RCCL's first ship with Internet access in the cabins.

Itineraries   See Appendix B.

Cabins   Large by RCCL standards, cabins are similar in size and decor to those aboard *Vision*-Class ships. Enhancements include larger closets and beds with rounded corners to leave more floor space. All cabins offer telephone, television, electronic minibar, hair dryers, and twin beds convertible to queen.

Specifications Standard inside cabins, including the 138 Category G with atrium views encompass 150 square feet. The 757 cabins with private veranda (50 percent of the total) have 180-square-foot interiors plus a 4.5-by-8.8-foot balcony. 26 wheelchair-accessible.

Dining *Voyager*'s main dining room is actually three: the Carmen, La Boheme, and Magic Flute restaurants connected by a grand staircase. Decor includes a 15-foot crystal chandelier, an antique harp, and gilded marble pillars. Seats—for almost 2,000 people—offer views of the staircase and main floor or the ocean.

Other dining venues are Portofino, an upscale Italian restaurant for dinner (reservations only); Windjammer Cafe, the Lido restaurant for breakfast, lunch, and dinner; Cafe Promenade, for continental breakfast, all-day pizzas, and specialty coffees; Island Grill, with a display kitchen, casual dinner; SeaSide Diner, a 1950s all-day/all-night eatery with indoor/outdoor seating and jukebox music; and Sprinkles, with around-the-clock ice cream and yogurt. There's a Johnny Rockets, which is wildly popular. In the beginning, the restaurant charged the chain's normal prices, but the cruise line received so many complaints that they dropped the charges on a trial basis. Stay tuned.

Facilities and Entertainment In addition to the ice-skating rink and television studio, *Voyager* has one of the most impressive showrooms afloat. The 1,347-seat La Scala Theater, inspired by Milan's famous opera house, rises through five decks and has a stage trimmed with gold leaf, a domed ceiling with hand-painted murals, and boxes with satin bunting.

Voyager also offers the $1 million Aquarium Bar with 50 tons of water in four huge saltwater aquariums; Spinners, a revolving gambling arcade with an interactive roulette wheel that players sit in to play; and Casino Royale, cruising's largest casino. Also aboard are a cigar and brandy lounge, champagne bar, English pub, Schooner Bar, and a two-deck-tall library. The Scoreboard sports bar carries events live on large monitors. Alongside the glass bridge spanning the Royal Promenade is The Vault, a two-deck-high late-night disco. And sitting atop of *Voyager* is High Notes, a jazz club offering nightly performances. Also high on the ship is a chapel where weddings are performed.

Voyager's conference center seats up to 400 people and can be converted into six smaller rooms and a boardroom. Also available are a multimedia screening room, video conferencing, classrooms, and space for exhibition/

trade shows. Business services provide typing, copying, and computer access.

Sports, Fitness, and Beauty   The 15,000-square-foot health center offers exercise equipment. The Solarium and spa occupy 10,000 square feet. On the ship's smoke stack is cruising's first rock-climbing wall. Novices and experienced climbers alike are well briefed in advance and participants work in teams. For most passengers, it's their first rock-climbing experience, and they love it! Other outdoor facilities include a nine-hole golf course, driving range, golf simulators, inline skating track, and basketball/volleyball court. Also available are Sea Quest dive and snorkel shop and the 19th Hole golf bar. Little wonder that one passenger, upon touring the *Voyager* remarked, "This sure is a guy's ship."

Children's Facilities   RCCL has expanded its children's facilities considerably with Adventure Ocean. It provides age-specific programs: Aquanauts (3–5 years), Explorers (6–8 years), Voyagers (9–12 years), and Optix (teenagers). The latter have a day/nightclub with computers, soda bar, DJ, and dance floor. Paint and Clay is a crafts area for young children; Kids Deck has deck checkers, shuffleboard, and tic-tac-toe; Challenger's Arcade is a virtual-reality game center; and Virtual Submarine provides underwater virtual-reality entertainment for all ages. The Computer Lab has 14 stations with games for amusement and education. Adventure Beach, for families, has swimming pools, a water slide, and water games and is convenient to SeaSide Diner.

Postscript   Passengers have responded to *Voyager* enthusiastically, and almost anyone would enjoy a week on this ship. But you need to understand that it's not cruising in the traditional sense. The ship is the destination; her itinerary is almost immaterial. Like we said, the *Voyager* is cruise ship as entertainment.

RO Cruises, Inc./Royal Olympic Cruises

805 Third Avenue, New York, NY 10022-7513
(212) 688-7555; (800) 872-6400 (United States)
(800) 368-3888 (Canada); fax (212) 688-2304
www.royalolympiccruises.com

Type of Ships   Small and midsize oceanliners.

Type of Cruises   Quality, low-key, destination-oriented, short cruises in Greek Isles, Eastern Mediterranean, and South America; longer cruises on less traveled paths in homey ambience.

Cruise Line's Strengths
- friendliness and personal warmth of the crew
- relaxed ambience
- Greek hospitality
- innovative itineraries
- cultural programs and quality guides

Cruise Line's Shortcomings
- aging fleet (except for *Olympic Voyager*)
- small cabins and limited facilities on smaller ships
- dissimilarity in combined fleets

Fellow Passengers   In winter, when the ships sail Western Hemisphere itineraries, 80 percent of passengers are age 55 and older and have the time, means, and inclination for long cruises. They are mature, modestly affluent, seasoned travelers, many retired or semiretired, with some sense of adventure. Destinations, quality experiences, and value are priorities. Most are college-educated and enjoy shipboard enrichment programs and shore excursions. Over 50 percent come from Florida, California, New York, and Texas and have annual household income of $75,000+. Most are frequent cruisers; up to 50 percent may be repeaters.

In summer, when the ships are in the Mediterranean, the passenger mix is international, with 40 percent from Australia, Mexico, South America, France, and Italy, and 60 percent from the United States and Canada.

They have household income of $50,000+. Average age is 40+. They range from newlyweds to retirees, plus families with children. Americans usually have been to Europe and have cruised before. Attractions of the Mediterranean appeal equally to honeymooners seeking romantic destinations, religious groups tracing the "footsteps of St. Paul," and amateur historians visiting places they studied in school.

Recommended For   Moderately affluent, adventurous travelers seeking a different kind of experience in refined, conservative ambience, who expect the level of service, comfort, and amenities found in good hotels; value-conscious travelers who prefer to stay in cozy local hotels but want an English-speaking environment; people interested in Greek culture and cuisine; experienced cruisers who enjoy the style of traditional oceanliner.

Not Recommended For   Party-seekers, night owls, those wanting big-ship action; unsophisticated travelers; people wanting to be entertained, and those with only slight interest in history.

Cruise Areas and Seasons   South America, Amazon, Orinoco, Caribbean, Panama Canal in winter; Italy, Egypt, Greek Isles, Eastern Mediterranean, Black Sea, spring–fall; transatlantic, April and November.

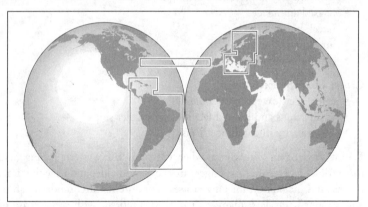

The Line   In 1995, Sun Line Cruises, one of the most respected Greek-owned cruise lines, and rival Epirotiki Line, one of Greece's oldest and largest lines, merged, forming a new company, Royal Olympic Cruises, which trades on the NASDAQ.

Sun Line was founded in the mid-1950s by a Greek family whose patriarch, the late Ch. A. Keusseoglou, had been head of Home Lines. Sun Line was a pioneer, introducing some of the first ships designed specifically for cruising that eliminated class distinctions and provided large public rooms and outdoor areas for relaxation and sports. Itineraries included lesser-known islands of the Eastern Caribbean a decade before other lines discov-

ered them, and combined Eastern Caribbean islands with a cruise on the
Orinoco or Amazon Rivers or the Panama Canal and offered cruises timed
for the spring equinox at Chichen Itza in the Yucatán. Sun Line was first in
1985 to offer Halley's Comet cruises (which were copied by almost everyone with a ship) and other solar eclipse–watching cruises in 1998 and 1999.
Many lines have added bigger ships, but Royal Olympic's remain small and
intimate. Most crew members are Greek and Filipino; many count 20 or
more years of service. The line has many repeaters. Traditionally, most of its
cruises are sold in the United States through companies that package them
as two-week vacations with tours of Greece, the Holy Land, and the Eastern Mediterranean, combining hotel stays with a cruise.

Two years after the merger, Royal Olympic began building two 840-
passenger ships. The first, *Olympic Voyager,* debuted in June 2000, the second is scheduled for 2001. Designed with an innovative "fast monohull," the
vessels are meant to be the speediest (up to 29 knots), most time-efficient
cruise ships afloat—a potential advantage in planning itineraries.

In 1998, the line changed its North American marketing name to RO
Cruises Inc. and purchased the *Olympic Countess* (former *Cunard Countess*)
and *World Renaissance* from the Awani Group of Indonesia. Then in 1999,
having suffered serious dislocations due to the war in Kosovo, ROC found
a white knight in Louise Cruise Lines, a Cyprus-based hotel, cruise, and
ferry operator and ROC competitor in the Eastern Mediterranean. Louise
first bought the 50 percent share of ROC owned by the Keusseoglou family and a slice of Potomeanos's holdings to gain controlling interest and has
been negotiating for the balance.

The Fleet	Built/Renovated	Tonnage	Passengers
*Odysseus**	1962/88/95	12,000	485
Olympic Countess	1976/91/96	18,000	840
Olympic Voyager	2000	25,000	840
Olympic Explorer	2001	25,000	840
Stella Oceanis	1965/93	5,500	300
Stella Solaris	1953/94	18,000	620
Triton	1971/76/91/96	14,000	620
World Renaissance	1966/91/96	12,000	455

Odysseus is on charter through 2003 and is not included in this edition.

Style   To sail on Royal Olympic's ships is to bide a while in a Greek town
at sea. Staff and crew serve guests with the natural ease of people at home,
and passengers are treated as valued friends, not tourists. The ships' moderate size contributes to the genial shipboard atmosphere. And the ships are

still traditional enough that you get a passenger list. The desire to experience Greek life and culture is delightfully contagious, and the ships offer many ways to satisfy it, from authentic Greek food to lessons in Greek dances and language. Every day, passengers can be heard practicing the latest tidbit of conversational Greek to the cheerful encouragement of crew and staff. The highlight of each cruise is Greek Night, with traditional Greek music and dancing by crew members.

In keeping with fitness trends, some ships offer spa cuisine. And for its high number of single women passengers, there's a host program on some long winter cruises.

Distinctive Features   Greek Night. Maya Equinox cruise. Host program on some longer cruises. Precruise purchase of shore excursions at savings.

	HIGHEST	LOWEST	AVERAGE
PER DIEM	$435	$123	$259

The above per diems are calculated from the cruise line's non-discounted *cruise only* fares on standard accommodations. Per diems vary by season, by cabin, and by cruise areas.

Rates   Ports charges are additional.

Special Fares and Discounts   Early-bird discounts. Low cruise-only rates, depending on itinerary and cabin category.
- Third/Fourth Persons: Yes.
- Children's Fare: Yes.
- Single Supplement: 150 percent, except suites; guaranteed share available.

Packages
- Air/Sea: Yes.
- Pre/Post: Yes. Summer Greek Islands/Mediterranean cruises can be combined with land packages for vacations of a week or longer.

Past Passengers   Passengers are registered as Royal Circle members after their first cruise and receive special mailings, discounts, and upgrades on selected sailings.

The Last Word   For travelers turned off by big, glitzy ships and their impersonal nature, Royal Olympic offers a refreshing option. The line provides the quality of traditional cruising with the comfort and warmth of Greek hospitality. Repeaters say it's like coming home; many return to the same ship year after year. With new owners and new ships, it's too early to know what direction ROC's future will take. Stay tuned.

Royal Olympic Cruises Standard Features

Officers Greek.

Staff Dining, Cabin, Cruise/Greek and Filipino.

Dining Facilities One main dining room for all meals and informal buffet breakfast and lunch served poolside. *Solaris* and *Olympic Voyager* have indoor/outdoor lido cafes with breakfast, lunch, and late-night buffets. *Olympic Voyager,* poolside pizza service.

Special Diets Low-salt, low-fat diets available. Kosher diets are accommodated after written request two weeks before departure.

Room Service 24 hours. Butler service in suites on *Olympic Voyager.*

Dress Code Comfortable, casual clothing during day; evening after 6 p.m. varies. *Solaris* 10- to 12-day cruises, 3 formal evenings, 2 informal, and remaining evenings casual.

Cabin Amenities Telephone, dual-channel radio, private bathroom, and a locking drawer for valuables. Television, *Solaris* top three categories and all cabins on *Olympic Voyager.*

Electrical Outlets 220 AC (110 AC razors only); 110 AC *Olympic Countess, World Renaissance.*

Wheelchair Access *Olympic Voyager,* four cabins.

Recreation and Entertainment Lounge with nightly dancing to orchestra, cabaret acts, passengers' talent show, Greek Night, masquerade. Bridge, backgammon, bingo, dance classes. *Olympic Voyager,* pizza bar, nightclub, casino, piano bar, cigar room, business center, library, card room.

Sports and Other Activities Swimming pool (two-section pool on *Solaris;* two pools on *World Renaissance*), exercise classes, shuffleboard, Ping-Pong. *Olympic Countess,* paddle tennis, putting green, driving range; outdoor pool with Jacuzzi.

Beauty and Fitness Beauty salon and barber shop. *Olympic Countess, World Renaissance, Olympic Voyager,* fitness center, exercise equipment, exercise classes, sauna. *Olympic Voyager,* spa, whirlpools.

Other Facilities Boutique; laundry service, no dry cleaning; medical services; religious service; ship-to-shore telephone service.

Children's Facilities None.

Theme Cruises Intermittently.

Smoking No pipes and cigars in dining room or lounge during show time. Smoking areas assigned in dining room.

ROC Suggested Tipping Per person per day, $9. Tips are pooled and divided among ship employees. On *Solaris,* tips can be paid by credit card when passenger settles final bills.

Credit Cards For cruise payment and on-board charges: American Express, Discover, MasterCard, and Visa.

Stella Solaris	Quality ❼	Value B
Registry: Greece	Length: 544 feet	Beam: 72 feet
Cabins: 329	Draft: 25.8 feet	Speed: 22 knots
Maximum Passengers:	Passenger Decks: 8	Elevators: 3
620	Crew: 320	Space Ratio: 29

The Ship   The *Stella Solaris* combines the facilities and amenities of a large ship with the atmosphere of a small oceanliner. She epitomizes traditional cruising with gracious service, quality, and warm Greek hospitality. Built in 1973, the ship has trim, flowing lines. Fine-tuned for North Americans, *Solaris* nonetheless feels European. You sense Old World charm when you step into the dignified, dark wood–paneled Main Foyer. No soaring atriums or lavish showrooms here. Rather, continental refinement is evident in furnishings and decor shipwide.

The cruise line has done a remarkable job of preserving *Solaris*'s character for more than four decades, replacing fabrics and fixtures as needed, but retaining original colors and patterns. The result is a comfortably sophisticated environment. A major renovation completed in 1995 resulted in an enhanced and redecorated main show lounge, enlarged casino, upgraded boutique, enlarged and upgraded spa and gym, new carpets in public areas, and redecorated cabins—all while preserving the ship's personality. Televisions are found in the top three categories of cabins. Passengers can orient themselves quickly because the main public rooms and dining room are on the Solaris Deck, which runs the full length of the ship. Most of the rooms are open and airy. Extra-high ceilings add to her spaciousness, and large windows connect passengers with the sea.

The Mediterranean-style main lounge is decorated in deep red and brown and hung with scenes from Greek mythology worked in bronze. The piano bar at the stern is a popular gathering spot for cocktails or private parties. A card and reading room on Boat Deck provides a quiet refuge; on Sapphire Deck, the large theater accommodates movies and concerts.

Itineraries   See Appendix B.

Cabins   Eleven price categories are distributed throughout the ship. Most cabins are large and decorated in pastels. Comfortable furnishings usually include twin beds, a dresser with lock drawers, large mirror, and coffee table. The three top categories include large, deluxe suites with separate sitting areas and bathrooms with tub and shower. All cabins and suites have telephones and multichannel music systems. Television is available in the top three categories. Nearly two thirds have bathrooms with tub and shower. Storage space is ample. Room service is available 24 hours a day; the menu is limited.

Specifications 79 inside cabins, 250 outside; 66 suites (6 with double beds). Standard dimensions, 189 square feet. 225 with twin beds (none convert to double); 79 with upper and lower berths; no singles; no wheelchair-accessible.

Dining The spacious dining room is first-class in decor, service, and cuisine. By day, light streams through windows on both sides of the long room. In evening, subdued lighting captures the spirit of the gathering. Tablecloth colors change with the evening's theme, but tables are always set with Royal Doulton china, Italian silverware, French crystal, and fresh flowers. Breakfast and lunch are open seatings; dinner has two assigned seatings. Most tables accommodate four or six persons; in smoking and nonsmoking sections are tables for two. Food and service are continental but designed to cater to American tastes. Unlike most cruise ships, *Solaris* does its own provisioning. Everything is prepared from scratch on board.

Lunch and dinner offer many choices and include low-fat and low-calorie items. Greek specialties, such as moussaka, are on the menu frequently, and genuine Greek salad is almost always available.

Topside, the indoor/outdoor lido cafe is the place for breakfast, lunch, and late-night buffets, midmorning bouillon, and afternoon tea. Passengers who prefer informality eat outside at umbrella-shaded tables by the ship's dual pools, or they take their trays one flight down to the Boat Deck and eat in old-fashioned wooden deck chairs. The deck has a wraparound promenade popular for jogging and strolling.

Service One factor contributing immensely to *Solaris*'s character is the remarkably large number of longtime crew members. The Greek staff deliver gracious, top-notch professional service with a personal touch, exemplifying Greece's tradition of hospitality.

Best of all are the pride and pleasure the crew take in their jobs—particularly in discovering and catering to passengers' preferences. For example: A recent passenger asked for a double cappuccino with breakfast the first morning, and the waiter delighted in bringing one each day without prompting.

Solaris's large number of repeat cruisers most often attribute their loyalty to the ship to its staff and crew and the warm atmosphere they create. Many request the same dining room and cabin attendants.

Facilities and Entertainment Cabaret-style entertainment features vocalists, magicians, dancers, and comedians. There's dance music in the main lounge after the show and in the disco.

A highlight of each cruise is Greek Night, when dinner features Greek specialties, and costumed officers and crew perform Greek song and dance (with passenger participation). Music features George Bouritas on bouzouki and the ship's excellent dance orchestra.

Activities and Diversions   The daily agenda, delivered under the cabin door, includes the usual: fitness classes, bridge tournaments, arts and crafts, dance lessons, backgammon, bingo, and movies.

Enrichment programs include destination lectures. Amazon cruises are accompanied by Loren McIntyre, who is credited with discovering the most remote source of the river. The Mayan equinox cruise also has extensive on-board lectures.

Sports, Fitness, and Beauty   The ship's two-section swimming pool is surrounded by an area for lounging, shuffleboard, and table tennis. Aerobics classes are offered for all ages and fitness levels. The gym has exercise bicycles, step machine, slant boards, and free weights. Walkers and joggers frequent the promenade deck (seven times around is slightly over a mile). Also aboard are a beauty salon, barber shop, sauna, and massage facilities.

Shore Excursions   Comprehensive shore excursions are described in literature accompanying cruise documents. Some can be reserved in advance. Tour companies working with *Solaris* are well organized and use comfortable buses with large windows. Tours generally allow time to explore on one's own. Most cruises highlight local culture and history. For example, on Amazon cruises, a folkloric performance is staged at the Manaus Opera House; on the Maya cruise, passengers go to Chichen Itza to see the Feathered Serpent's descent during the equinox.

In the Aegean, Black Sea, and Mediterranean, where the ship spends more than half the year, *Solaris* provides a tour of antiquity by sea, docking once or twice a day. The line's guide, describing the places visited, is well written and illustrated and makes a fine souvenir.

Touring schedules in the Eastern Mediterranean are very full; cruises can be quite tiring. Time to linger over meals or lounge aboard ship is scarce, unless you pass up some sight-seeing and shopping. Two guides aboard each cruise prepare passengers for ports and to escort them ashore. Royal Olympic has combined its cruise itineraries with land tours to create holidays of 7 to 21 days.

Stella Oceanis	Quality ❸	Value C
Registry: Greece	Length: 3540 feet	Beam: 53 feet
Cabins: 159	Draft: 17 feet	Speed: 16 knots
Maximum Passengers:	Passenger Decks: 6	Elevators: 1
300	Crew: 150	Space Ratio: 12

The Ship   Built in 1965, *Stella Oceanis* is a smaller version of *Stella Solaris*. Comfortable, functional, and well run, the ship is well suited for Greek Isles and Eastern Mediterranean cruises and offers excellent shore excursions and guides.

Public rooms include Minos Lounge (similar to the main lounge on *Solaris,* but a third its size), for dancing and entertainment; the Club, a small writing room; a small casino and shop; and Aphrodite Dining Room, which features open seating at breakfast and lunch, then two seatings for dinner. At sea, the center of activity is poolside on Sun Deck, where a daily hot and cold lunch buffet with Greek specialties is served.

The popular Plaka Taverna one flight down serves as a bar, movie theater, lecture room, and site of the midnight buffet and late-night disco. Also on Lido Deck are a beauty salon, barber shop, and promenade almost circling the ship. Cuisine and service are outstanding, combining the line's Greek heritage with continental selections.

Itineraries   See Appendix B.

Cabins   The ship has six categories. The majority of cabins are outside and rather simply furnished. Each has a private bathroom with shower, telephone, and dual-channel radio. Thirty-eight deluxe cabins have private baths with tubs.

Specifications   46 inside cabins, 113 outside; 6 suites. Standard dimensions, 130 square feet. 127 with twin beds (none convertible to double); 17 upper/lower berths; no singles; none wheelchair-accessible.

Postscript   *Stella Oceanis* is a comfortable, well-run ship suitable for short, destination-oriented itineraries. Most days are spent in port. Cruises are very port-intensive, some with two ports in a day. They should not be viewed as a cruise in the usual sense, rather as a tour of Greek and Mediterranean islands by sea.

Greek tour guides are among the world's best. They are university graduates and must meet very high standards to qualify. They are proud of their nation and eager for travelers to benefit from their extensive knowledge.

Hence, shore excursions are comprehensive tours and can be tiring. Pace yourself. In busy summer months, the line tries to deliver its passengers to popular sites before the competition arrives, even if it means an early-morning call. Most travelers are grateful for it. The port-intensive itineraries are most appreciated by those particularly interested in Greek history and antiquity.

Readers planning to cruise on the *Oceanis* should review the entire section on ROC for a full picture of the cruise experience on its ships.

Triton	Quality ❷	Value C
Registry: Greece	Length: 486 feet	Beam: 71 feet
Cabins: 325	Draft: 21 feet	Speed: 22 knots
Maximum Passengers:	Passenger Decks: 7	Elevators: 2
620	Crew: 315	Space Ratio: 20

The Ship   Built in 1971 as the *Cunard Adventurer,* the ship was bought by Norwegian Cruise Line in 1976, which refurbished and renamed her *Sunward II.* In 1991, she was acquired by Epirotiki Lines, which renovated her before introducing her as *Triton* in 1992. Public rooms, including the dining room, and recreational facilities are on the top decks.

The ship's facilities include a showroom, nightclub, four bars/lounges, casino, beauty/barber shop, boutique, and movie theater. *Triton* has wide teak decks and a large outdoor swimming pool with expansive deck area; adjacent is the fitness center.

A light and bright dining room offers two seatings for three meals and serves continental, Pacific Rim and spa cuisine, and Greek specialties. The service is cheerful and attentive; the ambience, friendly.

Itineraries   See Appendix B.

Cabins   Most cabins are on the bottom three decks and are available in eight categories. Cabins are small and narrow but attractive. Standard outside cabins have two lower beds; most are convertible to a queen-size bed. All are furnished with desk/dresser and chair and have a bathroom with shower.

Specifications   112 inside cabins, 223 outside; 32 deluxe. 299 with twin beds, convertible to double; 4 with upper and lower berths; no singles; none are wheelchair-accessible.

One of ROC's larger ships, *Triton* offers more facilities than most. She's a good value and is popular with budget-minded Europeans.

Olympic Countess	Quality ❸	Value C
Registry: Greece	Length: 537 feet	Beam: 75 feet
Cabins: 423	Draft: 19 feet	Speed: 18.5 knots
Maximum Passengers:	Passenger Decks: 7	Elevators: 2
840	Crew: 350	Space Ratio: 22

The Ship   Built by Cunard for informal, warm-weather cruising, *Cunard Countess* was acquired by Royal Olympic in January 1998 and renamed *Olympic Countess.* Aging but comfortable, she appeals to those seeking traditional cruising with port-intensive and unusual itineraries. Almost all public rooms are on the three highest decks. Lounges are large and geared to a busy program of daytime and evening entertainment.

She was renovated in 1996 and has tasteful, contemporary decor. The spacious Main Square lobby contains the purser's office, tour excursion office, and boutique.

Itineraries   See Appendix B.

Cabins   Accommodations are compact and comfortable, but are showing their age. There are 12 categories. About 60 percent of standard cabins are outside; all have phone, two-channel radio, baths with shower, and ample closet space. Twin beds are usually in an L configuration. Some cabins have a third lower bed, some a third upper berth; a few have one bed and one folding lower berth.

Higher-category cabins are roomier and have windows rather than portholes, sofa or chairs, television, VCR, minibar, twin beds, and bathrooms with tub and shower. Several cabins are equipped for the disabled, but some public areas, such as the pool, aren't wheelchair-accessible.

Specifications   152 inside, 271 outside, including 26 suites.

Dining   The windowed main dining room is pleasant but neither flashy nor elegant. The informal buffet, in an unusual arrangement, is on the same deck. The dining room has two seatings for three meals. The casual, open-air cafe serves early-morning pastries and a light breakfast, mid-morning bouillon, and light luncheon.

Facilities and Entertainment   Port-intensive itineraries curtail daytime shipboard activities. In the evenings, major production shows are presented in the comfortable main lounge, which also has a black marble dance floor and a large bar. An inside/outside lounge on the same deck offers outdoor shows and dancing, which is popular with passengers and the cruise staff.

The nightclub showcases live bands and a DJ playing Top 40 hits. By day, when there aren't aerobics classes and craft lessons, the lounge is a quiet refuge. The topside lounge is a three-in-one nightclub, piano bar, and forward observation lounge. The piano bar has after-dinner entertainment nightly. The glass-enclosed Art Nouveau casino shares the space, offering slot machines, poker, and roulette. The ship also has a video game room, movie theater/meeting room, quiet library, and beauty/barber shop.

Sports, Fitness, and Beauty Facilities include a paddle tennis court and golf driving range. The popular lido pool has two Jacuzzis, a bar, and a sunbathing area. Nearby is the fitness center, offering a Life Fitness Cardio-Fitness Center, mirrored wall, ballet barre, and sauna. A short jogging track is above the pool.

World Renaissance	Quality ❸	Value C
Registry: Greece	Length: 482 feet	Beam: 69 feet
Cabins: 262	Draft: 23 feet	Speed: 16 knots
Maximum Passengers:	Passenger Decks: 8	Elevators: 1
455	Crew: 235	Space Ratio: 27

The Ship The *World Renaissance* was built in 1966 by Paquet French Cruises as its flagship, *Renaissance*. Royal Olympic's predecessor, Epirotiki, bought her. Small and yachtlike, she nonetheless has spacious rooms with wood paneling and generous deck space. The ship, renovated in 1996, has 262 cabins including 15 suites. There are 182 outside doubles and 80 inside ones, plus 1 inside single. Facilities include El Greco Grand Salon, the pleasant main lounge; two heated outdoor pools; Xenia Tavern, an intimate setting for classical concerts and nightclub entertainment; a casino; card room/library; theater/conference room; gym, sauna, beauty salon, and boutique; and an infirmary. Laundry service is available. The dining room serves three meals a day. Continental fare and Greek specialties are featured.

Olympic Voyager	(Preview)	
Registry: Luxembourg	Length: 590 feet	Beam: 84 feet
Cabins: 420	Draft: 24 feet	Speed: 29 knots
Maximum Passengers:	Passenger Decks: 6	Elevators: 4
926	Crew: 360	Space Ratio: 30

The Ship Royal Olympic's new ships, built in Germany, are the first brand-new vessels for the line. *Olympic Voyager,* the first of two and the line's new flagship, was launched in June 2000; her sister, *Olympic Explorer,* follows in 2001. The well-known Athens-based firm of A & M Katzourakis Architects & Designers has created the interiors, with help from an impressive group of artists.

Among the ships' highlights are that 70 percent of the cabins are outside (including 48 suites) and that the vessel is built on a much-heralded, hydrodynamic "fast monohull" design with a sleek bow and graceful profile that enables her to achieve a cruising speed of over 29 knots, permitting less time in transit, more time in port, and the ability to reach more ports on a weekly itinerary, thus creating itineraries that no others can perform. From a technical perspective, the hull's contour delivers significantly reduced fuel consumption, and despite the ship's high speed, it's remarkably stable, with no more than a normal amount of vibration and engine noise.

Olympic Voyager has an extensive and unusual art collection that includes the works of calligrapher Rosella Gaavaglia, ceramist Ignazio Moncada, and painters Aldo Mondino, Erietta Vordoni, and Michaelis Katzourakis, among other notable artists. Each artist was commissioned to create works for specific public rooms and cabins.

Elegant yet comfortable, *Olympic Voyager*'s interior decor is fresh and modern yet classic with extensive use of cherry wood paneling and glass, as well as decks named for Greek gods. Helios, the top deck, has the swimming pool, an outdoor pizza bar, and the Jade Spa aft and the Sky Lounge forward, serving as an observation lounge by day and the disco by night. The deck also has the Sky suites.

Apollo Deck has most of the public rooms, including the indoor/outdoor Garden Restaurant at the stern and the Alexander the Great, the main lounge, at the bow. In between, there are the Cigar Club, the casino, shops, the Athena Library, a card and game room, and a piano bar.

Selene Deck is anchored by the Selene Dining Room at the stern and ocean view cabins and suites amidships, along with the reception area. Other facilities include a coffee bar, beauty salon, two shops, and a very large and well-equipped infirmary.

For her maiden season, *Olympic Voyager* sails in the Eastern Mediterranean on a seven-day/three-continent cruise—Europe, Asia, Africa—an itinerary that would take other cruise ships ten days or longer to complete. After a transatlantic cruise departing from Greece in late November, the ship will have her home port in Fort Lauderdale, from where she spends the winter sailing a series of 11-, 12-, and 17-day Amazon and Orinoco River Cruises and two 11-day Maya Equinox cruises. *Olympic Voyager* will be the only ship sailing round-trip on two-week cruises to the Amazon from Fort Lauderdale. In keeping with Royal Olympic's traditional reputation, an onboard enrichment features distinguished experts and scholars in anthropology, archaeology, astronomy, and international politics to enhance the cruise experience.

Itineraries   See Appendix B.

Cabins   Accommodations include Sky suites on Apollo Deck, each encompassing 375 square feet, with floor-to-ceiling sliding glass doors leading to a private balcony, and Bay Window suites, 215 square feet, located forward on Selene Deck. Both categories have bath with tub and shower and butler service. The Junior suites, 183 square feet, have walk-in closets. Some of the Junior suites accommodate four people. Venus and Dionysus Decks hold the Junior suites and the majority of standard cabins. The balance are on the lower Neptune Deck. Standard outside and inside cabins measuring 140 square feet seem small by today's standards on new ships, but they are well laid out and functional. However, the Bay Window suites are outstanding. They have an alcove with three large floor-to-ceiling windows projecting out over the sea. The 12 veranda suites on the top deck are very roomy, have deep balconies furnished with table and chairs, and two lounge chairs for sunning. All cabins have twin beds convertible to doubles; minibars, safe, three-channel radio, direct-dial phone, interactive television, hair dryers, and 24-hour room service. The outside cabins on Neptune, the lowest deck, have large portholes. The aft cabins on Neptune and Dionysus Decks may be the least desirable because of possible noise from the engines.

Specifications   48 suites, including 12 with verandas; 16 Bay Window and 20 Junior suites; 244 standard outside cabins, including 4 wheelchair-accessible; and 126 standard inside doubles.

Dining   The Selene Dining Room at the stern on Selene Deck has windows on three sides providing a lovely panorama of the ship's wake. Meals are served in two seatings at tables for two, four, six, and eight—all set far apart to assure quiet, ease of movement, and a certain amount of privacy.

The Garden Lounge, the ship's attractive buffet restaurant with curving banquettes, large windows, and a rich red carpet, offers seating both inside and out and can double as a casual lounge during the day. In the pool area, there's a pizza station beneath a lovely tented awning.

Facilities and Entertainment   Entertainment on board is mostly presented in the modest one-level Alexander the Great Lounge, where you'll find small-scale song-and-dance productions and music and magic acts. An attractive Piano Bar, set amidships along a central winding corridor, is the ship's main social hub and offers a comfortable (if often smoky) spot to relax.

The Anemos nightclub, perched above the bridge on the topmost deck, serves as a 270-degree observation lounge by day. One level below, there's a comfortable cigar room with fantastic lounge-style couches. The ship's small casino, immediately next door, is bisected by the two-level reception atrium. On one side are 44 slot machines; on the other, a bar, four poker tables, and roulette—it's safe to say gamblers are not Royal Olympic's core target audience.

The small gym is equipped with steps, stationary bicycles, treadmills, and weights, but it's not particularly attractive (half the exercise machines face away from the room's few windows—which sort of negates the advantage of having the windows in the first place). Fortunately, the adjoining spa has a pleasant environment and an extensive range of treatments at prices that are lower than aboard many ships. These include massages, sauna, Swiss showers, facials, Turkish bath, mud bath, and other treatments. The ship offers a variety of full-day spa packages from $105 to $218. A card room and a library with three computers round out the public rooms. There are no special facilities for children. The ship's deck space is limited; no promenade encircles the ship and some deck space along the side with lifeboats is unappealing and rather useless.

Postscript   While most cruise lines are building bigger and bigger ships for the mass market or more and more luxurious small ones for the most affluent travelers, Royal Olympic was willing to break out of the pack and deliver a truly unique, innovative, midsize cruise ship and offer cruises at reasonable prices. The line took a big gamble in building the *Olympic Voyager* and her sister ship, both for their size and their new technology, but judging from the positive response from passengers, it was a wise choice that should serve the line well. All in all, the ship sets a stylish new tone for Royal Olympic. There are a few small problems which we expect the line will solve in time. For instance, signage is all but absent in the stair towers, making it almost impossible to tell which deck you're on.

Seabourn Cruise Line

(a division of Cunard Line, Ltd.)
6100 Blue Lagoon Drive, Suite 400, Miami, FL 33126
(305) 463-3000; (800) 929-9391; fax (305) 463-3010
www.seabourn.com

Type of Ships   Small and midsize modern, ultraluxurious oceanliners.

Type of Cruises   Top-of-the-line luxury cruises on worldwide itineraries.

Cruise Line's Strengths
- impeccable service
- luxurious accommodations
- exclusivity
- ship size/maneuverability
- open-seating dining
- cuisine
- worldwide itineraries

Cruise Line's Shortcomings
- limited activities on small ships
- limitations on use of water sports facilities on small ships
- poor positioning of outdoor pool
- room service breakfast

Fellow Passengers   Sophisticated, discriminating, well-heeled, experienced travelers; 80 percent from North America; others are from Europe and elsewhere. Age varies, depending on season and destinations. Most are 50 and older; some are young professionals—doctors, lawyers, entrepreneurs—and honeymooners. They come mainly from the Northeast, Florida, California, and Chicago area. Fifty percent or more are repeaters. Passengers on shorter cruises, such as in the Caribbean, are likely to be active business owners and professionals, some semiretired; the mix could include a childless couple in their 30s or multigenerational families ages 4–70. Passengers are likely to have sailed on other luxury vessels and stayed in five-star hotels. They know and understand quality; their expectations are high and their judgment tough.

Seabourn Goddess passengers are affluent—successful business people, high-level managers, entrepreneurs, professionals. They're new money, experienced with luxury, self-assured but not stuffy, active but not fitness fanatics. They range from mid-30s to mid-60s or older; almost all are couples and likely to be on a honeymoon or celebration cruise. They are more likely to care about enjoying fine dining and fine wines and living the good life than delving into the refinements. About half have sailed on the ships before, and, depending on itinerary, about half will be North Americans with the remainder Europeans.

Recommended For Sophisticated, seasoned travelers accustomed to the best; affluent passengers whose first priority is service; those who seek exclusivity; yacht owners who want to leave the driving to others; those who shun big-ship, glitzy cruises; first-timers who seek and can afford small-ship ambience; honeymooners with rich parents; anyone who has won the lottery.

Not Recommended For Those unaccustomed to luxury or a sophisticated environment; anyone uncomfortable in a fancy restaurant or five-star European hotel; flashy dressers, late-night revelers, inexperienced travelers, children.

Cruise Areas and Seasons Caribbean, Panama Canal, South America, Asia in winter. Europe, Mediterranean, Black Sea, Norwegian fjords, Baltic, British Isles in spring/summer. New England, Canada, Caribbean, South Asia, East Africa, Indian Ocean in autumn.

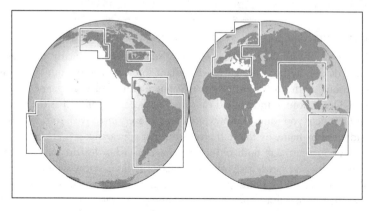

The Line Founded in 1987 by Norwegian industrialist Atle Brynestad, Seabourn Cruise Line's goal has always been to offer the world's most luxurious cruises and most elegant ships afloat, setting new standards and appealing to the most discriminating travelers. Seabourn quickly won enough fans with its first ship, *Seabourn Pride,* to complete a second one. Seabourn's posh ships with sleek, yachtlike profiles are small enough to be exclusive yet large enough to be spacious and offer most facilities of a large ship. The ambience is carefree elegance. Cruises follow the sun on worldwide itineraries that circle the globe in a year's time.

Dubbed the "Rolls Royce of the cruise industry," Seabourn is a privately held company, 50 percent owned by its founder and 50 percent by Carnival Cruise Line. In 1996, with the demise of Royal Viking and Royal Cruise lines, Seabourn acquired the *Royal Viking Queen,* which was originally intended to be the third Seabourn ship. Then, in March 1998, Carnival and a group of Norwegian investors acquired Cunard and merged it with Seabourn but retained the two lines as separate brands. Cunard's *Sea Goddess* twins (renamed *Seabourn Goddess*) and the *Royal Viking Sun* (renamed *Seabourn Sea*) are now part of Seabourn's fleet. With the purchase of Cunard, Carnival has become a major player in the luxury market, with a 58 percent market share.

The Fleet	Built/Renovated	Tonnage	Passengers
Seabourn Goddess I	1984/95/97	4,250	116
Seabourn Goddess II	1985/95	4,250	116
Seabourn Legend	1991/96/2000	10,000	204
Seabourn Pride	1988/2000	10,000	204
Seabourn Spirit	1989/2000	10,000	204
Seabourn Sun	1988/93/96/99	38,000	758

Style   Elegant but not stuffy, glamorous but not glitzy, Seabourn ships are like tony private clubs. Quality is key, starting with a nearly effortless embarkation and a white-gloved attendant to escort you to your suite (as luxurious as the brochure promises), where fruit and champagne await you. Decor exudes understated elegance. Service is as polished as the silver with which you dine—always attentive, never intrusive. You will be addressed by name by the staff after your first appearance.

Seabourn attracts both old-money travelers who disdain mainstream cruise ships and newly rich who appreciate the line's status symbolism. It also caters to stressed-out professionals and others seeking privacy. Whatever their background, they're affluent enough to be accustomed to a high level of service and style without excessive fuss.

Days at sea are for relaxing. Dress and atmosphere are informal, and time is unstructured. The usual announcements, pool games, and contests are absent. In fact, a Seabourn cruise is so low-key, you may need to read your daily agenda to know what's happening. Each cruise has one or two special events meant to be highlights. It might be a special concert in an unusual location for Seabourn passengers only; a visit to a private island, marina, or estate; or a sporting event. Evenings aboard ship are more formal; fine dining is the day's highlight. On evenings when you prefer to relax, a full-course dinner will be served en suite.

"As You Like It," described as the ultimate in vacation flexibility, gives passengers freedom to choose from varied options. Passengers can tailor their cruise with separate and independently priced cruise fares, air-travel options, pre- and postcruise tours, hotel, and transfers. For air, the choices are Seabourn's air program with preselected carriers, economy, business, first-class, or the Concorde; the cruise line's independent air program, booked through Seabourn; or a chartered Gulfstream to and from the ship anywhere in the world.

The three ships acquired from Cunard have very different origins but are similar in style to Seabourn, particularly the *Seabourn Goddess* twins. *Seabourn Sun* differences result from its larger size.

Distinctive Features   Unusual care for solo passengers. Foldout water sports marina. Personalized stationery, walk-in closets, complimentary self-service laundry/dryer. "As You Like It" booking options; golf program with Wide World of Golf. *Seabourn Sun:* air-conditioned tenders and same-level access, pool with swim-up bar, gold-plated bathroom fixtures in penthouse suites, and cruising's first croquet court.

	HIGHEST	LOWEST	AVERAGE
PER DIEM	$797	$273	$509

The above per diems are calculated from the cruise line's non-discounted *cruise only* fares on standard accommodations. Per diems vary by season, by cabin, and by cruise areas.

Rates   Tips are included; port charges are additional. Prestocked minibar in cabins (*Seabourn Sun,* suites only); wine with meals.

Special Fares and Discounts   Advance-purchase discounts of 10 percent for 12 months and 5 percent for 6 months on cruise only when paid in full. Other savings available on second-cabin purchase by family or friends, and two or more successive cruises. Repeaters get discount of 10 percent or more. Cruises designated on the line's calendar with $ offer price breaks; some may be positioning voyages.

- Worldfare: Advance purchase of 41 cruising days for $12,000 to 99 days for $26,500.

- Third Person: 25 percent of per-person published tariff.
- Children's Fare: Same as third person rate.
- Single Supplement: 140–200 percent of per-person double-occupancy basic suite, depending on cruise. *Seabourn Sun,* 125–140 percent; *Seabourn Goddess I* and *II,* none available.

Packages
- Air/Sea: Yes. First- and business-class upgrades at extra charge. Special Concorde fare package.
- Others: Yes.
- Pre/Post: Yes. Many basic air/sea packages include one hotel night in the departure city; extensions available in all major gateways.

Past Passengers   Former Seabourn and Cunard passengers may receive reciprocal benefits during the postmerger transition. Inquire. Members receive fare reductions for accumulated days of sailing, ranging from 25 percent after 28 days to a free 14-day cruise after 140 days. For a second Seabourn cruise, members get free trip cancellation/interruption insurance, plus other insurance and medical coverage. Up to 30 percent off for early payment.

Seabourn Goddess past passengers receive certificates for a 10 percent discount on their next cruise for each cruise of six or more days they recruit among friends and family, and every friend or family member gets a 10 percent discount on their next cruise. Past passengers can use up to four certificates (40 percent discount) on their next *Seabourn Goddess* cruise.

The Last Word   To compete in the growing ultra-deluxe market, Seabourn widened its price range and offers much more flexibility. The per diems on some sampler and promotional cruises are no more than those of mainstream cruises. In any year, Seabourn visits more than 300 ports in over 100 countries. Very few cruise lines can match those numbers. If you can afford the price, you're unlikely to find any finer cruising—even on your own yacht.

SEABOURN STANDARD FEATURES

Officers Norwegian.

Staff Dining/European; Cabin/Scandinavian; Cruise/British, European, and American.

Dining Facilities Two open-seating restaurants—one more formal, the other a casual indoor/outdoor cafe. *Seabourn Sun,* one dining room with single seating for three meals; alternative Italian restaurant. En suite dining. Complimentary wine.

Special Diets On request.

Room Service 24 hours, cabin menu and full-service.

Dress Code By day, casual but conservative, comfortable. Dinner is a dressy affair, informal (jacket and tie for men) or formal (two black-tie evenings on one-week cruise; four formal dinners on two-week cruise).

Cabin Amenities Television with CNN, ESPN; financial fax service; VCR, direct-dial telephone; marble bathroom with twin sinks (one on *Legend*) , tub and shower, deluxe toiletries, hair dryer, bathrobes, walk-in closet, minirefrigerator; safe. Stocked bar on all but *Sun.*

Electrical Outlets 110/220 AC.

Wheelchair Access Four suites. *Sun,* four cabins, wide bathroom doors, bathtubs with grab bars.

Recreation and Entertainment Three lounges with entertainment/dance music nightly; cabaret, classical music concerts, folkloric performances in ports of call; weekly dinner-dance; casino; cruise-related lectures. *Sun,* card room, bingo, bridge, dance lessons, gentlemen hosts, nightclub, four bars/lounges.

Sports and Other Activities Water sports marina, outdoor pool, deck sports; bridge instructor/lessons; enrichment programs. *Sun,* golf simulator, two pools.

Beauty and Fitness Several saunas, outdoor whirlpools, small gym, exercise classes, beauty salon, spa with massage, beauty treatments. *Sun,* walking/jogging deck.

Other Facilities Self-service laundry, laundry/dry cleaning; library; boutique; hospital; nondenominational religious services. *Sun,* medical facility, book and video library, concierge. *Goddess,* valet, Bvlgari shops.

Children's Facilities None; children under age 18 must be accompanied by parent or adult with written permission. *Sun,* youth counselors seasonally.

Theme Cruises Golf, classical music, food and wine, others.

Smoking Public rooms are designated as nonsmoking. One lounge is a smoker for after dinner. *Sun,* designated areas in public rooms.

Seabourn Suggested Tipping No-tipping-required policy.

Credit Cards For cruise payment and on-board charges: American Express, Diners Club, Discover, MasterCard, Visa.

Seabourn Legend	Quality ⑨	Value B
Seabourn Pride	Quality ⑨	Value B
Seabourn Spirit	Quality ⑨	Value B

Registry: Norway	Length: 439 feet	Beam: 63 feet
Cabins: 106	Draft: 16 feet	Speed: 18 knots
Maximum Passengers:	Passenger Decks: 6	Elevators: 4
204	Crew: 140	Space Ratio: 49

The Ships   In this age of glitzy ships, the Seabourn triplets (they are nearly identical) are the epitome of understatement. Clean lines, fine fabrics, and subtle styling are meant to soothe. Passengers board through a lobby that instantly reveals the ships' character. Quietly elegant, the small atrium spans five decks with a double circular stairway accented by brass railings and etched glass. A glass dome above illuminates the stairs and adjacent hallways with diffused natural light. Apricot and mauve carpeting complements blush marble and wood used throughout the vessel. The sense of space and serenity is immediate and is among the ships' most appealing features.

Public rooms occupy all of the two top levels and are aft on the two center decks. The dining room is on the lowest passenger level. All three ships are being given a stem to stern multi-million dollar renovation, along with the addition of French balconies to 36 suites, a computer learning center, a cigar humidor, and an expanded gym, among other improvements. Work on *Seabourn Pride* was completed in June 2000; *Legend* and *Spirit* will undergo similar treatment, to be completed in mid-December.

The main showroom, Magellan Lounge (King Olav on *Legend;* Amundsen Lounge on *Spirit*), has a stage and dance floor. It is the site of daytime lectures and evening entertainment. In the lobby area are the tour desk, cruise director's office, writing room, and computer center.

One flight up is a second entertainment lounge, which is cleverly glass-partitioned in three sections: a small casino with roulette, blackjack, and slot machines; an informal bar; and a piano lounge used for activities, socializing, daytime parties, and predinner cocktails. After dinner, it's a nightclub. There's also a small book-and-video library.

The first of the two top levels contains the sports and spa deck and indoor/outdoor Veranda Cafe. Another flight up is the Constellation Lounge (Midnight Sun on *Legend;* Horizon Lounge on *Spirit*). The beautiful observation area has sloping floor-to-ceiling windows and is the nicest of the public rooms. Surprisingly, it's underused, despite a radar screen linked to the bridge, huge globe, and computerized wall display showing weather conditions, itineraries, maps, and charts. Early-bird continental breakfast and afternoon tea are served here—both stellar times for ocean panoramas. Reference material on shore excursions, board games, and puzzles are available. A bar outside serves morning bouillon and is a popular gathering spot in fair weather. A promenade used by walkers and joggers connects the bar to a sunning deck.

Seabourn plans major renovations and redesign of some public rooms for all three ships in 2000. The most significant is the addition of French balconies to suites to be completed on the *Seabourn Pride* in May, *Seabourn Spirit* in November, and *Seabourn Legend* in December.

Itineraries   See Appendix B.

Cabins   Accommodations—all spacious, outside suites—are among the ships' finest features. Even standard Seabourn Suites are large. Their practical design maximizes space, and appointments—wall coverings, carpets, draperies, bed covers of fine, lightly textured fabrics—enhance harmony and elegance. After the current renovations are completed, virtually every element—carpets, drapes, bedspreads, and upholstery—will be new, and lighting will be improved.

They have well-defined sitting and sleeping sections. The roomy conversation area has a sofa, two chairs, and a coffee table that can be transformed into a dining table. Two cushioned stools provide extra seating for guests. The sitting area is next to a five-foot-wide picture window placed low enough that you can lie in bed and watch the passing scenery. The window has a mechanical shade operated by a switch near the desk and a device to automatically clean the outside.

On *Seabourn Pride,* 36 of the ship's 104 suites now have French balconies in place of the five-foot picture window. The balconies consist of two full-length sliding glass doors opening onto a narrow, Riviera-style balcony with a waist-high glass and teak balustrade. The sliding doors can be opened to enjoy sea breezes without cutting into the interior space of the room. *Pride*'s balconies, located on decks five and six, are an improved design over the prototype installed in *Seabourn Legend* last year. (The prototype used three panels of glass, requiring more framing that interrupted views.) By mid-December, 36 suites on *Spirit* and on *Legend* will also be fitted with the new balconies. In the ships' tariff, these suites are designated by categories B2 and B3 and their locations are shown on deck plans.

A curtain separating the sitting and sleeping areas can be drawn to put sleepers in darkness. Beds can be configured as twins or a queen. The bedroom section has a long dresser/desk and a large, lighted mirror.

A wall-mounted minirefrigerator and bar is stocked with two bottles of spirits or wine that you select when you book. Replenishments cost extra. Mineral water and soft drinks are free. The bar contains Norwegian crystal glassware. On the opposite wall is a pull-out writing desk, containing your personalized stationery and a small sewing kit. The cabinet conceals a remote-controlled television with CNN, ESPN, and other stations, plus a VCR. A radio plays four music channels. The walk-in closet contains extra shelf space and a safe.

The marble bathroom has twin sinks (*Legend,* one sink), mirrored storage shelves, a large tub, and a shower. Thick terry robes, a hair dryer, and toiletries are supplied.

Cabin doors have a thoughtful touch: a brass clamp to hold the daily agenda, messages, and menus. A hall-side door can be used to convert adjacent standard suites into doubles.

Sixteen larger suites are in four configurations. Classic suites have queen beds only, a larger sitting area, and a small veranda. Regal suites have a separate bedroom and living room, two bathrooms (one with shower and one with tub), a table with four chairs, two walk-in closets, and two sofas. Two owner's suites are the largest and have small private verandas.

Specifications   All suites: 88 standard suites *Seabourn* (90, *Legend/ Spirit*), 2 classic with verandas, 4 regal (8, *Legend/Spirit*), 4 owner's with verandas, 36 with French balconies. Standard dimensions, 277 square feet. 102 with twins (convertible to queen); no singles. 4 wheelchair-accessible.

Dining   Fine dining is central to a Seabourn cruise, and the choices are diverse. For any meal, dine when and with whom you like in The Restaurant dining room or the casual Veranda Cafe, an indoor/outdoor venue for buffet breakfast, lunch, and dinner. Both offer open seating. Or, dine en suite; a 24-hour cabin menu is available, or a meal from the dining room menu will be served course by course. Morning bouillon is served in the Sky Bar, afternoon tea with cucumber sandwiches in the Constellation Lounge.

Seabourn says it spends more on food than any other line does. The emphasis is on fresh ingredients, such as seafood, fruits, and vegetables, obtained in ports. Breads, pastries, and ice cream are prepared on board.

Menus, changed daily and repeated on a 60-day cycle, offer three appetizers, two soups, two salads, four entrees, four desserts, cheese, and ice cream. Generally, dishes are creative and sophisticated. You will find a familiar fettuccine alfredo, but you may be tempted by seared reindeer or grilled marlin with strawberry and cilantro sauce. Vegetarian and lean specialties are available.

Menu entrees are cooked to order, and presentation is outstanding. Suggested wines are usually moderately priced; the wine list is more elaborate. Wine is available by the glass. Caviar available by request.

The Restaurant is a pretty room dressed in pastels where tables are set with Wedgwood china, fine crystal, silverware, and fresh flowers. Most tables seat four or six, but twos, eights, and tens are available.

Breakfast and lunch appeal most to those who prefer a quiet environment and full service. Dinner is a lavish, somewhat formal affair. Two evenings each week call for formal attire, and for all but casual nights, dress suitable for fine dining in New York City or Paris is expected.

Service is unfailingly superb. In fact, service in The Restaurant is the best, most professional we have encountered on any cruise ship. Alas, the food doesn't always match it. Signature dishes at dinner are fabulous, but breakfast and lunch are uneven, and cold croissants for breakfast a disappointment.

At least once each cruise is a dinner dance in The Restaurant. Unlike on other cruise ships, singles are invited to join an officer's table or one hosted by management or a social-staff member. An invitation will be slipped under your door almost daily unless you indicate that you prefer to dine alone.

The informal, convivial atmosphere of Veranda Cafe makes it the most popular choice for breakfast and lunch or for dinner after a long shore excursion. The lively cafe bustles with people and conversation indoors. Outside, tables are set under protective awnings. In fair weather, the deck is one of the most delightful dining places anywhere.

The breakfast buffet offers fruit, fresh breads and pastries, smoked fish, cheeses, and eggs, pancakes, and waffles are made to order. The lunch buffet includes salads, made-to-order pasta, hot and cold seafood, chicken and meats, or grilled fish or meat on request. Hard to resist are the daily surprises: guacamole, an Asian buffet, or a cheese and dessert bar. The homemade ice cream is a passenger favorite. But these aren't your ordinary self-service buffets. An army of attentive stewards take drink orders, assist you with your plate, and bring seconds.

Normally on one evening, Veranda Cafe becomes a trattoria with a special menu and lively music. The meal and the evening are wonderful and very popular. Reserve early.

A 24-hour room-service menu has standard fare (sandwiches, soups, salad, and cheese plates), or a five-course dinner will be served one or two dishes at a time. But unless you need privacy or a break from the dress code (particularly after a long shore excursion), room service is never as good as The Restaurant.

Service   Most passengers rate service as the single best feature—and with good reason: it's impeccable. Shipwide, the thoroughly professional staff is gracious and attentive, but never intrusive. The Norwegian captain and officers, European hotel staff, Scandinavian stewardesses, and British and American cruise and social staff work harmoniously and are visibly proud of their ship. The ships' small size lends them to personalized service impossible on larger ships. The luxury setting offers more opportunities to provide good service, and the high crew-to-passenger ratio enables staff to deliver it.

The ship's no-tipping policy appeared to work very well, but we've recently been told that it's being modified to allow staff to accept tips. We thought it was the result of the line's lowering its cruise prices (20 percent or more), but we were wrong. Gratuities are still included in the cruise price. We hope the change won't impact service.

Facilities and Entertainment   Evening entertainment is tony, designed for sophisticated people. The ship's small orchestra plays easy listening and dance music in the Club, or a pianist/vocalist performs at the cocktail hour. Evening cabaret and variety shows staged in the Magellan Lounge are usually very good. They feature the cruise director and three or four social-staff members. Lounge seats are slightly tiered, providing excellent sight lines.

A classical concert or program by a young artist may be offered, or The Restaurant becomes a supper club with dancing.

The casino offers roulette, blackjack, slot machines, and gaming lessons.

Activities and Diversions   The daily agenda isn't taxing but might include a cooking demonstration; afternoon lecture by a well-known person from the arts, academia, politics, or show business; port talks; bridge lessons or play; a session with a golf pro; art class; galley tour, wine-and-cheese party; ice cream social; or folkloric show. A movie on one of Seabourn's other cruises—and a not-too-subtle sales pitch—may be presented. Not on the schedule are bingo, horse racing, pool games, or costume parties.

The Nautilus Room, an underwater viewing area, offers a glass window for watching the ocean below. But the view from the upper-deck observatory might prove more interesting.

The library is thinly stocked with books and movie videos. The boutique beckons to shoppers. The Computer Learning Center, now with five computers, is offering classes daily. In the Observation Lounge, a humidor cabinet was installed at the rear of the room and cigar tastings are held nightly.

Or, you can do nothing at all. If the weather is fair, you'll probably be out on deck, relaxing, snoozing, or soaking in the Jacuzzi. Some places offer protection in hot or cool weather.

Sports, Fitness, and Beauty   Decks have ample space for sunning and a teak promenade for walking or jogging. Whirlpools and a small, deep swimming pool are in a peculiar spot near the Veranda Cafe—the pool is often shaded by the ship's superstructure, inhibiting swimmers.

The ships have a water sports platform with a 30-by-30-foot steel-meshed cage that drops into the sea, creating a protected saltwater pool. A teak border provides a launch area for paddleboats, windsurfers, and sailboats. Two high-speed boats pull water skiers or transport snorkelers and divers to choice locations. Although the ships try to use these marinas at least once a week, rough water may preclude it.

Fitness facilities were upgraded substantially with the gym enlarged slightly and most of the equipment replaced and new cabinets and lockers added. Daily stretch and exercise classes at varied workout levels, individual training, sauna, and steam rooms are available. The beauty salon offers beauty treatments, such as toning, body wrap, and herbal massage.

Children's Facilities   Although Seabourn doesn't offer the ideal family vacation, it's a testimony to staff that three children younger than nine years old reported having the time of their lives on a recent cruise.

Shore Excursions   Excursions are well organized and orchestrated by an experienced, knowledgeable staff. On a Norwegian fjord cruise, the briefing was the most thorough heard on any but expedition-type cruises accompanied by specialists. There's no push to sell excursions, and even off-the-shelf motorcoach tours tend to be pricey. Information on excursions is sent to passengers before their cruise.

Each cruise offers one or two events designated as Signature Series shore excursions. They often are a cruise highlight but may have limited space. For example, a recent Norwegian voyage offered a concert of Edvard Grieg's music at his lakeside home near Bergen presented by Norway's foremost pianist and interpreter of Grieg's music.

Theme Cruises   In conjunction with Wide World of Golf, Seabourn offers golf cruises with play at prestigious private clubs worldwide. Each trip includes up to six rounds of golf and costs $610–1,555 per player. Included are greens fees, carts, caddies, transfers, golf bag cover, bag handling, tournament awards, and tour escort. "Seabourn School at Sea" is available on some sailings. The program, designed for beginners to advanced golfers, includes seminars and private lessons from a professional using video equipment and a swing analyzer.

Other themed cruises are offered, with such topics as wine or music.

Seabourn Goddess I	Quality ⑨	Value C
Seabourn Goddess II	Quality ⑨	Value C

Registry: Norway	Length: 344 feet	Beam: 47 feet
Cabins: 58	Draft: 14 feet	Speed: 16.5 knots
Maximum Passengers:	Passenger Decks: 5	Elevators: 1
116	Crew: 89	Space Ratio: 37

The Ships   For years, the opening picture in the *Seabourn Goddess* brochure showed the ship in the background as a white-gloved waiter wades through the water to deliver chilled champagne to a passenger floating on a mat by shore. Improbable? Yes, but it could happen. All you need is money and attitude.

Seabourn Goddess is the good life—the ultimate sybaritic fantasy: luxurious surroundings, gourmet food, lazy days, spa indulgence, romantic evenings, and servers catering to your every whim.

The *Seabourn Goddess* twins (formerly *Sea Goddess*) were designed to offer the most exclusive, luxurious vacations at sea. They trade on unabashed snob appeal, offering highly personalized service and an unregimented atmosphere that makes passengers feel as if they're in an exclusive private club.

(Sea Goddess Cruises, launched in 1984, was the first boutique cruise line, as those with small luxury ships are known. The ultra-deluxe ships set the standard for luxury in the 1980s, introducing the all-suite concept to cruise ships. Cunard acquired the twins in 1986. After Carnival and an investors group bought Cunard in 1998, *Sea Goddess I* and *II* were moved to Seabourn and renamed.)

Cabins, decor, itineraries, cuisine, service, and activities were planned to meet the expectations of a select group of very affluent people. Over the years, the ships attracted loyal fans and achieved a niche in the luxury market that no competitor has duplicated. With few passengers and a high ratio of staff, exclusivity and highly personalized service are assured.

Camaraderie among passengers develops quickly, friendships blossom, and a clubby atmosphere grows. By the second day, you'll recognize virtually everyone. By the end of the week, you probably have met them all.

The ships' interiors are sophisticated, understated, and elegant. Decor employs the highest quality fabrics, Oriental rugs, marble, fine wood, and brass. Contemporary art and huge bouquets of flowers are accents.

The luxury of a *Goddess* cruise begins before you leave home. About a month before departure, passengers receive a velvet box containing a leather passport case, luggage tags, and a preference request form. They're asked to specify spirits they want in their suite (included in the tab and replenished on request), books and magazines they prefer, and their choice of twin or double bed. They're advised that private tours or golf and tennis can be arranged at ports, and they're are invited to request appointments in the hair salon or for massage.

Itineraries   See Appendix B.

Cabins   All accommodations are suites of identical size. Smaller than cabins found on some newer luxury ships, they are nonetheless comfortable and beautifully appointed. The bedroom and sitting room can be divided by a curtain. The sleeping area is next to a large window. Some people prefer this (the lounge in suites often is beside the window) because it avoids guests' walking through one's bedroom. The lounge has a sofa, chair, and coffee table (convertible to a dining table). Suites have small bathrooms with tub and shower. They're stocked with ample toiletries, thick towels, and terry robes. There are three full-length closets, but they're small.

All cabins have telephone, stereo, refrigerator, remote-control television, VCR, key-card door lock, safe, good lighting, and a bar stocked to your preferences. Arriving passengers find a bowl of fruit and fresh flowers. Cabin attendants are European; they're cheerful and efficient.

Specifications   58 outside suites; dimensions, 205 square feet. All suites with twin beds convertible to double; no singles. Wheelchair-accessible cabins available.

Dining   *Seabourn Goddess*'s luxury is most apparent in its dining experience. The Dining Salon, a sea of pink and white tranquility, offers one open seating for three meals. Tables for two are accommodated as easily as for eight.

Dinner is leisurely, the atmosphere stylish, sophisticated, and romantic. Piano music plays softly. Tables are set with fine china, crystal, and fresh flowers. Beautifully presented entrees are prepared to order and served with premium wines and champagne. House wines (no additional charge) are excellent. Other wines are available at additional cost.

Seabourn Goddess fans insist the cuisine is the best aboard any cruise ship. Menus are imaginative and varied. Entrees range from the traditional to the exotic (medallions of reindeer). Caviar seems to come from a bottomless source; foie gras and truffles are also used liberally. Ingredients are fresh, often purchased locally, and meats are the highest quality. If no entree tempts you, you're encouraged to request something not on the menu.

Buffet breakfast and lunch are served at the casual, umbrella-shaded Outdoor Cafe. Room service can provide full meals—course by course—around the clock. Caviar at 3 a.m.? No problem.

Service   Pampering is the hallmark of a *Seabourn Goddess* cruise. Your every wish or whim is cheerfully granted. Some passengers make outrageous requests to see if they can be fulfilled. They can.

Most dining and cabin staff are Europeans—polished, professional, and personable. A service charge is included in the cruise price, and tipping has been discouraged. But that policy may be changing, we're told. If true, we hope it won't affect service.

Facilities and Entertainment   Activities and entertainment are low-key and minimal. *Goddess* passengers do not need entertainment; many choose the ships because they have few scheduled activities.

The Main Salon all-purpose lounge is site for exercise classes, meetings, and evening cocktails and dancing. Afternoon tea is served in the smaller Club Salon. Some passengers have a nightcap in the piano bar; others visit the small casino or browse the library (300 videos available).

Sports, Fitness, and Beauty   The ships are best in warm weather when life on the poolside teak decks is relaxed from sunrise to sunset. White-jacketed waiters tend to passengers' every need. A stern platform can be lowered to water level for snorkeling, swimming, and other sports. The ships carry windsurfing boards and speed boats for water skiing.

The Steiner Spa has a minigym. It's staffed by a fitness professional who schedules ability-specific exercise sessions and is available for consultation. Spa cuisine is served at lunch and dinner.

Seabourn Sun	Quality ⑧	Value C
Registry: Bahamas	Length: 673 feet	Beam: 95 feet
Cabins: 380	Draft: 23.5 feet	Speed: 21.4 knots
Maximum Passengers:	Passenger Decks: 8	Elevators: 4
758	Crew: 450	Space Ratio: 51.3

The Ship   *Seabourn Sun* (former *Royal Viking Sun*) was the prize of Cunard's purchase of Royal Viking in 1994. After Carnival and a Scandinavian investors group bought Cunard in 1998, Cunard and Seabourn Cruise Line merged, and the *Sun* was moved to Seabourn and renamed following a $15 million renovation in 1999.

Of all the ships introduced in the 1980s, *Seabourn Sun* lived up to her predictions of elegance and innovation. Finnish-built, she is one of cruising's most spacious ships. Penthouse suites are palatial; standard cabins are as large as other ships' suites. Treats include walk-in closets, beautiful, comfortable lounges, a swim-up bar in the main pool, a lap pool, a spa, and a golf simulator of famous courses; and some unusual features like same-level jetways for easy access to docks or tenders; air-conditioned tenders with lavatories and catamaran hulls for stability; and two high-speed, man-overboard boats.

Clean lines and uncluttered decor reflect the ship's Scandinavian origins. Fine wood and high-quality fabrics are used throughout the ship. Public rooms and facilities are on two center and two top decks. Cabins are spread over seven decks. During the recent renovations, all public areas were updated and all of the staterooms refurbished. The biggest changes are an elaborate new spa, a new outdoor seating area for the Garden Cafe, an expanded computer learning center, upgraded golf facilities, and a reconfigured Midnight Sun Lounge.

Itineraries   See Appendix B.

Cabins   A dozen categories offer four accommodations types: penthouse suites, deluxe, and standard outside and inside cabins. All but 25 cabins are outside and have large windows. Penthouse suites and deluxe cabins (more than a third of accommodations) have verandas. Cabins have pastel decor and dark wood cabinets with a mirrored dresser/desk. All have television, VCR, three-channel radio, phone, minirefrigerators, locking drawers, walk-in closets (cruising's first), and robes. Almost all have bathrooms with tub and shower. All but a few have twin beds convertible to kings, and most have a small sitting area with love seat, table, and chair. Two decks have launderettes. Room service is available 24 hours.

The largest, most luxurious suites are on the top two decks and have butler service. Dividers separate the bedroom and sitting areas. The owner's suite has a whirlpool bath surrounded by picture windows facing the sea—a first.

Specifications   25 inside cabins, 355 outside including suites; 18 penthouse suites; 1 owner's suite; 122 with verandas; 48 deluxe. Standard dimensions, 191 square feet. 368 cabins with 2 lower beds, convertible to doubles; 2 with single lower bed; 2 singles; 4 wheelchair-accessible.

Dining   *Sun*'s redecorated dining room stretches two thirds of the length of the Promenade Deck. It is divided into three sections: forward, middle, and aft. The most desirable section, aft, has large windows on three sides, providing a panorama of sea and scenery. The forward section is smaller and more intimate. Both sections have raised center areas that offer sea views regardless of table location. The middle section is narrow but is connected by a winding staircase to the popular Compass Rose Room and bar one deck above. All passengers are served in one seating with assigned tables for dinner, and in open seatings for breakfast and lunch. Tables, most seating six, eight, or ten people, are set with fresh flowers, fine china, crystal, and silverware. A few tables for two or four are often by the windows.

Superb cuisine is the ship's hallmark. Menus offer specialties from around the world, supplemented with fresh ingredients from each port of call. A chef's special menu, with suggested wines, is featured nightly. The full dinner menu offers three appetizers, three soups, two salads, sorbet, four entrees (fish, chicken, veal, beef), vegetable selections, cheese, three desserts, ice cream, and fruit. A light menu lists calorie counts.

The handsome Venezia, a reservations-only alternative restaurant done in dark woods, blues, greens, and burgundies, has its own galley and features Italian and continental cuisine. Tables can be arranged for two, four, six, or more with advance notice. Red and white wines selected by the sommelier are poured by the glass and are complimentary.

The Garden Room and Cafe is the alternative venue for buffet breakfast and lunch. Located aft on the bridge deck, it has been expanded with a teak-floor outdoor area resembling a sidewalk cafe. Buffet choices are varied and good, but service could be better. A wall of windows overlooks the deck and sea. Food may be taken onto the adjacent deck. Just forward of the Garden Cafe at the Pool Bar, hot dogs, hamburgers, and sandwiches—precooked and reheated—are served; speedy but not very appealing.

The 60-seat Venezia alternative restaurant features Italian cuisine. Specials are added daily to the extensive menu. Reservations are required (no additional cost), but passengers are limited to one per cruise. They can, however, join a standby list.

Service   Officers are Norwegian, friendly, and open. Most dining and hotel staff are northern European. Dining room service is spotty. On a recent cruise, one group of waiters forgot to serve dessert. Cabins attendants—pleasant and thoughtful, efficient and thorough—are young Scandinavian women.

Facilities and Entertainment   Norway Deck might be called the entertainment deck. It is anchored at both ends by lounges and in between you'll find a casino, a cigar and pipe lounge, an espresso bar, a movie theater, a computer center, a card room, the library, and boutiques.

Entertainment is not *Seabourn Sun*'s strong suit. Norway Lounge, the main lounge, accommodates all passengers at one time. It has a stage, bandstand, and dance floor. Daytime activities in the room may include a lecture or bingo. In evening, there might be a classical concert, production show, dancing to big band music, headliner entertainment, or the captain's party. Typical of ships built in the 1980s, the lounge has a low ceiling and poor sight lines from seats in the rear.

In the Midnight Sun Lounge, dressed with dark blue fabric and black leather, matching the black granite and mahogany bar, passengers enjoy afternoon parlor games or evening drinks when it becomes a piano bar. Later, it's a nightclub with cabaret and comedy.

The casino was enlarged by removing the bar to make room for additional slot machines and roulette, craps, and blackjack tables. Just outside the casino is the Espresso Bar (formerly the Wine Bar), one of the ship's most popular spots, which leads to the handsome Oak Room, reminiscent of a men's club, with leather chairs in a wood-paneled setting. It's a cozy daytime retreat and popular for after-dinner drinks. The builders spent more than $100,000 to ensure the safety of the room's wood-burning fireplace, but it has never been used. The U.S. Coast Guard withdrew its approval—such is the caprice of bureaucrats.

The Compass Rose Room, opposite the casino and Espresso Bar, is one of the *Sun*'s loveliest rooms, decorated in soft sea green, blue, and rose and offering a wall of windows with seaviews. The cocktail lounge offers piano music, premium wines by the glass from a cruvinet, and the midnight buffet. Stairs lead to the dining room below.

Stella Polaris Lounge above the bridge is an observation lounge with 180 degrees of wraparound windows facing the bow. It's popular for watching a transit of the Panama Canal or viewing the fjords of Norway. On days at sea, it's the scene for tea with white-glove service; in evening, it's a romantic setting for music and moonlight.

Activities and Diversions   *Seabourn Sun* offers an excellent program of port and theme lectures featuring distinguished speakers on topics ranging from art and antiques to wine and world affairs. The Starlight Theatre screens films twice daily and is used for lectures and meetings.

The *Sun*'s computer center has been expanded and now has ten computers for passengers' use. They can send e-mail for $5 per 5,000 bytes; incoming e-mail is free. The Dickens Library has diverse reading material. The card room nearby can be divided for private parties. Smart boutiques occupy an arcade.

Sports, Fitness, and Beauty   A wind-sheltered swimming pool on Bridge Deck has a whirlpool and swim-up bar and is ringed by a sunning area. Its location away from other sport facilities is unusual.

Outdoors are shuffleboard, Ping-Pong, and quoits. A teak deck for walking or jogging wraps the Promenade Deck. The ship's golf club and pro shop area now has a more sophisticated video course simulator that features virtual play on 12 famous courses around the world. Free onboard seminars and clinics are offered, and there is a putting green and driving cage located on the top deck. The ship offers a series of golf courses through out the year.

The ship's most heralded upgrade is the expand Spa du Soleil. The aft pool was moved further back to create a lap pool with two whirlpools and make room for a glass-enclosed fitness facility with toning and cardiovascular equipment. Spa treatment areas, designed with a classic Roman theme, boasts nine treatment rooms and an array of body treatments and a hair salon. Also available are sauna and beauty salon. The salon and spa packages are pricey.

Shore Excursions   Excursions are as varied as the ship's itineraries. Information is sent to passengers before they cruise. The ship's excursion desk is a full-service travel office.

Postscript   Despite the improvements, the ship does not have the elegance or high level of service of Seabourn's smaller ships. Seabourn expects to overcome the *Sun*'s size by having two levels of service. Passengers in the owner's and penthouse suites—about the total number of passengers on Seabourn's smaller ships—get the personal Seabourn-type service with butlers. Essentially, however, this ship will appeal to those who want the advantages of a larger vessel and could be a good choice for first-time cruisers who want a high level of service but are uncertain about sailing on small ships.

Silversea Cruises

110 East Broward Boulevard, Ft. Lauderdale, FL 33301
(954) 522-4477; (800) 722-6655; fax (954) 522-4499
www.silversea.com

Type of Ships   Ultraluxury, all-suite, small ships.

Type of Cruises   Luxurious cruises on worldwide itineraries.

Cruise Line's Strengths
- luxurious all-suite accommodations, most with verandas
- ship size/maneuverability
- open-seating dining
- cuisine
- impeccable service
- worldwide itineraries
- congenial atmosphere
- comprehensive, all-inclusive prices

Cruise Line's Shortcomings
- somewhat staid evening activities and entertainment
- shallow draft in rough seas

Fellow Passengers   Diverse demographically, Silversea passengers are experienced cruisers. Many have made the rounds of the luxury ships. Well-traveled and outgoing, passengers range from young professionals in their 30s to lively 80-year-olds. The majority are older than 50; most are American. Couples are the rule. Passengers come from throughout the United States, and Silversea has a sizable European following. Although Silversea is a young line, a remarkable number of passengers are repeaters.

Recommended For   Sophisticated, knowledgeable travelers who prefer a finely crafted ship and low-key atmosphere to the glitz and games of big ships; those who appreciate details and expect exacting service amid casual elegance.

Not Recommended For   Those for whom subtle luxury and attention to detail are unimportant; anyone uncomfortable among non-Americans. Late-night revelers or children.

Cruise Areas and Seasons   Africa, Seychelles, Madagascar, Mediterranean, Baltic, Canada, New England, Far East, China, Australia, New Zealand, South Pacific, South America, Caribbean, World Cruise, seasonally.

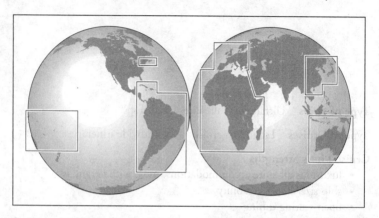

The Line   Silversea Cruises was created in the early 1990s by the Lefebvre family of Rome with the Vlasov Group of Monaco, commercial and passenger shipping families that previously owned Sitmar Cruises. The line targets the ultraluxury market. The name was chosen to suggest quality and luxury and the romance of the sea.

The Italian-built fleet of identical twins were launched in 1995. Silversea took the luxury market by storm with reasonable pricing, uncompromising service, and possibly the nicest accommodations afloat. The ultra-deluxe, six-deck ships' space ratio of 55.74 is among the highest of any cruise ship. Big-ship facilities, a comfortable small-ship atmosphere, and all-suite accommodations are offered at lower per diems than their competitors'. The ships are substantially larger than their direct competitors, but their biggest advantage is their high number of cabins with verandas. Prices aim to be the most comprehensive in luxury cruising. They cover airfare, transfers, port taxes, travel insurance, beverage service (liquors and nonalcoholic drinks), selected wines at lunch and dinner, in-suite hors d'oeuvres and full meals, a special shoreside event on some sailings, baggage handling, gratuities, and deluxe precruise accommodations.

The competition has modified its product to emulate Silversea, but few can rival the combination of deluxe accommodations and seamless hospitality. Service, provided by European crews, is flawless. The ratio of crew to passengers is 0.66 to 1.

Cruises involve two famous names: Le Cordon Bleu and *National Geographic Traveler* magazine. Menu selections were created by the famed cooking school in conjunction with the line's Chef de Cuisine. On select cruises with Cordon Bleu tie-in, regional specialties are highlighted, and demonstrations of cooking and table settings are presented. Photographers and journalists of *National Geographic* join noted experts to lecture on some cruises, and a library offers *National Geographic* articles, CD-ROMs, maps, and other information. Silversea will offer its first around-the-world cruise from January to May 2001.

Silversea was scheduled to launch *Silver Shadow,* the first of two new ships in September 2000. The new twins are about a third larger—25,000 tons—and will carry about a third more passengers than the line's present ships. The space ratio (exceeding 63) will be one of the highest of any cruise ship. The design is similar, but with enhancements based on passengers' comments: larger bathrooms and closets, more top-grade suites, 80 percent of cabins with verandas, poolside dining venue, computer center, cigar lounge, and larger spa and fitness center. The ships are being built at the T. Marrotti Shipyard in Italy, where the first two ships were built; the second, *Silver Whisper,* is scheduled for delivery in June 2001. The line holds options for two more ships. Silversea has also entered into an agreement to help plan and to staff and market the *ResidenSea,* the new luxury apartment ship, dubbed "The World," which is scheduled to debut in late 2001.

The Fleet	Built/Renovated	Tonnage	Passengers
Silver Cloud	1994	16,800	296
Silver Wind	1994	16,800	296
Silver Shadow	2000	25,000	388
Silver Whisper	2001	25,000	388

Style   Sparkling clean, impeccably maintained, and luxurious in an understated way consistent with fine yachts, the ships offer elegance undisturbed by pretense or formality. From boarding to disembarking, passengers are attended by a crew that makes a genuine effort to know each individual and anticipate their every need. This attention is direct and friendly, not suffocating or obsequious.

Suites are exceptionally comfortable and exceed their representation in the line's brochure. Public areas are inviting and elegant. Structured activities are available, but they tend toward the relaxing and cerebral. Announcements, games, and contests are the exception rather than the rule.

At sea and in port, days are casual. Evenings are low-key but dressier. Most cruises include a "Silversea Experience" signature event—usually an excursion with dining and drinks in a beautiful setting, perhaps a private island, private club, or deserted coast.

Silversea attracts gregarious and adventuresome passengers. Although the atmosphere is social and conducive to meeting new friends, dozens of delightful nooks offer solitary time.

Distinctive Features   All-suite accommodations; comprehensive air/sea travel with personalized service at intermediate travel stops; all-inclusive prices. Silversea Experience on most sailings. Moderate single supplements. Golf program. Bvlgari boutiques and bath amenities.

	HIGHEST	LOWEST	AVERAGE
PER DIEM	$985	$507	$735

The above per diems are calculated from the cruise line's non-discounted *cruise only* fares on standard accommodations. Per diems vary by season, by cabin, and by cruise areas.

Rates   Tips, on-board beverages, including select wine and spirits, round-trip airfare with upgrades to business class available, all transfers, and port charges are included.

Special Fares and Discounts   Bonus of 15 percent when final payment is made six months before sailing. Ten percent discount for booking four months before sailing, 5 percent for booking three months before. Advance-purchase discounts cannot be combined with the advance-payment bonus. Combining consecutive voyages offers substantial savings.

- Third Person: Approximately 50 percent of the Vista or Veranda Suite per-person published rate.
- Single Supplement: 125 percent, 150 percent, 175 percent of per-person double-occupancy basic suite, depending on cruise.

Packages
- Air/Sea: All cruises packaged with economy-class air; upgrades available for an additional charge, but still at special rates.
- Pre/Post: Extensive pre- and postcruise tours. Many air/sea packages include one or more hotel nights in the departure or termination city; extensions are available.

Past Passengers   Past passengers automatically become members of the Venetian Society, named to reflect the line's Italian ownership. On their second voyage, members receive a silver pin bearing the society's winged-lion emblem, a symbol of Venice. After they have sailed for 100-, 200-, and 500-plus days, they receive sapphire, emerald, and diamond pins, respectively. Members also receive a newsletter three times yearly containing information on special discounts. Other benefits include shipboard events hosted by the captain. Members get fare reductions of 5, 10, and 15 percent, combinable with early-booking incentives, advance-payment bonus, and consecutive-cruise savings. Members may bring friends in an additional suite at that savings. They also receive $250 or $500 shipboard credits and a credit to their Society account for the days their friends cruise. Members may accrue days toward a free cruise.

The Last Word   Silversea is about as good as its gets. It's hard to fault the accommodations, service, or food, and not having to pay extra for beverages or worry about tipping is a big plus. Itineraries are creative, nonrepetitive, and worldwide, calling on many ports seldom visited by cruise ships. Officers and crew are actively involved in providing highly personalized, caring service. The ships are intelligently designed with inviting public areas, and there's never a sense of crowding. If there are shortcomings, they are in the lack of innovative daily programs or evening entertainment that makes it worth staying up past 10:30 p.m. And though Silversea Cruises remains a good value for those who can afford it, the cruise line can no longer boast about its prices.

SILVERSEA CRUISES STANDARD FEATURES

Officers Italian.

Staff Dining/European; Cabin/European; Cruise/British and American.

Dining Facilities All meals served at one seating in restaurant; indoor/outdoor cafe for casual breakfast and lunch. Alternative dining specialty dinners on most evenings. En suite dining.

Special Diets Available on request.

Room Service 24 hours, cabin menu and full-service dining room menu.

Dress Code Casual, informal, or formal. By day, casual but conservative; comfortable. Dinner is a more dressy affair. Informal (jacket, no tie for men) or formal (two black-tie or dark suit evenings on one-week cruise; four formal dinners on two-week cruise).

Cabin Amenities Stocked bar, minirefrigerator; television with CNN, VCR, direct-dial telephone; Italian marble bathroom with sink, tub, and shower, Bvlgari toiletries, hair dryer, bathrobes, walk-in closet, safe.

Electrical Outlets 110/220 AC.

Wheelchair Access Limited.

Recreation and Entertainment Three lounges with entertainment/dance music nightly; cabaret, classical music concerts, folkloric performances in ports of call; nightly dancing; casino; cruise-related lectures.

Sports and Other Activities Outdoor pool, deck sports; bridge instructor/lessons; enrichment programs.

Beauty and Fitness Two saunas, two outdoor whirlpools, small gym, exercise classes, beauty salon, spa with massage, beauty treatments.

Other Facilities Self-service laundry, laundry/dry cleaning; library with books and video; Bvlgari boutique; hospital; nondenominational religious services.

Children's Facilities None; children under age 18 must be accompanied by parent or adult with written permission.

Theme Cruises Le Cordon Bleu food, wine; golf; opera; *National Geographic Traveler.*

Smoking Public rooms are designated as nonsmoking except for lounges.

Silversea Suggested Tipping No-tipping policy.

Credit Cards For cruise payment and on-board charges: American Express, Diners Club, MasterCard, Visa.

Silver Cloud / Silver Wind	Quality ⑩	Value C
Registry: Bahamas/Italy	Length: 514 feet	Beam: 70 feet
Cabins: 148	Draft: 18 feet	Speed: 20.5 knots
Maximum Passengers:	Passenger Decks: 6	Elevators: 4
296	Crew: 210	Space Ratio: 56.8

The Ships   The Silversea twins are the antithesis of the floating hotels that dominate cruising. Elegance is anchored in simplicity, clean lines, earth-tone fabrics, and polished wood and brass. The decor is styled to soothe.

The entry lobby surprises with its modest proportions. No six-story atrium here. The feeling is of boarding a yacht. The nine-deck ship's lay-out is simple. On topmost Deck 9 are an observation lounge and jogging/walking track that circles the ship. It overlooks the pool on Deck 8, which also contain the bridge, twin whirlpools, pool bar, and Panorama Lounge with indoor and outdoor seating. The lounge offers live music and dancing and is the late-night venue. Beside it, the library stocks books, magazines, periodicals, and videos; it's open around-the-clock, unlike on many ships.

On Decks 4–7, all cabins are forward, all public areas aft. Elevators and a circular stairwell are aft of amidships. Deck 7 offers the fitness center, spa, and beauty salon. Aft is the Terrace Cafe for informal dining and breakfast and lunch buffets. On Deck 6 are the main lobby, travel desk, reception desk, card and conference room, and showroom, which is large enough for small production shows but small enough to be intimate. It's the primary venue for dancing and events such as the captain's reception.

Deck 5 has a Bvlgari boutique, sundries shop, casino, and The Bar, where the showroom audience gathers. The Restaurant, on Deck 4, serves three meals in a plush setting. Public areas are extensive for ships of this size. Dozens of quiet places throughout the ship invite reading or watching the water.

Itineraries   See Appendix B.

Cabins   The spacious, all-outside suites are among the ships' signature features. Suites provide twin beds convertible to queen, walk-in closet, sitting area with loveseat, coffee table and side chairs, writing desk, dressing table with hair dryer, marble bathroom with full-size tub and shower, stocked refrigerator and cocktail bar, entertainment center with remote-controlled satellite television and VCR, and direct-dial telephone. A curtain separates the sleeping and living areas. Seventy-five percent of the 148 suites have private, teak verandas; the remainder provide picture windows. All suites are decorated in light earth tones or pastel blues with nautical trim of polished wood and brass. In addition to standard veranda suites at 295 square feet and standard vista suites (without verandas) at 240-square-feet, the ships offer deluxe suites ranging from 541 to 1,314 square feet.

Extras boost the accommodations into the ultra-deluxe category: pure cotton Frette bed linens and robes, down pillows, personalized stationery, fresh fruit, large umbrellas in the closets, complimentary shoeshine, and 24-hour room service.

Specifications   102 veranda suites, 34 vista suites, 3 silver suites (541 square feet), 2 royal suites (1,031 square feet in the 2-bedroom configuration), 2 grand suites (1,314 square feet with 2 bedrooms), and 1 owner's suite (827 square feet). 2 wheelchair-accessible. No singles.

Dining   The main dining room, called The Restaurant, is reminiscent of an exclusive club. Tables are set with Villeroy & Boch china, Christofle silver, linen, and Schott crystal. Draped picture windows flank the elegant room, and a domed center section adds to its spaciousness. A small marble dance floor allows for occasional dinner dances. Though formal, The Restaurant is also comfortable, relaxed, and unpretentious.

Passengers aren't assigned seating times or tables; they may eat any time during published hours. Lunch and breakfast buffets in the Terrace Cafe provide an informal option. No late-night buffet is offered. Room service is available 24 hours and is delivered with the same attention to detail characteristic of the dining room. Service at all venues is outstanding.

Carrying fewer passengers enables Silversea ships to cook dishes to order, as in a restaurant. (However, we have received complaints from some passengers that the kitchen isn't as accommodating as the line claims, or as it should be for this price, or as some competitors are.)

The line's affiliation with Le Cordon Bleu results in the culinary academy's participation in menu planning and food-focused cruises. Interestingly, Silversea also provides for picky eaters, health-conscious diners, and the meat-and-potatoes set. Only the finest ingredients are used, regardless of how simple or complex the dish. Meat eaters in search of a cruise ship that can prepare a good steak, chop, or prime rib will find nirvana here. Menus offer three appetizers, a pasta, two soups, two salads, sherbet, three main courses, and usually a grilled selection. In addition are a "Light and Healthy" and a vegetarian entree. The dessert menu is separate. Several wines chosen to accompany each evening meal are included in the cruise price.

The food is excellent in quality and presentation, but for those unaccustomed to rich sauces, creams, and oils, it can be a little overwhelming—

although you can order meals without creams or sauces. Freshness of ingredients is not a problem. One day, returning to ship aboard the tender, we were assaulted by an unexpected smell. Peering around the bulkhead, we discovered a grinning chef with a huge string of fish just purchased from local fishermen—a luxury that could never be provided on a large ship. The casual Terrace Cafe high on the stern offers a commanding view of the sea. A wall of windows faces the sheltered outside dining area. Tables are always set with china, crystal, and silver. Buffet waiters take orders for drinks and hot entrees. Theme dinners take diners through eight delectable regions of Italy plus cuisine of the cruise's area. Several times each cruise, the Terrace Cafe offers a special multicourse meal on a reservations basis. These meals provide a change of scenery and let chefs re-create traditional European fine dining.

Service Passenger ratings place service in a dead heat with accommodations as Silversea's best feature. We can't imagine how the service could be better. Without exception, the staff is professional and attentive, but never intrusive; friendly without being familiar; and thoroughly gracious in the European manner. Working harmoniously, officers and crew form a highly effective and responsive team. A concierge is available for special services. Silversea ships' size lends itself to more personalized service than larger ships can offer. There's also more opportunity in the luxurious setting to provide good service. Extensive training and a high 0.66 to 1 crew-to-passenger ratio combine to make Silversea service an industry standard-setter. There's no tipping. Period.

Facilities and Entertainment In the evening, the ship's small orchestra plays easy listening and dance music in The Bar, and a pianist or vocalist duo perform in the Panorama Lounge. The casino offers roulette, blackjack, slot machines, and gaming lessons. Evening entertainment in the Main Lounge spotlights individual entertainers and production shows by a six-member group. All passengers can be accommodated in the steeply tiered, two-level room. It's decorated in dark reds and blues. Murals of sinuous women add an Art Deco touch. Most sight lines are good. Late-night entertainment consists of audience-participation games, dancing, and piano music in the Panorama Lounge.

Activities and Diversions Activities in the next-day's program, delivered nightly to your suite, are more mainstream than you might expect on an ultraluxury cruise, but they prove that even the pampered and sophisticated play bingo! A typical day might include an early power walk with the fitness instructor, a visit to the bridge, a lesson about computers or multimedia, aerobics, wine tasting by the sommelier, a bridge lecture; bingo, backgammon, shuffleboard competition; water volleyball; golf putting competition; afternoon tea; team trivia; and line dancing lessons. In the evening there's music for dancing before and after dinner and evening entertainment—a variety show, comedy, and magic. Experts lecture on the cruise area, and a folkloric show might be staged by locals. A morning port talk will include a sales pitch for tours. Doing nothing is an option. Room service simplifies sleeping in. In fair weather, you'll probably be on deck, relaxing in a lounge chair or soaking in the Jacuzzi. There are ample places in shade or sheltered from wind. In foul weather, a video movie or reading in your suite might amuse.

Sports, Fitness, and Beauty   The pool deck has a large swimming pool, plentiful sunbathing space, two whirlpools and a pool bar. Blue-and-white striped chair cushions create a nautical atmosphere. The uppermost deck has an Astroturf-carpeted promenade for walking or jogging. The modest fitness center is well equipped with Lifecycles, a Stairmaster, and free weights. One or more daily stretch and exercise classes for various workout levels is offered; individual training is available. Adjacent is the spa offering sauna, steam rooms, and beauty treatments. A comprehensive new program of fitness, beauty, and spa treatments crafted for Silversea by Mandara Spa, an international spa specialist, was recently introduced. It uses naturally blended treatments and Balinese techniques, incorporating its signature blend of exotic, traditional, and cutting-edge health and beauty programs, offering a wide array of treatments, including such unusual indulgences as a Hot Lava Rock Massage and a Japanese Honey Steam Wrap.

The cruise lines offers Silver Links, a golf program involving 59 top courses in 26 countries around the world where passengers can during their cruise. The packages provide a seamless program with prearranged transportation, greens fees, carts, course descriptions, hosts, on-board parties, and more—for a fee.

Children's Facilities   Children are rare on Silversea cruises, and no children's facilities or programs are offered. The occasional child receives lots of attention and generally enjoys the cruise. The nice pool and all-included drinks and snacks help.

Shore Excursions   Shore excursions are administered efficiently on board, and the line has a good batting average with them. Silversea passengers' expectations that excursion operators will provide the same level of service they receive aboard ship may be unrealistic in some regions of the world, no matter how hard the cruise lines tries. This problem is, of course, not unique to Silversea; only that the contrast from the ship to the land operation is sometimes sharper.

Excursion sales are low-key, and some cruise directors do an excellent job of matching passengers with the tours most suited to their tastes. Even off-the-shelf motorcoach tours tend to be pricey. Passengers receive shore-excursion information before they depart.

Venetian Society cruises (about half of all) include one "Silversea Experience," a special shore excursion showcasing an area's culture. This may be a private tour or dinner in an extraordinary location. For example, the line has hosted wine tastings at private chateaux and dinner at a palace in St. Petersburg.

Theme Cruises   In conjunction with Le Cordon Bleu cooking academy, Silversea offers L'Art Culinaire cruises emphasizing food and wine. Other cruises, designed with *National Geographic Traveler,* emphasize nature and culture and are accompanied by magazine editors and photographers. Golf cruises cover 47 courses in 22 countries. Also available are fly-fishing and opera cruises. Inquire before booking about your special interest.

Postscript   Silversea cruises are elegant but not stuffy, and the ships, an ideal size: large enough to have sizable swimming pools, ample deck space, and varied public rooms, but small enough to sail up rivers, allow camaraderie among passengers, and offer open-seating dining. Ships are beautiful, service impeccable, and itineraries a cruise-lover's dream.

Silver Shadow / Silver Whisper   (Preview)

Registry: Bahamas	Length: 597 feet	Beam: 81 feet
Cabins: 194	Draft: 19.6 feet	Speed: 20.5 knots
Maximum Passengers:	Passenger Decks: 7	Elevators: 5
384	Crew: 287	Space Ratio: 64.4

The Ships   The first of Silversea's new ultraluxury ships, *Silver Shadow* is scheduled for delivery in September 2000. Her twin, *Silver Whisper,* will follow in June 2001. The noted Norwegian architectural team of Petter Yran and Bjorn Storbraaten, designers of *Silver Cloud* and *Silver Wind,* have created the ships, which are slightly larger and accommodate 100 more passengers than the line's first ships. Otherwise, they're similar to their sister ships. Their passenger space ratio of 64.4 is one of the highest of any cruise ship.

Silversea's hallmarks—veranda suites, single-seating dining, en suite dining, Christofle silverware, monogrammed Frette bed linens, down pillows, Bvlgari bath amenities—will be found aboard the new ships.

Among new features will be The Grill, a casual poolside dining venue. The bistro-style Terrace Cafe, popular on the current fleet for breakfast and lunch buffets, will offer regional Italian specialties in the evening. Silversea's partnership with Le Cordon Bleu will continue aboard the new ships.

Other new features will be a computer center, conference center, and cigar lounge, The Humidor by Davidoff, a Swiss-based purveyor of fine cigars and luxury merchandise. Designed in traditional English smoking club style with a humidor room, the lounge seats 25 and will offer complimentary cognacs and cordials, along with cigars. Another new feature is Le Champagne, an elegant wine and champagne bar designed in collaboration with Moet & Chandon, the famous champagne maker and Silversea's own house champagne. Located adjacent to the Terrace Cafe and cigar club, Le Champagne, which can accommodate up to 24 guests, is intended to be a sophisticated gathering place for before and after dinner drinks, as well as a versatile venue for private wine tastings and dinner parties. The decor of the room is similar to The Humidor with rich woods and warm tones, but with lighter furnishings and a more open floor plan. Its decor will also incorporate accents of Moet & Chandon's signature emblem—the crossed red ribbon which wraps the neck of each bottle of champagne; and a mosaic of etched glass with famous quotes about champagne from great figures in history such as Winston Churchill and Voltaire. A larger spa will offer beauty and massage treatments, sauna and steam rooms, and a full line of exercise equipment. Adjacent will be the Observation Lounge.

The ships also have show lounges, boutiques, swimming pools, and whirlpools.

Cabins Each vessel has 194 outside suites (more than 80 percent of them with private teak verandas): 2 Owner's Suites, 4 Grand Suites, 13 Silver Suites, 2 Medallion Suites, 134 Veranda Suites, 35 Vista Suites (no veranda), and 2 wheelchair-accessible cabins with verandas. Larger suites, such as the Owner's, Grand, and Silver Suites, are amidships.

A standard Veranda Suite measures a spacious 349 square feet, including veranda, and has a walk-in closet and large bathroom with telephone, double-basin vanity, full bath and shower, and separate toilet. Self-service laundry facilities will be available.

Star Clippers, Inc.

4101 Salzedo Avenue, Coral Gables, FL 33146
(800) 442-0551; (305) 442-0550; fax (305) 442-1611
www.star-clippers.com

Type of Ships   Replicas of nineteenth-century clipper sailing ships.

Type of Cruises   Casual, active, sports-oriented, sailing under canvas to out-of-the-way places.

Cruise Line's Strengths
- traditional sailing with some cruise ship comforts
- camaraderie
- ship size/maneuverability
- itineraries

Cruise Line's Shortcomings
- meager port information
- potential language/cultural collisions among passengers
- small cabins

Fellow Passengers   International mix. About half are American, Canadian, and Latin American; the other half European, particularly Germans, including non–English speakers. The average age is 45, but some cruises have 20- and 30-year-olds. The majority are couples, usually including about a dozen newlyweds.

As many as 50 percent may be repeaters, attracted by sailing on a square rigger. Many appreciate the beauty and authenticity of the clipper ships and have no interest in nightclubs, casinos, and glitter aboard mainstream cruise ships, which they probably have shunned.

Recommended For   Independent, active travelers who seek light adventure and off-the-beaten-track itineraries, small-ship devotees, stressed-out urbanites, honeymooners and romantics captivated by the notion of sailing on a tall ship. Also, avid sailors, water sports enthusiasts, experienced cruisers weary of crowded large ships, and conservationists who appreciate environmentally friendly travel aboard ships that use their engines only when necessary. It's a great experience for children seven and older who mix well with adults.

Not Recommended For Those seeking gourmet cuisine, pampering, around-the-clock activity, and resort facilities of a superliner. Physically impaired travelers.

Cruise Areas and Seasons Caribbean, South Asia, winter; Mediterranean, summer; transatlantic and trans–Indian Ocean, April and October.

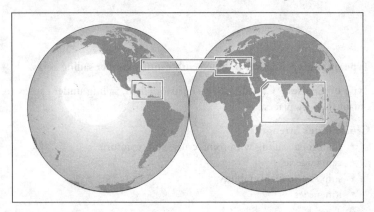

The Line Launched in 1991, Star Clippers is the dream come true of Swedish shipping entrepreneur Mikael Krafft, whose passion for sailing and building yachts and love of the clipper ship (one of America's greatest inventions, he says) led him to create an unusual cruise line with replicas of the sleek, mid-nineteenth-century trading ships. Called greyhounds of the sea, they were the fastest ships afloat until the arrival of the steam age in the late 1860s.

About 100 feet longer than the original clippers and equipped with the latest marine technology, these clippers combine the romance of yesteryear's sailing with some modern amenities. They offer the excitement of manning an authentic square rigger and cruising out-of-the-way waters of the Caribbean, Mediterranean, or South Asia.

The success of Star Clippers' twins lead the line to build a third ship. Said to be the world's largest sailing vessel, she entered service in March 2000.

The Fleet	Built/Renovated	Tonnage	Passengers
Star Clipper	1991	2,298	170
Star Flyer	1992	2,298	170
Royal Clipper	1999	5,000	224

Style Cruises have the freewheeling spirit of a private yacht and are intended to fit between budget-priced Windjammer Barefoot Cruises and pricey Windstar Cruises. They're designed for active, healthy folks who want their travel to be interesting, educational, and fun. Daytime dress is very casual (shorts and deck shoes); evenings are a bit dressier. Cabins are average size; public rooms few, but the teak decks are roomy.

Cruises offer island-hopping in a laid-back atmosphere with varied options at each port of call. The clippers can anchor in bays where large cruise ships cannot go. Launches take passengers to isolated beaches and places for scuba diving, snorkeling, and other water sports.

After a week's cruise, you will know on a first-name basis many passengers and most of the crew, who are both deck hands and sports instructors. You can help hoist the sails or laze about on deck watching the canvas and the sea. Itineraries ensure daylight cruising under sail. The environment is great for families with children ages 7–17.

Distinctive Features The ship and helping sail it. Captain's daily briefings. PADI certification.

	HIGHEST	LOWEST	AVERAGE
PER DIEM	$400	$193	$297

The above per diems are calculated from the cruise line's non-discounted *cruise only* fares on standard accommodations. Per diems vary by season, by cabin, and by cruise areas.

Rates Port charges are additional.

Special Fares and Discounts Ten percent discount on published rates for booking 120 days in advance on selected cruises.
- Single Fare: Guaranteed rate, depending on season, with cabin assigned two weeks before departure.
- Single Supplement: 150 percent of published fare.

Packages
- Air/Sea: Yes.
- Others: Honeymoon.
- Pre/Post: Yes.

Past Passengers Membership cards for the Past Passengers Club are sent after your voyage. Members receive special discounts and a bottle of champagne in their cabins on boarding and are placed on the ship's VIP list.

The Last Word Star Clippers provides an unusual experience on unique ships that are modern and comfortable, yet steeped in tradition. More affordable than *Sea Cloud* and more upscale than windjammers, Star Clippers' ships are more authentic than those of Club Med or Windstar. Yet, they definitely aren't for everyone.

The ships cannot readily accommodate disabled passengers and aren't for people who want mainstream cruising's comforts and options. English is the ships' language, but announcements are likely in other languages, depending on passenger makeup.

Language can become a problem when English speakers are outnumbered by non–English speakers. Communicating may be difficult, and some may feel left out of activities. The language problem varies with staff; some are more careful to translate.

STAR CLIPPERS STANDARD FEATURES

Officers European.

Staff Dining, Cabin/International; Cruise/Swedish, Australian, and Hungarian.

Dining Facilities One dining room for three meals with open, unassigned seating. Light breakfast, occasional buffet lunch, hors d'oeuvres served on deck at 5 p.m.

Special Diets Inquire in advance. Vegetarian, low-calorie standard on menus.

Room Service None.

Dress Code Relaxed and casual. Walking shorts, bathing attire with cover-up, skirts, slacks for daytime; slacks with polo or casual shirts, no jackets required for men in evening.

Cabin Amenities Radio, hair dryer, safe, cellular-satellite phone; movies, ports of call videos, and music; bathrooms with showers; upper category with whirlpool bath and minirefrigerator.

Electrical Outlets 110 AC.

Wheelchair Access None.

Recreation and Entertainment Piano bar with entertainer, outdoor deck bar for dancing and local entertainment, library/writing room, backgammon, and bridge.

Sports and Other Activities Two outdoor pools; water sports and equipment; sailing dinghies, windsurfers, water skiing, underwater viewing craft, waterjet launches, and inflatables carried on board. Learn-to-sail and dive certification programs.

Beauty and Fitness No beauty/barber service. Daily exercise sessions.

Other Facilities Dining room doubles as conference room; audiovisual equipment. Nurse on seven-day cruises; doctor and nurse on transatlantic. Ship's officers trained in emergency medicine.

Children's Facilities None; younger than age 18 must be accompanied by adult.

Theme Cruises None.

Smoking No smoking in cabins. At first briefing, captain emphasizes that smoking is allowed on deck or in rear of dining room.

Star Clippers Suggested Tipping Per person per day, cabin steward, $3; waiter and busboy, $5; 12.5 percent added to bar bills.

Credit Cards For cruise payment and on-board charges: American Express, MasterCard, and Visa.

Star Clipper / Star Flyer Quality ⑦   Value A

Registry: Luxembourg	Length: 360 feet	Beam: 50 feet
Cabins: 85	Draft: 18.5 feet	Speed: 17 knots
Maximum Passengers:	Passenger Decks: 4	Elevators: None
170	Crew: 72	Space Ratio: 15

The Ships   *Star Clipper* and *Star Flyer* are identical, with four masts and square-rigged sails on the forward mast—a Barquentine configuration—with a total of 16 sails (36,000 square feet of dacron). They are manned, not computerized, and are capable of attaining speeds up to 19 knots. A diesel engine is in reserve for calms and maneuvering in harbors.

At 226 feet, they are among the tallest ships and the first true sailing vessels to be classified by Lloyd's Register of Shipping since 1911. Built in Belgium, they comply with the latest safety regulations for passenger vessels on worldwide service.

The ships have four passenger decks; all but eight cabins are on the lower two. Public spaces, which were recently refurbished, are on the top two. There, amid sails and rigging, every Walter Mitty begins to salivate with anticipation. They can help hoist the sails or watch in wonder. The ships are generally under sail from late evening to the following mid-morning. Under normal conditions, they use the engine only to maneuver in port. For true salts and romantics, balmy tropical air filling the white sails against a star-filled sky is the essence of bliss. Many stay up half the night savoring it.

Itineraries   See Appendix B.

Cabins   Small but comfortable, cabins are carpeted, air-conditioned, and tastefully furnished with a counter/desk and built-in seat, large mirror, wood paneling, brass lamps, and prints of sailing scenes. Two portholes admit light. Under-bed storage holds luggage or scuba gear, and closet and drawer space is adequate for informal cruising.

Most cabins are outside and have twin beds convertible to a double. They have multichannel radio, phone, hair dryer, safe, ceiling-mounted television/video monitor (videotapes are available from the library in English and German), and 24-hour news prepared in British English, American English, Canadian English, and German. Each version includes news of interest to that group.

Bathrooms are very small. They have marble-trimmed fixtures and showers. Eight top-category cabins have whirlpool bathtubs, hair dryers, and minirefrigerators stocked at cruise's start (occupants pay for restocks). These cabins open onto the deck; some people may feel that decreases their privacy. Cabin service is limited to cleaning. Inside cabins are sold only when the ship is full. Aft cabins on lower decks should be avoided due to engine noise.

Specifications 6 inside cabins, 78 outside; no suites. Standard dimensions, 120 square feet. 66 cabins with 2 lower beds (convertible to queen); 18 cabins with fixed double beds; 8 cabins accommodate third passenger; 4 inside cabins have uppers and lowers; no singles.

Dining Clipper Dining Room, resplendent with shining brass and etched glass, is rather formal for such an informal ship. Seating is at tables for six among or around a forest of columns, and banquettes along the walls by portholes. All passengers and officers are accommodated at one open seating. When the ship is full, the room is crowded.

The buffet breakfast has made-to-order omelets; lunch has a different pasta daily and a self-service salad bar. A light, early-morning breakfast and occasional lunch buffet are also served on deck.

Dinner selections include beef, chicken, and fish; vegetables; cheeses; and desserts. The food is plentiful but appeals mostly to those with minimal interest in epicurean delights. During a week, food can range from adequate to good, but not gourmet. The menu emphasizes fresh ingredients, fruit, salads, vegetables, and seafood. Recently, the line's new executive chef has begun upgrading the food and menus. Stay tuned.

Wines are available at reasonable prices. For example: Robert Mondavi Cabernet Sauvignon, $26 per bottle, and house wine, Cuvee Lupe Cholet, France, red or white, $3.50 per glass.

Service Officers and deck crew are friendly, energetic, and easygoing. They mix freely and easily with passengers, helping create the ship's relaxed atmosphere. The dining and hotel staff is low-key and congenial.

Facilities and Entertainment A small, U-shaped piano lounge wraps the landing of the stairway between the main deck and dining room. It has brass-framed panoramic windows and small tables with cushioned banquettes that seat about two dozen people. The skylight overhead is actually the transparent bottom of a pool on the sun deck. A pianist or vocalist entertains before and after dinner.

Swinging doors connect to the outdoor Tropical Bar. Depending on the hour, it's a social center, meeting area, stage (where the captain speaks daily), spot for light breakfast or buffet lunch, or dance floor (taped music or electronic keyboard). There's no casino.

Activities and Diversions   Passengers might be found playing back-gammon or bridge.

The teak-paneled library/writing room resembles an English club, with large brass-framed windows, paintings of nautical scenes, and a non-working fireplace (snuffed by the U.S. Coast Guard). Furnished with card tables and comfortable chairs, it's a reception desk at boarding and a small meeting room. A good selection of popular fiction, travel, and coffee-table books is stocked. A tiny shop sells film and souvenirs. The dining room converts to a meeting room with screen projectors and video monitors for port lectures.

The captain and cruise director hold "story time," an informal briefing, on deck in late afternoon or the morning before arriving in port. Passengers congregate around the open bridge, where they can hear the captain and his mates at work and watch the sails being raised and lowered. Many lend a hand with the rigging, but few hang in for the full cruise.

Sports, Fitness, and Beauty   There are two tiny outdoor pools, one filled with fresh water and one with seawater. Beginning scuba lessons are offered at the forward pool.

Exercisers can walk from the stern to the bow around the open parts of the main and sun decks. At 8 a.m. daily, one of the water sports teams leads a half-hour aerobics session.

In the Caribbean and South Asia, water sports are a more important element of the cruise. The ships carry sailing dinghies, windsurfers, underwater viewing craft, boats for water skiing and skis, snorkel gear (issued for cruise duration), scuba equipment for certified divers, volleyballs, and oversized, solid-surface kadima paddles for beach sports. The ships might anchor in a remote cove or off a deserted beach and shuttle passengers to and from shore for snorkeling, sailing, windsurfing, and swimming.

The sports and recreational staff includes multilingual instructors. Snorkeling is organized almost daily in the Caribbean. Certified divers with C cards can join trips to reefs and underwater wrecks. A $40-per-dive charge covers air tank refill, personal supervision, and transport by Zodiac.

Three dive programs are available: a resort course, $79; PADI certification, $195 for those with documentation that they've completed classroom requirements; and full PADI certification course, $295. For the latter, the line recommends divers spread the course over a two-week cruise.

Shore Excursions   Guided tours (usually $30–40) focus on a destination's architectural, historical, and environmental points of interest and are likely to be more interesting than those offered by mainstream ships. Fewer passengers and unusual itineraries help ensure more stimulating, personalized tours for participants.

The ships tie up in port as seldom as possible. Patented stabilizing tanks keep the ship steady at anchor. Tender service is offered every half-hour until sailing time, usually around 6 p.m.

Royal Clipper	**(Preview)**	
Registry: Luxembourg	Length: 439 feet	Beam: 54 feet
Cabins: 112	Draft: 18.5 feet	Speed: 20 knots
Maximum Passengers:	Passenger Decks: 5	Elevators: None
228	Crew: 100	Space Ratio: NA

The Ship Star Clippers' third ship made her debut in July 2000 as the world's largest sailing vessel. The new clipper's gross tonnage is about 5,000 tons—more than twice that of *Star Clipper* or *Star Flyer*. She's about a third longer than those ships. Her capacity is 228 passengers, compared to 170 on the other two.

Royal Clipper, estimated to cost more than $75 million, is a five-masted full rigger with 42 sails, most of them square. She will be certified to cross all oceans and to sail on 7- and 14-day itineraries.

The new vessel is more upscale than her sisters and will introduce many new features. The ship has three outdoor swimming pools. The oval, center pool has a glass bottom, which allows light into the three-deck atrium below. A circular staircase, links the atrium with lounges, cabins, and public rooms. Other facilities include a hairdresser, spa, exercise room, and library.

The bilevel dining room accommodates all passengers at a single seating for meals. Below the bridge is an observation lounge with wraparound windows. On the main deck are the purser's office, a large piano lounge, an indoor/outdoor bar, and library. Captain Nemo's Lounge, on the lowest passenger deck, has 16-inch portholes looking out on marine life day and night. A hydraulically controlled water sports platform will offer an inflatable 16-foot raft for swimmers.

After the hull was finished, the ship was completed in Holland. The interior designs have been created by Donald Starkey of London, a noted megayacht interior designer. The new ship has two diesel engines in a single propeller shaft and a bow thruster and controllable pitch propeller that will virtually eliminate underwater drag when she is sailing.

Itineraries See Appendix B.

Cabins Of the 112 cabins, the 90 doubles, each with 150 square feet, are 35 percent larger than those on sister ships, and 26 have a third fold-down bed. There are two deck cabins of 125 square feet and six inside cabins of

100 square feet. Sixteen deck suites, each with 200 square feet, have private verandas and bathrooms with whirlpool tubs. Two owner's suites measure 320 square feet each and have a private entrance; butler service is provided.

Royal Clipper is spending her maiden summer in the Mediterranean, sailing from Cannes, and winter in the Caribbean, sailing from Barbados. She will offer transatlantic voyages in October/November and April/May. Some technical features and amenities will enable her to sail to the Baltic and other areas her sister ships have not cruised.

Windstar Cruises

300 Elliott Avenue West, Seattle, WA 98119
(206) 281-3535; (800) 258-7245; fax (206) 281-0627
www.windstarcruises.com

Type of Ships   Deluxe sailing yacht/cruise ships.

Type of Cruises   Low-key, laid-back, yet luxurious, for active, affluent travelers with cosmopolitan tastes for offbeat corners in sunny climes.

Cruise Line's Strengths
- appealing lifestyle
- private yacht exclusivity on small ships
- cabins
- romantic escape
- water sports

Cruise Line's Shortcomings
- evening activity
- port-intensive itineraries with minimal time under canvas

Fellow Passengers   The mix is broader than generally perceived. Not all drive BMWs and Porsches: 40 percent have Jeeps and Fords, and 77 percent of those are the family version rather than sports model. Passengers range from 20–80 in age, but the majority are 35–65 years old and the median age is 48. Incomes differ, and they might be first-time or experienced cruisers. Despite many differences, they share one aspect in common—a lifestyle preference, even if they can not enjoy it 365 days of the year. Passengers are likely to be well traveled; from the United States, Europe, and Latin America, and about 75 percent are professionals—lawyers, doctors, business executives—and probably work in high-pressure jobs. The remainder are apt to be retirees from similar pressure cookers, plus a few honeymooners. Fifty percent read business and professional magazines more than lifestyle or fashion ones. They are active and enjoy individual and low-energy sports, such as golfing, walking, and swimming.

Recommended For   Active, affluent, Type-A individualists, 25–75 years old, who really mean it when they say they want to chill out; those who wouldn't be caught dead on a mainstream cruise ship; divers and others who enjoy water sports in moderation; experienced cruisers looking for something different; those attracted by the romance of sailing ships who want upscale luxury.

Not Recommended For   Anyone who prefers large ships, thrives on action, or enjoys wearing fancy clothes; those who need to be entertained, don't relate to a sophisticated ambience; those who prefer a burger to brûlée.

Cruise Areas and Seasons   Caribbean, year-round; Mexico and Costa Rica, winter; Mediterranean, spring–fall; transcanal and transatlantic, April and October; Asia, New Zealand, Fiji, year-round.

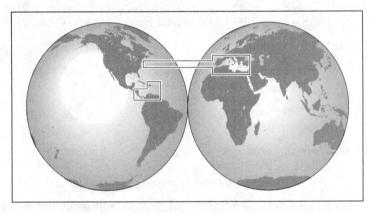

The Line   Four masts in a row, each with enormous triangular sails and as tall as a 20-story building, tower above a deck one and a half times the length of a football field and half its width. The great sails are manned by computers designed to monitor the direction and velocity of the wind to keep the ship from heeling more than six degrees. The sails can be furled in less than two minutes.

This ship is a windcruiser, which on its introduction in 1985 was called the most revolutionary vessel since the introduction of the steamship. The vessel uses wind power alone up to 50 percent of the time at sea, depending on itinerary; electrical power and back-up propulsion are provided by three diesel-electric engines. The ship marries the romance and tradition of sailing with the comfort and amenities of a cruise ship. Its all-outside cabins are larger, better designed, and better appointed than most standard cabins on mainstream cruise ships. The French-built vessels' shallow draft enables them to call at less visited ports, private marinas, and secluded beaches. They are fitted with a water sports platform at the stern that folds out to give direct access to the sea. Windstar Cruises was acquired by Holland America Line in 1987, and the next year both companies were purchased by Carnival Cruise Lines. Windstar continues to operate as a separate entity. In 1997, Windstar bought the five-masted *Club Med 1,* one of two identical ships in the Club Med fleet that are larger versions of Windstar's ships. Renamed *Wind Surf* and remodeled, she entered Windstar service in 1998.

In 2000, Windstar returned to year-round cruising in Asia with new itineraries around New Zealand and expects to add Fiji for 2001.

The Fleet	Built/Renovated	Tonnage	Passengers
Wind Song	1987	5,350	148
Wind Spirit	1988	5,350	148
Wind Star	1986	5,350	148
Wind Surf	1990/98/00	14,745	312

Style   Laid-back, romantic, and informal, the cruises combine the atmosphere of a private yacht with the amenities and services of a cruise ship. From the outset, the ships have offered exclusivity because of their size, ambience, and the people they attract: upscale professionals who can afford a luxury cruise but want a less structured environment and more unusual vacation than is available on traditional cruises.

The ships are wonderfully quiet under sail; you can hear the ocean wash the hull and the sails snap as wind fills them. Passengers visit the open bridge to see how everything works. The captains—their hands never far from the wheel—usually give eager passengers a few minutes at the helm.

There's a casual elegance and easygoing informality about the ship and its occupants. Regardless of age, passengers seem to blend easily; by week's end, they're good friends. Pressure to keep a schedule is nonexistent. *You* decide how to spend your day. Even ardent Type-A personalities can unwind.

Distinctive Features   The ship. Water sports platform; use of most sports gear free. A passenger lucky enough to hook a fish on a deep-sea outing can have it cooked by the chef.

	HIGHEST	LOWEST	AVERAGE
PER DIEM	$566	$246	$531

The above per diems are calculated from the cruise line's non-discounted *cruise only* fares on standard accommodations. Per diems vary by season, by cabin, and by cruise areas.

Rates   Port charges and tips are included.

Special Fares and Discounts   Booking six months in advance saves up to 50 percent. Windstar frequently offers two-for-one promotions. Other discounts are on a quarterly basis.

Passengers receive added benefits through a Windstar agreement with Preferred Hotels and Resorts Worldwide, which includes some of the world's leading hotels, among them Mansion on Turtle Creek in Dallas and the Peninsula in Hong Kong. They receive a free hotel night for every seven days of cruising or a $125-per-person shipboard credit for every five-night stay at a Preferred hotel.

• Single Supplement: 175 percent of the published per-person rate.

Packages
• Air/Sea: Yes.
• Others: Yes.
• Pre/Post: Yes.

Past Passengers   The Foremast Club is open to all who take a Windstar cruise. They receive a newsletter and other literature highlighting new itineraries and special discounts, including two-for-one savings on select cruises.

The Last Word   On our first Windstar cruise, having expected passengers on the level of royalty, the ones who seemed to be enjoying themselves most were a blue-collar couple from Massachusetts on their second honeymoon—and first cruise. A Windstar cruise is a relaxing, romantic escape, but the perception more than the reality seems to put it out of reach in price and ambience for most people. Although it's definitely a way to impress your friends, deciding whether this cruise is for you shouldn't be based on price (although you get a lot for your money), but on the type of cruise it offers. Those who relate to it think it's heaven; those who don't would probably be bored. If you need more convincing, Windstar has a video and CD-ROM available through Vacations on Video at (602) 483-1551; They also have a helpful, newly designed interactive Web site.

Our only complaint is that Windstar's itineraries are so port-intensive they leave little time for passengers to enjoy the ships, particularly under sail. Windstar recently added a day at sea to some Mediterranean cruises. We think two would have been better.

Windstar, like her sister company, Holland America Line, has a "no-tipping-required" policy. It supposedly means staff cannot solicit tips but can accept them. We think that's confusing, especially to first-time cruisers who already worry excessively about tipping. Further, tipping should never be "required." Period. It should be a passenger's prerogative. So, why does Windstar pretend? If it wants passengers to tip, it should say so.

WINDSTAR STANDARD FEATURES

Officers British, some Norwegians and Dutch.

Staff Dining, Cabin/Indonesian and Filipino; Cruise/American, British, and some Scandinavian hostesses.

Dining Facilities One open-seating restaurant; outdoor cafe for breakfast and lunch buffet featuring traditional and tropical specialties; occasional barbecues on the beach. *Wind Surf,* lunch, dinner in Bistro.

Special Diets Sail Light menus with low-calorie, heart-smart, and vegetarian selections. Advance notice requested for others.

Room Service 24 hours.

Dress Code Casual and elegantly casual.

Cabin Amenities Color television, VCR, CD player, three-channel radio; international direct-dial telephone; safe; minibar and refrigerator; hair dryer and terry robe.

Electrical Outlets 110 AC (220 *Wind Surf*).

Wheelchair Access None. Seeing-eye dogs have been permitted.

Recreation and Entertainment Piano bar, casino, lounge with local musicians or ship's band, library, videocassette/CD library.

Sports and Other Activities Water sports platform for sailboats, windsurfers, motorized inflatables, water skiing, scuba diving; snorkeling equipment carried on board; saltwater pool. Charge for diving.

Beauty and Fitness Beauty salon; hot tub/Jacuzzi, sauna, masseuse, fitness room with weight-training equipment. Spa on *Wind Surf.*

Other Facilities Laundry; doctor, infirmary.

Children's Facilities None. Children's videos.

Theme Cruises Wine, culinary, life-enrichment on some repositioning cruises, which are packaged with air fare and pre-/postcruise hotel packages.

Smoking Allowed in designated areas, but not in dining room.

Windstar Suggested Tipping Tipping-not-required policy.

Credit Cards For cruise payment and on-board charges: American Express, Discover, MasterCard, Visa, travelers cheques. No cash system on board.

Wind Song	Quality ⑨	Value C
Wind Spirit	Quality ⑨	Value C
Wind Star	Quality ⑨	Value C

Registry: Bahamas	Length: 440 feet	Beam: 64 feet
Cabins: 74	Draft: 13.5 feet	Speed: 8–12 knots
Maximum Passengers:	Passenger Decks: 4	Elevators: None
148	Crew: 81/91	Space Ratio: 36

The Ships   The triplets are identical inside and out. If not for their itineraries, they would be difficult to tell apart. Throughout, the tasteful appointments are well designed and inviting. They have the feel of a sailing ship—wood and leather, portholes, and nautical blue and white—yet they're modern, with expanses of windows creating spaciousness and spacestation–white walls adorned with contemporary art.

Because the number of passengers is small, boarding is speedy. You're greeted with a glass of champagne or chilled fruit drink and escorted to the main lounge to complete paperwork. Then, you're escorted to your cabin, where your luggage should be waiting.

The cabins, gym, and sauna are on the bottom two of four passenger decks. The third deck contains a main lounge and dining salon—both handsome. Through a lounge skylight, passengers have dramatic views of the majestic sails overhead. You'll also find a tiny casino, boutique, and beauty salon. The top deck offers a swimming pool, bar, and veranda lounge.

Itineraries   See Appendix B.

Cabins   With the exception of the owner's suite, cabins are identical: large and outside. Larger than those on mainstream cruise ships, these well-designed, nicely appointed cabins make optimum use of space and are fitted with twin beds or a queen-size bed.

The marriage of tradition and technology is apparent in cabins. Each has twin portholes with brass fittings and wood cabinetwork, including a foldout vanity with makeup mirror. Modern amenities include remote-control television, VCR, international direct-dial telephone, CD player, safe, and minibar stocked daily with beer, wine, spirits, and soft drinks. (*Note:* Drinks are expensive. A beer, for example, costs $5.) Bathrooms have showers, teak decking, well-lighted mirrors, hair dryers, terry robes, and adequate storage.

Specifications 74 outside cabins; 1 suite with queen-size bed. Standard dimensions, 185 square feet. 73 with twin beds (convertible to queen); 11 (20 on *Wind Star*) with third berths; no singles; no wheelchair-accessible.

Dining The teak-lined dining room—in nautical design with rope-wrapped pillars—has low ceilings and subdued lighting, giving it an intimate atmosphere. Seating is open, restaurant-style. Emphasis on food is less than on mainstream vessels, though the line is working to improve the fare. Cuisine that has been uneven, ranging from super to ordinary, is now getting good reviews, we're happy to report.

Menus by celebrity chef Joachim Splichal of Patrina and Pinot Bistro in Los Angeles, whose French cooking incorporates light California style, match Windstar's casual style of cruising. The line serves California wines to complement the cuisine; tastings are offered. "Sail Light" menus by Jeanne Jones, who developed the spa menus for Canyon Ranch and the Pritiken Center, also are available.

Coffee, tea, juices, and breakfast rolls are served poolside for early risers. Breakfast in the glass-enclosed veranda offers tropical fruits and freshly baked breads. Afternoon tea on the pool deck with finger sandwiches and pastries is popular.

In the Caribbean, a highlight is the pool deck barbecue, serving grilled lobster tails, shrimp, and other seafood accompanied by music from a local band.

Room service is available 24 hours a day.

Service The captain and European officers are affable, accessible, and visible, inviting passengers to watch the ship in operation, visiting with them, and participating in activities when possible. They welcome questions. Cabin staff and most restaurant personnel are Indonesian; deck stewards, bar personnel, and section captains are Filipino. All get very high marks.

Facilities and Entertainment Nightlife is low-key and minimal. The tiny casino has blackjack tables, a Caribbean stud poker table, and slot machines. An easy-listening trio plays nightly for dancing in the lounge. Topside, rock by video plays in the disco. You also can watch a movie in your cabin; a selection of videos is available at the reception desk. A Caribbean night showcases a reggae band, and passengers young and old dance on the pool deck.

Activities and Diversions Windstar ships don't have scheduled daily activities. You set your own schedule, make your own activity—independently or with new friends. That's what this cruise is all about. Days are passed sunbathing, reading, deep-sea fishing, swimming, and watching the ship's operation. (Readers should bring their books; selection aboard is limited.) Ship's television features two current movies daily, plus satellite news around the clock.

Sports, Fitness, and Beauty Water sports from the ships' foldout platform more than compensates for the absence of on-board sports. Furthermore, the ships' shallow draft enables them to stop at less visited ports and secluded beaches and coves. On Caribbean more than Mediterranean cruises, water sports are a main attraction. Carried aboard are sailboats, windsurf boards, snorkeling and diving equipment (including tanks), and Zodiacs (inflatable boats) to take passengers snorkeling, scuba diving, water skiing, and deep-sea fishing. Except for Scuba, gear is available free of charge. Scuba (one tank dive) costs $65 (divers must show certification). Beginning dive lessons are available. Dive masters and water sports directors are well qualified, personable, and eager to help. Snorkeling and scuba trips and lessons are organized daily. When the ships anchor off deserted islands, passengers often must wade from Zodiacs to the beach.

Each ship has a fitness room with some exercise equipment, sauna, and masseuse; Jacuzzis are on the pool deck. The beauty salon offers aromatherapy.

Shore Excursions Most excursions are half-day tours with an emphasis on tropical gardens, national parks, and other natural attractions. Prices are on the high side, costing $17–89. Excursions at St. Kitts in the Caribbean, for example, include a rain forest hike and horseback riding. In the Mediterranean, sight-seeing is emphasized.

Wind Surf	Quality ❼	Value C
Registry: Bahamas	Length: 617 feet	Beam: 59 feet
Cabins: 154	Draft: 16 feet	Speed: 12 knots
Maximum Passengers: 312	Passenger Decks: 6	Elevators: 2
	Crew: 185	Space Ratio: 34

The Ship *Wind Surf,* acquired by Windstar Cruises in 1997, is the former *Club Med 1,* a larger version of the Windstar trio. After extensive remodeling, the ship was rechristened *Wind Surf* and entered Windstar service in 1998.

During renovations, 31 deluxe suites were created, reducing the ship's capacity some, although it remains double that of her Windstar sisters. Reducing the number of passengers was intended to offset the ship's larger size, which dilutes the intimate Windstar experience. The suites are about double the size of already spacious standard cabins. A spa was also added.

The ship offers a complimentary water sports program and has a fully equipped conference center with meeting facilities for up to 118 people. Public rooms include the Wind Surf Lounge piano bar; a library well stocked with CDs, books, and videos; casino; signature shop; and fitness center. The captain maintains an open bridge. Also available are 24-hour room service, laundry service, and a doctor's office.

Itineraries   See Appendix B.

Cabins   The deluxe outside cabins encompass 188 square feet each and offer queen-size beds (convertible to twins) and a sitting area. They are similar in layout and decor to standard cabins on Windstar's other ships. All have television, VCR, CD player, safe, minibar and refrigerator, and direct-dial telephone. The bathroom has a shower, hair dryer, toiletries, and terry robe.

The 31 new ocean-view suites in selected areas of top decks measure 376 square feet. Their decor, in maroon and cream, is accented by teak wood, linen wall coverings, and original art. Each suite has a queen bed convertible to twins and a sofa bed. A curtain can be pulled across the bedroom to separate it from the living room for dining. In addition to standard amenities, suites boast his-and-her bathrooms with shower, teak flooring, plush towels and robes, and vanity lighting.

Specifications   31 deluxe outside suites; 123 outside cabins with queen beds (convertible to twins) and sitting area. Standard cabin dimensions, 188 square feet. Some cabins have third berth; some side-by-side have adjoining private door.

Dining   The ship's two dining rooms—The Restaurant and the smaller Bistro—accommodate all passengers at one sitting with no assigned seats. Menus for both were developed by Joachim Splichal, chef at Patina and Pinot Bistro, top Los Angeles restaurants. Passengers have the opportunity to dine in both during a cruise. Light and vegetarian menus are available. The Verandah Cafe serves breakfast and lunch.

The Bistro, Windstar's first alternative restaurant, is modeled after Splichal's Pinot Bistro. Splichal and his partner, Octavio Becerra, developed 132 recipes for The Bistro. The ship offers one of few rotisserie dining service at sea. Lighting, linens, china, waiter uniforms, and artwork distinguish it from The Restaurant.

Sports, Fitness, and Beauty   The 10,000-square-foot WindSpa, operated by Steiner, has a staff of ten and offers three kinds of treatments. Health and exercise includes aerobics, yoga, and other exercise classes; a water aerobics pool; and a fitness room with trainers. Pampering includes Swedish, deep tissue, sports, and other massage; aromatherapy; hair care; manicures, pedicures, and facials; and hand, foot, and spa bath treatments. Purification treatments include herbal wraps, algae and fango body masks, and mineral baths. Services can be purchased in advance or on board; they cost $259–699 per person. The Windstar brochure outlines options.

Wind Surf has a water sports platform and equipment similar to that on the Windstar trio, two saltwater pools, and two hot tubs.

Postscript   The most consistent complaint has been the ship's high, steep gangway, inconvenient for even the agile. But now the problem is scheduled to be remedied during the ship's November 2000 dry dock by lowering the entry/exit from Deck 4 to Deck 2. The conversion will require eliminating two cabins. The heavily promoted spa disappointed some, and exercise equipment in the fitness room needs updating.

Shipboard service got mixed reviews. Some problems might result from inadequate staffing for this caliber of ship. Room service could not fulfill its menu's claim of 24-hour availability for some basic items. In contrast, reports on service and food in the bistro were much better. However, a special request for chocolate crème brûlée made 24 hours in advance was denied. The chef said, "While we could do it on the smaller ships, we can't on this one."

Affluent clients attracted to Windstar for casual elegance, small ships, fewer passengers, and the chance to sail with passengers of similar means and interests will find that *Wind Surf* is different. One passenger observed, "*Wind Surf* is too large to get the true feeling of a yacht. It's more of a cruise ship experience than a sailing experience."

World Explorer Cruises

555 Montgomery Street, Suite 1400
San Francisco, CA 94111-2544
(415) 820-9200; (800) 854-3835; fax (415) 820-9292
www.wecruise.com

Type of Ship   Classic oceanliner.

Type of Cruises   Educational, port-intensive, light adventure.

Cruise Line's Strengths
- destinations
- exceptional lectures on Alaska
- cultural presentations
- warm, informal atmosphere
- friendly, efficient staff and crew
- 16,000-volume library
- value

Cruise Line's Shortcomings
- aging ship
- so-so cuisine

Fellow Passengers   From May–September, mature, experienced travelers older than age 50, retired couples, seniors, and some families with school-aged children embark on Alaska cruises. They're friendly, unpretentious people of varied means who don't seek casinos or glitzy revues. They would rather watch whales and glaciers and attend cultural shows and seminars. They hail from throughout the United States and Canada.

Most are well educated, well read, curious, good sports who participate enthusiastically in activities and excursions. They're interested in nature, culture, and learning, and they know how to have fun. They play bridge, games, and quizzes. They're physically and mentally active, regardless of age. Spring and fall Semester at Sea programs accept a limited number of adults who may study for credit or audit courses. Most are veteran travelers who fit the profile of Alaska passengers.

Recommended For Travelers seeking an experience focused on learning about the areas visited; those who prefer Bach to rock and enjoy the informal, friendly milieu of a small ship.

Not Recommended For Gamblers, snobs, flashy types, those who like to dress up, foodies, the fastidious; those who perceive a lack of value in the absence of luxury.

Cruise Areas and Seasons Alaska in summer; South America, Africa, and Asia, spring and fall Semester at Sea voyages; Caribbean/Central America in January.

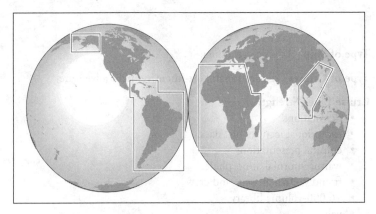

The Line Since 1978, World Explorer has offered in-depth cruises of Alaska in the summer. Other seasons, she's a floating campus for two 100-day voyages with the Semester at Sea program sponsored by the nonprofit Institute for Shipboard Education in cooperation with the University of Pittsburgh. A ten-day Caribbean cruise in early January separates the two programs. The institute adds top lecturers for the Alaska and Caribbean cruises to those the cruise line supplies and a fully qualified faculty and curriculum for about 600 students each semester. The ship (former *Enchanted Seas*) is on charter from Commodore Cruises.

The Fleet	Built/Renovated	Tonnage	Passengers
Universe Explorer	1957/1995	23,500	731

Style World Explorer's advertising theme, "Come for the Wildlife, not the Nightlife," sums up a cruise on *Universe Explorer*. It offers Alaska-by-immersion with emphasis on art, history, flora, fauna, culture, and geography. The in-depth program offers lecturers, visits to off-the-beaten-path ports, adventurous shore excursions, and intimate interaction with Alaska. Amid serious study is ample time for fun.

Because the ship is friendly and small, passengers get to know each other. The unpretentious, intellectual atmosphere is campuslike—more elderhostel than cruise. Passengers seem to have sincere affection for the ship and crew.

Home to university students when she is not cruising in Alaska, amenities are basic. Dress is casual and comfortable, even at dinner; jeans are the norm. Despite the ship's shortcomings, the atmosphere appeals to more affluent travelers with refined tastes. Every cruise features cultural entertainment, such as piano and classical concerts.

Distinctive Features   Educational program; world's largest library at sea.

	HIGHEST	LOWEST	AVERAGE
PER DIEM	$256	$147	$196

The above per diems are calculated from the cruise line's non-discounted *cruise only* fares on standard accommodations. Per diems vary by season, by cabin, and by cruise areas.

Rates   Port charges are additional.

Special Fares and Discounts   Passengers who book 5 months in advance get a $75 merchandise certificate for a 9-day cruise ($100 for a 14-day cruise) on gear from TravelSmith's catalog.
- Third Passenger: $395. Third and fourth passengers free on some cruises in cabins with two full-fare passengers.
- Single Supplement: 145 percent of categories 3–9.
- Up to 20 percent off brochure rates for AARP members.

Packages
- Air/Sea: Yes.
- Others: None.
- Pre/Post: Vancouver hotel and sight-seeing.

Past Passengers   No club or special deals.

The Last Word   This budget cruise ship is not recommended for everyone. But for those who want a learning vacation and friendship in an informal atmosphere on a small ship, the Alaska experience can be absolutely delightful. Even those who prefer a more deluxe setting could have a good experience if they take advantage of the outstanding lectures, excursions, and entertainment. Many well-educated, well-traveled passengers who have cruised on luxury ships praise the experience. The 100-day Semester at Sea is the ultimate educational travel experience for nonmatriculating adults.

WORLD EXPLORER CRUISES STANDARD FEATURES

Officers International.

Staff Dining, Cabin/Filipino; Cruise/American.

Dining Facilities Breakfast is open seating; lunch and dinner have two assigned seatings in the dining room. Breakfast and lunch, open seating in the Harbor Grill. Classical music often at dinner.

Special Diets Basic requests can be handled with advance notice.

Room Service None.

Dress Code Casual. Warm clothing and walking shoes for excursions and glacier watching. Rain gear and rubber-soled shoes are useful, as are binoculars. Gentlemen may want a jacket for dinner, but the only dress-up times are captain's parties, when ties and jackets for men and dresses or pantsuits for women are appropriate.

Cabin Amenities Private bath with showers; top category with bathtub.

Electrical Outlets 110 AC. Hair dryers may be used in cabins.

Wheelchair Access Some doorways have raised thresholds; elevator does not reach Bali Deck cabins.

Recreation and Entertainment Four bars in six lounges; including one for lectures, presentations on art, history, geology, botany, biology, and culture of Alaska. Nightly entertainment, including classical and folk music, opera performers, movies, talent shows, and dances. Movie theater.

Sports and Other Activities Swimming pool (not used in Alaska), basketball, volleyball, Ping-Pong, walking on upper promenade decks, animal- and bird-watching on deck at any time. Impromptu viewings of the northern lights (*aurora borealis*). Bingo, horse racing, and games.

Beauty and Fitness Beauty salon and barber shop, massage, fitness center featuring a variety of weight and exercise equipment.

Other Facilities 16,000-volume library, gift shop, medical unit.

Children's Facilities Youth center, youth counselors who plan special activities, children's prices for shore excursions.

Theme Cruises None.

Smoking No smoking in dining room; other areas, designated.

World Explorer Suggested Tipping Per person per day, cabin steward, $3; dining room stewards, $3; busboy, $2; 15 percent added to bar bill.

Credit Cards For cruise and on-board ship account payments: American Express, Discover, MasterCard, and Visa.

Universe Explorer	Quality ❸	Value A
Registry: Panama	Length: 617 feet	Beam: 84 feet
Cabins: 369	Draft: 28 feet	Speed: 18 knots
Maximum Passengers:	Passenger Decks: 7	Elevators: 3
731	Crew: 300	Space Ratio: 33

The Ship The *Universe Explorer* has had more lives than a cat. First as the *Brasil,* she sailed to South America for the old Moore-McCormack Lines; then she passed to Holland America as the *Volendam* and *Liberté* (with three more name changes in between), and to other lines as the *Canada Star, Queen of Bermuda,* and more recently, as Commodore Cruises' *Enchanted Seas.*

The ship has a variety of public rooms and lounges and ample deck space. Public rooms are in good condition, and the air conditioning functions well, considering the ship's age. Most public rooms are on the Promenade Deck, which runs the full length of the ship from the library at the fore to the pool at the stern. Side decks are teak and spacious, but they don't encircle the ship. The limited number of elevators requires long walks from some cabins.

Unique to a ship of this category is *Explorer*'s library, boasting more than 16,000 volumes. The newest addition is a hands-on exhibit of Alaskan native artifacts on loan from the Sheldon Jackson Museum in Sitka.

The *Explorer* has a fitness center, youth center, self-service laundry, theater, beauty shop, and medical clinic. Despite the ship's age, passengers seem little concerned about decor.

Itineraries See Appendix B.

Cabins The ship has large cabins that serve it well on long cruises, but some have seen better days. Most cabins are comfortable with ample closets and storage space for two, perhaps three people. They're cramped for four. More than 75 percent are outside; most top-priced cabins have bathrooms with tubs; others have showers only. Some bathrooms have a bidet. Water is steaming hot, and bathrooms are spotless. The usual amenities are provided. Electrical outlets are limited; one accommodates a hair dryer.

Bedside reading lights provide ample illumination. Noise appears to be more of a problem on lower levels, where passengers hear cleaning noises from the crew and the engines' humming. Lifeboats obstruct views from some cabins on Boat and Sun Decks; the deck plan notes these. Cabins on the lowest deck have no elevator access.

The ship has nine categories of cabins. Accommodations could be aptly described as collegiate-looking, like student quarters rather than cruise-ship cabins. Some are small and plain with twin beds and collapsible upper berths. Mattresses, bed coverings, and pillows are new in all, and all are equipped with color television and direct-dial telephones. Baby cribs are available.

Specifications   80 inside cabins, 293 outside; 32 with double bed, 4 with kings; 1 single. Standard dimensions, inside or outside, 152 square feet; deluxe and superior, 191–293 square feet. Variety of configurations: some twins with upper and lower berths; 169 with twin beds convertible to doubles; some connecting cabins. 70 cabins have bathtubs.

Dining   The Dining Room has open seating for breakfast, but lunch and dinner have two seatings with assigned tables. Guest string quartets play at dinner. Tables for two are available on request.

The menu's catch of the day—probably halibut or salmon—doesn't taste fresh. The menu also lists Asian and Italian selections, and all-American favorites—prime rib to baked Alaska. Asian specialties, including a festive Chinese dinner, are popular, as are the lunchtime salad bar and pasta. Some passengers find the menu limited; others say it's quite good.

A continental breakfast buffet in a glass-enclosed area of Promenade Deck attracts early birds. Harbor Grill nearby offers a full buffet breakfast and lunch, afternoon tea with finger sandwiches, and the late-night snack (about 10:45 to 11:45 p.m.) with hot dishes and desserts.

Service   Captain and crew are excellent and help create a wonderfully warm, one-big-family atmosphere. The Filipino staff, in particular, is genuinely nice and accommodating.

Facilities and Entertainment   Entertainment in harmony with Alaska's natural beauty is scheduled nightly. It might include classical musicians, an opera singer, or cabaret and pop vocalists. A recognized entertainer is featured on each cruise. The ship's five-piece orchestra plays dance music in the evenings. The theater presents first-run films. A passenger talent show is possible.

Computer instruction by teachers from SeniorNet is free with SeniorNet membership ($35), which also provides 125 Learning Centers nationwide; a newsletter; discounts on books, software, and hardware; and invitations to meetings.

Activities and Diversions   The most distinctive feature of World Explorer cruises is the lively lecture series in Alaska by guest experts, most with doctorates. Each day, lectures cover some aspect of Alaska—history, wildlife, geology, anthropology, art, botany, biology, or culture—often accompanied by videos, films, and slides. Rangers from the U.S. Forest Service in Sitka, Alaska (who board all cruise ships entering the bay) and geologists provide running commentary on the awesome sight. Sue Coleman, known for her Alaska-inspired art, or another artist is on board to give classes, normally three sessions per two-week voyage. The ship also has a 16,000-volume library, ostensibly the largest afloat.

At most any time, narrated animal- and bird-watching might take place on deck (bring binoculars). Also available: impromptu viewings of the northern lights, bingo, games, and horse racing. Days at sea provide an opportunity to browse in the library and enjoy fellow passengers.

Sports, Fitness, and Beauty   A fitness center, beauty/barber shop, Ping-Pong, and massage are available. The swimming pool and volleyball and basketball aren't available on Alaska cruises.

The line has teamed with Active Adventure Specialty Tours of Aurora, Colorado, to offer "Bike and Hike Alaska" escorted tours in eight ports of call. They suit all cycling levels and can be individually tailored. Packages start at $45 per day. The cruise line has details.

Children's Facilities   A youth center (one of the classrooms) is on Sun Deck. Counselors are aboard every summer cruise to provide children's activities. Some shore excursions offer children's prices.

Shore Excursions   More than 50 innovative and varied excursions are summarized (with prices) in a 50-page booklet sent to passengers a month before they cruise. Excursions range from rafting through moderate rapids to helicopter flights to glaciers where participants walk the ice in traction boots. It's helpful to be familiar with options before boarding.

More sedate outings visit local museums and galleries and pan for gold. All aim to add to passengers' understanding of Alaska. A Sitka favorite is visiting the Alaska Raptor Rehabilitation Center.

Expert lecturers may accompany excursions. The average of nine hours in each port allows time to make more than one outing at some stops.

Postscript   Expert lectures, cultural entertainment, and shore excursions make the World Explorer cruise in Alaska an unusual, well-rounded experience at affordable prices that, for the right people, offsets the ship's shortcomings. For information on the Semester at Sea program, contact: Institute for Shipboard Education, 811 William Pitt Union, University of Pittsburgh, Pittsburgh, PA 15260; phone (800) 854-0195 or (412) 648-7490; fax (412) 648-2298.

Other Cruise Lines and Their Ships

In addition to the 30 lines and 146 ships in the American mainstream of cruising already profiled in this section, another group of lines, with ships based mostly in Europe, may be of interest to readers. Space doesn't allow the same in-depth treatment, but generally they're small to midsize ships operated in the European tradition for Europeans. Their very interesting itineraries visit places many Americans would need an atlas to find. Ships have English-speaking staff, although the majority of passengers are Europeans speaking other languages. A few operate from U.S. or Asian ports.

The degree of luxury varies widely. Some are luxury vessels launched only in the last year or so; others are vintage ships renovated and forming a flotilla of new cruise lines.

Cruises appeal particularly to those who have traveled the main routes often and are looking for new destinations or a new environment in which to return to places seen previously. They also appeal to those who might never consider a typical cruise ship, preferring to explore less traveled waters.

Also described are a few lines and ships that cater mainly to the U.S. market but weren't profiled in depth for other reasons, including they're sold mainly through tour companies in combination with larger tour programs, they're under charter much of the year, or we had difficulty obtaining information.

Note: In the parentheses after the ship's name, the "Key" provides information pertaining to the number of cabins and passengers; officers and crew; and the ship's length and tonnage.

(Key: Cabins/Passengers; Officers/Crew; Ship Length/Tonnage)

Cape Canaveral Cruise Line

7099 N. Atlantic Avenue, Cape Canaveral, FL 32920
(321) 783-4052; (800) 910-SHIP
www.capecanaveralcruise.com

Dolphin IV (294/588; Greek/International; 501 ft./13,007 tons)
    The line was launched in 1996 after acquisition of *Dolphin IV* from the former Dolphin Cruise Line (since merged with Premier Cruises). The smallest ship in Bahamas service, *Dolphin IV* has a coziness and friendliness that passengers seem to like. She's well suited for her short cruises from Port Canaveral to the Bahamas and Key West that cater to budget-minded, first-time cruisers.

    Built in 1956 as a combination passenger-cargo ship, *Dolphin IV* was sold to a Portuguese company in 1966, renamed *Amelia Del Mello,* then sold to Greek interests in 1972 and rebuilt as a cruise ship. She plied the Mediterranean as the *Ithaca* for Ulysses Lines, as *Dolphin IV* of Paquet Cruises, and in 1984, became Dolphin Cruise Line's first ship. A major 1991 renovation gave her reflective metal ceilings, mirrored walls, and enlarged facilities.

Facilities and cabins are on six decks. Promenade Deck contains the main public rooms: lounge, showroom, library/video room, casino, disco, boutique, hair salon, spa, video game room, children's playroom, pool, and lido dining area. Topside, Sun Deck offers large lounging areas.

The six cabin categories range from inside cabins with upper and lower berths to junior suites with sitting rooms and full baths. More than half the cabins are outside, and most are furnished with twin beds, radio, and phone, but no television. The tastefully decorated rooms are small but adequate for two people on short cruises. Inside cabins are often more spacious than outside ones. Most have minimal storage space; bathrooms have a small shower and small toiletries shelf.

Barbizon Dining Room, cozy and nicely decorated in pinks and other soft colors, has two seatings for three meals. Live piano music accompanies dinner. Breakfast and lunch buffets are available in the Miramar cafe, and a barbecue grill is near the lido swimming pool.

Itineraries   See Appendix B.

Classical Cruises

132 East 70th Street, New York, NY 10021
(212) 794-3200; (800) 252-7745; fax (212) 774-1544
www.classicalcruises.com

Classical Cruises specializes in educational and cultural cruises, using a variety of well-known deluxe and luxury ships. Programs are designed for well-traveled, destination-oriented individuals who want a learning experience but don't want to forgo comfort. Itineraries span the world and include exotic and typical destinations. Lecturers and academics knowledgeable about the destination accompany cruises.

Callisto (17/34; Greece/European; 161 ft./431 tons)
The small luxury yacht is Classical Cruises' newest acquisition. Built in Germany, the ship has undergone a comprehensive renovation and refurbishment prior to its debut in September 2000. The ship has 17 outside cabins, each with large panoramic windows, a spacious lounge, a dining room accommodating all passengers at one open seating, and al fresco dining on two decks. There is piano bar, two broad decks for sunbathing, and a swimming platform at the vessel's stern. All cabins are air-conditioned and have full- or queen-sized beds, marble bath, radio, telephone, refrigerator, and television with VCR. The three-deck ship has a draft of 12 feet and a speed of 14 knots. It is equipped with Zodiac landing crafts. The bridge is outfitted with state-of-the-art navigational and communications equipment.

Rates start at $2,995 per person and include a five-day cruise, two nights in Athens at the Hotel Grande Bretagne with breakfast, airfare between Athens and Samos, tours of Athens and Sounion, shore excursions, house wines, and soft drinks. In 2001, there are three itineraries: Greek Islands; circumnavigation of Crete; and Egypt, the Red Sea, and Israel.

Clelia II (42/84; Greek/European; 290 ft./4,077 tons)

Formerly *Renaissance IV,* the *Clelia II* is a small, all-suite luxury vessel with roomy public rooms, sophisticated decor, and ample facilities. The five-deck ship has two lounges, a well-stocked library, beauty salon, steam bath, pool, Jacuzzi, medical facilities, and gym. The elegant dining room, in light wood and marble, has open seating for all meals. Breakfast and lunch buffets are served outdoors. Also available are a room-service menu, in-cabin meals from the restaurant during dining hours, and an 11 p.m. snack. Evening entertainment may be lectures, music, movies, and videos.

The spacious cabins, all with sea views, are paneled in dark wood and furnished with twin or queen-size beds. They have a sitting area or living room with vanity/desk, sofa, side chair, coffee table, refrigerator, television, radio, and VCR. Storage space is ample. Bathrooms are small and have showers only. Deluxe apartments and penthouse suites are available, some with two bathrooms and balconies.

Classical Cruises leases *Clelia II* for 11 months each year from its private owner; a French company operates the vessel; and Travel Dynamics, an incentive travel company, supplies the cruise director and tour managers. Cruises explore the Mediterranean and Africa, focusing on history, archaeology, architecture, and nature. Guest lecturers are usually from leading U.S. museums and universities. Prices include port charges and shore excursions.

Classical Cruises' other ships are the 48-passenger *Halcyon,* which sails the Adriatic Sea's Dalmatian coast, Tunisia, and the Eastern Mediterranean; and the 44-passenger *Panorama,* sailing the Eastern Mediterranean.

Itineraries   See Appendix B.

Cuba Cruise Corporation

13 Hazelton Avenue, Toronto, Ontario, M5R 2El
(800) 387-1387; (416) 964-2569; fax (416) 964-3416
www.cubacruising.com

La Habana (215/440; European/North American; 429 feet/20,000 tons)

On November 16, Cuba Cruise Corporation is scheduled to launch year-round three- and four-night voyages from Nassau to Havana on *La Habana,* focusing on Cuban life and culture. The cruises are being offered in association with Blyth & Company Travel, a Canadian company which specializes in educational and adventure travel and has been conducting tours to Cuba since 1978.

The three-night cruise departs Nassau on Thursday; the four-night one leaves on Sunday. On board, there will be Cuban entertainment and lectures and briefings about Cuba. Land programs include Havana by Night, walking tours of Old Havana, a reception in one of Ernest Hemingway's favorite bars, and opportunities to meet with Cuban students, professors, professional groups, and artists. Rates start at $595 per person, double occupancy. Port taxes are additional. Children under 12 years of age sharing a cabin with parents receive a 30% discount. Special airfares to Nassau are available from over 20 U.S. cities.

The ship has several lounges and bars and its own cigar maker. Cabins and suites are on three decks. Cuisine will feature Cuban dishes as well as continental and light fare. The ship has a beauty salon, fitness center, boutique, Internet access, and email service. Bikes for rent will be carried on board. The ship also has a doctor and nurse.

According to Cuba Cruises, the cruises are structured so that unlicensed American citizens can participate without violating U.S. law, providing they observe certain requirements. Passengers expenses in Cuba will be paid by a separate organization, one that promotes people-to-people contact, which will act as the Cuban "host" of the American passengers, enabling them to travel lawfully on a "fully hosted" basis provided they spend no money in Cuba. The cruise line claims it will assure that American passengers comply with all applicable U.S. legal restrictions. *Note:*

Itineraries   See Appendix B.

EuroCruises

33 Little West 12th Street, New York, NY 10014-1314
(212) 691-2099; (800) 688-3876; fax (212) 366-4747
www.eurocruises.com

EuroCruises is a U.S. company specializing in European cruises. It represents more than 30 oceangoing ships and riverboats—all European-owned and -managed. The cruises span the continent, from Portugal to Russia and from the Mediterranean to the Arctic. Though the majority sail between early spring and late fall, some cruises visit the Mediterranean, Canary Islands, and Caribbean in winter.

Included here are the lines and ships EuroCruises represents that offer ocean cruises, mainly of the Baltic, North Cape, Norwegian fjords, and Mediterranean. For EuroCruises' river voyages, see Part Three, Cruising Alternatives. In all cases, EuroCruises can provide brochures on ships and itineraries; these include deck plans and ships' features.

Fred Olsen Lines (EuroCruises)

Black Prince (450/238; European/Filipino; 465 ft./11,200 tons)

Built in 1966 and renovated in 1996, the ship caters to Britons. It sails on 9–49-night cruises from Dover, England, year-round, to the African coast, Canary Islands, Baltic Sea, Norwegian coast, Caribbean, Mediterranean, and Middle East. The ship—a good choice for gregarious travelers age 50 and older—has a gym, pool, sauna, beauty salon, disco, and casino and provides international entertainment and sports.

Black Watch (437/897; Norwegian/International; 630 ft./28,492 tons)

Formerly the *Royal Viking Star,* the much-loved *Black Watch* was judged too small and too old to compete in the U.S. market and was sold to Fred Olsen Lines and given an $8 million refurbishment.

Black Watch cabins come in a bewildering number of configurations. Thirty-nine are singles. Though most are small, all are nicely appointed. Ninety percent are outside with portholes, picture window, or private veranda. Baths are well designed but very plain. All cabins have televisions and phones, and many have refrigerators.

The ship's public areas are exceptional. The library is among cruising's largest and most splendidly appointed. (Unfortunately, it's only open a couple of hours each day.) Contiguous is an equally impressive card and game room. Both rooms display artifacts from earlier ships named *Black Watch.* Observation lounges overlook the bow and stern. Both provide live music well into the night. A third lounge adjoins the main showroom; decor honors the Scottish Black Watch Regiment.

The clubby Braemar Room, a large lounge adjacent to the dining room, is packed with brightly colored stuffed chairs. It's given over entirely to the British passion for tea, which is available around the clock.

Well-designed public areas continue outside with a promenade that encircles the ship. Also available are pools, Jacuzzis, bars, cafes, and outdoor areas (some covered) for sunning or relaxing.

Entertainment is professional, varied, and appealing to a range of ages and backgrounds. It puts to shame the offerings aboard many superliner competitors. During a recent voyage, we enjoyed Las Vegas–style production shows, an incredibly talented opera company, an illusionist, a comic, a celebrity vocalist, and classical music concerts. Lounges, the casino, and the Star Night Club dance venue bustle into the wee hours. Theme cruises are varied.

For an American, the greatest pleasure aboard *Black Watch* is meeting Britons—delightful, interested, and interesting. Many hours are spent with new English, Scottish, and Irish friends exploring the subtleties that make our cultures so similar yet so different. Some misunderstandings of idiom and accent are uproarious: Announcement of a "folkloric presentation" was heard by the Americans as a "full colonic presentation" . . . We couldn't wait! Because the British are gracious and friendly, being the minority was a special pleasure.

Itineraries   See Appendix B.

First European Cruises

95 Madison Avenue, Suite 1203, New York, NY 10016
(888) 98-EUROPE or (888) 983-8767; (212) 779-7168
www.first-european.com

Known in Europe as Festival Cruises and purchased by P&O Lines in 2000, First European Cruises operates three classic, midsize liners—and a new 1,200-passenger superliner—year-round in the Mediterranean and Northern Europe and the Caribbean in winter. Cruises are designed for the European, middle-income mass market of many nationalities. They will interest Americans who feel comfortable with other cultures or who speak one or two European languages. Staff is multilingual and speaks English, but most passengers do not.

First European maintains high standards of cleanliness and service. Some experienced American passengers have judged the food the best they have had on any cruise ship. Vessels are crowded and the cabins small, but the atmosphere is relaxed and unpretentious. Fare reductions and a children's program attract families during school vacations.

The cruise line plans to add four new ships in the next four years: two each for 1,500 passengers, and the second two each for 2,000 passengers.

Azur (360/720; Greek/International; 465 ft./15,000 tons)
   Built in 1971 and refurbished in 1996, the *Azur* has seven passenger decks with one nonsmoking dining room, several lounges and bars, two swimming pools, a cinema, casino, sports and fitness center, disco, karaoke bar, and children's room. Cabins have radio, phone, and bathrooms with shower. There are 24 suites.

Flamenco (401/800; Greek/European; 535 ft./17,000 tons)
   Formerly the *Southern Cross* of CTC Cruise lines, she was acquired in 1997, given an $8 million refurbishing, and renamed *Flamenco*. The ship has one nonsmoking dining room, a variety of lounges and bars, show-room, casino, shop, library, and gym. Exercise classes and massage are available. Cabins are small but have private baths with shower, radio, and closed-circuit television for movies.

Mistral (598/1,200; French/International; 708 ft./47,900 tons)
   Delivered in June 1999, the French-built *Mistral* flies the French flag. She is based in Genoa, sailing on cruises to the Greek Isles. Two similar

ships, the 1,500-passenger, 58,600-ton *European Vision,* will join the fleet in June 2001 and sail the Greek Isles, Egypt, and Israel from Genoa; and *European Dream,* will come online in April 2002.

The eight-passenger decks of the *Mistral*—named after European cities—have two restaurants, a theater, casino, conference center, piano bar, library/card room, beauty parlor, boutique, shopping arcade, show lounge, cigar bar, fitness center and spa with thalassotherapy center, sauna/massage, and two swimming pools. The ship also boasts a complete dialysis care unit.

The *Mistral's* 598 cabins include 80 suites with balconies. She has 297 standard outside and 221 standard inside cabins, and 2 wheelchair-accessible. The ship's capacity can be increased by 490 passengers when Pullman or sofa beds are used. The crew numbers 450.

Built at the same shipyard and with the same interior decors as the *Mistral,* the new ships will have some enhancements, such as a dedicated conference and Internet center, virtual reality games, golf driving range, children's splash pool, an additional outdoor restaurant, and a higher number of suites with private balconies. *European Vision* will sail in the Eastern Mediterranean from June to November; from December to April she will be based in Cancun cruising on a brand-new itinerary for the line.

First European will introduce two more ships—80,000 tons, 2,000 passengers—in 2003 and 2004.

Itineraries See Appendix B.

Global Quest (formerly OdessAmerica)
50 Glen Street, Suite 206, Glen Cove, NY 11542
676-4500; (800) 221-3254; fax (516) 676-4820
www.globalquesttravel.com

The line, formed in 1991 as OdessAmerica, is a joint venture between the Black Sea Shipping Company of Odessa, Ukraine, and International Cruise Center of Mineola, New York. BLASCO dates to 1833 and is the largest shipping company in the former Soviet Union, and one of the world's largest. It has 15 passenger ships and more than 300 cargo vessels.

Global Quest represents a variety of cruises and offers cruises of the Indian Ocean, Galápagos Islands, Adriatic Sea, Chilean archipelago, European and Russian rivers. See further listings in Part Three.

Royal Star (111/220; European/Swiss; 367 ft./6,179 tons)
Royal Star has five decks, air-conditioned cabins, pool, library, entertainment, casino, and health club. She sails from Mombasa on Indian Ocean/East African cruise/land tours in conjunction with the African Safari Club.

Itineraries   See Appendix B.

Golden Sun Cruises

40 East 52nd Street, 20th Floor
New York, NY 10022-5911
(212) 223-3222; (877) 244-8004; fax (212) 223-1081
www.goldensuncruises.com

Golden Sun Cruises is a joint venture between Dolphin Hellas Shipping, which owns the 560-passenger *Aegean I* (280/560; Greek/Greek; 461 ft./11,563 tons) and Artica Lines, which owns the 225-passenger *Arcadia* (129/225; Greek; 367 ft./4,842 tons) and a third ship, the 920-passenger *Aegean Spirit* (335/664; 579 ft./16,495 tons). The line offers three-, four-seven-, and fourteen-day cruises of the Greek isles. All three ships are air-conditioned; each has one swimming pool, gym and sauna, hair salon, shops, casino, library, several lounges and bars, dining room, and elevators.

Itineraries   See Appendix B.

Hebridean Island Cruises

Griffin House, Broughton Hall, Skipton, North Yorkshire BD23 3AN
011 44 1756 704704; (800) 659-2648; fax 011 44 1756 704794
www.hebridean.co.uk

Hebridean Princess (50 passengers; British/Scottish; 235 ft./1,420 tons)
    Built in 1964 to carry 600 passengers, the ship was redesigned in 1994 to carry only 50 passengers in the style of a deluxe country inn. Accommodations vary from singles with shared facilities to suites. The ship has a lounge, restaurant, library of books and videos, and shop. She visits lochs, estuaries, and Scotland's Inner and Outer Hebrides islands.

Hebridean Spirit (40/80; British/Scottish; 300ft./4,200 tons)
    In July 2000, Hebridean Island cruises bought the *MegaStar Capricorn* from Star Cruises, Asia's largest cruise line, and plans to rename her *Hebridean Spirit* when the vessel is delivered in November. The ship will be given a $4.7 million renovation and will be redesigned to accommodate 70–80 guests (down from 114 passengers now) in a style similar to the *Hebridean Princess*. The new ship, an ocean-going vessel, will enable Hebridean Island to cruise in new waters and plans to offer itineraries for North European and Mediterranean destinations in summer and the Indian Ocean in winter. Brits account for 84% of the line's passengers with 50% repeaters.

Itineraries See Appendix B.

Kristina Cruises (EuroCruises)

Kristina Regina (136/220; Finnish/Finnish; 320 ft./4,295 tons)

The ship, which has a receptive audience among well-traveled Americans, sails on three- to ten-night cruises from May to August in Scandinavia and Russia. She has an English-speaking staff, several bars and lounges, library, sauna, and sun decks. Dining is at one seating; menus vary. Her small size enables her to dock within walking distance of town centers. One of her most popular cruises, White Sea–White Nights, sails to the Polar Circle from Helsinki in late June.

Kristina Brahe (57/80; Finnish/Finnish; 190 ft./1,105 tons)

This four-deck, expedition-style ship is the largest operating on the Saimaa Canal. Built in Chicago in 1943, she served as a submarine destroyer on Africa's west coast during World War II. Afterward, she sailed under the Norwegian flag. In 1974, she was renovated, renamed *Kristina Brahe,* and Finnish flagged. Acquired by new owners in 1985, she has been extensively renovated. Outside cabins in Category A have private bath; other categories offer wash basins in cabins and shared bath facilities. She has two restaurants, Sun Deck, and shop. Six-night cruises in July depart Helsinki for St. Petersburg. An eight-day package includes round-trip airfare from New York.

Itineraries See Appendix B.

Mediterranean Shipping Cruises

420 Fifth Avenue, New York, NY 10018-2702
(212) 764-4800; (800) 666-9333; fax (212) 764-1486
www.msccruisesusa.com

Part of a Swiss group operating a global fleet of 87 container ships, Mediterranean Shipping Cruises acquired three of its four cruise ships in less than four years. One of the largest cruise lines in the Mediterranean, the firm has expanded its itineraries to South Africa and South America. With Italian staff and ambience, the ships offer classic cruises with good food and service.

Melody (549/1,076; Italian; 671 ft./36,500 tons)

Formerly the *Star/Ship Atlantic* of Premier Cruise Lines, *Melody* was acquired in 1997 by MSC. She has several lounges, a showroom, piano bar, disco, casino, fitness center, two outdoor pools, and beauty salon. Cabins are moderate size and have radio, direct-dial telephone, and private bathrooms. MSC's largest cruise ship, *Melody* sails the Caribbean in winter.

Monterey (290/576; Italian; 563 ft./21,051 tons)

Built in 1952 and refurbished in 1991 and 1997, *Monterey* once belonged to Matson Line and sailed for Aloha Pacific Cruises. The steam-operated vessel has been well maintained and is a pleasant older ship with a fine style and a friendly crew. She complies with new safety requirements. The classic, Art Deco vessel gleams with brass and polished mirrors and has two swimming pools, fitness center with two whirlpools, sauna, hospital, library, beauty salon, boutiques, casino, disco, and two elevators. The attractive dining room offers two seatings. Cabins on the top three decks are large and have private bathrooms. Handicapped-accessible cabins are available. Most passengers are middle-income Italian and British, age 55 and older.

Rhapsody (379/768; Italian; 541 ft./16,852 tons)

Built in 1977 as *Cunard Princess, Rhapsody* was refurbished in 1995 after purchase by MSC, and once more in 1997. Facilities include a swimming pool, whirlpool, fitness center, conference room, library, cafe, bars, casino, video arcade, cinema, beauty and barber shops, and medical center. Two elevators and dry cleaning services are available. A comfortable ship enhanced by a friendly atmosphere, she offers international cuisine with an Italian emphasis. It's served in the window-lined Meridian Dining Room at two seatings. Cabins are small with limited storage space and thin walls; all have private bathrooms. Passengers are middle-income Europeans older than 50. They tend to be smokers. *Rhapsody* spends summer in the Aegean and late fall in Israel and the Middle East.

Itineraries   See Appendix B.

Peter Deilmann Cruises

1800 Diagonal Road, Suite 170, Alexandria, VA 22314
(703) 549-1741; (800) 348-8287; fax (703) 549-7924
www.deilmann-cruises.com

Peter Deilmann Cruises' *Deutchland,* launched in 1998, was built as a traditional luxury liner in the grand European style. She has three restaurants and a promenade deck and accommodates 650 passengers in a variety of mostly outside staterooms. The ship is intended for German-speaking patrons. They will enjoy German food and German music and entertainment. All announcements and tours are conducted in German. There are some English-speaking staff aboard.

(For Peter Deilmann River Cruises, designed for English-speaking patrons as well as Europeans, see Part Three: Cruising Alternatives.)

Regal Cruises

P.O. Box 1329, Palmetto, FL 34220
(941) 721-7300; (800) 270-SAIL; fax (941) 723-0900
www.regalcruises.com

Regal Empress (667/1,180; European/International; 612 ft./23,000 tons)

Built in 1953 and formerly with Greek Line and Commodore Cruises, this handsome ship was refurbished once in 1993 and more recently in 1997.

The ship's interior is quite cut up, reflecting changes made by her various owners over the years. Some public rooms, however, show the ship's high quality when she was built. Most outstanding is the dining room, which has fine woods, etched glass, and some original murals. Steak, lobster, and other choices sure to appeal to the ship's budget audience are quite good for the price. The main showroom offers entertainment nightly; viewing is difficult when the ship sails full. Lounges include the Mermaid, which has a bar and dance floor; casino; and unusual disco created in the former theater.

The promenade deck is enclosed. Also available are an outdoor pool, two whirlpools, Jacuzzi, skeet shooting, shuffleboard, gym, beauty salon, boutique, small playroom, and library with comfortable reading chairs.

There are 453 outside cabins and 214 inside. Configurations vary widely. Most cabins have one upper berth. Bathrooms are small with shower only. Only suites have television.

In summer, *Regal Empress* offers budget cruises to New England and Canada from New York and short, party cruises to nowhere. The balance of the year, she sails to the Western and Eastern Caribbean and Panama Canal from Tampa Bay. Party cruises attract young urbanites; longer trips along the New England coast appeal to couples and families. The atmosphere changes remarkably between the two types of cruises. You'll get your money's worth, but make no mistake: This lady has seen better days.

Itineraries   See Appendix B.

Renaissance Cruises

1800 Eller Drive, Suite 300, P.O. Box 29009
Ft. Lauderdale, FL 33302-9009
(954) 463-0982; (800) 425-9553; fax (954) 759-7719
www.renaissancecruises.com

Renaissance VII–VIII (50–57/100–114; Italian/European; 290–297 ft.)
R1, R2, R3, R4, R5, R6, R7, R8 (316/684; Italian/European; 594 ft./30,200 tons)

In 1989, Renaissance Cruises launched the first of eight small, deluxe ships intended to blanket the world. The plan didn't work out, and only two of the ships now sail for Renaissance. Meanwhile, the line chartered or took space on other ships to meet demand for its eastern Mediterranean cruises while it built eight 684-passenger ships. The first and second, *R1* and *R2,* made their debut in 1998; *R3* and *R4* in 1999; *R5* and *R6* in 2000; and *R7* and *R8* in February 2001.

The line combines round-trip airfare from the United States, a hotel package, and a cruise at surprisingly low prices. They're promoted almost exclusively through an aggressive direct-mail program.

Renaissance VII–VIII from the original fleet, are small, luxurious, Italian-built ships finished in fine woods with lovely appointments and all-suite cabins. Facilities include a restaurant, lounge, piano bar, pool, casino, Jacuzzi, and beauty salon. They have a sports platform and carry water sports equipment.

The new, spacious *R* ships have eight passenger decks and offer single, open-seating dining in a choice of four restaurants: a steak house, an Italian restaurant, a clublike restaurant with pizzeria and barbecue grill, and a formal restaurant (although the line doesn't schedule formal nights). Other facilities include a cabaret and main lounge, several bars, casino, sports club with live ESPN, pool and bar, shops, library, beauty salon, spa, gym with Nautilus and other equipment, jogging track, and self-service launderette.

About 66 percent of cabins have private verandas. Cabins range from 30 inside of 159 square feet and 67 standard outside of 162 square feet, to 10 deluxe suites with 325 square feet plus balcony. The majority are 170 veranda cabins with 172 square feet. All have television with CNN, mini-safe, telephone, breakfast table, vanity, full-length mirror, and bath with shower.

R1, *R2, R5,* and *R6* sail on 11-day Eastern or Western Mediterranean cruise tours that include round-trip airfare from New York and pre- and post-cruise hotel stays, priced from $1,299. *R3* and *R4,* based in Tahiti, are the largest ships cruising French Polynesia year-round. Deployment of other new ships hasn't been announced.

In winter season, *Renaissance VII* and *VIII* will return to their popular East African cruise-tours. In autumn and spring, the ships offer 11-day Riviera cruise-tours, which include two-night hotel stays in both Barcelona and Rome, a five-day cruise, and round-trip airfare from New York, from $3,499. June through August, the ships sail on 13-day Russia and Scandinavia cruise-tours, which include two-night hotel stays in both Stockholm and Copenhagen, a seven-day cruise, and round-trip airfare from New York, from $3,999.

Passengers are transported on Renaissance's own plane. Business- and first-class upgrades are available. Passengers paying in full within five days of booking get discounts.

Itineraries   See Appendix B.

SPECIAL EXPEDITIONS

(See "Adventure and Cultural Cruises" in Part Three: Cruising Alternatives.)

Star Cruises

391B Orchard Road, No. 13-01, Ngee Ann City, Tower B,
Singapore 0923
(65) 733-6988; fax (65) 733-8622
www.starcruises.com

Malaysian-based Star Cruises is a phenomenon in Far Eastern cruising. Launched in 1993 with 2 ships, it grew quickly to a fleet of 11 ships despite the Asian financial crisis in 1998, and by 2000 with the purchase of Norwegian Cruise Lines and Orient Lines with their 8 ships, was tied with P&O/Princess as the third largest cruise line in the world. The line has captured 70 percent of the cruise market in Asia-Pacific, carrying over 1 million passengers over the first five years, and has won eight awards for its cabins and facilities. On all ships, there is no tipping.

The Star fleet consists of three brands: Star, SuperStar, and MegaStar, but it has two more under construction or planned. *Libra*-class 91,000-ton megaships *SuperStar Libra* and *SuperStar Scorpio* (recently earmarked for NCL and will be renamed) are scheduled for delivery in 2001 and 2002, and the 112,000-ton *Sagittarius*-class to follow in 2003 and 2004. By 2004, Star/NCL will have a fleet of 23 ships.

Star Cruises is owned by Malaysia's Genting International, a publicly traded investment group.

Star Aquarius (713/1,900) and *Star Pisces* (700/2,192; Scandinavian/ International; 574 ft./40,000 tons)

The two *Star* ships are former Baltic ferries designed for the regional Asian market. The ships sail on short cruises from Hong Kong and Singapore, catering largely to families and first-time cruisers. The ships are exceedingly well maintained; each has no fewer than ten food and beverages options. Child-care facilities are extensive. Activities and entertainment are geared to the whole family, with karaoke, Ping-Pong and other sports, a library, spa, boutiques, and big-name performances. The line earns high marks for its food and incredibly friendly crew.

The SuperStar Series is comprised of *SuperStar Gemini, SuperStar Leo, SuperStar Virgo, SuperStar Aries,* and *SuperStar Taurus.*

SuperStar Gemini (400/900; International; 532 ft./19,089 tons)

Built in 1992 in Spain for more than $100 million, *SuperStar Gemini* (the former *Crown Jewel*) was the first of the *SuperStar* group launched in 1995 and offers deluxe, traditional seven-night cruises from Singapore to

Southeast Asian ports with a crew of 470. She is designed to appeal to the fly-cruise markets of Australia, Europe, the United States, and Canada. Her itineraries also appeal to experienced Asian cruisers, who prefer longer cruises. Most passengers are European and Australian; the balance are from Japan, Taiwan, and Hong Kong.

SuperStar Leo (982/1,964; International/International; 887 ft./76,800 tons) was added in late 1998, and her twin, *SuperStar Virgo,* in 1999. They are the largest and first world-class megaships in the Asia-Pacific market, and they set new standards with extensive facilities for those who prefer activity-filled cruises. The vessels have a high crew-to-passenger ratio of one to two. They have a standard dining room and eight other dining venues. Two serve Chinese and Japanese cuisine, another offers Southeast Asian specialties. Unusual features include a public observation area of the bridge, with videos detailing bridge and engine operations. They offer a casino, spa and fitness center, shops, and children's facilities. The ships' cruising speed is a zippy 24 knots, enabling them to include four to six ports of call on a seven-night itinerary.

In 1997, Star bought the luxurious *Europa* for $75 million. She joined the fleet as *SuperStar Aries* in 1999, after a multimillion-dollar refit and refurbishment. The all-suite, 38,000-ton ship carries 600 passengers and is suited to around-the-world cruises. She is considered to be one of the best cruise ships in the world. *SuperStar Taurus* (formerly NCL's *Leeward*) offers short and long cruises from Japan, Korea, and China. *SuperStar Taurus*'s arrival completed Star Cruises' Asian geographical coverage from Kobe in the north to Singapore in the south.

MegaStar Taurus and *MegaStar Aries* (36/72; International/International; 270 ft./3,264 tons)

MegaStar is the most deluxe of Star's brands. Its ships, formerly *Aurora I* and *II,* are among the most luxurious small ships built in the 1990s. Each carries only 72 passengers and 80 crew members and is usually chartered to corporations, groups, or wedding parties.

MegaStar Sagittarius and *MegaStar Capricorn* (135 passengers; 4,200 tons)

Star Cruises has sold these two ships to other lines, but they will remain with Star on charter through March 2001.

Itineraries See Appendix B.

Swan Hellenic Cruises

631 Commack Road, Suite 1A, Commack, NY 11725
(631) 858-1270; (877) 219-4239; fax (631) 858-1279
www.swanhellenic.com

Minerva (194/300; British/Filipino, Ukrainian; 436 ft./12,500 tons)

Minerva, the new ship of Swan Hellenic, is aptly named for the Roman goddess of wisdom: Her cruises are dedicated to education, culture, and the arts, and exploration.

Decorated to resemble an English country house, the small ship's lounges and public rooms are comfortably furnished with patterned upholstery and leather couches and chairs. Artwork was purchased at country house auctions.

The main dining room and buffet-style cafe offer open seating. Both have indoor or outdoor service. Menu selections are well prepared and presented. A full English breakfast and afternoon tea are served. Servers are courteous, unobtrusive, and eager to please.

Facilities also include the Wheeler bar, the beauty center, an auditorium, a smoking room, a card room, sauna, swimming pool, and a library with several thousand books. Promenade Deck is unobstructed and encircles the ship.

Cabins include standard singles and doubles, deluxe and superior singles and doubles, and suites. The latter have separate sitting areas and bathrooms with tubs and showers. Four cabins are handicapped-accessible, and there are four single cabins as well. All cabins have televisions, phones, fax, terry robes, mirrored closets, and private bathrooms.

Minerva sails on itineraries ranging from the Mediterranean to the Far East. Guest lecturers provide background on ports of call. Talks are in English. Fares include most excursions and gratuities.

Swan Hellenic, which is owned by P&O Cruises, parent company of Princess Cruises, has a large following in the United Kingdom, Australia, Canada, and the United States. The line caters to travelers (most age 50 or older) who are intellectually curious and interested in art and culture of destinations they visit.

Itineraries   See Appendix B.

Part Three

Cruising Alternatives

River and Barge Cruises

A river cruise is not only a different way to see a country; it's a different country you will see. Whether you sail down the Danube or the Yangtze, up the Hudson or the Nile, or float on European channels or the Erie Canal, the cruise will be a new travel experience, even if you have visited the same area by land.

The river cruise most familiar to U.S. travelers is probably steamboating on the Mississippi, but there are many kinds of river cruises, their character shaped by the locale and nature of the waterway. An adventure cruise on the Amazon, for example, is quite different from barging in Burgundy. Nonetheless, river cruises share certain characteristics, and all are light years from an ocean cruise.

For starters, boats (a vessel is a *ship* on the ocean, but a *boat* on a river) on river cruises are small. Most carry 100–200 passengers, although some of the new riverboats accommodate 250 or more, and Delta Queen's *American Queen* takes 400 passengers. Barges that glide along small canals and waterways are much smaller, usually taking about 12 and never more than 24 passengers.

The small size of vessels and the nature of the waterways provide an intimate look at the cruise locale, heightening the sense of place and history in a way oceanliners never can. The destination, not the boat, is the main attraction on a river cruise.

Cabins are small but comfortable. The ambience is informal, the dress casual. Except on some large riverboats, nightly entertainment is absent. Passengers are left to their own devices, and many rediscover the pleasure of conversation and friendship.

RIVER AND BARGE CRUISES IN EUROPE

River cruises are available on major rivers worldwide, but the largest selection is in Europe—Rhine, Rhône, Seine, Danube, Volga—where rivers have been thoroughfares of commerce and culture for centuries.

European cruises—most between April and November—take you to the great cities through beautiful scenery laced with ancient forts, mighty cathedrals, and storybook castles. They dock in the heart of a different town each day. Tours are available, but most passengers can easily sight-see on their own.

River cruises reveal Europe the way it was meant to be seen. Almost all historic buildings were built facing the river, so when the boat docks in front of Pillnitz Palace on the Elbe, for example, passengers enter the way guests of Augustus the Strong would have entered centuries ago.

Some itineraries overnight in port, allowing passengers to attend local shows or dine ashore. Others sail at night so passengers wake refreshed for the next day of sight-seeing.

More than a dozen companies offer such cruises; one of the oldest, KD River Cruises of Europe, is typical. Its fleet of ten ships sails the length of the Rhine, as well as the Elbe, Moselle, Seine, Saône, and Rhône. Recently the line added the Danube and Rhine-Main-Danube Canal, which linked the North and Black Seas for the first time in 1994.

River boats and barges have completely different styles. Canals and smaller rivers deep in the countryside are traversed by barges gliding gently through some of the most beautiful and historic areas of England and the Continent. The pace is so leisurely (three or four miles per hour) that passengers can get off to walk in the woods or bike in the village and not be left behind. The tortoise's pace, the utter peace and relaxation, are for some the best vacation they ever had. For others, it's like watching grass grow.

By day, passengers lounge on deck, play cards, read, and watch the boat navigate the locks. They can walk or bike, discovering interesting places and friendly people, and reboard at the next lock. The price usually includes a choice of guided tours by minibus or bicycle to nearby castles, wineries, and medieval towns.

Hotel barges, as they are known, are like floating country inns. They vary in size, carrying from 6 to 51 passengers on cruises of 3, 6, or 13 days. Cabins are small and bathrooms are tiny, but the barges, such as those of French Country Waterways, are luxurious. Many, like Country Waterways, serve outstanding gourmet cuisine prepared by Cordon Bleu chefs. Regional wines, normally included in the cruise price, flow generously. The atmosphere is very informal—and very romantic.

Dozens of boats and barges cruise Europe. The season runs April through October. Here's a sampling with U.S. offices or representatives.

Note that several companies offer the same boats; agreements may not be exclusive.

(Key: Cabins/Passengers; Officers/Crew; Vessel Length)

Abercrombie & Kent International, Inc.

1520 Kensington Rd., Suite 212, Oak Brook, IL 60523-2141
(630) 954-2944; (800) 323-7308; fax (630) 954-3324
www.abercrombiekent.com
(Also see Abercrombie & Kent International under "Yangtze River Cruises," "Nile River Cruises," and "Amazon River Cruises," all later in this chapter.)

Actief (6/11; British; 100 ft.). Three to six nights, upper Thames.

Alouette (3/6; French/British; 98 ft.). Six nights in Burgundy and Franche Comté.

Anacoluthe (26/51; French; 210 ft.). Six nights, Seine and Yonne from Paris.

Caprice (11/21; French/British; 128 ft.). Six nights in Franche Comté and eastern Burgundy.

Cézanne (52/102; French; 356 ft.). Seven nights in Provence and Burgundy.

Chanterelle (14/24; British/French; 128 ft.). Six nights in the Upper Loire Valley.

Chardonnay (27/50; French; 260 ft.). Six nights on the Saône.

Fleur de Lys (4/7; French/British; 129 ft.). Six nights in Burgundy and Franche Comté.

Hirondelle (4/8; French/British; 128 ft.). Six nights in Burgundy and Franche Comté.

L'Abercrombie (11/22; French/British; 128 ft.). Six nights in central Burgundy.

L'Impressioniste (6/12; French; 128 ft.). Six nights in upper Burgundy (beginning April 2001).

Lafayette (12/22; British/French; 128 ft.). Six nights in lower Burgundy.

Libellule (10/20; British/French; 128 ft.). Six nights in Champagne.

Litote (10/20; British/French; 128 ft.). Six nights in northern Burgundy.

Lorraine (11/22; French/British; 128 ft.). Six nights in Alsace-Lorraine.

Marjorie II (6/12; Flemish; 128 ft.). Six nights on Seine and Yonne in France. Also sails on Saône in Burgundy and to Holland for tulip season.

Mirabelle (12/24; French; 128 ft.). Six nights on the Saône.

Napoleon (6/12; French; 129 ft.). Six nights on Rhône in Provence.

Princess Royale (12/22; French; 170 ft.). Six nights in Holland and Belgium.

Roi Soleìl (3/6; Dutch; 98 ft.). Six nights in Provence on Canal du Midi.

Scottish Highlander (4/8; Scottish; 117 ft.). Six nights on the Caledonian Canal.

Shannon Princess (7/12; Irish; 105 ft.). Six nights on the River Shannon.

The Barge Lady

101 West Grand Ave., Suite 200, Chicago, IL 60610
(312) 245-0900; (800) 880-0071; fax (312) 245-0952
www.bargelady.com

Variety of barges on canals of France, Holland, Belgium, Scotland, Ireland, and Great Britain; golf and wine-tasting cruises featured.

Etoile de Champagne

88 Broad St., Boston, MA 02110
(617) 426-1776; (800) 280-1492; fax (617) 426-4689
www.etoiledechampagne.com

Etoile de Champagne (6/13; Dutch; 128 ft.). Seven days, Holland, Belgium, France, and Mosel Valley; May–October.

EuroCruises

33 Little West 12th St., Suite 106, New York, NY 10014
(212) 691-2099; (800) 688-3876; fax (212) 366-4747
www.eurocruises.com

EuroCruises, a U.S. tour company, specializes in European cruises, especially unusual, off-the-beaten-track itineraries. More than 30 riverboats and oceangoing ships—all European-owned and -managed—are represented. River cruises cover all corners of the continent, from Portugal to Russia; most operate early spring to late fall.

Below are the river cruise lines and boats that EuroCruises represents. For EuroCruises' portfolio of oceangoing cruises, see the section in Part Two, "Other Cruise Lines and Their Ships." EuroCruises can provide details on all vessels and itineraries; brochures show deck plans and describe the ships' features.

Delphin Cruises (EuroCruises)

Delphin Queen (76/196; Ukrainian; 372 ft.). German-managed, this ship has three bars, a dance hall, sauna, massage, beauty salon, and two whirlpools. The restaurant accommodates all passengers at one seating. Varied entertainment is offered. The cuisine ranges from classic dishes to regional specialties. Vegetarian and light dishes are available. Ship sails on 7-night Danube cruises April–October; and two Danube Delta cruises and a 9- or 12-night Oltenita/Passau cruise in August.

Europe Cruise Line (EuroCruises)

Rhine Princess (60/120; Dutch/European; 273 ft.). The deluxe boat was reconstructed in 1992. All cabins have private bath; half have shower, half have bathtub. Restaurant has two seatings with Dutch and German theme dinners. Boat sails eight-day cruises on Rhine and Moselle between Basel and Amsterdam every other Sunday, May–September; special four-night tulip-time cruise in March and April; and eight-day castles and vineyards cruise from Frankfurt to Cologne.

Prussian Princess (69/144; German; 363 ft.). Ship has two bars, lounge, gift shop, library, laundry, beauty salon, and conference facilities. Cabins have air-conditioning, bath with shower, intravessel phone, radio, hair dryers, and bathrobe. Sails on 14-night Amsterdam–Budapest cruises, plus a "Grand Cruise" in July and August that includes the Main, Rhine, and Danube.

Gota Canal (EuroCruises)

Wilhelm Tham (60 passengers), *Juno* (60 passengers), *Diana* (60 passengers). Cruising Sweden's Gota Canal aboard a vintage steamer is one of northern Europe's unique experiences. Lavish daily luncheons include fine smorgasbords with fresh gravlax (salmon), sherried herring, caviar-stuffed eggs, reindeer meat, and cloudberry jam. Four- to six-day cruises, Gothenburg/Stockholm, May–September.

Leisure Cruises (EuroCruises)

Viking Peterhof (119/190; Swiss/Russian; 424 ft.). Comfortable, German-built ship (renovated in 1999) sails Russian inland waters. All cabins are outside; cruise staff speaks English. Two itineraries for 11- and 12-night cruises between St. Petersburg and Moscow, mid-May–September. Most shore excursions included.

Provence Line (EuroCruises)

Cézanne (53/102; French/French; 356 ft.). Boat has two Jacuzzis, sun deck, lounge, nightclub, bar, boutique, and fitness center. Meals of classic French and Italian cuisine prepared by a master chef are served at a single seating. All cabins are outside and have two convertible sofa beds (suites have double beds), a wardrobe closet, bedside tables, desk, air-conditioning, satellite television, SATCOM telephone, safe, and large bathroom with marble vanity. Two itineraries for seven-night Avignon–Lyon cruises are available April–mid-October.

Reiseburo Mittelthurgau (EuroCruises)

Normandie (53/120; French and British; 290 ft.). All cabins are outside and have air-conditioning, television, bathroom with shower, and a large window that opens. Seven-night cruises between Paris and Honfleur, April–October.

Arlène (53/120; French; 290 ft.). All 53 outside cabins aboard the Swiss-managed *Arlène* have twin beds, separate shower and toilet, and air-conditioning. The restaurant serves French cuisine at one sitting. Seven-night cruises between Paris and Honfleur, April–October.

Venezia (52/105; 270 ft.). The Swiss-registered *Venezia* offer seven-night cruises on the Po River between Venice and Cremona, April–October. All 52 cabins are spacious and comfortable with large sliding windows. The ship has a panorama lounge with bar, a sun deck, and a souvenir shop. Shore excursions are optional.

Peter Deilmann Cruises

1800 Diagonal Rd., Suite 170, Alexandria, VA 22314
(703) 549-1741; (800) 348-8287; fax (703) 549-7924
www.deilmann-cruises.com

This European line markets eight riverboats and *Lili Marleen,* a barquentine launched in 1994. Its luxury oceanliner, *Deutschland,* made her debut in 1998. The line is adding a ninth river boat, the 92-passenger *Casanova,* in April 2001, sailing from Venice on Italy's Po River through October.

Cézanne (53/102; French; 356 ft.). See under Provence Line above.

Danube Princess (95/200; Austrian/German; 364 ft.). Facilities include outdoor swimming pool, single-seating dining room, two bars, conference room, library, gift shop, and beauty salon. Cabins have private bathrooms, telephone, radio, and television. The ship sails 7-day Danube cruises March–October from Munich to Austria, Hungary, and Slovakia; and 10- and 11-day Black Sea cruises.

Dresden (54/110; European/German; 304 ft.). Facilities include single-seating dining room, bar, gift shop, beauty salon, fitness equipment, sauna, library, infirmary, and laundry room. All cabins have private shower and toilet, telephone, radio, and television. *Dresden* sails seven-day Elbe cruises from Hamburg or Dresden to Meissen, Magdeburg, and Wittenberg.

Katharina (41/79; German; 272 ft.). Double- and twin-bedded cabins with French doors on upper deck, picture windows on lower deck. Various itineraries on the Elbe River between Potsdam and Prague.

Königstein (31/58; German; 221 ft.). Seven-night cruises on the Elbe, Havel, Vltava, and Oder Rivers to historic German and Czech cities and towns.

Mozart (100/204; International; 396 ft.). The deluxe boat has large, all-outside cabins with spacious private bathrooms, television, minibar, hair dryer, and telephone. Facilities include an indoor swimming pool, whirlpool, sauna, and fitness center. From March to October, the boat sails seven-day Danube cruises departing on Sunday from Passau and calling at Bratislava, Budapest, Kalocza, Esztergom, Duernstein, and Melk. Several classical music summer cruises are scheduled.

Princesse de Provence (71/148; German/European; 363 ft.). Large cabins have private bathrooms, hair dryer, telephone, and radio. Facilities include fitness area, single-seating dining room, two bars, conference room, library, infirmary, and gift shop. March–November, the boat sails seven-day cruises round-trip from Lyon up the Saône River and down the Rhône to Arles, Chateauneuf-du-Pape, Viviers, Trevoux, and Avignon.

Prussian Princess (69/144; Austrian/German; 363 ft.). The deluxe boat offers spacious outside cabins with full-length French doors on the upper deck and picture windows on the lower. All cabins have private bathrooms, telephone, radio, and hair dryer. Facilities include single-seating dining room, lounge, two bars, library, dance floor, fitness area, conference room, boutique, and beauty salon. The boat sails seven-day cruises on the Rhine and Moselle Rivers and Main-Danube Canal between Amsterdam and Basel; round-trip from Frankfurt or Amsterdam through German, Belgian, and Dutch canals.

European Waterways

140 E. 56th St., New York, NY 10022
(212) 688-9489; (800) 217-4447; fax (212) 688-3778
www.europeanwaterways.com

Anjodi, La Joie de Vivre, La Reine Pedauque, La Belle Epoque, L'Impressioniste, Rosa, L'arte de Vivre, Laa Bon Vivant (5–6/10–12; French/French and English; 98–128 ft.). Six nights, rivers and canals of France.

Stella (4/8; French/French and English; 102 ft.). Six nights, between Amsterdam and Brussels during spring tulip season; canals of Alsace-Lorraine.

European Waterways also represents a medley of barges and riverboats for 6–14 passengers on the Shannon River in Ireland, Thames and other waterways of Britain, and Burgundy and other canals of France. Seven-day cruises on *Shannon Princess* can be geared to special interests, such as golf, sport fishing, equestrian, culinary, cycling, wildlife, and poetry. European Waterways also represents the luxury sailing ship *Sea Cloud* (see "Sailing

Ships") and Temptress Cruises, which offers itineraries in Belize and Costa Rica (see "Adventure and Cultural Cruises").

French Country Waterways

P.O. Box 2195, Duxbury, MA 02331

(781) 934-2354; (800) 222-1236; fax (781) 934-9048

Esprit (9/18; French/English; 128 ft.). Cote d'Or wine region (Burgundy Canal, Saône River, Canal du Centre from Dijon to St. Leger-sur-Dheune).

Horizon II (6/12; French/English; 128 ft.) Upper Burgundy (Burgundy Canal from Tonnerre to Venarey-les-Laumes).

Liberté (4/8; French/English; 100 ft.) Western Burgundy region (Canal du Nivernais from Auxerre to Clamecy).

Nenuphar (6/12; French/English; 128 ft.). Upper Loire region (Canal du Briar and Canal du Loing from Chatillon-sur-Loire to Samois-sur-Seine).

Princess (4/8; French/English; 128 ft.). Champagne, Moselle Valley, and Alsace-Lorraine regions.

Global Quest (formerly OdessAmerica)

50 Glen St., Suite 206, Glen Cove, NY 11542

(516) 676-4500; (800) 221-3254; fax (516) 676-4820

www.globalquesttravel.com

This company represents a variety of vessels, which cruise in five general areas: Europe; Russia, Ukraine, and Siberia; Danube; Galápagos and South America; and East Africa/Indian Ocean. Information on the latter two areas are found in the next section, "Adventure and Cultural Cruises."

"Europe by River" is the company's umbrella for 12 modern riverboats, all similar in size and holding 150–200 passengers and with all outside cabins, swimming pool, whirlpool, library, lounge, bar, and dining room serving international cuisine. They offer cruise/tour combinations of the Po, Elbe, Rhône, Saône, Rhine, Danube, Saar, Moselle, Main, Neckar, and Seine.

Lenin, Litvinov, Rybalko, Victor Glushkov (270 passengers; Russian or Ukrainian; 424 ft.). All outside cabins, informal atmosphere, local entertainment, and guest lecturers on history and culture. On these 14-day voyages, passengers arrive in a different port each morning and have most of the day for sight-seeing (guided tours optional). Boats sail from May to September on the rivers, lakes, and canals connecting Moscow and St. Petersburg. On three nights each in Moscow and St. Petersburg, passengers sleep aboard and can take guided shore excursions. *Viktor Glushkov* offers 11- and 12-day cruises connecting three nations on the Black Sea and Danube delta: Ukraine, Romania, and Bulgaria. A Turkey extension is available. Ports with guided tours include Kiev, Sevastopol, Yalta, Odessa, Rousse, Braila, and Tulcea.

Lev Tolstoy, Anton Chekhov (210 passengers; Russian; 380 ft.). *Lev Tolstoy* is among the newest, more upscale additions to the Russian waterways fleet. Its 11/12-day itineraries, June–September, are similar to other vessels', with shorter (2-night) stays in Moscow and St. Petersburg. Also cruises through Siberia. *Anton Chekhov,* built in 1978 and refurbished in 1993, cruises the Yenisey River.

Rousse, Volga, Deltastar, Amadeus I, II (73–236 passengers; European; 347–370 ft.). Danube cruises of 4 to 12 days, link central and southeastern Europe, the Balkans, and Black Sea with cruise/tour options from Amsterdam to Prague for many of the nine countries sharing the waters. Itineraries include entertainment, guest lecturers, and shore excursions. Ships have all outside cabins, informal atmosphere, and regional cuisine. Ports may include Passau, Budapest, Vienna, Bratislava, Tulcea, and Weissenkirchen. *Amadeus I* and *II* have a library, sun deck, and heated pools.

GT Corporate Cruises

2610 East 16th St., Brooklyn, NY 11235
(718) 934-4100; (800) 828-7970; fax (718) 934-9419
www.cruise-russ.com

Russ (332 passengers; Russian; 425 ft.). Fifteen-day tour of waterways connecting Moscow and St. Petersburg. Nine ports of call, including four days in Moscow and four in St. Petersburg. May–September.

Inland Voyages

c/o McGregor Travel, 112 Prospect St., Stamford, CT 06901
(203) 978-5010; (800) 786-5311; fax (203) 978-5027

Luciole (8/14; Belgian, French/British, French; 100 ft.). Six nights, Canal de Bourgogne or the Nivernais from Montbard.

KD River Cruises of Europe

USA East: 2500 Westchester Ave., Purchase, NY 10577
(914) 696-3600; (800) 346-6525; fax (914) 696-0833
USA West: 323 Geary St., Suite 603, San Francisco, CA 94102
(800) 858-8587; fax (415) 392-8868
www.rivercruises.com

This line sails the length of the Rhine, Elbe, Moselle, Seine, Saône, and Danube Rivers and the Rhine-Main-Danube Canal linking the North and Black Seas. In 2000, it was bought by Viking River Cruises, a Swiss company, which recently opened an office in the United States. With the acquisition, Viking now operates 26 riverboats.

Arlène, Normandie (104 passengers; French/International; 290 ft.). Inland waterways of France. Rhône and Saône *(Arlène)*, and Seine *(Normandie)*.

Austria, Britannia, Deutschland, Heinrich Heine, Italia, Theodor Fontane (50–92/104–184; German/German, International; 290–361 ft.). 2–12 nights, Rhine, Moselle, Main Rivers; 8 days, Rhine, Main, and Danube Canal (*Heinrich Heine*).

Clara Schumann (62/128; German/German, International; 312 ft.). Five to seven days, Elbe River, including regions of Saxony and Prussia.

Helvetia (72/140) Seven nights, Rhine and Moselle between Basel and Amsterdam. *William Tell* (50/100), seven nights, Danube between Regensburg and Budapest. Both boats operated by Triton Reisen, a KD subsidiary.

Le Boat

10 South Franklin Turnpike, Suite 204B, Ramsey, NJ 07446
(201) 236-2333; (800) 922-0291; fax (201) 236-1214
www.leboat.com

Le Boat specializes in barge charters and self-drive canal boats on canals in Britain, Scotland, France, Holland, Ireland, and Germany; and yacht charters worldwide.

Sea Cloud Cruises, Inc.

32–40 North Dean St., Englewood, NJ 07631
(201) 227-9404; (888) 732-2568; fax (201) 227-9424
www.seacloud.com

River Cloud (49/98; European; 360 ft.) Launched in 1996, the splendidly appointed *River Cloud* is one of the finest boats on European waterways. Interiors convey 1930s luxury reminiscent of the Orient Express. She offers the impeccable service and fine cuisine for which her famous sister ship, *Sea Cloud,* is known.

The elegant dining room serves meals in a single, open seating in a relaxed, friendly atmosphere. Breakfast and lunch are buffet-style; dinner is served at tables. Menus feature continental specialties and complimentary fine wines, beer, and soft drinks.

The centerpiece of the handsome lounge encircled by windows at the bow is a seven-foot Steinway grand piano. It's much in use during afternoon tea and music cruises when renowned pianists and opera stars are aboard. Amenities include a library, boutique, hair salon, exercise room, sauna, putting green, and large-scale chessboard. All cabins have telephone, radio, television, air-conditioning, safe, and marble bathrooms with showers and hair dryers.

The Dutch-built *River Cloud* sails on the Rhine, Main, Moselle, and Danube, April–October. The cruises are also sold through Dailey-Thorp

Travel of New York, (212) 307-1555; Abercrombie & Kent, (800) 323-7308; European Waterways, (800) 217-4447; and other U.S. companies.

River Cloud II (44/88; European; 338 ft.), designed to cruise Italy's historic Po River between Cremona and Venice, will sail seven-night itineraries with the debarkation port alternating each week. *River Cloud II* is scheduled to be launched in 2000; the line's other new ship, *Sea Cloud II,* is expected to join the fleet in April 2001.

River Cloud II's public rooms include a lounge and library, restaurant, boutique, and hair salon. The air-conditioned ship has 15 junior suites with windows and 29 double-bed cabins with portholes. All have direct-dial telephone, television with video player, radio and music channels, minibar, emergency button, and bath with shower, hair dryer, bathrobes, and toiletries. A fruit basket, half-bottle of champagne, bottled water, and soft drinks are replenished daily.

A typical cruise would include two nights in Venice, cruising the lagoon to the islands of Murano, Burano, Torcello, and Chioggia, before entering the Po. Other ports and sites to be visited include Taglio di Po, the Abbey of Pomposa, Ferrara, Mantua, Verona, and Parma. Shore excursions will include the Violin Museum in Boretto, where passengers will hear a private Stradivarius recital.

Swan Hellenic Cruises

631 Commack Road, Suite 1A, Commack, NY 11725
(631) 858-1270; (877) 219-4239; fax (531) 858-1279
www.swanhellenic.com

River holidays (on the *Cézanne* or *Swiss Crystal*) are accompanied by expert guest speakers. Fares include excursions and tips. Summer cruises explore waterways of Russia and Central Europe in small, chartered riverboats. Cruises are 8–15 days and can be combined with pre- and postcruise tours. Reservations can be made through API, a U.S.-based consortium of travel agents, (800) 402-4API, or direct at Swan Hellenic's London office on its toll-free number, (877) 219-4239, between 4 a.m. and 12:30 p.m. EST.

Viking River Cruises/U.S. Division

21820 Burbank Blvd. Woodland Hills, CA 91367
www.vikingrivercruises.com

A Switzerland-based company offering European and Russian cruises, Viking River Cruises has itineraries of 3 to 14 nights on the Rhine, Danube, Oder, Po, Seine, Rhône, Volga, and Dnjepr Rivers. Its newly established U.S. division is offering all-inclusive programs created specifically for English-speaking passengers on the Elbe, Danube, Rhine, and Moselle and ranging from 4 to 14 nights.

YANGTZE RIVER CRUISES IN CHINA*

The Chinese aptly call the Yangtze *Changjiang* (long river). Rising from the Tibetan plateau, it plunges through mountain passes into Sichuan to form a border between Hubei and Hunan before reaching the fertile plains of Jiangsu and Shanghai, a journey of almost 4,000 miles.

The Yangtze (a local name) is more than a scenic wonder. It was the site of epic battles in the second century B.C., and archaeological excavations suggest that the area was a cradle of Chinese civilization.

The river remains the great highway of central China, carrying passenger ferries, patrol boats, and barges piled with coal, limestone, timber, and cement. Small freighters deliver supplies to towns built into the cliffs and collect the fruit grown in terraced orchards.

The river is always busy, especially as it narrows into gorges. There, traffic control is essential, and cruise ship captains are in telephone contact with shore pilot stations as they steer the shallow-draft vessels between gravel shoals.

The Three Gorges: Qutang, Wu, Xiling

Qutang Gorge, also known as Wind Box Gorge, is five miles long, but never wider than 490 feet. Limestone cliffs erupt on either side in sheer walls up to 4,000 feet tall. The cliff face is pitted with caves, and the remains are visible of an old towpath—the only way through the gorge before the biggest boulders were cleared from the river.

Less than an hour after leaving the Qutang, cruise ship passengers enter 25-mile-long Wu Gorge. Its cliffs are so high and steep that the sun rarely touches the water. Twelve peaks dominate. According to myth, they're a goddess and her handmaidens who chose to be turned to stone to stand sentinel over the river.

Midway through the gorge is the border between Sichuan and Hubei Provinces. The exit from the gorge is only 164 feet across, the narrowest part of the river.

It takes another day for cruise ships to reach Xiling Gorge, the longest canyon, which winds 47 miles through small gorges amid fierce rapids. On either side are examples of the mountains beyond mountains of classic Chinese scenery.

Three Gorges Dam

Three Gorges Dam is under construction at Sandouping, at the eastern mouth of the gorges. It's massive. The dam wall will be almost two miles long and 607 feet tall. Behind it a lake will stretch 373 miles and cover 418 square

*This section, Yangtze River Cruises in China, was written by Shann Davies

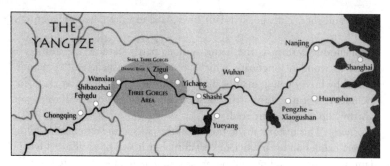

miles, inundating most of the Xiling and half of the Wu Gorges. A million or more people must be evacuated after the dam's completion in 2009.

Supporters say the $34 billion dam will control flooding and generate 84.7 billion kilowatt hours a year for Shanghai and the Lower Yangtze Basin. Opponents say it will destroy the environment and build a reservoir of toxic silt in an earthquake-prone region. Either way, it adds poignancy to a Yangtze cruise.

Cruise boats take a specially created detour around the dam wall under construction.

The first westerners to sail up the Yangtze River were British colonial administrators, who established the inland port of Hankow (now part of Wuhan) in the 1840s. The most adventurous continued into the sparsely populated wilderness upstream and found the Three Gorges.

Transport was by sailing ships, which were hauled by teams of trackers through raging rapids and over great boulders until English trader Archibald Little pioneered steamship service from Wuhan, finally reaching Chongqing (formerly Chungking) in 1898. The voyage remained extremely hazardous until the 1950s, when the Chinese blasted away the largest boulders.

Regular cruises through the gorges were introduced in the early 1980s and became an established part of many all-China itineraries. The gorges are on the 120-mile (192-km) stretch of river between Baidicheng and Yichang. Some itineraries between Chongqing and Yichang reduce the trip by a day and night. However, it has often proved difficult to arrange air or land transfers to or from Yichang. Most cruises thus cover the full 850-mile (1,370-km) section between Chongqing and Wuhan.

Shore Excursions (Upstream or Downstream)

Shennong Stream/Daning River Gorges   All cruises offer a side trip up one of the Yangtze's tributaries for a closer look at the natural grandeur. Excursions feature fast-flowing, crystal-clear streams with shifting, pebbled shoals and sheer cliffs pocked with caves, clad in waterfalls, and encrusted with ferns.

Shennong Stream is the better option, partly because the journey is taken in wooden longboats, which are steered, pushed, and sometimes hauled by husky young men of the Tujia minority. The half-day excursion includes a visit to a Tujia-style house, where local dance is performed and worthwhile souvenirs are sold.

Zigui   This historic town, poised on the cliffs at the entrance to Xiling Gorge, exudes an air of ancient certainty, but it will be swallowed by the dam. Only one building will be preserved: The temple dedicated to Chu Yuan, the scholar statesman who drowned himself in 278 B.C. in protest of his government's policy, will be moved downstream with the population. Travelers will lose a town whose main street is packed with sidewalk kitchens, vegetable stalls, al fresco hairdressers, one-room tailors, an alley of pool tables, and a storefront video game center.

Shashi/Jingzhou   Upstream from Wuhan, this bustling port contains the remains of a royal capitol from the seventh century B.C. Some original walls are maintained, and the museum contains a 2,000-year-old mummy.

Yueyang Tower   This gold-tiled pavilion on the Hunan banks of the river, upstream from Wuhan, was built in 716 as a military lookout. It was later expanded to provide a belvedere over scenic Dongting Lake.

Fengdu   Near the western entrance of Qutang Gorge, this ancient cliff town is reputed to be where people's spirits go after death. To placate unhappy and potentially dangerous phantoms, a temple sells "passports to hell" and other souvenirs.

Shibaozhai   The cliffside town, between Chongqing and the first gorge, has a 12-story red pagoda and hilltop temple.

Cruise Lines and Ships

About 40 ships offer cruises through the Yangtze gorges. The majority are Chinese-owned and marketed internationally by China Merchants Changjiang Cruise Company, with offices in Hong Kong (1607 Wing On Centre, 111 Connaught Road, Hong Kong).

A new generation of vessels caters to travelers whose interest has been fueled by reports that the gorges' days are numbered. These ships operate on regular itineraries designed to allow passage through the gorges during daylight. The timing concerns produce shore excursions that are conveniently located, interesting, varied, and appropriate to the area's history. The season lasts from late February to early December. Summer is extremely hot; in winter, the water level is low and temperatures are below freezing. There are almost weekly departures of the four-day, three-night downstream cruise from Chongqing and the five-day, four-night upstream trip from Wuhan.

Abercrombie & Kent International, Inc.
1520 Kensington Rd., Suite 212, Oak Brook, IL 60523
(630) 954-2944; (800) 323-7308; fax (630) 954-3324
www.abercrombiekent.com

East King, East Queen (78/156; Chinese; 300 ft.).

The twin boats *East King* and *East Queen* (operating April–October) are the fastest and most modern on the route. All cabins are a spacious 183 square feet and have picture windows, minibars, satellite television, international direct-dial telephones, safes, terry robes, hair dryers, and well-designed bathrooms. There are two suites, which can be combined with a tea lounge for seminars, groups, or small meetings. The main dining room serves western and Chinese meals. Public facilities include a nightclub, five karaoke rooms, an enclosed observation deck with cafe, a business center, and a 100-seat function room. Recreational facilities include a swimming pool, card rooms, gym, and sauna.

Regal China Cruises
57 W. 38th St., New York, NY 10018
(212) 768-3388; (800) 808-3388; fax (212) 768-4939
www.regalchinacruises.com

Princess Sheena, Princess Jeannie, Princess Elaine (134 cabins, 10 suites/ 258 passengers; Chinese; 424 ft.).

These German-built boats—the longest on the river—are managed by Regal China Cruises, a Sino-American joint venture. They offer a ballroom, bar, sun deck, business center, and health club with sauna, gym, and practitioner of acupuncture and qigong. The two dining rooms offer river views. The main restaurant serves buffets of western and Chinese cuisine; the other offers Chinese table service or a buffet.

Standard cabins are rather small (121 square feet) but have direct-dial phone, radio, television, air-conditioning, and bathrooms with showers. Only superior-category cabins have a separate shower stall. The ten suites are spacious, with separate sitting areas, kitchenettes, and bathrooms with tubs. Ten staterooms are specifically designated for single travelers.

The ships offers a variety of Chinese cultural programs, lectures, and activities, including mah-jongg, classical Chinese entertainment, and lessons in Chinese shadow boxing, t'ai chi, card games, and calligraphy. Local artisans demonstrate kite making, jewelry design, and other crafts daily. Passengers can also experience Chinese acupuncture or acupressure. The ships have American cruise directors versed in Chinese history, language, and culture. They lecture throughout every cruise, particularly during sailing through the gorges and before shore excursions.

March to November, the ships sail upstream on five-night cruises from

Wuhan to Chongqing and downstream on three-night cruises from Chongqing to Wuhan.

Victoria Cruises
57-08 Thirty-Ninth Ave., Woodside, NY 11377
(212) 818-1680; (800) 348-8084; fax (212) 818-9889
www.victoriacruises.com

Victoria I, II, III, IV, Victoria Yangtze Pearl, Victoria Yangtze Princess, Victoria Blue Whale, Victoria Blue Angel (77/154; Chinese).

Victoria Cruises, a New York–based Sino-American joint venture, sails vessels with the wedding-cake look and character of Mississippi riverboats. Each has four decks and an observation area and offers single-seating dining with Chinese and western cuisine.

All standard cabins (155 square feet) are outside. They have two lower berths, picture windows, and private bathrooms with shower. Three grades of suites all have bathtubs. Facilities include a business center, cocktail lounge, game room, health clinic, beauty salon, gift shop, and reading room.

In 1999, Victoria added the eastern Yangtze between Shanghai and Wuhan to its popular Three Gorges cruises on the western Yangtze. Stops at Nanjing, Yangzhou, Huangshan, and Lushan include numerous scenic and historic sites. Passengers can sail the river's entire navigable length or book segments (4–11 days). Western cruise directors lecture about China and the Yangtze, and a river guide offers narrative about sights.

Other Yangtze River Cruises

Several other U.S.-based companies offer Yangtze cruises. All include the cruises as part of longer China itineraries ranging from 12 to 24 days.

Collette Tours	(800) 832-4656	www.collettetours.com
Grand American Travels	(800) 868-6686	www.chinavacation.com
Japan & Orient Tours	(800) 377-1080	www.jot.com
Maupintour	(800) 255-4266	www.maupintour.com
Orient Flexi-pax	(800) 545-5540	www.orientflexipax.com
Pacific Bestour	(800) 688-3288	www.bestour.com
Pacific Delight	(800) 221-7179	www.pacificdelighttours.com
SITA World Travel	(800) 421-5643	www.sitatours.com
TBI Tours	(800) 223-0266	www.generaltours.com
Travcoa	(800) 992-2003	www.travcoa.com
Uniworld	(800) 733-7820	www.uniworldasiacruises.com
Visits Plus	(800) 321-3235	www.visitsplus.com

OTHER ASIAN RIVERS

Orient Express Cruises
c/o Orient Express Hotels
1155 Avenue of the Americas, New York, NY 10036
(800) 524-2420; fax (630) 954-3324
www.orient-expresstrains.com

Road to Mandalay (71/126; European/Burmese; 305 ft.). The unusual cruises in Myanmar (formerly Burma) are offered by Orient Express Trains and Cruises, the company that operates the famous Orient Express. The boat sails from early September to mid May on three- to seven-night itineraries on the Irrawaddy (Ayeyarwady) River between Mandalay and Pagan. The cruises are part of a package departing from Bangkok, Thailand, with round-trip flights to Yangon. The German-built *Road to Mandalay*, a deluxe cruiser, previously sailed the Rhine and Elbe. Before starting these cruises in 1996, the boat was renovated. Facilities include a pool, large sun deck, observation lounge, and several bars. The dining room accommodates all passengers in a single seating and serves international and Asian cuisine. The three cabin types include some singles. All have private bath and air-conditioning. Doubles have twin beds; larger cabins have a sitting area. Per person, double occupancy for three-night cruises range from $1,500 for a standard cabin to $3,160 for state cabin and include internal flights within Myamnar, transfers, and sight-seeing.

Two 10-night adventures have been added in mid-August to a little-known region north of Mandalay to beyond Bhamo, stopping just short of the China border. Unlike the tranquil flood plains surrounding the lower Irrawaddy, the northern landscape changes as the ship enters the Three Narrows region, marked with lush forests and towering cliffs. Rates per person, double occupancy, range from $3,995 for a superior cabin to $4,970 for a state cabin.

NILE RIVER CRUISES

No trip to Egypt is complete without a cruise on the Nile. It is the perfect way to enjoy the Egyptian countryside as well as to see ancient temples and monuments because the most famous sites are clustered along the great river. Your first view of the Nile snaking through the desert will illustrate dramatically why the river has been so important throughout Egypt's history. Quite literally, Egypt without the Nile would not exist. Beyond the green ribbon—the land irrigated by the Nile—the desert stretches endlessly into the horizon. The Nile flows so gently that ships glide as though unmoving. Riverbanks, always near, give passengers an intimate view of rural life in upper Egypt. Along the riverbanks and in the fields of the green valley, Egyptians live today much as they have for thousands of years. Life and land have a continuity bridging the centuries, as visitors will see from the ancient drawings on the temple and tomb walls and the present scenes of the countryside. They are scenes from the beginning of time. The sense of tranquility is an overwhelming sensation throughout the Nile cruise and is a total contrast from the roar and clamor of Cairo—the juxtaposition makes the pastoral setting of the Nile Valley all the more remote.

Itineraries

Those beginning their cruise in Upper Egypt may travel from Cairo to Luxor or Aswan by plane, train, or road. They can begin their trip in Aswan and cruise to Luxor or do the reverse. We recommend the former, as the trip then saves the best for last: climaxing with sight-seeing at Karnak and the Valley of the Kings at Luxor.

Aswan was the capital of Nubia in ancient times and an important trading place. Today, it's primarily a winter resort and the administrative center for the High Dam and surrounding region. Aswan is dotted with antiquities. The most important is the Temple of Philae—one of many temples saved from the High Dam's waters—on an island in the river. The botanical gardens, also on an island, and the Agha Khan's mausoleum are standard stops on the popular excursion made by *felucca,* the graceful sailboats of the Nile.

From Aswan, Nile steamers sail downstream (north) to Luxor, stopping at Kom Ombo, Edfu, and Esna—sites of temples dating from the Ptolemaic or Greek period. One temple has a wall carving bearing the only known likeness of Queen Cleopatra. Luxor is the modern town next to the ancient city of Thebes, capital of Egypt for most of its illustrious early history. Boats dock on the east bank near the Etap and Winter Palace hotels, both walking distance from Luxor Temple and a short carriage ride to the colossal Karnak Temple. A full-day excursion visits the west bank to the Valley of the Kings, where tombs of Tutankhamen and other pharaohs were found; the Valley of the Queens; and the Tombs of the Nobles, which contain important art.

Many cruises also sail north to the Temples of Dendera and Abydos, considered the most important temple in Egypt for its artwork. A limited number of cruises sail beyond Abydos on longer itineraries, stopping at Tel al Amarna, capital of revolutionary pharaoh Akhenaton and his beautiful wife, Nefertiti; Minya, central Egypt's largest town; and Beni Hassan, site of tombs containing drawings showing ancient Egyptians at play.

Lake Nasser/Abu Simbel

Construction of Aswan High Dam created Lake Nasser, which stretches more than 300 miles south from Aswan to the Sudanese border. As waters rose, the famous temple of Abu Simbel was moved to higher ground in a colossal 1950s international project. For decades, visitors flew or drove to see Abu Simbel. Now, they can go by Nile steamer, departing from the south side of the dam. (See Misr Travel below.)

Nile Steamers

Nile steamers are small and cozy, friendly and clublike. Some accommodate as few as 20; the largest carries 152 passengers. Cabins, smaller than those on standard cruise ships, are well appointed and comfortable. Most have twin lower beds (some have pull-down bunks for a third person), dressing table or nightstand, closet, and private bathroom with shower. Boats holding 80 or more passengers have lounges for reading and relaxing, a bar, sun deck, dining room with table service, and evening entertainment. Laundry service is available. Some offer Ping-Pong or a tiny swimming pool.

The boat's small size limits its recreational and entertainment facilities, but these aren't important on a Nile cruise, where antiquities and scenery are the attractions. "Roaming" room is surprisingly ample. Deck chairs invite lounging and watching history float by.

Newer vessels are four- and five-star and offer three- to five-night cruises between Luxor and Aswan. Some add Abydos and Dendera and feature cruises of six or seven nights plus optional land excursions.

Nile cruises are divided into three seasons (prices include all meals, service, taxes, and guided sight-seeing).

High season (October–April) per person per night: Five-star boats range from $130–200; four-star, $75–140. Shoulder season (May and September): 15 percent off high-season rates. Low season (June–August): 50 percent off high-season rates.

Although prices are lower in summer and many boats are air-conditioned, the heat in sight-seeing areas can be intense. Large groups walking generate dust in which it's difficult to breath; a dust mask or handkerchief over the mouth is helpful. Boat food usually is quite good. Be very careful, however, to eat only fruits and vegetables that can be peeled.

More than 200 boats or Nile steamers offer cruises. Unless you have the opportunity to inspect a vessel yourself, book only with established companies. Five-star boats operated by Hilton International, Mena House Oberoi, Meridian, Movenpick, Sheraton, and Sonesta are the main ones used by major U.S. tour companies.

If you arrive in Egypt without reservations and decide to cruise, make inquiries and reservations through the managing company's office in Cairo, where cabin space is controlled. If you wait until you arrive in Luxor or Aswan to find space, you must walk among ships and ask the boat manager if room is available.

If you have ample time, however, the latter method lets you see the ship, its cabins, and cleanliness (important, especially on boats less than five stars) before booking. And, if you're good at bargaining, you may negotiate a price better than you might have received in advance in Cairo.

A partial list of companies and Nile steamers follows.

(Key: Cabins/Passengers; Officers/Crew; Vessel Length)

Abercrombie & Kent International, Inc.

1520 Kensington Rd., Suite 212, Oak Brook, IL 60523
(800) 323-7308; fax (630) 954-3324
www.abercrombiekent.com

Sun Boat III (20 cabins); *Sun Boat IV* (42 cabins). Cruises of 5 to 8 days between Luxor and Aswan are part of an all-Egypt tour; Egypt and Kenya safari; or Egypt/Israel tour of 10–20 days.

Esplanade Tours

581 Boylston St., Boston, MA 02116
(617) 266-7465; (800) 426-5492; fax (617) 262-9829
www.ebitravel.com

Monarch, Regency, Regina, and *Royale* (51/102; Egyptian; 238 ft.). The luxury quartet, owned and operated by Travcotels of Egypt, are fully air-conditioned. Each has 49 double cabins and 2 singles and suites. Also lounges, bars, panoramic windows, single-seating dining room, two sun decks, swimming pool, gift shop, beauty salon, and laundry facilities. Cabins measure 230 square feet; suites have 380 square feet. All have television, video, minifridge, and bathrooms with shower, toilet, bidet, and hair dryer. Three-, four-, and seven-night cruises depart from Luxor or Aswan.

Mena House Oberoi Hotels/Misr Travel

Pyramids Road, Giza, Cairo, Egypt
20-2-383-3222; fax 20-2-383-7777

Sheherayar (74 cabins), *Shehrazah* (74 cabins), *Oberoi Philae* (58/105 cabins), and *Nephtis* (60/144 cabins) are operated by Oberoi Hotels, an international chain with hotels in Cairo and Aswan. The *Oberoi Philae* resembles a paddlewheeler. Each cabin has floor-to-ceiling sliding glass doors leading to private balconies. Jacket and tie are required for men at dinner. All ships sail on three- to six-night cruises between Luxor and Aswan.

Misr Travel

630 Fifth Ave., Suite 1460, New York, NY 10111
(212) 582-9210; (800) 223-4978; fax (212) 332-2609

Eugenie (50/100); *Nubian Sea* (60/120); *Kasr Ibrim* (60/120). Three and four nights on Lake Nasser. Boats have outside cabins with private baths. The four-night program sails south from Aswan on Monday and ends at Abu Simbel on Friday; three-night cruises sail north on Friday from Abu Simbel to Aswan. The highlight is a daylight visit to Abu Simbel. A special feature is a candlelight dinner on deck in front of the floodlit temple of Ramses II. The price is about $150 per person, double occupancy, in winter; lower in off-season. All meals and shore excursions are included.

Misr Travel, a quasi-governmental travel agency of Egypt, owns the boats operated by Oberoi, Sheraton, and other companies with hotels in Egypt. These include Movenpick's *Radamis* (67 cabins), Pyramisa's *Champillon* (67 cabins), and Meridien Hotel's *Anni* (76/152) and *Aton* (34 suites, 14 cabins). The latter is one of the most luxurious Nile boats. All offer three- to seven-night cruises departing from Luxor and Aswan.

Sheraton Nile Cruises/Misr Travel
630 Fifth Ave., Suite 1460, New York, NY 10111
(212) 582-9210; (800) 22-EGYPT; fax (212) 332-2609
Hotep, Tut (76/152; Egyptian; 72 ft.). Three, four, and seven nights between Luxor and Aswan.

Nabila Nile Cruises
605 Market St., Suite 507, San Francisco, CA 94105
(800) 443-NILE; fax (415) 979-0163
www.nabilatours.com
Ramses King of Thebes, Ramses King of the Nile, Queen of Sheeba, King of the Nile, Queen Nabila of Abu Simbel, Ramses II (40–83/78–154; Egyptian; 172–234 ft.). Four-night, five- and eight-day cruises from Luxor to Aswan.

Sonesta International Hotels Corporation
200 Clarendon St. (41st floor of John Hancock Building)
Boston, MA 02116
(617) 421-5400; (800) SONESTA (766-3782)
Or, 4 El Tayaran Street, Nasr City, Cairo, Egypt
011-202 262-8111; fax 263-5731
www.sonesta.com
Nile Goddess (65/136; Egyptian); *Sun Goddess* (58 cabins and 4 suites; Egyptian). Four–six nights between Luxor and Aswan.

U.S. AND CANADIAN RIVER CRUISES

The Mississippi has the best-known river cruises, but there are others— and new companies and cruises are added every year. Spectacular scenery is the main attraction. In the Northeast, the favorite season is autumn, with its brilliant foliage.

(Key: Cabins/Passengers; Officers/Crew; Vessel Length)

American Canadian Caribbean Line
(See Part Two: Cruise Lines and Their Ships.)

American West Steamboat Company
2 Union Square, Suite 4343, Seattle, WA 98101
(206) 292-9606; (800) 434-1232; fax (206) 340-0975
www.columbiarivercruise.com
 Queen of the West (73/165; American; 230 ft.). This deluxe paddle-wheeler is the first vessel of a company created by owners of Alaska's Glacier Bay Tours and Cruises. Inaugurated in 1995, the boat offers four- to seven-night cruises (March–December) on the Columbia, Snake, and Willamette Rivers from Portland, Oregon. All shore excursions are included in the price.

Cruise West
(See Part Two: Cruise Lines and Their Ships.)

Delta Queen Steamboat Company
(See Part Two: Cruise Lines and Their Ships.)

Ecomertours Nord-Sud
(See "Adventure and Culture Cruises" later in Part Three.)

International Expeditions, Inc.
One Environs Park, Helena, AL 35080
(800) 633-4734; fax (205) 428-1714
www.ietravel.com
 Sea Bird (70 passengers, 152 ft.) departs from Juneau, Alaska, on eight-day cruises (June–August). The deluxe yacht approaches glaciers, explores inlets, and showcases Alaska's coastal wildlife. Naturalist/guides escort frequent trips ashore and excursions in small craft.

RiverBarge Excursion Lines
201 Opelousas Ave., New Orleans, LA 70114
(504) 365-0022; (888) 456-2206; fax (504) 365-0000
www.riverbarge.com
 River Explorer (100/200; American; 297 ft.). Similar in concept to European barges, *River Explorer* was the first of its kind when it was inaugurated in 1998. A modern, American-built, -flagged, and -crewed hotel-barge, the vessel consists of two 295-foot custom-built barges connected and propelled by a 3,000-horsepower towboat. The forward barge contains public rooms, including a dining room accommodating all passengers at a single, open seating for all meals; a two-deck showroom; exercise and

games area; library; gift shop; and Pilot House Lounge, a re-creation of a river pilothouse complete with equipment and windows overlooking the bow. Art depicting river exploration decorates public areas.

The aft barge contains all 100 cabins, each measuring 200 square feet. All are outside and have picture windows. Upper-deck cabins have balconies. All have twin or super queen-size beds, satellite television, VCRs, telephones with computer ports, minirefrigerators, coffeemakers, irons, and bathrooms with tubs. Features include a never-empty cookie jar and 24-hour coffee service.

River Explorer sails from New Orleans on four- to ten-day excursions along the Mississippi River, its tributaries, and intracoastal waters. Each of seven itineraries focuses on a geographic region on the Mississippi, Ohio, Missouri, and Cumberland Rivers; Atchafalaya basin; and Gulf Intracoastal Waterway.

Prices begin at $795 per person, twin, for a four-day excursion. Taxes, port charges, most shore activities, and tipping are included. Alcoholic beverages cost extra.

St. Lawrence Cruise Lines/Canadian River Cruise Vacations
253 Ontario St., Kingston, Ontario, Canada K7L 2Z4
(613) 549-8091; (800) 267-7868; fax (613) 549-8410
www.stlawrencecruiselines.com

Canadian Empress (32/66; Canadian; 108 ft.). Four, five, and six nights on the St. Lawrence and Ottawa Rivers. Boarding ports include Kingston, Ottawa, Montreal, and Quebec City. Some cruises allow booking an additional whale-watching package in the Saguenay River area.

AMAZON RIVER CRUISES

Many mainstream ships with South American itineraries include an Amazon River cruise. They enter on the Atlantic delta and sail upriver to Manaus. The river is very wide; any intimate view must be obtained aboard small crafts on tributaries. More exotic regions of the upper Amazon are reached mainly from Iquitos, Peru. Many companies offering tours from the United States use the same boats on the Amazon; vessels' descriptions appear the first time they're named.

(**Key: Cabins/Passengers; Officers/Crew; Vessel Length**)

Abercrombie & Kent International, Inc.
1520 Kensington Rd., Suite 212, Oak Brook, IL 60523
(630) 954-2944; (800) 323-7308; fax (630) 954-3324
www.abercrombiekent.com

Explorer sails in March and April, leaving Belem, Brazil, on a 17-day cruise of the Amazon and its tributaries to Iquitos, Peru, and a second, upper-Amazon leg from Manaus to Iquitos. The latter leg also is available as a ten-day trip from Peru. (See Part Two: Cruise Lines and Their Ships.)

Ecotour Expeditions, Inc.

P.O. Box 128, Jamestown, RI 02835-0128
(800) 688-1822; fax (401) 423-9630
www.naturetours.com

Tucano (9/16; Peruvian; 80 ft.) has wood-paneled walls, a large observation deck, a living room, and a balcony. Seventy-six windows showcase the forest. All cabins have private bathrooms with shower, toilet, and sink.

Seven- to eleven-day cruises depart Miami year-round. The nature-oriented trips on the Amazon and tributaries are accompanied by naturalists.

Explorers Travel Group L.L.C.

One Main Street, Suite 304, Eatontown, NJ 07724
(800) 631-5650; fax: (732) 542-9420
www.explorerstravelgroup.com

The tour company offers various Amazon adventures aboard the riverboats described below. They depart from Iquitos on two- to seven-night cruises on the upper Amazon. Explorers also uses the *Tucano,* listed under Ecotour Expeditions.

Amazon Clipper (8/16; Peruvian; 65 ft.). Two-night cruises explore the tributaries to bird-watch, fish for piranha, and visit Ecopark, a wildlife rehabilitation sanctuary. *Clipper*'s cabins have private bathrooms, bunk berths, and nighttime air-conditioning. Facilities include covered saloon, bar, dining area, library, and fully equipped kitchen. Local cuisine is served, mainly fresh fish. Mineral water is provided.

Amazon Explorer (8/16; Peruvian; 85 ft.). Three- or six-night round-trip cruises upriver from Iquitos. The steel-constructed boat has a small air-conditioned lounge, dining room/bar, and sun deck. The cabins are outside doubles with bunk beds; all are air-conditioned and have private bath/shower.

Arca (29/32; Peruvian; 98 ft.). Three to six nights, upper Amazon. The air-conditioned, steel-hull riverboat operates between Iquitos and the twin cities of Tabatinga, Brazil, and Leticia, Colombia. She offers ten twin-bedded cabins with upper/lower berths and three triples with lower beds. All cabins have private bath and shower. The boat has a lounge/bar and covered and uncovered deck areas.

Marcelita (26/52; Peruvian; 192 ft.). New ship built in 1999 has dining room, bar, and library. All cabins are twins done in Amazon hardwoods with air-conditioning and private bathroom and shower.

Rio Amazonas (21/40; Peruvian; 146 ft.). Three- to six-night explorations of the upper Amazon, sailing downriver on Sunday from Iquitos to the twin cities of Tabatinga, Brazil, and Leticia, Colombia; upriver on Wednesday from Leticia. Itineraries can be combined. The ship has an air-conditioned dining room and library, covered and uncovered deck areas, and Jacuzzi/hot tub. Upper deck cabins have picture windows and private bathroom with shower. Sun deck cabins are larger, offering three twin beds, closet, and chair.

Fourth Dimension Tours
71-01 South West 99th Ave., Suite 106, Miami, FL 33173
(305) 279-0014; (800) 343-0020; fax (305) 273-9777
www.4thdimension.com
   Amazon Clipper (8/16; Peruvian; 65 ft.). See description above.

International Expeditions, Inc.
1 Environs Park, Helena, AL 35080
(800) 633-4734; fax (205) 428-1714
www.ietravel.com
   La Esmeralda (16 passengers; 91 ft.), *La Turmalina* (26 passengers; 110 ft.), *La Amatista* (28 passengers; 125 ft.), *La Malaquita* (8 passengers/ 100 ft.). These exploratory vessels sail from Iquitos, past the start of the Amazon, exploring its tributaries. These include the Ucayali, Marañon, or Tapiche Rivers, viewed from excursion craft and on foot along jungle trails. Naturalists/guides accompany outings. All cabins have private facilities and air-conditioning. Eight-day cruises, weekly departures throughout the year.

Ladatco Tours
3006 Aviation Ave., Suite 4C, Coconut Grove, FL 33133
(305) 854-8422; (800) 327-6162; fax (305) 285-0504
www.ladatco.com
   Amazon Clipper (8/16; Peruvian; 65 ft.). Two-deck riverboat refurbished for overnight touring. Cabins have bunk beds, private bath, and air-conditioning. Three- to four-day cruises, departing Monday and Wednesday from Manaus, on the Amazon and Negro Rivers; or a six-day cruise combining the two. Multilingual local guide accompanies.
   Rio Amazonas (See above). Six-day cruises, round-trip, departing Sunday from Iquitos. Three-night cruises available. Itinerary includes birdwatching, jungle walk, and fishing in the Ataquari River.

Marco Polo Vacations, Inc. and Galápagos Cruises, Inc.
11440 West Bernardo Court, Suite 161, San Diego, CA 92127
(800) 421-5276; fax: (858) 451-8472
www.marcopolovacations.com; www.amazonvacations.com

Desafio. Three-night cruises year-round depart from Manaus to the Amazon and tributaries accompanied by multilingual naturalist. Continental and Brazilian cuisine served buffet-style. Three-day Tucano program includes jungle walk to explore flora. The four-day Maguari program visits the Samauma village in the Ana-vilhanas Islands and sails to the "wedding of the waters," where the Negro and Solimoes meet to form the Amazon.

Tara Tours
6595 North West 36th St., Suite 306A, Miami, FL 33166
(305) 871-1246; (800) 327-0080; fax (305) 871-0417
www.taratours.com

Arca or *Rio Amazonas* (see above). Seven-night Amazon packages year-round from Miami to Iquitos include boat trips and one night at the Hotel Turistas, with jungle walks, visits to native villages, and English-speaking naturalists. Also, optional Lima–Cuzco–Machu Picchu cruise available on request.

Adventure and Cultural Cruises

Whether it is called an adventure or expedition cruise or an educational or cultural cruise is a matter of definition on which few people agree. And although there are differences, there are also similarities, particularly in the type of person to whom they appeal—namely, experienced travelers who prefer an intellectually stimulating or educational environment when they travel and do not need (or want) the activities and entertainment typical of mainstream cruises. They prefer the hands-on learning that adventure and educational cruises provide and the companionship of like-minded travelers.

Ships offering adventures or expeditions generally are informal and small, accommodating fewer than 150 passengers. Their small size enables them to visit places large ships cannot go. Vessels providing educational or cultural cruises might be larger and more formal. In all cases, the itineraries, which tend to be two weeks or longer, and opportunity to learn from experts are the main attractions.

A few adventure ships are deluxe, but most are comfortable workhorses that safely ply icy waters or jungle rivers. They have cozy, functional cabins; friendly service; and good food, served at one open seating, often family-style. Dress is casual. Most ships maintain an open bridge.

Cruises are almost always seasonal to take advantage of optimum weather and wildlife conditions. On board, passengers attend lectures by specialists and have time to enjoy fellow shipmates. Ports are likely to be remote and passengers travel by Zodiac boats to the most inaccessible areas, often making wet landings where no docks are available.

On shore, participants view wildlife and scenery, hike into coastal forests, or encounter remote cultures. Not all cruises require heavy exertion—many are light adventure, nothing more than a short walk. In the evening, staff naturalists and guest lecturers recap the day's excursion in well-attended sessions. On educational or cultural cruises, lecturers are more likely to be historians, anthropologists, museum authorities, and area specialists. Many such trips are sponsored by universities and museum groups, often as an alumni fund-raiser.

Destinations might be world-renowned sites visited by general tours, but participants on cultural cruises get in-depth information and excursions led by experts rather than the commercial guides that regular cruise lines use. Participants also are likely to attend cultural and folklore events. It isn't unusual for adventure and cultural cruises to overlap in their activities, particular those offering light adventure (or "soft" adventure, the unappealing term the travel trade uses). Not only do these cruises appeal to the same type of people, they also may appeal to the same people.

Expedition cruises don't require physical training, but participants should be in good condition and able to endure some exertion. More important, they need to be flexible in temperament as well as body. They should be good sports, keep a sense of humor, and be ready to forgo comforts occasionally. Adventure or expedition cruises take participants off the beaten path worldwide. They tend to be more expensive than mainstream cruises because fewer people share the cost and because it costs more to operate a ship in remote areas. Also, shore excursions are included, and lecturers must be accommodated in cabins that otherwise would draw revenue.

Participants tend to be strong environmentalists who expect fellow travelers to share their views. They like to be outdoors, are active, well traveled, well educated, intellectually curious, affluent, perhaps semiretired professionals age 50 or older. They belong to a museum or natural history group. They probably read *Audubon, National Geographic,* or *Smithsonian* magazine, watch public television, and support the local zoo.

Following is a representative list of companies offering adventure or expedition/educational/cultural cruises. They provide brochures, usually with deck plans of vessels they use, and descriptions of itineraries. Being specialists, they usually can answer questions with more firsthand authority than a travel agent or cruise line can.

Note: Regarding Galápagos, in an effort to prevent overcrowding at certain visitor sites, the Galápagos National Park Service has revised the itineraries of many tour boats. Check with the tour company for the latest information.

(Key: Cabins/Passengers; Officers/Crew; Vessel Length)

Abercrombie & Kent International, Inc.
(See Part Two: Cruise Lines and Their Ships.)

Explorer sails to Antarctica, the Falklands, South Georgia, and the Chilean fjords in astral summer, and offers Amazon cruises in March and April. Small boats are chartered for Galápagos cruises.

Alaska's Glacier Bay Tours & Cruises/Voyager Cruise Line
(See Part Two: Cruise Lines and Their Ships.)

American Safari Cruises
19101 36th Ave. W #201, Lynnwood, WA 98036
(888) 862-8881; (425) 776-4700; fax (425) 776-8889
www.americansafaricruises.com

Formed in 1996, American Safari Cruises offers nature-oriented adventure cruises for affluent travelers on two 120-foot small, luxury yachts: *Safari Spirit* with 6 cabins for 12 passengers and *Safari Quest* with 11 cabins for 21 passengers. Three basic Alaska itineraries offer off-the-beaten-track, close-up experiences of wildlife or scenery viewing at a leisurely pace with the pampering of a luxury cruise. In 2000, the line initiated three- and four-day fall cruises out of San Francisco to the heat of the California wine country.

All cabins on both vessels are outside and deluxe. Each is furnished with a queen bed or two twin beds (except for one cabin with one twin on *Safari Quest*), television with VCR, and private bathroom with shower or tub. Amenities include evening turndown service, terrycloth robes, and fresh flowers.

The main gathering spot is a salon furnished with comfortable couches and chairs. A self-service bar separates the dining area and salon. The salon opens onto the sports platform, where passengers can board a launch or two-passenger kayak or fish off the stern. A spiral staircase links all public decks, the library and lounge, and the bridge. A promenade circles the entire yacht. Both yachts have a top-deck hot tub for an under-the-stars spa experience.

On Alaskan itineraries, binoculars, rain jackets, and rubber boots are provided. A skilled and personable expedition leader accompanies each cruise and serves in lieu of a cruise director. A trained naturalist, the expedition leader organizes hikes, kayak explorations, and identifies wildlife enroute. In the evenings and when appropriate during the day, the expedition leader lectures on the flora, fauna, geology, and the history of the areas visited. Praised by passengers as caring, enthusiastic, and knowledgeable, the expedition leader elevates the experience from a luxury cruise to a horizon expanding voyage of discovery.

Food aboard American Safari cruises is as good as it gets on a cruise ship. Each day the chef joins the passengers to discuss the menu and to describe special dishes to be prepared. Early-bird breakfast of fresh fruit, pastries, cereal, juices, and hot beverages starts at 6 a.m. with a full service cooked-to-order breakfast available at 8 a.m. A full-course lunch is served at 1 p.m. Hors d'oeuvres are offered nightly during the cocktail hour preceding dinner at 7 p.m. Two entrees are offered each evening—usually fresh local seafood as well as chicken, lamb, or beef. Wine with meals and all other alcoholic beverages are included in the price of the cruise. The wine selection is stellar, as are the upscale labels in the well-stocked bar. Beer drinkers will love the draft beers from an Alaskan prize winning microbrewery.

The yachts travel in daytime for wildlife viewing and scenic exploration. In late afternoon, they anchor in a scenic secluded cove or bay for the night, offering further discovery on foot or by Zodiacs.

Sighting wildlife—whales, porpoises, harbor seals, black bears, brown bears, sea lions, bald eagles, cormorants, herons, sandhill cranes, oystercatchers, and gulls—is all but guaranteed. The yachts are small enough that the captain can change course immediately to approach something for closer inspection. Long Alaskan summer days allow kayaking, whale-watching by Zodiacs, and hiking until late evening.

All meals, excursions, and events on American Safari cruises are strictly informal. Jeans, khakis, and shorts, along with outdoor gear appropriate to the cruise venue and time of year, are all you need. Though the expedition leader has lots of activities on tap each day, the decision to participate is strictly yours. Hot tubbing, reading, napping, and watching movies on your cabin VCR are some of the alternatives available. Each ship also offers an aerobic exercise machine.

Three itineraries explore remote areas and small villages: an 11-day Inside Passage Explorer between Vancouver and Juneau, prices start at $3,695 per person, double; 8-day All-Alaska Adventurer cruise between Juneau to Sitka, from $4,695 per person, double; and the Southeast Alaska Discoverer, Juneau to Prince Rupert, which sails the length of Tracy Arm and follows humpback whales to their summer feeding in Frederick Sound, from May–September, from $5,195 per person, double. Prices cover shore excursions, including flight-seeing, unlimited use of kayaks, guided nature walks, fishing from the yacht, all private transfers, and open bar. Port charges and tips are extra. Both ASC vessels are also available for private charter.

Although a luxury product, American Safari cruises represent an exceptional value, offering a highly personalized and intimate private yacht experience for less than most upscale cruises of comparable length. Indeed, with early booking discounts and the inclusion of wine, liquor, and all shore excursions in the price of the cruise, American Safari cruises are among the most affordable luxury cruises afloat.

American Safari passengers are typically over 40 years old, well educated, and adventurous, individuals who revel in learning and discovery and who enjoy making new friends. As concerns the latter, life aboard an American Safari cruise is, after all, an intimate experience, one that practically insures that you will become well acquainted with your fellow passengers.

For October and November 2000, the line launched three- and four-night Wine Country cruises, departing from San Francisco and exploring the Napa Valley and Bay area. The program includes tours at private villas, exclusive dining in winery caves, and on-board wine tastings and lectures conducted by experts.

Classical Cruises (See the section in Part Two, "Other Cruise Lines and Their Ships.")

Clipper Cruises (See Part Two: Cruise Lines and Their Ships.)

Canodros, S.A.

Luis Urdaneta 1418 y Ave. del Ejercito, Guayaquil, Ecuador
011-5934-285711; fax 011-5934-287651
U.S.: (800) 327-9854; www.canodros.com

Galápagos Explorer II (50/100; Ecuadorian; 295 ft.) The luxury, all-suite ship, built in 1990 as the *Renaissance III,* sails three-, four-, and seven-night cruises weekly in the Galápagos Islands. Cruises can be combined with three or more nights at Kapawi Ecological Reserve, an unusual native Indian–owned and –operated deluxe base camp in the Amazon.

Ecuadorian-owned and operated, the ship has classic lines and interiors throughout. Cabins, all with sitting rooms, are air-conditioned and have queen or two twin beds, telephone, television for VCR use, refrigerator-bar, full-length wardrobe, marble bath, and 110-volt electric outlets. Also aboard are an outdoor pool and Jacuzzi, boutique, and doctor for minor illness or mishaps.

The elegant, nonsmoking restaurant offers one informal, open seating. International and Ecuadorian cuisine is served; special diets can be accommodated. A lunch buffet is served on deck. Staff will prepare additional dishes on request. All bar drinks—including bottled water—are complimentary; only name wines, champagne, and minibar contents cost extra. Cruise price also includes twice-daily tours escorted by naturalists.

The ship always anchors offshore, and passengers are tendered on dinghies for dry or wet landings. In keeping with the company's environmental commitment, all soaps, detergents, and shampoo used on board are biodegradable. The ship produces its own fresh water and is equipped with a sewage treatment system to minimize environmental impact. Chlorine isn't used on board. Paper and nontoxic solids are incinerated, metal cans are compacted for recycling, and nonbiodegradable trash is returned to port.

Ecomertours Nord-Sud Inc.

606 des Ardennes, Rimouski, Quebec G5L 3M3 Canada
(418) 724-6227; (888) 724-8687; fax (418) 724-2527
www.ecomertours.com

Echo des Mers (20/44; Canadian; 170 ft.) offers five-, seven-, or eight-day nature-oriented cruises of the St. Lawrence River and estuary from mid-June to mid-September. The small, expedition-style boat departs from Rimouski-East, a port 188 miles east of Quebec City, for Anticosti Island at the mouth of the St. Lawrence and the Mingan archipelago. The Mingan Islands are said to have the world's highest concentration of sea-carved limestone monoliths. Travelers view marine mammals, birds, and flora of the islands and visit villages on Quebec's lower north shore.

A seven-day eco-cruise, introduced in 1999 and planned for summer of 2000, visits the National Parks of Eastern Quebec along the St. Lawrence River to Saguenay–St. Lawrence Marine Park, the Mingan Islands National Park Reserve, and Forillon National Park in the Gaspe. A bilingual biologist-guide leads talks, discussions, and observation of whales and birds. Ecomertours is a member of Bas-Saint-Laurent Marine Mammal Ecowatch Network, Biosphere de Montreal, and Environment Canada.

Two other itineraries—one for bird-watching and the other for whale-watching—depart in July. Seabirds of the St. Lawrence concentrate on the Mingan Islands, St. Mary's Islands near Harrington Harbour, the eastern point of Anticosti Island at Gull's Cliffs, and Bonaventure Island in Gaspe.

The three-deck *Echo des Mers,* built in 1966 and refurbished in 1997, has 20 cabins fitted with a double bed or two twin beds and 2 cabins with twins that bunk four persons. Twelve cabins have private bathroom with shower; eight have shared bathroom. Two small dining rooms accommodate all passengers at one open seating. Breakfast is buffet-style, but lunch and dinner have table service. Menus offer two main courses of regional cuisine highlighting seafood bought from local fishermen. The boat has a small lounge, bar, and a lecture/reading room. Massages are available. Prices range from about $835 per person quad to about $1,520 per person double in the best accommodation. Transportation at stopovers is included. The company can arrange itineraries of two to eight days for special-interest charters, such as bird-watching, kayaking, and diving.

Ecoventura S.A. (See Galápagos Network, below.)

Esplanade Tours (See Part Three, and "Nile River Cruises.")

Fourth Dimension Tours
71-01 South West 99th Ave., Suite 106, Miami, FL 33173
(305) 279-0014; (800) 343-0020; fax (305) 273-9777
www.4thdimension.com

Santa Cruz (See Galápagos Cruises.) Six-, seven-, and ten-night programs from Miami to Ecuador, including four nights in Quito; and four- and seven-day Galápagos cruises. The company also uses *Delphin II, Corinthian, Flamingo,* and *Galápagos Explorer II.*

Galápagos Cruises c/o Adventure Associates
13150 Coit Rd., Suite 110, Dallas, TX 75240
(972) 907-0414; (800) 527-2500; fax (972) 783-1286
www.ecuadorable.com

Adventure Associates is the U.S. representative of Quito-based Metropolitan Touring, Ecuador's leading tour company and the oldest company offering Galápagos cruises. Ships are well run and have excellent naturalist-guides.

Isabela II (20/40; Ecuadorian; 166 ft.). Completely renovated in February 2000, the ship's new look includes an enlarged reception area, a redesigned library, and a new multimedia system for briefings and lectures. The mahogany-paneled dining room and library along with the bar-lounge and cabins were totally refurbished. The redesigned sun deck now has a bar, observation area for whale- and dolphin-watching, and a solarium. The ship offers satellite telephone, fax service, and, in the future, Internet access. She sails from Baltra on Tuesdays and Fridays on three-, four- and seven-night cruises of the Galápagos Islands; rates range from $1,140 to $2,660 in low season (March 16–June 14, September 1–October 31, November 21–December 20) and $1,270 to $2,955 in high season. Children under age 12 get a 50 percent discount year-round. Prices do not include Ecuador/Baltra flights or National Park entrance fee.

Santa Cruz (40/90; Ecuadorian; 230 ft.). Three-, four-, and seven-night Galápagos cruises. The ship, renovated in 1998, is one of the largest and most comfortable sailing in Galápagos waters. Food and service are good, and the ship is well run. All cabins were refitted and feature singles, doubles, or suites. The ship is carpeted and air-conditioned, with a large dining room, cocktail lounge, bar, library, Jacuzzi, and spacious decks. Three-day cruises visit the southern islands; four-day tours visit the central and northern groups. The two can be combined. Naturalist-guides, trained and licensed by Galápagos National Park, give nightly briefings on the next day's visit and accompany passengers on excursions. Groups are limited to 20 people.

Galápagos Network
76303 Blue Lagoon Dr., Suite 140, Miami, FL 33126
(305) 262-6264; (800) 633-7972; fax (305) 262-9609
www.ecoventura.com

The tour company, affiliated with a group of privately owned companies in Ecuador, offers year-round, three- to seven-night cruises in the Galápagos Islands on its fleet of small vessels. Cruises are designed for the well-educated, well-traveled, and those eager to learn about nature, ecology, and environmental issues. The boats' size allows them to visit remote islands. Naturalist-guides lecture and lead walks. Passengers are ferried to the islands by launches.

Three-night cruises visit the southern islands of Española (Hood), Floreana, and Santa Cruz. Four-night trips visit the central and northern islands of Bartolome, Plazas, Santiago (James), Tower, and Santa Cruz. All vessels depart from San Cristóbal island and can be chartered. Passengers can snorkel year-round and scuba dive on designated cruises. Pre- and postcruise packages in Ecuador are available.

Corinthian (24/48; Ecuadorian; 195 ft.). Built in the United States, the vessel has a spacious dining room, three bars, large television, library, Jacuzzi, and sun deck. Cabins are air-conditioned and have private bathrooms. Ship departs every Monday and Thursday.

Eric, Flamingo, Letty (10/20; Ecuadorian; 83 ft.). Built in 1993, *Letty* is the newest of three luxury yachts. All are air-conditioned. Cabins have private bathrooms, VCR, and stereo equipment. *Letty* departs on Monday and Thursday; the others depart on Tuesdays and Fridays. At least four hours per day are spent on each island. The boats are well suited for families or groups. New seven-night itineraries include the western islands of Fernandina and Isabela, as well as Española, Tower, Santa Cruz, Bartolome, South Plaza, Floreana, Santa Fe, and Santiago. In addition, passengers lunch at a ranch on Santa Cruz.

Galápagos Yacht Cruises c/o Galápagos, Inc.
7800 Red Rd., Suite 112, South Miami, FL 33143
(305) 665-0841; (800) 327-9854; fax (305) 661-1457

Cruz del Sur, Dorado, Estrella del Mar (6–8/12–16; Ecuadorian; 75–80 ft.). Small boats sail from San Cristóbal, *Dorado* sails from Baltra with stops at the main Galápagos islands and others where larger ships don't go.

Yolita (6/12; Ecuadorian; 17 ft.). Three-, four-, and seven-night cruises from San Cristóbal to Islas Lobos, Española, Punta Suarez, Gardener, Darwin Station, North Seymour, Baltra, Bachas, Rabida, Puerto Egas, Bartolome, Sullivan, Islas Plazas, Santa Fe, and Santa Cruz.

Global Quest (formerly OdessAmerica)
50 Glen St., Suite 206, Glen Cove, NY 11542
(516) 676-4500; (800) 221-3254; fax (516) 676-4820
(516) 747-8880; fax (516) 747-8367
www.globalquesttravel.com

Ambassador I (53/86; Ecuadorian; 296 ft.) has 40 outside cabins, 13 inside cabins, and is air-conditioned. It has a lounge, library, pool, lido bar, and single-seating dining room where American and continental cuisine with Ecuadorian specialties is served. The ship sails on three-, four-, and seven-night cruises year-round from Baltra to the Galápagos Islands and visits Española, Santa Cruz, Bartolome, Isabela, Santiago, and Floreana islands. Visitors go ashore in 20-foot boats carrying 20 people, including 2 crew members and a guide. Passengers may wade ashore. Twelve-day cruises include stayovers in Quito, Ecuador.

Eclipse (48; Ecuadorian; 210 ft.). Built in 1998, the boat has a swimming pool, library/video room, shop, bar and observation deck. Sails on seven-day itinerary in the Galápagos.

Royal Star (111/200; German; 472 ft.). Most cabins are outside, with air-conditioning, bathroom with shower, and phone. Some triples and quads available. One dining room with two seatings; cuisine is international with local specialties. Safari/cruise packages include 4–8 days to Kenya and 16–23-day cruise/land tour from Mombasa to Zanzibar and Mahe in the Seychelles.

Skorpios I, II, III (74–130; Chilean; 215–230 ft.). Built between 1988 and 1995 to U.S. standards, the ships have all outside cabins with television; one or two dining rooms and lounges, depending on the ship; and an open bar. From September to May, they sail six-day cruises combined with land packages of southern Chile between Puerto Montt to the San Rafael Lagoon—a total of 800 miles through channels, fjords, and archipelagos. Remote villages, Ice-Age glaciers, and the historic city of Castro are highlights.

Terra Australis (62/108; Chilean; 213 ft.). U.S. built, this ship is classified under the strict safety rules of the American Bureau of Shipping. She has large, all outside cabins with air-conditioning and heat, radio, telephone, and private bathroom; library, lounge, and bar; and a dining room serving good food accompanied by Chilean wines. She sails from October to April on 7- and 12-day cruises from Punta Arenas through the Strait of Magellan and Chile's inland waterways, visiting Beagle Channel, Puerto Williams, and Ushuaia, Argentina, the southernmost town in the world.

International Expeditions, Inc.
One Environs Park, Helena, AL 35080
(800) 633-4734; fax (205) 428-1714
www.ietravel.com

Eric, Flamingo, Letty, Corinthian, Galápagos Islands Cruises. (See Galápagos Network, above.)

Kleintours
Avenue Shyris 1000, Quito, Ecuador
(888) 50-KLEIN; tel/fax (305) 444-2940
www.kleintours.com.ec

Two small vessels, *Coral I* and *Coral II* (20- and 22-passenger capacity). Three-, four-, and seven-day cruises are available. Three-day cruises depart on Monday; four-day cruises, Thursday. Three-night cruise start at $763 in low season (May, June, September) and $895 in high season.

Lifelong Learning
101 Columbia Ste. 150, Aliso Viejo, CA 92656
(949) 362-2900

The tour company offers cultural and adventure cruises for a well-traveled clientele on either part or full charter of well-known ships, such as Hapag-Lloyd's *Hanseatic* and Radisson Seven Seas' *Song of Flower,* to exotic destinations around the globe, on itineraries often designed by the company. The voyages are accompanied by lecturers who are experts on the regions visited and usually include several days touring in the departure city. Examples for 2001 on the *Hanseatic* are a 14-day cruise to Namibia and South Africa, departing March 7, beginning with 4 days in Namibia, rounding the Cape of Good Horn, and ending in Durban, South Africa. Prices start at $8,975, including internal air transport, all shore excursions, port charges, and gratuities. Airfare from the United States is additional. The next leg, a 20-day voyage, spends 3 nights in Capetown before departing from Durban and visits Madagascar and the Seychelles.

Lindblad Expeditions

720 Fifth Ave., New York, NY 10019
(212) 765-7740; (800) 397-3348; fax (212) 265-3770
www.expeditions.com

The globe-roaming, four-ship company was founded by Sven-Olof Lindblad, son of the late Lars-Eric Lindblad, who pioneered modern expedition cruising. In 1969 he launched the *Lindblad Explorer,* designed to take travelers to remote areas in comfort and safety. Lindblad Expeditions describes its mission as "providing travelers with a more thoughtful way to see the world, avoiding crowded destinations, and seeking out natural ones." A wide selection of light adventure cruises in various parts of the world are offered.

Caledonian Star (68/110; Scandinavian/International; 293 ft.) offers off-the-beaten-track cruises through Europe and Asia. In late October–November, she sails from Turkey to Aqaba; from December–March, in South America and Antarctica; and in April and May, the Red Sea and Mediterranean. From May to August, she cruises from Lisbon to Dartmouth, England, around the British Isles, along the Norwegian fjords to Spitsbergen. Afterward, the ship offers a combination of Scotland and the Baltic to St. Petersburg, returning to Amsterdam.

Polaris (41/80; Swedish/Filipino and Swedish; 238 ft.) offers Galápagos cruises year-round. Ten-day land and sea itineraries are accompanied by outstanding naturalists, such as Dr. Lynn Fowler, who has conducted wildlife research in the area for 20 years.

Sea Bird, Sea Lion (36/70; American; 152 ft.). Four–15-day cruises of Alaska's Inside Passage; Columbia and Snake Rivers to Hells Canyon, Idaho; San Juan Islands; and an annual cruise to Baja California and the Sea of Cortés timed for optimum whale-watching.

The company occasionally charters other ships and operates cruises for universities or groups.

Marine Expeditions
890 Yonge St., Third Floor, Toronto, Ontario, Canada M4W 3P4
(416) 964-9069; (800) 263-9147; fax (416) 964-2366
www.marineex.com

The company, founded in 1992, has a fleet of three Russian expedition vessels with "ice capability." The moderately priced expeditions are designed for well-traveled passengers with a sense of adventure. From November to March, the ships, which are also sold in the United States through Global Quest, offer 8- and 10-night Antarctic expedition cruises; 14-night, Antarctica and Falklands; and 18-night, adding South Georgia. The ships' small size enables them to cruise waters inaccessible to large vessels. Zodiacs carry passengers close to wildlife and natural wonders where the ships cannot go. All expeditions are accompanied by experts who lecture and may guide.

Marine Adventurer (Akademik Ioffe) and *Marine Voyager (Akademik Segei Vavilov)* (40/80; Russian/North American; 384 ft.). Expedition cruises visit Antarctica and the Falklands during winter, with 8–18 nights aboard ship.

Marine Discovery (Alla Tarasova) (50/120; Russian/North American; 328 ft.). November–March: Chile, Antarctica, and the Falklands; April: 7- or 12-night Amazon cruise; June–September: 6–11 nights Great Britain, Iceland, Greenland, and Newfoundland; also 7 nights to the Arctic.

Melanesian Tourist Services Limited
Coastwatchers Avenue, P.O. Box 707, Madang, 511 Papua New Guinea
(310) 785-0370; fax (310) 785-0314
www.meltours.com

Melanesian Discoverer (21/35–54; New Guinean; 117 ft.). Four- and five-night cruises on the Sepik River, five-night cruises to Irian Jaya, and seven-night cruises of Melanesian islands, including the Trobriands, Rabaul, and Kavieng.

Metropolitan Touring (See Galápagos Cruises, above.)

Orient Lines (See Part Two: Cruise Lines and Their Ships.)

Quark Expeditions
980 Post Rd., Darien, CT 06820
(203) 656-0499; (800) 356-5699; fax (203) 655-6623
www.quark-expeditions.com

The tour company, a pioneer in Arctic and Antarctic expedition cruises, handles a group of Russian-built ships, all with Russian officers and crew. They're accompanied by an expedition leader, assistant expedition leader, lecturers, and Zodiac pilots who may be from the United States, Europe, or South America, depending on destinations and their expertise. Antarctica departures include a combination of Antarctic Peninsula, Weddell Sea, South Georgia, Falkland Islands, Chilean fjords, Ross Sea, New Zealand, and Australian subantarctic islands. Some depart from Cape Town. Some ships sail around the Arctic Circle and to the North Pole. Quark Expeditions publishes excellent brochures describing the itineraries; deck plans are included.

Professor Multinovsky (49/28; Russian; 226 ft.) has a lounge, bar, library, lecture room, two dining rooms, sauna, gift shop, and infirmary. November–March, Antarctic Peninsula, South Shetlands, South Georgia, and the Falklands round-trip to Ushuaia. June–August, British Isles, Faroes, Hebrides, Iceland, Greenland, Baffin, and Hudson Bay.

Akademik Sergei Vavilov (40/80; Russian; 384 ft.). The ship has a lounge, bar, library, lecture room, dining room, sauna, gift shop, and infirmary. November–March, Antarctic Peninsula, South Shetlands, South Georgia, and the Falklands round-trip to Ushuaia.

Kapitan Dranitysn (53/102; Russian/Russian and European; 437 ft.) has a lounge, bar, library, dining room, lecture room, gift shop, infirmary, gym, sauna, pool, and two helicopters. From July to September the icebreaker circumnavigates the Arctic, starting and ending in Murmansk. The voyage can be taken in one of four segments: Greenland, from Lonyearbyen, Norway, to Sondre Stromfjord; High Arctic, Sondre Stromfjord to Resolute; Northwest Passage, Resolute to Provideniya; and Northeast Passage, Provideniya to Lonyearbyen. Voyages to the Antarctic Peninsula, Weddell Sea, and South Atlantic Islands from November through February.

Kapitan Khlebnikov (61/108; Russian; 402 ft.). Antarctic icebreaker. Same itinerary as *Kapitan Dranitysn,* above.

Yamal (56/106; Russian; 500 ft.). One of the world's most powerful icebreakers, the ship has a lounge, bar, library, gift shop, infirmary, dining room, lecture room, gym, sauna, pool, and two helicopters. She departs on 15-day expeditions round-trip from Murmansk to the geographic North Pole. Optional excursions beneath Polar Ice Cap aboard "Mir" Deep-Sea submersibles are available.

Society Expeditions
2001 Western Ave., Suite 300, Seattle, WA 98121
(206) 728-9400; (800) 548-8669; fax (206) 728-2301
www.societyexpeditions.com

After the line's ship, *World Discoverer,* had to be scuttled following an accident in the Solomon Islands in spring 2000, Society Expeditions purchased another expedition ship in summer 2000 and expects to continue offering its roster of exotic, nature-oriented worldwide cruises

The new ship, also to be named *World Discoverer*, is a 12-year-old vessel holding 160 passengers. All cabins are outside with the standard ones starting at an unusual 200 square feet in size and ranging up to 396 square feet for each of the ten largest suites. There are also 8 veranda suites. The ice-hardened vessel will sail with the same staff that was on the previous ship.

Traditionally, Society Expeditions cruises, ranging from 6 to 21 days, are accompanied by experts who give daily shipboard lectures and act as guides. The line plans to start its new season in November with Antarctica cruises, followed (as in the past) with South America, French Polynesia, Society and Easter Islands, Fiji, and Papua New Guinea; and in the summer, cruises to Alaska and the Bering Strait, Russian Far East, and above the Arctic Circle.

Southern Heritage Expeditions

6033 West Century Blvd., No. 1270, Los Angeles, CA 90045
(310) 338-1538; (800) 421-3326; fax (310) 215-9705
www.heritage-expeditions.com

Akademik Shokaskiy (20/46; Russian; 236 ft.), built for research, is an ice-strengthened vessel suited for cruising the subantarctic islands of New Zealand and Australia, and the Antarctic. She carries Zodiac-type landing craft. The dining room serves international cuisine and doubles as a lecture room with television and VCR. Also available are a library/card room, bar, sauna, and doctor. Cruises depart November–February from New Zealand's southernmost town, Invercargill, on six itineraries.

Svalbard Polar Travel (EuroCruises)

303 West 13th St., New York, NY 10014
(212) 691-2099; (800) 688-3876; fax (212) 366-4747

Brand (40/60; Norwegian; 175 ft.) entered service in 1998 and cruises the arctic Spitsbergen northwest coast on five-day itineraries.

Polarstar (10/25; Norwegian; 152 ft.). Built in 1948, the small ice-breaker offers an unusual eight-day expedition to the northernmost parts of Norway's North Pole archipelago, which can be reached only by an expedition ship. Cabins for two and three people; each cabin has a basin; showers and bath facilities are communal. Late June–mid-August, she departs Saturdays from Tromso, Norway. Weather and ice conditions determine route and landing sites.

Temptress Adventure Cruises

6100 Hollywood Blvd., Suite 202, Hollywood, FL 33024
(305) 643-4040; (800) 336-8423; fax (305) 643-6438
www.temptresscruises.com

Adventure cruises of Costa Rica, Belize, and Panama combine natural history and light adventure. Snorkeling, diving, kayaking, sportfishing, and water skiing are available. Trained counselors lead children's programs.

Temptress Voyager (33/63; Costa Rican; 174 ft.) has all outside cabins with private bathroom and air-conditioning. She sails on five- and seven-night Belize and Guatemala cruises departing from Belize City and seven-day Panama cruises.

Temptress Explorer (50/99; Costa Rican; 185 ft.) cruises in Costa Rica on five- and seven-day itineraries that can be combined. Cabins are outside with private bath and air-conditioning. Built in Seattle for this route, the ship is designed for navigation of rivers and bays but has the stability of a heavier vessel.

Voyager Cruise Line (See Alaska's Glacier Bay Tours & Cruises in Part Two: Cruise Lines and Their Ships.)

Wilderness Travel
1102 Ninth St., Berkeley, CA 94710
(510) 558-2488; (800) 368-2794; fax (510) 558-2489
www.wildernesstravel.com

The adventure tour company offers Galápagos programs almost year-round, some with up to three departures monthly. They combine cruises on small yachts with hiking in areas not usually covered by conventional excursions. The company also has a combination of the Galápagos and Upper Amazon River. Solar eclipse cruises in Zimbabwe are offered, the next in 2001.

Norwegian Coastal Cruises and Other Cruise Ferries

The craggy coast of Norway, deeply indented like the fingers on your hand, was carved eons ago by massive glaciers. Crevices, which we call fjords, can be ten miles long. From their dark, mirrorlike waters rise almost vertical cliffs, and awesome mountains climb to several thousand feet on each side.

Often at the head of fjords are snow-capped peaks. In some places, glaciers inch toward the North Sea. Along the shores are lilliputian fishing villages and isolated farmhouses. Farther up the mountains are lodges where hikers bed down in summer and Olympic hopefuls fine-tune their skiing in winter.

The setting is beautiful; late May through early autumn are ideal for cruising. Most major lines with ships in Europe offer Norwegian fjord cruises. Each itinerary differs slightly, but the program is essentially the same: departing from Copenhagen, Oslo, or Bergen and going as far north as Trondheim, Norway's original capital and third-largest city, or Tromso, the largest town north of the Arctic Circle. Others continue to the North Cape, the northernmost point in Europe, and to Spitsbergen, a group of islands studded with massive glaciers. Another way to cruise the coast—the way Norwegians do—is on the Norwegian Coastal Express.

NORWEGIAN COASTAL VOYAGE*

Eleven working passenger-cargo ships, known as the *Hurtigruten* ("fast route" in Norwegian), operate a daily passenger and cargo service from Bergen to 35 ports on Norway's coast, well beyond the North Cape to Kirkenes, near the Russian border.

A Norwegian institution since 1893, the ships operate year-round through all weather and are a lifeline for the people in small, often isolated communities along the way. The vessels are transportation for locals and haul cargo ranging from automobiles and farm equipment to frozen fish.

The ships also carry tourists who may board and disembark at any port. Many visitors, however, take the 2,500-mile round-trip voyage as a 12-day cruise. Others sail one-way and return by road or air. (*Note:* Some open-water passages can be rough; passengers should come prepared.)

Time in port varies from as little as 15 minutes to several hours. There are shore excursions (about $20–40) at a few ports and more costly trips that leave the ship in one port, travel inland, and rejoin it in another.

The best time to make the trip is mid-May to July, the period with 24

*The remainder of this chapter was written by Theodore W. Scull.

hours of daylight. Some travelers prefer the quieter months of spring and fall. Summer sailings fill quickly, although space is often available at short notice. During the off-season, cabins are plentiful.

In the height of summer, some stretches are crowded with deck passengers, especially between the mainland and islands. Generally, about half of the passengers are local commuters, the balance an international mix. There are usually many English-speaking people. Announcements are made in the languages required by passenger makeup. Meals are served at two seatings when traffic warrants. Breakfast and lunch are buffet-style. Dinner is from a set menu; tables are reserved. Dietary requests should be made when booking. Continental and Norwegian dishes are served. Lunch offers the widest selection of hot and cold foods. Because of hefty taxes, alcoholic beverages are expensive—$6 for a beer is common. Entertainment is limited to the gorgeous scenery, enlivened by commentary, good conversation, cargo handling, and the festive occasion of crossing the Arctic Circle. The line provides an excellent guidebook. In summer, the newest ships might have a band for dancing.

Norwegian Coastal Voyages/Bergen Line markets the service in North America. The service has 11 ships in 3 classifications: new, mid-generation, and traditional.

New Ships

The *Kong Harald, Nordkapp, Nordlys, Nordnorge, Polarlys,* and *Richard With,* all completed since 1993, add to the *Hurtigruten* the concept of the cruise ferry with its greater comfort (well established and popular in Baltic waters). Large and boxy (390 feet long and 63 feet wide), the ships take as many as 490 passengers in relatively roomy accommodations. Cargo is handled via ramps.

The modern cabins are mostly outside. They have foldaway beds and two lower berths, audio channels, automated wake-up calls, tiled baths with showers, and hair dryers.

Public rooms have the fashionable look of modern cruise ships, with rich fabrics, thick carpets, and ample use of brass, glass, and veneers. A top-deck, wraparound observation lounge contains a cocktail lounge/bar. A middle deck offers a cocktail lounge, library/card room, conference rooms, souvenir shop, playroom, video arcade, 24-hour cafeteria, 240-seat restaurant, and private dining room. Also aboard are a sauna, small gym, and passenger laundry.

Mid-Generation Ships

The *Midnatsol, Narvik,* and *Vesteraalen,* built in 1982–83, carry up to 320 passengers. Cabins are smaller and plainer, but most are outside and all have private bathrooms with showers. The ships' have a forward-facing observation lounge and glass-enclosed top-deck lounge. Freight and vehicles are handled via roll-on ramps.

Traditional Ships

Harald Jarl and *Lofoten,* built in 1960 and 1964, respectively, have 169 and 223 berths in very small outside and inside cabins, some without private facilities. The best cabins sell fast.

Cargo and vehicles are loaded by crane. The ships possess rich character and have paneled lounges, lovely decorative features, and teak decks. Their hulls are battered from thousands of dockings.

Both have two forward-facing lounges; the upper is nonsmoking. The restaurant spans the ship's width. A cafeteria and lounge are used mainly by short-run passengers.

One other traditional ship, the 179-passenger *Nordstjernen* (built in 1956), offers eight-day summer cruises from Tromso to Spitsbergen and the North Cape.

On the Coastal Express

Billed as the World's Most Beautiful Voyage, especially when the weather cooperates, the Coastal Express offers relaxed and informal adventure. Aboard the *Harald Jarl,* the feeling is that of a small country hotel. On the first morning at sea, a sheer mountain wall plunges into the narrow channel, and, to port, Norwegian Sea breakers pile up against low-lying islands.

At a briefing, the courier reminds everyone that this is a working ship and that local passengers will be boarding and leaving at each port. The diesel engine throbs rhythmically in the background. At Bodo, a city at the northern end of Norway's main rail line, about 100 passengers board for the six-hour crossing to the Lofoten Islands. A crane swings aboard an automobile, whole fish, bundles of evergreen saplings, and building materials.

During brief port calls, you can walk briskly to the main shopping street to buy souvenirs and newspapers. On a recent trip, during the stop at Harstad, passengers attended a short worship service in a fortress church. There are visits to the North Cape promontory, an excursion from Kirkenes (turnaround port) to the Russian border, and a cruise into the Trollfjord, a one-mile passage between vertical rock cliffs bubbling with falling water. The new moon reflects in the turning basin as the captain revolves his ship in a tight half circle. (*Seabourn Pride* is among the few regular cruise ships small enough to make this maneuver.) By voyage's end, round-trip passengers have shared a 2,500-mile feast of dramatic scenery, shore visits, fresh food, and constantly changing weather.

EUROPEAN CRUISE FERRIES

Cruise ferry is an inadequate term for a sophisticated breed of ship that takes passengers on overnight sea voyages but provides most of the comforts and amenities of a deluxe liner. Still, that's the name. And cars, recreational vehicles, and large trucks are indeed below deck.

Operating throughout northern Europe, the ferries crisscross the Baltic and North Seas, linking cities such as Copenhagen and Oslo, Stockholm and Helsinki, Newcastle and Bergen. Creative train-ferry itineraries often include the Eurail pass network. Most passengers are Scandinavians (Danish, Finnish, Norwegian, Swedish), are traveling to visit Scandinavian friends and relations, or are simply cruising. Germans are the second most numerous among passengers. North Sea sailing attracts Britons.

Larger, newer ships offer varied restaurants. Options include quality à la carte dining, a 60-item smorgasbord, and simpler (cheaper) cafeteria meals. The *Silja Europa* has a McDonald's. After-dinner entertainment includes cabarets, dancing, gambling, and films. There are children's playrooms, video arcades, saunas, and duty-free shopping (purchases roll to check-out in supermarket carts). English is widely spoken.

Cabins vary from well-appointed rooms with windows and cruise-ship amenities to large family cabins with private showers. Most accommodations are away from activity and noise of public rooms.

The following lines are represented in North America. They offer the most extensive routes and some of the newest and most sophisticated ships. However, they're only a sampling of a wider network spanning all European seas, including the Mediterranean. Most major intercity services are year-round. Ships occasionally may change routes or be sold.

Color Line

Norwegian-based Color Line offers North Sea sailings between Bergen and Stavanger, Norway, and Newcastle, England; between Oslo, Norway, and Kiel, Germany; and between Oslo or Kristiansand, Norway, and Hirtshals in northern Denmark. In 1997, several fast, short sea routes opened between the northern Danish port of Skagen and southern Norwegian ports of Larvik and Moss.

The largest and most impressive of its ships are the *Kronprins Harald* and the *Princesse Ragnhild* on the Oslo–Kiel route, which leaves daily from either port for the 20-hour overnight run. The ships enter and leave Oslo via the scenic Oslofjord (a two-hour stretch). Most passengers are German or Norwegian.

The Fleet	Built/Renovated	Tonnage	Passengers
Christian IV	1982	15,064	2,000
Color Festival	1986/1992	34,314	1,937
Kronprins Harald	1987	31,914	1,432
Peter Wessel	1981/1988	29,704	2,180
Princesse Ragnhild	1981/1992	38,500	1,875
Silvia Ana	1996	7,505	1,200
Skagen	1975/1982	12,333	1,238

Sailings from Newcastle connect two to three times weekly in Bergen with Norwegian Coastal Express evening northbound departures.

Scandinavian Seaways (DFDS)

Danish-owned Scandinavian Seaways (DFDS) operates cruise ferries between England and Denmark; England and Sweden; England and Germany; England and the Netherlands; Denmark and Sweden; and Denmark and Norway.

The Fleet	Built/Renovated	Tonnage	Passengers
Admiral of Scandinavia	1976	18,888	1,032
Crown of Scandinavia	1994	35,498	2,026
Dana Anglia	1978	14,000	1,235
King of Scandinavia	1975/1988	15,800	1,175
Prince of Scandinavia	1975	15,794	1,525
Princess of Scandinavia	1975	15,794	1,525
Queen of Scandinavia	1981	25,941	1,535

The largest ships operate between Copenhagen and Oslo, with scenic departures from both cities at 5 p.m. and arrival about 9 the next morning. The northbound route from Copenhagen passes Hamlet's Castle at Helsingor, calls at Helsingborg (Sweden), and enters the Oslofjord at dawn. Two-night round-trip cruises are popular from Oslo and Copenhagen. They give passengers time ashore between the morning arrival and late-afternoon departure. The Copenhagen pier is adjacent to the central business district, and the Oslo pier is a short bus ride from the city's center.

DFDS departs year-round from Harwich, England, reached by boat train from London. It has three year-round overnight services to Esbjerg on the Danish west coast, with connecting boat train service to Copenhagen, Gothenburg (Sweden), and Hamburg, from where trains connect to all of Germany. Seasonal sailings operate from Newcastle to Gothenburg, Hamburg, and Amsterdam.

Silja Line

Operating the world's largest cruise ferries, Silja Line is the best-known Scandinavian ferry company. The ships are cities at sea; some carry as many as 3,000 passengers.

The Fleet	Built/Renovated	Tonnage	Passengers
Finnjet	1977	25,908	1,602
Silja Europa	1993	59,914	3,000
Silja Festival	1986/1992	34,414	1,740
Silja Scandinavia	1992	35,285	2,400
Silja Serenade	1990	58,376	2,700
Silja Symphony	1991	58,376	2,700
SuperSeaCat IV	2000	n.a.	752
Wasa Queen	1975/1992	16,546	1,400

Though busy, they're designed to avert crowding and long queues. Cruise ship–style atriums are the centerpiece; nearby are eateries, lounges, and bars for all incomes. The prestige route is Stockholm to Helsinki. A ship leaves each port at 6 p.m. every night year-round (the sun shines until 10 p.m. or later in summer, this being the Land of the Midnight Sun) and arrives the next day at 8:30 a.m. The two-hour passage through the Stockholm archipelago is a highlight; to enjoy the entire transit, be up about 6:30 a.m. The ship docks conveniently next to central Helsinki; passengers on the two-night round-trip have the day ashore. Extended stopovers are easily arranged. Arrival in Stockholm is equally convenient.

The overnight Stockholm to Turku, Finland, route is offered daily. A companion daylight service takes about 11 hours.

The fastest single-hull ship in northern Europe is the gas turbine *Finnjet,* whose 23-hour summer schedule between Helsinki and Rostock, Germany, calls for speeds of 30 knots. In the off-season, the ship operates a more relaxed schedule.

In April 2000, the line introduced the even faster *SuperSeaCat IV* on Baltic service between Helsinki, Finland, and Tallinn, Estonia. The new $30 million ship cruises at 37.8 knots and takes 1.5 hours to make the crossing. The 328-foot monohull carried 752 passengers, 164 cars, and 4 motorcoaches. Facilities include a bar and cafeteria, 50-seat business-class lounge, shop, and observation area.

Viking Line

The red-hulled ships of Viking Line, Silja Line's main competitor, cruise similar routes. The Stockholm-to-Turku daylight voyage calls at Marie-hamn in the beautiful Åland Islands, about halfway between Sweden and Finland. The Stockholm–Helsinki route may be taken as two-night round-trip cruises that include two dinners and two breakfasts.

The Fleet	Built/Renovated	Tonnage	Passengers
Amorella	1988	34,384	2,112
Cinderella	1989	46,398	2,500
Gabriella	1992	35,150	2,420
Isabella	1989	34,384	2,112
Mariella	1985	37,799	2,500
Rosella	1986	10,757	750

INFORMATION AND RESERVATIONS

Norwegian Coastal Voyages/ Bergen Line
405 Park Ave., New York, NY 10022
319-1300; (800) 323-7436; fax (212) 319-1390
www.bergenline.com

DFDS Seaways (USA) Inc.
Cypress Creek Business Park, 6555 NW 9th Ave., No. 207
Ft. Lauderdale, FL 33309
(800) 533-3755; fax (954) 491-7958
www.seaeurope.com; www.europeonsale.com

Nordic Saga Tours (for Color Line)
4215 21st Ave. West, Seattle, WA 98199
(800) 848-6449; 206-301-9129; fax. 206-301-9087
www.nordicsaga.com
The tour operator also represents Scandinavian Seaways, Fjord Line, and other European cruise ferries.

Borton Overseas (for Viking Line)
5412 Lyndale Ave. South, Minneapolis, MN 55419
822-4640; (800) 843-0602; fax. (612) 822-4755
www.bortonoverseas.com

Freighters

The following information was adapted with permission from "Setting Sail by Freighter," by Dave G. Houser and Rankin Harvey, published as a special issue of *Cruises & Tours* magazine.

INTRODUCTION TO FREIGHTER TRAVEL

Freighter travel may be the least understood segment of the cruise industry. You don't read or hear much about it, and cargo lines that offer passenger service rarely advertise in the mainstream media. Many travel agents lack experience and expertise in booking freighter cruises.

Freighters roam the globe, visiting famous and exotic ports. They offer a carefree, informal environment conducive to total relaxation, and they cost much less than conventional cruise ships.

Before the post–World War II boom in air travel and cruises, freighters were a significant mode of international travel. Expanding air routes, lower fares, and the growth of the cruise industry gradually relegated freighter travel to a minor niche in the cruise market.

Cargo lines have recognized a revival of interest. Some have introduced combined container and passenger vessels that can accommodate larger numbers of passengers. About 100 traditional freighters, which carry 4–12 passengers, are in service. Most are enjoying brisk bookings and operate at capacity during peak seasons.

FREIGHTERS: DEFINING THE BREED

What exactly is a freighter? First, let's say what it is not. A modern freighter isn't a rusty tramp steamer sailing on a mission of intrigue or romance as popularized in movies and novels. The vast majority of cargo vessels today are less than 20 years old. Trim and handsome, they're loaded with sophisticated navigation and communication equipment. Most are containerized, that is, their freight is carried in large metal containers resembling boxcars systematically stacked below and above decks.

The International Conventions and Conferences on Marine Safety defines the passenger-carrying freighter as a vessel principally engaged in transporting goods that is licensed to carry a maximum of 12 passengers. Those licensed to carry more than 12 are defined as combination cargo-passenger ships. The latter must meet stricter safety standards and carry more staff, including a doctor. They also have the advantage of gaining preferred docking privileges over ordinary freighters.

Nowadays, nearly all cargo ships run on fixed schedules along established routes. The exceptions are in so-called tramp service. Tramps don't sail regular routes or schedules and can be hired to haul almost anything, anywhere, anytime. A few take passengers.

Why People Choose Freighters

Traveling by freighter offers a rare opportunity to truly get away from it all. There are no crowds, no planned activities, no lines, no dress code, and no hoopla. The atmosphere aboard a freighter is relaxed and unstructured. Passengers can be as active or as lazy as they choose.

Freighters are for travelers who want to see the world on their own terms and at their own pace. Most are veteran travelers who have become bored or disillusioned with conventional tours, cruises, and popular vacation destinations. Their sense of adventure and yearning for discovery demand something different. A glance at freighter itineraries reveals ports that would be impractical or prohibitively expensive to visit any other way.

Freighter travelers recognize good value, and, on a per diem basis, there's no better travel value than freighters. With careful research and planning, you can roam the world for months aboard a freighter for about $100 per day.

Some people are attracted by the camaraderie they enjoy with fellow passengers. Sailing with usually no more than a dozen like-minded, well-informed veteran travelers in a low-key, relaxing atmosphere is their ideal travel environment and often leads to lasting friendships.

Is Freighter Travel for You?

Judging from the high rate of repeat bookings, once a freighter traveler, always a freighter traveler. If you haven't tried it but you've read this far, you may be a good candidate.

You must have plenty of time. Most folks just can't get away for a 30-, 60-, or 90-day voyage. For that reason alone, the majority of freighter travelers are retirees, teachers and professors, self-employed professionals, and occasionally an artist or writer. Common characteristics include an extensive travel background, love of the sea, preference for independent travel, and abhorrence of hoopla.

Wherever on this planet your imagination might roam, chances are you can go there on a freighter. Some more exotic and popular routes (round-trip from the United States) include: East Africa from the Gulf Coast (60–70 days), East or West Coast to New Zealand/Australia (45–75 days), around the world from Los Angeles (84 days), Marquesas Islands from Tahiti (16 days), Mediterranean from East or Gulf Coast (33–70 days), and South America from East or Gulf Coast (44–52 days).

Accommodations and Facilities

The majority of cargoliners have spacious, comfortable accommodations equal to and often better than those aboard cruise ships. Normally they're in a multistory superstructure at the stern. Cabins have showers and sometimes bathtubs. In most cases they're air-conditioned and tastefully furnished. Often, they have taped music, service phones, VCRs, minifridges, and picture windows rather than portholes.

Comfy, smartly decorated lounges invite card games, conversation, and evening cocktails. Most vessels have large-screen televisions and an extensive library of videotapes. Many cargoliners have small swimming pools, exercise rooms, and saunas for officer and passenger use, and plenty of deck space for walking.

An open bridge policy seems to prevail among freighters; you're welcome to watch officers and crew in action except during critical maneuvers, such as docking. On most freighters, in fact, passengers are free to go almost anywhere they please.

Pampering is not part of the program. Basic services are handled by a small contingent of stewards who usually double as cabin boys and waiters. A washer and dryer are generally available for passenger use. Phone and fax services are always available in emergencies, but policies on casual use vary.

Ships carrying more than 12 passengers have a doctor on board and generally have a small hospital or treatment center. But medical services aboard freighters carrying 12 or fewer passengers are limited. All, however, carry basic medical supplies, and someone aboard will be trained in first aid. In case of serious illness, the captain will contact the nearest ship or shore station with a doctor available for advice. In a grave emergency, the victim will be transferred to a ship with appropriate medical facilities or be put ashore at the nearest port. Costs incurred in medical evacuation and treatment are the passenger's responsibility.

In view of this, you're advised to take out travel health insurance with medical evacuation coverage and to carry more than enough of any medications you require.

Dining and Food

Every freighter has a comfortable dining room shared by officers and passengers. Dining is the day's special event and an opportunity to socialize. Most officers are congenial, eager to please, and happy to share their knowledge of the ship, the sea, and the world. Most freighter food is of good restaurant quality, well-prepared, and plentiful. Menus often feature the national cuisine of the ship's and/or officers' origin.

Breakfast and lunch are usually buffet-style, whereas dinners are served at tables, often in four or five courses. Coffee and tea are available anytime, and between-meal snacks are provided. Beer, wine, and liquor is available on most ships. It may be necessary for you to BYOB.

PLANNING YOUR FREIGHTER VOYAGE

The majority of freighters book up early, especially for peak summer months. Start early yourself—six months or more—to get your choice of ship and routing; a year ahead is not unusual on popular voyages.

Planning, booking, and confirming your voyage can take much longer than you imagined. Depending on itinerary, you may have to obtain travel documents, such as visas, make arrangements concerning your home or business, get physical checkup, and decide on trip and travel health insurance options.

First, consult a current issue of *Ford's Freighter Travel Guide* (19448 Londelius St., Northridge, CA 91324; phone (818) 701-7414), a comprehensive, twice-yearly guide listing almost all passenger-carrying freighter itineraries. Your local university library may have a copy. A subscription costs $24 (plus $1.98 sales tax for California residents). Single copies are $15.95.

As a smart second step, join TravLtips Cruise and Freighter Association (P.O. Box 580188, Flushing, NY 11358; (800) 872-8584; membership costs $20 per year per couple or $35 for two years). You'll connect with this loose-knit group of 28,000 freighter and offbeat-cruising buffs and receive bimonthly issues of *TravLtips,* the association magazine; periodic issues of *Roam the World by Freighter,* which includes members' reports of voyages; access to the association's travel planning and reservation services; and member-only invitations on special and unusual cruises. TravLtips and California-based Freighter World Cruises (180 S. Lake Ave., No. 335, Pasadena, CA 91101; (626) 449-3106) can help you select a vessel or voyage and book it, plus handle air and other travel arrangements.

Many cargo lines are represented by similar specialized agents. These services can be a real blessing, particularly to first-timers, because booking passage on a freighter is not quick and easy.

You need lead time. Because freighter schedules are prone to change, some lines require waitlisting (no charge) until firm schedules are released. Only then will waiting passengers be given an option on a cabin. A deposit—usually 10–20 percent—is required only after a cabin option is accepted. Final payment is usually due 45–60 days before sailing.

During the months before sailing, the departure date may shift a few days and the routing may change. (For example, you may be going to Wellington rather than Auckland.) This proves the value of having an experienced agent to keep you informed of changes and to help deal with them and your need for flexibility in schedule and attitude.

Every freighter company has its own policies affecting passengers. Most have literature outlining these policies and describing their ships and itineraries. Obtain such materials through your travel agent or directly from the line, and read all thoroughly—including the fine print. Pay particular attention to the company's cancellation policy, and take it into account when you consider trip cancellation insurance.

Some lines offer single cabins; others charge a single supplement, usually less than 50 percent.

Because freighters are working vessels, most lines won't accept preteen children for passage. Those that do usually charge the adult fare for children. Pets aren't permitted.

Fewer than 40 nations require U.S. citizens to carry visas, but those that do include Australia and Brazil—countries frequented by passenger-carrying freighters.

Your Health

Cargo lines require passengers age 65 or older to present a certificate of good health from their doctor before booking can be completed. Review your itinerary with your physician regarding risk of disease or infection and any immunizations or protective medicines needed. Up-to-the-minute immunization recommendations are available from the Centers for Disease Control's 24-hour fax hotline in Atlanta: (888) 232-3299. You'll need a touchtone phone and fax machine to receive faxed messages. You may also check for information on the CDC Web site at www.cdc.gov/travelershealth.

Clothing and Essentials

Packing for a 90-day freighter voyage should be no different from selecting gear and garments for a 10-day trip. Nor should it weigh more; cargo lines, unlike cruise lines, aren't obligated to provide baggage service. Don't bring more than you can handle.

Casual attire is the rule. It's possible there might be a special occasion calling for dressier clothes, or that restaurants ashore may require them. For every day, bring low-heeled, nonskid, rubber-soled shoes. They're essential for safe maneuvering aboard ship in rough seas. Be prepared for about any kind of climate. Light wraps (even in the tropics) and rain gear are essential.

Foul weather is almost a certainty during any long voyage, and many freighter veterans pack a lightweight, two-piece rain suit (parka and pants), and rubber boots. They also are handy for wading through the dust and residue that cakes bulk-loading docks. Bring binoculars, reading material (don't overdo; most ships have extensive libraries), washcloths, and facial tissue.

Electrical current on most foreign-flagged freighters is 220/250 AC. You'll need a voltage converter and plug adapter to use your appliances. Funds for shipboard expenses should be in U.S. currency. Traveler's cheques are generally accepted, but very few lines take credit cards or personal checks.

Most lines say they have no policy on tipping. A few say their stewards who serve passengers get extra pay and suggest that tipping be reserved for exceptional or special service. The norm seems to be $1.50 per person per day to the room steward and an equal amount to the dining steward.

Smoking is allowed on nearly all freighters because many officers and crew members smoke. A few lines bar smoking in dining rooms. The majority of officers and crew who smoke are courteous around nonsmoking guests, and most passengers say smoking isn't a big problem.

Freighter Travel Agents

The following is a sampling of freighter lines and routes. For more information, call the following agencies to request brochures of complete offerings.

Freighter World Cruises
180 South Lake Ave., Suite 335, Pasadena, CA 91101
(626) 449-3106; fax (626) 449-9573
www.freighterworld.com

TravLtips
163-07 Depot Rd., P.O. Box 580188, Flushing, NY 11358
(718) 939-2400; (800) 872-8584; fax (718) 939-2047
www.travltips.com

FREIGHTER TRAVEL DIRECTORY

The following directory is in two parts. The first provides information on nine cargo lines, their vessels departing from North American ports, and their booking contacts (addresses/phone are listed at the section's end). The asterisk indicates that the agent can arrange ancillary requirements, including air transportation (in some cases, air/sea package), hotel, transfers, hiring a car, sight-seeing, and travel insurance. The second part, Freighter Routing Directory, is organized by departure ports and gives a line's voyage duration and price range. Itineraries are available from cargo lines and sources cited previously. Information is subject to change.

Bank Line

Two ships (registry: Isle of Man; officers and crew: British/Bangladeshi), on tramp itineraries from Philadelphia, PA, between ports in Southeast Asia, via the Panama Canal, or to Europe and Indonesia via Suez and Singapore, returning to Philadelphia via the Panama Canal.

Agent: Freighter World Cruises.*

Clydebank (built 1974) and *Forthbank* (built 1973) each carry nine passengers. One owner's cabin, three double cabins, one single cabin.

Blue Star Line

Five ships (registry: Bahamas; officers and crew: British/Filipino), regular service from U.S. ports to Australia and New Zealand.

Agent: TravLtips.*

American Star, Melbourne Star, Queensland Star, and *Sidney Star* (built 1972) each carry ten passengers in four double and two single cabins. *Columbia Star* (built 1980) carries 12 passengers in ten cabins (sold double or single occupancy). All ships have cabins with bath and shower (some also have tub), passenger laundry, pantry, bar/lounge, television/VCR, library, and some exercise equipment. *Columbia Star* also has an exercise room. Age limit: 79 (medical certificate required).

Chilean Line

Two ships (registry: Liberia; officers and crew: Indian/Chilean) cruising between the U.S. Gulf Coast and the East Coast of South America.

Agent: Freighter World Cruises.*

Lircay, Laja (built 1978) each carry 12 passengers in four double and four single cabins. All have private bath and shower. Both ships have a lounge with television/VCR. Age limit: 82.

Columbus Line

Six ships (ownership: German; registry: Liberia; officers and crew: German), regular service from Los Angeles, CA, and Savannah, GA, to Australia and New Zealand.

Agent: Freighter World Cruises.*

Columbus America, Columbus Australia, and *Columbus Canada* (built 1971) each carry 12 passengers in three double and six single cabins.

Columbus Victoria, Columbus Queensland, and *Columbus California* (built 1978) carry eight passengers in four double cabins.

All vessels have larger than ordinary cabins with view windows, private bath/shower, and refrigerator. Large, nicely furnished lounge, library, bar, swimming pool, deck chairs. Age limit: 79.

DSR (Deutsche Seereederei Rostock)

Six ships (registry: Germany; officers and crew: German), regular service from New York to the Orient.

Agent: Freighter World Cruises.*

Pacific Senator, Patmos Senator, DSR Atlantic, Palermo Senator, Choyang Elite, and *DSR America* (built 1992). Six to eight passengers carried in nice double, single, and owner's cabins. All have bath, shower, refrigerator. Ship has lounge with radio, television and VCR, tape deck, sauna, swimming pool. Age limit: 79.

Ivaran Lines

Two container ships (registry: Bahamas; officers and crew: Norwegian/International), regular service from U.S. Gulf Coast to South America.

Agent: Ivaran Agencies.*

Americana (built 1988) carries 80 passengers in 2 suites, 20 double cabins, 8 outside and 10 inside singles. All have bath and shower, television and VCR, minibar, refrigerator, telephone, and safe. Ship has lounge with dance floor, cocktail bars, minicasino, library, hair stylist, sauna, pool, health club, and hospital. Light entertainment. No age limit.

San Antonio (built 1994) carries 12 passengers in three double and six single cabins. All have bath and shower, television/VCR, and refrigerator. Ship has lounge, sun deck, and swimming pool. Age limit: 79.

Leonhardt & Blumberg

Two ships (registry: Germany; officers and crew: German/South Sea islanders from Kiribati Islands), service between the U.S. East Coast and U.S. West Coast via Far East and Suez Canal.

Agent: Freighter World Cruises.*

Dagmar Maersk and *Doerthe Maersk* (built 1996) carry three passengers in one double and one single cabin. All have private bath and shower. Vessel has a lounge, elevator, and pool. Age Limit: 80.

Martime Reederei

One ship (registry: Cyprus; officers and crew: German), regular service from U.S. West Coast to Australia and Fiji.

Agent: Freighter World Cruises.*

Cielo di Los Angeles (built 1994) carries six passengers in one double twin and two double cabins. All have refrigerators and private bath and shower. Ship is fully air-conditioned and offers a self-serve laundry, lounge/bar, exercise room, sauna, and pool. Age limit: 79.

Mineral Shipping

Three ships (registry: Singapore; officers and crew: Croatian); one ship (registry: Bahamas; officers and crew: Croatian) in regular service from Savannah, GA, and on tramp itineraries in Mediterranean and sometimes to Brazil and Venezuela.

Agent: Freighter World Cruises.*

Christiane (built 1982) carries 12 passengers in nice accommodations with bath and shower. On the *Patty,* four single cabins adjoin in pairs with shared bathroom. Each vessel has a lounge with television/VCR; all but *Patty* have pools. Age limit: 82.

NSB (Niederelbe Schiffahrtsgesellschaft Buxtehude)

Sixteen ships (registry: Liberia; officers and crew: German/Filipino), four in around-the-world service from Long Beach, CA; seven in around-the-world service from Charleston, SC; four in service between the U.S. East Coast and U.S. West Coast via Far East and Suez Canal; one in service from Los Angeles, CA, to New Zealand and Australia.

Agent: Freighter World Cruises.*

IBN Sina, California Senator, London Senator, and *Hong Kong Senator* (built 1994) carry eight passengers in three double suites and two single cabins, all with private bath and shower. Ships have lounge, laundry, sauna, fitness room, indoor pool, and outdoor pool. Age limit: 79.

Contship Germany (built 1992); *Contship France* (1993); *Contship Singapore, Contship Ticino, Contship Lavagna, Contship Italy* (all 1994); and *Contship Europe* (1995). Each carries ten passengers in one owner's suite and four double cabins, all with private bath and shower. Ships have lounge, laundry, exercise room, sauna, and indoor pool. Age limit: 79.

Sea-Land Endeavour, Sea-Land Initiative, and *Sea-Land Mistral* (built 1996) carry eight passengers in four suites, each with refrigerator and private bath and shower. All offer a lounge, laundry, exercise room, and sauna. Age limit: 79.

Direct Currawong (built 1990) carries ten passengers in one owner's cabin and four double cabins, each with private bath and shower. Ship has lounge, laundry, exercise room, sauna, and indoor swimming pool. Age limit: 79.

Projex Line

One ship (registry: Germany; officers and crew: German and Polish/ Filipino), service from the U.S. West Coast to Mediterranean via Panama Canal.

Agent: Freighter World Cruises.*

Mel Europe (built 1997) carries eight passengers in four double cabins with sitting area, refrigerator, and private bath and shower. Ship has lounge, laundry, game room, exercise room, and pool. Age limit: 79.

Schlüter Line

One ship (registry: Cyprus; officers and crew: German/Filipino), service from Long Beach, CA, to Far East.

Agent: Freighter World Cruises.*

Choyang Phoenix (built 1996) carries four passengers in two double cabins. Each has separate sitting area, television/VCR, refrigerator, and private bath and shower. Vessel has lounge, exercise room, and indoor pool. Age limit: 79.

FREIGHTER ROUTING DIRECTORY

Routings are listed by destination from North American ports. Prices are per person per day and reflect the starting rates for *high season* travel. Off-season travel is often less expensive. The term *Southern ports* refers to those that embark into the Caribbean Sea.

Around the World

NSB Vessels depart from Eastern ports for West Indies, South Pacific, Southern Asia, Middle East, Mediterranean, and Western Europe. Voyages are 100–105 days. Rates start at $90 per day, per person, double occupancy; $115 per day, single. Plus $293 per person port taxes, insurance, and customs fees. Rates vary by ship.

Leonhardt & Blumberg Daily rates start at $100 per person, double occupancy; $110, single. Add $306 per person port taxes, insurance, and customs fees.

Westbound: Vessels depart West Coast for Orient, Far East, South Pacific, Mediterranean, Atlantic Canada, return to East Coast ports.

Eastbound: Vessels depart Eastern ports for Mediterranean, Middle East, Far East, return to West Coast ports.

Australia, New Zealand, Far East, Pacific, and Orient

Bank Line Vessels depart from East Coast for South Pacific, return to East Coast. One-way segments available. Double- and single-occupancy rates start at $95.

Blue Star Line One-way segments and "Fly-Sail" packages available. Rates start at $82 per day, per person, double occupancy; $97, single.

East Coast Service: Embark from Eastern ports for New Zealand and Australia, return to East Coast.

West Coast Service: Depart from Los Angeles for South Pacific, New Zealand, and Australia, return by same route.

Columbus Line   One-way segments and air/sea packages available. Rates begin at $105 per day, per person, double occupancy; $125, single.

East Coast Service: Depart from East Coast and Southern ports for New Zealand, Australia, and Caribbean, return to East Coast.

West Coast Service: Embark from West Coast for New Zealand, Australia, and South Pacific, return to West Coast.

DSR   Vessels depart from West Coast for Orient and Far East, return to West Coast. Daily rates start at $105 per person, double occupancy, $112, single. Add $213 for taxes, fees, and insurance.

NSB   Depart from West Coast for New Zealand and Australia, return to West Coast. Daily per person, double-occupancy rates start at $85; single, $100. Add $293 taxes, insurance, and fees.

Schlüter Line   Offers segments of routes, with per diem adjustments in fare, but passengers must maintain themselves ashore.

"Orient Express": Vessels depart from East Coast for Mediterranean, Middle East, South Pacific, Far East, and Orient, and return along similar route to East Coast ports. Double- and single-occupancy rates start at $85 per person, per day.

West Coast Service: Departs West Coast for Orient, Far East, and South Pacific, returns to West Coast. Double-occupancy rates start at $105 per person, per day; $121, single. Add $263 port taxes, insurance, and fees.

Central and South America, and the Caribbean

Chilean Line   Vessels depart Southern ports for Central and South America, return to Southern ports. Daily rates start at $100 per person, double occupancy; $110, single.

Ivaran Lines   Segments often available.

Caribbean and Central America: Departs Southern ports to Central America and Caribbean, returns to Southern ports, often on shorter itinerary (three weeks). Rates start at $160 per person, per day.

South America: Ships depart Southern ports to South America. Rates begin at $135 per person, per day, single or double.

Leonhardt & Blumberg   Ships depart East Coast for South America, return to East Coast. Prices begin at $90 per person, per day, double occupancy; $100, single. Add $213 for taxes, insurance, and customs.

Maritime Reederei   Round trips from both East and West coasts to South America. Daily rates begin at $100 per person, double occupancy; $110, single. Rates vary by ship. Add $263 taxes and insurance.

Africa

Bank Line   Ships depart from East Coast to Western Africa, South Africa, South America, Caribbean, return to East Coast. Not all listed ports will be called each sailing. Rates start at $110 per person, per day, double occupancy; $121, single.

Mediterranean

Projex Line   Ships depart West Coast for Caribbean and Mediterranean and return to West Coast. Daily rates begin at $100 per person, per day, double occupancy; $110, single.

Northern Europe

Mineral Shipping   Vessels depart East Coast, travel to northern Europe, sometimes Mediterranean, return to different East Coast port. One-way, round-trip available. Daily rates begin at $80 per person for single or double occupancy. Round-trip passengers must deposit $1,000 for emergency repatriation.

Note to Readers

Because of space limitations, we have included only freighters departing from U.S. ports. However, many others depart from ports in other countries.

Sailing Ships

Another group of ships offers a totally different cruise experience, combining a casual atmosphere and congenial company in the most romantic of all sea adventures: sailing under canvas. These ships range from an eight-passenger catamaran to windjammers that sail the coast of Maine and through the Caribbean. Three lines with sailing vessels—Club Med, Star Clippers, and Windstar—are included with mainstream companies in Part Two: Cruise Lines and Their Ships. In two cases, their product is a hybrid; with all three, it's a more sophisticated product than that offered by the traditional sailing vessels listed below.

(Key: Cabins/Passengers; Officers/Crew; Vessel Length)

Club Med (See Part Two: Cruise Lines and Their Ships.)

Coastal Cruises
P. O. Box 798, Camden, ME 04843
(207) 785-5670; (800) 992-2218
www.schoonermaryday.com
Mary Day (15/29; American; 90 ft.), a two-masted schooner, sails on four- and six-day cruises along the Maine coast, June–October.

Compagnie des Isles du Ponant
c/o Tauck Tours, 276 Post Rd., Westport, CT 06880
(203) 226-6911; (800) 788-7885; fax (203) 454-3081
www.tauck.com
Le Ponant (32/60; French/European; 289 ft.), a luxury yacht like *Wind Star,* is under charter by Tauck Tours, which offers cruises in the Caribbean in winter, including the Panama Canal, and Costa Rica and the Mediterranean in summer, usually sold in a land/sea package. The four-masted vessel's size allows entry into less visited ports and bays.

Dirigo Cruises
39 Waterside Ln., Clinton, CT 06413
Tel/fax (860) 669-7068
The company has 16 sailing ships, which are found in Europe, the British Isles, Maritimes of Nova Scotia, Caribbean, Galápagos, New Zealand, Tonga, and other South Seas islands.
Cuan Law, Lammer Law (9/18; American/American and Chilean; 105 ft.), two of the world's largest trimarans, sail six-night itineraries in the British Virgin Islands from Tortola (*Cuan Law*), and seven-night tours of the Galápagos Islands from San Cristóbal (*Lammer Law*).
Harvey Gamage (12/27; American; 95 ft.). Seven-day winter cruises from

St. Thomas to the United States and British Virgin Islands. In summer, three-night cruises between Bath, Maine, and Boston.

Regina Chatarina (8/22; British; 105 ft.), a two-masted lugger (schooner), sails from the Virgin Islands to Grenada on week-long Caribbean cruises. In summer, Canadian maritime voyages.

Soren Larson (9/18; British; 105 ft.), a two-masted brigadine, sails 3- to 33-day itineraries ranging from Panama, Miami, Halifax, Amsterdam, London, and Dartmouth.

Maine Windjammer Association
P.O. Box 1144P, Blue Hill, Maine 04614
(800) 807-WIND
www.sailmainecoast.com

Formed in 1977, the Maine Windjammer Association is made up of 13 privately owned and operated traditional tall ships that once belonged to commercial fleets. They delivered everything from fish and granite to coal and Christmas trees along U.S. coasts. The two- and three-masted schooners range from 64 to 132 feet long. Eight are National Historic Landmarks, some older than 100 years.

The windjammers offer three- to six-day cruises from mid-May to October, departing Rockland, Rockport, and Camden in Maine. With more than 3,000 islands, the Maine coast is one of the best and most beautiful sailing areas anywhere. Ships sail by day, about 10 a.m. to 3 p.m., and anchor each night at a deserted inlet or quiet port or village where passengers can go ashore. Passengers may participate in all aspects of sailing, from hoisting sails and taking the wheel to helping in the galley.

Meals are served family-style and include fresh seafood, roasts, garden salads, chowder, and homemade breads and desserts. A lobster bake on an island is featured on every six-day trip and most three-day cruises. Accommodations are simple: single, double, or triple cabins with comfortable mattresses, fresh linens, and plenty of blankets. Vessels provide running water and hot showers. Shipboard life is relaxed and informal.

Each windjammer carries 20–44 passengers and a crew of 4–10. Cruises are ideal family vacations, appropriate for all ages. (Check with individual captains regarding children. The minimum age for most is 12 or 14 years; however, *Isaac H. Evans* accepts children as young as 8 years old.) Some windjammers have theme cruises. The tall ships gather annually for an all-day race in which passengers can participate.

Cruise cost is about $115–130 per person, per day. Charter rates are available. All vessels undergo rigorous U.S. Coast Guard inspections and carry ship-to-shore radios and electronic navigational devices.

Air transportation is available to departure ports via Portland International Jetport, with limousine service to the Rockland/Camden area. Commuter air service is available from Boston, and buses run from Boston and Portland. All vessels offer free parking.

Member vessels are *American Eagle, Angelique, Grace Bailey, Heritage, Isaac H. Evans, J&E Riggin, Lewis R. French, Mary Day, Mercantile, Nathaniel Bowditch, Stephen Taber, Timberwind,* and *Victory Chimes.* The association provides descriptive brochures.

Peter Deilmann Cruises

1800 Diagonal Rd., Suite 170, Alexandria, VA 22314
(703) 549-1741; fax (703) 549-7924

Lili Marleen (25/50; German/European; 249 ft.), launched in 1994, is a re-creation of a nineteenth-century three-masted barquentine, a sailing vessel with one square-rigged mast and two gaff- or schooner-rigged masts. The ship has a lounge decorated with polished hardwoods and nautical paintings. The restaurant accommodates all passengers at one seating; cuisine is international with local specialties. There are three bars and a small library.

Lili Marleen has 25 twin outside cabins (2 standard, 20 superior, and 3 deluxe, which measure 108 square feet). They're decorated with burled wall finishes and pastel fabrics and have a sofa bed (convertible to double bed), upper Pullman berth, large wardrobe, safe, table and chair, sideboard, radio, and international dial phone. The tiled bathroom has a shower, hair dryer, and bathrobes. Laundry service and fax and telex are available. The ship sails on 7–12-day Canary Islands cruises, 7-, 9-, and 10-day Eastern and Western Mediterranean cruises, and a Persian Gulf cruise from Abu Dubai to Sharjah and Muscat.

Sea Cloud Cruises, Inc.

32-40 North Dean St., Englewood, NJ 07631
(201) 227-9404; (888) 732-2568; fax (201) 227-9424
www.seacloud.com

Sea Cloud (34/69; International; 360 ft.), one of the world's most luxurious sailing ships, was built as a wedding present by financier E. F. Hutton for his bride, Marjorie Merriweather Post. The ship has 34 air-conditioned cabins with phone, safe, hair dryer, and bathrobes. The elegant dining room accommodates all passengers at one seating; complimentary wines are served at lunch and dinner. A library and boutique are available.

The four-masted barque sails on different itineraries year-round. She plies the Eastern Caribbean in winter and the Mediterranean during the remainder of the year and is marketed by several U.S. companies. The same company owns the luxurious *River Cloud,* which sails European rivers (see "River and Barge Cruises in Europe").

Sea Cloud II (48/96; International; 384 ft.). The legendary *Sea Cloud* will get a mate in April 2001. The $40 million vessel is conventionally rigged with three masts (rather than *Sea Cloud*'s four), and her more than 3,000 square yards of sail are manually operated. Modern with the highest safety standards, the vessel is traditional in appearance and offers opulent 1930s decor. Forty-eight luxurious cabins range from 130 to 236 square feet; two owner's suites each contain 300 square feet. Large deck areas and a swimming platform provide plentiful outside space. The ship has a bar, library with panoramic views, restaurant with large windows, sauna, and gymnasium.

Her all-weather cruising ability sets her apart from *Sea Cloud,* which is generally restricted to sunny climes. *Sea Cloud II* is expected to cruise the North Sea and Baltic in summer, the Mediterranean in autumn, and South America in winter.

Star Clippers, Inc. (See Part Two: Cruise Lines and Their Ships.)

Victory Chimes
P.O. Box 1401, Rockland, ME 04841
(207) 265-5651; (800) 745-5651
www.victorychimes.com
Victory Chimes (18/40; American; 170 ft.), a three-masted schooner, is the largest windjammer under the U.S. flag. From June to September, she sails three- and six-day cruises along the 3,478-mile coast of Maine. In the early part of the 20th century, the ship hauled cargo up the Atlantic Coast. Although she has been refurbished, she looks the same as she did almost a century ago. She has all outside cabins, some for two and others for four, with opening portholes, bunk beds, and hot and cold water.

Windjammer Barefoot Cruises
1759 Bay Rd., P.O. Box 190120, Miami Beach, FL 33119
(305) 672-6453; (800) 327-2601; fax (305) 674-1219
www.windjammer.com
For sailors ages 7–70 with good sea legs and a Captain Mitty spirit, Windjammer Barefoot Cruises offers a chance to stand watch at the wheel or climb the mast and live out your fantasies. The line has a fleet of famous tall ships, including those once owned by Aristotle Onassis, the duke of Westminster, and financier E. F. Hutton. Most cabins have bunk beds, private facilities, and steward service. Itineraries are super, including the Grenadines (often called the world's most beautiful sailing waters) and less visited destinations in the Eastern and Southern Caribbean. Most cruises are six days; some have different southbound and northbound legs that can be combined.

Amazing Grace (96 passengers; British/West Indian; 234 ft.) is the fleet's only freighter. She offers 13-day cruises between Freeport, Bahamas, and Grenada.

Flying Cloud (33/66; British/West Indian; 208 ft.), built in France in 1935, offers a honeymoon suite paneled with stained-glass windows. Teak decks, rosewood-paneled benches, and a charthouse give the look of an old privateer. Couples can marry aboard *Flying Cloud;* the package includes cabin, champagne, flowers, wedding certificate, souvenir photograph, and a 50 percent anniversary discount.

Six-day Caribbean cruises depart from Tortola to some of the following (depends on wind): Salt Island, Virgin Gorda, Beef Island, Green Cay, Sandy Cay, Norman Island, Deadman's Bay, Cooper Island, Jost Van Dyke, and Peter Island.

Legacy (61/122; American/West Indian; 294 ft.), built in 1959, was a meteorological research and exploration vessel for the French government. She was acquired by Windjammer in 1989, stripped to her hull, and converted into a four-masted tall ship, debuting in 1998.

The well-designed vessel has her original portholes, wide stairways, hand-carved South American wood, and custom interiors. All cabins are air-conditioned and have private bathrooms with showers. They're simply decorated and have wooden wardrobes, full-length mirrors, and either bunk, double, or twin beds (some have sofa beds). The most luxurious cabin, Burke's Berth, has a platform double bed, entertainment center, bar, and picture windows.

The top deck, with its large bar, local bands, and hermit crab races, is action central. The captain gives a morning briefing here on the day's activities.

Meals are family-style in the dining room, which is air-conditioned. A small lounge contains the only television and VCR, along with books and games. *Legacy* is Windjammer's only ship to offer Junior Jammers Kids Club, a summer program of chaperoned activities for children age six and older.

Legacy departs every Monday from San Juan on alternating six-day itineraries, calling at Culebra, St. Croix, St. John, St. Thomas, and Jost Van Dyke; or Culebra, St. Croix, Virgin Gorda (Spanish Town and Leverick Bay), St. John, and Vieques (a nighttime call for kayaking in the phosphorescent bay).

Mandalay (72 passengers; British/West Indian; 236 ft.) is queen of the fleet. Formerly the yacht of financier E. F. Hutton and an oceanographic research vessel of Columbia University, she has three masts and 22,000 square feet of sail. Under Hutton's ownership, she was considered the world's most luxurious private yacht. When she retired in 1981 from Columbia, nearly half the existing knowledge of the ocean floor had been gathered by the ship.

Mandalay offers 6-day cruises from Grenada to Puerto la Cruz, plus 13-day cruises from Grenada to Antigua and other excursions to the Windward and Leeward Islands.

Polynesia (52/126; British/West Indian; 248 ft.), a legendary fishing schooner, has been featured in articles in *National Geographic* magazine and television productions.

She was added to the Windjammer fleet in 1975 after extensive remodeling. Twelve deck cabins, 40 regular cabins, and 2 admiral suites, all double occupancy, were constructed. All have private bathrooms and showers, wood paneling, and tile floors. Three bachelor quarters, each accommodating six, were built for people traveling alone or with their families. New plumbing, air-conditioning, and a teak deck were installed. The curved stern contains a specially designed dining salon with large tables, each depicting an island on *Polynesia*'s itinerary. The mascot parrot oversees the ship's slot machine.

Probably the most popular Windjammer ship, *Polynesia* offers monthly singles' cruises, as well as other theme cruises. She sails six-day Caribbean itineraries from St. Maarten to St. Barts, St. Kitts, Saba, Nevis, Prickly Pear, Anguilla, and Montserrat, depending on wind.

Yankee Clipper (65 passengers; British/West Indian; 197 ft.). In 1927, German industrialist Alfred Krupp built the ship as the *Cressida,* probably the world's only armor-plated private yacht.

Adolf Hitler was aboard during World War II to award the Iron Cross to a U-boat commander. She was confiscated as a war prize and commandeered by the U.S. Coast Guard. After the war, she was acquired by the wealthy Vanderbilt family, renamed *Pioneer,* and sailed off the West Coast. Joining Windjammer's fleet in 1965, she was rechristened *Yankee Clipper.* Extensive remodeling gave her a third mast, continuous upper deck, and cabins with private bathrooms and showers. She's one of the fastest tall ships.

Yankee Clipper offers six-day Caribbean cruises, leaving Grenada for Petit St. Vincent, Bequia, Mayreau, Palm Island, Union Island, Young Island, or Carriacou.

Windstar Cruises (See Part Two: Cruise Lines and Their Ships.)

Zeus Tours and Cruises
551 Fifth Ave., Suite 1001, New York, NY 10176
(212) 221-0006; (800) 447-5667; fax (212) 764-7912
www.zeustours.com

The Zeus Group, which marked its 50th year of operation in 1998, offers eastern Mediterranean and South American cruises in its own and chartered vessels. *Zeus I–III* (24/48; Greek/European and American; 174 ft.) sail on seven-day Mediterranean itineraries in summer. The group also offers 12-day Greek Isles cruises aboard the sail-cruiser *Galileo Sun*. The yacht has a bar-lounge and 18 air-conditioned cabins with private bath and telephone. Windsurfing, snorkeling, and fishing equipment are available.

Cruise Ships Index

(Key: A/Adventure; E/Europe; EC/European Cruise Ferries; F/Freighter;
G/Galápagos; GR/Greek Islands; M/Mainstream;
NC/Norwegian Coastals; O/Others; R/River; SS/Sailing Ship)

Ship	Cruise Line	Type	Page
Actief	Abercrombie & Kent	R	579
Admiral of Scandinavia	Scandinavian Seaways (DFDS)	EC	621
Adventurer of the Seas	Royal Caribbean International	M	485
Akademik Ioffe	(see *Marine Adventurer*)	A	613
Akademik Segei Vavilov	(see *Marine Voyager*)/	A	613, 614
	Quark Expeditions		
Akademik Shokalskiy	Southern Heritage	A	615
Alla Tarasova	(see *Marine Discovery*)	A	613
Alouette	Abercromie & Kent	R	579
Amadeus I, II	Global Quest	R	585
Amazing Grace	Windjammer Barefoot Cruises	SS	640
Amazon Clipper	Explorers Travel Group L.L.C./	R	600, 601
	Fourth Dimension Tours/Ladatco		
Amazon Explorer	Explorers Travel Group L.L.C.	R	600
Ambassador I	Global Quest	A/G	610
American Eagle	Maine Windjammer Assoc.	SS	638
American Queen	Delta Queen Steamboat	R	315
	Company		
American Star	Blue Star Line	F	630
Americana	Ivaran Lines	F	631
Amorella	Viking Line	EC	623
Amsterdam	Holland America Line	M	350
Anacoluthe	Abercrombie & Kent	R	579
Angeline	Maine Windjammer Assoc.	SS	638

Ship	Cruise Line	Type	Page
Anjodi	European Waterways/ Barge France	R	583
Anni	Misr Travel	R	597
Anton Chekhov	Reiseburo Mittelthurgau (EuroCruises)/Global Quest	R	585
Arca	Explorers Travel Group L.L.C./ Tara	R	600, 602
Arcadia	P&O Cruises	M	403
Arlène	Reiseburo Mittelthurgau (EuroCruises)/KD River Cruises of Europe	R	582, 586
Aton	Misr Travel	R	597
Aurora	P&O Cruises	M	405
Austria	KD River Cruises of Europe	R	586
Azur	First European Cruises	E	567
Big Red Boat I (Oceanic)	Premier Cruises	M	417
Big Red Boat II (Edinburgh Castle)	Premier Cruises	M	420
Big Red Boat III (Island Breeze)	Premier Cruises	M	421
Black Prince	Fred Olsen Lines (EuroCruises)	E	566
Black Watch	Fred Olsen Lines (EuroCruises)	E	566
Brand	Svalbard Polar Travel (EuroCruises)	A	615
Britannia	KD River Cruises of Europe	R	586
Caledonian Star	Lindblad Expeditions	A	612
California Senator	NSB	F	632
Callisto	Classical Cruises	R/O	563
Canadian Empress	St. Lawrence Cruise Lines	R	598
Cape Cod Light	Delta Queen Steamboat Company	R	319
Cape May Light	Delta Queen Steamboat Company	R	319
Caprice	Abercrombie & Kent	R	579
Carnival Destiny	Carnival Cruise Lines	M	178
Carnival Legend	Carnival Cruise Lines	M	183
Carnival Pride	Carnival Cruise Lines	M	183
Carnival Spirit	Carnival Cruise Lines	M	183
Carnival Triumph	Carnival Cruise Lines	M	178

Ship	Cruise Line	Type	Page
Carnival Victory	Carnival Cruise Lines	M	178
Caronia	Cunard	M	301
Celebration	Carnival Cruise Lines	M	175
Century	Celebrity Cruises	M	195
Cézanne	Abercrombie & Kent/ Provence Line (EuroCruises)	R	579, 581
Champillon	Misr Travel	R	597
Chanterelle	Abercrombie & Kent	R	579
Chardonnay	Abercrombie & Kent	R	579
Choyang Elite	DSR	F	631
Choyang Phoenix	Schlüter Line	F	633
Christian IV	Color Line	EC	621
Christiane	Mineral Shipping	F	632
Cielo di Los Angeles	Martime Reederei	F	631
Cinderella	Viking Line	EC	623
Clara Schumann	KD River Cruises of Europe	R	586
Clelia II	Classical Cruises	A	564
Clipper Adventurer	Clipper Cruise Line	M	212
Clipper Odyssey	Clipper Cruise Line	M	214
Club Med 2	Club Med	SS	222
Clydebank	Bank Line	F	630
Color Festival	Color Line	EC	621
Columbia Queen	Delta Queen Steamboat Company	R	318
Columbia Star	Blue Star Line	F	630
Columbus America	Columbus Line	F	630
Columbus Australia	Columbus Line	F	630
Columbus California	Columbus Line	F	630
Columbus Canada	Columbus Line	F	630
Columbus Queensland	Columbus Line	F	630
Columbus Victoria	Columbus Line	F	630
Contship Europe	NSB	F	632
Contship France	NSB	F	632
Contship Germany	NSB	F	632
Contship Italy	NSB	F	632
Contship Lavagna	NSB	F	632
Contship Singapore	NSB	F	632
Contship Ticino	NSB	F	632
Corinthian	Galápagos Network	A/G	609
CostaAllegra	Costa Cruise Lines	M	249

Ship	Cruise Line	Type	Page
CostaAtlantica	Costa Cruise Lines	M	256
CostaClassica	Costa Cruise Lines	M	244
CostaMarina	Costa Cruise Lines	M	249
CostaRiviera	Costa Cruise Lines	EC	257
CostaRomantica	Costa Cruise Lines	M	244
CostaVictoria	Costa Cruise Lines	M	252
Crown Dynasty	Commodore Cruise Line	M	262
Crown Odyssey	Orient Lines	M	391
Crown of Scandinavia	Scandinavian Seaways (DFDS)	EC	621
Crown Princess	Princess Cruises	M	434
Cruz del Sur	Galápagos Yacht Cruises	A/G	610
Crystal Harmony	Crystal Cruises	M	285
Crystal Symphony	Crystal Cruises	M	285
Cuan Law	Dirigo Cruises	SS	636
Dagmar Maersk	Leonhardt & Blumberg	F	631
Dana Anglia	Scandinavian Seaways (DFDS)	EC	621
Danube Princess	Peter Deilmann Cruises	R	582
Dawn Princess	Princess Cruises	M	440
Delphin Queen	Delphin Cruises (EuroCruises)	R	580
Delta Queen	Delta Queen Steamboat Company	R	310
Deltastar	Global Quest	R	585
Desafio	Marco Polo	R	602
Deutchland	Peter Deilmann Cruises	M	571
Deutschland	KD River Cruises of Europe	R	586
Direct Currawong	NSB	F	632
Disney Magic	Disney Cruise Line	M	326
Disney Wonder	Disney Cruise Line	M	326
Doerthe Maersk	Leonhardt & Blumberg	F	631
Dolphin IV	Cape Canaveral Cruise Line	M	562
Dorado	Galápagos Yacht Cruises	A/G	610
Dresden	Peter Deilmann Cruises	R	582
DSR America	DSR	F	631
DSR Atlantic	DSR	F	631
East King	Abercrombie & Kent	R	590
East Queen	Abercrombie & Kent	R	590
Echo des Mers	Ecomertours Nord-Sud	A	607
Eclipse	Global Quest	G	610
Ecstasy	Carnival Cruise Lines	M	167
Elation	Carnival Cruise Lines	M	167

Ship	Cruise Line	Type	Page
Enchanted Capri	Commodore Cruise Line	M	235
Enchanted Isle	Commodore Cruise Line	M	231
Enchantment of the Seas	Royal Caribbean International	M	481
Eric	Galápagos Network	A/G	610
Esprit	French Country Waterways	R	584
Estrella del Mar	Galápagos Yacht Cruises	A/G	610
Etoile de Champagne	Etoile de Champagne	R	580
Eugenie	Misr Travel	R	596
Executive Explorer	Alaska's Glacier Bay Tours and Cruises	A	130
Explorer	Abercrombie & Kent	M/A/R	118, 600, 604
Explorer of the Seas	Royal Caribbean International	M	485
Fantasy	Carnival Cruise Lines	M	167
Fascination	Carnival Cruise Lines	M	167
Finnjet	Silja Line	EC	622
Flamenco	First European Cruises	M	567
Flamingo	Galápagos Network	A/G	609
Fleur de Lys	Abercrombie & Kent	R	579
Flying Cloud	Windjammer Barefoot Cruises	SS	640
Forthbank	Bank Line	F	630
Gabriela	Viking Line	EC	623
Galápagos Explorer II	Canodros	G	607
Galaxy	Celebrity Cruises	M	195
Galileo Sun	Zeus Tours and Cruises	SS	642
Golden Princess	Princess Cruises	M	445
Grace Bailey	Maine Windjammer Assoc.	SS	638
Grand Princess	Princess Cruises	M	445
Grande Caribe	American Canadian Caribbean	M	144
Grande Mariner	American Canadian Caribbean	M	144
Grandeur of the Seas	Royal Caribbean International	M	481
Hanseatic	Lifelong Learning	M	612
Harvey Gamage	Dirigo Cruises	SS	636
Hebridean Princess	Hebridean Island Cruises	E	569
Hebridean Spirit	Hebridean Island Cruises	M	569
Heinrich Heine	KD River Cruises of Europe	R	586
Helvetia	KD River Cruises of Europe	R	586
Heritage	Maine Windjammer Assoc.	SS	638
Hirondelle	Abercrombie & Kent	R	579
Holiday	Carnival Cruise Lines	M	175

Ship	Cruise Line	Type	Page
Legend of the Seas	Royal Caribbean International	M	481
Lenin	Global Quest	R	584
Letty	Galápagos Network	A/G	609
Lev Tolstoy	Global Quest	R	585
Lewis R. French	Maine Windjammer Assoc.	SS	638
Libellule	Abercrombie & Kent	R	579
Liberté	French Country Waterways	R	584
Lili Marleen	Peter Deilmann Cruises	SS	638
Lircay	Chilean Line	F	630
Litote	Abercrombie & Kent	R	579
Litvinov	Global Quest	R	584
London Senator	NSB	F	632
Lorraine	Abercrombie & Kent	R	579
Luciole	Inland Voyages	R	585
Maasdam	Holland America Line	M	339
Majesty of the Seas	Royal Caribbean International	M	473
Mandalay	Windjammer Barefoot Cruises	SS	640
Marcelita	Explorers Travel Group L.L.C.	R	600
Marco Polo	Orient Lines	M	387
Mariella	Viking Line	EC	623
Marine Adventurer	Marine Expeditions	A	613
Marine Discovery	Marine Expeditions	A	613
Marine Voyager	Marine Expeditions	A	613
Marjorie II	Abercrombie & Kent	R	579
Mary Day	Coastal Cruises/Maine Windjammer Assoc.	SS	636, 638
MegaStar Aries	Star Cruises	M	575
MegaStar Taurus	Star Cruises	M	575
Mel Europe	Projex Line	F	632
Melanesian Discoverer	Melanesian Tourist Services	A	613
Melbourne Star	Blue Star Line	F	630
Melody	Mediterranean Shipping Cruises	M	570
Merchantile	Maine Windjammer Assoc.	SS	638
Mercury	Celebrity Cruises	M	195
Millennium	Celebrity Cruises	M	199
Minerva	Swan Hellenic Cruises	O	576
Mirabelle	Abercrombie & Kent	R	580
Mississippi Queen	Delta Queen Steamboat Company	R	314
Mistral	First European Cruises	E	567

Ship	Cruise Line	Type	Page
Polarstar	Svalbard Polar Travel (EuroCruises)	A	615
Polynesia	Windjammer Barefoot Cruises	SS	641
Prince of Scandinavia	Scandinavian Seaways (DFDS)	EC	621
Princess	French Country Waterways	R	584
Princess Elaine	Regal China Cruises	R	591
Princess Jeannie	Regal China Cruises	R	591
Princess of Scandinavia	Scandinavian Seaways (DFDS)	EC	621
Princess Sheena	Regal China Cruises	R	591
Princesse de Provence	Peter Deilmann Cruises	R	583
Princesse Ragnhild	Color Line	EC	621
Princesse Royale	Abercrombie & Kent	R	580
Professor Multinovsky	Quark Expeditions	A	614
Prussian Princess	Europe Cruise Line (EuroCruises)/ Peter Deilmann Cruises	R	581, 583
QE2	Cunard	M	297
Queen Nabila of Abu Simbel	Nabila Nile Cruises	R	597
Queen of Scandinavia	Scandinavian Seaways (DFDS)	E	621
Queen of Sheeba	Nabila Nile Cruises	R	597
Queen of the West	American West Steamboat Company	R	598
Queensland Star	Blue Star Line	F	630
R1–R8	Renaissance Cruises	M	572
Radamis	Misr Travel	R	597
Radisson Diamond	Radisson Seven Seas Cruises	M	456
Ramses II	Nabila Nile Cruises	R	597
Ramses King of the Nile	Nabila Nile Cruises	R	597
Ramses King of Thebes	Nabila Nile Cruises	R	597
Regal Empress	Regal Cruises	M	572
Regal Princess	Princess Cruises	M	434
Regency	Esplanade Tours	R	596
Regina	Esplanade Tours	R	596
Regina Chatarina	Dirigo Cruises	SS	637
Rembrandt	Premier Cruises	M	414
Renaissance VII–VIII	Renaissance Cruises	M	572
Rhapsody	Mediterranean Shipping Cruises	M	570

Ship	Cruise Line	Type	Page
Rhapsody of the Seas	Royal Caribbean International	M	481
Rhine Princess	Europe Cruise Line (EuroCruises)	R	581
Rio Amazonas	Explorers Travel Group L.L.C./Ladatco/Tara Tours	R/A	601, 602
River Cloud	Sea Cloud Cruises	R	586
River Cloud II	Sea Cloud Cruises	R	587
River Explorer	RiverBarge Excursion Lines	R	598
Road to Mandalay	Orient Express Cruises	R	593
Roi Soleìl	Abercrombie & Kent	R	580
Rosella	Viking Line	EC	623
Rotterdam	Holland America Line	M	350
Rousse	Global Quest	R	585
Royal Clipper	Star Clippers, Inc.	M	543
Royal Princess	Princess Cruises	M	431
Royal Star	Global Quest	M	568, 610
Royale	Esplanade Tours	R	596
Russ	GT Corporate Cruises	R	585
Rybalko	Global Quest	R	584
Ryndam	Holland America Line	M	339
Safari Quest	American Safari Cruises	R	604
Safari Spirit	American Safari Cruises	R	604
San Antonio	Ivaran Lines	F	631
Santa Cruz	Galápagos Cruises/Fourth Dimension Tours	A/G	608, 609
Scottish Highlander	Abercrombie & Kent	R	580
Sea Bird	Lindblad Expeditions	A	612
Sea Bird	International Expeditions	R	598
Sea Cloud	Sea Cloud Cruises	A/G/SS	638
Sea Cloud II	Sea Cloud Cruises	A/G/SS	639
Sea Goddess I	(see *Seabourn Goddess I*)	M	516
Sea Goddess II	(see *Seabourn Goddess II*)	M	516
Sea Lion	Lindblad Expeditions	A	612
Sea Princess	Princess Cruises	M	440
Seabourn Goddess I	Seabourn Cruise Line	M	516
Seabourn Goddess II	Seabourn Cruise Line	M	516
Seabourn Legend	Seabourn Cruise Line	M	510
Seabourn Pride	Seabourn Cruise Line	M	510
Seabourn Spirit	Seabourn Cruise Line	M	510
Seabourn Sun	Seabourn Cruise Line	M	518

Ship	Cruise Line	Type	Page
SeaBreeze	Premier Cruises	M	422
Sea-Land Endeavour	NSB	F	632
Sea-Land Initiative	NSB	F	632
Sea-Land Mistral	NSB	F	632
Sensation	Carnival Cruise Lines	M	167
Seven Seas Mariner	Radisson Seven Seas Cruises	M	466
Seven Seas Navigator	Radisson Seven Seas Cruises	M	463
Shannon Princess	Abercrombie & Kent/ European Waterways	R	580, 583
Sheherayar	Mena House Oberoi Hotel	R	596
Shehrazah	Mena House Oberoi Hotel	R	596
Sidney Star	Blue Star Line	F	630
Silja Europa	Silja Line	EC	622
Silja Festival	Silja Line	EC	622
Silja Scandinavia	Silja Line	EC	622
Silja Serenade	Silja Line	EC	622
Silja Symphony	Silja Line	EC	622
Silver Cloud	Silversea Cruises	M	529
Silver Shadow	Silversea Cruises	M	533
Silver Whisper	Silversea Cruises	M	533
Silver Wind	Silversea Cruises	M	529
Silvia Ana	Color Line	EC	621
Skagen	Color Line	EC	621
Skorpios I–III	Global Quest	A	611
Song of Flower	Radisson Seven Seas Cruises	M	458
Soren Larson	Dirigo Cruises	SS	637
Sovereign of the Seas	Royal Caribbean International	M	473
Spirit of '98	Cruise West	M	271
Spirit of Alaska	Cruise West	M	274
Spirit of Columbia	Cruise West	M	274
Spirit of Discovery	Cruise West	M	272
Spirit of Endeavour	Cruise West	M	277
Spirit of Glacier Bay	Cruise West	M	276
Spirit of Oceanus	Cruise West	M	278
Splendour of the Seas	Royal Caribbean International	M	481
Star Aquarius	Star Cruises	M	574
Star Clipper	Star Clippers, Inc.	M	540
Star Flyer	Star Clippers, Inc.	M	540
Star Pisces	Star Clippers, Inc.	M	574
Statendam	Holland America Line	M	339

Ship	Cruise Line	Type	Page
Stella	European Waterways/ Barge France	R	583
Stella Oceanis	Royal Olympic Cruises	M	497
Stella Solaris	Royal Olympic Cruises	M	494
Stephen Taber	Maine Windjammer Assoc.	SS	638
Sun Boat III–IV	Abercrombie & Kent	R	596
Sun Goddess	Sonesta International Hotels	R	597
Sun Princess	Princess Cruises	M	440
SuperSeaCat IV	Silja Line	EC	622
SuperStar Aries	Star Cruises	M	575
SuperStar Gemini	Star Cruises	M	574
SuperStar Leo	Star Cruises	M	575
SuperStar Taurus	Star Cruises	M	575
SuperStar Virgo	Star Cruises	M	575
Temptress Explorer	Temptress Cruises	A	616
Temptress Voyager	Temptress Cruises	A	616
Terra Australis	Global Quest	A	611
Theodor Fontane	KD River Cruises of Europe	R	586
Timberwind	Maine Windjammer Assoc.	SS	638
Triton	Royal Olympic Cruises	M	498
Tropicale	Carnival Cruise Lines	M	182
Tucano	Ecotour Expeditions	R	600
Tut	Sheraton Nile Cruises/ Misr Travel	R	597
Universe Explorer	World Explorer Cruises	M/A	559
Veendam	Holland America Line	M	339
Venezia	Reiseburo Mittelthurgau (EuroCruises)	R	582
Victoria	P&O Cruises	M	401
Victoria Blue Angel	Victoria Cruises	R	592
Victoria Blue Whale	Victoria Cruises	R	592
Victoria I–IV	Victoria Cruises	R	592
Victoria Yangtze Pearl	Victoria Cruises	R	592
Victoria Yangtze Princess	Victoria Cruises	R	592
Victory Chimes	Maine Windjammer Assoc./ Victory Chimes	SS	638, 639
Viking Peterhof	Leisure Cruises (EuroCruises)	R	581
Viking Serenade	Royal Caribbean International	M	480
Viktor Glushkov	Global Quest	R	584

Ship	Cruise Line	Type	Page
Vision of the Seas	Royal Caribbean International	M	481
Volendam	Holland America Line	M	354
Volga	Global Quest	R	585
Voyager of the Seas	Royal Caribbean International	M	485
Wasa Queen	Silja Line	EC	622
Westerdam	Holland America Line	M	346
Wilderness Adventurer	Alaska's Glacier Bay Tours and Cruises	A	132
Wilderness Discoverer	Alaska's Glacier Bay Tours and Cruises	A	132
Wilderness Explorer	Alaska's Glacier Bay Tours and Cruises	A	134
Wilhelm Tham	Gota Canal (EuroCruises)	R	581
William Tell	KD River Cruises	R	586
Wind Song	Windstar Cruises	M	550
Wind Spirit	Windstar Cruises	M	550
Wind Star	Windstar Cruises	M	550
Wind Surf	Windstar Cruises	M	552
World Discoverer	Society Expeditions	A	615
World Renaissance	Royal Olympic Cruises	M	500
Yamal	Quark Expeditions	A	614
Yankee Clipper	Windjammer Barefoot Cruises	SS	641
Yolita	Galápagos Yacht Cruises	A/G	610
Yorktown Clipper	Clipper Cruise Line	M	210
Zaandam	Holland America Line	M	354
Zenith	Celebrity Cruises	M	190
Zeus I–III	Zeus Tours and Cruises	SS	642

Appendix B

Cruise Ship Itineraries

Abercrombie & Kent International, Inc.

Explorer   **Home Port** Varies with itinerary

December–February, 14–20 nights, Antarctica. Tour programs depart/end in Santiago or Buenos Aires; cruise between Ushuaia and Stanley, Falkland Islands or round trip Ushuaia. December, "Circumnavigation of South Georgia and Falkland Islands"; "Antarctica and Falkland Islands"; January "Antarctica"; February, "Ice Cruise" (sails farther into the area than cruise ships generally go) followed by "Antarctica, Falklands, and South Georgia."

April–May, 16 and 17 nights, "River Sea," a nearly 2,300-mile voyage from Belem up the Amazon to Iquitos, Peru, or reverse. Can be taken between Manaus and Iquitos for 10 or 11 nights. Extensions to Machu Picchu and other South American destinations available.

June–July, 15 and 16 nights, "Maritime Britain" from Edinburgh to London via Dundee, Orkneys, Shetlands, Hebrides, Rum, Skye, Iona, Staffa, St. Kilda, Isle of Man, Waterford, Ireland, and Scilly Isles. "Secrets of the Celts," reverse itinerary with more port calls in Ireland. July–August, 18 nights "White Nights" to Arctic and White Sea round trip from Oslo, includes Norwegian Fjords, Solovetsky Islands, and Arkhangelsk in the Russian Arctic. August, "Viking Shores," 12 nights, Oslo to Edinburgh, includes Norwegian Fjords, Lofoten Islands, Shetlands, and Orkneys.

September, 8 nights, "Vintage Ports," pre-cruise stay in Paris, sail from Bordeaux to Lisbon visiting ports in Spain and Portugal. Followed by 35 nights, "Lost Islands of the Atlantic," Santa Cruz de Tenerife to Falkland Islands with stops in Cape Verde, Ascension, St. Helena, Tristan de Cuhna, Nightingale Island, Gough Island, and South Georgia.

Alaska's Glacier Bay Tours and Cruises/Voyager Cruise Line

Executive Explorer   **Home Ports** Seattle, Juneau, Ketchikan

Early May–early September, 7 nights, between Ketchikan and Juneau (northbound or southbound) calling at Kake (Tlingit Native village), Sitka, Haines, Skagway, plus natural areas such as Glacier Bay National Park, Misty Fjords, Tracy Arm. Passengers overnight in embarkation port before boarding. Repositioning cruises April 29 and September 8 between Seattle and Alaska.

Wilderness Adventurer   **Home Ports** Juneau, La Paz

Mid-May–early September, 7 nights, soft-adventure cruises round trip from Juneau. Passengers overnight in Juneau before boarding. Unlike standard itineraries, route takes ship mostly to uninhabited wilderness, where passengers use ship's sea kayaks or are ferried ashore in Zodiacs to hike. Aside from scheduled visits to Glacier Bay National Park, Tracy Arm Fjord, and Chichagoff, Baranof, and Admiralty Islands, itinerary flexible, allowing captain to choose area based on weather and water conditions, passenger interest, whale or wildlife sightings. Port calls are limited to isolated communities such as tiny Elfin Cove (summer population 30–35) or Warm Springs Bay.

January–March, ship sails on 6-night soft-adventure itineraries in Mexico's Sea of Cortés, round trip from La Paz, to uninhabited or lightly inhabited islands and coves for kayaking, snorkeling, and hiking. Ports include seventeenth-century mission town of Loreto and motorcoach excursion to Bahia Magdalena, an area said to offer Pacific coast's best whale-watching. Positioning cruises at beginning and end of Alaska and Baja seasons.

Wilderness Discoverer   **Home Ports** Seattle, Juneau, Sitka

Mid-May–mid-September, 7 nights, Alaska between Juneau and Sitka, calling at Tracy Arm, Skagway, Glacier Bay National Park, and Baranof Island. May 6 and September 16, positioning cruises between Seattle and Alaska.

Wilderness Explorer   **Home Ports** Seattle, Juneau, Glacier Bay

Mid-May–late August, 6 nights, active adventure itineraries from Glacier Bay. Passengers fly to Glacier Bay to join the ship and spend 4 days there and in Icy Strait, with most daylight hours sea kayaking or hiking. Cruise price includes round trip air transport between Juneau and Glacier Bay. Positioning cruises between Seattle and Glacier Bay, May 3 and August 29.

American Canadian Caribbean Line

Grande Caribe   **Home Ports**   Warren, RI, others vary with itinerary

Winter, 11 nights, Caribbean and Panama Canal cruises: Virgin Islands; or St. Maarten/Antigua; or Antigua/Grenada; or Trinidad/Orinoco Delta/ Curaçao. Panama Canal from Panama City calling at Colon, San Blas, Portobello, Panama Canal, Tobago, Isla del Rey, Contadora, Point Alegre, Darien Jungle, Balboa. March 30, 2001, 9 nights from Panama City to Belize.

May–November, 5–15 nights, exploring New England, Canadian Maritimes, Gaspé Peninsula, St. Lawrence Seaway, Saguenay River, Erie Canal. Erie Canal/Fall Foliage cruises along inland waterways of New York, New England, and Canada between Rhode Island and Quebec City.

Spring and Fall, 14-night positioning cruises along East Coast Inside Passage between Warren, RI and Florida.

Grande Mariner   **Home Ports**   Warren, RI, others vary with itinerary

Winter, 7 and 11 nights, Caribbean and Bahamas cruises: St. Maarten/ Antigua; or Virgin Islands; or Bahamas/Eleuthera/Exuma Cays; or Bahamas/ Exuma Cays.

April, May and November, 12- and 14-night East Coast Inside Passage cruises between Rhode Island and Florida.

June–October, 5–15 nights, New England Islands; or Erie Canal/ Saguenay River; or Saguenay/Gaspé/Nova Scotia/Maine. Erie Canal/Fall Foliage cruises along inland waterways of New York, New England, and Canada between Rhode Island and Quebec City.

Niagara Prince   **Home Ports**   Warren, RI; others vary with itinerary

December–January, 11 nights, Belize/Roatan; or Belize/Barrier Reef/ Guatemala. February, 7 nights, Florida/Tampa/Titusville.

March, 7-night, Colonial Intracoastal Waterway between Florida and South Carolina. April–May, Florida/Titusville/Tampa or between Chicago and New Orleans on the Mississippi.

June–October, 6–15 nights, round trip from Chicago, calling at Holland, Manistee, Mackinac Island, Sturgeon Bay, and Milwaukee; or between Warren and Chicago via Erie Canal and Great Lakes. Erie Canal/ Fall Foliage cruises along inland waterways of New York, New England, and Canada between Rhode Island and Quebec City. November 5, 2001, 14 nights, positioning cruise, East Coast Inside Passage from Warren to Florida.

American Hawaii Cruises/United States Lines

Independence (AHC)   **Home Ports** Kahului, Maui

Repositions November 4, 2000 from Honolulu to Kahului, Maui, on 7-night cruise. Afterward, year-round, 7 nights, departing Kahului at 9 p.m. Saturday; Sunday at sea; Monday, Hilo, Hawaii; Tuesday, Kona, Hawaii; Wednesday, Honolulu, Oahu; Thursday, Nawiliwili, Kauai, arriving 4 p.m., remaining until 4 p.m. Friday. Returns to Kahului on Saturday morning.

Patriot (USL)   **Home Port** Honolulu

Beginning December 9, 2000, year-round, 7 nights, departing Honolulu at 9:15 p.m. Saturday; Sunday at sea arriving in evening at Kauai and remaining overnight; Monday evening, departs for Kahului, Maui, arriving Tuesday morning and remaining overnight. Sails Wednesday evening for Hilo and Kona, Hawaii, returning to Honolulu on Saturday morning.

Cape Canaveral Cruise Line

Dolphin IV   **Home Port** Port Canaveral

Year-round, 2 nights to Freeport, 4 nights to Freeport and Key West. Special 6-night "Real Millennium" cruise, December 27, 2000 to Freeport, Nassau and Key West.

Carnival Cruise Lines

Carnival Conquest   **Home Port** To be announced
Enters service, Fall 2002.

Carnival Destiny   **Home Port** San Juan

September 2000–December 2002, 7 nights, alternating Southern Caribbean, round trip from San Juan. "Dutch Treat" calls at St. Thomas/St.John, St. Lucia, Curaçao, Aruba. "European Delight" visits St. Thomas/St. John, Antigua, Guadeloupe, Aruba.

Carnival Legend (Debuts 2002)   **Home Port** To be announced

Carnival Pride (Debuts late 2001)   **Home Port** To be announced

Carnival Spirit   **Home Ports** Miami, Vancouver

Spring and Fall, 2001 and 2002, 14–17 nights, Panama Canal positioning cruises between Miami and San Diego and May 20, 2001, 3-night Pacific Coastal from San Francisco to Vancouver.

Fall 2001, 2002; Spring 2002, 2003; 12 nights, Hawaii between Honolulu (overnight) and Ensenada or Vancouver to Lahaina, Maui (overnight); Nawiliwili, Kauai; Hilo and Kona, Hawaii.

Summer 2001 and 2002, 7-night Alaska between Vancouver and Seward to Ketchikan, Endicott Arm, Juneau, Skagway, Lynn Canal, Sitka, College Fjord northbound; College Fjord, Valdez, Hubbard Glacier, Juneau, Skagway, Lynn Canal, Ketchikan southbound.

September 2001, 2002 and May, 2002, 7-night round trip from Vancouver to Juneau, Glacier Bay, Skagway and Ketchikan.

Winter 2001–2002 and November, December 2002, 8 nights, alternating Western and Southern Caribbean, from Miami to St.Maarten, Barbados, Martinique or Belize City; Limon, Costa Rica; Colon, Panama.

Carnival Triumph   **Home Port** Miami

Year-round, Saturday, 7 nights, alternating Eastern and Western Caribbean, from Miami to San Juan, St. Thomas, St. Croix; or, Playa del Carmen, Cozumel, Grand Cayman, Ocho Rios.

Carnival Victory   **Home Ports** Miami, New York

October–May, Sunday, 7 nights, alternating Eastern and Western Caribbean from Miami to San Juan, St. Croix, St. Thomas; or, Playa del Carmen, Cozumel, Grand Cayman, Ocho Rios.

Late May, 4 nights, Canada from Boston to Halifax and Saint John. June–September, 4 and 5 nights, Canada from New York to Halifax or Halifax and Saint John. September, 7 nights, Fall Foliage, Canada/New England from New York to Boston, Portland, Sydney and Halifax, Nova Scotia.

Celebration   **Home Port** Galveston

Year-round, 4 nights, from Galveston, Texas on alternate Thursdays to Playa del Carmen/Cozumel; or 5 nights, departing alternate Mondays and Saturdays to Cozumel, Calica/Cancún. Both have 2 days at sea.

Ecstasy   **Home Port** Miami

Year-round, 3 and 4 nights, Bahamas and Western Caribbean, from Miami. 3-night cruise departs Friday to Nassau; 4-night departs Monday to Key West and Playa del Carmen/Cozumel; both have one day at sea.

Elation   **Home Port** Los Angeles

Year-round, 7 nights, Mexican Riviera, every Sunday from Los Angeles to Puerto Vallarta, Mazatlan, Cabo San Lucas.

Fantasy   **Home Port** Port Canaveral

Year-round, 3 and 4 nights, Bahamas cruises from Port Canaveral. 3 nights departs Thursday to Nassau; 4 nights departs Sunday to Freeport and Nassau; both have one day at sea.

Fascination   **Home Port** San Juan

Year-round, 7 nights, Eastern/Southern Caribbean from San Juan on Saturday to St. Thomas, St. Maarten, Dominica, Martinique, Barbados. This island sampler is one of Carnival's best itineraries, particularly for those on first Caribbean visit, reflecting Caribbean's cultural diversity and offering contrasts between highly developed St. Thomas and St. Maarten and less traveled Dominica, historical Barbados, and seductive Martinique.

Holiday   **Home Port** Los Angeles

Year-round, 3 and 4 nights, Baja California from Los Angeles. 3 nights departs Friday to Ensenada; 4 nights departs Monday to Catalina Island and Ensenada. Both have one full day at sea.

Imagination   **Home Port** Miami

Year-round, 4 and 5 nights, Western Caribbean from Miami. 4 nights, alternate Thursdays to Key West and Playa del Carmen/Cozumel; 5 nights has 2 itineraries: Alternate Mondays to Grand Cayman and Calica/Cancún; alternate Saturdays to Grand Cayman and Ocho Rios.

Inspiration   **Home Port** New Orleans

Year-round, 7 nights from New Orleans on Sundays to Montego Bay, Grand Cayman, Playa del Carmen/Cozumel.

Jubilee   **Home Port** Tampa

Year-round, 4 and 5 nights, Western Caribbean from Tampa. 4 nights, alternate Thursdays to Key West, Playa del Carmen, Cozumel with one day at sea; 5 nights, on alternate Mondays and Saturdays replaces Key West with Grand Cayman and 2 days at sea.

Paradise   **Home Port** Miami

Year-round, 7 nights, alternating Eastern and Western Caribbean from Miami on Sundays to Nassau, San Juan, St. Thomas; or Playa del Carmen/Cozumel, Grand Cayman, Ocho Rios. Both 3 days at sea.

Sensation   **Home Port** Tampa

Year-round, 7 nights, Western Caribbean from Tampa on Sundays to Grand Cayman, Playa del Carmen, Cozumel, New Orleans. 3 days at sea.

Tropicale   **Home Port** Ft. Lauderdale

November 22, 2000–January 31, 2001, 10 nights, Panama Canal from Ft. Lauderdale to Aruba, Cartagena, Colombia; partial transit of Panama Canal to Gatun Lake; Limon, Costa Rica; and Key West.

From February 2001, year-round, 7 nights, Western Caribbean from Ft. Lauderdale to Key West, Belize City, Playa del Carmen, Cozumel and Progreso (Merida) with 2 days at sea.

Celebrity Cruises

Century   **Home Port** Ft. Lauderdale

Year-round, 7 nights, alternating Eastern and Western Caribbean, from Ft. Lauderdale on Saturdays to San Juan, St. Thomas, St. Maarten, Nassau; or, Ocho Rios, Grand Cayman, Cozumel, Key West. Both have 2 days at sea.

Galaxy   **Home Ports** San Juan, Stockholm

October 2000–April 2001, 7 nights, Southern Caribbean, departing Saturdays from San Juan to St. Croix, St. Lucia, Barbados, Antigua, St. Thomas. One day at sea.

April and September, 14 and 15 nights, transatlantic, San Juan–Stockholm and Amsterdam–San Juan.

May–September 7 nights, Baltic round trip from Stockholm to Helsinki, St. Petersburg, Rostock (for Berlin), Germany; Visby/Gotland, Sweden. September, 12 nights, Baltic from Stockholm to Amsterdam.

October 2001–March 2002, 7 nights, Southern Caribbean, round trip from San Juan on Fridays to St. Thomas, St. Kitts, Barbados, Aruba.

Horizon   **Home Ports** Aruba, New York

November–December 2000, 7 nights, Caribbean from Aruba to St. Thomas, St. Kitts, St. Lucia, Barbados. January–April 2001 and November 2001–March 2002, alternates with Panama Canal itinerary to Colon, Panama; Puerto Limon, Costa Rica; San Blas Islands; Cartagena, Colombia.

May–October, 7 nights, from New York on Saturdays to Bermuda, calling at Hamilton and St. George. April and October, positioning cruises Aruba–San Juan; San Juan–New York and New York–Aruba.

Infinity   **Home Ports** Vancouver, San Juan

February 3, inaugural, 14 nights, Panama Canal from Ft. Lauderdale to Key West, Cozumel, Puerto Limon, Puerto Caldera, Acapulco, Cabo San Lucas, ending in San Diego. Repeats February 24; reverse itinerary, March 10. February and April, 10–11 nights, Hawaii, Ensenada–Honolulu or reverse, calls at Kailua, Kona, and Hilo, Hawaii; Nawiliwili, Kauai; and Lahaina, Maui.

May, 10 nights, Alaska from San Francisco to Vancouver, calling at Seattle, Victoria, Sitka, Skagway, Juneau, Ketchikan, and Inside Passage.

May–September, 7 nights, Alaska Inside Passage cruises from Vancouver to Juneau, Skagway, Haines, Hubbard Glacier, and Ketchikan. September, 9 nights, Vancouver to San Diego via Ketchikan, Juneau, Victoria, and San Francisco and 13 nights, Panama Canal from San Diego to San Juan.

October 2001–April 2002, 7 nights, Southern Caribbean round trip from San Juan on Saturdays to St. Croix, St. Lucia, Barbados, Antigua, St. Thomas.

Mercury   **Home Port** Varies with itinerary

November 2000–March 2001 and December 2001–March 2002, 10–15 nights, South America; Ft. Lauderdale–La Guaira (Caracas); La Guaira–Rio de Janeiro; Rio–Valparaiso (Santiago); Valparaiso–Buenos Aires and reverse; round trip Buenos Aires; Buenos Aires–La Guaira (2001) and Valparaiso–Rio; Rio–La Guaira (2002); La Guaira–Ft.Lauderdale.

March–April and November, 7–10 nights, Eastern and Western Caribbean cruises from Ft. Lauderdale. April, 14 nights, positioning Panama Canal cruise, Ft. Lauderdale–San Diego and 11 nights, Pacific Coast/Alaska, San Diego–Vancouver.

May–September, 7 nights, Alaska, alternating north and southbound between Vancouver and Seward on Fridays via Inside Passage, Ketchikan, Juneau, Skagway, Hubbard Glacier, Valdez, College Fjord. Sitka replaces Valdez on southbound sailings. September 14 and 21, 7 nights, Alaska Inside Passage round trip from Vancouver.

September–October, 11 and 12 nights, Hawaii, Vancouver–Honolulu; Honolulu–Ensenada. October–November, 14 nights, Panama Canal, San Diego–Ft. Lauderdale and reverse.

Millennium   **Home Ports** Ft. Lauderdale, Barcelona, Istanbul

November 2000–April 2001, 7 nights, alternating Eastern and Western Caribbean from Ft. Lauderdale on Sundays to San Juan, Catalina Island, St. Thomas, Nassau; or, Key West, Calica, Cozumel, Grand Cayman. April and September, 13 and 14 nights, transatlantic from Ft. Lauderdale to Barcelona and reverse.

May–September, 12 nights, between Barcelona and Istanbul, visiting Monte Carlo, Rome, Naples, Athens, Haifa, Alexandria and Kusadasi; or, Malta, Naples, Rome, Corsica, and Monte Carlo. September, 7 nights, Western Mediterranean round trip from Barcelona to Malta, Naples, Rome, Corsica, Villefranche.

October 2001–April 2002, 7 nights, round trip from Ft. Lauderdale on Sundays to San Juan, Catalina, St. Thomas, and Nassau.

Summit   **Home Port** Ft. Lauderdale

October 2001–April 2002, 10 and 11 nights, Western, Southern, and Eastern Caribbean round trip from Ft. Lauderdale to Key West, Cozumel, Puerto Limon, Colon, Colombia, Aruba, Grand Cayman; or, St. Maarten, St. Lucia, Barbados, St. Kitts, St. Thomas.

Zenith   **Home Ports** Ft. Lauderdale, New York

November 2000–April 2001, 10–11 nights Eastern/Southern Caribbean from Ft. Lauderdale to St. Maarten, St Lucia, Barbados, Antigua, St. Thomas; or, Curaçao, La Guaira (Caracas), Grenada, Barbados, Martinique, St. Thomas.

April–October, 7 nights, Bermuda, from New York on Saturdays to Hamilton and St. George with 2 days at sea. April and October, 7 and 8 nights, positioning cruises Ft. Lauderdale–San Juan; San Juan–New York and New York–Barbados; Barbados–Tampa.

Winter 2001–2002, 7 nights, Western Caribbean, round trip from Tampa on Sundays to Key West, Grand Cayman, Cozumel, Costa Maya.

Classical Cruises

Callisto   **Home Port**   Varies with itinerary

January–March, 9-night cruise-tours, Egypt, Jordan and Red Sea, 2 days in Cairo, fly to Luxor for 2 days, board Callisto, visit Aqaba and Petra, Jordan; Eilat and Negev, Israel; Sharm el Sheikh and Hurghada, Egypt; return to Cairo for overnight.

April–May, 9 nights, Circumnavigate Crete, round trip from Heraklion to Aghios Nicolaos, Kritsa, Lato, Gournia, Sitia, Kato Zakros, Aghia Galini, Sfakia, Gramvousa, Kastelli, Chania, Rethimnon.

June–October, 8-night Greek Islands with 2 days in Athens, sail to Delos, Mykonos, Santorini, Amorgos, Patmos, Kusadasi (Ephesus), Samos.

Clelia II   **Home Port**   Varies with itinerary

December 2000–January 2001, 26-night cruise-tour, Cairo–Mumbai (Bombay). January, 19 nights, India, tour of Delhi, Agra, Jaipur; sail from Madras to Sri Lanka, Madurai, Cochin, Mangalore, Goa, and Mumbai. February 11, 18 nights, India/Arabia from Mumbai to Kuwait; February 26, 13 nights, Fabled Kingdoms and Modern Nations, from Kuwait to Muscat visiting Iran, Kuwait, Bahrain, Qatar, Dubai, United Arab Emirates. April, 14 nights, Greece, Crete, Turkey from Athens to Istanbul. April 26 and September 11, 14 nights, Turkey, Malta, Italy, Greece from Istanbul to Athens. May, 11 nights, Mediterranean, Athens to Barcelona and 9 nights, Barcelona to Rome. June, 12 nights, Croatia, Corfu, Greece, Turkey from Venice to Istanbul. October 5, 67 nights, circumnavigation of Africa, round trip from Athens, available in 3 segments, Athens–Maputo, Mozambique (for Victoria Falls National Park, Zimbabwe); Maputo–Accra, Ghana; Accra–Athens.

Halcyon   **Home Port**   Varies with itinerary

January–February, 13 nights, Timbuktu and the Rivers of West Africa from Bamako, Mali–Dakar, Senegal. March, 10 nights, Madrid and Andalusia, from Madrid to Ronda, Spain. April, 10 nights, Sicily circumnavigation from Palermo. June, 8 nights, Tuscany, round trip from Porto Ercole (near Rome). July, 9 nights, Italy cruise-tours with 3 days in Rome, sail to Sorrento, Amalfi, and Capri. September–October, Dalmatian Coast between Dubrovnik, Croatia, and Venice. October–November, the Peloponnese, Greece cruise-tour with 3 days in Athens before sailing.

Panorama   **Home Port** Varies with itinerary

June–July, 8 nights, Scotland, cruise-tour, 2 days in Edinburgh, round trip from Oban sailing to Barra, Isles of Lewis, Skye, Mull, and Iona. August, 8 nights, Channel Islands, coastal England and Brittany, round trip from Southampton; and 8 nights, Southampton to Le Havre, Cherbourg, St. Malmo, Roscoff, Belle-île, La Pallice, Bordeaux. October, 10 nights, Turkey.

Clipper Cruise Line

Clipper Adventurer   **Home Port** Varies with itinerary

December 2000, 15 and 17 days, Exploring Antarctica and The Falklands and Antarctica. March 8, 2001, 13 days, Colonial Brazil from Rio de Janeiro to Fortaleza. April, 12 and 13 days, Western Mediterranean and Portugal. May 2, 15 days, Western Europe from Lisbon to Dover.

May–July, 12 and 14 days, Britain, Ireland, Normandy, and Baltic. August–September, 11, 15, 16 days, Iceland, Greenland, Maritime Canada, U.S. East Coast. October, 13 and 17 days, Amazon, Colonial Brazil, and coastal South America. November, December 2001, 17 and 23 days, Falklands, Antarctica, and South Georgia.

Clipper Odyssey   **Home Port** Varies with itinerary

December 2000–March 2001, 12–18 nights, New Zealand, Australia, Great Barrier Reef, Spice Islands, and Bali.

April–May, 14 and 16 nights, Philippines, Taiwan, Japan, and China. July–August, 11–16 nights, Russian Far East, Aleutian Islands, Alaska, Kamchatka Peninsula, Kuril Islands, Japan. September, 14 nights, Japan and China; 17 nights, China and Vietnam. October–November, 14–19 nights, Southeast Asia, Bali, and back to Australia.

Nantucket Clipper   **Home Port** Varies with itinerary

December–February, 7 nights, Jewels of the Lesser Antilles round trip from Antigua to St. Kitts, Saba, St. Eustatius, St. Barts, Anguilla, St. Martin.

March, April, 7 nights, Intracoastal between Jacksonville and Charleston. April, 14 nights, Colonial America and Civil War Battlefields from Jacksonville to Washington, D.C./Alexandria, and 7 nights, Washington D.C. to New York City.

June–October, 7 and 14 nights, New England, Maritime Canada, St. Lawrence Seaway & Thousand Islands, Great Lakes, Hudson River, Chesapeake Bay. October, 11 nights, Colonial Heritage on Intracoastal Waterway from Washington to Jacksonville.

Yorktown Clipper   **Home Port** Varies with itinerary

December 2000–March 2001, 7 and 8 nights, Southern Caribbean and Orinoco River, including Curaçao, Bonaire, Isla Margarita, Trinidad, Tobago, Grenada, Mayreau, Bequia, St. Lucia, Dominica, Nevis, St. Kitts.

March–April, November–December, 8 and 11 nights, Costa Rica, Darien Jungle, Panama Canal, then north to Copper Canyon and Seas of Cortez, in conjunction with South Orient Express train.

May–September, 7–12 nights, British Columbia, Southeast Alaska, Pacific Northwest, and Canadian Rockies in conjunction with the Rocky Mountaineer Train. October, 5 nights, Inland Waterways of Northern California from Redwood City to Sausalito, Sacramento, Napa Valley, and San Francisco.

Club Med

Club Med 2   **Home Ports** Martinique, Cannes

Winter, 7 days, Caribbean, from Martinique on 5 alternating itineraries: St. Lucia, Tobago Cays, Bequia, Mayreau, Barbados, and Carriacou; or Los Roques, Blanquilla, Carriacou, Barbados, Mayreau; or Les Saintes, St. Barts, Virgin Gorda, Jost Van Dyke, St. Thomas, St. Kitts; or St. Lucia, Union, Grenada, La Blanquilla, Trinidad, Mayreau; or Les Saintes, St. Maarten, Tintamarre, San Juan, Virgin Gorda, St. Kitts.

Summer, 3, 4, 7 days, French and Italian Rivieras, Greek Isles, Turkey, and Spain. Positioning cruises in April and October.

Commodore Cruise Line/Crown Cruise Line

Crown Dynasty   **Home Ports** Aruba, Baltimore, Philadelphia

November 4, 2000–April 14, 2001, 7 nights, Southern Caribbean from Aruba on Saturdays to Curaçao, Soufriere and Castries, St. Lucia; Barbados; Grenada, and Bonaire.

May to November, 7 nights, Bermuda from Baltimore or Philadelphia.

Spring and Fall positioning cruises between Baltimore and Aruba. Fall, New England/Canada: to be announced.

Enchanted Capri   **Home Port** New Orleans

Year-round from New Orleans; 5 nights, Western Caribbean on Sundays, to Playa del Carmen/Cozumel and Progreso, Mexico; 2 nights, weekend "Cruise to Nowhere" on Fridays.

Enchanted Isle   **Home Port** New Orleans

Year-round, 7 nights, Western Caribbean, from New Orleans on Saturdays to Playa del Carmen, Cozumel, Grand Cayman, Montego Bay, with 3 days at sea. January 27, March 24, October 6, Roatan, Honduras, and Belize, replace Grand Cayman and Montego Bay.

April and September, 14 nights, Panama Canal from New Orleans to Cozumel, Roatan, San Andres, partial Canal transit to Gatun Lake, Cartagena, Aruba, and Ocho Rios.

December 2000 and 2001, 10 and 11 nights, Caribbean between New Orleans and San Juan to St. John/St.Thomas, St. Maarten, Antigua, Guadeloupe, St. Kitts; or St. Croix, St. Lucia, Grenada, Aruba, Ocho Rios, Cozumel.

Costa Cruise Lines

CostaAllegra   **Home Port** Genoa

May–November, 11, 12 nights, Eastern Mediterranean or Atlantic Islands from Genoa to Naples, Catania, Egypt, Israel, Cyprus, and Greece or Barcelona, Casablanca, Canary Islands, Madeira, and Malaga. May, 11 nights, Black Sea and Greek Islands, round trip from Genoa. Winter, South America, sold to South Americans only.

CostaAtlantica   **Home Ports** Ft. Lauderdale, Venice

November 3, 2000, 14 nights, transatlantic, Genoa to Ft. Lauderdale. November 2000–April 2001 and 2001–2002, 7 nights, alternating Eastern and Western Caribbean from Ft. Lauderdale on Sundays to San Juan, St. Thomas/St. John, Catalina Island/Casa de Campo, Nassau; or, Key West, Playa del Carmen/Cozumel, Ocho Rios, Grand Cayman.

April 29, Ft. Lauderdale to Genoa followed by positioning cruise, Genoa to Venice. May–November, 7 nights, Eastern Mediterranean from Venice on Sunday to Bari, Katakolon, Kusadasi, Istanbul, Athens. Positioning cruise from Venice to Genoa, followed by November 23, transatlantic cruise, Genoa to Ft. Lauderdale.

CostaClassica   **Home Port** Venice

To be stretched in winter and re-enter service in April in Europe. April–November, 7 nights, Eastern Mediterranean, from Venice on Monday to Greek Isles and Dubrovnik, Croatia.

CostaMarina   **Home Port** Copenhagen

June–September, 7 nights, Copenhagen on Sundays to either the Baltic and Russia or Norway and the Fjords.

Winter, South America, sold to South Americans only.

CostaRomantica   **Home Ports** Amsterdam, Guadeloupe

June–September, 10–14 nights from Amsterdam to either Norwegian Fjords, North Cape, and Spitzbergen or the Baltic and Russia. Spring and fall positioning cruises between Amsterdam and Genoa. October, 12 nights, Egypt, Israel, and Greece from Genoa.

Winter, Caribbean cruises from Guadeloupe, sold in Europe only.

CostaVictoria   **Home Ports** Ft. Lauderdale, Genoa

November 17, 2000, 16-night transatlantic, Genoa to Ft. Lauderdale. December 3 and 11, 5 nights, Western Caribbean from Ft. Lauderdale to Playa del Carmen/Cozumel and Grand Cayman. December, 7 and 8 nights, Eastern or Western Caribbean, December from Ft. Lauderdale.

January–April, 7 nights, alternating Eastern and Western Caribbean from Ft. Lauderdale on Sunday to either San Juan, St. Thomas/St. John, Catalina Island/Casa de Campo, Nassau, or Key West, Playa del Carmen/Cozumel, Ocho Rios, Grand Cayman. April 22, transatlantic from Ft. Lauderdale to Genoa.

May–November, 7 nights, Western Mediterranean from Genoa on Sunday to Naples; Palermo, Sicily; Tunis, Tunisia; Majorca, Barcelona, Marseille. November 17, transatlantic, Genoa to Ft. Lauderdale.

Cruise West

Spirit of Alaska   **Home Ports** Portland, Juneau

March–May, September–October, 7 nights, Columbia and Snake rivers round trip of 1,000 miles from Portland to Astoria and Cannon Beach, through Columbia Gorge to twin cities of Clarkston, Washington and Lewiston, Idaho. River cruises offer migratory birds, flowers, fresh greenery in spring; sunshine and warm water in summer; bright foliage in Columbia River Gorge in autumn.

May–September, 7 nights, Inside Passage, between Juneau and Ketchikan.

Spirit of Columbia   **Home Ports** Seattle, Whittier

March–May, September–October, 7 nights, British Columbia and Pacific Northwest Islands, round trip from Seattle to Vancouver, Howe Sound, Princess Louisa Inlet, Gulf Islands, Victoria, San Juan Islands and La Conner artists' community.

May–September, 3–4 nights, Prince William Sound, round trip from Whittier.

Spirit of Discovery   **Home Ports** Seattle, Portland

March–May, September–October, 7 nights, Columbia and Snake Rivers, round trip from Portland (See Spirit of Alaska for description).

May–September, 7 nights, Inside Passage between Juneau and Ketchikan.

Spirit of Endeavour   **Home Ports** Seattle, Juneau, San Francisco,
Cabo San Lucas

May–September, 7 nights, Inside Passage between Seattle and Juneau including and Glacier Bay.

Late September–late November, 3 and 4 nights, California wine country, round trip from San Francisco to Sonoma, Napa Valley, Sacramento River Delta, Sacramento.

December–March, 3, 4 nights, Sea of Cortés between Cabo San Lucas and La Paz, Baja, or 7 nights, round trip from Cabo San Lucas north along eastern Baja coast to Isla Espiritu Santo, Bahia Concepcion; Mulege, a palm-shaded oasis, Loreto, Baja capital until 1829; and La Paz. "Wildlife Safari" departures call at Puerto Escondido, where passengers cross to Pacific side for whale-watching. March 31, 8 nights, Cabo San Lucas to Los Mochis, same ports plus Isla Angel de la Guarda, Isla Tiburon, Guaymas. Reverse itinerary, April 7. Positioning cruises between San Diego and Cabo San Lucas, December 9, 2000, April 14, 2001, and December 8, 2001. Prices include shore excursions. Optional pre- and post-cruise Copper Canyon tours available with most sailings.

Spirit of Glacier Bay   **Home Ports**   Seattle, Whittier, Portland

March–May, September–October, 7 nights, Columbia and Snake Rivers, round trip from Portland. (See *Spirit of Alaska* for description.)

May–September, 3 and 4 nights, from Whittier to Prince William Sound, College Fjord, Columbia Glacier, Harriman Fjord, and Blackstone Bay.

Spirit of '98   **Home Ports**   Seattle, Juneau, Cabo San Lucas

May–September, 7 nights, between Seattle and Juneau including Inside Passage and Glacier Bay. September–October, 7 nights, Columbia and Snake Rivers, round trip from Portland. (See *Spirit of Alaska* for description.) November–December, 3–4 nights, California wine country, round trip from San Francisco to Sonoma, Napa Valley, Sacramento River Delta, Sacramento.

January–February 3, 4 nights, Sea of Cortes, between Cabo San Lucas and La Paz. Wednesday, 3 nights, to Bonanza Beach and Loreto; Saturday, 4 nights, calls at Bahia Concepcion/Mulege also. February–March, 7 nights, Sea of Cortes round trip from Cabo San Lucas, north along eastern Baja coast to Isla Espiritu Santo, Bahia Concepcion; Mulege, a palm-shaded oasis, Loreto, and La Paz. "Wildlife Safari" departures call at Puerto Escondido, where passengers cross to Pacific side for whale-watching. January 6 and April 4, 7 nights, positioning cruises between San Diego and La Paz. Prices include shore excursions. Optional pre- and post-cruise Copper Canyon tours available with most sailings.

Spirit of Oceanus   **Home Ports**   Juneau, Victoria, Seward

May, 32 nights, positioning cruise, Singapore to Whittier, available in 4 segments: Singapore/Hong Kong; Hong Kong/Tokyo; Petropavlovsk/Whittier.

June 9, inaugural Alaska season. 7 or 10 nights, Island Seas, from Victoria to Juneau visiting Prince Rupert; Metlakatla, only Tsimshian Indian community in Alaska; Wrangell, Petersburg, Misty Fjords, whale-watching in Frederick Sound, Tracy Arm, and Sitka via Peril Strait and Sergius Narrows—waterways inaccessible to larger ships. 10 nights, Glacier Seas, from Whittier to Victoria via Prince William Sound and Inside Passage with visit to Copper River fishing village of Cordova, Sitka, Juneau, and one night at anchor in Thomas Bay near Petersburg.

Winter season, to be announced.

Crystal Cruises

Crystal Harmony   **Home Port**   San Francisco, others vary with itinerary

January–late March, 11–16 nights, South America, from Ft. Lauderdale to Buenos Aires followed by Cape Horn cruises between Buenos Aires and Valparaiso; then, Amazon cruises, Buenos Aires to Manaus with overnight in Rio for Carnival; and Manaus to Ft. Lauderdale.

March, May, August, September, and October to year end, 7–17 nights, Panama Canal, Caribbean, Mexican Riviera.

May–August, 12 nights, Alaska and Canada round trip from San Francisco.

September–October, 11 nights, New England and Canada, between New York and Montreal. October, 11 nights, U.S. East Coast and Caribbean from New York to San Juan.

Crystal Symphony   **Home Port**   Varies with itinerary

January, 7 nights, Mexican Riviera, round trip from Los Angeles, followed by 104 night, 2001 World Cruise from Los Angeles to London with calls at 38 ports in 31 countries, including 9 inaugural calls, on a transpacific route to Hong Kong, Southeast Asia, East, Southern, and West Africa to Southampton. Four segments of 24–28 days available.

April–June and August–September, Mediterranean and Western Europe from London, Barcelona, Rome, Venice, or Athens. June–July Baltic from London, Copenhagen, or Amsterdam.

October–mid-November, circumnavigation of Africa from Rome in two segments; 24 nights, Rome–Cape Town via Suez, and 22 nights, Cape Town–Lisbon. November 25, 11 nights, transatlantic, Lisbon to Ft. Lauderdale followed by December, 15 and 14 nights, Panama Canal cruises, Ft. Lauderdale–Los Angeles; Los Angeles–San Juan.

Cuba Cruise Corporation

La Habana   **Home Port** Nassau

Year-round beginning November 2000, 3 and 4 nights, Nassau to Havana, with educational/cultural shore excursion program; "Havana Getaway," Thursday, 3 nights, arrives in Havana Friday afternoon, departs Saturday at noon. "Cuba Getaway," Sunday, 4 nights, arrives in Havana Monday afternoon, departs Wednesday at noon. (Americans legally can take these cruises as they are with a hosted group, provided they do not spend money in Cuba or purchase Cuban goods on board the ship. Some individuals also qualify under a "general license" category.)

Cunard Line, Ltd.

Caronia   **Home Ports** Southampton, others vary with itinerary

January–April, 14, 18, 23 nights, South America: Ft. Lauderdale–Valparaiso; Valparaiso–Rio de Janeiro and reverse; Valparaiso–Ft. Lauderdale; Ft. Lauderdale–Manaus and reverse. April, 14 nights, transatlantic positioning from Ft. Lauderdale to Hamburg.

May–July, 12 and 15 nights, Western Europe; Norwegian Fjords; Iberia and Baltic. July, 18 days, transatlantic, Southampton to New York, via Norway, Faeroe Islands, Iceland, Maritime Canada.

August–October, 4 departures from New York; 12 and 18 nights, New England, Canada and Bermuda, Colonial South. October, 14 nights, transatlantic from New York to Southampton calling at Bermuda, Azores, Lisbon. October, 10 nights, Madeira, Canary Islands round trip from Southampton, and Southampton–Cape Town and reverse. December, round trip from Southampton; 3 nights to Guernsey; Christmas/New Year, 19 nights to La Coruna, Morocco, Canary Islands, Madeira, Lisbon.

QE2   **Home Ports** New York, Southampton, others vary with itinerary

January 5–April 20, 104 nights, World Cruise, round trip from New York in 8 segments. Sails via Panama Canal and South Pacific to Australia, Southeast Asia, China, India, Suez Canal to Europe, ending with transatlantic from Southampton to New York. April, 13 nights, Floating Jazz Festival, transatlantic from New York to Ft. Lauderdale, Madeira, Lisbon, Le Havre, Southampton.

May 3–October 4, 6, 7 nights, transatlantic crossings between Southampton and New York. Some crossings include an additional European port, all have a theme. Can be combined with one-way on the Concorde. *QE2* has garage and kennels for automobiles, motorcycles and pets. Crossings from Southampton or New York are interspersed with other cruises: 12 nights Europe/Mediterranean; 12 nights British Isles/Norwegian

Fjords; 11 nights, Canada/New England; 12 nights Iberia/Bordeaux; 6 nights Bermuda/Newport.

October–November, 12 nights, Madeira/Canary Islands round trip from Southampton, and 14, 15 nights, Southampton–Cape Town and reverse. December 11, 11 nights, 6th annual Blues Cruise, Southampton to Amsterdam, Madeira, Tenerife, Ft. Lauderdale. Christmas/New Year, 14 nights, Caribbean Islands Holiday round trip from Ft. Lauderdale.

Delta Queen Coastal Cruises

Cape May Light, Cape Cod Light   **Home Port** Varies with itinerary
Inaugural season, Spring–Summer 2001, 7 and 14 nights, U.S. East Coast, Colonial America, New England, Hudson River, Maritime Canada, Gaspé Peninsula, Saguenay River, St. Lawrence Seaway, Welland Canal, Great Lakes, calling at ports not visited by large cruise ships—Mystic Seaport, Martha's Vineyard, Annapolis, West Point, Campobello Island, Buffalo, Niagara Falls, Toronto, Ottawa.

Delta Queen Steamboat Company

American Queen   **Home Port** New Orleans
Year-round, except early February, 4–8 nights, Mississippi River. September/ October also sails on Ohio, Illinois, Arkansas, and Tennessee rivers. Most cruises are round trip from New Orleans or to Memphis. Cruises also depart from St. Paul, St. Louis, Cincinnati, and Chattanooga. Themes include Culinary Cruise, Big Band, Gardens of the River, Spring Pilgrimage, Fall Foliage, and Old Fashioned Holidays.

Columbia Queen   **Home Port** Portland, OR
Year-round, 8 nights (with pre-cruise hotel night in Portland), Columbia, Snake, and Willamette rivers from Portland, with stops in Astoria, Cannon Beach, Columbia River Gorge, Pendleton, and Clarkston, where passengers take a jet boat excursion through Hell's Canyon, and end with visit to Timberline Lodge at 6,000 feet on Mount Hood. Tour to Mount St. Helena is one of 18 included shore excursions on region's history and culture.

Delta Queen   **Home Port** New Orleans
Year-round from mid-February, 3–11 nights, Mississippi, Ohio, Cumberland, Tennessee, Illinois, and Intracoastal waterway. New for July 2001: Tombigbee from St. Louis to Mobile and Nashville. Cruises depart from New Orleans, Memphis, Little Rock, Cincinnati, Chattanooga, St. Louis, Chicago, and Galveston. Many theme cruises include Jazz Celebration, Spring Pilgrimage, Civil War, Kentucky Derby, Big Band, Sternwheel Regatta, Fall Foliage, and Old Fashioned Holidays. June 24, Great Steamboat Race, 11 nights, is a competition from New Orleans to St. Louis.

Mississippi Queen   **Home Port** New Orleans

Year-round from January, 3–11 nights, Mississippi, Ohio, Cumberland, Tennessee, Kanawha, and Illinois rivers. Cruises depart New Orleans, Memphis, Chattanooga, Nashville, Cincinnati, and Louisville. Theme cruises include Big Band, Veterans Reunion, Spring Pilgrimage, Mark Twain, Fall Foliage, and Old Fashioned Holidays. June 24, Great Steamboat Race, 11 nights, from New Orleans to St. Louis.

Disney Cruise Line

Disney Magic   **Home Port** Port Canaveral

Year-round, 7 nights, round trip from Port Canaveral on Saturdays to St. Maarten, St. Thomas (with excursions to St. John), and Castaway Cay, Disney's private island in Abacos, 3 days at sea.

Disney Wonder   **Home Port** Port Canaveral

Year-round, 3 or 4 nights, round trip from Port Canaveral. 3 nights on Thursdays, to Nassau for the day and evening and day at Castaway Cay. 4 nights on Sundays, add a day at sea or Freeport, Grand Bahama Island. 7-day packages combine cruise and visit to Walt Disney World in Orlando.

First European Cruises

Azur   **Home Ports** Genoa, Venice

Year-round, 10, 11, and 12 nights, Eastern Mediterranean, round trip from Venice October–April; from Genoa, April–October with cruises between Genoa and Venice in January, April and October. Calls at ports in Greece, Israel, Egypt, and Italy. On 12-night cruises from Genoa, June–August, passengers may join ship in Barcelona, the first port of call. Cruise then visits Catania, Sicily; Katakolon, Greece; Alexandria and Port Said, Egypt; Ashdod, Israel; Piraeus (Athens), Corinth Canal and Rome. Christmas/New Year cruise, 11 nights, round trip from Venice.

Bolero   **Home Ports** Santo Domingo, Savona

Winter charter for cruises from Santo Domingo. April, 16 nights, transatlantic from Santo Domingo to Savona via San Juan, Guadeloupe, Martinique, Barbados, Madeira, Malaga, and Marseille.

April 28–November 17, 7 nights, round trip from Savona to Barcelona, Mallorca, Tunis, Malta, Palermo, Sicily, Rome. April 23, 5 night cruise to Barcelona, Mallorca, Corsica, Rome. December 6, 15 nights, transatlantic Genoa to Santo Domingo, via Almeria, Malaga, Madeira, Barbados, Guadeloupe, Antigua, Tortola.

Flamenco   **Home Ports** Savona, Kiel

Winter, 11 nights, Canary Islands, round trip from Savona via Almeria, Malaga, Madeira, Tenerife, Lanzarote, Safi, Casablanca, Alicante, and Marseille. May 19, 4 nights, round trip from Savona to Menorca, Mallorca, Ibiza, Barcelona. May 23 and September 15, positioning cruises, 10 nights, between Genoa and Kiel.

June–mid-September, 7 nights, Fjords or Baltic, round trip from Kiel to either Visby, Stockholm, Tallin, St. Petersburg, Copenhagen; or Flaam, Gudvangen, Molde, Andalsness, Hellesylt, Geirganger, Bergen, Copenhagen. December 21, 7-night Christmas cruise, round trip from Genoa to Naples, Malta, Tunis, Palermo, Rome. December 27, 11-night New Year cruise to Canary Islands.

Mistral   **Home Ports** Guadeloupe, Venice, Genoa

Winter, 7 nights, Caribbean, round trip from Guadeloupe to either St. Maarten, Tortola, St. Barts, Dominica, Antigua, Barbuda; or, Martinique, Trinidad, Grenada, Barbados, St. Lucia, Barbuda. June–November, 7 nights, Greek Islands, round trip from Venice, to Pireo, Kusadasi, Heraklion, Delphi, Dubrovnik.

November 11, 12 nights, Lebanon/Syria from Venice to Genoa; November 22, 11 nights, Egypt/Libya round trip from Genoa. April 5 and December 6, 15 nights, positioning cruises between Genoa and Guadeloupe.

European Vision   **Home Ports** Genoa, Cancun

July 1–November 18, 7 nights, inaugural season, Greek Islands, round trip from Genoa to Naples, Katakolon, Santorini, Mykonos, Rhodes, Gythion. December 5, 17 nights, transatlantic, Genoa to Cancun.

December–April, 7 nights, Caribbean, round trip from Cancun to Costa Rica, San Andres, Montego Bay, Grand Cayman, Playa del Carmen/Cozumel.

European Dream   **Home Port** To be announced

Enters service April 2002

Fred Olsen Lines (EuroCruises)

Black Prince   **Home Ports** Dover, Southampton

November–March, 13–35 nights, Canary Islands and Caribbean round trip from Southampton or Dover.

April, September–November, 13–23 nights, Eastern and Western Mediterranean round trip from Dover.

June–July, 7–13 nights, North Cape, Baltic, Norway from Dover.

Black Watch   **Home Ports** Southampton, Dover, Barbados

January–March, 69 nights, circumnavigation of South America, available in 3 segments: 18 nights, Southampton–Rio de Janeiro; 27 nights, Rio–Lima; 24 nights, Lima–Southampton.

March–May and September, 11–15 nights, Canary Islands, Iberia, Mediterranean round trip from Dover and Southampton.

May–August, 8–15 nights, Norway, North Cape, Baltic, Spitsbergen round trip from Dover. October, 15 nights, transatlantic positioning, Dover–St. Lucia.

October–December, 14 nights, Caribbean and Amazon from Barbados, St. Lucia, and Santo Domingo.

Global Quest (formerly OdessAmerica)

Royal Star   **Home Port** Mombasa

Year-round, 17–25 days, East Africa/Indian Ocean, from Mombasa, cruise/land tours in conjunction with African Safari Club. Destinations include Kenya and South Africa with stops at Zanzibar, Mayotte, and Nosy Bé.

Golden Sun Cruises

Aegean I   **Home Port** Piraeus

November 2000–March 2001, 7 nights, Greek Islands and Eastern Mediterranean round trip from Piraeus to Heraklion, Cyprus; Port Said, Egypt; Ashdod, Israel; Rhodes.

Summer to be announced.

Aegean Spirit   **Home Ports** Piraeus, Las Palmas

December 2000–March 2001, 7 nights, Canary Islands and North Africa, round trip from Las Palmas to Lanzarote, Agadir, Madeira (overnight), La Palma, Tenerife.

Summer to be announced.

Arcadia   **Home Port** Piraeus

To be announced.

Hebridean Island Cruises

Hebridean Princess   **Home Port** Varies with itinerary

Scotland's "Highlands and Islands" including the Inner and Outer Hebrides, Orkney, Iona, Rhum, Muck, Eigg, Lewis, Skye, and Staffa and the Norwegian Fjords and coastal ports, including Bergen.

Hebridean Princess   **Home Port** To be announced

After November, North European and Mediterranean in summer; Indian Ocean in winter. Specific ports of call to be announced.

Holland America Line

Amsterdam   **Home Ports** Ft. Lauderdale, others vary with itinerary

January–March; November–December, 10 nights, Panama Canal between Ft. Lauderdale and Puerto Caldera via Half Moon Cay (HAL's private Bahamian island), St. Thomas/St. John, Curaçao, San Juan del Sur (Nicaragua) or reverse. December 29, New Year cruise calls at Cartagena, Columbia, San Blas instead of St. Thomas/St. John.

April and August, 16 night, transatlantic, Ft. Lauderdale–Rome; Copenhagen–New York. April–May, 12 nights, Western Mediterranean and Europe from Rome or Lisbon.

June–August, 12 nights, Baltic, British Isles, Iceland, or Norwegian Fjords from Copenhagen or London (Harwich).

September–October, 7, 10 nights, Canada/New England from New York or Montreal.

January–April 2002, maiden World cruise.

Maasdam   **Home Port** Ft. Lauderdale

January–April; November–December, 7 nights, Western Caribbean from Ft. Lauderdale every Sunday to Playa del Carmen/Cozumel, Grand Cayman, Ocho Rios, Half Moon Cay.

Late April–late October, alternates with Eastern Caribbean to Nassau, San Juan, St. Thomas/St. John, and Half Moon Cay.

Noordam   **Home Ports** Tampa, Copenhagen, others vary with itinerary

January–April and December, 14 nights, Southern Caribbean, round trip from Tampa to San Juan, St. Thomas/St. John, Guadeloupe, Barbados, St. Lucia, Margarita, Bonaire, Aruba, Grand Cayman. April and November, 12, 14 nights, transatlantic, Tampa–Lisbon (April), Rome–Tampa (November).

April 27–May 17; September 22–November 11, 10 nights, Mediterranean from Istanbul, Rome, or Lisbon.

May–September, 10 nights, Baltic round trip from Copenhagen to Tallinn, Estonia; St. Petersburg (overnight); Helsinki; Stockholm and Kalmar, Sweden; Warnemunde (Berlin), Copenhagen (overnight). May and September, 14 nights, Western Europe between Rome and Copenhagen.

Rotterdam   **Home Ports** Venice, others vary with itinerary

January 4, 14 nights, Panama Canal from Ft. Lauderdale to Los Angeles. January–April, 99 nights, World Cruise, from Los Angeles to New York via Peru, across South Pacific to New Zealand, Australia, Southeast Asia, through Suez to Europe, transatlantic to Ft. Lauderdale and New York. Available in 14 segments of 14–36 nights.

May–November, 14 nights, Eastern and Western Mediterranean, Black Sea or Holy Land, between Venice and Barcelona or Istanbul. April and

November, 14/12 or 22 nights, transatlantic, between Ft. Lauderdale and Barcelona. December, 10 or 14 nights, Southern Caribbean round trip from Ft. Lauderdale.

Ryndam   **Home Ports** Vancouver, others vary with itinerary

January–February, November–December, 17 nights, Cape Horn between Valparaiso, Chile, and Rio de Janeiro. January, April, November, 17 nights, South America between Ft. Lauderdale and Valparaiso and San Diego–Valparaiso (November).

April, 20 nights, Panama Canal from Ft. Lauderdale to Seattle available in 12- to 19-night segments.

May–September, 7 nights, Alaska, between Vancouver and Seward via Ketchikan, Juneau, Sitka, and Hubbard Glacier or Glacier Bay. Valdez included on some northbound cruises. Two Inside Passage cruises, round trip from Vancouver in May and September, include Glacier Bay and Skagway/Haines in place of Sitka.

September 28, 3 nights, Pacific Coast, Vancouver–San Diego. October, 7, 10 nights, Mexico/Sea of Cortes, round trip from San Diego.

Statendam   **Home Ports** San Diego, Vancouver

October–April, alternating 10-night Mexico and 15-night Hawaii cruises, round trip from San Diego, calling at Cabo San Lucas, Mazatlan, Acapulco, Zihuatanejo, Puerto Vallarta with 4 days at sea; or, Hilo, Honolulu, Kauai, Lahaina, Kona, and Ensenada.

May–September, 7 nights, Alaska, between Vancouver and Seward via Ketchikan, Juneau, Sitka, Hubbard Glacier or Glacier Bay. Valdez included on some northbound cruises.

May and September, 4 and 3 night Pacific Coast between San Diego and Vancouver. September 29, Hawaii and Mexico cruises resumes.

Veendam   **Home Ports** Ft. Lauderdale, Vancouver

October–April, 7 nights, Southern Caribbean from San Juan on Fridays, to Santo Domingo, Barbados, Martinique, St. Maarten, St.Thomas/St. John.

May–September, 7 nights, Alaska, between Vancouver and Seward via Ketchikan, Juneau, Sitka, Hubbard Glacier or Glacier Bay; Valdez on some northbound cruises. Two Inside Passage cruises in September, round trip Vancouver include Glacier Bay and Skagway/Haines in place of Sitka.

April and October, 14 nights, Panama Canal from Aruba to Los Angeles or Vancouver (April) and San Francisco to San Juan (October). Southern Caribbean from San Juan resume in October.

Volendam   **Home Ports** Ft. Lauderdale, Vancouver

October–April, 10 night, Southern Caribbean, round trip from Ft. Lauderdale to Bonaire, Isla de Margarita, St. Lucia, St. Kitts, St.Thomas/St. John,

Nassau; or, Curaçao, La Guaira, Trinidad, Martinique, St.Thomas/St. John, Half Moon Cay.

May–September, 7 nights, Alaska, from Vancouver on Mondays to Juneau, Skagway/Haines, Glacier Bay, and Ketchikan.

April and October, 21 and 20 nights, Panama Canal between Ft. Lauderdale and Vancouver. Available in 12–19 night segments.

October, Southern Caribbean from Ft. Lauderdale resume.

Westerdam   **Home Ports** Ft. Lauderdale, Vancouver

October–December 2000, 7 night, Eastern Caribbean from Ft. Lauderdale.

January–April, alternating 8 and 5 nights, Eastern Caribbean from Ft. Lauderdale to Nassau, San Juan, Philipsburg, St.Thomas/St. John, Half Moon Cay; or, Key West, Half Moon Cay, Nassau.

May–September, 7 nights, Alaska, from Vancouver on Thursdays to Juneau, Skagway/Haines, Glacier Bay, Ketchikan.

April and October, 19 and 18 nights, positioning Panama Canal/ Mexican Riviera between Ft. Lauderdale and Vancouver. Available in shorter segments.

Zaandam   **Home Ports** Ft. Lauderdale, Vancouver

October–April, 10 nights, Southern Caribbean, round trip from Ft. Lauderdale to Bonaire, Isla de Margarita, St. Lucia, St. Kitts, St.Thomas/St. John, Nassau; or, Curaçao, La Guaira, Trinidad, Martinique, St.Thomas/St. John, Half Moon Cay.

May–September, 7 nights, Alaska, from Vancouver on Saturdays, to Juneau, Skagway/Haines, Glacier Bay and Ketchikan.

April and September/October, 22 nights, Panama Canal between Ft. Lauderdale and Vancouver, available in shorter segments.

October, Southern Caribbean cruises from Ft. Lauderdale resume.

Kristina Cruises (EuroCruises)

Kristina Regina   **Home Port** Helsinki

June–August, 3 nights, visa free cruises to St. Petersburg, round trip from Helsinki. June 4, 11 nights, Baltic States and June 27, 14 nights, White Sea-White Nights cruise to Murmansk, North Cape, Lofoten Islands, Norwegian Fjords, both round trip from Helsinki.

Mediterranean Shipping Cruises

Melody   **Home Ports** Ft. Lauderdale, Genoa

December 27, 2000, 17 nights, transatlantic from Genoa to Ft. Lauderdale followed by 12-night cruises, round trip from Ft. Lauderdale to St.Thomas, Antigua, Grenada, St. Lucia, Guadeloupe, Tortola, Nassau; or,

Montego Bay, Cartagena, San Blas Islands, partial Panama Canal transit to Gatun Lake, Puerto Limon, Key West.

April 11, 18 nights, transatlantic from Ft. Lauderdale to Genoa. April–October, 7 nights, round trip from Genoa every Sunday to Naples, Palermo, Tunis, Mallorca, Barcelona, and Marseille. October and November, 12 nights, round trip from Genoa to Syria, Lebanon, Egypt, Crete; or, Spain, Madeira, Canary Islands, Morocco.

Monterey **Home Ports** Durban, Genoa

November 5, 2000, 22 nights, Genoa to Durban via Suez Canal and East Africa. November–April, 2–10 nights, Durban to nowhere, Portuguese Island, Cape Town, Bazaruto, Madagascar, or Mauritius.

April 8, 22 nights, from Cape Town to Genoa via West Africa, Atlantic Islands, Morocco and Spain.

April 28–October 23, Eastern Mediterranean round trip, 11 nights, from Genoa to Naples, Alexandria, Port Said, Ashdod, Kusadasi, Patmos, Piraeus, Capri. May 9, Sept. 20, Oct. 12 for 11 nights, to Spain, Madeira, Canary Islands, Morocco. May 31 for 11 nights, to Malta, Tunisia, Greece, Corsica. August 4 for 14 nights, to Morocco, Canary Islands, Madeira, Gibraltar and Spain.

Rhapsody **Home Ports** Rio de Janeiro, Venice, Genoa

November 15, 2000, 18 nights, transatlantic from Genoa to Rio de Janeiro; December 9–February 24, 2001, 7 nights, "Tropical Brazil" round trip from Rio on Sundays to Porto Seguro, Salvador, Arraial Beach, and Buzios. March 3 transatlantic, 18 nights, from Rio de Janeiro to Genoa.

April, May 10, October, 11 nights, round trip from Genoa to Western Mediterranean, Middle East, or to Canary Islands.

May 26–September 22, 7 nights, Eastern Mediterranean, round trip from Venice on Sundays, to Bari, Katakolon, Kusadasi, Patmos, Rhodes, and Dubrovnik.

Norwegian Cruise Line

Norway **Home Port** Miami

Through March 31, 2001, 7 nights, Eastern Caribbean from Miami on Saturdays to St. Maarten, St. John, St. Thomas, Great Stirrup Cay (NCL's private island); 3 days at sea.

April 7, 8 nights, Western Caribbean to Grand Cayman, Roatan Bay Islands, Cozumel, Great Stirrup Cay, 3 days at sea.

Year-round from April 15, 2001, alternating 2-night cruises on Friday to Great Stirrup Cay and 5-night cruises on Sundays to Grand Cayman and Cozumel, 2 days at sea.

Norwegian Dream   **Home Ports**   Dover, Buenos Aires, Valparaiso, others vary with itinerary

Winter, 2000–2001, 2001–2002, 14 nights, Cape Horn/Strait of Magellan between San Antonio, Chile and Buenos Aires. December and March, positioning cruises between San Antonio and Miami. Summer, 2001 and 2002, 12 nights, Baltic Capitals, round trip from Dover.

October–November, 12 nights, Eastern Mediterranean, Black Sea or transMediterranean from Athens or Istanbul.

April, December, 16 and 17 nights, transatlantic, Miami–Rome, or Barcelona–Miami. April, September, 12 nights, Western Europe, Rome–Dover, and Dover–Athens.

Norwegian Majesty   **Home Ports**   San Juan, Boston

Winter, 7 nights, Southern Caribbean, round trip from San Juan on Sundays, 2000–2001, to Aruba, Curaçao, Tortola, St. Thomas; or, St. Lucia, Antigua, St. Maarten, St. Croix, St. Thomas.

2001–2002, to Martinique, Antigua, St. Maarten, Tortola, St. Thomas; or, St. Lucia, Barbados, Dominica, St. Kitts, St. Croix.

Summer, 2001 and 2002, 7 nights, Bermuda, round trip from Boston on Sundays, to St. George's for 4 days with 2 days at sea. April and October positioning cruises between San Juan and Boston.

Norwegian Sea   **Home Ports**   Miami, New York, Montreal

January 15–April 27, 2001, Bahamas, round trip from Miami on Mondays, 4 nights, to Key West, Great Stirrup Cay, Nassau; and Fridays, 3 nights, to Nassau and Great Stirrup Cay.

November 5, 2001–April 12, 2002, Bahamas and Mexico, round trip from Miami on Mondays, 4 nights, to Key West and Cozumel; Fridays, 3 nights, to Nassau and Great Stirrup Cay. May, 7 nights, Bahamas, round trip from New York to Nassau and Great Stirrup Cay with 4 days at sea.

June–mid-September, 7 nights, New England, round trip from New York to Halifax, Bar Harbor, Boston, Martha's Vineyard, Newport. September–October, 7 nights, Canada/New England, between New York and Montreal. Spring and Fall, May 1, Nassau–New York, 5 nights positioning; October 21, 15 nights, Montreal–Miami.

Norwegian Sky   **Home Ports**   Miami, Seattle

November–April, 7 nights, alternating Bahamas/Eastern Caribbean and Bahamas/Western Caribbean from Miami to Nassau, San Juan, St. Thomas, Great Stirrup Cay; or, Grand Cayman, Ocho Rios, Nassau, Grand Stirrup Cay, 2 days at sea. April, 15 nights, Panama Canal positioning from Miami to San Diego via Grand Cayman, Cartagena, Costa Rica, Acapulco, Manzanillo, and Puerto Vallarta.

April 2001 and 2002, 6 nights, Pacific Coast, Ensenada to Seattle via San Francisco and Victoria, B.C.

April–September, 7 nights, Alaska, round trip from Seattle to Juneau, Skagway, Glacier Bay; or, Sawyer Glacier, Ketchikan, Victoria. September 23 cruise end in Vancouver.

October–November, 10 nights, Hawaii, Vancouver to Honolulu; round trip Honolulu to Kiribati and Hawaiian Islands; and Honolulu to Ensenada. November, 16 nights, Panama Canal, San Diego to Miami.

December 2001–April 2002, 7 nights, Eastern Caribbean, from Miami to St. Thomas, San Juan, Great Stirrup Cay, 3 days at sea.

Norwegian Sun **Home Port** Miami

September 10, 2001 inaugural sailing, 16 nights, transatlantic, Southampton to New York via Le Havre, Cobh, Glasgow, Iceland, Newfoundland, and Halifax.

September–October, 12 nights, Canada/New England, round trip from New York to Boston, Bar Harbor, Sydney, Corner Brook, Quebec City, Saguenay River, and Halifax. November, 14 nights, positioning, New York–Miami via Norfolk, Charleston, San Juan, St. Thomas, St. Maarten, Bonaire, Aruba.

November 2001–April 2002, 7 nights, Western Caribbean, round trip from Miami to Grand Cayman, Roatan, Belize City, and Cozumel.

Norwegian Wind **Home Ports** Miami, Vancouver, various in Asia

November 2000–April 2001, 7 nights, Western Caribbean from Miami to Grand Cayman, Roatan, Belize City, Cozumel, 2 days at sea. April, 17 nights, Panama Canal positioning cruise from Miami to San Francisco. April 24, 6 nights, Pacific Coastal, San Francisco to Vancouver via Astoria, Seattle, Victoria.

May–September, 7 nights, Alaska, round trip from Vancouver on Mondays via Inside Passage, Juneau, Skagway/Haines, Ketchikan, Glacier Bay, or Sawyer Glacier.

September 24, 22 nights, Vancouver to Beijing.

October–December, 7 and 11 nights, China and Southeast Asia between Hong Kong, Singapore, and Bangkok with land tour add-ons.

December 2001–April, 2002, 10–19 nights, South Pacific, from Singapore to Australia, New Zealand, and transpacific to Tahiti, Hawaii, and Vancouver.

Orient Lines

Crown Odyssey **Home Port** Varies with itinerary

November–December 2000, Southeast Asia cruises between Mumbai (Bombay), Singapore, and Hong Kong. January–February 2001, Australia/

New Zealand from Sydney, Cairns, and Auckland. February 22, 34 nights, transpacific, Auckland to Los Angeles, available in segments, Auckland–Papeete and Papeete–Los Angeles.

March, 16 nights, Panama Canal, Los Angeles to Ft. Lauderdale. April, 19 nights, transatlantic, Ft. Lauderdale to Barcelona. Late April–November, 12–18 nights, Greek Isles and Mediterranean cruises from Barcelona, Athens, Istanbul, or Rome.

Marco Polo   **Home Port** Varies with itinerary

January–February, 11–18 nights, Antarctica, (only 450 passengers allowed by authorities; ship's normal complement is 600–800). Includes lectures by scientists, wildlife viewing from Zodiacs, and visits to scientific stations. Series starts in Buenos Aires and calls at Falkland Islands; final cruise combines Antarctica with Chilean Fjords. Others cruises are round trip Ushuaia.

December 2000 and late-February, March, 2001, 13–35 nights, Round South America in five segments.

April 11, 18-night transatlantic, Barbados to Barcelona.

April, September, October, 11–19 nights, Mediterranean and Greek Isles cruises from Barcelona, Rome, Lisbon, Venice, and Istanbul with Western Europe positioning cruises between Dover and Rome, Lisbon, or Copenhagen.

May–September, 11–18 nights, Baltic and Norwegian Fjords cruises from Copenhagen or Stockholm. June, 17 nights, North Cape for Midsummer, from Copenhagen with midnight champagne celebration while cruising the North Cape.

P&O Cruises

Arcadia   **Home Ports** Southampton, Barbados

November 2000–April, 2001, 15 nights, round trip from Barbados to Caribbean, Panama Canal, or Amazon. April and October, 12 and 14 nights, transatlantic between Barbados and Southampton.

May–October, 4–16 nights, round trip from Southampton to Canary Islands, Iberia, Eastern and Western Mediterranean, Baltic, Norwegian Fjords, Arctic. November, cruises from Barbados resume.

Aurora   **Home Port** Southampton

January–April, 90 nights, World Cruise, westbound from Southampton via Caribbean and Panama Canal to Acapulco and San Francisco, to Hawaii and South Pacific to New Zealand and Australia, Japan, China, Hong Kong, Singapore, India, via Suez to Israel, Turkey, Barcelona, Southampton. 4–23 night segments available.

Round trip from Southampton for remainder of year: April, November, 17 and 22 nights, Caribbean; April, July, October–December, 12–17 nights, Canary Islands, Madeira, Portugal; May, August–October, 16–17 nights, Eastern Mediterranean/Holy Land; June–August 12–14 nights, Western Mediterranean; May, 13 nights, Baltic; June, 15 nights, Norwegian Fjords and Iceland; September, 9–10 nights, transatlantic between Southampton and Boston/New York. September 15 cruise visits Newport and Bar Harbor, Maine.

Oriana   **Home Port** Southampton

January–April, 92 nights, World Cruise, eastbound from Southampton to South Africa, Indian Ocean, Sri Lanka, Singapore, Bali, Australia, New Zealand, South Pacific, Vancouver, San Francisco, Acapulco, Guatemala, Panama Canal, Caribbean, Southampton. 15–23 nights segments available.

Round trip from Southampton for balance of year: April, May, August, October–November, 10–13 nights, Canary Islands, Madeira, Portugal. April, June, August–October, 13–14 nights, Western Mediterranean. May, November, 17–18 nights, Eastern Mediterranean/Black Sea/Holy Land. July, 16 nights, Adriatic. August, 13 nights, Baltic. June–July, 7 and 15 nights, Norwegian Fjords. June, September, 5 and 7 nights, France, Spain, Portugal, Guernsey. December, 23 nights, Caribbean.

Victoria   **Home Port** Southampton, Barbados, Venice

January–March, 15 nights, Caribbean, round trip from Barbados or between Barbados and New Orleans. March, 14 nights, transatlantic, Barbados–Southampton.

April–August, 10–15 nights, round trip from Southampton to Canary Islands, Western Mediterranean, Baltic, Norwegian Fjords/Iceland, North Cape. September, 23 nights, St. Lawrence and New England round trip from Southampton.

September, 12 nights, positioning, Southampton to Venice. October–November, 14–15 nights, Eastern Mediterranean, Holy Land, Black Sea, round trip from Venice. December, 15 nights, transatlantic from Malaga, Spain–Barbados. December, cruises from Barbados resumes.

Peter Deilmann Cruises

Deutschland   **Home Port** Varies with itinerary

November–December 2000, 13–16 nights, Africa: Mauritius–Cape Town; round trip Cape Town; Cape Town–Dakar, Senegal; Dakar–Jamaica.

January–March, 13–22 nights, Panama Canal and Round South America in segments: Jamaica–Balboa, Panama; Balboa–Valparaiso; Valparaiso–Rio de Janeiro; Rio de Janeiro–Manaus.

March, 15 nights, Amazon/transatlantic from Manaus to Canaries. April and September, 11, 13 and 9 nights, Western Europe positioning, Genoa–Lisbon; Lisbon–Cuxhaven, Germany; Kiel–Lisbon; Lisbon–Genoa.

Late May–July and September, 9–13 nights, Baltic round trip from Kiel, Germany. July–September, British Isles, Iceland, Norwegian Fjords from Cuxhaven, Germany. October–November 7, 11, 15 nights, Mediterranean/ Middle East from Genoa, Venice or Cyprus. November–December, 14–18 nights, Middle East, India, and Indian Ocean, Venice–Aqaba; Aqaba– Dubai; Dubai–Bombay; Bombay–Mauritius.

Premier Cruise Lines

Big Red Boat I (Oceanic)   **Home Port**   Port Canaveral

Year-round, 3–4 nights, Nassau and Salt Cay from Port Canaveral on Fridays and Mondays.

Big Red Boat II (Edinburgh Castle)   **Home Port**   Tampa

Winter, 7 nights, Western Caribbean from Tampa on Saturdays to Key West, Belize, Roatan, and Cozumel. Summer to be announced.

Big Red Boat III (IslandBreeze)   **Home Port**   Houston

Year-round, 7 nights, Mexico, from Houston on Saturdays to Veracruz, Playa del Carmen, and Cozumel (overnight).

Seabreeze   **Home Port**   Ft. Lauderdale

Year-round, 7 nights, Western Caribbean from Ft. Lauderdale on Sundays to Cozumel, Roatan, Belize, and Key West.

Rembrandt   **Home Port**   Port Canaveral

November 2000–April 2001, 7 nights, Eastern Caribbean from Port Canaveral on Sundays to Nassau/Salt Cay, San Juan, St. John/St. Thomas. Summer to be announced.

Princess Cruises

Crown Princess   **Home Ports**   Ft. Lauderdale, Copenhagen, Boston, Honolulu

November 2000–May 2001, 10 nights, Panama Canal, round trip from Ft. Lauderdale to Cartagena, partial Panama Canal transit, Puerto Limón, Grand Cayman, Cozumel, 4 days at sea. February 18 ports are Ocho Rios, Costa Rica, Cartagena, and Aruba. April 29, transatlantic from Ft. Lauderdale to Rome followed by 12-night Western Europe, Rome to Copenhagen.

May–August, 10 nights, alternating Scandinavia/Russia and Baltic Heritage cruises round trip from Copenhagen. August, transatlantic, Copenhagen–Boston followed by Canada/New England cruises round trip from Boston.

November, 15 nights, Panama Canal from Ft. Lauderdale to San Diego.
November–December, 12 nights, Hawaii and Tahiti; Ensenada–Honolulu;
Honolulu–Papeete and reverse; Honolulu–Ensenada.

Dawn Princess   **Home Ports** San Juan, Vancouver

October 2000–April 2001, 7 nights, Southern Caribbean, round trip from
San Juan to Curaçao, Isla Margarita, Martinique, St. Kitts, St. Thomas; or,
Trinidad, Barbados, Antigua, Tortola, St. Thomas. April, 21 nights,
Panama Canal/Mexican Riviera positioning from San Juan to Vancouver,
available in segments.

May–September, 7 nights, Alaska between Vancouver and Seward, visiting Ketchikan, Juneau, Skagway, Glacier Bay, College Fjord. September,
15 nights, Panama Canal, San Francisco–San Juan. October, Southern
Caribbean cruises from San Juan resume.

Golden Princess   **Home Ports** Barcelona, Istanbul, Ft. Lauderdale

May 16, inaugural, 12 nights, Southampton–Barcelona. May–September,
12 nights Mediterranean between Barcelona and Istanbul via Monte
Carlo, Florence/Pisa, Naples, Venice (overnight), Athens, Ephesus,
overnights onboard in Istanbul and Barcelona. September, 15 nights,
transatlantic, Barcelona–Ft. Lauderdale. Winter 2001–2002 from October, 7 nights, Eastern Caribbean, round trip from Ft. Lauderdale to
Princess Cays, St. Maarten, St. Thomas.

Grand Princess   **Home Port** Ft. Lauderdale

Year-round, 7 nights, Caribbean from Ft. Lauderdale on Sundays.

January–April 29 to St. Thomas, St. Maarten, Princess Cay with 3 days
at sea. May 6–September 30, alternates with a Western itinerary to
Princess Cay, Grand Cayman, Costa Maya, Cozumel. From October,
Western itinerary is offered every Sunday.

Ocean Princess   **Home Ports** San Juan, Vancouver, Ft. Lauderdale

October 2000–April 2001, 7 nights, Southern Caribbean, round trip from
San Juan to Barbados, St. Lucia, St. Kitts, St. Maarten, St. Thomas; or,
Aruba, Caraças, Grenada, Dominica, St. Thomas. April 29, 22 nights,
Panama Canal/Mexican Riviera from San Juan to Vancouver available in
segments.

May–September, 7 nights, Alaska between Vancouver and Seward, visiting Ketchikan, Juneau, Skagway, Glacier Bay, College Fjord. September 26
for 15 nights, Panama Canal positioning, San Francisco–Ft. Lauderdale.

From October, 10 nights, alternating Eastern and Southern Caribbean
round trip from Ft. Lauderdale to Princess Cays, St. Maarten, Antigua,
Barbados, St. Lucia, St. Thomas. Dominica, Isla Margarita, and Curaçao
replace Antigua and St. Lucia on Southern itinerary.

Pacific Princess   **Home Ports** New York, others vary with itinerary

November–December 2000, Holy Land from Rome, Istanbul, and Athens. January and March, 25 nights, West Africa positioning between Istanbul and Cape Town. January–March, 11 nights, East Africa and Africa/India from Cape Town or Mombasa. April, 29 days, four continents transatlantic from Istanbul to New York.

May–October, 7 nights, Bermuda round trip from New York to St. George's, Hamilton, and Royal Naval Dockyard.

November, 27 nights, New York–Cape Town, via Bermuda, Barbados, Trinidad, Devil's Island, Fortaleza, Abidjan, Accra, Walvis Bay, Luderitz, Cape Town. November–December, 24 nights, Cape Town–Athens via Suez Canal. December, 14 nights, Holy Land from Athens to Istanbul.

Regal Princess   **Home Ports** Vancouver, others vary with itinerary

November–December 2000 and February, 12–15 nights, Australia, New Zealand and South Pacific from Auckland and Sydney.

January, 12 nights, Tahiti–Hawaii; Hawaii–Tahiti; Tahiti–Sydney. March–April, 12–19 nights, Sydney–Singapore; Bangkok–Beijing; Beijing–Osaka; April and September, 19 nights, Alaska/Far East between Osaka and Vancouver.

May–September, 7 nights, Alaska, round trip from Vancouver via Inside Passage to Juneau, Skagway, Glacier Bay, and Sitka. October, 16 nights, Beijing–Bangkok. November, 19 nights, Bangkok–Sydney.

Royal Princess   **Home Port** Varies with itinerary

November 2000–February 2001, 14 nights, Cape Horn between Buenos Aires and Santiago, and Amazon from Buenos Aires–Manaus and Manaus–Ft. Lauderdale.

February–April, 72 nights, World Cruise from Ft. Lauderdale to Rome via the Panama Canal, South Pacific, New Zealand, Australia, Southeast Asia, India, Middle East, Suez Canal, and Holy Land. Not available in segments. May, 12 nights, Holy Land from Rome or Athens and Western Mediterranean round trip from Rome. June, 12 nights, Mediterranean/Atlantic, Rome–London.

June–August, British Isles, Scandinavia, Baltic, Iberia round trip from London. August 27, 14 nights, Northern Europe/transatlantic, London–New York.

September–October, 10 nights, Canada/New England between Montreal and New York. From November, 14–18 nights, South America, Ft. Lauderdale–Buenos Aires followed by Cape Horn/Strait of Magellan between Buenos Aires and Santiago.

Sea Princess   **Home Ports** Ft. Lauderdale, Vancouver, San Juan

October–April, 7 nights, Western Caribbean round trip from Ft. Lauderdale on Saturdays to Princess Cay, Ocho Rios, Grand Cayman, Cozumel; 2 days at sea. April, 15 nights, Panama Canal positioning to San Diego. April–May, 10 nights, Hawaii, Ensenada–Honolulu; Honolulu–Vancouver calling at Hilo and Kailua, Kona, Hawaii; Lahaina, Maui (overnight); and Kauai.

May–September, 7 nights, Alaska between Vancouver and Seward, visiting Ketchikan, Juneau, Skagway, Glacier Bay, College Fjord. September, 7 nights, Mexican Riviera, San Francisco–Acapulco. October, 10 nights, Panama Canal, Acapulco–San Juan.

From October, 7 nights, Southern Caribbean, round trip from San Juan to St. Thomas, Dominica, Grenada, Caraças, Aruba; St. Thomas, St. Maarten, St. Kitts, St. Lucia, Barbados, San Juan.

Sun Princess   **Home Ports** San Juan, Vancouver

October–April, 10 nights, Panama Canal between San Juan and Puerto Caldera, Costa Rica via St. Thomas, Dominica, Barbados, Aruba, Cartagena, Puntarenas. January 28 for 7 nights, Southern Caribbean round trip from San Juan. April 25 for 20 nights, Panama Canal/Mexican Riviera repositioning from San Juan to Vancouver available in segments.

May–September, 7 nights, Alaska between Vancouver and Seward, visiting Ketchikan, Juneau, Skagway, Glacier Bay, College Fjord. September, 15 nights, Panama Canal, Los Angeles–Ft. Lauderdale. From October, 10 nights, Caribbean/Panama Canal round trip from Ft. Lauderdale with partial Canal transit.

Radisson Seven Seas Cruises

Paul Gauguin   **Home Port** Papeete

Year-round, 7 nights, French Polynesia from Tahiti to Bora Bora, Tahaa or Huahine, Raiatea, and Moorea in Society Islands, with overnight at Rangiroa. December 1 for 14 nights, includes Marquesas Islands.

Radisson Diamond   **Home Ports** San Juan, others vary with itinerary

January–May and November–December, 4, 5, 7 nights, Caribbean from San Juan. February, 7 nights and December, 9 and 7 nights, Panama Canal from San Juan, Gamboa/Panama, Aruba, or Caldera.

April and November, 9 nights, transatlantic between San Juan and Madeira. April–October, 7, 9, 10 nights, Mediterranean from Nice, Rome, Athens, Istanbul, or Venice.

Seven Seas Mariner   **Home Ports** Ft. Lauderdale, Vancouver, others vary with itinerary

March inaugurals, 9 nights, Panama Canal from Ft. Lauderdale–Puerto Caldera or reverse. April and October, 9 nights, Bermuda, round trip from Ft. Lauderdale. May, 5 nights, and November, 7 and 10 nights, Caribbean from Ft. Lauderdale. May, November, December, 15 and 16 nights, Panama Canal between Ft. Lauderdale and Los Angeles.

Late May–September, Alaska, between Vancouver and Seward or round trip from Vancouver. September 5 for 11 nights, Alaska from Vancouver to San Francisco. September 16 for 26 nights, South Pacific round trip from San Francisco.

December, 9 nights, Mexican Riviera, round trip from Los Angeles. May and December, 1 night samplers from Los Angeles.

Seven Seas Navigator   **Home Ports** Ft. Lauderdale, others vary with itinerary

December–February 2001, 7–16 nights, Caribbean and Panama Canal from Los Angeles, Ft. Lauderdale, Puntarenas.

February–April, 58 nights, Grand Circle South America in four segments; 13 nights, Ft. Lauderdale–Callao, Peru; 17 nights, Callao–Buenos Aires; 28 nights, Buenos Aires–Manaus; 12 nights, Manuas–Ft. Lauderdale. April and November, 9 nights, transatlantic, Ft. Lauderdale–Madeira and Tenerife–Ft. Lauderdale.

April–late June, 6 and 7 nights, Western Mediterranean, from Rome or Barcelona. June 24 and August 31, 7 and 9 nights, Western Europe, Lisbon–Greenwich; Hamburg–Lisbon.

July–August, 7–10 nights, Baltic from Greenwich, Stockholm, or Copenhagen. September–October, Western Mediterranean and Eastern Mediterranean/Holy Land from Lisbon, Nice, Venice, Istanbul, Athens, Haifa, or Rome. November 11, 7 nights, pre-transatlantic from Barcelona–Tenerife.

November–December, 7 and 9 nights, Caribbean from Ft. Lauderdale and Palm Beach.

Song of Flower   **Home Port** Varies with itinerary

November 2000 positioning from Europe to Southeast Asia; 15 nights, Athens–Muscat, 14 nights, Muscat–Phuket.

Late November 2000–March 2001, 8–15 nights, Vietnam and Indonesia from Hong Kong, Phuket, Bali, Singapore, Bangkok. April, positions from Southeast Asia to Europe: 14 nights, Phuket–Muscat, 10 nights, Muscat–Aqaba, 10 nights, Aqaba–Istanbul.

May, September, October, 7–11 nights, Western Mediterranean from Istanbul, Rome, Monte Carlo, or Lisbon. May and September, 9 nights, French Coast, Lisbon–Rouen, and London–Lisbon. June and August, 9 nights, British Isles from Rouen, Edinburgh, or London. June–August, 7–11 nights, Baltic, Rouen, Stockholm, Copenhagen, and Hamburg. October, 7 nights, Eastern Mediterranean from Athens or Istanbul.

November, returns to Southeast Asia; 10 nights, Istanbul–Aqaba; 10 nights, Aqaba–Muscat; 17 nights, Muscat–Singapore. December, Vietnam cruises resume.

Regal Cruises

Regal Empress   **Home Ports** New York, Port Manatee

December 2000–May 2001, 3–11 nights, Western Caribbean from Port Manatee including Mayan Adventure to Progreso/Merida and Cozumel; Key West overnight to Cay Sal, Bahamas, and Key West; Mexico to Playa del Carmen, Cancun, Cozumel; special cruises December 23, February 18, March 4, 11, and April 1, 2001 to Progress (Merida), Cozumel, and Costa Maya, a new port 150 miles south of Cancun.

Panama Canal to Grand Cayman, partial Panama Canal transit, San Blas Islands, Puerto Limon, and San Andres, Colombia; Sunspree cruises, overnight to nowhere.

June–October, 5 and 2 nights round trip from New York: 5 nights, New England/Canada to Newport; Saint John, NB; Portland, Martha's Vineyard, alternates with 2-night Sunspree cruises to nowhere. July, two 7-night cruises to Nassau and Freeport. September, 12 nights, Fall Foliage to Newport, Bar Harbor, Corner Brook, NF; Quebec City; Charlottetown, PEI and Halifax, NS.

Renaissance Cruises

R1   **Home Ports** Athens, Istanbul

December 2000–February 2001, 27 nights, Istanbul–Eliat, Israel and reverse, with calls in Greece, Egypt, Crete, Cyprus, Jordan with a Suez Canal transit. Followed by year-round, 10- to 16-night cruise tours from Athens to Istanbul or reverse. Ports of call in the Greek Isles, Turkey, and on longer sailings, Egypt and Israel.

R2   **Home Ports** Barcelona, Venice

November–February, 50 nights, Athens–Bangkok and reverse, with shorter cruises: 30 nights, Athens to Singapore. Others to be announced. Followed by year-round, 10- to 16-night cruise tours from Venice to Barcelona or reverse.

R3 and *R4*   **Home Port** Papeete

Year-round, 11 and 14 nights, French Polynesia round trip from Tahiti to Moorea, Huahine, Raiatea, Bora Bora with longer cruises calling at Tahaa and Thai, the Vanilla Island.

R5   **Home Ports** Venice, Istanbul, Athens

Fall and Winter, 10- to 16-night cruise tours from Athens to Istanbul or reverse. Ports of call in the Greek Isles, Turkey, and on longer sailings, Egypt, and Israel.

Spring and Summer, 14 nights, Venice to Istanbul and reverse. Ports of call to be announced.

R6   **Home Ports** Barcelona, Lisbon, Stockholm, Dover

Fall and Winter, 14 and 25 nights, Canary Islands, from Barcelona to Lisbon and reverse. Spring and Summer, 16 nights, Stockholm to Dover and reverse. May and September, 16-night positioning cruises between Dover and Barcelona. Other shorter and longer itineraries may be scheduled during the year.

R7   **Home Ports** Athens, Istanbul, Stockholm, Dover

Fall and Winter, 14 nights, Athens to Istanbul and reverse.

Spring and Summer, 16 nights, Stockholm to Dover and reverse. May and September, 16-night positioning cruises between Dover and Athens. Some shorter and longer itineraries may be scheduled.

R8   **Home Port** To be announced

Enters service February 2001; itineraries to be announced.

Renaissance VII and VIII   **Home Ports** Mahe, Seychelles

November 2000–April 2001, 16-night cruise tours combine safari in Kenya with cruise to 5 ports in the Seychelles and 3-day tour in Egypt.

Royal Caribbean International

Adventure of the Seas   **Home Port** San Juan

November 18, 2001 inaugural. Year-round, 7 nights, Southern Caribbean from San Juan to Aruba, Curaçao, St. Maarten, St. Thomas.

Brilliance of the Seas   **Home Port** To be announced

Enters service July 1, 2002; itineraries to be announced.

Enchantment of the Seas   **Home Port** Miami

Year-round, 7 nights, alternating Eastern and Western Caribbean, from Miami to Key West, Playa del Carmen/Cozumel, Ocho Rios, Grand

Cayman, 2 days at sea (Costa Maya, Mexico replaces Ocho Rios from April 8, 2001 except on New Year's sailing); or, St. Maarten, St. Thomas/St. John, Nassau, 3 days at sea.

Explorer of the Seas **Home Port** Miami

October 28, 2000 inaugural. Year-round, 7 nights, Eastern Caribbean from Miami on Saturdays to Labadee (RCI's private resort), San Juan, Puerto Rico, St. Thomas. Nassau will be added to itinerary in April 2001.

Grandeur of the Seas **Home Port** San Juan

November 2000–April 2001, 7 nights, Southern Caribbean, round trip from San Juan on Saturday to Aruba, Curaçao, St. Maarten, St. Thomas. April 21, positions to Miami. April 28 for 14 nights, transatlantic, Miami–Barcelona. May, 7 nights, roundtrip from Barcelona to Villefranche (Nice/Cannes/Monte Carlo), Florence/Pisa, Rome, Naples, and Malta.

June–September, 7 nights, Barcelona to Rome followed by alternating Western and Eastern Mediterranean from Rome on Saturdays to Naples, Malta, Barcelona, Villefranche, Livorno (Florence/Pisa); or Katakolon, Rhodes, Kusadasi, Athens. September, 14 nights, transatlantic from Rome to Boston. September–October, 7 and 10 nights, Canada/New England, round trip from Boston. November–December, 10 and 11 nights, Circle Caribbean round trip from Miami.

Legend of the Seas **Home Port** Varies with itinerary

November 2000–May 2001, Royal Journeys from Athens to Auckland and return in 14–17 night segments: Athens–Mombasa; Mombasa–Bombay; Bombay–Singapore; round trip from Singapore; Singapore to Sydney; Sydney to Auckland; and reverse to Athens. May, 10 nights, Athens to Barcelona.

May, September and October, 12 nights, Mediterranean and Adriatic, round trip from Barcelona and positioning between Barcelona and Harwich.

June–August, 12 nights, Baltic or British Isles/Norway round trip from Harwich.

November, 7 nights, Barcelona to Athens. Afterwards, Royal Journeys resume, 13–16 nights: Athens–Dubai; Dubai–Singapore; round trip Singapore; Singapore–Sydney.

Majesty of the Seas **Home Port** Miami

Year-round, Bahamas from Miami, 3 nights on Fridays to Nassau, and Coco Cay (RCI private Bahamian island); 4 nights on Mondays adds Key West.

Monarch of the Seas **Home Ports** San Juan, Ft. Lauderdale

April 2000–September 2001, 7 nights, Southern Caribbean from San Juan on Sundays to St. Thomas, Antigua, Barbados, St. Lucia, St. Maarten.

October–December, 4 and 5 nights, alternating Western Caribbean itineraries, round trip from Ft. Lauderdale; 4 nights, alternating Thursdays to Key West and Cozumel, 5 nights, alternating Saturdays to Cozumel and Grand Cayman, 5 nights, alternating Mondays to Costa Maya, Cozumel, and Key West.

Nordic Empress **Home Ports** San Juan, New York

November 2000–April 2001, Caribbean from San Juan for 3-night cruises to St. Thomas and St. Maarten; 4 nights adds St. Croix.

May–October, 7 nights, Bermuda, round trip from New York every Sunday to Kings' Wharf and Hamilton. April and October, 9 and 8 nights, positioning between San Juan and New York.

October–December, 4, 5 nights, round trip from San Juan: 4 nights to St. Croix, St. Maarten, St. Thomas; new 5 nights to Tortola/Virgin Gorda, St. Maarten, Antigua; or, St. Kitts, St. Lucia, Barbados.

Radiance of the Seas **Home Ports** Vancouver, San Juan

April 7, inaugural, 14 nights, Panama Canal, Ft. Lauderdale to Los Angeles and 7-night Pacific Coastal, Ensenada to Seattle.

April–May and September–October, 3 and 4 nights, Vancouver and Victoria from Seattle, and 2-night positioning cruises between Seattle and Vancouver.

Late May–September, 7 nights, Alaska, round trip from Vancouver to Inside Passage, Juneau, Skagway, Haines, Hubbard Glacier, and Ketchikan.

October, 10 and 14 nights, Hawaii, Vancouver–Honolulu and Honolulu–Ensenada to Hilo, Kailua Kona, Lahaina, Maui, Kauai. November, 14 nights, Panama Canal from San Diego to San Juan.

November 2000–March 2002, 7 nights, Southern Caribbean round trip from San Juan to St. Thomas, St. Croix, St. Maarten, St. Lucia, and Barbados.

Rhapsody of the Seas **Home Port** Varies with itinerary

October 2000–April 2001, 7 nights, Mexican Riviera, round trip from Los Angeles (April 8 and 15 from San Diego) on Sundays to Cabo San Lucas, Mazatlan, Puerto Vallarta.

April–May, September–October, 10, 11 and 12 nights, Hawaii, between Ensenada and Honolulu or Honolulu and Vancouver calling at

Hilo, Kailua Kona, Lahaina, Maui, Kauai. May 13, 5 nights, Alaska, round-trip from Vancouver.

May–September, 7 nights, Alaska, between Vancouver and Seward via Hubbard Glacier, Sitka, Skagway, Juneau, Ketchikan. October, 14 nights, Panama Canal positioning from San Diego to Galveston.

October–December, 7 nights, round trip from Galveston on Sundays to Playa del Carmen, Cozumel, Grand Cayman, Key West. Holiday cruise December 23, to Grand Cayman, Montego Bay, Curaçao, Aruba; or reverse, December 30, Aruba–Tampa; Cozumel replaces Montego Bay.

January–February, 2002, 7 nights, Western Caribbean, round trip from Tampa to Costa Maya, Playa del Carmen, Cozumel, Grand Cayman, Key West. February 9, Mardi Gras cruise to New Orleans from Tampa.

February 22–March, 7 nights, Western Caribbean, round trip from New Orleans, same ports as Tampa cruises, without Key West.

Sovereign of the Seas   **Home Port** Port Canaveral

Year-round, 3–4 nights, Bahamas from Port Canaveral to Nassau and Coco Cay on Thursdays and Mondays.

Splendour of the Seas   **Home Ports** Santos, Buenos Aires, Barcelona, Venice

December 8, 2000, 15 nights, positioning from Miami to Santos (Sao Paulo), Brazil for 5, 7, 12 night cruises round trip from Santos or between Santos and Buenos Aires. These cruises cater to South American market. April 6, 14 nights, transatlantic, Recife, Brazil, to Lisbon. April and November, Canary Islands, between Lisbon and Barcelona.

May–October, 7 nights, Greek Isles, round trip from Venice. May and October, 7 nights, positioning between Barcelona and Venice and 4 night cruises round trip from Barcelona.

Viking Serenade   **Home Port** Los Angeles

To November 2, 2001, 3–4 nights, West Coast and Mexico, from Los Angeles on Friday to Ensenada (3 nights); Monday to Catalina Island, San Diego, and Ensenada (4 nights).

Vision of the Seas   **Home Ports** San Diego, Vancouver

December, 2000, April–May, September, and November 2001, 10 and 11 nights, Hawaii between Ensenada and Honolulu or Honolulu to Vancouver via Hilo; Kailua Kona; Lahaina, Maui; and Kauai. January, April, and October, 13–15 nights, Panama Canal between San Diego and Miami. January–April, 10, 11 nights, Circle Caribbean, round trip from Miami to Playa del Carmen, Cozumel, Grand Cayman, Ocho Rios, Aruba, Curaçao, plus Key West on 11-night cruise.

May–September, 7 nights, Alaska, round trip from Vancouver to Hubbard Glacier, Skagway/Haines, Juneau, Ketchikan, Misty Fjord.

November–December, 7 nights, Mexican Riviera round trip from San Diego to Puerto Vallarta, Mazatlan, and Cabo San Lucas.

Voyager of the Seas   **Home Port** Miami

Year-round, 7 nights, Western Caribbean, round trip from Miami every Sunday to Labadee, Ocho Rios, Cozumel. From April 2001, Grand Cayman will be added to itinerary.

RO Cruises, Inc./Royal Olympic Cruises

Olympic Countess   **Home Port** Piraeus

March–November, 3 and 4 nights, Greek Islands and Ephesus, round trip from Piraeus, 3-night Aegean Discovery departs Fridays for Mykonos, Rhodes, Patmos, Kusadasi; 4-night Aegean Classic on Mondays, same ports plus Crete and Santorini. Or, from Venice to the same port.

Olympic Explorer   **Home Port** Piraeus

May 12–October 27, inaugural season, Adriatic, Greek Isles, Turkey round trip from Piraeus on Saturdays to Corfu, Venice, Dubrovnik, Nafilion, Istanbul, Mykonos, and Santorini.

Olympic Voyager   **Home Ports** Piraeus, Ft. Lauderdale

December 2000–April, maiden year, 11, 12, 17 nights, South America, round trip from Ft. Lauderdale. Amazon cruises visit San Juan, Tortola, Barbados, cruise Amazon River, Boca da Valeria, Manaus (overnight) Santarem, Devil's Island, Trinidad, Martinique, St. Thomas. Orinoco cruises call at San Juan, Tortola, Barbados, cruise Orinoco River, Puerto Ordaz, Trinidad, Martinique, St. Thomas. Maya cruises visit Montego Bay, Honduras, Guatemala, Belize, Playa del Carmen, Cozumel, Key West. April 16, 12-night transatlantic from Ft. Lauderdale to Barcelona.

May–November, 7 nights, Three Continents, round trip from Piraeus on Saturdays to Santorini, Alexandria, Port Said, Ashdod, Rhodes, Istanbul, Kusadasi, and Mykonos.

Stella Oceanis   **Home Port** Heraklion

May–October, 3, 4 and 7 nights, Cretan Discovery; round trip from Heraklion for 7 nights on Mondays to Delos, Mykonos, Kusadasi, Patmos, Piraeus, Hydra, Rethymnon, Santorini, Amorgos, Kos, and Bodrum; available in 3- and 4-night segments on Mondays, Heraklion–Rethymnon, or Fridays, Rethymnon–Heraklion.

Stella Solaris   **Home Ports** Piraeus, Ft. Lauderdale

December 1, 2000, 21-night transatlantic, Piraeus to Ft. Lauderdale. December 22, 2000 and January 5, 2001, 8 nights, Panama Canal, between Ft. Lauderdale and San Diego.

January 19, 58 nights, Circle South America with unusually long stays in many ports: round trip from Ft. Lauderdale to Ocho Rios; San Andres; Port Limon; transit Panama Canal; Balboa; Manta, Ecuador (overnight); Salavery, Callao/Lima (4 days in port), Peru; Valparaiso/Santiago (2 days in port), Puerto Montt, Strait of Magellan, Punta Arenas, Cape Horn; Ushuaia, Puerto Madryn, Buenos Aires (2½ days in port); Montevideo; Rio de Janeiro (3 days in port), Salvador, Recife, Belem; Devil's Island, French Guiana; Trinidad; Barbados, St. Thomas. Available in 3 segments: 21 nights, Ft. Lauderdale–Santiago; 29 nights, Santiago–Rio; 19 nights, Rio–Ft. Lauderdale. March, 19 nights, transatlantic, Ft. Lauderdale–Piraeus (Athens).

April–October, 7 nights, Greece/Turkey, round trip from Piraeus on Fridays to Istanbul (overnight), Kusadasi, Patmos, Mykonos, Rhodes, Heraklion, and Santorini.

Triton   **Home Port** Rome

May–September, 7 nights, Greek Isles and Turkey round trip from Civitavecchia (Rome) on Saturdays to Messina, Katakolon, Santorini, Mykonos, Kusadasi, Patmos, Piraeus, Corinth Canal, and Itea. Or from Civitavecchia (Rome) to Venice via the same ports.

World Renaissance   **Home Port** Piraeus

March–November, 3 and 4 nights, Greek Islands and Ephesus, round trip from Piraeus, 3-night Aegean Discovery on Fridays to Mykonos, Rhodes, Patmos, Kusadasi (Ephesus); 4-night Aegean Classic on Mondays, same ports plus Crete and Santorini.

Seabourn Cruise Line

Seabourn Goddess I   **Home Ports** St. Thomas, others vary with
itinerary

November–April, 4–7 nights, from St. Thomas on itineraries to popular small islands; some can be combined with 2 or 3 nights at Frenchman's Reef on St. Thomas or Westin on St. John.

April–October, 7 nights, Mediterranean and Atlantic Isles, from Malaga, Nice, Rome, Venice, Athens, or Istanbul. April and November, 10 nights, transatlantic between St. Thomas and Canary Islands.

Seabourn Goddess II   **Home Ports** Barbados, others vary with itinerary

November–April, 4–7 nights, Southern Caribbean, from Barbados with New Year cruise from St. Thomas. Can be combined with 2 or 3 nights at Frenchman's Reef on St. Thomas or Westin on St. John. May–November, 7 nights, Mediterranean and Atlantic Isles, from Lisbon, Seville, Barcelona, Nice, Rome, Venice, Athens, Istanbul, or Malaga. April and November, 10 nights, transatlantic between Barbados and Canary Islands.

Seabourn Legend   **Home Port** Varies with itinerary

November–February, 22, 14 or 8 nights, Panama Canal, Mexican Rivera, from West Palm Beach to Acapulco and Los Angeles or reverse, ending in Ft. Lauderdale.

Late February–May, 7–15 nights, Eastern/Southern Caribbean from Ft. Lauderdale, San Juan, Barbados, West Palm Beach.

May–November, 7–14 nights, Mediterranean/Riviera, Western Europe, Scandinavia/Russia from Lisbon, Nice, Rome, Barcelona, Malaga, London, or Amsterdam. May and November, 9, 15 nights, transatlantic between San Juan and Lisbon (May) or Malaga (November).

Seabourn Pride   **Home Port** Varies with itinerary

January–April, 14–18 nights, South America, Ft. Lauderdale to Valparaiso; round trip from Valparaiso to Cape Horn; Valparaiso to Ft. Lauderdale; Ft. Lauderdale to Manaus; Manaus to Ft. Lauderdale.

May–August, 7–21 nights, Riviera, Western Europe, Scandinavia/ Russia, Norwegian Fjords, British Isles from Lisbon, London, Copenhagen, Barcelona, Malaga, or Lisbon. April and September, 18 and 21 nights, transatlantic from Ft. Lauderdale to Barcelona and London to New York (September).

Late September–November, 12 nights, Canada/New England and Colonial America, between New York and Montreal or New York to Nassau. November–December, 7–16 nights, Bahamas, Eastern Caribbean from Ft. Lauderdale, San Juan.

Seabourn Spirit   **Home Port** Varies with itinerary

January–March, 14–17 nights, Southeast Asia, featuring Vietnam from Hong Kong, Bangkok, and Singapore. Mid-March, 16 nights, Arabia, Red Sea via Suez to Israel.

April–November, 7–14 nights, Eastern Mediterranean, Greek Isles, Black Sea, Italy, French Riviera from Istanbul, Athens, Rome, Venice. November, 21-night cruise/safari, from Haifa to Mombasa or Mombasa to Singapore. December, 14 and 16 nights, Southeast Asia featuring Vietnam from Singapore and Hong Kong.

Seabourn Sun   **Home Port** Varies with itinerary

January–April, 99 nights, World Cruise, from San Francisco to Ft. Lauderdale via South Pacific to Australia, Southeast Asia, Middle East, Mediterranean, transatlantic. Available 9 to 80 nights in segments. April 19, 17 nights, Colonial South/New England/Canada from Ft. Lauderdale to Quebec City. Spring transatlantic.

   May–September, 7–16 nights, Italy, Western Europe, Norwegian Fjords, Scandinavia, and Russia from Barcelona, Naples, Rouen, Dover. September 5, 17 nights, transatlantic from Dover to Quebec City. September 22 for 16 nights, Quebec City to Ft. Lauderdale. October 8 for 34 nights, transatlantic/Europe round trip from Ft. Lauderdale to Atlantic Isles, Morocco, Spain, France, Italy, Corsica, and San Juan. November, December, 10 nights, Mexico, Caribbean, round trip from Ft. Lauderdale; Holiday Cruise, 19 nights, Panama Canal, Ft. Lauderdale to San Francisco.

Silversea Cruises

Silver Cloud   **Home Port** Varies with itinerary

November–April, 10–16 nights, Far East and South Pacific, from Singapore, Hong Kong, Sydney, Auckland, Bali, and Bangkok. May, 11–16 nights, Africa and India, from Singapore, Bombay, and Dubai. June–July and September–November, 7–14 nights, Mediterranean from Athens, Malta, Monte Carlo, Lisbon, Casablanca, Istanbul, Athens. August–September, 9–14 nights, Northern Europe from Rouen, Copenhagen, Edinburgh, and Dublin.

   Late November–December, 9, 15 and 16 nights, Africa and India, from Dubai and Mombasa ending in Cape Town.

Silver Shadow   **Home Port** Varies with itinerary

November–February, 7–18 nights, South America East Coast and Cape Horn from Rio de Janeiro, Buenos Aires, Ushuaia, and Valparaiso.

   March–April, Africa, 14 nights, Rio de Janeiro to Cape Town; 16 nights, Cape Town to Mombasa; 9 nights, round trip from Mombasa; 15 nights, Mombasa to Haifa.

   Late April–September, 7–14 nights, Mediterranean, from Istanbul, Rome, Barcelona, Lisbon, Nice, Venice, or Athens.

   October 10, 16 nights, Athens to Dubai; October 26, 14 nights, Dubai to Singapore. November–December, Southeast Asia and South Pacific from Singapore, Hong Kong, Bali, and Sydney.

Silver Wind   **Home Port** Varies with itinerary

January–April, 126 nights, World Cruise, Los Angeles to London via the Pacific to Sydney, Southeast Asia, India, Suez, Mediterranean, Western Europe. Available in 5 segments of 15 to 34 nights.

May–October, 7–14 nights, Western Europe, then Mediterranean from London, Lisbon, Barcelona, Monte Carlo, Rome, Athens, Istanbul, Malta, or Venice.

November, December 14–16 nights, from Haifa, Mombasa and Cape Town. December 20, Holiday cruise, 16 nights, South America/ Caribbean, Rio de Janeiro to Ft. Lauderdale.

Star Clippers, Inc.

Note: All ports may not be included on every Star Clipper cruise, as itineraries are subject to weather conditions and alterations by the captain, in search of calm sailing and best anchorages.

Royal Clipper   **Home Ports** Barbados, Cannes

October 2000–April 2001, 7 nights, Southern Caribbean, alternating cruises round trip from Barbados on Saturdays to Martinique, Iles des Saintes, Antigua, St. Kitts, Dominica, St. Lucia; or, Martinique, St. Lucia, Bequia, Tobago Cays, Grenada, and Grenadines. April and October, 21 nights, transatlantic between Barbados and Cannes.

May–October, 7 nights, Western Mediterranean, alternating cruises round trip from Cannes to Sardinia; Corsica; Livorno and Portovenere, Italy; and Monte Carlo; or, Hyeres Islands, Menorca, Mallorca, Barcelona, and Cap Creus, Spain; and St. Tropez. November, Southern Caribbean cruises from Barbados resume.

Star Clipper   **Home Ports** Antigua, Barbados, Rome

November 2000–April 2001, 7 nights, Southern Caribbean, alternating cruises round trip from St. Maarten on Sundays to St. Maarten, St. Barts, Nevis, Guadeloupe, Dominica, Ile de Saintes, Antigua; or, Anguilla, Sandy Cay or Jost van Dyke, Soper's Hole, Norman Island, Virgin Gorda, St. Kitts, and St. Barts. April and October, 26 and 22 nights, transatlantic, Antigua–Rome; Malaga–St. Maarten (October 27, with 7-night positioning, Rome–Malaga). May–October, 7 nights, Western Mediterranean, alternating cruises round trip from Rome on Saturdays to Paestun, Italy; Sicily, Aeolian Islands, Sorrento and Palmarola, Italy; or, Corsica, Monte Carlo, Portofino, Livorno, Elba.

November, Southern Caribbean cruises from St. Maarten resume.

Star Flyer   **Home Ports** Phuket, Athens

November 2000–March, 2001, 7 nights, Far East, alternating cruises, round trip from Phuket, Thailand on Saturdays, to Penang, Malaysia and Thai islands including Ko Lipe, Ko Khai Nok, Similan Islands, and Phang Nga/Ko Dam Hok; or, Ko Surin, Ko Miang, Ko Rok Nok, and Phi Phi Islands, Thailand; Langkawi, Malaysia and Phang Nga/Ko Dam Hok.

April and October, 37 and 35 nights, positioning between Athens and Phuket.

May–October, 7 nights, Eastern Mediterranean, alternating cruises, round trip from Athens on Saturdays, to Kusadasi, Bay of Roses, Turkey; Patmos, Mykonos, and Kea, Greece; or, Bodrum and Dalyhn River, Turkey; Rhodes, Santorini, and Hydra, Greece. November, Far East cruises from Phuket resume.

Star Cruises

MegaStar Aries   (chartered)

MegaStar Taurus   (chartered)

Star Aquarius   **Home Port** Laem Chabang, Thailand
October 2000–March, short cruises from Bangkok (Laem Chabang) to islands of Phu Quoc, Ko Samui, Ko Chang, and Ko Kong.
   Summer to be announced.

Star Pisces   **Home Port** Hong Kong
Year-round, 1 night to nowhere from Hong Kong catering to gamblers and first-time cruisers.

SuperStar Aries   **Home Ports** Fukuoka, Kobe, Pusan
October 2000–March, 3 and 4 nights, to Kobe and Fukuoka, Japan; Pusan and Cheju, South Korea. Passengers may embark in either Fukuoka, Kobe, or Pusan. Summer to be announced.

SuperStar Capricorn II   **Home Port** To be announced
Enters service 2004

SuperStar Gemini   **Home Port** Singapore
June 4, 2000–March, 7 nights, Andaman Sea, round trip from Singapore to Kuala Lumpur (Port Klang), Port Dickson, Penang, Langkawi Island, and Malacca, Malaysia, and Phuket, Thailand.
   Summer to be announced.

SuperStar Leo   **Home Port** Hong Kong
October 2000–April, 3 nights, round trip Hong Kong to Sanya and Haikou on Hainan Island, China and Halong Bay, Vietnam. An exclusive arrangement secured by Star Cruises will enable Chinese nationals to cruise with only border pass from Hainan Island to Halong Bay, thereby reducing the need to apply for a visa.
   Summer to be announced.

SuperStar Libra   **Home Port** To be announced
Enters service late 2001.

SuperStar Sagittarius II   **Home Port** To be announced
Enters service in 2003.

SuperStar Scorpio   **Home Port** To be announced
To be renamed and join NCL fleet in 2002.

SuperStar Taurus   **Home Port** Kobe
November 2000–March, short cruises from Kobe to Cheju and Pusan,
South Korea, or, to Pusan, South Korea and Beppu, Japan.
   Summer to be announced.

SuperStar Virgo   **Home Port** Singapore
October 2000–March, Malacca Straits, round trip from Singapore to
Phuket, Langkawi Island, Port Dickson, Kuala Lampur (Port Klang).
   Summer to be announced.

Swan Hellenic Cruises

Minerva   **Home Port** Varies with itinerary
Many cruise-tour packages available.
   November–December 2000, Middle East and India. January–February,
2001, 7–17 nights, India, Sri Lanka, and Southeast Asia from Calcutta,
Bangkok, Bali, Hong Kong. February–March, 9–15 nights, repositions to
Mediterranean via India and Middle East.
   April, 6–14 nights, Eastern Mediterranean from Cyprus or Istanbul.
May and July, 7–14 nights, Athens–Barcelona; Barcelona–London. June, 14
nights, Baltic, London–Copenhagen or reverse. July, 7–14 nights, London–
Venice. August–October, 7, 14 nights, Eastern Mediterranean, Black Sea,
Italy from Venice, Istanbul, Limnos, Izmir, Cyprus, or Crete. November,
14–19 nights, Middle East, Sri Lanka, India from Sardinia to Colombo, Sri
Lanka. Christmas/New Year, 14 or 19 nights, Sri Lanka to Singapore.

Windjammer Barefoot Cruises (See Part 3, Sailing Ships)

Amazing Grace   **Home Port** Varies with itinerary
Year-round, 12 nights, between Freeport and Trinidad, calling at Antigua,
Bequia, Conception, Cooper Island, Dominica, Dominican Republic,
Grand Turk, Great Inagua, Grenada, Iles des Saintes, Jost Van Dyke, Nevis,
Norman Island, Plana Cay, St. Barts, St. Kitts, St. Lucia, St. Maarten, Tor-
tola, and Virgin Gorda.

Flying Cloud **Home Port** Tortola

Year-round on Mondays, 5 nights, round trip from Tortola to Salt Island, Cooper Island, Virgin Gorda, and Jost Van Dyke or Cooper Island, Peter Island, Norman Island, and Virgin Gorda.

Legacy **Home Ports** St. Thomas, St. Lucia

Year-round, 5 nights, round trip from St. Thomas to Buck Island, Culebra, Jost Van Dyke, St. John's, Norman Island, St. Croix, Tortola, Vieques. Summer–Fall, 5 nights, round trip from St. Lucia to Barbados, Bequia, Grenada, Tobago, Soufriere, St. Vincent.

Mandalay **Home Ports** Antigua, Grenada, Puerto La Cruz

Winter–Spring, 12 nights, between Antigua and Grenada, or, 5 nights, round trip from Grenada on 5th Monday of month. Ports include Bequia, Canouan, Carriacou, Dominica, Grenada Iles des Saintes, Martinique, Mayreau, Nevis, St. Lucia, and St. Vincent. Summer–Fall, 5 nights, Venezuela, between Grenada and Puerto La Cruz, Venezuela on Sundays calling at Los Testigos, Chimana Segunda, Grenada, Arapo, and Playa Blanca.

Polynesia **Home Port** St. Lucia

Year-round on Mondays, 5 nights, round trip from St. Lucia: Winter–Spring to St. Maarten, St. Barts, Anguilla, Tintamarre, Saba; or, St. Maarten, St. Eustatius, Nevis, St. Kitts.

   Summer–Fall to St. Lucia, Martinique, Dominica, Guadeloupe, Iles des Saintes; or, St. Lucia, St. Vincent, Bequia, Mayreau, Canouan.

Yankee Clipper **Home Port** Grenada

Year-round on Mondays, 5 nights, round trip from Grenada to Bequia, Carriacou, Mayreau, and St. Vincent, or, Grenada, Bequia, Canouan, St. Vincent, and Union Island.

Windstar Cruises

Wind Song **Home Ports** Puerto Caldera, Athens, Auckland

December 2000–April, 7 nights, Costa Rica, round trip from Puerto Caldera on west coast to San Juan del Sur (Nicaragua), Flamingo, Quepos, San Josecitas, Curu, Tortuga.

   April–May, positions from Costa Rica to Athens in 6- to 14-night segments; Costa Rica–Barbados; Barbados–Lisbon; Lisbon–Monte Carlo; Monte Carlo–Rome–Athens.

   May–October, 7 nights, Greek Isles and Kusadasi between Athens and Istanbul. Late October–December, positions from Athens to Auckland in 14- to 18-night segments: Athens–Bombay; Bombay–Bali; Bali–Cairns; Cairns–Auckland.

December 2001–March, 10 nights, New Zealand between Auckland and Christchurch.

Wind Spirit   **Home Ports** St. Thomas, Athens, Puerto Caldera

November, 2000–April, 7 nights, Eastern Caribbean from St. Thomas to St. John, St. Martin, St. Barts, Tortola, Jost Van Dyke, and Virgin Gorda.

April–May, October–November, positioning from St. Thomas to Athens in 12–16-night segments: St. Thomas–Lisbon; Lisbon–Nice–Rome; Rome–Athens.

May–October, 7 nights, Greek Isles and Kusadasi between Athens and Istanbul. Late October–December, positioning from Athens to Costa Rica, 6- to 14-night segments: Athens–Rome–Monte Carlo; Monte Carlo–Lisbon; Lisbon–Barbados; Barbados–Panama Canal–Costa Rica.

December, takes over *Wind Song*'s Costa Rica itineraries from Puerto Caldera.

Wind Star   **Home Ports** Puerto Morelos (Cancun), Barcelona

November 2000–April, 7 nights, Belize, from Puerto Morelos to Roatan, Honduras, Belize (Goff's Cay, Coco Plum Caye, Laughing Bird Caye, Dangriga), and Cozumel.

April–May, positions from Puerto Morelos to Barcelona, 7- to 14-night segments: Puerto Morelos–Barbados; Barbados–Lisbon; Lisbon–Barcelona.

May–October, 7 nights, alternating between Barcelona–Nice and return; Barcelona–Lisbon and return. Can be combined to make a 14-night cruise.

November, positions from Barcelona to Puerto Morelos; Barcelona–Lisbon, 7 nights; Lisbon–Barbados, 14 nights; Barbados–Puerto Morelos, 14 nights. December, Belize cruises resume.

Wind Surf   **Home Ports** Barbados, Rome

November 2000–March, 7 nights, Eastern/Southern Caribbean round trip from Barbados, northbound to Nevis, St. Martin, St. Barts, Iles des Saintes, St. Lucia; or, southbound to Tobago, Bequia, Martinique, St. Lucia, Mayreau.

April, positions to Nice in 13- and 14-day segments; Barbados–Lisbon; Lisbon–Nice.

April–November, 7 nights, Mediterranean/French and Italian Rivieras alternating between Rome–Venice calling at Amalfi, Messina, Corfu, Dubrovnik, Rab Island (Croatia) or reverse. Rome–Nice calling at Corsica, Portoferraio, Portovenere, Portofino, San Tropez, and Monte Carlo or reverse. November, positions to Barbados in 14-night segments: Nice–Lisbon; Lisbon–Barbados. December, Caribbean cruises from Barbados resume.

World Explorer Cruises

Universe Explorer   **Home Ports** Vancouver, others vary

May 8–August 14, 14 nights, Alaska, round trip from Vancouver along Inside Passage to Wrangell, Juneau, Skagway (Haines option), Glacier Bay, Seward (Anchorage option), Valdez, Yakutat Bay/Hubbard Glacier, Sitka, Ketchikan, Victoria; or, Metlakatla, Juneau, Skagway, Hubbard Glacier, Seward, Kodiak, Glacier Bay, Sitka, Ketchikan, Victoria. Both itineraries have 3 days at sea and average of 9 hours in ports, longer than most Alaska cruises.

September–April, two University of Pittsburgh, 100-night Semester at Sea voyages; January 15–April 25 from Nassau to Cuba, Brazil, South Africa, Kenya, India, Malaysia, Vietnam, Hong Kong, Shanghai, Japan, ending in Seattle; September 10–December 19, from Seattle to Japan, Hong Kong, Vietnam, Malaysia, India, Suez, Egypt, Turkey, Tunisia, Casablanca, and Miami.

2001 Unofficial Guide to Cruises Reader Survey

If you would like to express an opinion about your cruise or this guidebook, complete the following survey and return to:

Unofficial Guide Reader Survey
P.O. Box 43673
Birmingham, AL 35243

Name of ship: Today's date:

Date, duration, and destination of cruise:

Please circle one of the following:

—*Was this your*   1st   2nd   3rd   4th   5th   6th or more cruise?

—*Would you take another cruise on this ship?*   Yes   No

—*Recommend it to a friend?*   Yes   No

—*Do you plan to cruise*   within a year   within next 3 years   longer?

—*Your age:*   teens   20s   30s   40s   50s   60s   70s   over 80

—*You are:*   employed   self-employed   retired

—*Line of work:*

Please score items below from 1 to 10 with 10 being the highest or best. Feel free to add your comments.

Value for money:

Total cruise experience:

Your overall impression of the ship *(appearance, appeal, furnishings and decor, cleanliness, sports and recreation facilities, consistency, comfort, boarding/disembarking procedures):*

Cruise director *(available, helpful, friendly):*

Cruise staff:

Dining room food *(choices, quality, taste, presentation):*

Breakfast and lunch buffet:

Dining room service:

Bar service:

Cabin *(size, layout, soundproofing, cleanliness, appearance, condition):*

Bathroom:

Cabin attendant *(service, attitude):*

Enrichment programs, lectures, games *(variety and quality)*:

Entertainment in the main lounge:

Entertainment in other lounges:

Children's programs:

Youth counselors:

Shore excursions *(guides, variety, advanced information, value)*:

Some more questions:

—Was the food quality better, worse, or about what you expected?

—Were wine and bar prices low, moderate, or high?

—Was the music level tolerable or too loud, especially by the pool?

—Were you bothered by announcements over the public address system?

—Was the promotion of shipboard shops low key, moderate, or hard sell?

—Was the lifeboat drill well executed?

—Did you choose your cruise for its itinerary?

—Which ports of call did you like best?

—Were port talks poor or helpful?

—Did the speakers plug specific shops?

—Was passenger information available prior to the cruise? in your cabin? during the cruise?

Your hometown:

How did you learn about your cruise?

How did you learn about this book?

Where did you buy your cruise?

When and where did you buy this book?

(Optional) If you are available for a telephone interview, please give us your name, address, telephone number, and a convenient time to call.

THANK YOU!